Contents

Origins: Beginnings of the Universe, Earth, and Life

From Chapter 2 of *Introduction to Oceanography*, Tenth Edition, Harold V. Thurman, Alan P. Trujillo.

Origins: Beginnings of the Universe, Earth, and Life

Courtesy of NASA and the Space Telescope Science Institute

Dense cluster of galaxies. The small circular swirls in this image represent distant galaxies, each of which is composed of large numbers of individual stars. The deepest view of the universe so far, astronomers use such images to study the history and development of the universe. To collect this image, the Advanced Camera for Surveys aboard NASA's Hubble Space Telescope peered for more than 13 hours through the center of one of the most massive galaxy clusters known, Abell 1689, which acted as a gravitational lens.

Key Questions

- How did the universe originate?
- What sequence of events led to the origin of Earth?
- Where did Earth's oceans come from?
- Did life on Earth begin in the oceans?
- How old is Earth?

The answers to these questions (and much more) can be found in the highlighted concept statements within this chapter.

"Beginnings; are apt to be shadowy."

—Rachel Carson, *The Sea Around Us* (1956)

Why does Earth have such an abundance of water—especially in the liquid form—when it is so scarce on most other bodies in the solar system? Where did Earth's water come from? How has the composition of our planet changed over time? What distribution of energy and mass were needed to create the right conditions for life to originate? Is an ocean essential to the origin of life? Unfortunately, some of these questions don't have definitive answers. In this chapter, we explore what is known about the origin of our universe, Earth, and life.

Origin of the Universe

Humans have always been fascinated by the stars, and some who took their stargazing seriously gradually figured out that not all the points of light visible in the night sky were the same. In fact, eight of the closest ones are not even stars; they are *planets* (*planetes* = wanderer), which were so named because they appeared to wander relative to the fixed background of distant stars. Earth and its eight neighboring planets orbit around an average sized star, the Sun, and comprise our **solar system**.

Our solar system lies about two-thirds of the way from the center of a huge spiral of stars called the **Milky Way galaxy** (*galaxias* = milky) (Figure 1a). The Milky Way galaxy contains more than 100 billion stars and gets its name because it is a broad band of faint light, giving it a milky appearance in the night sky. In fact, all the stars that can be seen at night with the naked eye belong to the Milky Way galaxy. Still, *Proxima Centauri*, the star nearest to the Sun, is more than 4×10^{13} (40 trillion) kilometers [2.5×10^{13} (25 trillion) miles] away. Figure 1b is an image of galaxy NGC 4414, a distant spiral **galaxy** that resembles our own, taken by NASA's Hubble Space Telescope.

The Milky Way is only one of numerous galaxies in the much larger **universe** (*universum* = whole), and it is smaller than most others are. On a clear night, if you look very carefully from a vantage point in the Northern Hemisphere, you might see a hazy patch of light within the constellation Andromeda. That patch is our nearest spiral neighbor, the Andromeda galaxy,[1] which

---

[1]The distant Andromeda galaxy is named after the constellation through which it can be seen from Earth.

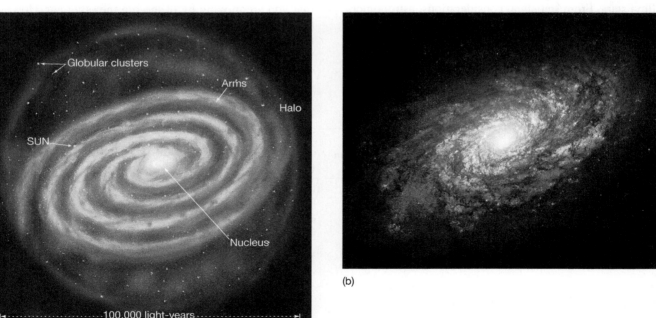

(a)

(b)

Courtesy of NASA and the Space Telescope Science Institute

Figure 1 The Milky Way and NGC 4414 galaxies.

(a) Artist's conception of the Milky Way galaxy, which is about 100,000 light-years across and has a central nucleus with spiral arms. Our solar system is located about two-thirds the distance from the center of the Milky Way galaxy.
(b) NASA Hubble Space Telescope image of galaxy NGC 4414, which is a spiral galaxy similar to the Milky Way.

is about 3×10^{19} kilometers (1.9×10^{19} miles) away. Powerful new telescopes have enabled astronomers to observe even more distant galaxies (see chapter-opening photo). Within 1×10^{22} kilometers (0.6×10^{22} miles) of our galaxy, in fact, there are at least 100 million others, and astronomers estimate that there are some 100 billion galaxies in the universe, each harboring an enormous number of stars.

Light-Year: An Astronomical Distance

To deal with the large distances involved in astronomy, astronomers have developed a handy unit for measuring distance: the **light-year**, which is equal to the distance light travels in one year. Measuring distance with a unit of time might seem illogical because most moving objects can move at a variety of speeds. Light, however, always travels at exactly the same speed of 299,792 kilometers (186,282 miles) per second, so each light-year is a constant distance. Astronomers have found that using light-years makes the expression of large (astronomical) distances much easier. For example, since light travels almost 10 trillion kilometers (6.2 trillion miles) in one year, Proxima Centauri is about 4 light-years from the Sun. For the rest of this chapter, light-years will be used for astronomical distances.

The Milky Way galaxy is 100,000 light-years in diameter (Figure 1a). Stars are much closer together near the center of the galaxy and much farther apart toward the edges. The central *nucleus* (*nucleos* = a little nut) of the galaxy is only about 10,000 to 15,000 light-years across and, within the Milky Way, there are approximately 100 billion stars. From statistical considerations, astronomers estimate that tens of millions of these stars have families of planets, and perhaps millions of these planets could be inhabited by intelligent creatures.

Moving Galaxies and the Redshift

By observing changes in the light radiating from these distant galaxies, astronomers have determined that nearly all of them are moving away from us. It has also been determined that the most distant galaxies are traveling more rapidly than the closest ones. In fact, speeds of more than 250,000 kilometers (155,000 miles) per second—which is 80% of the speed of light—have been deduced for these galaxies.

How can the speed of a distant galaxy be determined? A galaxy's speed can be calculated by measuring its shift in the pattern of light emission toward the red end of the spectrum—called a *redshift*. This effect is similar to how the pitch of an emergency vehicle siren changes as it approaches and passes you. Moreover, the greater the observed redshift, the faster the galaxy is moving, and as a result, the more distant it is from Earth (Figure 2).

It is important to remember that as the motion of celestial objects is observed from Earth, Earth is not standing still in space. Earth orbits the Sun at about 30 kilometers (18.6 miles) per second, and the solar system spins around at 220 kilometers (137 miles) per second as the Milky Way rotates in space. The Milky Way is also moving out from the center of the universe at high speed. We don't feel any of this motion, however, because everything that we perceive is moving at the same speed we are.

To illustrate this concept, imagine traveling in a car on a straight stretch of freeway. If another car is traveling nearby at the same speed as your car, you cannot perceive any change in distance between the vehicles. If you ignore the scenery passing by, you would be unable to determine that you are moving by observing the other car. However, if you see a car overtake your vehicle, you know it is traveling faster than you are. If the ride is perfectly smooth, you can't determine whether you are going

Constellation in which galaxy may be seen	Velocity km/s (mi/s)	Distance from sun (light-years)	Shift of absorption lines	
			Violet	Red
			(short wavelength)	(long wavelength)
Virgo	1,200 (745)	43,000,000	shift	
Corona Borealis	21,500 (13,351)	728,000,000	shift	
Hydra	61,000 (37,881)	1,960,000,000	shift	

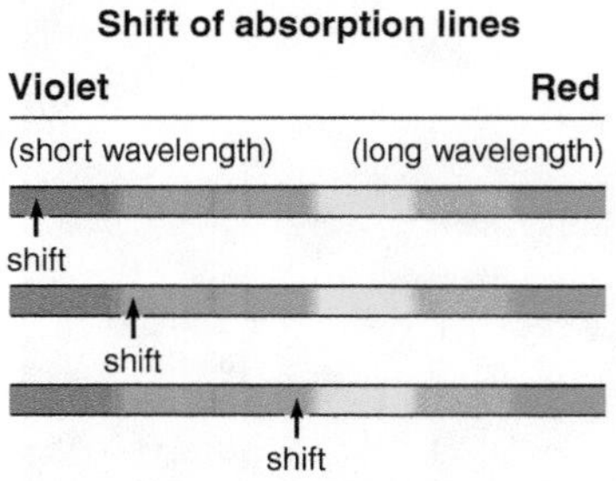

Figure 2 Motion of selected galaxies and the redshift.

Three galaxies moving away from the Sun show characteristic relationships between velocity, distance from the Sun, and the apparent shift of absorption lines toward the red end of the light spectrum (redshift) for a wavelength of violet light (*arrows*). For the closest galaxy (*top*), the redshift is minimal and the spectrum still represents violet light. However, in the more distant galaxies (*center* and *bottom*), the redshift increases to the blue and green portions of the visible spectrum—indicating that these galaxies are traveling at higher velocities.

100 kilometers (62 miles) per hour and being passed by a car going 140 kilometers (87 miles) per hour, or whether you are standing still and being passed by a car going 40 kilometers (25 miles) per hour. Note that *the change in the relative positions* of the two vehicles is the same in both instances.

The Big Bang

From our point of view on Earth, it appears that most of the galaxies in the universe are moving away from us. But if we remember that we are moving too, a more reasonable explanation is that we are riding along within an expanding universe. Astronomers have concluded that all galaxies are moving away from a center and from one another as if they were fragments from some ancient explosion. Unlike a bomb explosion, however, where pieces lose speed due to friction and gravity as they move away from the center, the pieces of the universe are actually *gaining* speed as they move away from the center. That's why the most distant galaxies are moving the fastest.

When did this explosion occur? If all of these galaxies are moving away from a central point, it might be reasoned that they all originated from a single large mass. If so, this origination time can be calculated from their speeds how long it has taken them to reach their present positions. In this way, astronomers estimate the age of the universe to be about 13.7 billion years old.

The idea of an exploding universe is called the **big bang theory**, which suggests that all matter originated as a dense, hot, supermassive ball with extremely high temperature and pressure conditions that underwent a cataclysmic explosion. According to the theory, elementary particles formed within the first one-billionth of a second; after one-hundredth of a second, neutrons, protons, and electrons formed. In about 25 minutes, the temperature dropped to 1 billion degrees, allowing neutrons and protons to combine to form atomic nuclei. At about 3000 degrees, nuclei attracted electrons to form the first *atoms* (*a* = not, *tomos* = cut). All matter began as atoms of hydrogen and helium, the two lightest elements.

After the blinding flash of the big bang, the universe plunged into a darkness called the Dark Ages, when there were no stars, no galaxies, and no light. After about 200 million years of darkness, stars began to form from the clouds of helium and hydrogen that moved outward from the central explosion. When these clouds became large enough, they started to contract and increase in temperature. As temperatures within the clouds became high enough, a process known as a **fusion** (*fusus* = to melt) **reaction** was initiated. A fusion reaction occurs when temperatures reach tens of millions of degrees and hydrogen atoms are converted to helium atoms, releasing large amounts of energy in the form of light.

At some point in its history, every star undergoes another contraction, and the helium is burned, producing carbon. With successive contractions, heavier elements such as oxygen, silicon, and iron are produced. When a star develops an iron core and contracts, it explodes, producing a *supernova* (*super* = great, *novus* = new). The material from this explosion contains many of the newly produced heavier elements. When this material is ejected into space, it forms interstellar clouds of gas and space dust that recombine to form new stars.

> The big bang, which occurred about 13.7 billion years ago, created the raw materials in the universe to produce galaxies, including the Milky Way galaxy, of which our solar system is a part.

? STUDENTS SOMETIMES ASK ...
I have a hard time buying into the idea of the universe starting as a "big bang." Did it really happen?

You're not the first to have this doubt. In fact, the name *big bang* was originally coined by cosmologist Fred Hoyle as a sarcastic comment on the believability of the theory. The big bang theory proposes that our universe began as a violent explosion, from which the universe continues to expand, evolve, and cool. Through decades of experimentation and observation, scientists have gathered substantial evidence that supports this theory. Despite this fact, the big bang theory, like all other scientific theories, can never be proved. It is always possible that a future observation will disprove a previously accepted theory. Nevertheless, the big bang has replaced all alternative theories and remains the only widely accepted scientific model for the origin of the universe.

Origin of the Solar System and Earth

Earth is the third of nine planets in our solar system that revolve around the Sun (Figure 3). Evidence suggests that the Sun and the rest of the solar system formed about 5 billion years ago from a huge cloud of gas and space dust called a **nebula** (*nebula* = a cloud). Astronomers base this hypothesis on the orderly nature of our solar system and the consistent age of meteorites (pieces of the early solar system). Using sophisticated telescopes, astronomers have also been able to observe distant nebula in various stages of formation (Figure 4).

The Nebular Hypothesis

According to the **nebular hypothesis** (Figure 5), all bodies in the solar system formed from an enormous cloud composed mostly of hydrogen and helium, with only a small percentage of heavier elements. As this huge accumulation of gas and dust revolved around its center,

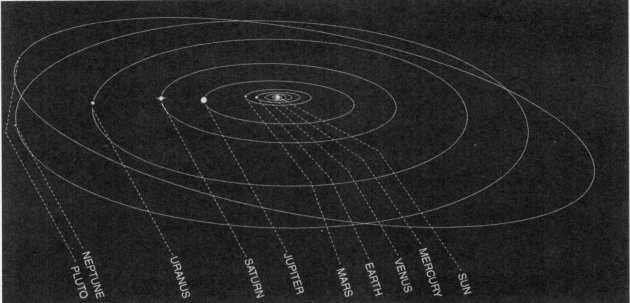

Reprinted by permission from Tarbuck, E. J., and Lutgens, F. K., Earth Science, 6th ed. (Fig. 19.1), Macmillan Publishing Company, 1991

(a)

Figure 3 The solar system.

(a) Orbits of the planets of the solar system, drawn to scale. **(b)** Relative sizes of the Sun and the planets. Distance not to scale.

the Sun began to form as the force of gravity concentrated particles. In its early stages, the diameter of the Sun may have equaled or exceeded the diameter of our entire solar system today.

As the nebular matter that formed the Sun contracted, small amounts of it were left behind in eddies, similar to whirlpools in a stream. The material in these eddies was the beginning of the **protoplanets** (*proto* = original, *planetes* = wanderer) and their orbiting satellites, which later consolidated into the present planets and their moons.

Protoearth

Protoearth looked very different from Earth today. It was a huge mass, perhaps 1000 times greater in diameter than Earth today and 500 times more massive. There were neither oceans nor any life on the planet. In addition, the structure of the deep Protoearth is thought to have been *homogenous* (*homo* = alike, *genous* = producing), which means that it had a uniform composition throughout. The structure of Protoearth changed, however, when its heavier constituents migrated toward the center to form a heavy core.

Throughout this process, meteorites from space bombarded Protoearth. Late in the stage of planetary formation, a large body about the size of Mars struck Earth. Planetary scientists believe that the object's rocky outer layer was propelled into orbit around Earth as the Moon, while its metallic interior remained with Earth.

Reprinted by permission from Tarbuck, E. J., and Lutgens, F. K., Earth Science, 6th ed. (Fig. 19.2), Macmillan Publishing Company, 1991

(b)

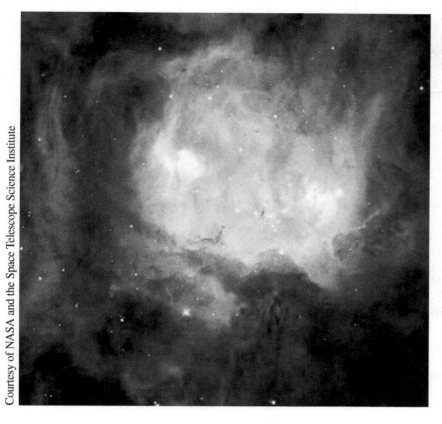

Courtesy of NASA and the Space Telescope Science Institute

Figure 4 The Ghost Head Nebula.

NASA's Hubble Space Telescope image of the Ghost Head Nebula (NGC 2080), which is a site of active star formation.

After Tarbuck, E. J., and Lutgens, F. K., The Earth: An Introduction to Physical Geology, 5th ed. (Fig. 1.10), Prentice Hall, 1996

Figure 5 The nebular hypothesis.

(a) A huge cloud of dust and gases (a nebula) contracts. (b) Most of the material is gravitationally swept toward the center, producing the Sun, while the remainder flattens into a disk. (c) Small eddies are created by the circular motion. (d) In time, most of the remaining debris forms the planets and their moons.

During this early formation of the protoplanets and their satellites, the Sun condensed into such a hot, concentrated mass that forces within its interior began releasing energy through atomic fusion. Recall that during a fusion reaction, hydrogen is converted to helium and large amounts of energy are released.

In addition to light energy, the Sun also emits ionized (electrically charged) particles that make up the solar wind. In the early stages of our solar system, the solar wind blew away the nebular gas that remained from the formation of the planets and their satellites. Eventually, these light gases were literally boiled away from the four inner planets as the planetary atmospheres were heated up by the Sun.

Meanwhile, the four protoplanets closest to the Sun (Mercury, Venus, Earth, and Mars) were heated so intensely by solar radiation that their initial atmospheres (mostly hydrogen and helium) boiled away. Much of this lost gas was captured by the larger planets beyond Mars: Jupiter, Saturn, Uranus, and Neptune. Additionally, the combination of ionized solar particles and internal warming of these protoplanets caused them to drastically shrink in size. As the protoplanets continued to contract, heat was produced deep within their cores from the spontaneous disintegration of atoms, called *radioactivity* (*radio* = radiation, *acti* = a ray).

> The nebular hypothesis suggests that Earth and all the bodies of the solar system were created by contraction of a cloud of gas and space dust.

Density Stratification

The release of internal heat became so intense that Earth's surface became molten. Once Earth became a ball of hot liquid rock, the elements were able to segregate according to their **densities**[2] in a process called **density stratification** (*strati* = a layer, *fication* = making). The highest-density materials (primarily iron and nickel) concentrated in the core, whereas lower and lower–density components (primarily rocky material) formed concentric spheres around the core. If you've ever noticed how oil-and-vinegar salad dressing settles out into a lower-density top layer (the oil) and a higher-density bottom layer (the vinegar), then you've seen how density stratification causes separate layers to form. Thus, Earth became a layered sphere based on density.

---

[2]Density is defined as mass per unit volume. An easy way to remember this is that density is a measure of *how heavy something is for its size*. For instance, an object that has a low density is light for its size (like a dry sponge, foam packing, or a surfboard). An object that has a high density is heavy for its size (like cement, most metals, or a large container full of water). Note that density has nothing to do with the *thickness* of an object: Some objects (like a stack of foam packing) can be thick but have low density.

The cutaway view of Earth's interior in Figure 6 shows that the high-density **core** can be divided into a solid *inner core* and a liquid *outer core*, both of which are composed of iron and nickel. Surrounding the core is the lower-density rocky **mantle** (a solid zone), and surrounding the mantle is the even lower-density **crust**. There are two kinds of crust—oceanic and continental. *Oceanic crust* underlies the ocean basins, has a higher density than continental crust, and is 4 to 10 kilometers (2.5 to 6.2 miles) thick. *Continental crust* underlies the continents, has a lower density than oceanic crust, and is 35 to 60 kilometers (22 to 37 miles) thick.

STUDENTS SOMETIMES ASK...
How do we know about the internal structure of Earth?

You might suspect that the internal structure of Earth has been sampled directly. However, humans have never penetrated beneath the crust! The internal structure of Earth is determined by using indirect observations. Every time there is an earthquake, waves of energy (called *seismic waves*) penetrate Earth's interior. Seismic waves change their speed and are bent and reflected as they move through zones having different properties. An extensive series of monitoring stations around the world detects and records this energy. The data are analyzed and used to work out the structure of Earth's interior.

Origin of the Atmosphere and the Oceans

Earth's geologic history began about 4.6 billion years ago, when the planet had cooled sufficiently for the crust to become solid. At that time, only a small fraction of Earth's original hydrogen and helium atmosphere remained, and there was still a lot of volcanic activity. Intense meteorite bombardment of the surface also continued until about 3.9 billion years ago.

Origin of the Atmosphere

Where did the atmosphere come from? Most likely, an early atmosphere was expelled from inside Earth by a process called **outgassing**. During the period of density stratification, the lowest-density material contained within Earth was composed of various gases. These gases rose to the surface and were expelled to form Earth's early atmosphere. What was the composition of these gases? They are believed to have been similar to the gases emitted from volcanoes, geysers, and hot springs today; mostly water vapor (steam), with small amounts of carbon dioxide, hydrogen, and other gases. The composition of this early atmosphere was not, however, the same composition as today's atmosphere. There was probably little free oxygen and nitrogen, but large amounts

Reprinted by permission from Tarbuck, E. J., and Lutgens, F. K., The Earth: An Introduction to Physical Geology, 4th ed. (Fig. 1.11), Macmillan Publishing Company, 1993

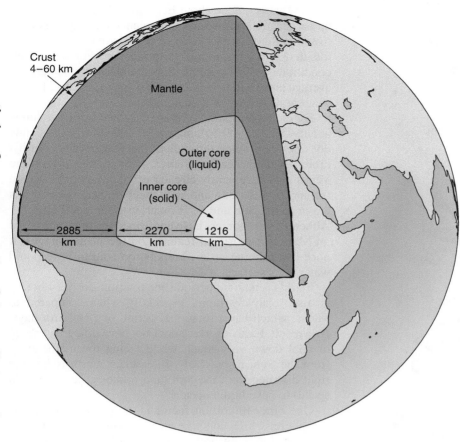

Crust
4–60 km

Mantle

Outer core
(liquid)

Inner core
(solid)

2885
km

2270
km

1216
km

Figure 6 Earth's internal structure.

A cutaway view of Earth's interior, showing the major subdivisions of Earth structure. The inner core (highest density), outer core, and mantle are drawn to scale, but the thickness of the crust (lowest density) is exaggerated about five times.

of carbon dioxide, water vapor, sulfur dioxide, and methane were present. The composition of the atmosphere changed over time because of the influence of life and possible changes in the mixing of material in the mantle.

Origin of the Oceans

Where did the oceans come from? Their origin is directly linked to the origin of the atmosphere. Figure 7 shows that as Earth cooled, the water vapor released to the atmosphere during outgassing condensed and fell to Earth. Evidence suggests that by at least 4 billion years ago, most of the water vapor from outgassing had accumulated to form the first permanent oceans on Earth.

Originally, Earth had no oceans. The oceans (and atmosphere) came from inside Earth as a result of outgassing and were present by at least 4 billion years ago.

STUDENTS SOMETIMES ASK...

You mentioned that the oceans came from inside Earth. However, I've heard that the oceans came from outer space as icy comets. Which one is true?

Comets, being about half water, were once widely held to be the source of Earth's oceans. During Earth's early development, space debris left over from the origin of the solar system bombarded the young planet, and there could have been plenty of water supplied to Earth. However, spectral analyses of the chemical composition of three comets—Halley, Hyakutake, and Hale-Bopp—during near-Earth passes they made in 1986, 1996, and 1997, respectively, revealed a crucial chemical difference between the hydrogen in comet ice and that in Earth's water. If comets supplied large quantities of water to Earth, much of Earth's water would still exhibit the telltale type of hydrogen identified in comets. Instead, this type of hydrogen is exceedingly rare in water on Earth. Assuming that the compositions of these three comets are representative of all comets, it seems unlikely that comets supplied much water to Earth.

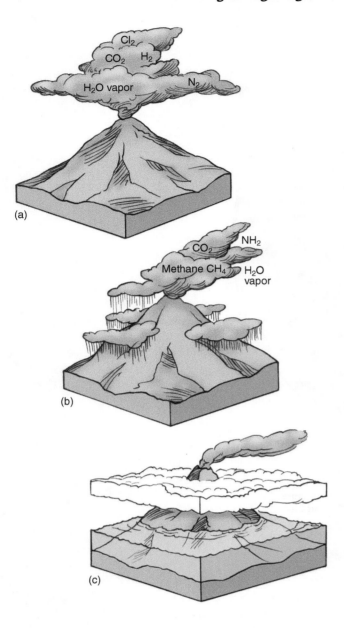

Figure 7 Formation of Earth's early atmosphere and oceans.

Early in Earth's history, widespread volcanic activity released large amounts of water vapor (H_2O vapor) and smaller quantities of various gases such as carbon dioxide (CO_2), chlorine (Cl_2), hydrogen (H_2), and nitrogen (N_2). This produced an atmosphere containing water vapor, carbon dioxide, methane (CH_4), and ammonia (NH_2). As Earth cooled, the water vapor **(a)** condensed into clouds and **(b)** fell to Earth's surface, where it accumulated to form the oceans **(c)**.

Oceans on Other Worlds?

Since our neighboring planets had a similar origin, it seems surprising that they do not have oceans while Earth does. What is unique about Earth that allowed it to develop an ocean? It turns out that a planet's average distance from the Sun and its rotational period are the critical factors in determining a planet's surface temperature. If both conditions are just right to allow the planet to maintain an average temperature between 0 and 100° C (32 to 212° F), water at its surface will be liquid.

For example, Earth's average distance from the Sun is about 150,000,000 kilometers (93,000,000 miles); this does not vary much throughout the year because Earth's orbital path is nearly circular. Even though Mars and Venus also have nearly circular orbits, Mars orbits much further from the Sun and so is much colder; Venus orbits closer to the Sun and so is much warmer (see Figure 3). Although astronomers have confirmed the presence of ice on Mars and erosional features on the planet suggest it once had running water, Mars is too cold to have liquid water at its surface.

Earth's rotational period (one rotation every 24 hours) is also relatively rapid, especially when compared to Venus, which has a rotational period of 244 Earth-days. As a result, Earth's surface does not have time to warm up or cool down very much while facing toward or away from the Sun, respectively. In essence, Earth is just the right distance from the Sun (and rotates at just the right speed) to have liquid oceans.

One other important factor is the presence of an atmosphere, which acts like an insulating blanket around a planet, blocking both incoming solar energy and escaping re-radiated energy. Even with Earth's fortuitous distance from the Sun and rotational period, its average surface temperature would be a chilly −21°C (−5.8°F) if not for the atmosphere. The heat-trapping effectiveness of an atmosphere depends on the gases it contains and the wavelengths of the solar and re-radiated energy. This warming phenomenon is referred to as the *greenhouse effect*. For example, greenhouse warming caused by the carbon dioxide-rich atmosphere on Venus further raises the temperature there, so any liquid water would have boiled away long ago. Greenhouse warming caused by Earth's atmosphere raises the average surface temperature to 14°C (57°F), ensuring that the oceans will neither freeze nor boil away.

Remarkably, some of the best prospects of finding liquid water within our solar system lie beneath the icy surfaces of some of Jupiter's moons. For instance, Europa is suspected to have an ocean of liquid water hidden under its outer covering of ice. Detailed images sent back to Earth from the *Galileo* spacecraft have revealed that Europa's icy surface is quite young and exhibits cracks apparently filled with dark fluid from below. This suggests that under its icy shell, Europa must have a warm, mobile interior—and perhaps an ocean. Because the presence of water in the liquid form is a necessity for life as we know it, there has been much interest in sending an orbiter to Europa—and eventually a lander capable of launching a robotic submarine—to determine if it too may harbor life.

The Development of Ocean Salinity

The relentless rainfall that landed on Earth's rocky surface dissolved many elements and compounds and carried them into the newly forming oceans. Even though Earth's oceans have existed since early in the formation of the planet, its chemical composition must have changed. This is because the high carbon dioxide and sulfur dioxide content in the early atmosphere would have created a very acidic rain, capable of dissolving grater amounts of minerals in the crust than occurs today. In addition, volcanic gases such as chlorine became dissolved in the atmosphere. As rain fell and washed to the ocean, it carried some of these dissolved compounds, which accumulated in the newly forming oceans.[3] Eventually, a balance between inputs and outputs was reached, producing an ocean with a chemical composition similar to today's oceans.

STUDENTS SOMETIMES ASK...
Are the oceans growing more or less salty or has their salinity remained constant over time?

We can answer this question by studying the proportion of water vapor to chloride ion, Cl^-, using ancient marine rocks. Chloride ion is important because it forms part of the most common salts in the ocean (e.g., sodium chloride, potassium chloride, and magnesium chloride). Also, chloride ion is produced by outgassing, like the water vapor that formed the oceans. Currently, there is no indication that the ratio of water vapor to chloride ion has fluctuated throughout geologic time, so it can be reasonably concluded that the oceans' salinity has been relatively constant through time.

Cycling and Mass Balance

If input from outer space is discounted, the elements that make up the atmosphere and the ocean must have come from within Earth's interior and been brought to the surface by volcanic activity. Can a whole ocean full of water come from volcanic eruptions? Is there enough chloride in volcanic emissions to account for all the chloride in the sea? These questions can be answered using simple mass balance calculations.

---

[3]Note that some of these dissolved components were removed or modified by chemical reactions between ocean water and rocks on the sea floor.

Source of Ocean Water

Studies have shown that the material brought to Earth's surface by volcanoes comes from the lower crust or the upper mantle. Let's start our examination of the source of ocean water by determining the mass of Earth's mantle.

Earth's mantle has a volume of 1.0×10^{27} cubic centimeters and an average density of 4.5 grams per cubic centimeter. The general equation is

$$\text{volume} \times \text{density} = \text{mass} \qquad (1)$$

To determine the mass of material in the mantle, we plug values into Equation (1):

$$(1.0 \times 10^{27} \text{ cm}^3) \times (4.5 \text{ g/cm}^3) = 4.5 \times 10^{27} \text{ grams} \qquad (2)$$

The same method can be used to determine the mass of water in the present-day oceans.

If all of the ocean's water came from the mantle, how much mass has been lost from the mantle? To answer this, we need to compare the mass of the ocean to the mass of the mantle before water loss (which equals present-day mantle mass plus the mass of ocean water). We calculate:

$$\frac{1.4 \times 10^{24} \text{ g}}{(4500 \times 10^{24} \text{ g}) + (1.4 \times 10^{24} \text{ g})} = 0.00031 \text{ or } 0.031\% \qquad (3)$$

Therefore, the mantle would need to have lost only 0.031% of its mass as water to produce Earth's oceans.

The next question to ask is how much water (by weight percent) Earth's mantle could have contained. To determine this, we need to find some analogous material that is similar in composition to the original mantle material. Probably the best analogs are silicate-containing stony meteorites, which are fragments of the early solar system that have remained largely unchanged. The average water content of these meteorites is about 0.5% by weight, which is about 16 times more than the 0.031% that was calculated as being necessary to account for the present oceans.

Additionally, recent laboratory studies of certain minerals subjected to conditions that simulate those deep within the planet suggest that there was enough water released from minerals in the mantle as Earth cooled to supply about five times the amount of water present in Earth's oceans. Therefore, the mantle could very easily have served as the source for water in Earth's oceans if there was a sufficient rate of escape from the mantle to the surface.

Recall that there have been oceans on Earth for about 4 billion years. If the amount of water in volcanic emissions is considered and an average rate of discharge over the last 4 billion years is assumed, calculations show that volcanoes have produced enough water vapor to fill the oceans more than 100 times. Even if 99% of

EXAMPLE 1

Given that the volume of seawater is 1.4×10^{24} grams and its average density is 1.0 grams per cubic centimeter, what is the ocean's mass?

We can plug values into Equation (1) to determine the answer:

$$(1.4 \times 10^{24} \text{ cm}^3) \times (1.0 \text{ g/cm}^3) = 1.4 \times 10^{24} \text{ grams}$$

The ocean's mass is 1.4×10^{24} grams.

this water were recycled, there would still be enough to account for the present-day oceans. Clearly, there is strong evidence that suggests Earth's mantle is a likely source of ocean water.

Sources of Salts in the Ocean

To understand the sources and processes that control the amount of salt in the ocean, let's look more closely at the chemical and physical weathering processes that break down rock. *Chemical weathering* releases elements contained in rock by dissolving them. *Physical weathering* breaks down rocks by various natural processes that crack, split, smash, pulverize, and grind rocks into smaller pieces.

Water carries both dissolved materials and solid particles from source areas toward the oceans. Although most dissolved materials make it to the oceans, larger solid particles often do not. Moreover, water flowing from the mountains toward the oceans encounters increasingly more gentle slopes, thereby losing velocity along the way. Because the size of particles that water can carry depends on its velocity, the larger particles are deposited relatively close to their source and may not make it to the ocean, whereas the finest particles are carried all the way to the ocean where they finally settle out in deep, quiet water.

Volcanic gases emitted into the atmosphere may also end up in the ocean. All gases dissolve to some extent in water. Chlorine, sulfur gases, and carbon dioxide in the atmosphere all dissolve in rain and thereby enter the ocean.

Element Mass Balances

In the preceding section, it was implied that all the material that is now sediment, all the dissolved salt in the ocean, and all the gases in the atmosphere are thought to have come from *primary crystalline rocks* of the solid Earth. If this is true, then one should be able to add up the masses for each of the elements in sediments, the oceans, and the atmosphere to see whether the total balances with what could have been weathered from primary crystalline rocks (Figure 8). In this context, the primary rocks, sediments, oceans and atmosphere are referred to as *reservoirs*.

Estimates for the total element masses in each reservoir are obtained by multiplying the volume of the reservoir by the average element concentration in the reservoir (similar to the calculation in Example 1). Mass estimates are most accurate for those reservoirs for which the volumes are known and in which the element concentrations are not highly variable, such that the average value is representative. Furthermore, ocean and atmosphere element mass estimates are much more accurate than the estimates for primary crystalline rocks and sediments because rocks and sediments are composed of a variety of different materials, so their properties are more difficult to estimate. Another difficulty in making these estimates is separating recycled material from primary material.

Nonetheless, for the most common elements in crystalline rocks (Na, Ca, K, Si, Mg, and Fe), the balance sheets agree well, within the error of the estimates. For certain elements (Cl, S, C [as CO_2], and N), it appears that large quantities have come from somewhere other than primary crystalline rock. These elements and compounds are found in the atmosphere, ocean, and sedimentary rocks in far greater amounts than would have been made available by chemical weathering of primary crystalline rocks and are called **excess volatiles** (*volatilis* = flying) (Table 1). This imbalance suggests that volcanic activity rather than surface weathering is the source for these elements. It also implies that volcanic activity is the source for the water in the oceans and atmosphere.

Figure 8 Geochemical balances.

All the material eroded from primary crystalline rocks (*left*) is accounted for by corresponding material in the atmosphere, oceans, and sediments (*right*), creating a balance of geochemical components.

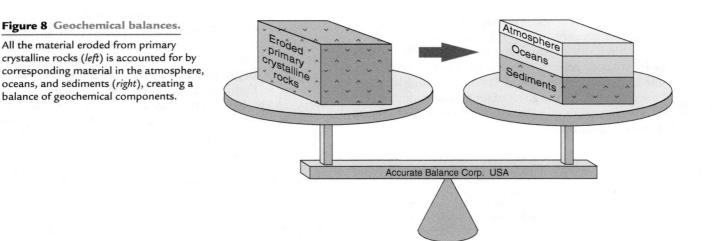

TABLE 1 **Excess volatiles (values are in grams $\times 10^{20}$).**

Compound or element:	H_2O	C as CO_2	Cl	N	S	H, B, Br, Ar, F, etc.
Found in:						
a. Atmosphere and ocean	14,600	1.5	276	39	13	1.7
b. Buried in sedimentary rocks	2,100	920.0	30	4	15	15.0
Total	16,700	921.5	306	43	28	16.7
Supplied by:						
a. Weathering of crystalline rocks	130	11.0	5	0.6	6	3.5
Difference of (found in) − (supplied by), which are known as *excess volatiles*	16,570	910.5	301	42.4	22	13.2

After Rubey, W. W. 1951; courtesy of the Geological Society of America

STUDENTS SOMETIMES ASK...

*Does Earth's continuing volcanic activity
(and outgassing) mean that the oceans
will gradually cover more and more of the surface?*

Not necessarily, because the surface area of the oceans depends directly on the volume of the basin in which they form. During the initial solidification of Earth's crust, there may have been no distinct continents or ocean basins. Instead, both may have formed gradually as the oceans themselves formed. If the continents formed gradually, then the capacity of the oceans' basins to hold water may have gradually increased, too. It is likely the surface area of the oceans has been relatively constant for a long period of geologic time and the only major change in the ocean's character has been an increase in depth.

Origin of Life

How did life begin on Earth? One recent hypothesis is that the organic building blocks of life may have arrived embedded in meteors, comets, or cosmic dust. Alternatively, life may have originated around **hydrothermal** (*hydro* = water, *thermo* = heat) **vents**—hot springs—deep in the ocean. Yet another idea is that life originated in rock material deep below Earth's surface.

According to the fossil record on Earth, the earliest known life forms were primitive bacteria that lived about 3.5 billion years ago. This record indicates that the basic building blocks for the origin of life came from materials already present on Earth. The oceans were the most likely place for these materials to interact and produce life.

A Working Definition of Life

What is life? It might seem easy to differentiate those that are living from the non-living, but the unusual nature of some life forms makes defining life a challenging task. Also, both living and nonliving things are composed of the same basic building blocks: atoms, which move continuously in and out of living and nonliving systems. This free exchange of identical components between life and nonlife is one of the factors that complicates attempts at formally defining life.

A simple definition of life is that it consumes energy from its environment. Using this definition, a car engine could probably be classified as alive. An engine, however, cannot self-replicate or otherwise reproduce itself, which is another key component of life.

Several other qualities are crucial in defining life. Water probably needs to be a part of a living organism because living things need a solvent for biochemical reactions—though ammonia might also work. A living thing probably has to have some sort of a membrane to distinguish itself from its environment. In addition, most living things tend to respond to stimuli or adapt to their environment. Lastly, life as we know it is carbon-based, since carbon is so useful in making chemical compounds. Because NASA's definition of life must encompass the potential of extraterrestrial life (Box 1), NASA have been using a fairly simple working definition of life: "Life is a self-sustained chemical system capable of undergoing Darwinian evolution." However, even this definition is problematic in that it would likely require observation of several successive generations over a considerable length of time to verify evolution in a life form.

A good working definition of life, then, should incorporate most of these ideas: that living things can capture, store, and transmit energy; they are capable of reproduction; they can adapt to their environment; and they change through time.

The Importance of Oxygen to Life

Oxygen, which comprises almost 21% of our present atmosphere, is essential to human life for two reasons. First, our bodies need oxygen to "burn" (*oxidize*) food, releasing energy to our cells. Second, oxygen in the form of **ozone** (*ozon* = to smell[4]) protects Earth's surface from most of the Sun's harmful ultraviolet radiation (which is why there is such concern over the development of an ozone hole over Antarctica).

---

[4]Ozone gets its name because of its pungent, irritating odor.

BOX 1   Research Methods in Oceanography

LIFE ON MARS?

Some material that has fallen to Earth is thought to have originated as fragments blasted off the surface of Mars from collisions with meteoroids. One of these fragments, which was discovered in Antarctica in 1984 and named meteorite ALH 84001, caused a great scientific controversy in 1996 when researchers from NASA reported they had found what appeared to be fossilized microbes within the meteorite. During study of the meteorite, scientists found unusual structures resembling those that are formed by terrestrial bacteria, although on a much smaller scale. If the structures could be confirmed as being produced by a life form, it would provide compelling evidence for life on Mars.

One group of skeptics immediately countered with the fact that the meteorite has been on Earth for thousands of years and had plenty of time to become contaminated by terrestrial life. Another group was skeptical as to the biologic origin of the evidence; they claimed it could have been created by inorganic processes. What tools can scientists use to tell the difference?

One of the signatures of terrestrial life is its preference for light *isotopes* (*iso* = same, *topos* = place) of elements. If an organism needs to use carbon, for example, it will preferentially use ^{12}C instead of ^{13}C; if it needs sulfur, it will use ^{32}S instead of ^{34}S, and so on. Thus, organic matter and other compounds generated by metabolic processes will be enriched in light isotopes relative to the surrounding environment. When an isotopic analysis of the meteorite was conducted, it did not show enrichment in light isotopes. But what if the life forms that evolved on Mars didn't preferentially use light isotopes?

The NASA scientists claimed unique chemical signatures found in the meteorite are indicative of production by a life form. Particularly, the presence of complex organic molecules called PAHs (polycyclic aromatic hydrocarbons) in the meteorite suggests the presence of a life form. PAHs, however, can result from nonbiologic processes and are even abundant in interstellar space. Other researchers analyzed the meteorite for the presence of amino acids, the building blocks of life, but could not find any. In addition, the extremely small size of the structures limits the possibility that they were produced by a life form. But could an entirely different type of life—one much smaller than those known on Earth that does not use amino acids—be present on Mars?

Although it appears unlikely that the unusual structures identified in Martian meteorite ALH 84001 were created by a life form, it highlights the question of whether scientists will be able to recognize life on other worlds. Mars seems to be a prime candidate for life because there is strong evidence that Mars once had liquid water at its surface, thereby fulfilling one of the most important conditions for life. Did life begin on Mars but die out when the water became trapped at the poles? Or, were other conditions never just right for life to form? Are Martian and Earth life forms both seeds from space—Earth's seed flourished, but Mars's seed died?

The existence of complex organic molecules across space, combined with the recent discovery of planets around other stars, makes it likely that the conditions conducive to life have developed in other solar systems as well. If so, perhaps there are many other worlds with life, some of them even evolving into intelligent civilizations

with which our civilization can communicate. To test this hypothesis, "listening" telescopes are being monitored, radio messages have been sent, and probes containing messages have been launched into space in hopes that another civilization on a different world might be looking and listening, too. One prominent effort in this regard is the Search for Extraterrestrial Intelligence in the Universe (SETI) Institute in Mountain View, California, which was established in 1984 to explore the origin, nature, and prevalence of life in the universe.

Although life has existed on Earth very nearly since its beginnings, the fossil record suggests it can survive here only temporarily. In the history of life on Earth, there have been many mass extinction events (one of the most famous is the Cretaceous–Tertiary event that wiped out the dinosaurs). Nonetheless, at least some life forms have managed to avoid demise and carry on, proving that life always seems to find a way to survive. The unanswered question is whether life could have originated and survived on a different world.

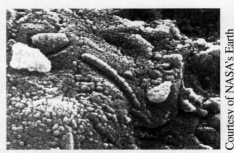

Courtesy of NASA's Earth Observatory

Close-up of Martian meteorite ALH 84001.

The tube-like structure in the middle of this photomicrograph is one of the controversial features of Martian meteorite ALH 84001. The structure is 0.5 micron long, where one micron equals one-millionth of a meter.

Fortunately, much of the energy represented by ultraviolet radiation is exhausted in the layer of the upper atmosphere called the *stratosphere* (*stratus* = to extend, *sphere* = a ball). Here, ozone (O_3) is created when ultraviolet light bombards oxygen molecules (O_2) and knocks some of them apart. Chemically, the reaction is:

$$O_2 + \text{ultraviolet light} \rightarrow O + O \qquad (4)$$

Each oxygen atom produced is very reactive and readily combines with another oxygen molecule to produce a molecule of ozone:

$$O_2 + O \rightarrow O_3 \qquad (5)$$

These two reactions occur so rapidly that oxygen molecules are essentially undetectable in the stratosphere.

In the process of forming ozone, oxygen molecules absorb ultraviolet radiation. Once ozone is created, it has the ability to block incoming ultraviolet radiation. Oxygen—either as O_2 or O_3—that is not bonded to other atoms is known as *free oxygen*.

Evidence suggests that Earth's early atmosphere (the product of outgassing) was different from Earth's initial hydrogen-helium atmosphere and different from the mostly nitrogen-oxygen atmosphere of today. The early atmosphere probably contained large percentages of water vapor and carbon dioxide and smaller percentages of hydrogen, methane, and ammonia, but very little free oxygen.

Why was there so little free oxygen in the early atmosphere? Oxygen may well have been outgassed, but oxygen and iron have a strong affinity for each other.[5] Iron occurs in two forms: ferrous iron (Fe^{2+}) and ferric iron (Fe^{3+}), with ferrous iron reacting readily with oxygen to produce ferric iron. Most of the iron in volcanic rocks at Earth's surface is ferrous, and there was probably sufficient iron in early volcanic rocks to chemically bind most of the oxygen that was outgassed. Thus, any oxygen released by volcanic activity was quickly used up in the conversion of ferrous iron to the ferric state, effectively removing it from the early atmosphere.

Without oxygen in Earth's early atmosphere, moreover, there would have been no ozone layer to block most of the Sun's harmful ultraviolet radiation. In fact, the lack of a protective ozone layer may have been a key component in influencing the development of life on Earth.

The First Organic Substances

The main elements in organic compounds and in living things are hydrogen, carbon, and, to a lesser extent, nitrogen. *Amino acids* and *nucleotides* are the two types of organic compounds that are the building blocks of living tissue on Earth. Only 20 different amino acids exist; there are only five nucleotides. From these, all of the more complex organic molecules are formed: *Proteins* form chains of amino acids in different combinations, and the nucleic acids *DNA* and *RNA* form chains of the five nucleotides.

One advantage of the absence of oxygen in the early atmosphere was the chemical stability of gases containing reduced carbon and nitrogen, such as methane and ammonia, as well as the more complex molecules that are produced from them. These gases formed by combination of the hydrogen, nitrogen, and carbon outgassed from the mantle.

In 1952, a 22-year old graduate student of chemist Harold Urey at the University of Chicago named **Stanley Miller** (Figure 9b) conducted a laboratory experiment that had profound implications about the development of life on Earth. In Miller's experiment, he exposed a mixture of carbon dioxide, methane, ammonia, hydrogen, and water (the components of the early atmosphere and ocean) to ultraviolet light (from the Sun) and an electrical spark (to imitate lightning) (Figure 9). After a few weeks, the clear water turned pink and then brown, indicating the formation of a large assortment of organic molecules including amino acids, which are the basic components of life. Perhaps, Miller suggested, this was how organic compounds were made on the ancient Earth before life existed.

Throughout the 1960s, scientists continued to work with equipment similar to that used by Miller and, using either electricity or ultraviolet radiation, succeeded in synthesizing all 20 types of amino acids and the five nucleotides. All of these compounds must have been present in the "primordial soup" of ocean water within which life arose.

Miller's now-famous laboratory experiment of a simulated primitive Earth in a bottle demonstrated that vast amounts of organic molecules could have been produced in Earth's early oceans. What is unclear, however, is precisely how this organic material developed into more complex molecular structures—such as proteins and DNA—that are intrinsic to life. For example, many of these small organic molecules occur as dissolved compounds in water and are separated from other molecules by layers of attached water molecules (called *hydration spheres*). In this setting, it would be incredibly difficult for small molecules to form complex chains. However, experiments have shown that evaporating or heating the primordial soup to remove the water—or allowing the organic compounds to settle out onto clay mineral surfaces—are ways in which these individual molecules could become linked into larger molecules.

Alternatively, some scientists have recently moved the primordial soup pot from the ocean surface to the deep sea floor, where there exist hot springs called hydrothermal vents. These hydrothermal vents spew murky, mineral-rich clouds of fluids into the ocean that could also have generated the right conditions to produce life's precursor molecules.

Whether created at the surface or in the deep ocean, the organic material must have become chemically

---

[5]As an example of the strong affinity of iron and oxygen, consider how common rust—a compound of iron and oxygen—is on Earth's surface.

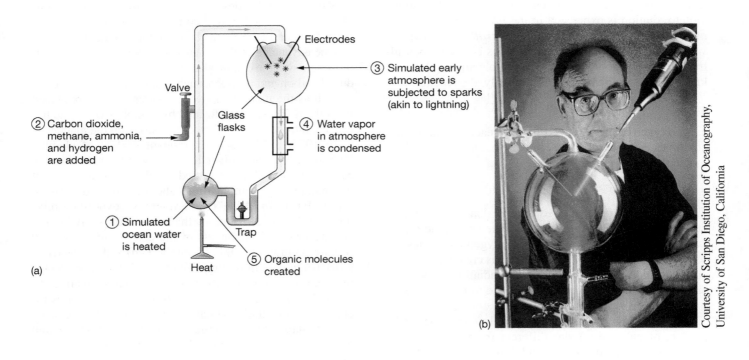

Electrodes

③ Simulated early
atmosphere is
subjected to sparks
(akin to lightning)

Valve

Glass
flasks

② Carbon dioxide,
methane, ammonia,
and hydrogen
are added

④ Water vapor
in atmosphere
is condensed

① Simulated
ocean water
is heated

Trap

(a)

Heat

⑤ Organic molecules
created

(b)

Courtesy of Scripps Institution of Oceanography,
University of San Diego, California

Figure 9 Creation of organic molecules.

(a) Laboratory apparatus used by Stanley Miller to simulate the conditions of the early atmosphere and the oceans. The experiment produced organic molecules and suggests that the basic components of life were created in the oceans. **(b)** Stanley Miller in 1999, with his famous apparatus in the foreground.

self-reproductive at some point. Further, it must have developed the ability to actively metabolize food and grow toward a characteristic size and shape dictated by internal molecular codes.

> Organic molecules were produced in a simulation of Earth's early atmosphere and ocean, suggesting that life most likely originated in the oceans.

The First Organisms

From a practical standpoint, there is an enormous increase in complexity from large organic molecules to a self-organized, replicating, living organism that is able to control and regulate its internal environment. One consideration is the amino acids that comprise proteins and the nucleotides that make up nucleic acids in organisms are linked in very specific orders. Under experimental conditions, chains of organic molecules can be produced, but they contain randomly ordered molecules.

Another consideration is that self-organization requires an organism to be physically separated from the external environment so that its internal chemistry can remain within certain limits, regardless of changes in the environment. The first living organisms were probably little more than simple membranes surrounding internal fluids that were very similar in composition to the pri-

mordial soup. The membrane had to allow needed molecules to enter the organism, waste products to leave the organism, and regulatory molecules (proteins) to be retained. The membrane also had to be easily mended after being split in two when the organism divided to form new individuals.

The very earliest forms of life were probably **heterotrophs** (*hetero* = different, *tropho* = nourishment). Heterotrophs require an external food supply, which was abundantly available in the form of nonliving organic matter in the ocean around them. *Fermenting* (*fermentum* = to boil) *bacteria* are modern-day examples of heterotrophic organisms. These bacteria obtain energy by breaking down complex organic molecules such as sugars and carbohydrates, which are obtained from their environment. Their waste products are simpler molecules such as ethyl alcohol and acetic acid. Humans utilize fermenting bacteria to create a variety of foods, including wine, beer, cheese, and vinegar.

The First Autotrophs

The **autotrophs** (*auto* = self, *tropho* = nourishment), which can manufacture their own food supply, evolved later and had a distinct advantage over heterotrophs. The first heterotrophs could only survive and increase their numbers if organic molecules were created rapidly enough by ultraviolet radiation or lightning strikes to keep pace with their expanding populations. They were also limited to living only within the nutrient-rich parts of the primordial soup that was the early oceans. Autotrophs, on the other hand, can prosper simply by making what they need wherever they can find raw materials in the presence of an energy source. Possible energy sources include chemical reactions that release energy, electricity (as was used in the Miller experimental apparatus), and sunlight.

The most abundant energy source available during the early stages of life was—and still is—sunlight. Although damaging short wavelength ultraviolet radiation provided the energy that synthesized the first organic molecules out of the primordial soup, organisms could not harness that energy without sustaining damage to their existing molecules. Since water naturally blocks ultraviolet radiation, the first organisms to use sunlight must have lived far enough below the water's surface to escape damage, yet close enough to the surface to take advantage of the non-damaging, longer wavelength visible light that penetrates to greater depths in the ocean.

The first autotrophs were probably similar to our present-day **anaerobic** (*an* = without, *aero* = air) **bacteria**, which live without atmospheric oxygen. They may have been able to derive energy from inorganic compounds at deep-water hydrothermal vents using a process called **chemosynthesis** (*chemo* = chemistry, *syn* = with, *thesis* = an arranging). In fact, the recent discovery of 3.2 billion year old microfossils of bacteria from deep-water marine rocks found in what is now

Australia supports the idea of a high-temperature origin of life on the deep ocean floor in the absence of light.

Photosynthesis and Respiration   Eventually, more complex single-celled autotrophs evolved. They developed a green pigment called *chlorophyll* (*chloro* = green, *phyll* = leaf), which captures the Sun's energy through **photosynthesis** (*photo* = light, *syn* = with, *thesis* = an arranging). In photosynthesis (Figure 10, *top*), plants capture light energy and store it as sugars. A chemical reaction in which energy is captured or absorbed is said to be *endothermic* (*endo* = inside, *thermo* = heat). In **respiration** (*respir* = to breathe) (Figure 10, *middle*), the sugars are oxidized with oxygen so their stored energy can be used to carry on the life processes of the plant or the animal that eats the plant. A chemical reaction that releases energy is said to be *exothermic* (*exo* = outside, *thermo* = heat).

Not only are photosynthesis and respiration chemically opposite processes, but they are also complementary because the products of photosynthesis (sugars and oxygen) are used during respiration and the products of respiration (water and carbon dioxide) are used in photosynthesis (Figure 10, *bottom*). Thus, autotrophs (algae and plants) and heterotrophs (most bacteria and animals) have developed a mutual need for each other.

The first photosynthesizers were probably similar to modern sulfur bacteria that use hydrogen sulfide as a source of hydrogen and carbon dioxide as a carbon source. Both of these compounds were abundant in Earth's early atmosphere and in the primordial soup (early ocean). The waste product of these photosynthe-

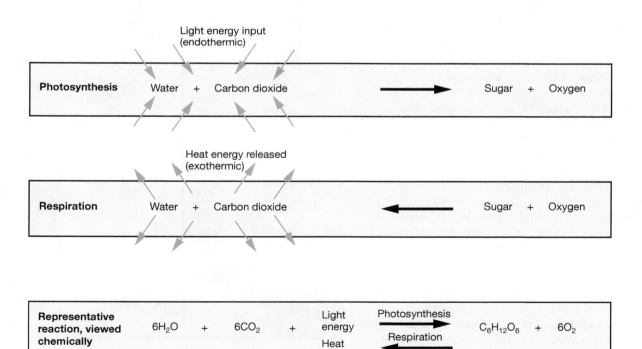

Figure 10 Photosynthesis (*top*), respiration (*middle*), and representative reactions viewed chemically (*bottom*).

sizing reactions is pure solid sulfur, which is excreted harmlessly by the organism. At some point, however, autotrophs evolved that could use water as a source of hydrogen. These organisms, ancestors of modern **cyanobacteria** (*kuanos* = dark blue), had a great advantage in that water was abundant everywhere. Just as the splitting of hydrogen sulfide produced sulfur as a waste product, the waste product of those reactions was free oxygen, which was toxic to many organisms.

What is the oldest evidence on Earth of photosynthesis? Rocks found in Greenland and dated at 3.8 billion years contain somewhat ambiguous chemical evidence that could have belonged to photosynthetic bacteria. Unfortunately, fossils from these rocks are not present, either because the rocks initially lacked fossils or because rocks this old have been so extensively altered. The oldest unequivocal evidence for primitive photosynthetic bacteria comes from fossilized remains of organisms recovered from rocks in northwestern Australia that formed on the sea floor 3.465 billion years ago (Figure 11). Some of these fossils resemble cyanobacteria, others resemble *coccoidal* (*coccus* = berry, *eidos* = like) *bacteria*, and some even look as if they were preserved in the act of dividing! Certainly, by 3.5 billion years ago, photosynthetic life was flourishing.

However, the oldest rocks containing iron oxide (rust)—an indicator of an oxygen-rich atmosphere—do not appear until about 2 billion years ago. Thus, photosynthetic organisms took at least 1.5 billion years to develop and begin producing abundant free oxygen in the atmosphere (Figure 12). At the same time, when a large amount of oxygen-rich (ferric) iron sank to the base of the mantle, it may have been heated by the core, risen as a plume to the ocean floor, and began releasing large amounts of oxygen about 2.5 billion years ago.

The Oxygen Crisis For anaerobic bacteria that had grown successfully in an oxygen-free world, all this oxygen was nothing short of a catastrophe! The increased atmospheric oxygen caused the ozone concentration in the upper atmosphere to build up, thereby shielding Earth's surface from ultraviolet radiation—and effectively eliminating anaerobic bacteria's food supply of organic molecules in the primordial soup. In addition, oxygen (particularly in the presence of light) is highly reactive with organic matter. When anaerobic bacteria are exposed to toxic oxygen and light, they are killed instantaneously. By 1.8 billion years ago, the atmosphere's oxygen content had increased to such a high level that it began causing the extinction of many anaerobic organisms. Nonetheless, descendants of such bacteria survive on Earth today in isolated microenvironments that are dark and free of oxygen, such as deep in soil or rocks, in garbage, and inside other organisms.

Cyanobacteria, however, evolved to exploit this new high oxygen environment. A metabolic pathway evolved that enabled these organisms to use oxygen to release energy from organic matter. They were the first organisms with the capacity for **aerobic** (*aero* = air) **respiration**; up until that time, respiration was strictly anaerobic. Because oxygen is so reactive with organic matter compared with the compounds metabolized in anaerobic respiration, it also yields much more energy. Compared with anaerobic respiration, aerobic respiration yields nearly *20 times* more energy—a fact that has led to its widespread use on Earth.

In early cyanobacteria, the same structures were used in photosynthesis and respiration, with photosynthesis occurring during the day and respiration occurring at night. Modern algae and plants can carry on both processes simultaneously because their cells have separate structures for the two processes: **mitochondria** (*mitos* = thread, *khondros* = grain) for respiration and **plastids** (*plastos* = molded) for photosynthesis. Mitochondria are also the site of respiration in animal cells, but those cells lack plastids and cannot synthesize organic matter. Although modern cells are much more complex than the cells of the cyanobacteria and their early contemporaries, the first critical steps in their design likely occurred at this time in Earth's history as a result of the oxygen crisis.

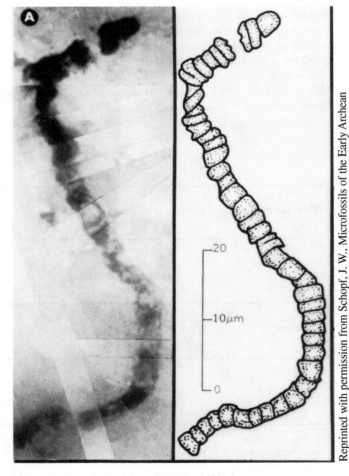

Reprinted with permission from Schopf, J. W., Microfossils of the Early Archean Apex Chert: New Evidence of the Antiquity of Life, Science 260:5108, 640–646. © 1993 American Association for the Advancement of Science

Figure 11 Earth's oldest fossilized life form.

Photomicrograph of fossilized bacteria (*left*) with interpretive drawing (*right*) from 3.465 billion year old rocks in northwestern Australia. Scale is in microns.

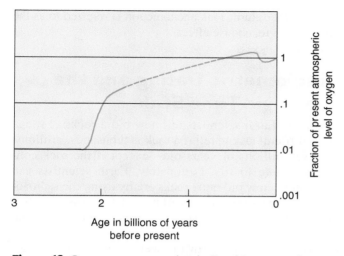

Figure 12 Oxygen concentration in Earth's atmosphere.

Concentration of atmospheric oxygen over the past 3 billion years based on data from geochemical and fossil evidence. The steep rise in oxygen about 2 billion years ago indicates the advent of photosynthesis. Dashed part of the curve indicates uncertainty.

Multicellular Life and Symbiosis

The earliest living organisms were **prokaryotic** (*pro* = before, *karuotos* = nuts) **cells**, which consisted of a single cell with no central nucleus and no internal membrane; as a result, the genetic material was loose within the cell. On the other hand, **eukaryotic** (*eu* = good, *karuotos* = nuts) **cells**, including modern plant and animal cells, contain membrane-bound nuclei, have complex membrane systems, and possess other intracellular bodies such as mitochondria and plastids. The central nucleus contains the genetic material of the cell, which is tightly coiled into structures called *chromosomes* (*khroma* = color, *soma* = a body). The oldest preserved eukaryotic cells are from single–celled organisms that lived about 1.4 to 1.6 billion years ago.

Remarkably, there seem to be no transitional forms between prokaryotic and eukaryotic cells. This fact and other chemical and genetic evidence have led evolutionary biologists to suggest that eukaryotic cells began as cooperative interactions between groups of bacteria. Mitochondria, for example, may have begun as predatory, oxygen-respiring bacteria that ate their hosts from the inside out. Eventually, these bacteria survived within their host without killing it and, at the same time, the host had the advantage of utilizing their metabolic byproducts as food. Similarly, plastids may have been photosynthesizing bacteria that were ingested by larger organisms and ended up surviving within the host and providing it with new organic matter as food. A relationship in which two or more organisms associate in a way that benefits at least one of them is called **symbiosis** (*sym* = together, *bios* = life). Symbiosis is such a successful adaptation that it is still employed today by many organisms.

How did symbiosis begin? Prokaryotic cells undergo simple division in order to reproduce. Sometimes, the division is incomplete and two cells remain attached to each other.[6] Scientists think that "mistakes" of this sort led to prokaryotic and eukaryotic multicellular organisms. With these colonial arrangements, member cells could become specialized for specific tasks, such as locomotion, sensing, photosynthesis, respiration, or reproduction. Another possibility is that primitive cells took up other cells initially as food but, instead of digesting them, the food provided other benefits to the host, so the host and the "food" entered into a symbiotic relationship. In addition, the swapping of single or multiple genes between organisms—called *lateral gene transfer*—could have provided organisms with new specialized traits that enabled them to succeed in their environment.

Moreover, eukaryotic cell colonies proved to be such an advantageous lifestyle that by about 1 billion years ago, all sorts of new eukaryotic organisms emerged. By 700 million years ago, numerous types of complex, multicellular, soft-bodied animals existed, which are the predecessors of all modern life that exists today.

Evolution and Natural Selection

Every living organism that inhabits Earth today is the result of **evolution** by the process of **natural selection** that has been going on since these early times. Evolution is the theory that groups of organisms adapt and change with the passage of time. Descendants differ morphologically and physiologically from their ancestors. Certain advantageous traits are naturally selected and passed on from one generation to the next. Evolution is the process by which various **species** (*species* = a kind) have been able to inhabit increasingly numerous environments on Earth.

As species adapted to Earth's various environments, they also modified the environments in which they lived. For example, when plants emerged from the oceans and inhabited the land, they changed it from a harsh and bleak landscape (much like the Moon's surface today) to one that was green and lush. The ocean changed, too, as vast quantities of dead organisms accumulated on the sea floor. Some of these accumulations have been turned into rock and uplifted onto continents, sometimes at high elevations. Because these rocks formed on the sea floor, there is much to be learned about the oceans of the past by studying them.

Changes to Earth's Environment

The development and successful evolution of photosynthetic organisms is greatly responsible for the world as

---

[6]Life forms in which a number of similar cells live attached together are called *colonies*.

we know it today (Figure 13). These organisms reduced the amount of carbon dioxide in the early atmosphere from relatively high levels to 0.037% today. At the same time, they increased the amount of free oxygen in the early atmosphere from very low levels to 21% today. The increasing level of oxygen, in turn, made it possible for most present-day animals to develop.

The remains of ancient plants and animals buried in oxygen-free environments have become the oil, natural gas, and coal deposits of today. These so-called *fossil fuels* provide over 90% of the energy currently used to power modern society. Humans depend not only on the food energy stored in today's plants but also on the energy stored in plants during the geologic past.

Because of increased burning of fossil fuels for home heating, industry, power generation, and transportation during the industrial age, the atmospheric concentration of carbon dioxide and other gases that help warm the atmosphere has increased, too. Many people are concerned that increased global warming will cause serious prob-

lems in the future. This phenomenon is referred to as the increased greenhouse effect.

Radiometric Dating and the Geologic Time Scale

How can Earth scientists tell how old a rock is? It can be a difficult task to tell if a rock is thousands, millions, or even billions of years old—except if the rock contains telltale fossils. Fortunately, Earth scientists can determine how old most rocks are by using the radioactive materials contained within rocks. In essence, this technique involves reading a rock's internal "rock clock."

Most rocks on Earth (as well as those from outer space) contain small amounts of radioactive materials such as uranium, thorium, and potassium. These radioactive materials spontaneously break apart or decay into atoms of other elements at predictable rates.

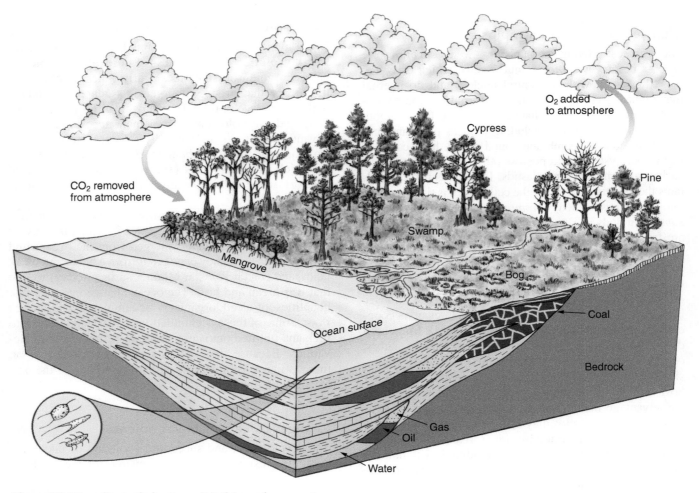

Figure 13 The effect of plants on Earth's environment.

As microscopic photosynthetic cells (*inset*) became established in the ocean, Earth's atmosphere was enriched in oxygen and depleted in carbon dioxide. As organisms died and accumulated on the ocean floor, some of their remains were converted to oil and gas. The same process occurred on land, sometimes producing coal.

Radioactive materials have a characteristic *half-life*, which is the time required for one-half of the atoms in a sample to decay to other atoms. The older the rock is, the more radioactive material will have been converted to decay product. Of course, this method works only if there is a *closed system*: that is, no decay product atoms are lost or gained, and the decay product atoms are clearly discernable from other atoms of the same element. Analytical instruments can accurately measure the amount of radioactive material and the amount of resulting decay product in rocks. By comparing these two quantities and knowing the rate of decay for a radioactive element, the age of the rock can thus be determined. Such dating is referred to as **radiometric** (*radio* = radioactivity, *metri* = measure) **age dating** and is an extremely powerful tool for determining the age of rocks.

For example, Figure 14 shows two locations where rocks contain small amounts of a particular type of radioactive uranium, which has a half-life of 713 million years and decays to a stable form of lead. Measurements at Location A indicate that half of the radioactive uranium has been converted to lead, its decay product. Thus, one half-life has elapsed and the rock is 713 million years old. At Location B, three-quarters of the original radioactive material has converted to its decay product, so the rock here must be older than that at Location A.

Two half-lives have elapsed and the rock is 1426 million (1.4 billion) years old. Using this method, hundreds of thousands of rock samples have been age dated from around the world.

The ages of rocks on Earth and the names of the geologic time periods are shown in the **geologic time scale** (Figure 15; see also Box 2). Initially, the divisions between geologic periods were based on major extinction episodes as recorded in the fossil record. As radiometric age dates became available, they were also included on the geologic time scale.

The time scale indicates Earth is 4.6 billion years old. The oldest known intact rocks on Earth, located in northwestern Canada, are 3.96 billion years old. In western Australia, however, geologists have recently discovered a 4.4 billion-year-old mineral fragment trapped within another rock. Starting with the origin of the first single-celled organisms about 3.5 billion years ago, the geologic time scale also shows important advances in the development of life forms on Earth.

> Earth scientists can accurately determine the age of most rocks by analyzing their radioactive components, some of which indicate that Earth is 4.6 billion years old.

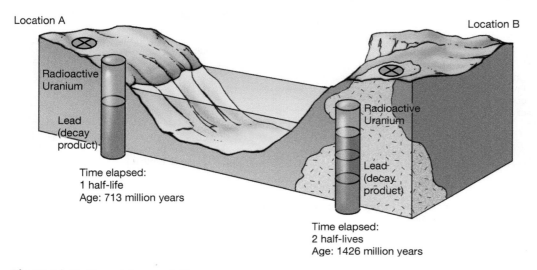

Figure 14 Radiometric age dating.

Locations A and B contain rocks with radioactive uranium that has a half-life of 713 million years and decays to lead. At Location A, one-half of the radioactive uranium has converted to lead, indicating that one half-life has elapsed so the rocks are 713 million years old. At Location B, three-quarters of the radioactive uranium has converted to lead, indicating that two half-lives have elapsed and that the rocks are 1426 million (1.4 billion) years old.

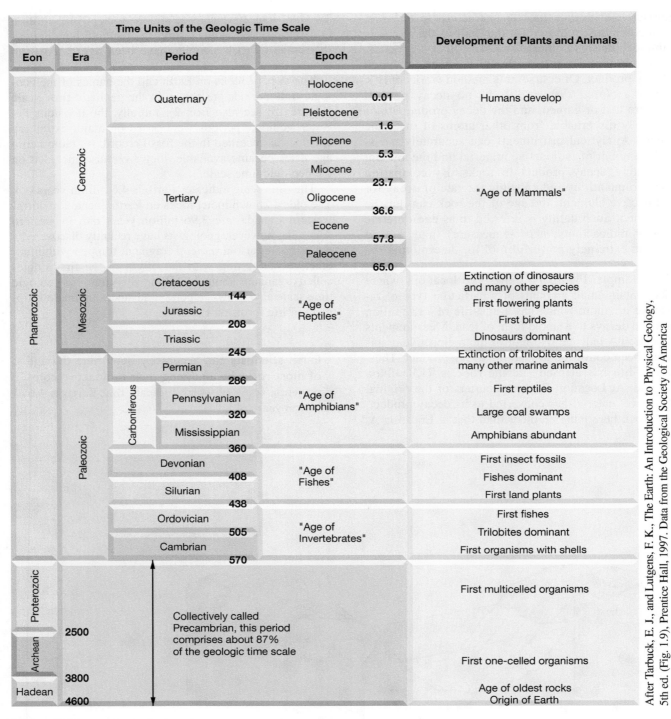

Figure 15 The geologic time scale.

Numbers on the time scale represent time in millions of years before the present; significant advances
in the development of plants and animals on Earth are also shown.

After Tarbuck, E. J., and Lutgens, F. K., The Earth: An Introduction to Physical Geology,
5th ed. (Fig. 1.9), Prentice Hall, 1997. Data from the Geological Society of America

BOX 2 Historical Feature
"DEEP" TIME

The time line of Earth history shown in Figure 2B indicates that Earth is 4.6 billion years old. It is difficult to comprehend how old Earth is, however, because 4.6 billion (that's 4600 million, or 4,600,000,000) is so enormous. To gain some idea of the immensity of a number in the billions, how high would a stack of one billion fresh one-dollar bills be (Table 2A)?

The problem with an example such as this is that the mind becomes immune to comprehending such large amounts of money—or any such large numbers. For instance, how long would it take to count to 4.6 billion if you counted one number every second for 24 hours a day, seven days a week, 365 days a year? The answer can be easily calculated, remembering that there are 60 seconds in a minute and 60 minutes in an hour. The rather surprising answer is given at the end of the Box if you need help.

TABLE 2A **Thickness of stacks of fresh one-dollar bills.**

Thickness of a stack of ...	Would be ...
100 fresh one-dollar bills	1 centimeter (0.4 inch) high
1000 fresh one-dollar bills	10 centimeters (4 inches) high
1,000,000 (one million) fresh one-dollar bills	100 meters (330 feet) high
1,000,000,000 (one billion) fresh one-dollar bills	100 kilometers (62 miles) high

Another way to try to visualize the enormity of geologic time is by representing its entirety with a roll of toilet paper.[7] If you use a standard 500-sheet roll and round off the age of Earth to 5 billion years, then each sheet on the roll represents 10 million years. As you unroll the paper, keep in mind that you are progressing through all of geologic time and that the last sheet on the roll (the last 10 million years) is about four times longer than the time humans have existed on Earth. In fact, all of recorded human history is represented by the last $1/2000$th of a sheet, and a long human lifetime of 100 years is only $1/100,000$th of a sheet! It is indeed humbling to realize how insignificant the length of time human existence on Earth has been.

Can one really imagine the space taken up by $1 billion, or the lifetimes it would take to count to 4.6 billion, or how many sheets of toilet paper have gone by in 4.6 billion years of Earth history? The same scale problem exists with visualizing millions or billions of years, often called "deep" time or geologic time. But keep trying, and maybe someday you will get a glimpse into the huge expanse of time represented by the geologic time scale. It will amaze you.

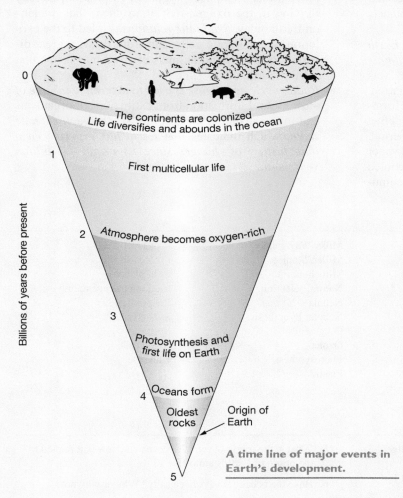

Billions of years before present

0
The continents are colonized
Life diversifies and abounds in the ocean

1
First multicellular life

2
Atmosphere becomes oxygen-rich

3
Photosynthesis and first life on Earth

4
Oceans form
Oldest rocks
Origin of Earth

5

A time line of major events in Earth's development.

Answer to question posed above: 4.6 billion seconds corresponds to 145.9 years (which amounts to about two human lifetimes!).

[7]Toilet paper has many advantages: It is something with which most people are familiar, it is inexpensive and readily available, it is long and linear (like geologic time), and it is even perforated into individual sheets.

Chapter in Review

- *Our galaxy, the Milky Way galaxy, is composed of numerous stars and is one of countless galaxies in the universe.* Galaxies are thought to be accumulations of debris from the *big bang*, the explosion that formed the universe about 13.7 billion years ago. Stars result from accumulation of gaseous masses that collapsed in on themselves, resulting in internal temperatures and pressures extreme enough to set off *fusion reactions*, burning hydrogen to produce helium. Stars give rise to heavier elements by successive expansions and contractions.

- *Our solar system, consisting of the Sun and nine planets, most likely formed from a huge cloud of gas and space dust called a nebula.* According to the *nebular hypothesis*, the nebular matter contracted to form the Sun, and the planets were formed from eddies of material that remained. The Sun, composed of hydrogen and helium, was massive enough and concentrated enough to emit large amounts of energy. The Sun also emitted ionized particles that swept away any nebular gas that remained from the formation of the planets and their satellites.

- *The Protoearth, more massive and larger than Earth today, was molten and homogenous.* The *initial atmosphere*, composed mostly of hydrogen and helium, was later driven off into space by intense solar radiation. The Protoearth began a period of rearrangement, forming a layered structure of core, mantle, and crust through *density stratification*. Also during this period, *outgassing* produced an early atmosphere rich in water vapor and carbon dioxide. Once Earth's surface cooled sufficiently, the water vapor condensed and accumu-

lated to give Earth its oceans. Rainfall on the surface dissolved compounds that, when carried to the ocean, made it salty.

- *Life is thought to have begun in the oceans.* Ultraviolet radiation from the Sun and hydrogen, carbon dioxide, methane, ammonia, and inorganic molecules from the oceans may have combined to produce carbon-containing molecules. Certain combinations of these molecules eventually produced *heterotrophic organisms* (which cannot make their own food) that were probably similar to present-day anaerobic bacteria. Eventually, *autotrophs evolved* that had the ability to make their own food through *chemosynthesis*. Later, some cells developed chlorophyll, which *made photosynthesis possible* and led to the development of plants.

- *Photosynthetic organisms altered the environment* by extracting carbon dioxide from the atmosphere and also by releasing free oxygen, which was lethal to many existing organisms. Eventually, *organisms evolved* that could use oxygen for respiration, thereby thriving in the oxygen-rich atmosphere that remains on Earth today. *Symbiotic relationships* led to the evolution of eukaryotic cells, and from these, a great diversity of plants and animals evolved into forms that inhabit Earth today.

- *Radiometric age dating is used to determine the age of most rocks.* Information from extinctions of organisms and from age dating rocks comprises the *geologic time scale*, which indicates that *Earth has experienced a long history of changes since its origin 4.6 billion years ago.*

Key Terms

Aerobic respiration	Eukaryotic cell	Milky Way galaxy	Prokaryotic cell
Anaerobic bacteria	Evolution	Miller, Stanley	Protoearth
Autotroph	Excess volatile	Mitochondria	Protoplanet
Big Bang theory	Fusion reaction	Natural selection	Radiometric age dating
Chemosynthesis	Galaxy	Nebula	Respiration
Core	Geologic time scale	Nebular hypothesis	Solar system
Crust	Heterotroph	Outgassing	Species
Cyanobacteria	Hydrothermal vent	Ozone	Symbiosis
Density	Light-year	Photosynthesis	Universe
Density stratification	Mantle	Plastid	

Questions and Exercises

1. How do the observed motions of galaxies support the big bang theory?
2. Discuss the origin of the solar system using the nebular hypothesis.
3. How was the Protoearth different from today's Earth?
4. What is density stratification, and how did it change the Protoearth?
5. What is the origin of Earth's oceans and how is it related to the origin of Earth's atmosphere?
6. Have the oceans always been salty? Why or why not?
7. Describe some basic characteristics of living things and list the order in which they evolved.

8. How does the presence of oxygen (O_2) in our atmosphere help reduce the amount of ultraviolet radiation that reaches Earth's surface?

9. What was Stanley Miller's experiment, and what did it help demonstrate?

10. Discuss photosynthesis and respiration, and explain their relationship to the chemical processes of storing and releasing energy by organisms.

11. As plants evolved on Earth, great changes in Earth's environment were produced. Describe some of the major changes caused by plants.

12. Earth has had three atmospheres (initial, early, and present). Describe the composition and origin of each one.

13. What events must have occurred for life to evolve?

14. Construct a representation of the geologic time scale, using an appropriate quantity of any substance (other than dollar bills or toilet paper). Be sure to indicate some of the major changes that have occurred on Earth since its origin.

MINERALS
BUILDING BLOCKS
OF ROCKS

From Chapter 1 of *Foundations of Earth Science*, Sixth Edition, Frederick K. Lutgens, Edward J. Tarbuck, Dennis Tasa.

MINERALS
BUILDING BLOCKS OF ROCKS

To assist you in learning the important concepts in this chapter, you will find it helpful to focus on the following questions:

1. What are minerals, and how are they different from rocks?

2. What are the smallest particles of matter? How do atoms bond?

3. How do isotopes of the same element vary, and why are some isotopes radioactive?

4. What are some of the physical and chemical properties of minerals? How can these properties be used to distinguish one mineral from another?

5. What are the eight elements that make up most of Earth's continental crust?

6. What is the most abundant mineral group? What do all minerals within this group have in common?

7. When is the term *ore* used with reference to a mineral? What are the common ores of iron and lead?

Crystal shape or habit is a basic mineral property. (Photo by Jeffry Scovil)

Earth's crust and oceans are the source of a wide variety of useful and essential minerals. Most people are familiar with the common uses of many basic metals, including aluminum in beverage cans, copper in electrical wiring, and gold and silver in jewelry. But some people are not aware that pencil lead contains the greasy-feeling mineral graphite and that bath powders and many cosmetics contain the mineral talc. Moreover, many do not know that drill bits impregnated with diamonds are employed by dentists to drill through tooth enamel, or that the common mineral quartz is the source of silicon for computer chips. In fact, practically every manufactured product contains materials obtained from minerals. As the mineral requirements of modern society increase, the task of locating new sources of useful minerals becomes more challenging.

In addition to the economic uses of rocks and minerals, all of the processes studied by geologists are in some way dependent on the properties of these basic Earth materials. Events such as volcanic eruptions, mountain building, weathering and erosion, and even earthquakes involve rocks and minerals. Consequently, a basic knowledge of rocks and minerals is essential to the understanding of all geologic phenomena.

MINERALS: BUILDING BLOCKS OF ROCKS

GEODe
EARTH SCIENCE

Earth Materials
▼ Minerals

We begin our discussion of Earth materials with an overview of **mineralogy** (*mineral* = mineral, *ology* = the

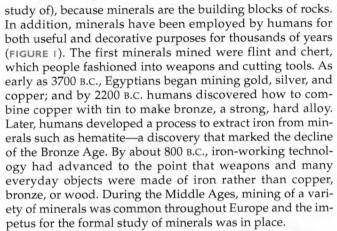

FIGURE 1 Collection of well-developed quartz crystals found near Hot Springs, Arkansas. (Photo by Jeff Scovil)

study of), because minerals are the building blocks of rocks. In addition, minerals have been employed by humans for both useful and decorative purposes for thousands of years (**FIGURE 1**). The first minerals mined were flint and chert, which people fashioned into weapons and cutting tools. As early as 3700 B.C., Egyptians began mining gold, silver, and copper; and by 2200 B.C. humans discovered how to combine copper with tin to make bronze, a strong, hard alloy. Later, humans developed a process to extract iron from minerals such as hematite—a discovery that marked the decline of the Bronze Age. By about 800 B.C., iron-working technology had advanced to the point that weapons and many everyday objects were made of iron rather than copper, bronze, or wood. During the Middle Ages, mining of a variety of minerals was common throughout Europe and the impetus for the formal study of minerals was in place.

The term *mineral* is used in several different ways. For example, those concerned with health and fitness extol the benefits of vitamins and minerals. The mining industry typically uses the word when referring to anything taken out of the ground, such as coal, iron ore, or sand and gravel. The guessing game known as *Twenty Questions* usually begins with the question, *Is it animal, vegetable, or mineral?* What criteria do geologists use to determine whether something is a mineral?

Geologists define **minerals** as *any naturally occurring inorganic solid that possesses an orderly crystalline structure and a well-defined chemical composition.* Thus, those Earth materials that are classified as minerals exhibit the following characteristics:

1. **Naturally occurring.** Minerals form by natural, geologic processes. Synthetic materials, meaning those produced in a laboratory or by human intervention, are not considered minerals.

2. **Solid substance.** Minerals are solids within the temperature ranges normally experienced at Earth's surface. For example, ice (frozen water) is considered a mineral, whereas liquid water and water vapor are not.

3. **Orderly crystalline structure.** Minerals are crystalline substances, which means their atoms are arranged in an orderly, repetitive manner (**FIGURE 2**). This orderly packing of atoms is reflected in the regularly shaped objects we call crystals. Some naturally occurring solids, such as volcanic glass (obsidian), lack a repetitive atomic structure and are not considered minerals.

4. **Well-defined chemical composition.** Most minerals are chemical compounds having compositions expressed by chemical formulas. In nature, however, it is not uncommon for some atoms within a crystal structure to be replaced by others of similar size without changing the internal structure or properties

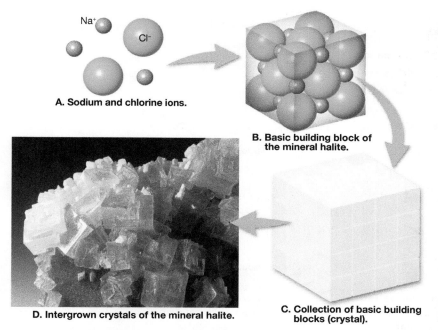

A. Sodium and chlorine ions.

B. Basic building block of the mineral halite.

C. Collection of basic building blocks (crystal).

D. Intergrown crystals of the mineral halite.

FIGURE 2 Illustration of the orderly arrangement of sodium and chloride atoms (ions) in the mineral halite. The arrangement of atoms into basic building blocks having a cubic shape results in regularly shaped cubic crystals. (Photo by Dennis Tasa)

crystalline solid like salt but which comes from sugarcane or sugar beets, is a common example of such an organic compound. However, many marine animals secrete inorganic compounds, such as calcium carbonate (calcite), in the form of shells and coral reefs. If these materials are buried and become part of the rock record, they are considered minerals by geologists.

In contrast to minerals, rocks are more loosely defined. Simply, a **rock** is any solid mass of mineral, or mineral-like, matter that occurs naturally as part of our planet. Some rocks are composed almost entirely of one mineral. A common example is the sedimentary rock *limestone,* which consists of impure masses of the mineral calcite. However, most rocks, like the common rock granite shown in **FIGURE 3**, occur as aggregates of several different minerals. The term *aggregate* implies that the minerals are joined in such a way that their individual properties are retained. Note that the mineral constituents of granite can be easily identified (Figure 3).

Some rocks are composed of nonmineral matter. These include the volcanic rocks *obsidian* and *pumice,* which are noncrystalline glassy substances, and *coal,* which consists of solid organic debris.

Although this chapter deals primarily with the nature of minerals, keep in mind that most rocks are simply aggregates of minerals. Because the properties of rocks are determined largely by the chemical composition and

of that mineral. Therefore, the chemical compositions of minerals may vary, but they do so *within specific, well-defined limits.*

5. **Generally inorganic.** Inorganic crystalline solids, such as ordinary table salt (halite), that are found naturally in the ground are considered minerals. Organic compounds, on the other hand, are generally not. Sugar, a

Granite
(Rock)

Quartz
(Mineral)

Hornblende
(Mineral)

Feldspar
(Mineral)

FIGURE 3 Most rocks are aggregates of one or more minerals. Shown here is a hand sample of the igneous rock granite and three of its major constituent minerals. (Photos courtesy E. J. Tarbuck)

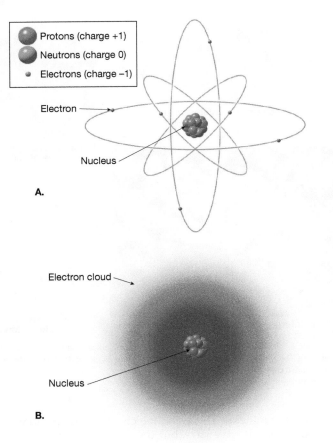

FIGURE 4 Two models of the atom. **A.** This simplified view of an atom has a central nucleus, consisting of protons and neutrons, encircled by high-speed electrons. **B.** Another model of an atom showing spherically shaped electron clouds (principal shells). Note that these models are not drawn to scale. Electrons are minuscule in size compared to protons and neutrons, and the relative space between the nucleus and electron shells is much greater than illustrated.

crystalline structure of the minerals contained within them, we will consider these Earth materials.

ATOMS: BUILDING BLOCKS OF MINERALS

When minerals are carefully examined, even under optical microscopes, the innumerable tiny particles of their internal structures are not discernable. Nevertheless, all matter, including minerals, is composed of minute building blocks called **atoms**—the smallest particles that cannot be chemically split. Atoms, in turn contain even smaller particles—*protons* and *neutrons* located in a central **nucleus** that is surrounded by *electrons* (**FIGURE 4**).

Properties of Protons, Neutrons, and Electrons

Protons and **neutrons** are very dense particles with almost identical masses. By contrast, **electrons** have a negligible mass, about 1/2000th that of a proton. For comparison, if a proton or a neutron had the mass of a baseball, an electron would have the mass of a single grain of rice.

Both protons and electrons share a fundamental property called *electrical charge*. Protons have an electrical charge of +1 and electrons have a charge of −1. Neutrons, as the name suggests, have no charge. The charge of protons and electrons are equal in magnitude, but opposite in polarity, so when these two particles are paired, the charges cancel each other. Since matter typically contains equal numbers of positively charged protons and negatively charged electrons, most substances are electrically neutral.

In illustrations, electrons are sometimes shown orbiting the nucleus in a manner that resembles the planets of our solar system orbiting the Sun (**FIGURE 4A**). However, electrons do not actually behave this way. A more realistic depiction shows electrons as a cloud of negative charges surrounding the nucleus (**FIGURE 4B**). Studies of the arrangements of electrons show that they move about the nucleus in regions called *principal shells*, each with an associated energy level. In addition, each shell can hold a specific number of electrons, with the outermost shell containing **valence electrons** that interact with other atoms to form chemical bonds.

Most of the atoms in the universe (except hydrogen and helium) were created inside massive stars by nuclear fusion and released into interstellar space during hot, fiery supernova explosions. As this ejected material cooled, the newly formed nuclei attracted electrons to complete their atomic structure. At the temperatures found at Earth's surface, all free atoms (not bonded to other atoms) have a full complement of electrons—one for each proton in the nucleus.

Elements: Defined by Their Number of Protons

The simplest atoms have only one proton in their nuclei whereas others have more than 100. The number of protons in the nucleus of an atom, called the **atomic number,** determines

Tendency to
lose outermost
electrons
to uncover full
outer shell

Noble
gases
(inert)

Tendency to fill
outer shell by
sharing electrons

Tendency
to gain
electrons
to make full
outer shell

Atomic number
Symbol of element
Atomic weight
Name of element

| 2 |
| He |
| 4.003 |
| Helium |

Metals
Transition metals
Nonmetals
Noble gases
Lanthanide series
Actinide series

VIII A

| 1 |
| H |
| 1.0080 |
| Hydrogen |

| 2 |
| He |
| 4.003 |
| Helium |

I A

II A

Tendency to lose electrons

III A IV A V A VI A VII A

3	4
Li	Be
6.939	9.012
Lithium	Beryllium

5	6	7	8	9	10
B	C	N	O	F	Ne
10.81	12.011	14.007	15.9994	18.998	20.183
Boron	Carbon	Nitrogen	Oxygen	Fluorine	Neon

11	12
Na	Mg
22.990	24.31
Sodium	Magnesium

III B IV B V B VI B VII B ⎯⎯ VIII B ⎯⎯ I B II B

13	14	15	16	17	18
Al	Si	P	S	Cl	Ar
26.98	28.09	30.974	32.064	35.453	39.948
Aluminum	Silicon	Phosphorus	Sulfur	Chlorine	Argon

19	20	21	22	23	24	25	26	27	28	29	30	31	32	33	34	35	36
K	Ca	Sc	Ti	V	Cr	Mn	Fe	Co	Ni	Cu	Zn	Ga	Ge	As	Se	Br	Kr
39.102	40.08	44.96	47.90	50.94	52.00	54.94	55.85	58.93	58.71	63.54	65.37	69.72	72.59	74.92	78.96	79.909	83.80
Potassium	Calcium	Scandium	Titanium	Vanadium	Chromium	Manganese	Iron	Cobalt	Nickel	Copper	Zinc	Gallium	Germanium	Arsenic	Selenium	Bromine	Krypton

37	38	39	40	41	42	43	44	45	46	47	48	49	50	51	52	53	54
Rb	Sr	Y	Zr	Nb	Mo	Tc	Ru	Rh	Pd	Ag	Cd	In	Sn	Sb	Te	I	Xe
85.47	87.62	88.91	91.22	92.91	95.94	(99)	101.1	102.90	106.4	107.87	112.40	114.82	118.69	121.75	127.60	126.90	131.30
Rubidium	Strontium	Yttrium	Zirconium	Niobium	Molybdenum	Technetium	Ruthenium	Rhodium	Palladium	Silver	Cadmium	Indium	Tin	Antimony	Tellurium	Iodine	Xenon

55	56	57 TO 71	72	73	74	75	76	77	78	79	80	81	82	83	84	85	86
Cs	Ba		Hf	Ta	W	Re	Os	Ir	Pt	Au	Hg	Tl	Pb	Bi	Po	At	Rn
132.91	137.34		178.49	180.95	183.85	186.2	190.2	192.2	195.09	197.0	200.59	204.37	207.19	208.98	(210)	(210)	(222)
Cesium	Barium		Hafnium	Tantalum	Tungsten	Rhenium	Osmium	Iridium	Platinum	Gold	Mercury	Thallium	Lead	Bismuth	Polonium	Astatine	Radon

87	88	89 TO 103
Fr	Ra	
(223)	226.05	
Francium	Radium	

57	58	59	60	61	62	63	64	65	66	67	68	69	70	71
La	Ce	Pr	Nd	Pm	Sm	Eu	Gd	Tb	Dy	Ho	Er	Tm	Yb	Lu
138.91	140.12	140.91	144.24	(147)	150.35	151.96	157.25	158.92	162.50	164.93	167.26	168.93	173.04	174.97
Lanthanum	Cerium	Praseodymium	Neodymium	Promethium	Samarium	Europium	Gadolinium	Terbium	Dysprosium	Holmium	Erbium	Thulium	Ytterbium	Lutetium

89	90	91	92	93	94	95	96	97	98	99	100	101	102	103
Ac	Th	Pa	U	Np	Pu	Am	Cm	Bk	Cf	Es	Fm	Md	No	Lw
(227)	232.04	(231)	238.03	(237)	(242)	(243)	(247)	(249)	(251)	(254)	(253)	(256)	(254)	(257)
Actinium	Thorium	Protactinium	Uranium	Neptunium	Plutonium	Americium	Curium	Berkelium	Californium	Einsteinium	Fermium	Mendelevium	Nobelium	Lawrencium

FIGURE 5 Periodic table of the elements.

its chemical nature. All atoms with the same number of protons have the same chemical and physical properties. Together, a group of the same kind of atoms is called an **element**. There are about 90 naturally occurring elements and 23 that have been synthesized.

You are probably familiar with the names of many elements including copper, iron, oxygen, and carbon. Since the number of protons identifies an element, all carbon atoms have 6 protons and 6 electrons. Likewise, any atom that contains 8 protons is an oxygen atom.

Elements are organized so that those with similar properties line up in columns. This arrangement, called the **periodic table**, is shown in **FIGURE 5**. Each element has been assigned a one- or two-letter symbol. The atomic numbers and masses are also included for each element.

Atoms of the naturally occurring elements are the basic building blocks of Earth's minerals. A few minerals, such as native copper, diamonds, and gold, are made entirely of atoms of only one element (**FIGURE 6**). However, most elements tend to join with atoms of other elements to form **chemical compounds**. Most minerals are chemical compounds composed of atoms of two or more elements.

FIGURE 6 Gold mixed with quartz. Gold, silver, copper, and diamonds are naturally occurring minerals composed entirely of atoms of a single element.

DID YOU KNOW?

Although wood pulp is the main ingredient for making newsprint, many higher grades of paper contain large quantities of clay minerals. In fact, each page of this textbook consists of about 25 percent clay (the mineral kaolinite). If rolled into a ball, this much clay would be roughly the size of a tennis ball.

WHY ATOMS BOND

Except for a group of elements known as the noble gases, atoms bond to one another under the conditions (temperatures and pressures) that occur on Earth.* Some atoms bond to form *ionic compounds*, some form *molecules*, and still others form *metallic substances*. Why does this happen? Experiments show that electrical forces hold atoms together and bond them to each other. These electrical attractions lower the total energy of the bonded atoms, which, in turn, generally makes them more stable. Consequently, atoms that are bonded in compounds tend to be more stable than atoms that are free (not bonded).

As was noted earlier, valence (outer shell) electrons are generally involved in chemical bonding. FIGURE 7 shows a shorthand way of representing the number of valence electrons. Notice that the elements in Group I have one valence electron, those in Group II have two valence electrons, and so on up to eight valence electrons in Group VIII.

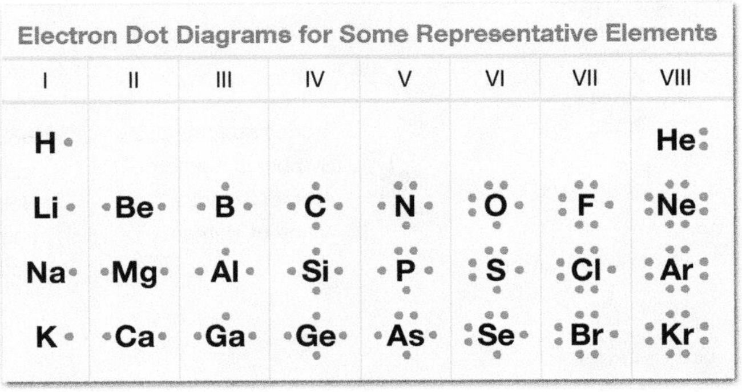

FIGURE 7 Dot diagrams for some representative elements. Each dot represents a valence electron found in the outermost principal shell.

Octet Rule

The noble gases (except helium) have very stable electron arrangements with eight valence electrons and, therefore, tend to lack chemical reactivity. Many other atoms gain, lose, or share electrons during chemical reactions to end up with electron arrangements of the noble gases. This observation led to a chemical guideline known as the **octet rule:** *Atoms tend to gain, lose, or share electrons until they are surrounded by eight valence electrons.* Although there are exceptions to the octet rule, it is a useful *rule of thumb* for understanding chemical bonding.

When an atom's outer shell does not contain eight electrons, it is likely to chemically bond to other atoms to fill its shell. A **chemical bond** is the transfer or sharing of electrons that allows each atom to attain a full valence shell of electrons. Some atoms do this by transferring all of their valence electrons to other atoms so that an inner shell becomes the full valence shell.

When the valence electrons are transferred between the elements to form ions, the bond is an *ionic bond*. When the electrons are shared between the atoms, the bond is a *covalent bond*. When the valence electrons are shared among all the atoms in a substance, the bonding is *metallic*. In any case, the bonding atoms get stable electron configurations, which usually consist of eight electrons in their outmost shells.

*Examples of noble gases are helium, neon, and argon. In each case, their outer shell of valence electrons is considered to be full and therefore they have little tendency to participate in chemical reactions.

Ionic Bonds: Electrons Transferred

Perhaps the easiest type of bond to visualize is the *ionic bond* in which one atom gives up one or more of its valence electrons to another atom to form **ions**—*positively and negatively charged atoms*. The atom that loses electrons becomes a positive ion, and the atom that gains electrons becomes a negative ion. Oppositely charged ions are strongly attracted to one another and join to form ionic compounds.

Consider the ionic bonding that occurs between sodium (Na) and chlorine (Cl) to produce sodium chloride, the mineral halite—common table salt. Notice in FIGURE 8A that sodium gives up its single valence electron to chlorine. As a result, sodium now has a stable configuration with eight electrons in its outermost shell. By acquiring the electron the sodium loses, chlorine—which has seven valence electrons—gains the eighth electron needed to complete its outermost shell. Thus, through the transfer of a single electron, both the sodium and chlorine atoms have acquired a stable electron configuration.

After electron transfer takes place, the atoms are no longer electrically neutral. By giving up one electron, a neutral sodium atom becomes positively charged (with 11 protons and 10 electrons). Similarly, by acquiring one electron, a neutral chlorine atom becomes negatively charged (with 17 protons and 18 electrons). We know that ions with like charges repel, and those with unlike charges attract. Thus, an **ionic bond** is the attraction of oppositely charged ions to one another, producing an electrically neutral compound.

FIGURE 8B illustrates the arrangement of sodium and chlorine ions in ordinary table salt. Notice that salt consists of alternating sodium and chlorine ions, positioned in such a manner that each positive ion is attracted to and sur-

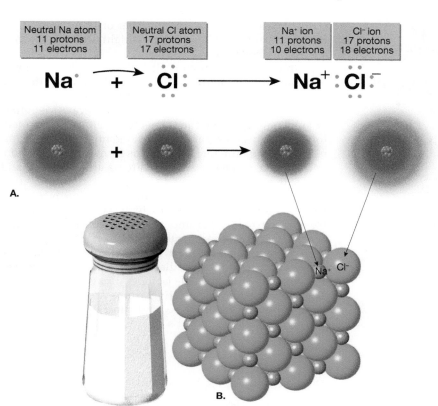

FIGURE 8 Chemical bonding of sodium chloride (table salt). **A.** Through the transfer of one electron in the outer shell of a sodium atom to the outer shell of a chlorine atom, the sodium becomes a positive ion and chlorine a negative ion. **B.** Diagram illustrating the arrangement of sodium and chlorine ions in table salt.

rounded on all sides by negative ions, and vice versa. This arrangement maximizes the attraction between ions with opposite charges while minimizing the repulsion between ions with identical charges. Thus, ionic compounds consist of an orderly arrangement of oppositely charged ions assembled in a definite ratio that provides overall electrical neutrality.

The properties of a chemical compound are dramatically different from the properties of the elements comprising it. For example, sodium is a soft silvery metal that is extremely reactive and poisonous. If you were to consume even a small amount of elemental sodium, you would need immediate medical attention. Chlorine, a green poisonous gas, is so toxic it was used as a chemical weapon during World War I. Together, however, these elements produce sodium chloride, a harmless flavor enhancer that we call table salt. When elements combine to form compounds, their properties change significantly.

Covalent Bonds: Electrons Shared

Sometimes the forces that hold atoms together cannot be understood on the basis of the attraction of oppositely charged ions. One example is the hydrogen molecule (H_2), in which the two hydrogen atoms are held together tightly and no ions are present. The strong attractive force that holds two hydrogen atoms together results from a **covalent bond**, *a chemical bond formed by the sharing of a pair of electrons between atoms.*

Imagine two hydrogen atoms (each with one proton and one electron) approaching one another so that their orbitals overlap (**FIGURE 9**). Once they meet, the electron configuration will change so that both electrons will mainly occupy the space between the atoms. In other words, the two electrons are shared by both hydrogen atoms and attracted simultaneously by the positive charge of the proton in the nucleus of each atom (Figure 9). The attraction between the electrons and both nuclei holds these atoms together. Although ions do not exist in hydrogen molecules, the force that holds these atoms together arises from the attraction of oppositely charged particles—protons in the nuclei and electrons shared by the atoms.

Metallic Bonds: Electrons Free to Move

In **metallic bonds**, the valence electrons are free to move from one atom to another so that all atoms share the available valence electrons. This type of bonding is found in metals such as copper, gold, aluminum, and silver, and in alloys such as brass and bronze. Metallic bonding accounts for the high electrical conductivity of metals, the ease with which metals are shaped, and numerous other special properties.

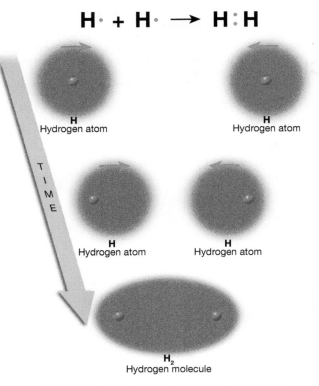

$$H \cdot + H \cdot \rightarrow H : H$$

Hydrogen atom   Hydrogen atom

Hydrogen atom   Hydrogen atom

H₂
Hydrogen molecule

FIGURE 9 Formation of a covalent bond between two hydrogen atoms (H) to form a hydrogen molecule (H_2). When hydrogen atoms bond, the electrons are shared by both hydrogen atoms and attracted simultaneously by the positive charge of the protons in the nucleus of each atom. The attraction between electrons and both nuclei holds (bonds) these atoms together.

DID YOU KNOW?

The purity of gold is expressed by the number of *karats*. Twenty-four karats is pure gold. Gold less than 24 karats is an alloy (mixture) of gold and another metal, usually copper or silver. For example, 14-karat gold contains 14 parts gold (by weight) mixed with 10 parts of other metals.

ISOTOPES AND RADIOACTIVE DECAY

The **mass number** of an atom is simply the total number of its protons and neutrons. All atoms of a particular element have the same number of protons, but may have varying numbers of neutrons. Atoms with the same number of protons, but different numbers of neutrons are **isotopes** of that element. Isotopes of the same element are labeled by placing the mass number after the element's name or symbol. For example, carbon has three well-known isotopes. One has a mass number of 12 (carbon-12), another has a mass number of 13 (carbon-13), and the third, carbon-14, has a mass number of 14. Since all atoms of the same element have the same number of protons, and carbon has six, carbon-12 also has

six neutrons to give it a mass number of 12. Carbon-14, on the other hand, has six protons plus eight neutrons to give it a mass number of 14.

In chemical behavior, all isotopes of the same element are nearly identical. To distinguish among them is like trying to differentiate identical twins, with one weighing slightly more than the other. Because isotopes of an element behave the same chemically, different isotopes often become parts of the same mineral. For example, when the mineral calcite forms from calcium, carbon, and oxygen, some of its carbon atoms are carbon-12 and some are carbon-14.

The nuclei of most atoms are stable. However, many elements do have isotopes in which the nuclei are unstable—carbon-14 is one example of an unstable isotope. In this context, *unstable* means that the nuclei change through a random process called **radioactive decay**. During radioactive decay, unstable isotopes radiate energy and emit particles. The rates at which unstable isotopes decay are measurable. Therefore, certain radioactive atoms are used to determine the ages of fossils, rocks, and minerals.

DID YOU KNOW?

One of the world's heaviest cut and polished gemstones is z 22,892.5-carat golden-yellow topaz. Currently housed in the Smithsonian Institution, this roughly 10-pound gem is about the size of an automobile headlight and could hardly be used as a piece of jewelry, except perhaps by an elephant.

PHYSICAL PROPERTIES OF MINERALS

GEODe
EARTH SCIENCE

Earth Materials
▼ Minerals

Each mineral has a definite crystalline structure and chemical composition that give it a unique set of physical and chemical properties shared by all samples of that mineral. For example, all specimens of halite have the same hardness, the same density, and break in a similar manner. Because a mineral's internal structure and chemical composition are difficult to determine without the aid of sophisticated tests and equipment, the more easily recognized physical properties are frequently used in identification.

Optical Properties

Of the many optical properties of minerals—luster, the ability to transmit light, color, and streak—are most frequently used for mineral identification.

FIGURE 10 The freshly broken sample of galena (right) displays a metallic luster, whereas the sample on the left is tarnished and has a submetallic luster. (Photo courtesy of E. J. Tarbuck)

Luster

The appearance or quality of light reflected from the surface of a mineral is known as **luster**. Minerals that have the appearance of metals, regardless of color, are said to have a *metallic luster* (FIGURE 10). Some metallic minerals, such as native copper and galena, develop a dull coating or tarnish when exposed to the atmosphere. Because they are not as shiny as samples with freshly broken surfaces, these samples are often said to exhibit a *submetallic luster*.

Most minerals have a *nonmetallic luster* and are described using various adjectives such as *vitreous* or *glassy*. Other nonmetallic minerals are described as having a *dull* or *earthy luster* (a dull appearance like soil), or a *pearly luster*

(such as a pearl, or the inside of a clamshell). Still others exhibit a *silky luster* (like satin cloth), or a *greasy luster* (as though coated in oil).

The Ability to Transmit Light

Another optical property used in the identification of minerals is the ability to transmit light. When no light is transmitted, the mineral is described as *opaque;* when light, but not an image, is transmitted through a mineral it is said to be *translucent*. When both light and an image are visible through the sample, the mineral is described as *transparent*.

Color

Although **color** is generally the most conspicuous characteristic of any mineral, it is considered a diagnostic property of only a few minerals. Slight impurities in the common mineral quartz, for example, give it a variety of tints including pink, purple, yellow, white, gray, and even black (FIGURE 11). Other minerals, such as tourmaline, also exhibit a variety of hues, with multiple colors sometimes occurring in the same sample. Thus, the use of color as a means of identification is often ambiguous or even misleading.

Streak

The color of the powdered mineral, called **streak,** is often useful in identification. A mineral's streak is obtained by rubbing it across a *streak plate* (a piece of unglazed porcelain) and observing the color of the mark it leaves (FIGURE 12).

FIGURE 11 Quartz. Some minerals, such as quartz, occur in a variety of colors. These samples include crystal quartz (colorless), amethyst (purple quartz), citrine (yellow quartz), and smoky quartz (gray to black). (Photo by E.J. Tarbuck)

FIGURE 12 Although the color of a mineral is not always helpful in identification, the streak, which is the color of the powdered mineral, can be very useful. (Photo by Dennis Tasa)

FIGURE 13 Although most minerals exhibit only one common crystal shape, some such as pyrite have two or more characteristic habits. (Photos by Dennis Tasa)

Although the color of a mineral may vary from sample to sample, its streak usually does not.

Streak can also help distinguish between minerals with metallic luster or nonmetallic luster. Metallic minerals generally have a dense, dark streak, whereas minerals with nonmetallic luster typically have a light-colored streak.

It should be noted that not all minerals produce a streak when using a streak plate. For example, if the mineral is harder than the streak plate, no streak is observed.

Crystal Shape or Habit

Mineralogists use the term **crystal shape** or **habit** to refer to the common or characteristic shape of a crystal or aggregate of crystals. A few minerals exhibit somewhat regular polygons that are helpful in their identification. For example, magnetite crystals sometimes occur as octahedrons, garnets often form dodecahedrons, and halite and fluorite crystals tend to grow as cubes or near cubes. While most minerals have only one common habit, a few have two or more characteristic crystal shapes such as the pyrite sample shown in FIGURE 13.

By contrast, some minerals rarely develop perfect geometric forms. Many, however, develop a characteristic shape useful for identification. Some minerals tend to grow equally in all three dimensions, whereas others tend to be elongated in one direction, or flattened if growth in one dimension is

suppressed. Commonly used terms to describe these and other crystal habits include *equant* (equidimensional), *bladed, fibrous, tabular, prismatic, platy, blocky,* and *botryoidal* (FIGURE 14).

Mineral Strength

How easily minerals break or deform under stress is determined by the type and strength of the chemical bonds that hold the crystals together. Mineralogists use terms including *tenacity, hardness, cleavage,* and *fracture* to describe mineral strength and how minerals break when stress is applied.

A. Bladed

B. Prismatic

C. Banded

D. Botryoidal

FIGURE 14 Some common crystal habits. **A.** *Bladed.* Elongated crystals that are flattened in one direction. **B.** *Prismatic.* Elongated crystals with faces that are parallel to a common direction. **C.** *Banded.* Minerals that have stripes or bands of color or texture. **D.** *Botryoidal.* Groups of intergrown crystals resembling a bunch of grapes.

DID YOU KNOW?

The name *crystal* is derived from the Greek (*krystallos*, meaning "ice") and was applied to quartz crystals. The ancient Greeks thought quartz was water that had crystallized at high pressures deep inside Earth.

Tenacity

The term **tenacity** describes a mineral's toughness, or its resistance to breaking or deforming. Minerals that are ionically bonded, such as fluorite and halite, tend to be *brittle* and shatter into small pieces when struck. By contrast, minerals with metallic bonds, such as native copper, are *malleable*, or easily hammered into different shapes. Minerals, including gypsum and talc, that can be cut into thin shavings are described as *sectile*. Still others, notably the micas, are *elastic* and will bend and snap back to their original shape after the stress is released.

Hardness

One of the most useful diagnostic properties is **hardness**, a measure of the resistance of a mineral to abrasion or scratching. This property is determined by rubbing a mineral of unknown hardness against one of known hardness, or vice versa. A numerical value of hardness can by obtained by using the **Mohs scale** of hardness, which consists of 10 minerals arranged in order from 1 (softest) to 10 (hardest), as shown in **FIGURE 15A**. The Mohs scale is a relative ranking, and it does not imply that mineral number 2, gypsum, is twice as hard as mineral 1, talc. In fact, gypsum is only slightly harder than talc, as **FIGURE 15B** indicates.

In the laboratory, other common objects can be used to determine the hardness of a mineral. These include a human fingernail, which has a hardness of about 2.5, a copper penny (3.5), and a piece of glass (5.5). The mineral gypsum, which has a hardness of 2, can be easily scratched with a fingernail. On the other hand, the mineral calcite, which has a hardness of 3, will scratch a fingernail but will not scratch glass. Quartz, one of the hardest common minerals, will easily scratch glass. Diamonds, hardest of all, scratch anything, including other diamonds.

Cleavage

In the crystal structure of many minerals, some atomic bonds are weaker than others. It is along these weak bonds that minerals tend to break when they are stressed. **Cleavage** (*Kleiben* = carve) is the tendency of a mineral to break (cleave) along planes of weak bonding. Not all minerals have cleavage, but those that do can be identified by the relatively smooth, flat surfaces that are produced when the mineral is broken.

The simplest type of cleavage is exhibited by the micas (**FIGURE 16**). Because these minerals have very weak bonds in one direction, they cleave to form thin, flat sheets. Some minerals have excellent cleavage in one, two, three, or more directions, whereas others exhibit fair or poor cleavage, and still others have no cleavage at all. When minerals break evenly in more than one direction, cleavage is described by

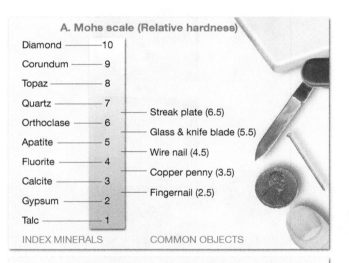

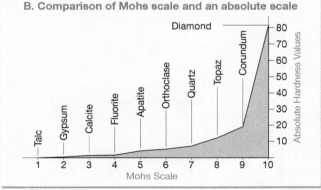

FIGURE 15 Hardness scales. **A.** Mohs scale of hardness, with the hardness of some common objects. **B.** Relationship between Mohs relative hardness scale and an absolute hardness scale.

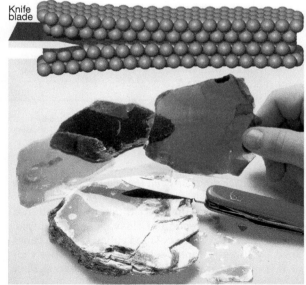

FIGURE 16 The thin sheets shown here were produced by splitting a mica (muscovite) crystal parallel to its perfect cleavage. (Photo by Breck P. Kent)

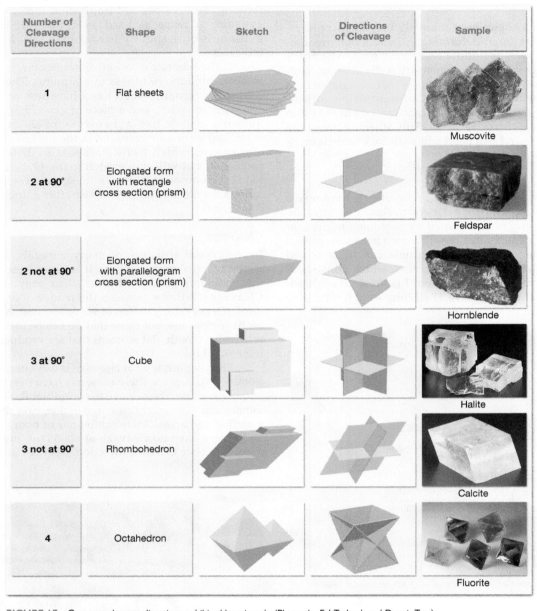

Number of Cleavage Directions	Shape	Sketch	Directions of Cleavage	Sample
1	Flat sheets			Muscovite
2 at 90°	Elongated form with rectangle cross section (prism)			Feldspar
2 not at 90°	Elongated form with parallelogram cross section (prism)			Hornblende
3 at 90°	Cube			Halite
3 not at 90°	Rhombohedron			Calcite
4	Octahedron			Fluorite

FIGURE 17 Common cleavage directions exhibited by minerals. (Photos by E. J. Tarbuck and Dennis Tasa)

the number of cleavage directions and the angle(s) at which they meet (FIGURE 17).

Each cleavage surface that has a different orientation is counted as a different direction of cleavage. For example, some minerals cleave to form six-sided cubes. Because cubes are defined by three different sets of parallel planes that intersect at 90-degree angles, cleavage is described as *three directions of cleavage that meet at 90 degrees*.

Do not confuse cleavage with crystal shape. When a mineral exhibits cleavage, it will break into pieces that all have the same geometry. By contrast, the smooth-sided quartz crystals shown in Figure 1 do not have cleavage. If bro-ken, they fracture into shapes that do not resemble one another or the original crystals.

Fracture

Minerals having chemical bonds that are equally, or nearly equally, strong in all directions exhibit a property called **fracture**. When minerals fracture, most produce uneven surfaces and are described as exhibiting *irregular fracture*. However, some minerals, such as quartz, break into smooth, curved surfaces resembling broken glass. Such breaks are called *conchoidal fractures* (FIGURE 18). Still other minerals exhibit fractures that produce splinters or fibers

FIGURE 19   Double refraction illustrated by the mineral calcite. (Photo by Chip Clark)

FIGURE 18   Conchoidal fracture. The smooth, curved surfaces result when minerals break in a glasslike manner. (Photo by E. J. Tarbuck)

that are referred to as *splintery* and *fibrous fracture*, respectively.

Density and Specific Gravity

Density, an important property of matter, is defined as mass per unit volume. Mineralogists often use a related measure called **specific gravity** to describe the density of minerals. Specific gravity is a unitless number representing the ratio of a mineral's weight to the weight of an equal volume of water.

Most common rock-forming minerals have a specific gravity of between 2 and 3. For example, quartz has a specific gravity of 2.65. By contrast, some metallic minerals such as pyrite, native copper, and magnetite are more than twice as dense as quartz. Galena, an ore of lead, has a specific gravity of roughly 7.5, whereas the specific gravity of 24-karat gold is approximately 20.

With a little practice, you can estimate the specific gravity of a mineral by hefting it in your hand. Ask yourself, does this mineral feel about as "heavy" as similar sized rocks you have handled? If the answer is "yes," the specific gravity of the sample will likely be between 2.5 and 3.

Other Properties of Minerals

In addition to the properties already discussed, some minerals can be recognized by other distinctive properties. For example, halite is ordinary salt, so it can be quickly identified through taste. Talc and graphite both have distinctive feels; talc feels soapy, and graphite feels greasy. Further, the streak of many sulfur-bearing minerals smells like rotten eggs. A few minerals, such as magnetite, have a high iron content and can be picked up with a magnet, while some

DID YOU KNOW?

Clay minerals are sometimes used as an additive to thicken milkshakes in fast-food restaurants.

varieties (lodestone) are natural magnets and will pick up small iron-based objects such as pins and paper clips (see Figure 25).

Moreover, some minerals exhibit special optical properties. For example, when a transparent piece of calcite is placed over printed text, the letters appear twice. This optical property is known as *double refraction* (FIGURE 19).

One very simple chemical test involves placing a drop of dilute hydrochloric acid from a dropper bottle onto a freshly broken mineral surface. Certain minerals, called carbonates, will effervesce (fizz) as carbon dioxide gas is released (FIGURE 20). This test is especially useful in identifying the common carbonate mineral calcite.

FIGURE 20   Calcite reacting with a weak acid. (Photo by Chip Clark)

DID YOU KNOW?

The mineral pyrite is commonly known as "fool's gold," because its golden-yellow color closely resembles gold. The name *pyrite* is derived from the Greek *pyros* ("fire"), because it gives off sparks when struck sharply.

MINERAL GROUPS

Earth Materials

▼ Minerals

Nearly 4000 minerals have been named, and several new ones are identified each year. Fortunately, for students who are beginning to study minerals, no more than a few dozen are abundant! Collectively, these few make up most of the rocks of Earth's crust and, as such, are often referred to as the **rock-forming minerals**.

Although less abundant, many other minerals are used extensively in the manufacture of products and are called *economic minerals*. Rock-forming minerals and economic minerals are not mutually exclusive groups. When found in large deposits, some rock-forming minerals are economically significant. One example is the mineral calcite, which is the primary component of the sedimentary rock limestone and has many uses including the production of cement.

It is worth noting that *only eight elements* make up the bulk of the rock-forming minerals and represent more than 98 percent (by weight) of the continental crust (**FIGURE 21**). These elements, in order of abundance, are oxygen (O), silicon (Si), aluminum (Al), iron (Fe), calcium (Ca), sodium (Na), potassium (K), and magnesium (Mg). As shown in Figure 21, silicon and oxygen are by far the most common elements in Earth's crust. Furthermore, these two elements readily combine to form the basic "building block" for the

most common mineral group, the **silicates**. More than 800 silicate minerals are known and they account for more than 90 percent of Earth's crust.

Because other mineral groups are far less abundant in Earth's crust than the silicates, they are often grouped together under the heading **nonsilicates.** Although not as common as silicates, some nonsilicate minerals are very important economically. They provide us with iron and aluminum to build our automobiles, gypsum for plaster and drywall for home construction, and copper wire that carries electricity and connects us to the Internet. Some common nonsilicate mineral groups include the carbonates, sulfates, and halides. In addition to their economic importance, these mineral groups include members that are major constituents in sediments and sedimentary rocks.

We first discuss the most common mineral group, the silicates, and then consider some of the prominent nonsilicate mineral groups.

Silicate Minerals

Every silicate mineral contains oxygen and silicon atoms. Except for a few minerals, such as quartz, most silicate minerals also contain one or more additional elements that join to produce an electrically neutral compound. These elements give rise to the great variety of silicate minerals and their varied properties.

All silicates have the same fundamental building block, the **silicon-oxygen tetrahedron.** This structure consists of four oxygen atoms surrounding a much smaller silicon atom, as shown in **FIGURE 22**. Thus, a typical hand-size silicate mineral specimen contains millions of these silicon-oxygen tetrahedra, joined together in a variety of ways.

In some minerals, the tetrahedra are joined into chains, sheets, or three-dimensional networks by sharing oxygen atoms (**FIGURE 23**). These larger silicate structures

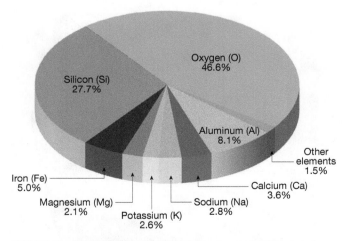

FIGURE 21 Relative abundance of the eight most common elements in the continental crust.

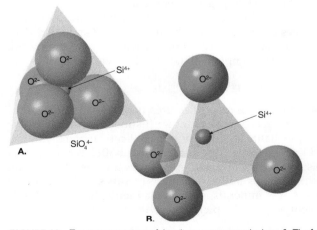

FIGURE 22 Two representations of the silicon-oxygen tetrahedron. **A.** The four large red spheres represent oxygen atoms, and the blue sphere represents a silicon atom. The spheres are drawn in proportion to the radii of the atoms. **B.** An expanded view of the tetrahedron that has an oxygen atom at each of the four corners.

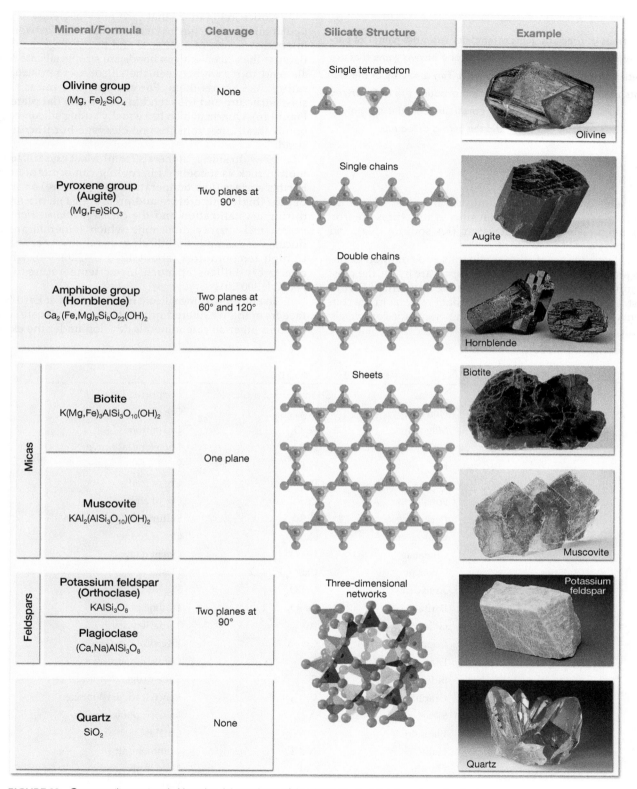

Mineral/Formula	Cleavage	Silicate Structure	Example
Olivine group $(Mg, Fe)_2SiO_4$	None	Single tetrahedron	Olivine
Pyroxene group (Augite) $(Mg,Fe)SiO_3$	Two planes at 90°	Single chains	Augite
Amphibole group (Hornblende) $Ca_2(Fe,Mg)_5Si_8O_{22}(OH)_2$	Two planes at 60° and 120°	Double chains	Hornblende
Micas — **Biotite** $K(Mg,Fe)_3AlSi_3O_{10}(OH)_2$	One plane	Sheets	Biotite
Micas — **Muscovite** $KAl_2(AlSi_3O_{10})(OH)_2$	One plane	Sheets	Muscovite
Feldspars — **Potassium feldspar (Orthoclase)** $KAlSi_3O_8$	Two planes at 90°	Three-dimensional networks	Potassium feldspar
Feldspars — **Plagioclase** $(Ca,Na)AlSi_3O_8$	Two planes at 90°	Three-dimensional networks	
Quartz SiO_2	None	Three-dimensional networks	Quartz

FIGURE 23 Common silicate minerals. Note that the complexity of the silicate structure increases down the chart.

DID YOU KNOW?

The names of precious gems often differ from the names of parent minerals. For example, *sapphire* is one of two gems that are varieties of the same mineral, *corundum*. Tiny amounts of the elements titanium and iron in corundum produce the most prized blue sapphires. When the mineral corundum contains chromium, it exhibits a brilliant red color and the gem is called *ruby*.

are then connected to one another by other elements. The primary elements that join silicate structures are iron (Fe), magnesium (Mg), potassium (K), sodium (Na), and calcium (Ca).

Major groups of silicate minerals and common examples are given in Figure 23. The *feldspars* are by far the most plentiful group, comprising more than 50 percent of Earth's crust. *Quartz,* the second most abundant mineral in the continental crust, is the only common mineral made completely of silicon and oxygen.

Notice in Figure 23 that each mineral *group* has a particular silicate *structure*. A relationship exists between this internal structure of a mineral and the *cleavage* it exhibits. Because the silicon-oxygen bonds are strong, silicate minerals tend to cleave between the silicon-oxygen structures rather than across them. For example, the micas have a sheet structure and thus tend to cleave into flat plates (see Figure 16). Quartz, which has equally strong silicon-oxygen bonds in all directions, has no cleavage but fractures instead.

How do silicate minerals form? Most crystallize from molten rock as it cools. This cooling can occur at or near Earth's surface (low temperature and pressure) or at great depths (high temperature and pressure). The *environment* during crystallization and the *chemical composition of the molten rock* mainly determine which minerals are produced. For example, the silicate mineral olivine crystallizes at high temperatures (about 1200°C [2200°F]), whereas quartz crystallizes at much lower temperatures (about 700°C [1300°F]).

In addition, some silicate minerals form at Earth's surface from the weathered products of other silicate minerals. Still other silicate minerals develop under the extreme

Table 1   Common Nonsilicate Mineral Groups

Mineral Group	Name	Chemical Formula	Economic Use
Oxides	Hematite	Fe_2O_3	Ore of iron, pigment
	Magnetite	Fe_3O_4	Ore of iron
	Corundum	Al_2O_3	Gemstone, abrasive
	Ice	H_2O	Solid form of water
Sulfides	Galena	PbS	Ore of lead
	Sphalerite	ZnS	Ore of zinc
	Pyrite	FeS_2	Sulfuric acid production
	Chalcopyrite	$CuFeS_2$	Ore of copper
	Cinnabar	HgS	Ore of mercury
Sulfates	Gypsum	$CaSO_4 \cdot 2H_2O$	Plaster
	Anhydrite	$CaSO_4$	Plaster
	Barite	$BaSO_4$	Drilling mud
Native elements	Gold	Au	Trade, jewelry
	Copper	Cu	Electrical conductor
	Diamond	C	Gemstone, abrasive
	Sulfur	S	Sulfa drugs, chemicals
	Graphite	C	Pencil lead, dry lubricant
	Silver	Ag	Jewelry, photography
	Platinum	Pt	Catalyst
Halides	Halite	$NaCl$	Common salt
	Fluorite	CaF_2	Used in steelmaking
	Sylvite	KCl	Fertilizer
Carbonates	Calcite	$CaCO_3$	Portland cement, lime
	Dolomite	$CaMg(CO_3)_2$	Portland cement, lime

FIGURE 24 Thick bed of halite (salt) at an underground mine in Grand Saline, Texas. (Photo by Tom Bochsler)

pressures associated with mountain building. Each silicate mineral, therefore, has a structure and a chemical composition that *indicate the conditions under which it formed.* Thus, by carefully examining the mineral makeup of rocks, geologists can often determine the circumstances under which they formed.

Important Nonsilicate Minerals

Although nonsilicates make up only about 8 percent of Earth's crust, some minerals, such as gypsum, calcite, and halite, are major constituents in sedimentary rocks. Furthermore, many others are important economically. Table 1 lists some of the nonsilicate mineral classes and a few examples of each. Some of the most common nonsilicate minerals belong to one of three classes of minerals—the carbonates (CO_3^{2-}), the sulfates (SO_4^{2-}), and the halides (Cl^{1-}, F^{1-}, B^{1-}).

The carbonate minerals are much simpler structurally than the silicates. This mineral group is composed of the carbonate ion (CO_3^{2-}) and one or more kinds of positive ions. The most common carbonate mineral is *calcite,* $CaCO_3$ (calcium carbonate). This mineral is the major constituent in two well-known rocks: limestone and marble. Limestone has many uses, including road aggregate, building stone, and the main ingredient in portland cement. Marble is primarily used decoratively in homes, businesses, and places of worship.

Two other nonsilicate minerals frequently found in sedimentary rocks are *halite* and *gypsum.* Both minerals are commonly found in thick layers that are the last vestiges of ancient seas that have long since evaporated (FIGURE 24).

Like limestone, both are important nonmetallic resources. Halite is the mineral name for common table salt (NaCl). Gypsum ($CaSO_4 \cdot 2H_2O$), which is calcium sulfate with water bound into the structure, is the mineral of which plaster and other similar building materials are composed.

Most nonsilicate mineral classes contain members that are prized for their economic value. This includes the oxides, whose members hematite and magnetite are important ores of iron (FIGURE 25). Also significant are the sulfides, which are basically compounds of sulfur (S) and one or more metals. Examples of important sulfide minerals include galena (lead), sphalerite (zinc), and chalcopyrite (copper). In addition, native elements, including gold, silver, and carbon (diamonds), plus a host of other nonsilicate minerals—fluorite (flux in making steel), corundum (gemstone, abrasive), and uraninite (a uranium source)—are important economically.

FIGURE 25 Two important ores of iron. **A.** Magnetite. **B.** Hematite. (Photos by E. J. Tarbuck)

A. Magnetite

B. Hematite

Gypsum, a white-to-transparent mineral, was first used as a building material in Anatolia (present-day Turkey) around 6000 B.C. It is also found on the interiors of the great pyramids in Egypt, which were erected in about 3700 B.C. Today, an average new American home contains more than 7 metric tons of gypsum in the form of 6000 square feet of wallboard.

MINERAL RESOURCES

Mineral resources are Earth's storehouse of useful minerals that can be recovered for use. Resources include already identified deposits from which minerals can be extracted profitably, called **reserves,** as well as known deposits that are not yet recoverable under present economic conditions or technology. Deposits assumed to exist based on geologic evidence are also considered mineral resources.

The term **ore** denotes useful metallic minerals that can be mined for profit. In common usage, the term is also applied to some nonmetallic minerals, such as fluorite and sulfur. However, materials used for such purposes as building stone, road paving, abrasives, ceramics, and fertilizers are not usually called ores; rather, they are classified as *industrial rocks and minerals.*

Recall that more than 98 percent of Earth's crust is composed of only eight elements. Except for oxygen and silicon, all other elements make up a relatively small fraction of common crustal rocks (see Figure 21). Indeed, the natural concentrations of most elements in crustal rocks are exceedingly small. A rock containing the average crustal percentage of a valuable element such as gold has no economic value, because the cost of extracting it greatly exceeds the value of the gold that could be recovered.

To have economic value, an element must be concentrated above the level of its average crustal abundance. For example, copper makes up about 0.0135 percent of the crust. For a deposit to be considered an ore of copper, it must contain a concentration that is about 100 times this amount. Aluminum, on the other hand, represents 8.13 percent of the crust and can be extracted profitably when found in concentrations only about four times its average crustal percentage.

It is important to realize that economic changes affect whether or not a deposit is profitable to extract. If demand for a metal increases and its price rises sufficiently, the status of a previously unprofitable deposit changes. Unprofitable deposits may also become profitable if improved mining techniques allow the material to be extracted at a lower cost. This situation was illustrated at the copper-mining operation located at Bingham Canyon, Utah, one of the largest open-pit mines on Earth (FIGURE 26). Mining was halted there in 1985 because obsolete equipment had driven the cost of extracting the copper beyond the selling price. The owners responded by replacing an antiquated 1000-car railroad with conveyor belts and pipelines for transporting the ore and waste. These devices achieved a cost reduction of nearly 30 percent and returned this mining operation to profitability.

THE CHAPTER IN REVIEW

• A *mineral* is a naturally occurring inorganic solid that possesses an orderly crystalline structure and a definite chemical composition. Most *rocks* are aggregates composed of two or more minerals.

• The building blocks of minerals are *elements*. An *atom* is the smallest particle of matter that still retains the characteristics of an element. Each atom has a *nucleus,* which contains *protons* and *neutrons*. Orbiting the nucleus of an atom are *electrons*. The number of protons in an atom's nucleus determines its *atomic number* and the name of the element. Atoms bond together to form a *compound* by either gaining, losing, or sharing electrons with another atom.

• *Isotopes* are variants of the same element but with a different *mass number* (the total number of neutrons plus protons found in an atom's nucleus). Some isotopes are unstable and disintegrate naturally through a process called *radioactive decay.*

• The properties of minerals include *crystal shape (habit), luster, color, streak, hardness, cleavage, fracture,* and *density* or *specific gravity.* In addition, a number of special physical and chemical properties (*taste, smell, elasticity, feel, magnetism, double refraction,* and *chemical reaction to hydrochloric acid*) are useful in identifying certain minerals. Each mineral has a unique set of properties that can be used for identification.

• Of the nearly 4000 minerals, no more than a few dozen make up most of the rocks of Earth's crust and, as such, are classified as rock-forming minerals. Eight elements (oxygen, silicon, aluminum, iron, calcium, sodium, potassium, and magnesium) make up the bulk of these minerals and represent more than 98 percent (by weight) of Earth's continental crust.

• The most common mineral group is the *silicates*. All silicate minerals have the *silicon-oxygen tetrahedron* as their fundamental building block. In some silicate minerals, the tetrahedra are joined in chains; in others, the tetrahedra are arranged into sheets or three-dimensional networks. Each silicate mineral has a structure and a chemical

FIGURE 26 Aerial view of Bingham Canyon copper mine near Salt Lake City, Utah. This huge open-pit mine is about 4 kilometers (2.5 miles) across and 900 meters (nearly 3000 feet) deep. Although the amount of copper in the rock is less than 1 percent, the huge volumes of material removed and processed each day (about 200,000 tons) yield significant quantities of metal. (Photo by Michael Collier)

composition that indicates the conditions under which it formed. The *nonsilicate* mineral groups include the *oxides* (e.g., magnetite, mined for iron), *sulfides* (e.g., sphalerite, mined for zinc), *sulfates* (e.g., gypsum, used in plaster and frequently found in sedimentary rocks), *native elements* (e.g., graphite, a dry lubricant), *halides* (e.g., halite, common salt, and frequently found in sedimentary rocks), and *carbonates* (e.g., calcite, used in portland cement and a major constituent in two well-known rocks: limestone and marble).

● The term *ore* is used to denote useful metallic minerals, such as hematite (mined for iron) and galena (mined for lead), that can be mined at a profit, as well as some nonmetallic minerals, such as fluorite and sulfur, that contain useful substances.

KEY TERMS

atom	covalent bond	habit	mass number
atomic number	crystal shape	hardness	metallic bonds
chemical bond	density	ionic bond	mineral
chemical compound	electron	ions	mineralogy
cleavage	element	isotope	mineral resource
color	fracture	luster	Mohs scale

neutron	periodic table	rock-forming minerals	tenacity
nonsilicate	proton	silicates	valence electrons
nucleus	radioactive decay	silicon-oxygen tetrahedron	
octet rule	reserve	specific gravity	
ore	rock	streak	

QUESTIONS FOR REVIEW

1. Briefly describe the five characteristics an Earth material should have in order to be considered a mineral.

2. Define the term *rock*.

3. List the three main particles of an atom and explain how they differ from one another.

4. If the number of electrons in an atom is 35 and its mass number is 80, calculate the following:
   a. the number of protons
   b. the atomic number
   c. the number of neutrons

5. What occurs in an atom to produce an ion?

6. What is an isotope?

7. Although all minerals have an orderly internal arrangement of atoms (crystalline structure), most mineral samples do not visibly demonstrate their crystal form. Why?

8. Why might it be difficult to identify a mineral by its color?

9. If you found a glassy-appearing mineral while rock hunting and had hopes that it was a diamond, what simple test might help you make a determination?

10. Table 1 lists a use for corundum as an abrasive. Explain why it makes a good abrasive in terms of the Mohs hardness scale.

11. Gold has a specific gravity of almost 20. If a five-gallon pail of water weighs about 40 pounds, how much would a five-gallon pail of gold weigh?

12. What are the two most common elements in Earth's crust?

13. What is the term used to describe the basic building block of all silicate minerals?

14. What are the two most common silicate minerals in Earth's crust?

15. List three nonsilicate minerals that are commonly found in rocks.

16. Contrast a mineral *resource* and a mineral *reserve*.

17. What might cause a mineral deposit that had not been considered an ore to become reclassified as an ore?

COMPANION WEBSITE

The *Foundations of Earth Science* Website uses the resources and flexibility of the Internet to aid in your study of the topics in this chapter. Written and developed by the authors and other Earth science instructors, this site will help improve your understanding of Earth science. Visit **www.mygeoscienceplace.com** in order to:

- **Review** key chapter concepts.
- **Read** with links to the ebook and to chapter-specific web resources.
- **Visualize** and comprehend challenging topics using learning activities in *GEODe: Earth Science*.
- **Test** yourself with online quizzes.

GEODe: EARTH SCIENCE

GEODe: Earth Science is a valuable and easy to use learning aid that can be accessed from your chapter's Companion Website **www.mygeoscienceplace.com.** It is a dynamic instructional tool that promotes understanding and reinforces important concepts by using tutorials, animations, and exercises that actively engage the student.

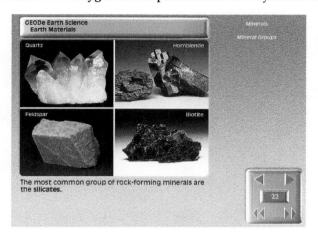

The most common group of rock-forming minerals are the silicates.

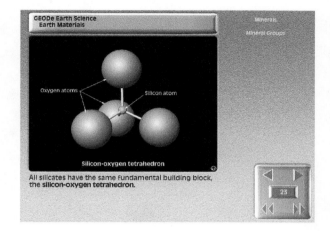

All silicates have the same fundamental building block, the silicon-oxygen tetrahedron.

ROCKS
MATERIALS OF
THE SOLID EARTH

From Chapter 2 of *Foundations of Earth Science*, Sixth Edition, Frederick K. Lutgens, Edward J. Tarbuck, Dennis Tasa.

ROCKS
MATERIALS OF THE SOLID EARTH

To assist you in learning the important concepts in this chapter, you will find it helpful to focus on the following questions:

1. What is the rock cycle and why is it important?

2. What are the three groups of rocks and the geologic processes involved in the formation of each?

3. What two criteria are used to classify igneous rocks?

4. What are the two major types of weathering and the processes associated with each?

5. What are the names and environments of formation for some common detrital and chemical sedimentary rocks?

6. What are the names, textures, and environments of formation for some common metamorphic rocks?

The mass of igneous rock challenging this climber originated deep beneath Earth's surface. (Photo by Cliff Leigh/Aurora Photos)

Why study rocks? Some rocks and minerals have great economic value. In addition, all Earth processes depend in some way on the properties of these basic Earth materials. Events such as volcanic eruptions, mountain building, weathering, erosion, and even earthquakes involve rocks and minerals. Consequently, a basic knowledge of Earth materials is essential to understanding most geologic phenomena.

Every rock contains clues about the environment in which it formed. For example, some rocks are composed entirely of small shell fragments. This tells Earth scientists that the rock originated in a shallow marine environment. Other rocks contain clues that indicate they formed from a volcanic eruption or deep in the Earth during mountain building (FIGURE 1). Thus, rocks contain a wealth of information about events that have occurred over Earth's long history.

We classify rocks into three groups—*igneous*, *sedimentary*, and *metamorphic*—based on the processes that created them. Before examining each group, we will view the *rock cycle*, which depicts the interrelationships among them.

EARTH AS A SYSTEM: THE ROCK CYCLE

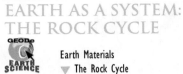

Earth Materials
▼ The Rock Cycle

Earth as a system is illustrated most vividly when we examine the rock cycle. The **rock cycle** allows us to see many of the interactions among the many components and processes of the Earth system (FIGURE 2). It helps us understand the origin of igneous, sedimentary, and metamorphic rocks and how they are connected. In addition, the rock cycle demonstrates that any rock type, under the right circumstances, can be transformed into any other type.

The Basic Cycle

We begin our discussion of the rock cycle with molten rock, called *magma*, which forms by melting that occurs primarily within Earth's crust and upper mantle. Once formed, a magma body often rises toward the surface because it is less dense than the surrounding rock. Occasionally magma

FIGURE 1 Rocks contain information about the processes that produce them. This large exposure of igneous rocks located in the Sierra Nevada of California, was once a molten mass found deep within Earth. (Photo by Brian Bailey/Getty Images)

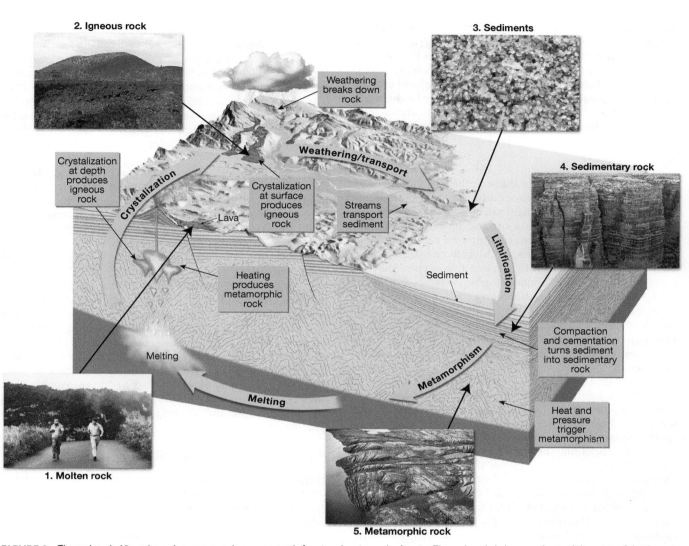

2. Igneous rock

3. Sediments

Weathering breaks down rock

Weathering/transport

4. Sedimentary rock

Crystalization at depth produces igneous rock

Crystalization

Crystalization at surface produces igneous rock

Streams transport sediment

Lava

Lithification

Sediment

Heating produces metamorphic rock

Compaction and cementation turns sediment into sedimentary rock

Melting

Metamorphism

Melting

Heat and pressure trigger metamorphism

1. Molten rock

5. Metamorphic rock

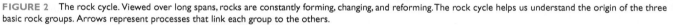

FIGURE 2 The rock cycle. Viewed over long spans, rocks are constantly forming, changing, and reforming. The rock cycle helps us understand the origin of the three basic rock groups. Arrows represent processes that link each group to the others.

reaches Earth's surface where it erupts as *lava*. Eventually, molten rock cools and solidifies, a process called *crystallization* or *solidification*. Molten rock may solidify either beneath the surface or, following a volcanic eruption, at the surface. In either situation, the resulting rocks are called *igneous rocks*.

If igneous rocks are exposed at the surface, they undergo *weathering*, in which the daily influences of the atmosphere slowly disintegrate and decompose rocks. The loose materials that result are often moved downslope by gravity, and then picked up and transported by one or more erosional agents—running water, glaciers, wind, or waves. Eventually, these particles and dissolved substances, called *sediment*, are deposited. Although most sediment ultimately comes to rest in the ocean, other sites of deposition include river floodplains, desert basins, swamps, and sand dunes.

Next, the sediments undergo *lithification*, a term meaning "conversion into rock." Sediment is usually lithified into *sedimentary rock* when compacted by the weight of overlying materials or when cemented as percolating groundwater fills the pores with mineral matter.

If the resulting sedimentary rock becomes deeply buried or is involved in the dynamics of mountain building, it will be subjected to great pressures and intense heat. The sedimentary rock may react to the changing environment by turning into the third rock type, *metamorphic rock*. If metamorphic rock is subjected to still higher temperatures, it may melt, creating magma, and the cycle begins again.

Although rocks may appear to be stable, unchanging masses, the rock cycle shows they are not. The changes, however, take time—sometimes millions or even billions of years. In addition, the rock cycle operates continuously around the globe, but in different stages depending on the location. Today, new magma is forming under the island of Hawaii, whereas the rocks that comprise the Colorado Rockies are slowly being worn down by weathering and erosion. Some of this weathered debris will eventually be carried to the Gulf of Mexico, where it will add to the already substantial mass of sediment that has accumulated there.

Alternative Paths

Rocks do not necessarily go through the cycle in the order that was just described. Other paths are also possible. For example, igneous rocks, rather than being exposed to weathering and erosion at Earth's surface, may remain deeply buried. Eventually, these masses may be subjected to the strong compressional forces and high temperature associated with mountain building. When this occurs, they are transformed directly into metamorphic rocks.

Metamorphic and sedimentary rocks, as well as sediment, do not always remain buried. Rather, overlying layers may be eroded away, exposing the once buried rock. When this happens, the material is attacked by weathering processes and turned into new raw materials for sedimentary rocks.

In a similar manner, igneous rocks that formed at depth can be uplifted, weathered, and turned into sedimentary rocks. Alternatively, igneous rocks may remain at depth where the high temperatures and forces associated with mountain building may metamorphose or even melt them. Over time, rocks may be transformed into any other rock type, or even into a different form of its original type. There are many paths that rocks may take through the rock cycle.

What drives the rock cycle? Earth's internal heat is responsible for the processes that form igneous and metamorphic rocks. Weathering and the transport of weathered material are external processes, powered by energy from the Sun. External processes produce sedimentary rocks.

IGNEOUS ROCKS: "FORMED BY FIRE"

Earth Materials
▼ Igneous Rocks

In the discussion of the rock cycle, we pointed out that **igneous rocks** form as *magma* cools and crystallizes. But what is magma and what is its source? **Magma** is molten rock generated by partial melting of rocks in Earth's mantle and in the lower crust in smaller amounts. This molten material consists mainly of the elements found in silicate minerals. Silicon and oxygen are the main constituents in magma, with lesser amounts of aluminum, iron, calcium, sodium, potassium, magnesium, and others. Magma also contains some gases, particularly water vapor, which are confined within the magma body by the weight (pressure) of the overlying rocks.

Once formed, a magma body buoyantly rises toward the surface because it is less dense than the surrounding rocks. Occasionally molten rock reaches the surface, where it is called **lava** (FIGURE 3). Sometimes, lava is emitted as fountains produced when escaping gases propel molten rock skyward. On other occasions, magma is explosively ejected from vents, producing a spectacular eruption such as the 1980 eruption of Mount St. Helens. However, most eruptions are not violent; rather, volcanoes more often emit quiet outpourings of lava.

Igneous rocks that form when molten rock solidifies *at the surface* are classified as **extrusive** or **volcanic** (after the Roman fire god Vulcan). Extrusive igneous rocks are abundant in western portions of the Americas, including the volcanic cones of the Cascade Range and the extensive lava flows of the Columbia Plateau. In addition, many oceanic islands, including the Hawaiian Islands, are composed almost entirely of volcanic igneous rocks.

Most magma, however, loses its mobility before reaching the surface and eventually crystallizes deep below the surface. Igneous rocks that *form at depth* are termed **intrusive** or **plutonic** (after Pluto, the god of the lower world in classical mythology). Intrusive igneous rocks remain at depth unless portions of the crust are uplifted and the overlying rocks stripped away by erosion. Exposures of intrusive igneous rocks occur in many places, including Mount Washington, New Hampshire; Stone Mountain, Georgia; the Black Hills of South Dakota; and Yosemite National Park, California (FIGURE 4).

From Magma to Crystalline Rock

Magma is a very hot, thick fluid, that contains solids (mineral crystals) and gases. The liquid portion of a magma body is composed of atoms that move about freely. As magma cools, random movements slow, and atoms begin to arrange themselves into orderly patterns—a process called *crystallization*. As cooling continues, numerous small crystals develop and atoms are systematically added to these centers of crystal growth. When the crystals grow large enough for their edges to meet, their growth ceases for lack of space. Eventually, all of the liquid is transformed into a solid mass of interlocking crystals.

The rate of cooling strongly influences crystal size. If a magma cools very slowly, it allows atoms to migrate over

FIGURE 3   Fluid basaltic lava emitted from Hawaii's Kilauea Volcano. (Photo by Photo Resource Hawaii/www.DanitaDelmont.com)

FIGURE 4   Mount Rushmore National Memorial, located in the Black Hills of South Dakota, is carved from the intrusive igneous rock granite. This massive igneous body cooled very slowly at depth and has since been uplifted and the overlying rocks stripped away by erosion. (Photo by Barbara A. Harvey/Shutterstock)

great distances. Consequently, *slow cooling results in the formation of large crystals.* On the other hand, if cooling occurs rapidly, the atoms lose their motion and quickly combine. This results in a large number of tiny crystals that all compete for the available atoms. Therefore, *rapid cooling results in the formation of a solid mass of small intergrown crystals.*

If a geologist encounters igneous rock containing crystals large enough to be seen with the unaided eye, it means it formed from molten rock, which cooled slowly at depth. But if the crystals can be seen clearly only with a microscope, the geologist knows that the magma cooled quickly, at or near Earth's surface.

If the molten material is quenched almost instantly, there is insufficient time for the atoms to arrange themselves into a crystalline network. Solids produced in this manner consist of randomly distributed atoms. Such rocks are called *glass* and are quite similar to ordinary manufactured glass. "Instant" quenching sometimes occurs during violent volcanic eruptions that produce tiny shards of glass called *volcanic ash.*

In addition to the rate of cooling, the composition of a magma and the amount of dissolved gases influence crystallization. Because magmas differ in each of these aspects, the physical appearance and mineral composition of igneous rocks vary widely. Nevertheless, it is possible to classify igneous rocks based on their *texture* and *mineral composition.*

What Can Igneous Textures Tell Us?

Texture describes the overall appearance of an igneous rock, based on the *size* and *arrangement* of its interlocking crystals. Texture is an important property because it allows geologists to make inferences about a rock's origin based on careful observations of crystal size and other characteristics. You learned that rapid cooling produces small crystals, whereas very slow cooling produces much larger crystals. As you might expect, the rate of cooling is slow in magma chambers lying deep within the crust, whereas a thin layer of lava extruded upon Earth's surface may chill to form solid rock in a matter of hours. Small molten blobs ejected from a volcano during a violent eruption can solidify in mid-air.

Igneous rocks that form rapidly at the surface or as small masses within the upper crust have a **fine-grained texture**, with the individual crystals too small to be seen with the unaided eye (FIGURE 5B). Common in many fine-grained igneous rocks are voids, called *vesicles*, left by gas bubbles that formed as the lava solidified (FIGURE 6). Rocks containing these voids are said to display a **vesicular texture**.

When large masses of magma solidify far below the surface, they form igneous rocks that exhibit a **coarse-grained texture**. These coarse-grained rocks have the appearance of a mass of intergrown crystals, roughly equal in size and large enough that individual minerals can be identified with the unaided eye. Granite is a classic example (FIGURE 5D).

A large mass of magma located at depth may require tens of thousands, even millions, of years to solidify. Because materials crystallize under different environmental conditions (temperature, pressure), it is possible for crystals of one mineral to become quite large before others even start to form. Should molten rock containing some large crystals move to a different environment—for example, by erupting at the surface—the remaining molten portion of the lava would cool more quickly. The resulting rock, which will have large crystals embedded in a matrix of smaller crystals, is said to have a **porphyritic texture** (FIGURE 5C).

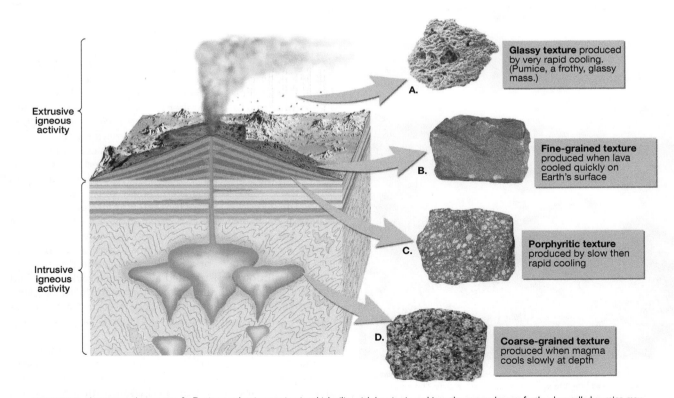

Glassy texture produced by very rapid cooling. (Pumice, a frothy, glassy mass.)

Fine-grained texture produced when lava cooled quickly on Earth's surface

Porphyritic texture produced by slow then rapid cooling

Coarse-grained texture produced when magma cools slowly at depth

FIGURE 5 Igneous rock textures. **A.** During a volcanic eruption in which silica-rich lava is ejected into the atmosphere, a frothy glass called pumice may form. **B.** Igneous rocks that form at or near Earth's surface cool quickly and often exhibit a fine-grained texture. **C.** A porphyritic texture results when magma that already contains some large crystals migrates to a new location where the rate of cooling increases. The resulting rock consists of large crystals embedded within a matrix of smaller crystals. **D.** Coarse-grained igneous rocks form when magma slowly crystallizes at depth. (Photos courtesy of E. J. Tarbuck)

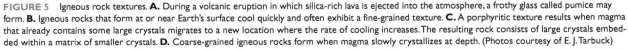

FIGURE 6 Scoria is a volcanic rock that is vesicular. Vesicles form as gas bubbles escape near the top of a lava flow. (Photo courtesy of E. J. Tarbuck)

During some volcanic eruptions, molten rock is ejected into the atmosphere, where it is quenched quickly. Rapid cooling may generate rock having a **glassy texture** (FIGURE 5A). Glass results when unordered atoms are "frozen in place" before they are able to unite into an orderly crystalline structure. In addition, magmas containing large amounts of silica (SiO_2) are more likely to form rocks that exhibit a glassy texture than those with a low silica content.

Obsidian, a common type of natural glass, is similar in appearance to a dark chunk of manufactured glass (FIGURE 7). Another volcanic rock that usually exhibits a glassy texture is *pumice*. Often found with obsidian, pumice forms when large amounts of gas escape from molten rock to generate a gray, frothy mass (FIGURE 8). In some samples, the vesicles

FIGURE 7 Obsidian, a natural glass, was used by Native Americans for making arrowheads and cutting tools. (Photo by E. J. Tarbuck; inset photo by Jeffrey Scovil)

FIGURE 8 Pumice, a glassy rock, is very lightweight because it contains numerous vesicles. (Photo by E. J. Tarbuck; inset photo by Chip Clark)

are quite noticeable, whereas in others, the pumice resembles fine shards of intertwined glass. Because of the large volume of air-filled voids, many samples of pumice will float in water (Figure 8).

Igneous Compositions

Igneous rocks are composed mainly of silicate minerals. Chemical analysis shows that silicon and oxygen—usually expressed as the silica (SiO_2) content of a magma—are by far the most abundant constituents of igneous rocks. These two elements, plus ions of aluminum (Al), calcium (Ca), sodium (Na), potassium (K), magnesium (Mg), and iron (Fe), make up roughly 98 percent by weight of most magmas. In addition, magma contains small amounts of many other elements, including titanium and manganese, and trace amounts of much rarer elements such as gold, silver, and uranium.

As magma cools and solidifies, these elements combine to form two major groups of silicate minerals. The *dark silicates* are rich in iron and/or magnesium and are relatively low in silica (SiO_2). *Olivine, pyroxene, amphibole,* and *biotite mica* are the common dark silicate minerals of Earth's crust. By contrast, the *light silicates* contain greater amounts of

DID YOU KNOW?

Quartz watches actually contain a quartz crystal to keep time. Before quartz watches, timepieces used some sort of oscillating mass or tuning fork. Cogs and wheels converted this mechanical movement to the movement of the hand. It turns out that if voltage is applied to a quartz crystal, it will oscillate with a consistency that is hundreds of times better for timing than a tuning fork. Because of this property, and modern integrated-circuit technology, quartz watches are now built so inexpensively that when they stop working, they are typically replaced rather than repaired. Modern watches that employ mechanical movements are very expensive indeed.

potassium, sodium, and calcium and are richer in silica than dark silicates. Light silicates include *quartz, muscovite mica,* and the most abundant mineral group, the *feldspars.* Feldspars make up at least 40 percent of most igneous rocks. Thus, in addition to feldspar, igneous rocks contain some combination of the other light and/or dark silicates listed earlier.

Classifying Igneous Rocks

Igneous rocks are classified by their texture and mineral composition. The texture of an igneous rock is mainly a result of its cooling history, whereas its mineral composition is largely a consequence of the chemical makeup of the parent magma and the environment of crystallization.

Despite their great compositional diversity, igneous rocks can be divided into broad groups according to their proportions of light and dark minerals. A general classification scheme based on texture and mineral composition is provided in FIGURE 9.

Granitic (Felsic) Rocks

Near one end of the continuum are rocks composed almost entirely of light-colored silicates—quartz and potassium feldspar. Igneous rocks in which these are the dominant minerals have a **granitic composition**. Geologists also refer to granitic rocks as being **felsic**, a term derived from *f*eldspar and *si*lica (quartz). In addition to quartz and feldspar, most granitic rocks contain about 10 percent dark silicate minerals,

usually biotite mica and amphibole. Granitic rocks are rich in silica (about 70 percent) and are major constituents of the continental crust.

Granite is a coarse-grained igneous rock that forms where large masses of magma slowly solidify at depth. During episodes of mountain building, granite and related crystalline rocks may be uplifted, where the processes of weathering and erosion strip away the overlying crust. Areas where large quantities of granite are exposed at the surface include Pikes Peak in the Rockies, Mount Rushmore in the Black Hills, Stone Mountain in Georgia, and Yosemite National Park in the Sierra Nevada (see Figure 4).

Granite is perhaps the best-known igneous rock (FIGURE 10), in part, because of its natural beauty, which is enhanced when polished, and partly because of its abundance. Slabs of polished granite are commonly used for tombstones, monuments, and countertops.

Rhyolite is the extrusive equivalent of granite and, likewise, is composed essentially of light-colored silicates (Figure 10). This fact accounts for its color, which is usually buff to pink or light gray. Rhyolite is fine-grained and frequently contains glass fragments and voids, indicating rapid cooling in a surface environment. In contrast to granite, which is widely distributed as large intrusive masses, rhyolite deposits are less common and generally less voluminous. Yellowstone Park is one well-known exception where extensive lava flows and thick ash deposits of rhyolitic composition are found.

Chemical Composition		Granitic (Felsic)	Andesitic (Intermediate)	Basaltic (Mafic)	Ultramafic
Dominant Minerals		Quartz Potassium feldspar Sodium-rich plagioclase feldspar	Amphibole Sodium- and calcium-rich plagioclase feldspar	Pyroxene Calcium-rich plagioclase feldspar	Olivine Pyroxene
TEXTURE	Coarse-grained	Granite	Diorite	Gabbro	Peridotite
	Fine-grained	Rhyolite	Andesite	Basalt	Komatiite (rare)
	Porphyritic	"Porphyritic" precedes any of the above names whenever there are appreciable phenocrysts			
	Glassy	Obsidian (compact glass) Pumice (frothy glass)			Uncommon
Rock Color (based on % of dark minerals)		0% to 25%	25% to 45%	45% to 85%	85% to 100%

FIGURE 9 Classification of the major groups of igneous rocks based on their mineral composition and texture. Coarse-grained rocks are plutonic, solidifying deep underground. Fine-grained rocks are volcanic, or solidify as shallow, thin plutons. Ultramafic rocks are dark, dense rocks, composed almost entirely of minerals containing iron and magnesium. Although relatively rare on Earth's surface, these rocks are believed to be major constituents of the upper mantle.

Texture	Composition		
	Granitic (Felsic)	**Andesitic** (Intermediate)	**Basaltic** (Mafic)
Course-grained (Intrusive)	Granite	Diorite	Gabbro
Fine-grained (Extrusive)	Rhyolite	Andesite	Basalt

FIGURE 10   Common igneous rocks. (Photos by E. J. Tarbuck)

Basaltic (Mafic) Rocks

Rocks that contain substantial dark silicate minerals and calcium-rich plagioclase feldspar (but no quartz) are said to have a **basaltic composition** (Figure 10). Basaltic rocks contain a high percentage of dark silicate minerals, so geologists also refer to them as **mafic** (from *ma*gnesium and *ferrum*, the Latin name for iron). Because of their iron content, basaltic rocks are typically darker and denser than granitic rocks.

Basalt, the most common extrusive igneous rock, is a very dark green to black, fine-grained volcanic rock composed primarily of pyroxene, olivine, and plagioclase feldspar. Many volcanic islands, such as the Hawaiian Islands and Iceland, are composed mainly of basalt (**FIGURE 11**). Further, the upper layers of the oceanic crust consist of basalt. In the United States, large portions of central Oregon and Washington were the sites of extensive basaltic outpourings.

The coarse-grained, intrusive equivalent of basalt is *gabbro* (Figure 10). Although gabbro is not commonly exposed at the surface, it makes up a significant percentage of the oceanic crust.

Andesitic (Intermediate) Rocks

As you can see in Figure 10, rocks with a composition between granitic and basaltic rocks are said to have an **andesitic** or **intermediate composition** after the common volcanic rock *andesite*. Andesitic rocks contain a mixture of both light- and dark-colored minerals, mainly amphibole and plagioclase feldspar. This important category of igneous rocks is associated with volcanic activity typically confined to continental margins. When magma of intermediate composition crystallizes at depth, it forms the coarse-grained rock called *diorite* (Figure 10).

Ultramafic Rocks

Another important igneous rock, *peridotite*, contains mostly the dark-colored minerals olivine and pyroxene and thus, falls on the opposite side of the compositional spectrum from granitic rocks (Figure 10). Because peridotite is composed almost entirely of dark silicate minerals, its chemical composition is referred to as **ultramafic**. Although ultramafic rocks are rare at Earth's surface, peridotite is believed to be the main constituent of the upper mantle.

How Different Igneous Rocks Form

Because a large variety of igneous rocks exist, it is logical to assume that an equally large variety of magmas also exist. However, geologists have observed that a single volcano may extrude lavas exhibiting quite different compositions. Data of this type led them to examine the possibility that magma might change (evolve) and thus, become the parent to a variety of igneous rocks. To explore this idea, a pioneering investigation into the crystallization of magma was carried out by N. L. Bowen in the first quarter of the 20th century.

mediate temperatures the minerals *amphibole* and *biotite* begin to crystallize.

During the last stage of crystallization, after most of the magma has solidified, the minerals *muscovite* and *potassium feldspar* may form (Figure 12). Finally, *quartz* crystallizes from any remaining liquid. Olivine and quartz are seldom found in the same igneous rock, because quartz crystallizes at much lower temperatures than olivine.

Analysis of igneous rocks provides evidence that this crystallization model approximates what can happen in nature. In particular, we find that minerals that form in the same general temperature range on Bowen's reaction series are found together in the same igneous rocks. For example, notice in Figure 12 that the minerals quartz, potassium feldspar, and muscovite, located in the same region of Bowen's diagram, are typically found together as major constituents of the igneous rock *granite.*

Magmatic Differentiation

Bowen demonstrated that different minerals crystallize from magma systematically. But how do Bowen's findings account for the great diversity of igneous rocks? During the crystallization process, the composition of magma continually changes. This occurs because as crystals form, they selectively remove certain elements from the magma, which leaves the remaining liquid portion depleted in these elements. Occasionally, separation of the solid and liquid components of magma occurs during crystallization, which creates different mineral assemblages. One such scenario, called **crystal settling**, occurs when the earlier formed minerals are denser (heavier) than the liquid portion and sink toward the bottom of the magma chamber, as shown in **FIGURE 13**. When the remaining molten material solidifies—either in place or in another location if it migrates into fractures in the surrounding rocks—it will form a rock with a chemical composition much different from the parent magma (Figure 13). The formation of one or more secondary magmas from a single parent magma is called **magmatic differentiation.**

At any stage in the evolution of a magma, the solid and liquid components can separate into two chemically distinct units. Further, magmatic differentiation within the secondary magma can generate other chemically distinct masses of molten rock. Consequently, magmatic differentiation and separation of the solid and liquid components at various stages of crystallization can produce several chemically diverse magmas and, ultimately, a variety of igneous rocks.

FIGURE 11   Basaltic lava flowing from Kilauea volcano, Hawaii. (Photo by Roger Ressmeyer/CORBIS)

Bowen's Reaction Series

In a laboratory setting, Bowen demonstrated that magma with its diverse chemistry crystallizes over a temperature range of at least 200°C unlike simple compounds (such as water), which solidify at specific temperatures. As magma cools, certain minerals crystallize first, at relatively high temperatures (top of **FIGURE 12**). At successively lower temperatures, other minerals begin to crystallize. This arrangement of minerals, shown in Figure 12, became known as **Bowen's reaction series**.

Bowen discovered that the first mineral to crystallize from a body of magma is *olivine*. Further cooling results in the formation of *pyroxene*, as well as *plagioclase feldspar*. At inter-

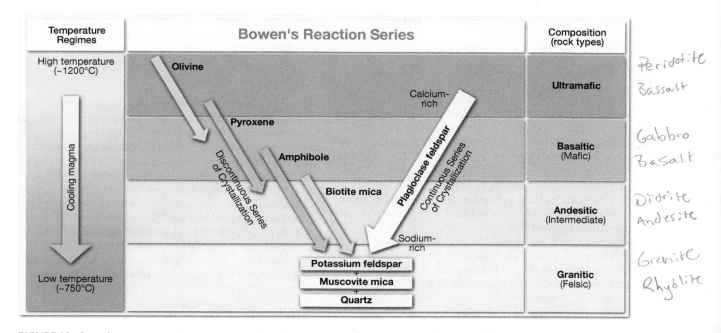

Peridotite
Bassalt

Gabbro
Basalt

Diorite
Andesite

Granite
Rhyolite

FIGURE 12 Bowen's reaction series shows the sequence in which minerals crystallize from a magma. Compare this figure to the mineral composition of the rock groups in Figure 9. Note that each rock group consists of minerals that crystallize in the same temperature range.

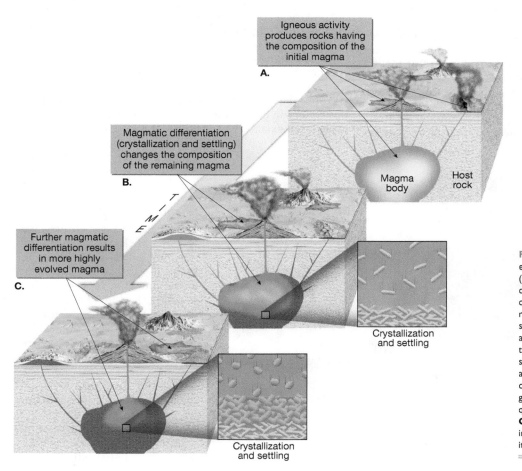

FIGURE 13 Illustration of how a magma evolves as the earlier formed minerals (those richer in iron, magnesium, and calcium) crystallize and settle to the bottom of the magma chamber, leaving the remaining melt richer in sodium, potassium, and silica (SiO_2). **A.** Emplacement of a magma body and associated igneous activity generates rocks having a composition similar to that of the initial magma. **B.** After a period of time, crystallization and settling change the composition of the melt, while generating rocks having a composition quite different from the original. **C.** Further magmatic differentiation in another more highly evolved its associated rock types.

WEATHERING OF ROCKS TO FORM SEDIMENT

Sculpturing Earth's Surface
▼ Weathering and Soils

All materials are susceptible to weathering. Consider, for example, the synthetic rock we call concrete. A newly poured concrete sidewalk is smooth, but many years later, the same sidewalk will appear chipped, cracked, and rough, with pebbles exposed at the surface. If a tree is nearby, its roots may grow under the sidewalk, heaving and buckling the concrete. The same natural processes that eventually break apart a concrete sidewalk also act to disintegrate natural rocks, regardless of their type or strength.

Why does rock weather? Simply, **weathering** is the natural response of Earth materials to a *new environment*. For instance, after millions of years of erosion, the rocks overlying a large body of intrusive igneous rock may be removed. This exposes the igneous rock to a whole new environment at the surface. This mass of crystalline rock, which formed deep below ground, where temperatures and pressures are high, is now subjected to very different and comparatively hostile surface conditions. In response, this rock mass will gradually change until it is once again in equilibrium, or balance, with its new environment. Such transformation of rock is what we call *weathering.*

In the following sections, we will discuss the two basic categories of weathering—mechanical and chemical. Mechanical weathering is the physical breaking up of rocks. Chemical weathering actually alters what a rock is, changing it into different substances. Although we will consider these two processes separately, keep in mind that they usually work simultaneously in nature. Furthermore, the activities of erosional agents—wind, water, and glaciers—that transport weathered rock particles are important. As these mobile agents move rock debris, they relentlessly disintegrate it further.

Mechanical Weathering of Rocks

When a rock undergoes **mechanical weathering**, it is broken into smaller and smaller pieces. Each piece retains the characteristics of the original material. The end result is many small pieces from a single large one. **FIGURE 14** shows that breaking a rock into smaller pieces increases the surface area available for chemical attack. An example is adding sugar to water. A chunk of rock candy will dissolve much more slowly than will an equal volume of sugar granules because of the vast difference in surface area. Hence, by breaking rocks into smaller pieces, mechanical weathering increases the amount of surface area available for chemical weathering.

In nature, three important physical processes break rocks into smaller fragments: frost wedging, sheeting, and biological activity.

Frost Wedging

If you leave a glass bottle full of water in a freezer too long, you will find the bottle fractured. The bottle breaks because liquid water has the unique property of expanding about 9 percent upon freezing. This is also the reason that poorly insulated or exposed water pipes rupture during frigid weather. You might also expect this process to fracture rocks in nature. After water works its way into cracks in the rock, it freezes, expands, and enlarges the openings (**FIGURE 15**). After many freeze-thaw cycles, the rock is broken into pieces.

This process is appropriately called **frost wedging** (Figure 15). Frost wedging is most pronounced in mountainous regions in the middle latitudes where a daily freeze-thaw cycle often exists. Here, sections of rock are wedged loose and may tumble into large piles called *talus* or *talus slopes* that often form at the base of steep rock outcrops (Figure 15).

Sheeting

When large masses of intrusive igneous rock are exposed by erosion, entire slabs begin to break loose, like the layers of an onion. This process, called **sheeting,** is thought to occur because of the great reduction in pressure that accompanies the removal of the overlaying rock (**FIGURE 16**). The outer layers expand more than the rock below and thus separate from the rock body. Granite is particularly prone to sheeting.

Continued weathering eventually causes the slabs to separate and spall off, creating

FIGURE 14 Chemical weathering can occur only to those portions of a rock that are exposed to the elements. Mechanical weathering breaks rock into smaller and smaller pieces, thereby increasing the surface area available for chemical attack.

FIGURE 15 Frost wedging. As water freezes, it expands, exerting a force great enough to break rock. When frost wedging occurs in a setting such as this, the broken rock fragments fall to the base of the cliff and create a cone-shaped accumulation known as talus. (Photo by Tom & Susan Bean)

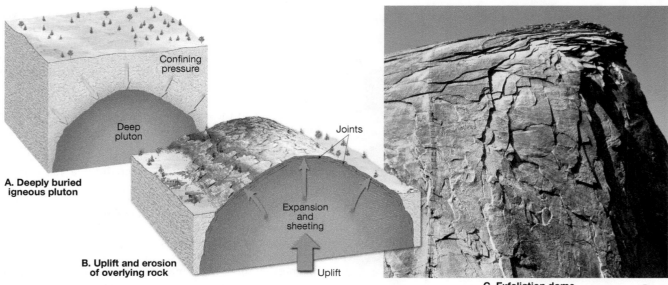

FIGURE 16 Sheeting is caused by the expansion of crystalline rock as erosion removes the overlying material. When the deeply buried pluton (**A**) is surface following uplift and erosion (**B**), the igneous mass fractures into thin slabs. The photo (**C**) is of the summit of Half Dome in Yosemite National F It is an exfoliation dome and illustrates the onionlike layers created by sheeting. (Photo by (Gary Moon/agefotostock)

exfoliation domes. Excellent examples of exfoliation domes include Stone Mountain, Georgia, and Half Dome in Yosemite National Park (Figure 16).

Biological Activity

Weathering is also accomplished by the activities of organisms, including plants, burrowing animals, and humans. Plant roots in search of water grow into fractures, and as the roots grow, they wedge the rock apart (**FIGURE 17**). Burrowing animals further break down the rock by moving fresh material to the surface, where physical and chemical processes can more effectively attack it.

Chemical Weathering of Rocks

Chemical weathering alters the internal structure of minerals by removing and/or adding elements. During this transformation, the original rock is altered into substances that are stable in the surface environment.

FIGURE 17 Root wedging widens fractures in rocks and aids the process of mechanical weathering. (Photo by Kristin Piljay)

Water is the most important agent of chemical weathering. Oxygen dissolved in water will *oxidize* some materials. For example, when an iron nail is found in the soil, it will have a coating of rust (iron oxide), and if the time of exposure has been long, the nail will be so weak that it can be broken as easily as a toothpick. When rocks containing iron-rich minerals (such as hornblende) oxidize, a yellow to reddish-brown rust will appear on the surface.

Carbon dioxide (CO_2) dissolved in water (H_2O) forms carbonic acid (H_2CO_3). This is the same weak acid produced when soft drinks are carbonated. Rain dissolves some carbon dioxide as it falls through the atmosphere, so normal rainwater is mildly acidic. Water in the soil also dissolves carbon dioxide released by decaying organic matter. The result is that acidic water is everywhere on Earth's surface.

How does rock decompose when attacked by carbonic acid? Consider the weathering of the common igneous rock, granite. Recall that granite is composed mainly of quartz and potassium feldspar. As the weak acid slowly reacts with crystals of potassium feldspar, potassium ions are displaced. *This destroys the mineral's crystalline structure.*

The most abundant products of the chemical breakdown of feldspar are clay minerals. Because clay minerals are the end product of chemical weathering, they are very stable under surface conditions. Consequently, clay minerals make up a high percentage of the inorganic material in many soils.

In addition to the formation of clay minerals, some silica (SiO_2) is dissolved from the feldspar structure and is carried away by groundwater. The dissolved silica will eventually precipitate to produce a hard, dense sedimentary rock (chert), fill pore spaces between mineral grains, or be carried to the ocean, where microscopic animals will build silica shells from it.

Quartz, the other main component of granite, is very resistant to chemical weathering. Because it is durable, quartz remains substantially unaltered when attacked by weak acid. As granite weathers, the feldspar crystals become dull and slowly turn to clay, releasing the once interlocked quartz grains, which still retain their fresh, glassy appearance. Although some quartz remains in the soil, much is transported to the sea and other sites, where it becomes sandy beaches and sand dunes.

To summarize, *the chemical weathering of granite produces clay minerals along with potassium ions and silica, which enter into solution.* In addition, durable quartz grains are freed.

Table 1 lists the weathered products of some of the most common silicate minerals. Remember that silicate minerals make up most of Earth's crust and are composed primarily of just eight elements. When chemically weathered, the silicate minerals yield sodium, calcium, potassium, and magnesium ions. These may be used by plants or removed by groundwater. The element iron combines with oxygen to produce iron-oxide compounds that give soil a reddish-brown or yellowish color. The three remaining elements—aluminum, silicon, and oxygen—join with water to produce clay minerals that become an important part of the soil.

Table I Products of weathering

Original Mineral	Weathers to Produce	Released into Solution
Quartz	Quartz grains	Silica (SiO_2)
Feldspar	Clay minerals	Silica (SiO_2) Ions of potassium, sodium, and calcium
Hornblende	Clay minerals	Silica (SiO_2)
	Iron minerals (limonite and hematite)	Ions of calcium and magnesium
Olivine	Iron minerals (limonite and hematite)	Silica (SiO_2) Ions of magnesium

Ultimately, the products of weathering form the raw materials for building sedimentary rocks, which we consider next.

SEDIMENTARY ROCKS: COMPACTED AND CEMENTED SEDIMENT

Earth Materials
▼Sedimentary Rocks

Recall the rock cycle, which shows the origin of **sedimentary rocks**. Weathering begins the process. Next, gravity and erosional agents (running water, wind, waves, and glacial ice) remove the products of weathering and carry them to a new location where they are deposited. Usually, the particles are broken down further during this transport phase. Following deposition, this **sediment** may become lithified, or "turned to rock." Commonly, *compaction* and *cementation* transform the sediment into solid sedimentary rock.

The word *sedimentary* indicates the nature of these rocks, for it is derived from the Latin *sedimentum*, which means "settling," a reference to a solid material settling out of a fluid. Most sediment is deposited in this fashion. Weathered debris is constantly being swept from bedrock and carried away by water, ice, or wind. Eventually, the material is deposited in lakes, river valleys, seas, and countless other places. The particles in a desert sand dune, the mud on the floor of a swamp, the gravels in a streambed, and even household dust are examples of sediment produced by this never-ending process.

The weathering of bedrock and the transport and deposition of the weathering products are continuous. Therefore, sediment is found almost everywhere. As piles of sediment accumulate, the materials near the bottom are compacted by the weight of the overlying layers. Over long periods, these sediments are cemented together by mineral matter deposited from water in the spaces between particles. This forms solid sedimentary rock.

Geologists estimate that sedimentary rocks account for only about 5 percent (by volume) of Earth's outer 16 kilometers (10 miles). However, the importance of this group of rocks is far greater than this percentage implies. If you sampled the rocks exposed at Earth's surface, you would find that the great majority are sedimentary (FIGURE 18). Indeed, about 75 percent of all rock outcrops on the continents are sedimentary. Therefore, we can think of sedimentary rocks as comprising a relatively thin and somewhat discontinuous layer in the uppermost portion of the crust. This makes sense because sediment accumulates at the surface.

It is from sedimentary rocks that geologists reconstruct many details of Earth's history. Because sediments are deposited in a variety of different settings at the surface, the rock layers that they eventually form hold many clues to past surface environments. They may also exhibit characteristics that allow geologists to decipher information about the method and distance of sediment transport. Furthermore, it is sedimentary rocks that contain fossils, which are vital evidence in the study of the geologic past.

Finally, many sedimentary rocks are important economically. Coal, which is burned to provide a significant portion of U.S. electrical energy, is classified as a sedimentary rock. Other major energy resources (petroleum and natural gas) occur in pores within sedimentary rocks. Other sedimentary rocks are major sources of iron, aluminum, manganese, and fertilizer, plus numerous materials essential to the construction industry.

Classifying Sedimentary Rocks

Materials accumulating as sediment have two principal sources. First, sediments may originate as solid particles from weathered rocks, such as the igneous rocks earlier described. These particles are called *detritus*, and the sedimentary rocks that they form are called **detrital sedimentary rocks** (FIGURE 19).

The second major source of sediment is soluble material produced largely by chemical weathering. When these dissolved substances are precipitated back as solids, they are called *chemical sediment*, and they form **chemical sedimentary rocks**. We will now look at detrital and chemical sedimentary rocks (Figure 19).

Detrital Sedimentary Rocks

Though a wide variety of minerals and rock fragments may be found in detrital rocks, clay minerals and quartz dominate. As you learned earlier, clay minerals are the most abundant product of the chemical weathering of silicate minerals, especially the feldspars. Quartz, on the other hand, is abundant because it is extremely durable and very resistant to chemical weathering. Thus, when igneous rocks such as granite are weathered, individual quartz grains are set free.

Geologists use particle size to distinguish among detrital sedimentary rocks. Figure 19 presents the four size categories for particles making up detrital rocks. When gravel-size particles predominate, the rock is called *conglomerate* if the sediment is rounded (FIGURE 20A) and *breccia* if the pieces are angular (FIGURE 20B). Angular fragments indicate that the particles were not transported very far from their source prior to deposition and so have not

FIGURE 18 Sedimentary rocks exposed at Capital Reef National Park, Utah. Sedimentary rocks are exposed at the surface more than igneous and metamorphic rocks. Because they contain fossils and other clues about the geologic past, sedimentary rocks are important in the study of Earth history. Vertical changes in rock types represent environmental changes through time. (Photo by Scott T. Smith/CORBIS)

had corners and rough edges abraded. *Sandstone* is the name given rocks when sand-size grains prevail (FIGURE 21). *Shale,* the most common sedimentary rock, is made of very fine-grained sediment (FIGURE 22). *Siltstone,* another rather fine-grained rock, is sometimes difficult to differentiate from rocks such as shale, which are composed of even smaller clay-size sediment.

Particle size is not only a convenient method of dividing detrital rocks; the sizes of the component grains also provide useful information about the environment in which the sediment was deposited. Currents of water or air sort the particles by size. The stronger the current, the larger the particle size carried. Gravels, for example, are moved by swiftly

flowing rivers, rockslides, and glaciers. Less energy is required to transport sand; thus, it is common in windblown dunes, river deposits, and beaches. Because silts and clays settle very slowly, accumulations of these materials are generally associated with the quiet waters of a lake, lagoon, swamp, or marine environment.

Although detrital sedimentary rocks are classified by particle size, in certain cases the mineral composition is also part of naming a rock. For example, most sandstones are predominantly quartz-rich, and they are often referred to as quartz sandstone. In addition, rocks consisting of detrital sediments are rarely composed of grains of just one size. Consequently, a rock containing quantities of both sand and

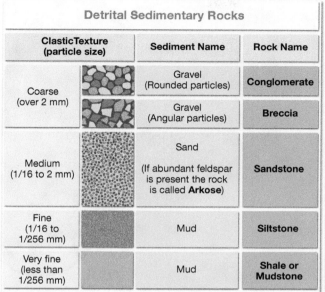

Detrital Sedimentary Rocks		
Clastic Texture (particle size)	Sediment Name	Rock Name
Coarse (over 2 mm)	Gravel (Rounded particles)	Conglomerate
Coarse (over 2 mm)	Gravel (Angular particles)	Breccia
Medium (1/16 to 2 mm)	Sand (If abundant feldspar is present the rock is called **Arkose**)	Sandstone
Fine (1/16 to 1/256 mm)	Mud	Siltstone
Very fine (less than 1/256 mm)	Mud	Shale or Mudstone

Chemical and Organic Sedimentary Rocks			
Composition	Texture	Rock Name	
Calcite, CaCO$_3$	Nonclastic: Fine to coarse crystalline	Crystalline Limestone	
Calcite, CaCO$_3$	Nonclastic: Fine to coarse crystalline	Travertine	
Calcite, CaCO$_3$	Clastic: Visible shells and shell fragments loosely cemented	Coquina	Biochemical Limestone
Calcite, CaCO$_3$	Clastic: Various size shells and shell fragments cemented with calcite cement	Fossiliferous Limestone	Biochemical Limestone
Calcite, CaCO$_3$	Clastic: Microscopic shells and clay	Chalk	Biochemical Limestone
Quartz, SiO$_2$	Nonclastic: Very fine crystalline	Chert (light colored) Flint (dark colored)	
Gypsum CaSO$_4$•2H$_2$O	Nonclastic: Fine to coarse crystalline	Rock Gypsum	
Halite, NaCl	Nonclastic: Fine to coarse crystalline	Rock Salt	
Altered plant fragments	Nonclastic: Fine-grained organic matter	Bituminous Coal	

FIGURE 19 Identification of sedimentary rocks. Sedimentary rocks are divided into two major groups, detrital and chemical, based on their source of sediment. The main criterion for naming detrital rocks is particle size, whereas the primary basis for distinguishing among chemical rocks is their mineral composition.

silt can be correctly classified as sandy siltstone or silty sandstone, depending on which particle size dominates.

Chemical Sedimentary Rocks

In contrast to detrital rocks, which form from the solid products of weathering, chemical sediments are derived from material that is carried in solution to lakes and seas. This material does not remain dissolved in the water indefinitely. When conditions are right, it precipitates to form chemical sediments. This precipitation may occur directly as the

DID YOU KNOW?

The most important and common material used for making glass is silica, which is usually obtained from the quartz in "clean," well-sorted sandstones.

A. **B.**

FIGURE 20 Detrital rocks made up of gravel-sized particles. **A.** *Conglomerate* (rounded particles) **B.** *Breccia* (angular particles). (Photos by E. J. Tarbuck)

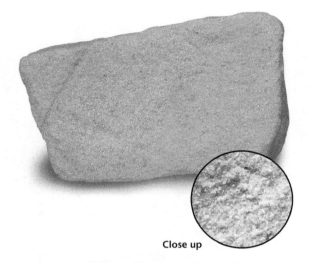

FIGURE 21   Quartz sandstone. After shale, sandstone is the most abundant sedimentary rock. (Photos by E. J. Tarbuck)

FIGURE 23   This rock, called *coquina*, consists of shell fragments; therefore, it has a biochemical origin. (Photos by E. J. Tarbuck)

result of physical processes, or indirectly through life processes of water-dwelling organisms. Sediment formed in this second way has a *biochemical* origin.

An example of a deposit resulting from physical processes is the salt left behind as a body of saltwater evaporates. In contrast, many water-dwelling animals and plants extract dissolved mineral matter to form shells and other hard parts. After the organisms die, their skeletons may accumulate on the floor of a lake or ocean.

Limestone is the most abundant chemical sedimentary rock. It is composed chiefly of the mineral calcite ($CaCO_3$). Ninety percent of limestone is biochemical sediment, while the remaining amount chemically precipitates from seawater.

One easily identified biochemical limestone is *coquina*, a coarse rock composed of loosely cemented shells and shell fragments (**FIGURE 23**). Another less obvious but familiar example is *chalk*, a soft, porous rock made up almost entirely of the hard parts of microscopic organisms that are no larger than the head of a pin (**FIGURE 24**).

Inorganic limestone forms when chemical changes or high water temperatures increase the concentration of calcium carbonate to the point that it precipitates. *Travertine*, the type of limestone that decorates caverns, is one example. Groundwater is the source of travertine that is deposited in caves. As water drops reach the air in a cavern, some of the carbon dioxide dissolved in the water escapes, causing calcium carbonate to precipitate.

Dissolved silica (SiO_2) precipitates to form varieties of microcrystalline quartz (**FIGURE 25**). Sedimentary rocks composed of microcrystalline quartz include chert (light color), flint (dark), jasper (red), and agate (banded). These chemical sedimentary rocks may have either an inorganic or biochemical origin, but the mode of origin is usually difficult to determine.

Very often, evaporation causes minerals to precipitate from water. Such minerals include halite, the chief component of *rock salt*, and gypsum, the main ingredient of *rock gypsum*. Both materials have significant commercial importance. Halite is familiar to everyone as the common salt used in cooking and seasoning foods. Of course, it has many other uses and has been considered important enough that people have sought, traded, and fought over it for much of human history. Gypsum is the basic ingredient of plaster of Paris. This material is used most extensively in the construction industry for "drywall" and plaster.

FIGURE 22   Shale is a fine-grained detrital rock that is, by far, the most abundant of all sedimentary rocks. Dark shales containing plant remains are relatively common. (Photo courtesy of E. J. Tarbuck)

FIGURE 24   White Chalk Cliffs, East Sussex, England. (Photo by Prisma/ Superstock)

A. Agate

B. Flint   **C.** Jasper   **D.** Arrowhead

FIGURE 25   *Chert* is a name used for a number of dense, hard rocks made of microcrystalline quartz. Three examples are shown here. **A.** *Agate* is the banded variety. (Photo by Jeffrey A. Scovil) **B.** The dark color of *flint* results from organic matter. (Photo by E. J. Tarbuck) **C.** The red variety, called *jasper*, gets its color from iron oxide. (Photo by E. J. Tarbuck) **D.** Native Americans frequently made arrowheads and sharp tools from chert. (Photo by LA VENTA/CORBIS/SYGMA)

In the geologic past, many areas that are now dry land were covered by shallow arms of the sea that had only narrow connections to the open ocean. Under these conditions, water continually moved into the bay to replace water lost by evaporation. Eventually, the waters of the bay became saturated and salt deposition began. Today, these arms of the sea are gone, and the remaining deposits are called **evaporite deposits**.

On a smaller scale, evaporite deposits can be seen in such places as Death Valley, California. Here, following rains or periods of snowmelt in the mountains, streams flow from surrounding mountains into an enclosed basin. As the water evaporates, *salt flats* form from dissolved materials left behind as a white crust on the ground (FIGURE 26).

DID YOU KNOW?

Each year, about 30 percent of the world's supply of salt is extracted from seawater. The seawater is pumped into ponds and allowed to evaporate, leaving behind "artificial evaporites," which are harvested.

Coal is quite different from other chemical sedimentary rocks. Unlike other rocks in this category, which are calcite- or silica-rich, coal is made mostly of organic matter. Close examination of a piece of coal under a microscope or magnifying glass often reveals plant structures such as leaves, bark, and wood that have been chemically altered but are still identifiable. This supports the conclusion that coal is the end product of the burial of large amounts of plant material over extended periods (FIGURE 27).

The initial stage in coal formation is the accumulation of large quantities of plant remains. However, special conditions are required for such accumulations, because dead plants normally decompose when exposed to the atmosphere. An ideal environment that allows for the buildup of plant material is a swamp. Because stagnant swamp water is oxygen-deficient, complete decay (oxidation) of the plant material is not possible. At various times during Earth history, such environments have been common. Coal undergoes successive stages of formation. With each successive stage, higher temperatures and pressures drive off impurities and volatiles, as shown in Figure 27.

Lignite and bituminous coals are sedimentary rocks, but anthracite is a metamorphic rock. Anthracite forms

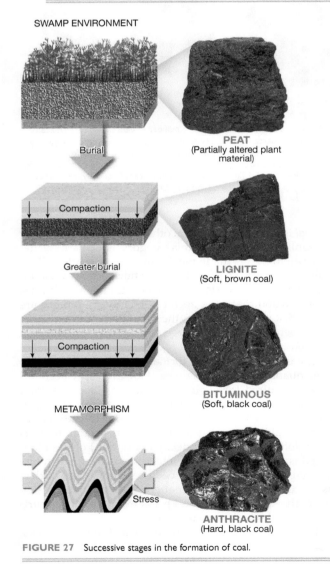

SWAMP ENVIRONMENT

Burial

PEAT
(Partially altered plant material)

Compaction

Greater burial

LIGNITE
(Soft, brown coal)

Compaction

METAMORPHISM

BITUMINOUS
(Soft, black coal)

Stress

ANTHRACITE
(Hard, black coal)

FIGURE 27   Successive stages in the formation of coal.

when sedimentary layers are subjected to the folding and deformation associated with mountain building.

In summary, we divide sedimentary rocks into two major groups: detrital and chemical. The main criterion for classifying detrital rocks is particle size, whereas chemical rocks are distinguished by their mineral composition. The categories presented here are more rigid than is the actual state of nature. Many detrital sedimentary rocks are a mixture of more than one particle size. Furthermore, many sedimentary rocks classified as chemical also contain at least small quantities of detrital sediment, and practically all detrital rocks are cemented with material that was originally dissolved in water.

Lithification of Sediment

Lithification refers to the processes by which sediments are transformed into solid sedimentary rocks. One of the most common processes is *compaction*. As sediments accumulate through time, the weight of overlying material compresses the deeper sediments. As the grains are pressed closer and closer, pore space is greatly reduced. For example, when clays are buried beneath several thousand meters of material, the volume of the clay may be reduced as much as 40 percent. Compaction is most significant in fine-grained sedimentary rocks such as shale, because sand and other coarse sediments compress little.

Cementation is another important means by which sediments are converted to sedimentary rock. The cementing materials are carried in solution by water percolating through the pore spaces between particles. Over time, the cement precipitates onto the sediment grains, fills the open spaces, and joins the particles. Calcite, silica, and iron oxide are the most common cements. Identification of the cementing material is simple. Calcite cement will effervesce (fizz) with dilute hydrochloric acid. Silica is the hardest cement and thus produces the hardest sedimentary rocks. When a sedimentary rock has an orange or red color, this usually means iron oxide is present.

FIGURE 28 Sedimentary environments. **A.** Ripple marks preserved in sedimentary rocks may indicate a beach or stream channel environment. (Photo by Marli Miller) **B.** Mud cracks form when wet mud or clay dries and shrinks, perhaps signifying a tidal flat or desert basin. (Photo by Gary Yeowell/Getty Images Inc.—Stone Allstock)

A

B

Features of Sedimentary Rocks

Sedimentary rocks are particularly important in the study of Earth history. These rocks form at Earth's surface, and as layer upon layer of sediment accumulates, each records the nature of the environment at the time the sediment was deposited. These layers, called **strata**, or **beds**, are the *single most characteristic feature of sedimentary rocks* (see Figure 18).

The thickness of beds ranges from microscopically thin to tens of meters thick. Separating the strata are *bedding planes*, flat surfaces along which rocks tend to separate or break. Generally, each bedding plane marks the end of one episode of sedimentation and the beginning of another.

Sedimentary rocks provide geologists with evidence for deciphering past environments. A conglomerate, for example, indicates a high-energy environment, such as a rushing stream, where only the coarse materials can settle out. By contrast, black shale and coal are associated with a low-energy, organic-rich environment, such as a swamp or lagoon. Other features found in some sedimentary rocks also give clues to past environments (**FIGURE 28**).

Fossils, the traces or remains of prehistoric life, are perhaps the most important inclusions found in some sedimentary rock. Knowing the nature of the life forms that existed at a particular time may help answer many questions about the environment. Was it land or ocean, lake or swamp? Was the climate hot or cold, rainy or dry? Was the ocean water shallow or deep, turbid or clear? Furthermore, fossils are important time indicators and play a key role in matching up rocks from different places that are the same age. Fossils are important tools used in interpreting the geologic past.

METAMORPHIC ROCKS: NEW ROCK FROM OLD

Earth Materials
▼ Metamorphic Rocks

Recall from the discussion of the rock cycle that metamorphism is the transformation of one rock type into another. **Metamorphic rocks** are produced from preexisting igneous, sedimentary, or even other metamorphic rocks. Thus, every metamorphic rock has a *parent rock*—the rock from which it was formed.

Metamorphism, which means to "change form," is a process that leads to changes in the mineralogy, texture (for example, grain size), and sometimes the chemical composition of rocks. Metamorphism takes place when preexisting rock is subjected to a physical or chemical environment that is significantly different from that in which it initially formed. In response to these new conditions the rock gradually changes until a state of equilibrium with the new environment is reached. Most metamorphic changes occur at the elevated temperatures and pressures that exist in the zone beginning a few kilometers below Earth's surface and extending into the upper mantle.

Metamorphism often progresses incrementally, from slight changes *(low-grade metamorphism)* to substantial changes *(high-grade metamorphism)*. For example, under low-grade metamorphism, the common sedimentary rock *shale* becomes the more compact metamorphic rock called *slate*. Hand samples of these rocks are sometimes difficult to distinguish, illustrating that the transition from sedimentary to metamorphic rock is often gradual and the changes can be subtle.

In more extreme environments, metamorphism causes a transformation so complete that the identity of the parent rock cannot be determined. In high-grade metamorphism, such features as bedding planes, fossils, and vesicles that may have existed in the parent rock are obliterated. Further, when rocks deep in the crust (where temperatures are high) are subjected to directed pressure, the entire mass may deform, producing large-scale structures, such as folds (**FIGURE 29**).

In the most extreme metamorphic environments, the temperatures approach those at which rocks melt. However, *during metamorphism the rock must remain essentially solid,* for if complete melting occurs, we have entered the realm of igneous activity.

Most metamorphism occurs in one of two settings:

1. When rock is intruded by magma, **contact** or **thermal metamorphism** may take place. In such a situation, change is caused by the rise in temperature within the host rock surrounding the mass of molten material.

2. During mountain building, great quantities of rock are subjected to directed pressures and high temperatures associated with large-scale deformation called **regional metamorphism**.

Extensive areas of metamorphic rocks are exposed on every continent. Metamorphic rocks are an important component of many mountain belts, where they make up a large portion of a mountain's crystalline core. Even the stable continental interiors, which are generally covered by sedimentary rocks, are underlain by metamorphic basement rocks. In all of these settings, the metamorphic rocks are usually highly deformed and intruded by igneous masses. Consequently, significant parts of Earth's continental crust are composed of metamorphic and associated igneous rocks.

DID YOU KNOW?

Some low-grade metamorphic rocks actually contain fossils. When fossils are present in metamorphic rocks, they provide useful clues for determining the original rock type and its depositional environment. In addition, fossils whose shapes have been distorted during metamorphism provide insight into the extent to which the rock has been deformed.

FIGURE 29 Folded and metamorphosed rocks in Anza Borrego Desert State Park, California. (Photo by A. P. Trujillo/APT Photos)

What Drives Metamorphism?

The agents of metamorphism include *heat, pressure (stress),* and *chemically active fluids.* During metamorphism, rocks are usually subjected to all three metamorphic agents simultaneously. However, the degree of metamorphism and the contribution of each agent vary greatly from one environment to another.

Heat as a Metamorphic Agent

Thermal energy (*heat*) is the most important factor driving metamorphism. It triggers chemical reactions that result in the recrystallization of existing minerals and the formation of new minerals. Thermal energy for metamorphism comes mainly from two sources. Rocks experience a rise in temperature when they are intruded by magma rising from below. This is called *contact* or *thermal metamorphism.* In this situation, the adjacent host rock is "baked" by the emplaced magma.

By contrast, rocks that formed at Earth's surface will experience a gradual increase in temperature as they are taken to greater depths. In the upper crust, this increase in temperature averages about 25°C per kilometer. When buried to a depth of about 8 kilometers (5 miles), where temperatures are between 150°C and 200°C, clay minerals tend to become unstable and begin to recrystallize into other minerals, such as chlorite and muscovite, that are stable in this environment. (Chlorite is a micalike mineral formed by the metamorphism of iron- and magnesian-rich silicates.) However, many silicate minerals, particularly those found in crystalline igneous rocks—quartz and feldspar, for example—remain stable at these temperatures. Thus, metamorphic changes in these minerals require much higher temperatures in order to recrystallize.

Confining Pressure and Differential Stress as Metamorphic Agents

Pressure, like temperature, also increases with depth as the thickness of the overlying rock increases. Buried rocks are subjected to *confining pressure*— similar to water pressure in that the forces are equally applied in all directions (**FIGURE 30 A**). The deeper you go in the ocean, the greater the confining pressure. The same is true for buried rock. Confining pressure causes the spaces between mineral grains to close, producing a more compact rock having greater density. Further, at great

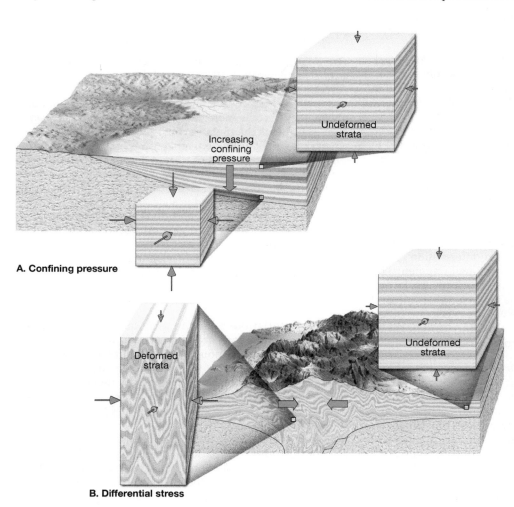

A. Confining pressure

B. Differential stress

FIGURE 30 Pressure (stress) as a metamorphic agent. **A.** In a depositional environment, as confining pressure increases, rocks deform by decreasing in volume. **B.** During mountain building, rocks subjected to differential stress are shortened in the direction that pressure is applied, and lengthened in the direction perpendicular to that force.

FIGURE 31 Deformed metamorphic rocks exposed in a road cut in the Eastern Highland of Connecticut. Imagine the tremendous force required to fold rock in this manner. (Photo by Phil Dombrowski)

depths, confining pressure may cause minerals to recrystallize into new minerals that display more compact crystalline forms.

During episodes of mountain building, large rock bodies become highly crumpled and metamorphosed (FIGURE 30B). The forces that generate mountains are unequal in different directions and are called *differential stress*. Unlike confining pressure, which "squeezes" rock equally in all directions, differential stresses are greater in one direction than in others. As shown in Figure 30B, rocks subjected to differential stress are shortened in the direction of greatest stress, and elongated, or lengthened, in the direction perpendicular to that stress. The deformation caused by differential stresses plays a major role in developing metamorphic textures.

In surface environments where temperatures are relatively low, rocks are *brittle* and tend to fracture when subjected to differential stress. Continued deformation grinds and pulverizes the mineral grains into small fragments. By contrast, in high-temperature environments, rocks are *ductile*. When rocks exhibit ductile behavior, their mineral grains tend to flatten and elongate when subjected to differential stress. This accounts for their ability to deform by flowing (rather than fracturing) to generate intricate folds (FIGURE 31).

Chemically Active Fluids

Fluids composed mainly of water and other volatiles (materials that readily change to gases at surface conditions), including carbon dioxide, are believed to play an important role in some types of metamorphism. Fluids that surround mineral grains act as catalysts to promote recrystallization by enhancing ion migration. In progressively hotter environments, these ion-rich fluids become correspondingly more reactive.

When two mineral grains are squeezed together, the parts of their crystalline structures that touch are the most highly stressed. Atoms at these sites are readily dissolved by the hot fluids and move to the voids between individual grains. Thus, hot fluids aid in the recrystallization of mineral grains by dissolving material from regions of high stress and then precipitating (depositing) this material in areas of low stress. As a result, *minerals tend to recrystallize and grow longer in a direction perpendicular to compressional stresses.*

When hot fluids circulate freely through rocks, ionic exchange may occur between adjacent rock layers, or ions may migrate great distances before they are finally deposited. The latter situation is particularly common when we consider hot fluids that escape during the crystallization of an intrusive mass of magma. If the rocks surrounding the magma differ markedly in composition from the invading fluids, there may be a substantial exchange of ions between the fluids and host rocks. When this occurs, the overall composition of the surrounding rock changes.

Metamorphic Textures

The degree of metamorphism is reflected in the rock's *texture* and *mineralogy*. (Recall that the term *texture* is used to describe the size, shape, and arrangement of grains within a rock.) When rocks are subjected to low-grade metamorphism, they become more compact and thus denser. A common example is the metamorphic rock slate, which forms when shale is subjected to temperatures and pressures only slightly greater than those associated with the compaction that lithifies sediment. In this case, differential stress causes the microscopic clay minerals in shale to align into the more compact arrangement found in slate.

Under more extreme conditions, stress causes certain minerals to recrystallize. In general, recrystallization encourages the growth of larger crystals. Consequently, many metamorphic rocks consist of visible crystals, much like coarse-grained igneous rocks.

Foliation

The term **foliation** refers to any planer (nearly flat) arrangement of mineral grains or structural features within a rock (FIGURE 32). Although foliation may occur in some sedimentary and even a few types of igneous rocks, it is a fundamental characteristic of regionally metamorphosed rocks—that is, rock units that have been strongly deformed, mainly by folding. In metamorphic environments, foliation is ultimately driven by compressional stresses that shorten rock units, causing mineral grains in preexisting rocks to develop parallel, or nearly parallel, alignments. Examples of foliation include the parallel alignment of platy minerals such as the micas; the parallel alignment of flattened pebbles; compositional banding in which dark and light minerals separate generating a layered appearance; and rock cleavage in which rocks can be easily split into tabular slabs.

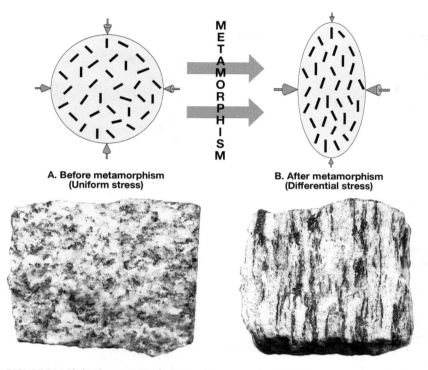

FIGURE 32 Under the pressures of metamorphism, some mineral grains become reoriented and aligned at right angles to the stress. The resulting orientation of mineral grains gives the rock a foliated (layered) texture. If the coarse-grained igneous rock (granite) on the left underwent intense metamorphism, it could end up closely resembling the metamorphic rock on the right (gneiss). (Photos by E. J. Tarbuck)

Nonfoliated Textures

Not all metamorphic rocks exhibit a foliated texture. Those that do not are referred to as **nonfoliated**, and typically develop in environments where deformation is minimal and the parent rocks are composed of minerals that exhibit equidimensional crystals, such as quartz or calcite. For example, when a fine-grained limestone (made of calcite) is metamorphosed by the intrusion of a hot magma body, the small calcite grains recrystallize to form larger interlocking crystals. The resulting rock, *marble*, exhibits large, equidimensional grains that are randomly oriented, similar to those in a coarse-grained igneous rock.

To review, metamorphic processes cause many changes in existing rocks, including increased density, growth of larger crystals, foliation (reorientation of the mineral grains into a layered or banded appearance), and the transformation of low-temperature minerals into high-temperature minerals (FIGURE 33). Further, the introduction of ions generates new minerals, some of which are economically important.

Common Metamorphic Rocks

Here is a brief overview of common rocks produced by metamorphic processes.

Rock Name			Texture	Grain Size	Comments	Original Parent Rock
Slate	Increasing	Metamorphism	Foliated	Very fine	Excellent rock cleavage, smooth dull surfaces	Shale, mudstone, or siltstone
Schist			Foliated	Medium to Coarse	Micaceous minerals dominate, scaly foliation	Shale, mudstone, or siltstone
Gneiss			Foliated	Medium to Coarse	Compositional banding due to segregation of minerals	Shale, granite, or volcanic rocks
Marble			Nonfoliated	Medium to coarse	Interlocking calcite or dolomite grains	Limestone, dolostone
Quartzite			Nonfoliated	Medium to coarse	Fused quartz grains, massive, very hard	Quartz sandstone
Anthracite			Nonfoliated	Fine	Shiny black rock that may exhibit conchoidal fracture	Bituminous coal

FIGURE 33 Classification of common metamorphic rocks.

Foliated Rocks

Slate is a very fine-grained foliated rock composed of minute mica flakes that are too small to be visible (**FIG-URE 34**). A noteworthy characteristic of slate is its excellent rock cleavage, or tendency to break into flat slabs. This property has made slate a useful rock for roof and floor tile, and billiard tables (**FIGURE 35**). Slate is usually generated by the low-grade metamorphism of shale. Less frequently, it is produced when volcanic ash is metamorphosed. Slate's color is variable. Black slate contains organic material; red slate gets its color from iron oxide; and green slate is usually composed of chlorite, a greenish micalike mineral.

Schists are strongly foliated rocks formed by regional metamorphism (Figure 34). They are platy and can be readily split into thin flakes or slabs. Many schists, like slates, originate from shale parent rock. However, schist forms under more extreme metamorphic conditions. The term *schist* describes the *texture* of a rock regardless of composition. For example, schists composed primarily of muscovite and biotite are called *mica schists*.

Gneiss (pronounced "nice") is the term applied to banded metamorphic rocks in which elongated and granular (as opposed to platy) minerals predominate (Figure 34). The most common minerals in gneisses are quartz and feldspar, with lesser amounts of muscovite, biotite, and hornblende. Gneisses exhibit strong segregation of light and dark silicates, giving them a characteristic banded texture. While still deep below the surface where temperatures and pressures are great, banded gneisses can be deformed into intricate folds.

Nonfoliated Rocks

Marble is a coarse, crystalline rock whose parent rock is limestone. Marble is composed of large interlocking calcite crystals, which form from the recrystallization of smaller grains in the parent rock. Because of its color and relative softness (hardness of only 3 on the Mohs scale), marble is a popular building stone. White marble is particularly prized as a stone from which to carve monuments and statues, such as the Lincoln Memorial in Washington D.C. (**FIGURE 36**). The parent rocks from which various marbles form contain impurities that color the stone. Thus, marble can be pink, gray, green, or even black.

Quartzite is a very hard metamorphic rock most often formed from quartz sandstone. Under moderate- to

DID YOU KNOW?

Because marble can be carved readily, it has been used for centuries for buildings and memorials. Examples of important structures whose exteriors are clad in marble include the Parthenon in Greece, the Taj Mahal in India, and the Washington Monument in the United States.

FIGURE 34 Common metamorphic rocks. (Photos by E. J. Tarbuck)

high-grade metamorphism, the quartz grains in sandstone fuse. Pure quartzite is white, but iron oxide may produce reddish or pinkish stains, and dark minerals may impart a gray color.

FIGURE 35   Because slate breaks into flat slabs, it has many uses. The larger image shows crates full of slate ready to be shipped from a quarry in England. (Photo by Alamy). In the inset photo, slate is used to roof a house in Switzerland. (Photo by E. J. Tarbuck)

A.

B.

FIGURE 36   Marble, because of its workability, is a widely used building stone. **A.** The white exterior of the Lincoln Memorial in Washington, D.C., is constructed mainly of marble that was quarried in Marble, Colorado. Inside, pink Tennessee marble was used for the floors, Alabama marble for the ceilings, and Georgia marble for Lincoln's statue. (Photo by Daniel Grill/iStockphoto) **B.** The exterior of India's Taj Mahal is constructed primarily of the metamorphic rock marble. (Holger Mette/Shutterstock)

THE CHAPTER IN REVIEW

• The three rock groups are igneous, sedimentary, and metamorphic. *Igneous rock* forms from *magma* that cools and solidifies in a process called *crystallization*. *Sedimentary rock* forms from the *lithification* of sediment. *Metamorphic rock* forms from rock that has been subjected to great pressure and heat in a process called *metamorphism*.

• Igneous rocks are classified by their *texture* and *mineral composition*.

• The rate of cooling of magma greatly influences the size of mineral crystals in igneous rock and thus its texture. The four basic igneous rock textures are (1) *fine-grained*, (2) *coarse-grained*, (3) *porphyritic*, and (4) *glassy*.

• Igneous rocks are divided into broad compositional groups based on the percentage of dark and light silicate minerals they contain. *Felsic rocks* (e.g., granite and rhyolite) are composed mostly of the light-colored silicate minerals potassium feldspar and quartz. Rocks of *intermediate* composition (e.g., andesite) contain plagioclase feldspar and amphibole. *Mafic rocks* (e.g., basalt) contain abundant pyroxene and calcium-rich plagioclase feldspar.

• The mineral makeup of an igneous rock is ultimately determined by the chemical composition of the magma from which it crystallized. N. L. Bowen showed that as magma cools, minerals crystallize in an orderly fashion at different temperatures. *Magmatic differentiation* changes the composition of magma and causes more than one rock type to form from a common parent magma.

• *Weathering* is the response of surface materials to a changing environment. *Mechanical weathering*, the physical disintegration of material into smaller fragments, is accomplished by *frost wedging*, sheeting, and *biological activity*. *Chemical weathering* involves processes by which the internal structures of minerals are altered by the removal and/or addition of elements. It occurs when materials are *oxidized* or *react with acid*, such as carbonic acid.

• *Detrital sediments* originate as solid particles derived from weathering and are transported. *Chemical sediments* are soluble materials produced largely by chemical weathering that are precipitated by either inorganic or biological processes. *Detrital sedimentary rocks*, which are classified by particle size, contain a variety of mineral and rock fragments, with clay minerals and quartz the chief constituents. *Chemical sedimentary rocks* often contain the products of biological processes or mineral crystals that form as water evaporates and minerals precipitate. *Lithification* refers to the processes by which sediments are transformed into solid sedimentary rocks.

• Common detrital sedimentary rocks include *shale* (the most common sedimentary rock), *sandstone*, and *conglomerate*. The most abundant chemical sedimentary rock is *limestone*, consisting chiefly of the mineral calcite. *Rock gypsum* and *rock salt* are chemical rocks that form as water evaporates.

• Some features of sedimentary rocks that are often used in the interpretation of Earth history and past environments include *strata* or *beds* (the single most characteristic feature), *bedding planes*, and *fossils*.

• Two types of metamorphism are (1) *regional metamorphism* and (2) *contact or thermal metamorphism*. The agents of metamorphism include *heat*, *pressure* (stress), and *chemically active fluids*. Heat is the most important because it provides the energy to drive the reactions that result in the *recrystallization* of minerals. Metamorphic processes cause many changes in rocks, including *increased density*, growth of *larger mineral crystals*, *reorientation of the mineral grains* into a layered or banded appearance known as *foliation*, and the formation of *new minerals*.

• Some common metamorphic rocks with a *foliated texture* include *slate*, *schist*, and *gneiss*. Metamorphic rocks with a *nonfoliated texture* include *marble* and *quartzite*.

KEY TERMS

andesitic (intermediate) composition
basaltic composition
Bowen's reaction series
chemical sedimentary rock
chemical weathering
coarse-grained texture
contact (thermal) metamorphism
crystal settling

detrital sedimentary rock
evaporite deposit
extrusive (volcanic)
felsic
fine-grained texture
foliation
fossil
frost wedging
glassy texture
granitic composition

igneous rock
intrusive (plutonic)
lava
lithification
mafic
magma
magmatic differentiation
mechanical weathering
metamorphic rock
metamorphism
nonfoliated texture

porphyritic texture
regional metamorphism
rock cycle
sediment
sedimentary rock
sheeting
strata (beds)
texture
ultramafic composition
vesicular texture
weathering

QUESTIONS FOR REVIEW

1. Explain the statement "One rock is the raw material for another" using the rock cycle.

2. If a lava flow at Earth's surface had a basaltic composition, what rock type would the flow likely be (see Figure 10)? What igneous rock would form from the same magma if it did not reach the surface but instead crystallized at great depth?

3. What does a porphyritic texture indicate about the history of an igneous rock?

4. How are granite and rhyolite different? The same? (See Figure 10.)

5. Relate the classification of igneous rocks to Bowen's reaction series.

6. If two identical rocks were weathered, one mechanically and the other chemically, how would the products of weathering for the two rocks differ?

7. How does mechanical weathering add to the effectiveness of chemical weathering?

8. How is carbonic acid formed in nature? What are the products when this acid reacts with potassium feldspar?

9. Which minerals are most common in detrital sedimentary rocks? Why are these minerals so abundant?

10. What is the primary basis for distinguishing among various detrital sedimentary rocks?

11. Distinguish between the two categories of chemical sedimentary rocks.

12. What are evaporite deposits? Name a rock that is an evaporite.

13. Compaction is an important lithification process with which sediment size?

14. What is probably the single most characteristic feature of sedimentary rocks?

15. What is metamorphism?

16. List the three agents of metamorphism and describe the role of each.

17. Distinguish between regional and contact metamorphism.

18. Which feature would easily distinguish schist and gneiss from quartzite and marble?

19. In what ways do metamorphic rocks differ from the igneous and sedimentary rocks from which they formed?

COMPANION WEBSITE

The *Foundations of Earth Science* Website uses the resources and flexibility of the Internet to aid in your study of the topics in this chapter. Written and developed by the authors and other Earth science instructors, this site will help improve your understanding of Earth science. Visit **www.mygeoscienceplace.com** in order to:

• **Review** key chapter concepts.

• **Read** with links to the ebook and to chapter-specific web resources.

• **Visualize** and comprehend challenging topics using learning activities in *GEODe: Earth Science*.

• **Test** yourself with online quizzes.

GEODe: EARTH SCIENCE

GEODe: Earth Science is a valuable and easy to use learning aid that can be accessed from your chapter's Companion Website **www.mygeoscienceplace.com.** It is a dynamic instructional tool that promotes understanding and reinforces important concepts by using tutorials, animations, and exercises that actively engage the student.

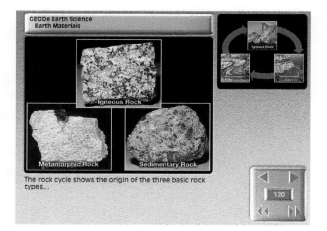

The rock cycle shows the origin of the three basic rock types...

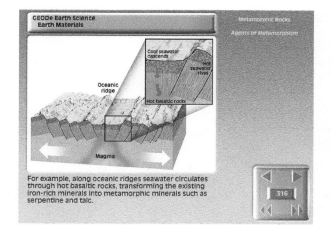

For example, along oceanic ridges seawater circulates through hot basaltic rocks, transforming the existing iron-rich minerals into metamorphic minerals such as serpentine and talc.

Mountain Building

From Chapter 10 of *Earth Science*, Twelfth Edition, Edward J. Tarbuck, Frederick K. Lutgens, Dennis Tasa.

Hiker in the Himalaya Mountains, Nepal. (Photo by Jimmy Chin)

ountains provide some of the most spectacular scenery on our planet (Figure 1). This splendor has been captured by poets, painters, and songwriters alike. Geologists believe that at some time all continental regions were mountainous masses and have concluded that the continents grow by the addition of mountains to their flanks. Consequently, as geologists unravel the secrets of mountain formation, they also gain a deeper understanding of the evolution of Earth's continents. If continents do indeed grow by adding mountains to their flanks, how do geologists explain the existence of mountains (the Urals, for example) that are located in the interior of a landmass? To answer this and related questions, this chapter attempts to piece together the sequence of events believed to generate these lofty structures. We begin our look at mountain building by examining the process of rock deformation and the structures that result.

Rock Deformation

GEODe
EARTH SCIENCE
Forces Within
▶ **Mountain Building**

Every body of rock, no matter how strong, has a point at which it will fracture or flow. **Deformation** (*de* = out, *forma* = form) is a general term that refers to all changes in the original shape and/or size of a rock body. Most crustal de-

formation occurs along plate margins. The lithosphere consists of large segments (plates) that move relative to one another. Plate motions and the interactions along plate boundaries generate forces that cause rock to deform.

When rocks are subjected to forces (stresses) greater than their own strength, they begin to deform, usually by folding, flowing, or fracturing (Figure 2). It is easy to visualize how rocks break, because we normally think of them as being

FIGURE 1 Mount Sneffels in the Colorado Rockies. (Photo by Gavrel Jecan/Art Wolfe, Inc.)

FIGURE 2 Deformed sedimentary strata at Stair Hole, near Lulworth, Dorset, England. These layers of Jurassic-age rock, originally deposited in horizontal beds, have been folded as a result of the collision between the African and European crustal plates. (Photo by Tom and Susan Bean, Inc.)

brittle. But how can rock masses be bent into intricate folds without being broken during the process? To answer this question, geologists performed laboratory experiments in which rocks were subjected to forces under conditions that simulated those existing at various depths within the crust.

Although each rock type deforms somewhat differently, the general characteristics of rock deformation were determined from these experiments. Geologists discovered that when stress is gradually applied, rocks first respond by deforming elastically. Changes that result from *elastic deformation* are recoverable; that is, like a rubber band, the rock will return to nearly its original size and shape when the force is removed. (The energy for most earthquakes comes from stored elastic energy that is released as rock snaps back to its original shape.) Once the elastic limit (strength) of a rock is surpassed, it either flows (*ductile deformation*) or fractures (*brittle deformation*). The factors that influence the strength of a rock and how it will deform include temperature, confining pressure, rock type, and time.

Temperature and Confining Pressure

Rocks near the surface, where temperatures and confining pressures are low, tend to behave like a brittle solid and fracture once their strength is exceeded. This type of deformation is called **brittle** (*bryttian* = to shatter) **failure** or **brittle deformation**. From our everyday experience, we know that glass objects, wooden pencils, china plates, and even our bones exhibit brittle failure once their strength is surpassed. By contrast, at depth, where temperatures and confining pressures are high, rocks exhibit *ductile* behavior. **Ductile deformation** is a type of solid-state flow that produces a change in the size and shape of an object without fracturing. Ordinary objects that display ductile behavior include modeling clay, bee's wax,

caramel candy, and most metals. For example, a copper penny placed on a railroad track will be flattened and deformed (without breaking) by the force applied by a passing train.

Ductile deformation of a rock—strongly aided by high temperature and high confining pressure—is somewhat similar to the deformation of a penny flattened by a train. Rocks that display evidence of ductile flow usually were deformed at great depth and may exhibit contorted folds that give the impression that the strength of the rock was akin to soft putty (Figure 2).

Rock Type

In addition to the physical environment, the mineral composition and texture of a rock greatly influence how it will deform. For example, crystalline rocks, such as granite, basalt, and quartzite, that are composed of minerals that have strong internal molecular bonds tend to fail by brittle fracture. By contrast, sedimentary rocks that are weakly cemented, or metamorphic rocks that contain zones of weakness, such as foliation, are more susceptible to ductile flow. Rocks that are weak and thus most likely to behave in a ductile manner when subjected to differential forces include rock salt, gypsum, and shale; limestone, schist, and marble are of intermediate strength. In fact, rock salt is so weak that it deforms under small amounts of differential stress and rises like stone pillars through beds of sediment that lie in and around the Gulf of Mexico.

Time

One key factor that researchers are unable to duplicate in the laboratory is how rocks respond to small amounts of force applied over long spans of *geologic time*. However, insights into the effects of time on deformation are provided in everyday settings. For example, marble benches have been known to sag under their own weight over a span of a hundred years or so, and wooden bookshelves may bend after being loaded with books for a relatively short period. In nature small stresses applied over long time spans surely play an important role in the deformation of rock. Forces that are unable to deform rock when initially applied may cause rock to flow if the force is maintained over an extended period of time.

Folds

Forces Within
▶ **Mountain Building**

During mountain building, flat-lying sedimentary and volcanic rocks are often bent into a series of wavelike undulations called **folds**. Folds in sedimentary strata are much like those that would form if you were to hold the ends of a sheet of paper and then push them together. In nature, folds come in a wide variety of sizes and configurations. Some folds are broad flexures in which rock units hundreds of meters thick have been slightly warped. Others are very tight microscopic structures found in metamorphic rocks. Size differences notwithstanding, most folds are the result of *compressional forces* that result in the shortening and thickening of the crust.

Types of Folds

The two most common types of folds are anticlines and synclines (Figure 3). An **anticline** is most commonly formed by the upfolding, or arching, of rock layers.* Anticlines are sometimes spectacularly displayed where highways have been cut through deformed strata (Figure 3A). Often found in association with anticlines are downfolds, or troughs, called **synclines**. Notice in Figure 3 that the limb of an anticline is also a limb of the adjacent syncline.

Depending on their orientation, these basic folds are described as *symmetrical* when the limbs are mirror images of

---

*By strict definition, an anticline is a structure in which the oldest strata are found in the center. This most typically occurs when strata are upfolded. Furthermore, a syncline is strictly defined as a structure in which the youngest strata are found in the center. This occurs most commonly when strata are downfolded.

FIGURE 3 Block diagram and photos showing the principal types of folded strata. **A.** The upfolded or arched structures are anticlines. The downfolds or troughs are synclines. Notice that the limb of an anticline is also the limb of the adjacent syncline. **B.** Anticlines and synclines exposed along a cliff on the Mediterranean island of Crete. (Photo by Marco Simoni/Robert Harding Picture Library Ltd./Alamy) **C.** Overturned fold in Alaska's Denali National Park. (Photo by Michael Collier)

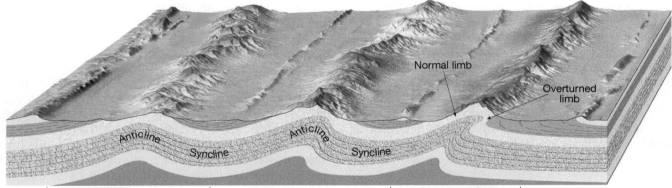

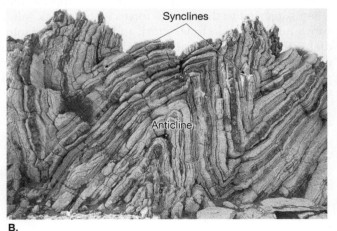

each other and *asymmetrical* when they are not. An asymmetrical fold is said to be *overturned* if one limb is tilted beyond the vertical (Figure 3C). An overturned fold can also lie on its side so that a plane extending through the axis of the fold would be horizontal. These *recumbent* folds are common in mountainous regions such as the Alps.

Folds do not continue forever; rather, their ends die out much like the wrinkles in cloth. Some folds *plunge* because the axis of the fold penetrates into the ground (Figure 4). As the figure shows, both anticlines and synclines can plunge. Figure 4 shows an example of a plunging anticline and the pattern produced when erosion removes the upper layers of the structure and exposes its interior. Note that the outcrop pattern of an anticline points in the direction it is plunging, whereas the opposite is true for a syncline. A good example of the kind of topography that results when erosional forces attack folded sedimentary strata is found in the Valley and Ridge Province of the Appalachians.

Although we have separated our discussion of folds and faults, in the real world folds are generally intimately coupled with faults. Examples of this close association are broad, regional features called *monoclines*. Particularly prominent features of the Colorado Plateau, **monoclines** are large, step-like folds in otherwise horizontal sedimentary strata (Figure 5). These folds appear to be the result of the reactivating of steeply dipping fault zones located in basement rocks beneath the plateau. As large blocks of basement rock were displaced upward along ancient faults, the comparatively ductile sedimentary strata above responded by folding. On the Col-orado Plateau, monoclines display a narrow zone of steeply inclined beds that flatten out to form the uppermost layers of large elevated areas, including the Zuni Uplift, Echo Cliffs Uplift, and San Rafael Swell. Displacement along these reactivated faults often exceeds 1 kilometer (0.6 mile).

Domes and Basins

Broad upwarps in basement rock may deform the overlying cover of sedimentary strata and generate large folds. When this upwarping produces a circular or elongated structure, the feature is called a **dome**. Downwarped structures having a similar shape are termed **basins**.

The Black Hills of western South Dakota is a large domed structure thought to be generated by upwarping. Here erosion has stripped away the highest portions of the upwarped sedimentary beds, exposing older igneous and metamorphic rocks in the center (Figure 6). Remnants of these once continuous sedimentary layers are visible, flanking the crystalline core of these mountains.

Several large basins exist in the United States. The basins of Michigan and Illinois have very gently sloping beds similar to saucers (Figure 7). These basins are thought to be the result of large accumulations of sediment, whose weight caused the crust to subside.

Because large basins usually contain sedimentary beds sloping at very low angles, they are usually identified by the age of the rocks composing them. The youngest rocks are found near the center, and the oldest rocks are at the flanks.

FIGURE 4 Plunging folds. **A.** Idealized view of plunging folds in which a horizontal surface has been added. **B.** View of plunging folds as they might appear after extensive erosion. Notice that in a plunging anticline the outcrop pattern "points" in the direction of the plunge, while the opposite is true of plunging synclines. **C.** Sheep Mountain, a doubly plunging anticline. (Photo by Michael Collier)

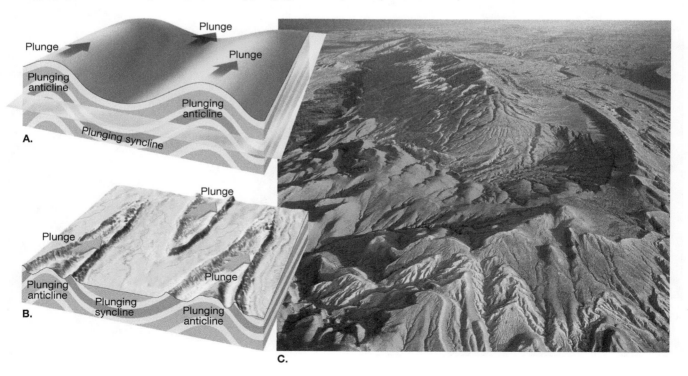

A.

B.

FIGURE 5 Monoclines are large step-like folds in sedimentary strata. **A.** Monocline located near Mexican Hat, Utah. (Photo by Tom Bean) **B.** This monocline consists of bent sedimentary beds that were deformed by faulting in the bedrock below. The thrust fault in this diagram is called a *blind thrust* because it does not reach the surface.

This is just the opposite order of a domed structure, such as the Black Hills, where the oldest rocks form the core.

Faults

GEODe
Forces Within
Mountain Building

Faults are fractures in the crust along which appreciable displacement has taken place. Occasionally, small faults can be recognized in road cuts where sedimentary beds have been offset a few meters, as shown in Figure 8. Faults of this scale usually occur as single discrete breaks. By contrast, large faults, like the San Andreas Fault in California, have displacements of hundreds of kilometers and consist of many interconnecting fault surfaces. These *fault zones* can be several kilometers wide and are often easier to identify from high-altitude photographs than at ground level.

FIGURE 6 The Black Hills of South Dakota, a large domal structure with resistant igneous and metamorphic rocks exposed in the core.

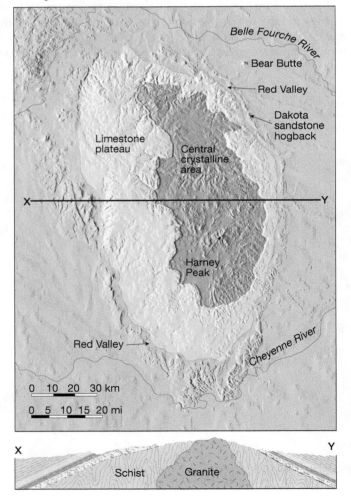

FIGURE 7 The bedrock geology of the Michigan Basin. Notice that the youngest rocks are centrally located, while the oldest beds flank this structure.

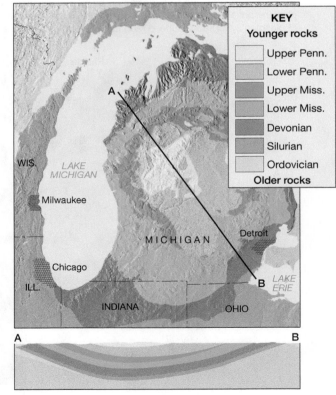

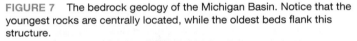

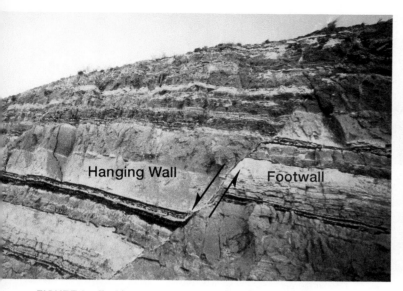

FIGURE 8 Faulting caused the vertical displacement of these beds located near Kanab, Utah. Arrows show relative motion of rock units. (Photo by Tom Bean)

Dip-Slip Faults

Faults in which the movement is primarily parallel to the inclination, or dip, of the fault surface are called **dip-slip faults**. Vertical displacements along dip-slip faults may produce long, low cliffs called **fault scarps** (*scarpe* = a slope).

It has become common practice to call the rock surface that is immediately above the fault the *hanging wall* and to call the rock surface below, the *footwall* (Figure 8). This nomenclature arose from prospectors and miners who excavated shafts and tunnels along fault zones because these are frequently sites of ore deposits. In these tunnels, the miners would walk on the rocks below the mineralized fault zone (the footwall) and hang their lanterns on the rocks above (the hanging wall).

Two major types of dip-slip faults are *normal faults* and *reverse faults*.

Normal Faults Dip-slip faults are classified as **normal faults** when the hanging wall block moves down relative to the footwall block (Figure 9A). Most normal faults have steep dips of about 60 degrees, which tend to flatten out with depth. However, some dip-slip faults have much lower dips, with some approaching horizontal. Because of the downward motion of the hanging wall block, normal faults accommodate lengthening, or extension, of the crust.

Normal faulting is prevalent at spreading centers where plate divergence occurs. A central block called a **graben** (*graben* = ditch) is bounded by normal faults and drops as the plates separate (Figure 10). These grabens produce an elongated valley bounded by relatively uplifted structures called **horsts**. An excellent example of horst and graben topography is found in the Basin and Range Province, a region that encompasses Nevada and portions of surrounding states (Figure 10). The crust has been elongated and broken to create more than 200 relatively small mountain ranges. Averaging about 80 kilometers (about 50 miles) in length, the ranges rise 900 to 1,500 meters (about 3,000 to 5,000 feet) above the adjacent down-faulted basins. Notice in Figure 10 that the dips of the normal faults in the Basin and Range Province decrease with depth and join together to form a nearly horizontal fault called a *detachment fault*. These detachment faults extend for several kilometers below the surface. They form a major boundary between the rocks below, which exhibit ductile deformation, and the rocks above, which demonstrate brittle deformation via faulting.

Fault motion provides geologists with a method of determining the nature of the forces at work within Earth. Normal faults indicate the existence of tensional forces that pull the crust apart. This "pulling apart" can be accomplished either by uplifting that causes the surfaces to stretch and break or by opposing horizontal forces.

Reverse and Thrust Faults **Reverse faults** and **thrust faults** are dip-slip faults in which the hanging wall block moves up relative to the footwall block (Figure 9B and C). Reverse faults have dips greater than 45 degrees, and thrust faults have dips less than 45 degrees. Because the hanging wall

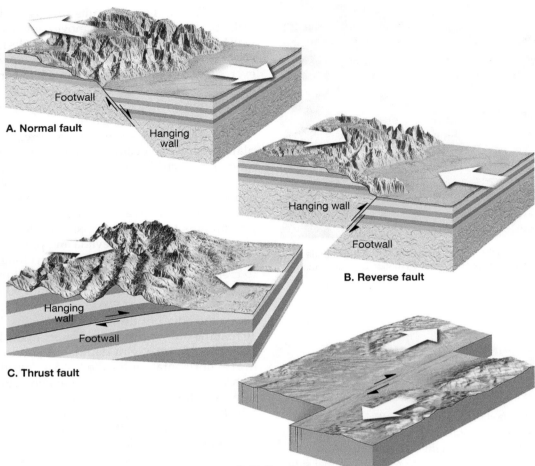

FIGURE 9 Block diagrams of four types of faults. **A.** Normal fault. **B.** Reverse fault. **C.** Thrust fault. **D.** Strike-slip fault.

FIGURE 10 Normal faulting in the Basin and Range Province. Here tensional stresses have elongated and fractured the crust into numerous blocks. Movement along these fractures has tilted the blocks, producing parallel mountain ranges called *fault-block mountains*. The downfaulted blocks (grabens) form basins, whereas the upfaulted blocks (horsts) are eroded to form rugged mountainous topography. In addition, numerous tilted blocks (half-grabens) form both basins and highlands. (Photo by Michael Collier)

block moves up and over the footwall block, reverse and thrust faults accommodate shortening of the crust.

Most high-angle reverse faults are small and accommodate local displacements in regions dominated by other types of faulting. Thrust faults, on the other hand, exist at all scales. In mountainous regions such as the Alps, Northern Rockies, Himalayas, and Appalachians, thrust faults have displaced strata as far as 100 kilometers (about 60 miles) over adjacent rock units. The result of this large-scale movement is that older strata end up overlying younger rocks.

Whereas normal faults occur in tensional environments, reverse and thrust faults result from strong compressional stresses. In these settings, crustal blocks are displaced *toward* one another, with the hanging wall being displaced upward relative to the footwall. Thrust faulting is most pronounced in subduction zones and other convergent boundaries where plates are colliding. Compressional forces generally produce folds as well as faults and result in a thickening and shortening of the material involved.

Strike-Slip Faults

Faults in which the dominant displacement is horizontal and parallel to the trend, or strike, of the fault surface are called **strike-slip faults** (Figure 9D). Because of their large size and linear nature, many strike-slip faults produce a trace that is visible over a great distance (Figure 11). Rather than a single fracture along which movement takes place, large strike-slip faults consist of a zone of roughly parallel fractures. The zone may be up to several kilometers wide. The most recent movement, however, is often along a strand only a few meters wide, which may offset features such as stream channels (see Figure B in Box 1). Furthermore, crushed and broken rocks produced during faulting are more easily eroded, often producing linear valleys or troughs that mark the locations of strike-slip faults.

The earliest scientific records of strike-slip faulting were made following surface ruptures that produced large earthquakes. One of the most noteworthy of these was the great San Francisco earthquake of 1906. During this strong earthquake, structures such as fences that were built across the San Andreas Fault were displaced as much as 4.7 meters (15 feet). Because the movement along the San Andreas causes the crustal block on the opposite side of the fault to move to the right as you face the fault, it is called a *right-lateral* strike-slip fault. The Great Glen fault in Scotland is a well-known example of a *left-lateral* strike-slip fault, which exhibits the opposite sense of displacement.

Many major strike-slip faults cut through the lithosphere and accommodate motion between two large crustal plates. This special kind of strike-slip fault is called a **transform** (*trans* = across, *forma* = form) **fault**. Numerous transform faults cut the oceanic lithosphere and link offset segments of oceanic ridges. Others accommodate displacement between continental plates that move horizontally with respect to each other. One of the best-known transform faults is California's San Andreas Fault (see Box 1). This plate-bounding fault can be traced for about 950 kilometers (600 miles) from the Gulf of California to a point along the Pacific Coast north of San Francisco, where it heads out to sea. Ever since its formation, about 29 million years ago, displacement along the San Andreas Fault has exceeded 560 kilometers (340 miles). This movement has accommodated the northward displacement of southwestern California and the Baja Peninsula of Mexico in relation to the remainder of North America.

Joints

Forces Within
▶ Mountain Building

Among the most common rock structures are fractures called **joints**. Unlike faults, joints are fractures along which *no appreciable displacement* has occurred. Although some joints have a random orientation, most occur in roughly parallel groups (Figure 12).

We have already considered two types of joints. Earlier we learned that *columnar joints* form when igneous rocks cool and develop shrinkage fractures that produce elongated, pillarlike columns. Also recall that sheeting produces a pattern of gently curved joints that develop more or less parallel to the surface of large exposed igneous bodies such as batholiths. Here the jointing results from the gradual expansion that occurs when erosion removes the overlying load.

In contrast to the situations just described, most joints are produced when rocks in the outermost crust are deformed. Here forces associated with crustal movements cause the rock to fail by brittle fracture. For example, when folding occurs, rocks situated at the axes of the folds are elongated and pulled apart to produce tensional joints. Extensive joint patterns can also develop in response to relatively subtle and often barely perceptible regional upwarping and downwarping of the crust. In many cases, the cause for jointing at a particular locale is not readily apparent.

FIGURE 11 Aerial view of strike-slip (right-lateral) fault in southern Nevada. The amount of offset is shown by the displacement of the black line. (Photo by Marli G. Miller)

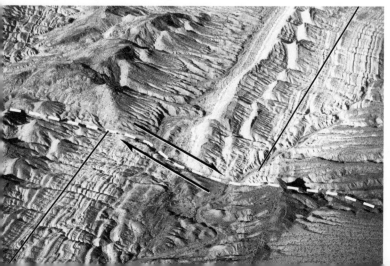

BOX 1 ▶ PEOPLE AND THE ENVIRONMENT

The San Andreas Fault System

The San Andreas, the best-known and largest fault system in North America, first attracted wide attention after the great 1906 San Francisco earthquake and fire. Following this devastating event, geologic studies demonstrated that a displacement of as much as 5 meters (3 feet) along the fault had been responsible for the earthquake. It is now known that this dramatic event is just one of many thousands of earthquakes that have resulted from repeated movements along the San Andreas throughout its 29-million-year history.

Where is the San Andreas fault system located? As shown in Figure A, it trends in a northwesterly direction for nearly 1,300 kilometers (780 miles) through much of western California. At its southern end, the San Andreas connects with a spreading center located in the Gulf of California. In the north, the fault enters the Pacific Ocean at Point Arena, where it is thought to continue its northwesterly trend, eventually joining the Mendocino fracture zone. In the central section, the San Andreas is relatively simple and straight. However, at its two extremities, several branches spread from the main trace, so that in some areas the fault zone exceeds 100 kilometers (60 miles) in width.

FIGURE A Map showing the extent of the San Andreas Fault system. Inset is an aerial view of the San Andreas Fault. (Photo by D. Parker/Photo Researchers)

FIGURE B Aerial view showing offset stream channel across the San Andreas Fault on the Carrizo Plain west of Taft, California. (Photo by Michael Collier)

Many rocks are broken by two or even three sets of intersecting joints that slice the rock into numerous regularly shaped blocks. These joint sets often exert a strong influence on other geologic processes. For example, chemical weathering tends to be concentrated along joints, and in many areas groundwater movement and the resulting dissolution in soluble rocks is controlled by the joint pattern (Figure 12). Moreover, a system of joints can influence the direction that stream courses follow.

Mountain Building

Forces Within
▶ **Mountain Building**

Like other people, geologists have been inspired more by Earth's mountains than by any other landforms (Figure 13). Through extensive scientific exploration over the last 150 years, much has been learned about the internal processes that generate these often spectacular terrains. The name for the processes

Over much of its extent, a linear trough reveals the presence of the San Andreas Fault. When the system is viewed from the air, linear scars, offset stream channels, and elongated ponds mark the trace in a striking manner. On the ground, however, surface expressions of the faults are much more difficult to detect. Some of the most distinctive landforms include long, straight escarpments, narrow ridges, and sag ponds formed by settling of blocks within the fault zone. Furthermore, many stream channels characteristically bend sharply to the right where they cross the fault (Figure B).

With the development of the theory of plate tectonics, geologists began to realize the significance of this great fault system. The San Andreas Fault is a transform boundary separating two crustal plates that move very slowly. The Pacific plate, located to the west, moves northwestward relative to the North American plate, causing earthquakes along the fault (Table A).

The San Andreas is undoubtedly the most studied of any fault system in the world. Although many questions remain unanswered, geologists have learned that each fault segment exhibits somewhat different behavior. Some portions of the San Andreas exhibit a slow creep with little noticeable seismic activity. Other segments regularly slip, producing small earthquakes, whereas still other segments seem to store elastic energy for hundreds of years and rupture in great earthquakes. This knowledge is useful when assigning earthquake-hazard potential to a given segment of the fault zone.

Because of the great length and complexity of the San Andreas Fault, it is more appropriately referred to as a "fault system." This major fault system consists primarily of the San Andreas Fault and several major branches, including the Hayward and Calaveras faults of central California and the San Jacinto and Elsinore faults of southern California (Figure 10.A). These major segments, plus a vast number of smaller faults that include the Imperial Fault, San Fernando Fault, and the Santa Monica Fault, collectively accommodate the relative motion between the North American and Pacific plates.

Ever since the great San Francisco earthquake of 1906, when as much as 5 meters of displacement occurred, geologists have attempted to establish the cumulative displacement along this fault over its 29-million-year history. By matching rock units across the fault, geologists have determined that the total accumulated displacement from earthquakes and creep exceeds 560 kilometers (340 miles).

TABLE A Major Earthquakes on the San Andreas Fault System

Date	Location	Magnitude	Remarks
1812	Wrightwood, CA	7	Church at San Juan Capistrano collapsed, killing 40 worshippers.
1812	Santa Barbara channel	7	Churches and other buildings wrecked in and around Santa Barbara.
1838	San Francisco peninsula	7	At one time thought to have been comparable to the great earthquake of 1906.
1857	Fort Tejon, CA	8.25	One of the greatest U.S. earthquakes. Occurred near Los Angeles, then a city of 4,000.
1868	Hayward, CA	7	Rupture of the Hayward fault caused extensive damage in San Francisco Bay area.
1906	San Francisco, CA	8.25	The great San Francisco earthquake. As much as 80 percent of the damage caused by fire.
1940	Imperial Valley	7.1	Displacement on the newly discovered Imperial fault.
1952	Kern County	7.7	Rupture of the White Wolf fault. Largest earthquake in California since 1906. Sixty million dollars in damages and 12 people killed.
1971	San Fernando Valley	6.5	One-half billion dollars in damages and 58 lives claimed.
1989	Santa Cruz Mountains	7.1	Loma Prieta earthquake. Six billion dollars in damages, 62 lives lost, and 3,757 people injured.
1994	Northridge (Los Angeles area)	6.9	Over 15 billion dollars in damages, 51 lives lost, and over 5,000 injured.

that collectively produce a mountain belt is **orogenesis**, (*oros* = mountain, *genesis* = to come into being). The rocks comprising mountains provide striking visual evidence of the enormous compressional forces that have deformed large sections of Earth's crust and subsequently elevated them to their present positions. Although folding is often the most conspicuous sign of these forces, thrust faulting, metamorphism, and igneous activity are always present in varying degrees.

Mountain building has occurred during the recent geologic past in several locations around the world. These young mountainous belts include the American Cordillera, which runs along the western margin of the Americas from Cape Horn to Alaska and includes the Andes and Rocky mountains; the Alpine-Himalaya chain, which extends from the Mediterranean through Iran to northern India and into Indochina; and the mountainous terrains of the western Pacific, which include volcanic island arcs such as Japan, the Philippines, and Sumatra. Most of these young mountain belts have come into existence within the past 100 million years. Some, including the Himalayas, began their growth as recently as 45 million years ago.

FIGURE 12 Chemical weathering is enhanced along joints in sandstone, near Moab, Utah. (Photo by Michael Collier)

In addition to these relatively young mountain belts, several chains of older mountains exist on Earth as well. Although these older structures are deeply eroded and topographically less prominent, they clearly possess the same structural features found in younger mountains. Typical of this older group are the Appalachians in the eastern United States and the Urals in Russia.

Over the years, several hypotheses have been put forward regarding the formation of Earth's major mountain belts. One early proposal suggested that mountains are simply wrinkles in Earth's crust, produced as the planet cooled from its original semimolten state. As Earth lost heat, it contracted and shrank. In response to this process, the crust was deformed similar to when the peel of an orange wrinkles as the fruit dries out. However, neither this nor any other early hypothesis was able to withstand careful scrutiny and had to be discarded.

Mountain Building at Subduction Zones

With the development of the theory of plate tectonics, a model for orogenesis with excellent explanatory power has emerged. According to this model, most mountain building occurs at convergent plate boundaries. Here, the subduction of oceanic lithosphere triggers partial melting of mantle rock, providing a source of magma that intrudes the crustal rocks that form the margin of the overlying plate. In addition, colliding plates provide the tectonic forces that fold, fault, and metamorphose the thick accumulations of sediments that have been deposited along the flanks of landmasses. Together,

FIGURE 13 This peak is part of the Karakoram Range in Pakistan. The Karakoram are part of the Himalayan system. (Photo by Art Wolfe)

You mentioned that most mountains are the result of crustal deformation. Are there areas that exhibit mountainous topography but have been produced without crustal deformation?

Yes. Plateaus—areas of high-standing rocks that are essentially horizontal—are one example of a feature that can be deeply dissected by erosional forces into rugged, mountainlike landscapes. Although these highlands resemble mountains topographically, they lack the structures associated with orogenesis. The opposite situation also exists. For instance, the Piedmont section of the eastern Appalachians exhibits topography that is nearly as subdued as that seen in the Great Plains. Yet, because this region is composed of deformed metamorphic rocks, it is clearly part of the Appalachian Mountains.

these processes thicken and shorten the continental crust, thereby elevating rocks that may have formed near the ocean floor, to lofty heights.

To unravel the events that produce mountains, researchers examine ancient mountain structures as well as sites where orogenesis is currently active. Of particular interest are active subduction zones, where lithospheric plates are converging. Here the subduction of oceanic lithosphere generates Earth's strongest earthquakes and most explosive volcanic eruptions, as well as playing a pivotal role in generating many of Earth's mountain belts.

The subduction of oceanic lithosphere gives rise to two different types of mountain belts. Where *oceanic lithosphere* subducts beneath an *oceanic plate*, an *island arc* and related tectonic features develop. Subduction beneath a *continental block*, on the other hand, results in the formation of a *continental volcanic arc* along the margin of the adjacent landmass. Plate boundaries that generate continental volcanic arcs are often referred to as *Andean-type plate margins.*

Island Arcs

Island arcs form where two oceanic plates converge and one is subducted beneath the other (Figure 14). This activity results in partial melting of the mantle wedge located above the subducting plate and eventually leads to the growth of a volcanic island arc on the ocean floor. Because they are associated with

subducting oceanic lithosphere, island arcs are typically found on the margins of an ocean basin, such as the Pacific—where the majority of volcanic island arcs are found. Examples of active island arcs include the Mariana, New Hebrides, Tonga, and Aleutian arcs.

Island arcs represent what are perhaps the simplest mountain belts. These structures result from the steady subduction of oceanic lithosphere, which may last for 100 million years or more. Somewhat sporadic volcanic activity, the emplacement of igneous bodies at depth, and the accumulation of sediment that is scraped from the subducting plate gradually increase the volume of crustal material capping the upper plate. Some mature volcanic island arcs, such as Japan, appear to have been built upon a preexisting fragment of crustal material.

The continued development of a mature volcanic island arc can result in the formation of mountainous topography consisting of belts of igneous and metamorphic rocks. This activity, however, is viewed as just one phase in the development of a major mountain belt. As you will see later, some volcanic arcs are carried by a subducting plate to the margin of a large continental block, where they become involved in a major mountain-building episode.

Mountain Building Along Andean-Type Margins

Mountain building along continental margins involves the convergence of an oceanic plate and a plate whose leading edge contains continental crust. Exemplified by the Andes

FIGURE 14 The development of a volcanic island arc due to the convergence of two oceanic plates. Continuous subduction along these Aleutian-type convergent zones results in the development of thick units of continental-type crust. Inset photo shows an aerial view of some of the many volcanic islands that make up the Aleutians. The lowermost cluster of summits, known as the Islands of Four Mountains, is home to Cleveland Volcano, one of the Aleutians' most active volcanoes. (Photo courtesy of NASA)

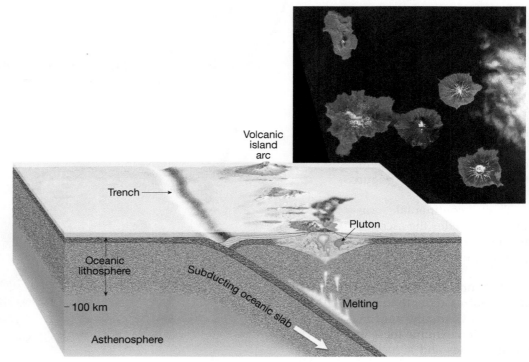

Mountains, an *Andean-type convergent zone* results in the formation of a continental volcanic arc and related tectonic features inland of the continental margin.

The first stage in the development of an idealized Andean-type mountain belt occurs prior to the formation of the subduction zone. During this period the continental margin is a **passive continental margin**; that is, it is not a plate boundary but a part of the same plate as the adjoining oceanic crust. The East Coast of North America provides a present-day example of a passive continental margin. Here, as at other passive continental margins surrounding the Atlantic, deposition of sediment on the continental shelf is producing a thick wedge of shallow-water sandstones, limestones, and shales (Figure 15A). Beyond the continental shelf, turbidity currents are depositing sediments on the continental slope and rise.

At some point the continental margin becomes active. A subduction zone forms and the deformation process begins (Figure 15B). A good place to examine an **active continental margin** is the west coast of South America. Here the Nazca plate is being subducted beneath the South American plate along the Peru–Chile trench. This subduction zone probably formed prior to the breakup of the supercontinent of Pangaea.

In an idealized Andean-type subduction, convergence of the continental block and the subducting oceanic plate leads to deformation and metamorphism of the continental margin. Once the oceanic plate descends to about 100 kilometers (60 miles), partial melting of mantle rock above the subducting slab generates magma that migrates upward (Figure 15B).

Thick continental crust greatly impedes the ascent of magma. Consequently, a high percentage of the magma that intrudes the crust never reaches the surface—instead, it crystallizes at depth to form plutons. Eventually, uplifting and erosion exhume these igneous bodies and associated

metamorphic rocks. Once they are exposed at the surface, these massive structures are called *batholiths* (Figure 15C). Composed of numerous plutons, batholiths form the core of the Sierra Nevada in California and are prevalent in the Peruvian Andes.

During the development of this continental volcanic arc, sediment derived from the land and scraped from the subducting plate is plastered against the landward side of the trench-like piles of dirt in front of a bulldozer. This chaotic accumulation of sedimentary and metamorphic rocks with occasional scraps of ocean crust is called an **accretionary wedge**

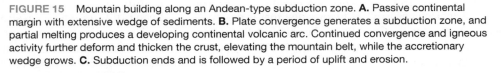

FIGURE 15 Mountain building along an Andean-type subduction zone. **A.** Passive continental margin with extensive wedge of sediments. **B.** Plate convergence generates a subduction zone, and partial melting produces a developing continental volcanic arc. Continued convergence and igneous activity further deform and thicken the crust, elevating the mountain belt, while the accretionary wedge grows. **C.** Subduction ends and is followed by a period of uplift and erosion.

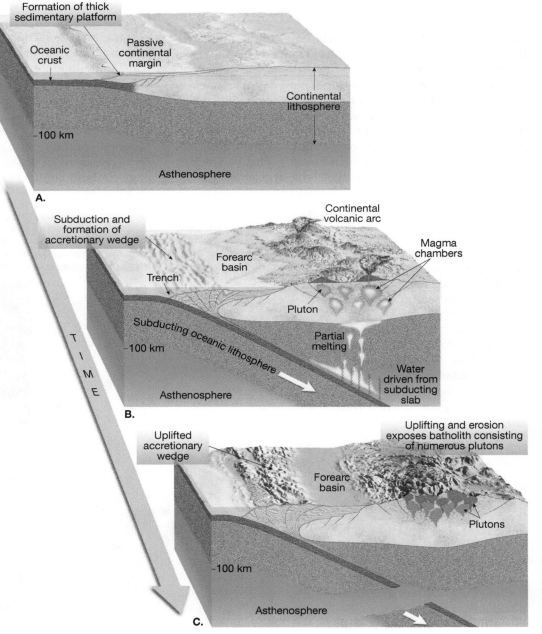

(Figure 15B). Prolonged subduction can build an accretionary wedge that is large enough to stand above sea level (Figure 15C).

Andean-type mountain belts are composed of two roughly parallel zones. The volcanic arc develops on the continental block. It consists of volcanoes and large intrusive bodies intermixed with high-temperature metamorphic rocks. The seaward segment is the accretionary wedge. It consists of folded and faulted sedimentary and metamorphic rocks (Figure 15C).

Sierra Nevada and Coast Ranges One of the best examples of an inactive Andean-type orogenic belt is found in the western United States. It includes the Sierra Nevada and the Coast Ranges in California. These parallel mountain belts were produced by the subduction of a portion of the Pacific Basin under the western edge of the North American plate. The Sierra Nevada batholith is a remnant of a portion of the continental volcanic arc that was produced by several surges of magma over tens of millions of years. Subsequent uplifting and erosion have removed most of the evidence of past volcanic activity and exposed a core of crystalline, igneous, and associated metamorphic rocks.

In the trench region, sediments scraped from the subducting plate, plus those provided by the eroding continental volcanic arc, were intensely folded and faulted into an accretionary wedge. This chaotic mixture of rocks presently constitutes the Franciscan Formation of California's Coast Ranges. Uplifting of the Coast Ranges took place only recently, as evidenced by the young unconsolidated sediments that still mantle portions of these highlands.

Collisional Mountain Ranges

Forces Within
▶ **Mountain Building**

As you have seen, when a slab of oceanic lithosphere subducts beneath a continental margin, an Andean-type mountain belt develops. If the subducting plate also contains a slab of continental lithosphere, continued subduction eventually carries the continental block to the trench. Oceanic lithosphere is relatively dense and readily subducts, but continental crust is composed of low-density material that is too buoyant to undergo subduction. Consequently, the arrival of the continental block at the trench results in a collision with the overriding continent. The result is crustal shortening and thickening to produce a mountain belt.

Mountain belts can develop as a result of the collision and merger of an island arc or some other small crustal fragment with a continental block, as well as from the collision and joining of two or more continents.

Terranes and Mountain Building

The process of collision and accretion (joining together) of comparatively small crustal fragments to a continental margin has generated many of the mountainous regions rimming

the Pacific. Geologists refer to these accreted crustal blocks as *terranes*. Simply, the term **terrane** refers to any crustal fragment that has a geologic history distinct from that of adjoining terranes. Terranes come in various shapes and sizes.

What is the nature of these crustal fragments, and from where do they originate? Research suggests that prior to their accretion to a continental block, some of the fragments may have been *microcontinents* similar to the present-day island of Madagascar, located east of Africa in the Indian Ocean. Many others were island arcs similar to Japan, the Philippines, and the Aleutian Islands. Still others are submerged crustal fragments, such as *oceanic plateaus*, which were created by massive outpourings of basaltic lavas associated with hot-spot activity (Figure 16).

Accretion and Orogenesis. The widely accepted view is that as oceanic plates move, they carry embedded oceanic plateaus, volcanic island arcs, and microcontinents to an Andean-type subduction zone. When an oceanic plate contains a chain of small seamounts, these structures are generally subducted along with the descending oceanic slab. However, thick units of oceanic crust, such as the Ontong Java Plateau, or a mature island arc composed of abundant "light" igneous rocks may render the oceanic lithosphere too buoyant to subduct. In these situations, a collision between the crustal fragment and the continent occurs.

The sequence of events that occurs when a mature island arc reaches an Andean-type margin is shown in Figure 17. Because of its buoyancy, a mature island arc will not subduct beneath the continental plate. Instead, the upper portions of these thickened zones are peeled from the descending plate and thrust in relatively thin sheets upon the adjacent continental block. In some settings continued subduction may carry another crustal fragment to the continental margin. When this fragment collides with the continental margin, it displaces the accreted island arc further inland, adding to the zone of deformation and to the thickness and lateral extent of the continental margin.

The North American Cordillera The idea that mountain building occurs in association with the accretion of crustal fragments to a continental mass arose principally from studies conducted in the North American Cordillera (Figure 18). Here it was determined that some mountainous areas, principally those in the orogenic belts of Alaska and British Columbia, contain fossil and paleomagnetic evidence indicating that these strata once lay nearer the equator.

It is now assumed that many of the other terranes found in the North American Cordillera were once scattered throughout the eastern Pacific, much as we find island arcs and oceanic plateaus distributed in the western Pacific today (Figure 16). Since before the breakup of Pangaea, the eastern portion of the Pacific basin (Farallon plate) has been subducting under the western margin of North America. Apparently, this activity resulted in the piecemeal addition of crustal fragments to the entire Pacific margin of the continent—from Mexico's Baja Peninsula to northern Alaska (Figure 18). In a like manner, many modern

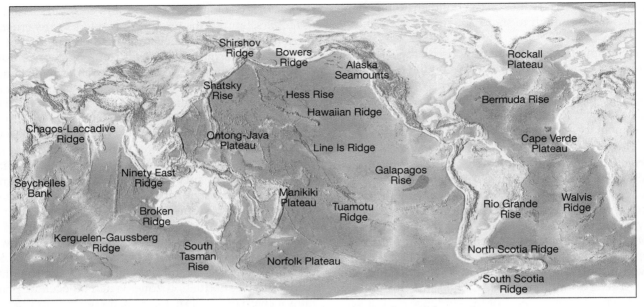

FIGURE 16 Distribution of present-day oceanic plateaus and other submerged crustal fragments. (Data from Ben-Avraham and others)

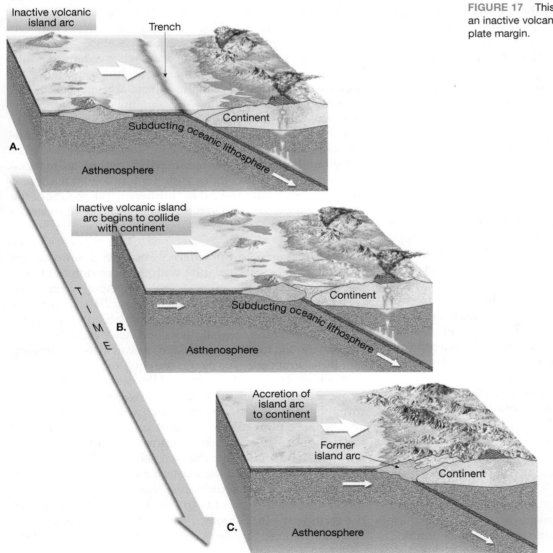

FIGURE 17 This sequence illustrates the collision of an inactive volcanic island arc with an Andean-type plate margin.

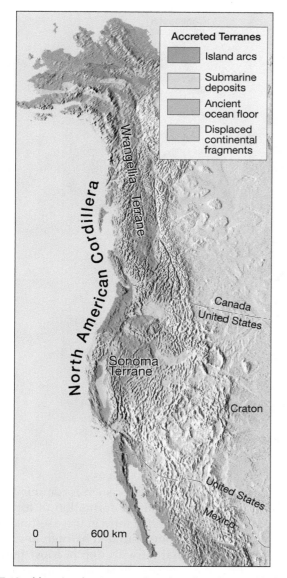

FIGURE 18 Map showing terranes thought to have been added to western North America during the past 200 million years. (Redrawn after D. R. Hutchinson and others)

microcontinents will eventually be accreted to active continental margins, producing new orogenic belts.

Continental Collisions

Continental collisions result in the development of mountains that are characterized by shortened and thickened crust. Thicknesses of 50 kilometers (30 miles) are common, and some regions have crustal thicknesses in excess of 70 kilometers (40 miles). In these settings, crustal thickening is achieved through folding and faulting.

We now take a closer look at two examples of collision mountains—the Himalayas and the Appalachians. The Himalayas are the youngest collision mountains on Earth and are still rising. The Appalachians are a much older mountain belt, in which active mountain building ceased about 250 million years ago.

The Himalayas The mountain-building episode that created the Himalayas began roughly 45 million years ago when India began to collide with Asia. Prior to the breakup of Pangaea, India was part of a Southern Hemisphere landmass that also included Australia. Upon splitting from that continent, India moved rapidly, geologically speaking, a few thousand kilometers in a northward direction.

The subduction zone that facilitated India's northward migration was located near the southern margin of Asia (Figure 19). Ongoing subduction along Asia's margin created an Andean-type plate margin that contained a well-developed volcanic arc and accretionary wedge. Eventually, the intervening ocean basin was consumed at the subduction zone and India collided with the Eurasian plate. The tectonic forces involved in the collision were immense and caused the more deformable materials located on the seaward edges of these landmasses to be highly folded and faulted (Figure 19). The shortening and thickening of the crust elevated great quantities of crustal material, thereby generating the spectacular Himalayan mountains (see Figure 13).

In addition to uplift, crustal thickening caused lower layers to become deeply buried and to experience elevated temperatures and pressures. Partial melting within the deepest and most deformed region of the developing mountain belt produced magma bodies that intruded and further deformed the overlying rocks. It is in such environments where the metamorphic and igneous core of a major mountain belt is generated.

The Appalachians The Appalachian Mountains provide great scenic beauty near the eastern margin of North America from Alabama to Newfoundland. The orogeny that generated this extensive mountain system lasted a few hundred million years and was one of the stages in the assembling of Pangaea. Our simplified scenario begins roughly 600 million years ago when an ocean body, which predated the North Atlantic (referred to as the ancestral North Atlantic), began to close. Two subduction zones probably formed. One was located seaward of the coast of Africa and gave rise to a volcanic arc similar to those that presently rim the western Pacific. The other developed adjacent to a continental fragment that lay off the coast of North America, as shown in Figure 20A.

Between 450 and 500 million years ago, the marginal sea located between this crustal fragment and North America began to close. The ensuing collision deformed the continental shelf and sutured the crustal fragment to the North American plate. The metamorphosed remnants of the continental fragment are recognized today as the crystalline rocks of the Blue Ridge and western Piedmont regions of the Appalachians (Figure 20B). In addition to the pervasive metamorphism, igneous activity placed numerous plutonic bodies along the continental margin, particularly in New England.

A second episode of mountain building occurred about 400 million years ago. The continued closing of the ancestral North Atlantic resulted in the collision of the developing volcanic arc with North America (Figure 20C). Evidence for this event is visible in the Carolina Slate Belt of the eastern Piedmont, which contains metamorphosed sedimentary and volcanic rocks characteristic of an island arc.

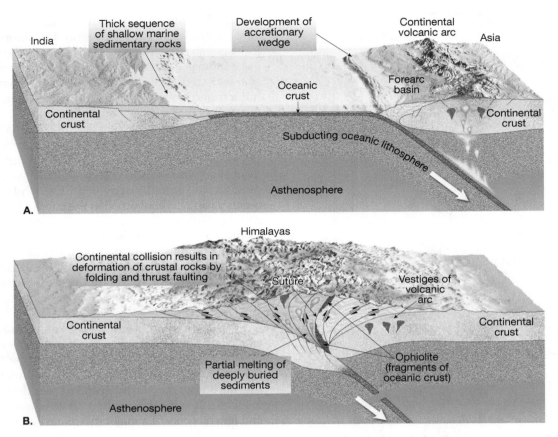

FIGURE 19 Illustration showing the collision of India with the Eurasian plate, producing the spectacular Himalayas.

The final orogeny occurred somewhere between 250 and 300 million years ago, when Africa collided with North America. This event displaced and further deformed the shelf sediments and sedimentary rocks that had once flanked the eastern margin of North America (Figure 20D). Today these folded and thrust-faulted sandstones, limestones, and shales make up the largely unmetamorphosed rocks of the Valley and Ridge Province.

Geologically speaking, shortly after the formation of the Appalachian Mountains, the newly formed supercontinent of Pangaea began to break into smaller fragments. Because the zone of rifting occurred east of the location where Africa collided with North America, a remnant of Africa remains "welded" to the North American plate.

Other mountain ranges that exhibit evidence of continental collisions include the Alps and the Urals. The Alps are thought to have formed as a result of a collision between Africa and Europe. The Urals, on the other hand, formed during the assembly of Pangaea when northern Europe and northern Asia collided.

Fault-Block Mountains

Most mountain belts, including the Alps, Himalayas, and Appalachians, form in compressional environments, as evidenced by the predominance of large thrust faults and folded strata.

However, other tectonic processes, such as continental rifting, can also produce uplift and the formation of topographic mountains. The mountains that form in these settings, termed **fault-block mountains**, are bounded by high-angle normal faults that gradually flatten with depth. Most fault-block mountains form in response to broad uplifting, which causes elongation and faulting. Such a situation is exemplified by the fault blocks that rise high above the rift valleys of East Africa.

Mountains in the United States in which faulting and gradual uplift have contributed to their lofty stature include the Sierra Nevada of California and the Grand Tetons of Wyoming (Figure 21). Both are faulted along their eastern flanks, which were uplifted as the blocks tilted downward to the west. Looking west from Owens Valley, California, and Jackson Hole, Wyoming, the eastern fronts of these ranges (the Sierra Nevada and the Tetons, respectively) rise over 2 kilometers (1.2 miles), making them two of the most imposing mountain fronts in the United States (Figure 21).

One of Earth's largest regions of fault-block mountains is the Basin and Range Province. This region extends in a roughly north-to-south direction for nearly 3,000 kilometers (2,000 miles) and encompasses all of Nevada and portions of the surrounding states, as well as parts of southern Canada and western Mexico. Here, the brittle upper crust has literally been broken into hundreds of fault blocks. Tilting of these faulted structures (half-grabens) gave rise to nearly parallel mountain ranges, averaging about 80 kilometers (50 miles)

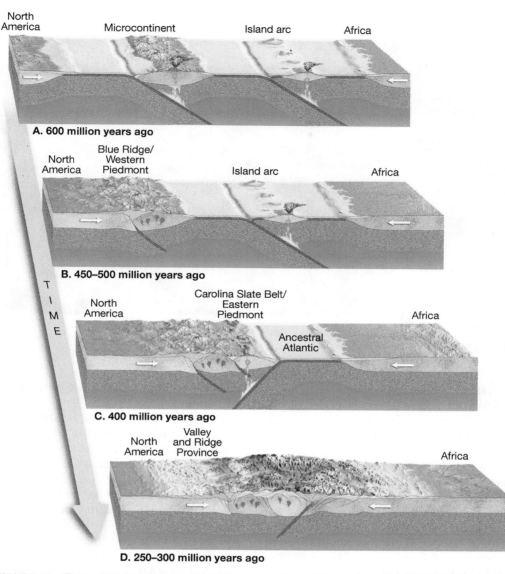

North America | Microcontinent | Island arc | Africa

A. 600 million years ago

North America | Blue Ridge/ Western Piedmont | Island arc | Africa

B. 450–500 million years ago

North America | Carolina Slate Belt/ Eastern Piedmont | Ancestral Atlantic | Africa

C. 400 million years ago

North America | Valley and Ridge Province | Africa

D. 250–300 million years ago

T I M E

FIGURE 20 These simplified diagrams depict the development of the southern Appalachians as the ancient North Atlantic was closed during the formation of Pangaea. Three separate stages of mountain-building activity spanned more than 300 million years. (After Zve Ben-Avraham, Jack Oliver, Larry Brown, and Frederick Cook)

in length, which rise above adjacent sediment-laden basins (see Figure 10).

Extension in the Basin and Range Province began about 20 million years ago and appears to have "stretched" the crust as much as twice its original width. High heat flow in the region, three times average, and several episodes of volcanism provide strong evidence that mantle upwelling caused doming of the crust, which in turn contributed to extension in the region.

Vertical Movements of the Crust

In addition to the large crustal displacements driven mainly by plate tectonics, gradual up-and-down motions of the continental crust are observed at many locations around the globe. Although much of this vertical movement occurs along plate margins and is associated with active mountain building, some of it is not.

Evidence for crustal uplift occurs along the West Coast of the United States. When the elevation of a coastal area remains unchanged for an extended period, a wave-cut platform develops. In parts of California, ancient wave-cut platforms can now be found as terraces hundreds of meters above sea level (Figure 22). Such evidence of crustal uplift is easy to find; unfortunately, the reason for uplift is not always as easy to determine.

Isostasy

Early workers discovered that Earth's less-dense crust floats on top of the denser and deformable rocks of the mantle. The concept of a floating crust in gravitational balance is called

FIGURE 21   The Grand Tetons of Wyoming are an excellent example of fault-block mountains. (Photo by Stefano Amantini/Alantide Phototravel/CORBIS)

isostasy (*iso* = equal, *stasis* = standing). One way to grasp the concept of isostasy is to envision a series of wooden blocks of different heights floating in water, as shown in Figure 23. Note that the thicker wooden blocks float higher than the thinner blocks.

Similarly, many mountain belts stand high above the surrounding terrain because of crustal thickening. These compressional mountains have buoyant crustal "roots" that extend deep into the supporting material below, just like the thicker wooden blocks shown in Figure 23.

Visualize what would happen if another small block of wood were placed atop one of the blocks in Figure 23. The combined block would sink until a new isostatic (gravitational) balance was reached. However, the top of the combined block would actually be higher than before, and the bottom would be lower. This process of establishing a new level of gravitational equilibrium is called **isostatic adjustment**.

Applying the concept of isostatic adjustment, we should expect that when weight is added to the crust, it will respond by subsiding, and when weight is removed, the crust will rebound. (Visualize what happens to a ship as cargo is being loaded and unloaded.) Evidence for crustal subsidence followed by crustal rebound is provided by Ice Age glaciers. When continental ice sheets occupied portions of North America during the Pleistocene epoch, the added weight of 3-kilometer-thick (nearly 2-mile-thick) masses of ice caused downwarping of Earth's crust by hundreds of meters. In the 8,000 years since the last ice sheet melted, uplifting of as much as 330 meters (1,000 feet) has occurred in Canada's Hudson Bay region, where the thickest ice had accumulated.

FIGURE 22   Former wave-cut platforms now exist as a series of elevated terraces on the west side of San Clemente Island off the southern California coast. Once at sea level, the highest terraces are now about 400 meters (1,320 feet) above it. (Photo by John S. Shelton)

FIGURE 23   This drawing illustrates how wooden blocks of different thicknesses float in water. In a similar manner, thick sections of crustal material float higher than thinner crustal slabs.

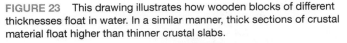

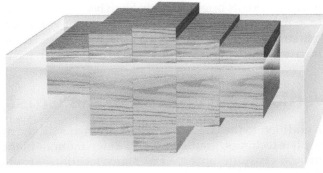

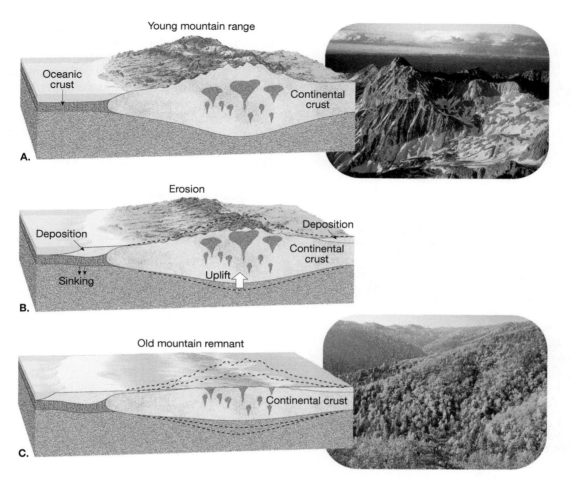

FIGURE 24 This sequence illustrates how the combined effect of erosion and isostatic adjustment results in a thinning of the crust in mountainous regions. **A.** When mountains are young, the continental crust is thickest. (Photo by Michael Collier) **B.** As erosion lowers the mountains, the crust rises in response to the reduced load. **C.** Erosion and uplift continue until the mountains reach "normal" crustal thickness. (Photo by Mark Karrass/CORBIS)

One of the consequences of isostatic adjustment is that as erosion lowers the summits of mountains, the crust will rise in response to the reduced load (Figure 24). However, each episode of isostatic uplift is somewhat less than the elevation loss due to erosion. The processes of uplifting and erosion will continue until the mountain block reaches "normal" crustal thickness. When this occurs, the mountains will be eroded to near sea level, and the once deeply buried interior of the mountain will be exposed at the surface. In addition, as mountains are worn down, the eroded sediment is deposited on adjacent landscapes, causing these areas to subside (Figure 24).

How High Is Too High?

Where compressional forces are great, such as those driving India into Asia, mountains such as the Himalayas result. But is there a limit on how high a mountain can rise? As mountaintops are elevated, gravity-driven processes such as erosion and mass wasting accelerate, carving the deformed strata into rugged landscapes. Just as important, however, is the fact that gravity also acts on the rocks within these mountainous masses. The higher the mountain, the greater the downward force on the rocks near the base. (Visualize a group of cheerleaders at a sporting event building a human pyramid.) At some point the rocks deep within the developing mountain, which are comparatively warm and weak, will

Students Sometimes ask . . .

What's the difference between a terrane and a terrain?

The term *terrane* is used to designate a distinct and recognizable series of rock formations that has been transported by plate tectonic processes. Since geologists who mapped these rocks were unsure where they came from, these rocks were sometimes called "exotic," "suspect," "accreted," or "foreign" terranes. Don't confuse this with the term *terrain*, which describes the shape of the surface topography or "lay of the land."

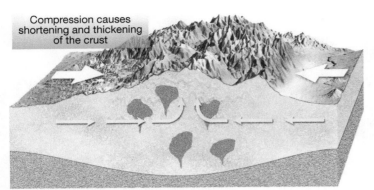

Compression causes shortening and thickening of the crust

A. Horizontal compressional forces dominate

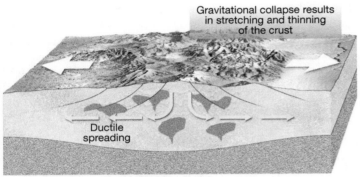

Gravitational collapse results in stretching and thinning of the crust

Ductile spreading

B. Gravitational forces dominate

FIGURE 25 Block diagram of a mountain belt that is collapsing under its own "weight." Gravitational collapse involves normal faulting in the upper, brittle portion of the crust and ductile spreading at depth.

begin to flow laterally, as shown in Figure 25. This is analogous to what happens when a ladle of very thick pancake batter is poured on a hot griddle. As a result, the mountain will experience a **gravitational collapse**, which involves normal faulting and subsidence in the upper, brittle portion of the crust and ductile spreading at depth.

You then might ask, What keeps the Himalayas standing? Simply, the horizontal compressional forces that are driving India into Asia are greater than the vertical force of gravity. However, once India's northward trek ends, the downward pull of gravity will become the dominant force acting on this mountainous region.

Chapter Summary

- *Deformation* refers to changes in the shape and/or volume of a rock body. Rocks deform differently depending on the environment (temperature and confining pressure), the composition of the rock, and the length of time stress is maintained. Rocks first respond by deforming *elastically* and will return to their original shape when the stress is removed. Once their elastic limit (strength) is surpassed, rocks either deform by ductile flow or they fracture. *Ductile deformation* is a solid-state flow that results in a change in size and shape of rocks without fracturing. Ductile deformation occurs in a high-temperature/high-pressure environment. In a near-surface environment, most rocks deform by *brittle failure*.

- Among the most basic geologic structures associated with rock deformation are *folds* (flat-lying sedimentary and volcanic rocks bent into a series of wavelike undulations). The two most common types of folds are *anticlines,* formed by the upfolding, or arching, of rock layers, and *synclines*, which are downfolds. Most folds are the result of horizontal *compressional stresses. Domes* (upwarped structures) and *basins* (downwarped structures) are circular or somewhat elongated folds formed by vertical displacements of strata.

- Faults are fractures in the crust along which appreciable displacement has occurred. Faults in which the movement

is primarily vertical are called *dip-slip faults*. Dip-slip faults include both *normal* and *reverse faults*. Low-angle reverse faults are called *thrust faults*. Normal faults indicate *tensional stresses* that pull the crust apart. Along spreading centers, divergence can cause a central block called a *graben*, bounded by normal faults, to drop as lithospheric plates separate.

- Reverse and thrust faulting indicate that *compressional forces* are at work. Large *thrust faults* are found along subduction zones and other convergent boundaries where plates are colliding.

- *Strike-slip faults* exhibit mainly horizontal displacement parallel to the fault surface. Large strike-slip faults, called *transform faults*, accommodate displacement between plate boundaries. Most transform faults cut the oceanic lithosphere and link spreading centers. The San Andreas Fault cuts the continental lithosphere and accommodates the northward displacement of southwestern California.

- *Joints* are fractures along which no appreciable displacement has occurred. Joints generally occur in groups with roughly parallel orientations and are the result of brittle failure of rock units located in the outermost crust.

- The name for the processes that collectively produce a mountain system is *orogenesis*. Most mountains consist of roughly parallel ridges of folded and faulted sedimentary and volcanic rocks, portions of which have been strongly metamorphosed and intruded by younger igneous bodies.

- Subduction of oceanic lithosphere under a continental block gives rise to an *Andean-type plate margin* that is characterized by a continental volcanic arc and associated igneous plutons. In addition, sediment derived from the land, as well as material scraped from the subducting plate, becomes plastered against the landward side of the trench, forming an *accretionary wedge*. An excellent example of an inactive Andean-type mountain belt is found in the western United States and includes the Sierra Nevada and the Coast Range in California.

- Mountain belts can develop as a result of the collision and merger of an island arc, oceanic plateau, or some other small crustal fragment to a continental block. Many of the mountain belts of the North American Cordillera were generated in this manner.

- Continued subduction of oceanic lithosphere beneath an Andean-type continental margin will eventually close an ocean basin. The result will be a *continental collision* and the development of compressional mountains that are characterized by shortened and thickened crust as exhibited by the Himalayas. The development of a major mountain belt is often complex, involving two or more distinct episodes of mountain building. Continental collisions have generated many mountain belts, including the Alps, Urals, and Appalachians.

- Although most mountains form along convergent plate boundaries, other tectonic processes, such as continental rifting, can produce uplift and the formation of topographic mountains. The mountains that form in these settings, termed *fault-block mountains*, are bounded by high-angle normal faults that gradually flatten with depth. The Basin and Range Province in the western United States consists of hundreds of faulted blocks that give rise to nearly parallel mountain ranges that stand above sediment-laden basins.

- Earth's less dense crust floats on top of the denser and deformable rocks of the mantle, much like wooden blocks floating in water. The concept of a floating crust in gravitational balance is called *isostasy*. Most mountainous topography is located where the crust has been shortened and thickened. Therefore, mountains have deep crustal roots that isostatically support them. As erosion lowers the peaks, *isostatic adjustment* gradually raises the mountains in response. The processes of uplifting and erosion will continue until the mountain block reaches "normal" crustal thickness. Gravity also causes elevated mountainous structures to collapse under their own "weight."

Key Terms

accretionary wedge	dome	horst	reverse fault
active continental margin	ductile deformation	isostasy	strike-slip fault
anticline	fault	isostatic adjustment	syncline
basin	fault-block mountains	joint	terrane
brittle failure (brittle deformation)	fault scarp	monocline	thrust fault
deformation	fold	normal fault	transform fault
dip-slip fault	graben	orogenesis	
	gravitational collapse	passive continental margin	

Review Questions

1. What is rock *deformation*?

2. How is *brittle deformation* different from *ductile deformation*?

3. List three factors that determine how rocks will behave when exposed to stresses that exceed their strength. Briefly explain the role of each.

4. Distinguish between *anticlines* and *synclines*, *domes* and *basins*, *anticlines* and *domes*.

5. How is a *monocline* different from an *anticline*?

6. The Black Hills of South Dakota are a good example of what type of structural feature?

7. Contrast the movements that occur along normal and reverse faults. What type of force is indicated by each fault?

8. Is the fault shown in Figure 8 a normal or reverse fault?

9. Describe a *horst* and a *graben*. Explain how a graben valley forms, and name one.

    What type of faults are associated with fault-block mountains?

11. How are reverse faults different from thrust faults? In what way are they the same?

12. The San Andreas Fault is an excellent example of a _____ fault.

13. How are joints different from faults?

14. In the plate tectonics model, which type of plate boundary is most directly associated with mountain building?

15. Briefly describe the development of a volcanic island arc.

16. The formation of mountainous topography at a volcanic

17. What is an *accretionary wedge*? Briefly describe its formation.

18. What is a *passive margin*? Give an example. Then give an example of an *active continental margin*.

19. In what way are the Sierra Nevada and the Andes similar?

20. How can the Appalachian Mountains be considered a collision-type mountain range when the nearest continent is 5,000 kilometers (3,000 miles) away?

21. How does the plate tectonics theory help explain the existence of fossil marine life in rocks atop mountains formed by continental collisions?

22. Define the term *terrane*. How is it different from the term *terrain*?

23. In addition to microcontinents, what other structures are thought to be carried by the oceanic lithosphere and eventually accreted to a continent?

The line before (item 16, partially cut): island arc, such as Japan, is considered just one phase in the development of a major mountain belt. Explain.

24. Briefly describe the major differences between the evolution of the Appalachian Mountains and the North American Cordillera.

25. Compare the processes that generate fault-block mountains to those associated with most other major mountain belts.

26. Give one example of evidence that supports the concept of crustal uplift.

27. What happens to a floating object when weight is added? Subtracted? How does this principal apply to changes in the elevation of mountains? What term is applied to the adjustment that causes crustal uplift of this type?

28. How does the formation and melting of Pleistocene ice sheets support the idea that the lithosphere tries to remain in isostatic balance?

Examining the Earth System

1. A good example of the interactions between Earth's spheres is the influence of mountains on climate. Examine the temperature graphs and annual precipitation amounts for the cities of Seattle and Spokane, Washington (Figure 26). Notice on the inset map that mountains (the Cascades) separate the two cities and that the general wind direction in the region is from west to east (the prevailing westerlies of the midlatitudes). Which city receives the greatest annual precipitation? Contrast the summer and winter temperatures that occur at each city. What influence have the mountains apparently had on Spokane's rainfall and temperature?

2. The Cascades have had a profound effect on the amount and type of plant and animal life (biosphere) that inhabit the region around Spokane and Seattle. Provide several specific examples to verify this statement.

FIGURE 26 Comparison of the average monthly temperatures and precipitation for Seattle and Spokane. Note that Seattle receives an average of 38.4 inches of precipitation per year while Spokane receives only 17 inches of precipitation on average.

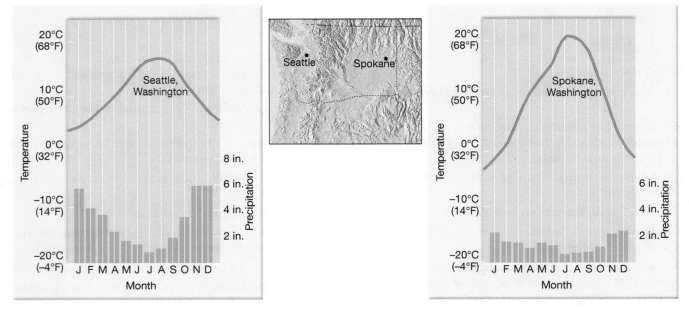

Online Study Guide

The *Earth Science* Website uses the resources and flexibility of the Internet to aid in your study of the topics in this chapter. Written and developed by Earth science instructors, this site will help improve your understanding of Earth science. Visit **www.mygeoscienceplace.com** and click on the cover of *Earth Science 12e* to find:

- Online review quizzes
- Critical thinking exercises
- Links to chapter-specific Web resources
- Internet-wide key term searches

GEODe: Earth Science

GEODe: Earth Science makes studying more effective by reinforcing key concepts using animation, video, narration, interactive exercises, and practice quizzes. A copy is included with every copy of *Earth Science 12e*

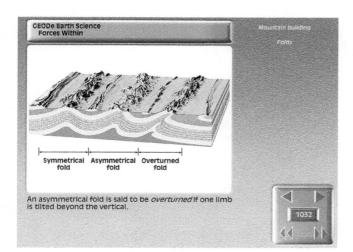

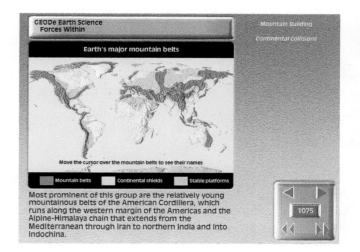

GEOLOGIC TIME

From Chapter 8 of *Foundations of Earth Science*, Sixth Edition, Frederick K. Lutgens, Edward J. Tarbuck, Dennis Tasa.

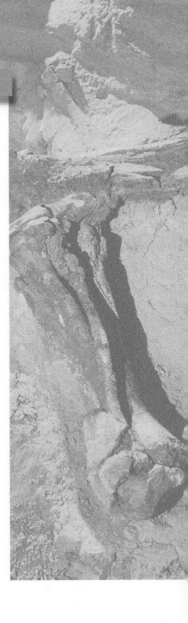

GEOLOGIC TIME

To assist you in learning the important concepts in this chapter, you will find it helpful to focus on the following questions:

1. What is the doctrine of uniformitarianism? How does it differ from catastrophism?

2. What are the two types of dates used by geologists when they interpret Earth history?

3. What are the basic laws, principles, and techniques used to establish relative dates?

4. What are fossils? What conditions favor the preservation of organisms as fossils?

5. How are fossils used to correlate rocks of similar ages that are in different places?

6. What is radioactivity, and how are radioactive isotopes used in radiometric dating?

7. What is the geologic time scale, and what are its principal subdivisions?

8. Why is it difficult to assign reliable numerical dates to samples of sedimentary rock?

Paleontologists excavating the remains of an Ice Age mammoth near Hot Springs in the Black Hills of South Dakota. These animals were prehistoric relatives of modern elephants. Fossils are important tools in deciphering Earth history.
(Photo by Phil Degginger Alamy)

In the eighteenth century, James Hutton recognized the immensity of Earth history and the importance of time as a component in all geologic processes. In the nineteenth century, others effectively demonstrated that Earth had experienced many episodes of mountain building and erosion, which must have required great spans of geologic time. Although these pioneering scientists understood that Earth was very old, they had no way of knowing its true age. Was it tens of millions, hundreds of millions, or even billions of years old? Rather, a geologic time scale was developed that showed the sequence of events based on relative dating principles. What were these principles? What part did fossils play? With the discovery of radioactivity and the development of radiometric dating techniques, geologists can now assign fairly accurate dates to many of the events in Earth history. What is radioactivity? Why is it a good "clock" for dating the geologic past? This chapter will answer these questions.

GEOLOGY NEEDS A TIME SCALE

In 1869, John Wesley Powell, who was later to head the U.S. Geological Survey, led a pioneering expedition down the Colorado River and through the Grand Canyon (FIGURE 1)*. Writing about the strata that were exposed by the downcutting of the river, Powell observed that "the canyons of this region would be a Book of Revelations in the rock-leaved Bible of geology." He was undoubtedly impressed with the millions of years of Earth history exposed along the walls of the Grand Canyon (FIGURE 2).

B.

A.

FIGURE 1   **A.** Start of the expedition from Green River station. A drawing from Powell's 1875 book. **B.** Major John Wesley Powell, pioneering geologist and the second director of the U.S. Geological Survey. (Courtesy of the U.S. Geological Survey, Denver)

Down the Great Unknown, a book by Edward Dolnick (HarperCollins, 2001), is a fascinating account of the journey.

Powell realized that the evidence for an ancient Earth is concealed in its rocks. Like the pages in a long and complicated history book, rocks record the geologic events and changing life forms of the past. The book, however, is not complete. Many pages, especially in the early chapters, are missing. Others are tattered, torn, or smudged. Yet, enough of the book remains to allow much of the story to be deciphered.

Interpreting Earth history is an important goal of geology. Like a modern-day sleuth, the geologist must interpret clues found preserved in the rocks. By studying rocks, especially sedimentary rocks, and the features they contain, geologists can unravel the complexities of the past.

Geologic events by themselves, however, have little meaning until they are put into a time perspective. Studying

FIGURE 2   This hiker is resting atop the Kaibab Formation, the uppermost layer in the Grand Canyon. Hundreds of millions of years of Earth history is contained in the strata that lay beneath him. This is a view of Cape Royal on the Grand Canyon's North Rim. (Photo by Michael Collier)

history, whether it be the Civil War or the Age of Dinosaurs, requires a calendar. Among geology's major contributions is a calendar called the *geologic time scale* and the discovery that Earth history is exceedingly long.

The geologists who developed the geologic time scale revolutionized the way people think about time and perceive our planet. They learned that Earth is much older than anyone had previously imagined and that its surface and interior have been changed over and over again by the same geologic processes that operate today.

SOME HISTORICAL NOTES ABOUT GEOLOGY

The nature of our Earth—its materials and processes—has been a focus of study for centuries. However, the late 1700s is generally regarded as the beginning of modern geology. It was during this time that James Hutton published his important work, *Theory of the Earth*. Prior to this time, a great many explanations about Earth history relied on supernatural events.

Catastrophism

In the mid-1600s, James Ussher, Anglican Archbishop of Armagh, Primate of All Ireland, published a work that had immediate and profound influence. A respected scholar of the Bible, Ussher constructed a chronology of human and Earth history in which he determined that Earth was only a few thousand years old, having been created in 4004 B.C. Ussher's treatise earned widespread acceptance among Europe's scientific and religious leaders, and his chronology was soon printed in the margins of the Bible itself.

During the 1600s and 1700s, the doctrine of **catastrophism** strongly influenced people's thinking about Earth. Briefly stated, catastrophists believed that Earth's varied landscapes had been fashioned primarily by great catastrophes. Features such as mountains and canyons, which today we know take great periods of time to form, were explained as having been produced by sudden and often worldwide disasters of unknowable causes that no longer operate. This philosophy was an attempt to fit the rate of Earth's processes to the prevailing ideas on Earth's age.

The Birth of Modern Geology

When James Hutton, a Scottish physician and gentleman farmer, published his *Theory of the Earth* in the late 1700s, he put forth a principle that is a pillar of geology today, **uniformitarianism**. It states that *the physical, chemical, and biological laws that operate today have also operated in the geologic past.* This means that the forces and processes that we observe presently shaping our planet have been at work for a very long time. Thus, to understand ancient rocks, we must first understand present-day processes and their results. This idea is commonly expressed by saying, "The present is the key to the past."

Prior to Hutton's *Theory of the Earth,* no one had effectively demonstrated that geologic processes occur over extremely long periods of time. However, Hutton persuasively argued that processes that appear weak and slow acting could, over long spans of time, produce effects that were just as great as those resulting from sudden catastrophic events. Unlike his predecessors, Hutton cited verifiable observations to support his ideas.

For example, when he argued that mountains are sculpted and ultimately destroyed by weathering and the work of running water, and that their wastes are carried to the oceans by processes that can be observed, Hutton said, "We have a chain of facts which clearly demonstrates that the materials of the wasted mountains have traveled through the rivers"; and further, "There is not one step in all this progress that is not to be actually perceived." He then went on to summarize these thoughts by asking a question and immediately providing the answer: "What more can we require? Nothing but time."

Geology Today

The basic tenets of uniformitarianism are just as viable today as in Hutton's day. We realize more strongly than ever that the present gives us insight into the past and that the physical, chemical, and biological laws that govern geologic processes remain unchanging through time. However, we also understand that the doctrine should not be taken too literally. To say that geologic processes in the past were the same as those occurring today is not to suggest that they always had the same relative importance or that they operated at precisely the same rate. Moreover, some important geologic processes are not currently observable, but evidence that they occur is well established. For example, we know that Earth has experienced impacts from large meteorites even though we have no human witnesses. Such events altered Earth's crust, modified its climate, and strongly influenced life on the planet.

The acceptance of the concept of uniformitarianism, however, meant the acceptance of a very long history for Earth. Although Earth's processes vary in their intensity, they still take a long time to create or destroy major landscape features. For example, geologists have established that mountains once existed in portions of present-day Minnesota, Wisconsin, Michigan, and Manitoba. Today, the region consists of low hills and plains. Erosion (processes that wear land away) gradually destroyed these peaks. Estimates indicate that the North American continent is being lowered at a rate of about 3 centimeters (1 inch) per 1000 years. At this rate, it would take 100 million years for water, wind, and ice to lower mountains that were 3000 meters (10,000 feet) high.

But even this time span is relatively short on the time scale of Earth history, because the rock record shows that Earth has experienced *many cycles* of mountain building and erosion. Concerning the ever-changing nature of Earth through great expanses of geologic time, Hutton made a statement that was to become his most famous. In concluding his classic 1788 paper published in the *Transactions of the Royal Society of Edinburgh,* he stated, "The results, therefore, of our present enquiry is, that we find no vestige of a beginning—no prospect of an end."

It is important to remember that although many features of our physical landscape may seem to be unchanging over the decades we might observe them, they are nevertheless changing, but on time scales of hundreds, thousands, or even many millions of years.

RELATIVE DATING—KEY PRINCIPLES

GEODe
EARTH SCIENCE

    Deciphering Earth History
    ▼ Relative Dating

The geologists who developed the geologic time scale revolutionized the way people think about time and perceive our planet. They learned that Earth is much older than anyone had previously imagined and that its surface and interior have been changed over and over again by the same geologic processes that operate today.

During the late 1800s and early 1900s, various attempts were made to determine Earth's age. Although some of the methods appeared promising at the time, none proved to be reliable. What these scientists were seeking was a **numerical date**. Such dates specify the actual number of years that

have passed since an event occurred. Today, our understanding of radioactivity allows us to accurately determine numerical dates for many rocks that represent important events in Earth's distant past. We will study radioactivity later in this chapter. Prior to the discovery of radioactivity, geologists had no accurate and dependable method of numerical dating and had to rely solely on relative dating.

Relative dating means that rocks are placed in their proper *sequence of formation*—which formed first, second, third, and so on. Relative dating cannot tell us how long ago something took place, only that it followed one event and preceded another. The relative dating techniques that were developed are valuable and still widely used. Numerical dating methods did not replace these techniques; they simply supplemented them. To establish a relative time scale, a few simple principles or rules had to be discovered and applied. Although they may seem obvious to us today, they were major breakthroughs in thinking at the time, and their discovery and acceptance were important scientific achievements.

Law of Superposition

Nicolaus Steno (1638–1686), a Danish anatomist, geologist, and priest, is credited with being the first to recognize a sequence of historical events in an outcrop of sedimentary rock layers. Working in the mountains of western Italy, Steno applied a very simple rule that became the most basic principle of relative dating—the **law of superposition**. The law simply states that in an undeformed sequence of sedimentary rocks, each bed is older than the one above it and younger than the one below. Although it may seem obvious that a rock layer could not be deposited unless it had something older beneath it for support, it was not until 1669 that Steno clearly stated the principle.

This rule also applies to other surface-deposited materials such as lava flows and beds of ash from volcanic eruptions. Applying the law of superposition to the beds exposed in the upper portion of the Grand Canyon (FIGURE 3), you can easily

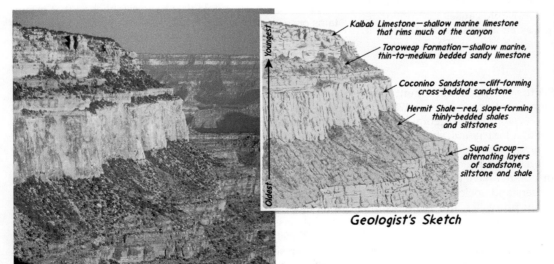

Geologist's Sketch

Kaibab Limestone—shallow marine limestone that rims much of the canyon

Toroweap Formation—shallow marine, thin-to-medium bedded sandy limestone

Coconino Sandstone—cliff-forming cross-bedded sandstone

Hermit Shale—red, slope-forming thinly-bedded shales and siltstones

Supai Group—alternating layers of sandstone, siltstone and shale

Youngest

Oldest

FIGURE 3 Applying the law of superposition to these layers exposed in the upper portion of the Grand Canyon, the Supai Group is oldest and the Kaibab Limestone is youngest. (Photo by E. J. Tarbuck)

FIGURE 4 Most layers of sediment are deposited in a nearly horizontal position. Thus, when we see rock layers that are folded or tilted, we can assume that they must have been moved into that position by crustal disturbances *after* their deposition. These folded strata are at Agio Pavlos on the Mediterranean island of Crete. (Photo by Marco Simoni/Robert Harding)

place the layers in their proper order. Among those that are shown, the sedimentary rocks in the Supai Group must be the oldest, followed in order by the Hermit Shale, Coconino Sandstone, Toroweap Formation, and Kaibab Limestone.

Principle of Original Horizontality

Steno is also credited with recognizing the **principle of original horizontality**. This principle simply states that most layers of sediment are deposited in a horizontal position. Thus, if we observe rock layers that are flat, it means they have not been disturbed and still have their *original* horizontality. The layers in the Grand Canyon illustrate this in Figure 2 and Figure 3. But if they are folded or inclined at a steep angle, they must have been moved into that position by crustal disturbances sometime *after* their deposition (**FIGURE 4**).

Principle of Cross-Cutting Relationships

When a fault cuts through other rocks, or when magma intrudes and crystallizes, we can assume that the fault or intrusion is younger than the rocks affected. For example, in **FIGURE 5**, the faults and dikes clearly must have occurred *after* the sedimentary layers were deposited.

This is the **principle of cross-cutting relationships**. By applying the cross-cutting principle, you can see that fault A occurred *after* the sandstone layer was deposited, because it "broke" the layer. However, fault A occurred *before* the conglomerate was laid down, because that layer is unbroken.

We can also state that dike B and its associated sill are older than dike A, because dike A cuts the sill. In the same manner, we know that the batholith was emplaced after movement occurred along fault B, but before dike B was formed. This is true because the batholith cuts across fault B, and dike B cuts across the batholith.

Inclusions

Sometimes inclusions can aid the relative dating process. **Inclusions** are fragments of one rock unit that have been enclosed within another. The basic principle is logical and straightforward. The rock mass adjacent to the one containing the inclusions must have been there first in order to provide the rock fragments. Therefore, the rock mass containing inclusions is the younger of the two. **FIGURE 6** provides an example. In part A, we know that the intrusive igneous rock is younger because it contains inclusions of the surrounding rock. In part C, the inclusions of intrusive igneous rock in the adjacent sedimentary layer (above

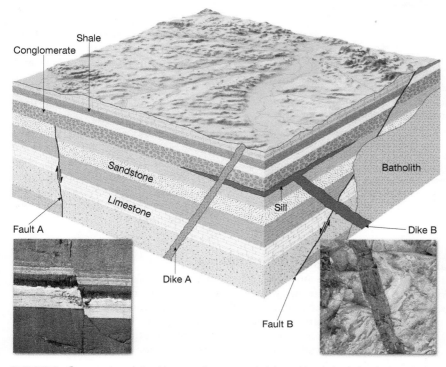

FIGURE 5 Cross-cutting relationships are an important principle used in relative dating. An intrusive rock body is younger than the rocks it intrudes. A fault is younger than the rock layers it cuts.

representing certain spans of geologic time. However, no place on Earth has a complete set of conformable strata.

Throughout Earth history, the deposition of sediment has been interrupted again and again. All such breaks in the rock record are termed *unconformities*. An **unconformity** represents a long period during which deposition ceased, erosion removed previously formed rocks, and then deposition resumed. In each case, Earth's crust has undergone uplift and erosion, followed by subsidence and renewed sedimentation. Unconformities are important features because they represent significant geologic events in Earth history. Moreover, their recognition helps us identify which intervals of time are not represented by strata and are missing from the geologic record.

The rocks exposed in the Grand Canyon of the Colorado River represent a tremendous span of geologic history. It is a wonderful place to take a trip through time. The canyon's colorful strata record a long history of sedimentation in a variety of environments—advancing seas, rivers and deltas, tidal flats, and sand dunes. But the record is not continuous. Unconformities represent vast amounts of time that are not accounted for in the canyon's layers. FIGURE 7 is a geologic cross section of the Grand Canyon. Refer to it as you read about three basic types of unconformities: angular unconformities, disconformities, and nonconformities.

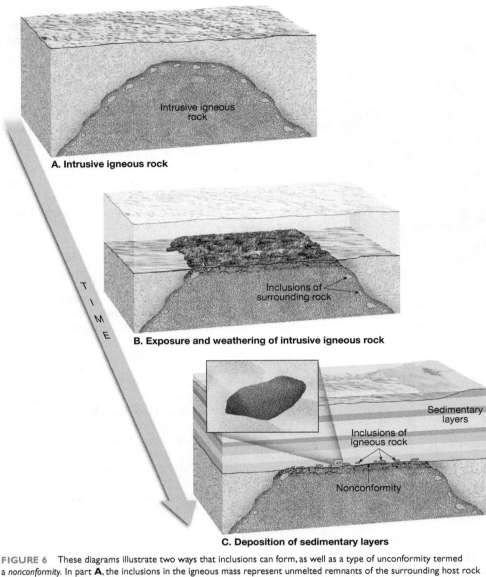

A. Intrusive igneous rock

B. Exposure and weathering of intrusive igneous rock

C. Deposition of sedimentary layers

FIGURE 6 These diagrams illustrate two ways that inclusions can form, as well as a type of unconformity termed a *nonconformity*. In part **A**, the inclusions in the igneous mass represent unmelted remnants of the surrounding host rock that were broken off and incorporated at the time the magma was intruded. In part **C**, the igneous rock must be older than the overlying sedimentary beds because the sedimentary beds contain inclusions of the igneous rock. When older intrusive igneous rocks are overlain by younger sedimentary layers, a *nonconformity* is said to exist. The inset shows a close-up of an inclusion of igneous rock in a younger host rock.

the line labeled "nonconformity") indicate that the sedimentary layer was deposited on top of an eroded igneous mass rather than being intruded from below by a mass of magma that later crystallized.

Unconformities

When we observe layers of rock that have been deposited essentially without interruption, we call them **conformable**. Many areas exhibit conformable beds

Angular Unconformity

The most easily recognized unconformity is **angular unconformity**. It consists of tilted or folded sedimentary rocks that are overlain by younger, more flat-lying strata. An angular unconformity indicates that during the pause in deposition, a period of deformation (folding or tilting) as well as erosion occurred. The steps in FIGURE 8 illustrate this process.

When James Hutton studied an angular unconformity in Scotland more than 200 years ago, it was clear to him that it

FIGURE 7   This cross section through the Grand Canyon illustrates the three basic types of unconformities. An angular unconformity can be seen between the tilted Precambrian Unkar Group and the Cambrian Tapeats Sandstone. Two disconformities are marked, above and below the Redwall Limestone. A nonconformity occurs between the igneous and metamorphic rocks exposed in the inner gorge and the sedimentary strata of the Unkar Group. A nonconformity, highlighted by a photo, also occurs between the rocks of the inner gorge and the Tapeats Sandstone.

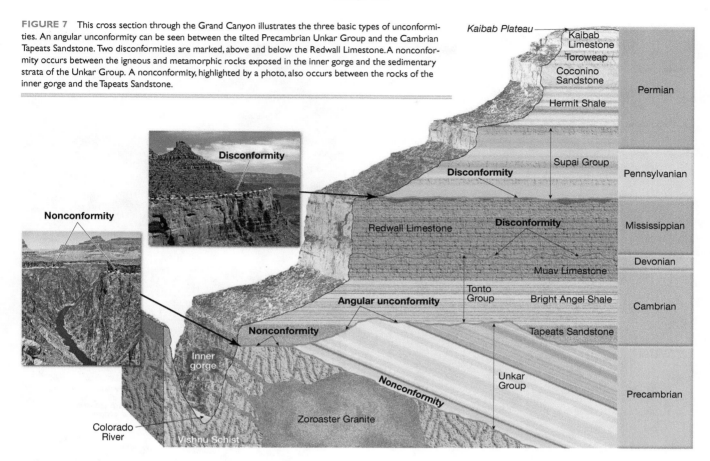

represented a major episode of geologic activity (FIGURE 9). He also appreciated the immense time span implied by such relationships. Later, when a companion wrote of their visit to the site, he stated that, "The mind seemed to grow giddy by looking so far into the abyss of time."

Disconformity

When contrasted with angular unconformities, **disconformities** are more common but usually far less conspicuous because the strata on either side are essentially parallel. Many disconformities are difficult to identify because the rocks above and below are similar and there is little evidence of erosion. Such a break often resembles an ordinary bedding plane. Other disconformities are easier to identify because the ancient erosion surface is cut deeply into the older rocks below. Two disconformities are labeled on the geological cross section of the Grand Canyon in Figure 7.

Nonconformity

The third basic type of unconformity is **nonconformity**. Here, the break separates older metamorphic or intrusive

igneous rocks from younger sedimentary strata (see Figure 6). Just as angular unconformities and disconformities imply crustal movements, so, too, do nonconformities. Intrusive igneous masses and metamorphic rocks originate far below the surface. For a nonconformity to develop, a period of uplift and the erosion of overlying rocks must occur. Once exposed at the surface, the igneous or metamorphic rocks are subjected to weathering and erosion prior to subsidence and the renewal of sedimentation.

Applying Relative Dating Principles

By applying the principles of relative dating to the hypothetical geologic cross section shown in FIGURE 10, the rocks and the events in Earth history they represent can be placed into their proper sequence. The statements within the figure summarize the logic used to interpret the cross section. In this example, we establish a relative time scale for the rocks and events in the area of the cross section. Remember, we do not know how many years of Earth history are represented, nor do we know how this area compares to any other.

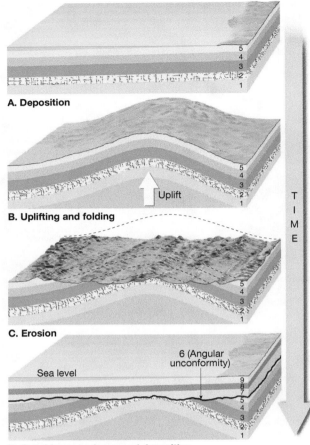

A. Deposition

B. Uplifting and folding

Uplift

C. Erosion

Sea level

6 (Angular unconformity)

D. Subsidence and renewed deposition

T I M E

FIGURE 8 Formation of an angular unconformity. An angular unconformity represents a period during which deformation and erosion occurred.

Above the unconformity lie gently dipping beds of redish sandstone and conglomerate

Angular unconformity

Rock hammer

Below the unconformity lie nearly vertical sandstones and shales

Geologist's Sketch

FIGURE 9 This angular unconformity at Siccar Point, Scotland, was first described by James Hutton more than 200 years ago. (Photo by Marli Miller)

CORRELATION OF ROCK LAYERS

To develop a geologic time scale that applies to the entire Earth, rocks of similar age in different regions must be matched up. Such a task is referred to as **correlation**. Within a limited area, correlating the rocks of one locality with those of another may be done simply by walking along the outcropping edges. However, this may not be possible when a bed is not continuously exposed. Correlation over short distances is often achieved by noting the position of a rock layer in a sequence of strata. Or, a layer may be identified in another location if it consists of very distinctive or uncommon minerals.

By correlating the rocks from one place to another, a more comprehensive view of the geologic history of a region is possible. **FIGURE 11** shows the correlation of strata at three sites on the Colorado Plateau in southern Utah and northern Arizona. No single locale exhibits the entire sequence, but correlation reveals a more complete picture of the sedimentary rock record.

Many geologic studies involve relatively small areas. Such studies are important in their own right, but their full

DID YOU KNOW?

The *word fossil* comes from the Latin *fossilium*, which means "dug up from the ground." As originally used by medieval writers, a fossil was *any* stone, ore, or gem that came from an underground source. In fact, many early books on mineralogy are called books of fossils. The current meaning of fossil came about during the 1700s.

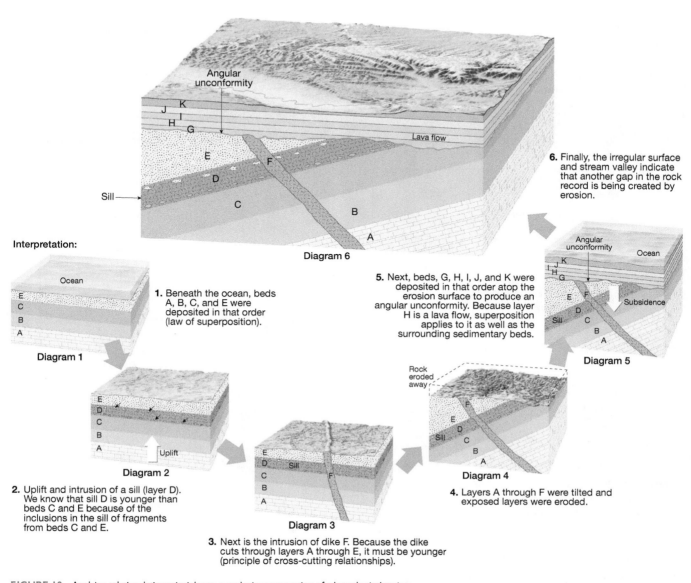

Interpretation:

Diagram 1

1. Beneath the ocean, beds A, B, C, and E were deposited in that order (law of superposition).

Diagram 2

2. Uplift and intrusion of a sill (layer D). We know that sill D is younger than beds C and E because of the inclusions in the sill of fragments from beds C and E.

Diagram 3

3. Next is the intrusion of dike F. Because the dike cuts through layers A through E, it must be younger (principle of cross-cutting relationships).

Diagram 4

4. Layers A through F were tilted and exposed layers were eroded.

Diagram 5

5. Next, beds, G, H, I, J, and K were deposited in that order atop the erosion surface to produce an angular unconformity. Because layer H is a lava flow, superposition applies to it as well as the surrounding sedimentary beds.

Diagram 6

6. Finally, the irregular surface and stream valley indicate that another gap in the rock record is being created by erosion.

FIGURE 10   Applying relative dating principles to a geologic cross section of a hypothetical region.

value is realized only when the rocks are correlated with those of other regions. Although the methods just described are sufficient to trace a rock formation over relatively short distances, they are not adequate for matching rocks that are separated by great distances. When correlation between widely separated areas or between continents is the objective, geologists must rely on fossils.

FOSSILS: EVIDENCE OF PAST LIFE

Fossils, the remains or traces of prehistoric life, are important inclusions in sediment and sedimentary rocks. They are important basic tools for interpreting the geologic past. The scientific study of fossils is called **paleontology**. It is an

interdisciplinary science that blends geology and biology in an attempt to understand all aspects of the succession of life over the vast expanse of geologic time. Knowing the nature of

DID YOU KNOW?

People frequently confuse paleontology and archaeology. Paleontologists study fossils and are concerned with *all* life forms in the geologic past. By contrast, archaeologists focus on the material remains of past human life. These remains include both the objects used by people long ago, called *artifacts*, and the buildings and other structures associated with where people lived, called *sites*.

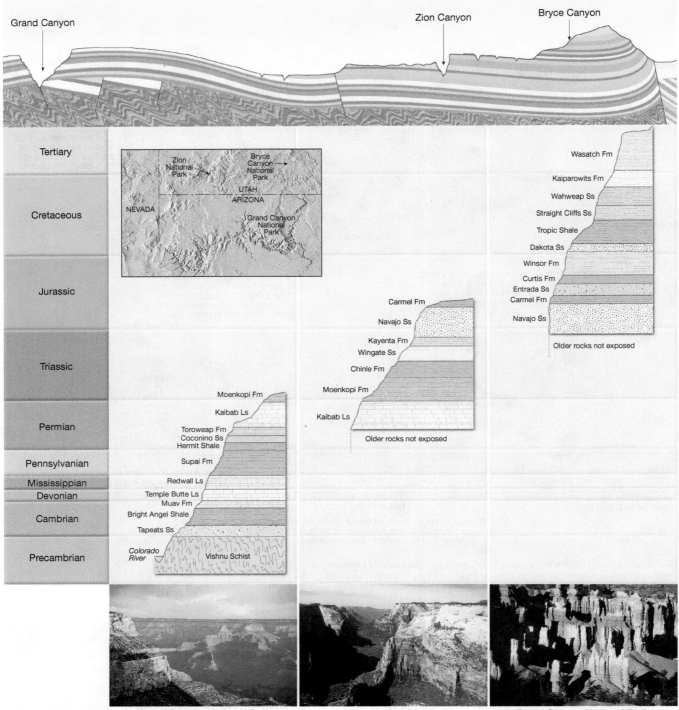

FIGURE 11 Correlation of strata at three locations on the Colorado Plateau allows for a more complete view of the extent of sedimentary rocks in the region. (After U.S. Geological Survey. Insert photos E. J. Tarbuck)

the life forms that existed at a particular time helps researchers understand past environmental conditions. Further, fossils are important time indicators and play a key role in correlating rocks of similar ages that are from different places.

Types of Fossils

Fossils are of many types. The remains of relatively recent organisms may not have been altered at all. Such objects as teeth, bones, and shells are common examples. Far less common are entire animals, flesh included, that have been preserved because of rather unusual circumstances. Remains of prehistoric elephants called mammoths that were frozen in the Arctic tundra of Siberia and Alaska are examples, as are the mummified remains of sloths preserved in a dry cave in Nevada.

Given enough time, the remains of an organism are likely to be modified. Fossils often become *petrified* (literally, "turned into stone"), meaning that the small internal cavities and pores of the original structure are filled with precipitated mineral matter (**FIGURE 12A**). In other instances *replacement* may occur. The cell walls and other solid material are removed

and replaced with mineral matter. The microscopic details of the replaced structure are sometimes faithfully retained.

Molds and casts constitute another common class of fossils. When a shell or other structure is buried in sediment and then dissolved by underground water, a *mold* is created. The mold faithfully reflects only the shape and surface marking of the organism; it does not reveal any information concerning its internal structure. If these hollow spaces are subsequently filled with mineral matter, *casts* are created (**FIGURE 12B**).

A type of fossilization called *carbonization* is particularly effective in preserving leaves and delicate animal forms. It occurs when fine sediment encases the remains of an organism. As time passes, pressure squeezes out the liquid and gaseous components and leaves behind a thin residue of carbon (**FIGURE 12C**). Black shales deposited as organic-rich mud in oxygen-poor environments often contain abundant carbonized remains. If the film of carbon is lost from a fossil preserved in fine-grained sediment, a replica of the surface, called an *impression*, may still show considerable detail (**FIGURE 12D**).

FIGURE 12 There are many types of fossilization. Six examples are shown here. **A.** Petrified wood in Petrified Forest National Park, Arizona. **B.** This trilobite photo illustrates mold and cast. **C.** A fossil bee preserved as a thin carbon film. **D.** Impressions are common fossils and often show considerable detail. **E.** Insect in amber. **F.** Coprolite or fossil dung. (Photo A by Bernhard Edmaier/Photo Researchers, Inc.; Photos B, D, and F by E. J. Tarbuck; Photo C courtesy of Florissant Fossil Beds National Monument; Photo E by Colin Keates/Dorling Kindersly Media Library)

Delicate organisms, such as insects, are difficult to preserve, and consequently they are relatively rare in the fossil record. They must not only be protected from decay, but also not be subjected to any pressure that would crush them. One way in which some insects have been preserved is in *amber,* the hardened resin of ancient trees. The fly in FIGURE 12E was preserved after being trapped in a drop of sticky resin. Resin sealed off the insect from the atmosphere and protected the remains from damage by water and air. As the resin hardened, a protective pressure-resistant case formed.

In addition to the fossils already mentioned, there are numerous other types, many of them only traces of prehistoric life. Examples of such indirect evidence include the following:

1. Tracks—animal footprints made in soft sediment that was later lithified.
2. Burrows—tubes in sediment, wood, or rock made by an animal. These holes may later become filled with mineral matter and preserved. Some of the oldest-known fossils are believed to be worm burrows.
3. Coprolites—fossil dung and stomach contents that can provide useful information pertaining to food habits of organisms (FIGURE 12F).
4. Gastroliths—highly polished stomach stones that were used in the grinding of food by some extinct reptiles.

Conditions Favoring Preservation

Only a tiny fraction of the organisms that have lived during the geologic past have been preserved as fossils. The remains of an animal or plant are normally destroyed. Under what circumstances are they preserved? Two special conditions appear to be necessary: rapid burial and the possession of hard parts.

When an organism perishes, its soft parts are usually quickly eaten by scavengers or decomposed by bacteria. Occasionally, however, the remains are buried by sediment. When this occurs, the remains are protected from the environment where destructive processes operate. Rapid burial, therefore, is an important condition favoring preservation.

In addition, animals and plants have a much better chance of being preserved as part of the fossil record if they have hard parts. Although traces and imprints of soft-bodied animals such as jellyfish, worms, and insects exist, they are not common. Flesh usually decays so rapidly that preservation is exceedingly unlikely. Hard parts such as shells, bones, and teeth predominate in the record of past life.

DID YOU KNOW?

Even when organisms die and their tissues decay, the organic compounds (hydrocarbons) of which they were made may survive in sediments. These are called *chemical fossils.* These hydrocarbons form oil and gas, but some residues can persist in the rock record and be analyzed to determine the kinds of organisms they are derived from.

Because preservation is contingent on special conditions, the record of life in the geologic past is biased. The fossil record of those organisms with hard parts that lived in areas of sedimentation is quite abundant. However, we get only an occasional glimpse of the vast array of other life forms that did not meet the special conditions favoring preservation.

Fossils and Correlation

The existence of fossils had been known for centuries, yet it was not until the late 1700s and early 1800s that their significance as geologic tools was made evident. During this period, an English engineer and canal builder, William Smith, discovered that each rock formation in the canals he worked on contained fossils unlike those in the beds either above or below. Further, he noted that sedimentary strata in widely separated areas could be identified—and correlated—by their distinctive fossil content.

Based on Smith's classic observations and the findings of many geologists who followed, one of the most important and basic principles in historical geology was formulated: *Fossil organisms succeed one another in a definite and determinable order, and, therefore, any time period can be recognized by its fossil content.* This has come to be known as the **principle of fossil succession**. In other words, when fossils are arranged according to their age by applying the law of superposition to the rocks in which they are found, they do not present a random or haphazard picture. To the contrary, fossils document the evolution of life through time.

For example, an Age of Trilobites is recognized quite early in the fossil record. Then, in succession, paleontologists recognize an Age of Fishes, an Age of Coal Swamps, an Age of Reptiles, and an Age of Mammals. These "ages" pertain to groups that were especially plentiful and characteristic during particular time periods. Within each of the ages, subdivisions are based on certain species of trilobites, and certain types of fish, reptiles, and so on. This same succession of dominant organisms, never out of order, is found on every major landmass.

Once fossils were recognized as time indicators, they became the most useful means of correlating rocks of similar ages in different regions. Geologists pay particular attention to certain fossils called **index fossils**. These fossils are widespread geographically and are limited to a short span of geologic time, so their presence provides an important method of matching rocks of the same age. Rock formations, however, do not always contain a specific index fossil. In such situations, groups of fossils, called *fossil assemblages,* are used to establish the age of the bed. FIGURE 13 illustrates how an assemblage of fossils can be used to date rocks more precisely than could be accomplished by the use of only one of the fossils.

In addition to being important and often essential tools for correlation, fossils are important environmental indicators. Although much can be deduced about past environments by studying the nature and characteristics of sedimentary rocks, a close examination of the fossils present can usually provide a great deal more information.

For example, when the remains of certain clam shells are found in limestone, the geologist can assume that the region

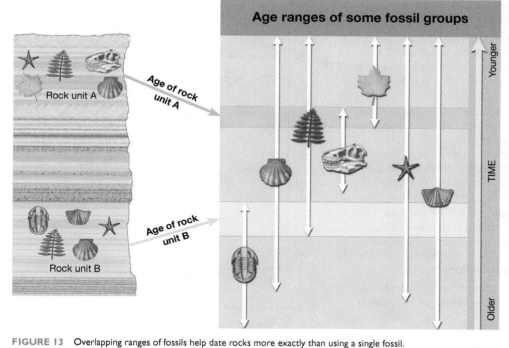

Age ranges of some fossil groups

Rock unit A

Age of rock unit A

Rock unit B

Age of rock unit B

Younger

TIME

Older

FIGURE 13   Overlapping ranges of fossils help date rocks more exactly than using a single fossil.

past. We know that Earth is about 4.6 billion years old and that the dinosaurs became extinct about 65.5 million years ago. Dates that are expressed in millions and billions of years truly stretch our imagination because our personal calendars involve time measured in hours, weeks, and years. Nevertheless, the vast expanse of geologic time is a reality, and it is radiometric dating that allows us to measure it accurately. In this section, you will learn about radioactivity and its application in radiometric dating.

Reviewing Basic Atomic Structure

Each atom has a *nucleus* containing protons and neutrons and the nucleus is orbited by electrons. *Electrons* have a negative electrical charge, and *protons* have a positive charge. A *neutron* is actually a proton and an electron combined, so it has no charge (it is neutral).

The *atomic number* (the element's identifying number) is the number of protons in the nucleus. Every element has a different number of protons in the nucleus and thus a different atomic number (hydrogen = 1, oxygen = 8, uranium = 92, etc.). Atoms of the same element always have the same number of protons, so the atomic number is constant.

Practically all (99.9 percent) of an atom's mass is found in the nucleus, indicating that electrons have practically no mass at all. By adding together the number of protons and neutrons in the nucleus, the *mass number* of the atom is determined. The number of neutrons in the nucleus can vary. These variants, called *isotopes,* have different mass numbers.

To summarize with an example, uranium's nucleus always has 92 protons, so its atomic number always is 92. But its neutron population varies, so uranium has three isotopes: uranium-234 (number of protons + neutrons = 234), uranium-235, and uranium-238. All three isotopes are mixed in nature. They look the same and behave the same in chemical reactions.

Radioactivity

The forces that bind protons and neutrons together in the nucleus are usually strong. However, in some isotopes, the nuclei are unstable because the forces binding protons and neutrons together are not strong enough. As a result, the nuclei spontaneously break apart (decay), a process called **radioactivity**. What happens when unstable nuclei break apart?

was once covered by a shallow sea, because that is where clams live today. Also, by using what we know of living organisms, we can conclude that fossil animals with thick shells capable of withstanding pounding and surging waves must have inhabited shorelines. On the other hand, animals with thin, delicate shells probably indicate deep, calm offshore waters. Hence, by looking closely at the types of fossils, the approximate position of an ancient shoreline may be identified.

Further, fossils can indicate the former temperature of the water. Certain present-day corals require warm and shallow tropical seas like those around Florida and the Bahamas. When similar corals are found in ancient limestones, they indicate that a Florida-like marine environment must have existed when they were alive. These are just a few examples of how fossils can help unravel the complex story of Earth history.

DATING WITH RADIOACTIVITY

GEODe

EARTH SCIENCE

Deciphering Earth History
▽ Radiometric Dating

In addition to establishing relative dates by using the principles described in the preceding sections, it is also possible to obtain reliable numerical dates for events in the geologic

Three common types of radioactive decay are illustrated in **FIGURE 14** and are summarized as follows:

1. *Alpha particles* (α particles) may be emitted from the nucleus. An alpha particle consists of 2 protons and 2 neutrons. Consequently, the emission of an alpha particle means (a) the mass number of the isotope is reduced by 4, and (b) the atomic number is decreased by 2.

2. When a *beta particle* (β particle), or electron, is given off from a nucleus, the mass number remains unchanged, because electrons have practically no mass. However, because the electron has come from a neutron (remember, a neutron is a combination of a proton and an electron), the nucleus contains one more proton than before. Therefore, the atomic number increases by 1.

3. Sometimes an electron is captured by the nucleus. The electron combines with a proton and forms an additional neutron. As in the last example, the mass number remains unchanged. However, because the nucleus now contains one less proton, the atomic number decreases by 1.

An unstable (radioactive) isotope is referred to as the *parent*. The isotopes resulting from the decay of the parent

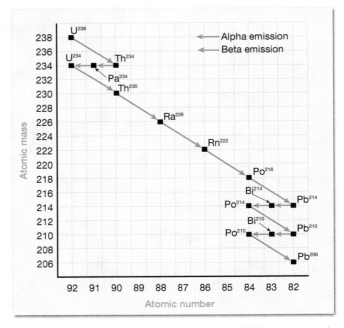

FIGURE 15 The most common isotope of uranium (U-238) is an example of a radioactive decay series. Before the stable end product (Pb-206) is reached, many different isotopes are produced as intermediate steps.

are the *daughter products*. **FIGURE 15** provides an example of radioactive decay. When the radioactive parent, uranium-238 (atomic number 92, mass number 238), decays, it follows a number of steps, emitting eight alpha particles and six beta particles before finally becoming the stable daughter product lead-206 (atomic number 82, mass number 206).

Certainly among the most important results of the discovery of radioactivity is that it provides a reliable method of calculating the ages of rocks and minerals that contain particular radioactive isotopes. The procedure is called **radiometric dating.** Why is radiometric dating reliable? The rates of decay for many isotopes have been precisely measured and do not vary under the physical conditions that exist in Earth's outer layers. Therefore, each radioactive isotope used for dating has been decaying at a fixed rate ever since the formation of the rocks in which it occurs, and the products of decay have been accumulating at a corresponding rate. For example, when uranium is incorporated into a mineral that crystallizes from magma, there is no lead (the stable daughter product) from previous decay. The radiometric "clock" starts at this point. As the uranium in this newly formed mineral disintegrates, atoms of the daughter product are trapped and measurable amounts of lead eventually accumulate.

Half-Life

The time required for one half of the nuclei in a sample to decay is called the **half-life** of the isotope. Half-life is a common way of expressing the rate of radioactive disintegration. **FIGURE 16** illustrates what occurs when a radioactive parent decays directly into its stable daughter product. When the

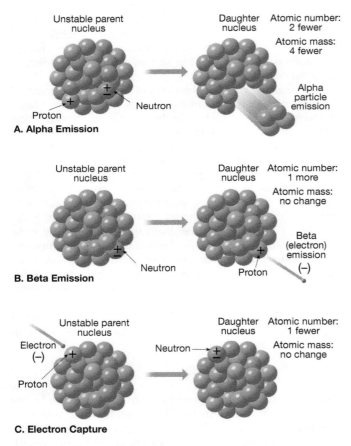

FIGURE 14 Common types of radioactive decay. Notice that in each case, the number of protons (atomic number) in the nucleus changes, thus producing a different element.

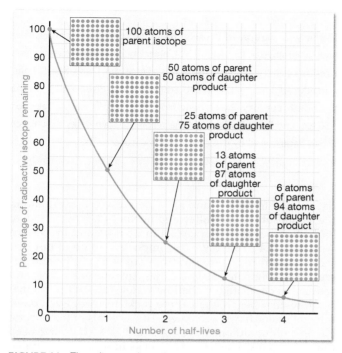

FIGURE 16 The radioactive decay curve shows change that is exponential. Half of the radioactive parent remains after one half-life. After a second half-life, one-quarter of the parent remains, and so forth.

Table 1 Radioactive isotopes frequently used in radiometric dating

Radioactive Parent	Stable Daughter Product	Currently Accepted Half-Life Values
Uranium-238	Lead-206	4.5 billion years
Uranium-235	Lead-207	713 million years
Thorium-232	Lead-208	14.1 billion years
Rubidium-87	Strontium-87	47.0 billion years
Potassium-40	Argon-40	1.3 billion years

years old, but potassium-40 is more versatile. Although the half-life of potassium-40 is 1.3 billion years, analytical techniques make possible the detection of tiny amounts of its stable daughter product, argon-40, in some rocks that are younger than 100,000 years. Another important reason for its frequent use is that potassium is abundant in many common minerals, particularly micas and feldspars.

It is important to realize that an accurate radiometric date can be obtained only if the mineral remained a closed system during the entire period since its formation. A correct date is not possible unless there was neither the addition nor loss of parent or daughter isotopes. This is not always the case. In fact, an important limitation of the potassium-argon method arises from the fact that argon is a gas, and it may leak from minerals, throwing off measurements.

Remember that although the basic principle of radiometric dating is simple, the actual procedure is quite complex. The analysis that determines the quantities of parent and daughter must be painstakingly precise. In addition, some radioactive materials do not decay directly into the stable daughter product. As you saw in Figure 15 uranium-238 produces 13 intermediate unstable daughter products before the fourteenth and final daughter product, the stable isotope lead-206, is produced.

Dating with Carbon-14

To date very recent events, carbon-14 is used. Carbon-14 is the radioactive isotope of carbon. The process is often called **radiocarbon dating**. Because the half-life of carbon-14 is only 5,730 years, it can be used for dating events from the historic past as well as those from very recent geologic history. In some cases, carbon-14 can be used to date events as far back as 75,000 years.

DID YOU KNOW?

One common precaution against sources of error in radiometric dating is the use of cross checks. This simply involves subjecting a sample to two different methods. If the two dates agree, the likelihood is high that the date is reliable. If an appreciable difference is found, other cross checks must be employed to determine which, if either, is correct.

quantities of parent and daughter are equal (ratio 1:1), we know that one half-life has transpired. When one-quarter of the original parent atoms remain and three-quarters have decayed to the daughter product, the parent/daughter ratio is 1:3, and we know that two half-lives have passed. After three half-lives, the ratio of parent atoms to daughter atoms is 1:7 (one parent atom for every seven daughter atoms).

If the half-life of a radioactive isotope is known and the parent–daughter ratio can be determined, the age of the sample can be calculated. For example, assume that the half-life of a hypothetical unstable isotope is 1 million years and the parent–daughter ratio in a sample is 1:15. Such a ratio indicates that four half-lives have passed and that the sample must be 4 million years old.

Radiometric Dating

Notice that the *percentage* of radioactive atoms that decay during one half-life is always the same: 50 percent. However, the *actual number* of atoms that decay with the passing of each half-life continually decreases. As the percentage of radioactive parent atoms declines, the proportion of stable daughter atoms rises, with the increase in daughter atoms just matching the drop in parent atoms. This fact is the key to radiometric dating.

Of the many radioactive isotopes that exist in nature, five have proved particularly important in providing radiometric ages for ancient rocks (Table 1). Rubidium-87, uranium-238, and uranium-235 are used for dating rocks that are millions of

Carbon-14 is continuously produced in the upper atmosphere as a consequence of cosmic-ray bombardment. Cosmic rays, which are high-energy particles, shatter the nuclei of gas atoms, releasing neutrons. Some of the neutrons are absorbed by nitrogen atoms (atomic number 7), causing their nuclei to emit a proton. As a result, the atomic number decreases by 1 (to 6), and a different element, carbon-14, is created (**FIGURE 17A**). This isotope of carbon quickly becomes incorporated into carbon dioxide, which circulates in the atmosphere and is absorbed by living matter. As a result, all organisms contain a small amount of carbon-14, including yourself.

While an organism is alive, the decaying radiocarbon is continually replaced, and the proportions of carbon-14 and carbon-12 remain constant. Carbon-12 is the stable and most common isotope of carbon. However, when any plant or animal dies, the amount of carbon-14 gradually decreases as it decays to nitrogen-14 by beta emission (**FIGURE 17B**). By comparing the proportions of carbon-14 and carbon-12 in a sample, radiocarbon dates can be determined.

Although carbon-14 is useful in dating only the last small fraction of geologic time, it has become a valuable tool for anthropologists, archaeologists, and historians, as well as for geologists who study very recent Earth history. In fact, the development of radiocarbon dating was considered so important that the chemist who discovered this application, Willard F. Libby, received a Nobel prize.

Importance of Radiometric Dating

Radiometric dating methods have produced literally thousands of dates for events in Earth history. Rocks exceeding 3.5 billion years in age are found on all of the continents. Earth's oldest rocks (so far) are gneisses from northern Canada near Great Slave Lake that have been dated at 4.03 billion years (b.y.). Rocks from western Greenland have been

dated at 3.7 to 3.8 b.y., and rocks nearly as old are found in the Minnesota River Valley and northern Michigan (3.5 to 3.7 b.y.), in southern Africa (3.4 to 3.5 b.y.), and in western Australia (3.4 to 3.6 b.y.). It is important to point out that these ancient rocks are not from any sort of "primordial crust" but originated as lava flows, igneous intrusions, and sediments deposited in shallow water—an indication that Earth history began *before* these rocks formed. Even older mineral grains have been dated. Tiny crystals of the mineral zircon having radiometric ages as old as 4.3 b.y. have been found in younger sedimentary rocks in western Australia. The source rocks for these tiny durable grains either no longer exist or have not yet been found.

Radiometric dating has vindicated the ideas of Hutton, Charles Darwin, and others who inferred that geologic time must be immense. Indeed, modern dating methods have proved that there has been enough time for the processes we observe to have accomplished tremendous tasks.

THE GEOLOGIC TIME SCALE

Deciphering Earth History
▼ Geologic Time Scale

Geologists have divided the whole of geologic history into units of varying magnitude. Together, they comprise the **geologic time scale** of Earth history (**FIGURE 18**). The major units of the time scale were delineated during the nineteenth century, principally by scientists in Western Europe and Great Britain. Because radiometric dating was unavailable at that time, the entire time scale was created using methods of relative dating. It was only in the twentieth century that radiometric dating permitted numerical dates to be added.

Structure of the Time Scale

The geologic time scale divides the 4.6-billion-year history of Earth into many different units and provides a meaningful time frame within which the events of the geologic past are arranged. As shown in Figure 18, **eons** represent the greatest expanses of time. The eon that began about 542 million years ago is the **Phanerozoic**, a term derived from Greek words meaning "visible life." It is an appropriate description because the rocks and deposits of the Phanerozoic eon contain abundant fossils that document major evolutionary trends.

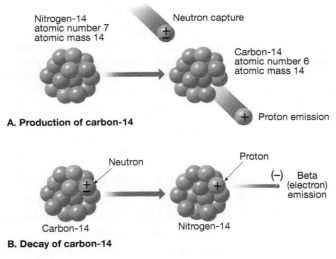

A. Production of carbon-14

Nitrogen-14
atomic number 7
atomic mass 14

Neutron capture

Carbon-14
atomic number 6
atomic mass 14

Proton emission

Neutron

Proton

Carbon-14

Nitrogen-14

(−) Beta (electron) emission

B. Decay of carbon-14

FIGURE 17 **A.** Production and **B.** decay of carbon-14. These sketches represent the nuclei of the respective atoms.

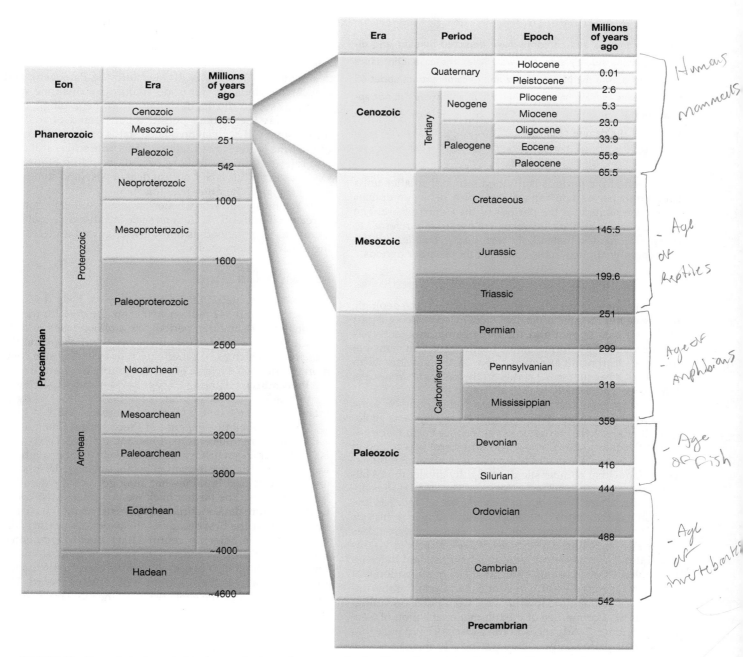

FIGURE 18 The geologic time scale. Numbers on the time scale represent time in millions of years before the present. The numerical dates were added long after the time scale had been established using relative dating techniques. The Precambrian accounts for more than **88 percent** of geologic time. The time scale is a dynamic tool. Advances in the geosciences require that updates be made from time to time. This version was updated in July 2009.

Another glance at the time scale shows that eons are divided into **eras**. The three eras within the Phanerozoic are the **Paleozoic** ("ancient life"), the **Mesozoic** ("middle life"), and the **Cenozoic** ("recent life"). As the names imply, these eras are bounded by profound worldwide changes in life forms.

Each era of the Phanerozoic eon is divided into units known as **periods**. The Paleozoic has seven and the Mesozoic and Cenozoic each have three. Each of these periods is characterized by a somewhat less profound change in life forms as compared with the eras.

Although movies and cartoons have depicted humans and dinosaurs living side by side, this was never the case. Dinosaurs flourished during the Mesozoic era and became extinct about 65 million years ago. Humans and their close ancestors did not appear on the scene until the late Cenozoic, more than 60 million years *after* the demise of dinosaurs.

Each of the periods is divided into still smaller units called **epochs**. As you can see in Figure 18, seven epochs have been named for the periods of the Cenozoic era. The epochs of other periods, however, are not usually referred to by specific names. Instead, the terms *early, middle,* and *late* are generally applied to the epochs of these earlier periods.

Terminology and the Geologic Time Scale

There are some terms that are associated with the geologic time scale but are not "officially" recognized as being a part of it. The best known and the most common example is *Precambrian*—the informal name for the eons that came before the current Phanerozoic eon. Although the term *Precambrian* has no formal status on the geologic time scale, it has been traditionally used as though it did.

Hadean is another informal term that is found on some versions of the geologic time scale and is used by some geologists. It refers to the earliest interval (eon) of Earth history—before the oldest known rocks. When the term was coined in 1972, the age of Earth's oldest rocks was about 3.8 billion years. Today that number stands at slightly greater than 4 billion, and, of course, is subject to revision. The name *Hadean* derives from *Hades* Greek for *underworld*—a reference to the "hellish" conditions that prevailed on Earth early in its history.

Effective communication in the geosciences requires that the geologic time scale consist of standardized divisions and dates. So, who determines which names and dates on the geologic time scale are "official"? The organization that is largely responsible for maintaining and updating this important document is the International Committee on Stratigraphy (ICS), a committee of the International Union of Geological Sciences*. Advances in the geosciences require that the scale be periodically updated to include changes in unit names and boundary age estimates.

For example, the geologic time scale shown in Figure 18 was updated as recently as July 2009. After considerable dialogue among geologists who focus on very recent Earth history, the ICS changed the date for the start of the Quaternary period and the Pleistocene epoch from 1.8 million to 2.6 million years ago. Who knows, perhaps by the time you read this, other changes will have been made.

*To view the current version of the ICS time scale, go to http://www.stratigraphy.org. *Stratigraphy* is the branch of geology that studies rock layers (strata) and layering (stratification), thus its primary focus is sedimentary and layered volcanic rocks.

If you were to examine a geologic time scale from just a few years ago, it is quite possible that you would see the Cenozoic era divided into the Tertiary and Quaternary periods. However, on more recent versions the space formerly designated as Tertiary is divided into the Paleogene and Neogene periods. As our understanding of this time span changed, so too did its designation on the geologic time scale. Today the Tertiary period is considered as an "historic" name and is given no official status on the ICS version of the time scale. Nevertheless, many time scales still contain references to the Tertiary period, including Figure 18. One reason for this is that a great deal of past (and some current) geological literature uses this name.

For those who study historical geology, it is important to realize that the geologic time scale is a dynamic tool that continues to be refined as our knowledge and understanding of Earth history evolves.

Precambrian Time

Notice that the detail of the geologic time scale does not begin until about 542 million years ago, the date for the beginning of the Cambrian period. The 4 billion years prior to the Cambrian is divided into two eons, the *Archean* and the *Proterozoic,* which are divided into four eras. It is also common for this vast expanse of time to simply be referred to as the **Precambrian**. Although it represents about 88 percent of Earth history, the Precambrian is not divided into nearly as many smaller time units as is the Phanerozoic eon.

Why is the huge expanse of Precambrian time not divided into numerous eras, periods, and epochs? The reason is that Precambrian history is not known in great enough detail. The quantity of information geologists have deciphered about Earth's past is somewhat analogous to the detail of human history. The farther back we go, the less we know. Certainly, more data and information exist about the past 10 years than for the first decade of the twentieth century; the events of the nineteenth century have been documented much better than the events of the first century A.D., and so on. So it is with Earth history. The more recent past has the freshest, least disturbed, and most observable record. The farther back in time the geologist goes, the more fragmented the record and clues become.

Some scientists have suggested that the Holocene epoch has ended and that we have entered a new epoch called the *Anthropocene*. It is considered to be the span, beginning in the early 1800s, in which the global environmental effects of increased human population and economic development have dramatically transformed Earth's surface. Although used currently as an informal metaphor for human-caused global environmental change, a number of scientists feel that there is merit in recognizing the Anthropocene as a new "official" geologic epoch.

DIFFICULTIES IN DATING THE GEOLOGIC TIME SCALE

Although reasonably accurate numerical dates have been worked out for the periods of the geologic time scale (see Figure 18), the task is not without difficulty. The primary problem in assigning numerical dates is the fact that not all rocks can be dated by radiometric methods. For a radiometric date to be useful, all minerals in the rock must have formed at about the same time. For this reason, radioactive isotopes can be used to determine when minerals in an igneous rock crystallized and when pressure and heat created new minerals in a metamorphic rock.

However, samples of sedimentary rock can only rarely be dated directly by radiometric means. A sedimentary rock may include particles that contain radioactive isotopes, but the rock's age cannot be accurately determined because the grains that make up the rock are not the same age as the rock in which they occur. Rather, the sediments have been weathered from rocks of diverse ages (FIGURE 19).

Radiometric dates obtained from metamorphic rocks may also be difficult to interpret, because the age of a particular mineral in a metamorphic rock does not necessarily represent the time when the rock initially formed. Instead, the date may indicate any one of a number of subsequent metamorphic phases.

If samples of sedimentary rocks rarely yield reliable radiometric ages, how can numerical dates be assigned to sedimentary layers? Usually the geologist must relate them to datable igneous masses, as in FIGURE 20. In this example, radiometric dating has determined the ages of the volcanic ash bed within the Morrison Formation and the dike cutting the Mancos Shale and Mesaverde Formation. The sedimentary beds below the ash are obviously older than the ash, and all the layers above the ash are younger (principle of superposition). The dike is younger than the Mancos Shale and the Mesaverde Formation but older than the Wasatch Formation because the dike does not intrude the Tertiary rocks (cross-cutting relationships).

From this kind of evidence, geologists estimate that a part of the Morrison Formation was deposited about 160 million years ago, as indicated by the ash bed. Further, they conclude that the Tertiary period began after the intrusion of the dike, 66 million years ago. This is one example of literally thousands that illustrates how datable materials are used to "bracket" the various episodes in Earth history within specific time periods. It shows the necessity of combining laboratory dating methods with field observations of rocks.

FIGURE 19 A useful numerical date for this conglomerate is not possible because the gravel that composes it was derived from rocks of diverse ages. (Photo by E. J. Tarbuck)

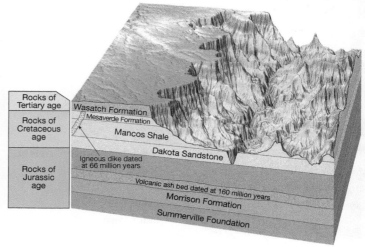

FIGURE 20 Numerical dates for sedimentary layers are usually determined by examining their relationship to igneous rocks. (After U.S. Geological Survey)

THE CHAPTER IN REVIEW

• During the seventeenth and eighteenth centuries, *catastrophism* influenced the formulation of explanations about Earth. Catastrophism states that Earth's landscapes have been developed primarily by great catastrophes. By contrast, *uniformitarianism,* one of the fundamental principles of modern geology advanced by *James Hutton* in the late 1700s, states that the physical, chemical, and biological laws that operate today have also operated in the geologic past. The idea is often summarized as "the present is the key to the past." Hutton argued that processes that appear to be slow acting could, over long spans of time, produce effects that were just as great as those resulting from sudden catastrophic events.

• The two types of dates used by geologists to interpret Earth history are (1) *relative dates,* which put events in their *proper sequence of formation*, and (2) *numerical dates,* which pinpoint the *time in years* when an event took place.

• Relative dates can be established using the *law of superposition, principle of original horizontality, principle of cross-cutting relationships, inclusions,* and *unconformities.*

• *Correlation,* matching up two or more geologic phenomena of similar ages in different areas, is used to develop a geologic time scale that applies to the entire Earth.

• *Fossils* are the remains or traces of prehistoric life. The special conditions that favor preservation are *rapid burial* and the possession of *hard parts* such as shells, bones, or teeth.

• Fossils are used to *correlate* sedimentary rocks that are widely separated by using the rocks' distinctive fossil content and applying the *principle of fossil succession.* The principle of fossil succession states that fossil organisms succeed one another in a definite and determinable order, and, therefore, any time period can be recognized by its fossil content.

• Each atom has a nucleus containing *protons* (positively charged particles) and *neutrons* (neutral particles). Orbiting the nucleus are negatively charged *electrons*. The *atomic number* of an atom is the number of protons in the nucleus. The *mass number* is the number of protons plus the number of neutrons in an atom's nucleus. *Isotopes* are variants of the same atom, but with a different number of neutrons and hence a different mass number.

• *Radioactivity* is the spontaneous breaking apart (decay) of certain unstable atomic nuclei. Three common forms of radioactive decay are (1) emission of an alpha particle from the nucleus, (2) emission of a beta particle (or electron) from the nucleus, and (3) capture of an electron by the nucleus.

• An unstable *radioactive isotope*, called the *parent,* will decay and form *daughter products*. The length of time for one-half of the nuclei of a radioactive isotope to decay is called the *half-life* of the isotope. If the half-life of the isotope is known, and the parent–daughter ratio can be measured, the age of a sample can be calculated.

• The *geologic time scale* divides Earth history into units of varying magnitude. It is commonly presented in chart form, with the oldest time and event at the bottom and the youngest at the top. The principal subdivisions of the geologic time scale, called *eons,* include the *Archean* and *Proterozoic* (together, these two eons are commonly referred to as the *Precambrian*), and, beginning about 542 million years ago, the *Phanerozoic*. The Phanerozoic (meaning "visible life") eon is divided into the following eras: *Paleozoic* ("ancient life"), *Mesozoic* ("middle life"), and *Cenozoic* ("recent life").

• A significant problem in assigning numerical dates to units of time is that *not all rocks can be dated radiometrically*. A sedimentary rock may contain particles of many ages that have been weathered from different rocks that formed at various times. One way geologists assign numerical dates to sedimentary rocks is to relate them to datable igneous masses, such as dikes and volcanic ash beds.

KEY TERMS

angular unconformity	epoch	Mesozoic era	Precambrian
catastrophism	era	nonconformity	radioactivity
Cenozoic era	fossil	numerical date	radiocarbon dating
conformable	fossil succession, principle of	original horizontality, principle of	radiometric dating
correlation	geologic time scale	paleontology	relative dating
cross-cutting relationships, principle of	half-life	Paleozoic era	superposition, law of
disconformity	inclusions	period	unconformity
eon	index fossil	Phanerozoic eon	uniformitarianism

QUESTIONS FOR REVIEW

1. Contrast the philosophies of *catastrophism* and *uniformitarianism*. How did the proponents of each perceive the age of Earth?

2. Distinguish between numerical dates and relative dates.

3. What is the law of superposition? How are cross-cutting relationships used in relative dating?

4. When you observe an outcrop of steeply inclined sedimentary layers, what principle allows you to assume that the beds became tilted *after* they were deposited?

5. Refer to Figure 5 and answer the following questions:
   a. Is fault A older or younger than the sandstone layer?
   b. Is dike A older or younger than the sandstone layer?
   c. Was the conglomerate deposited before or after fault A?
   d. Was the conglomerate deposited before or after fault B?
   e. Which fault is older, A or B?
   f. Is dike A older or younger than the batholith?

6. A mass of granite is in contact with a layer of sandstone. Using a principle described in this chapter, explain how you might determine whether the sandstone was deposited on top of the granite or the granite was intruded into the sandstone after the sandstone was deposited.

7. Distinguish among angular unconformity, disconformity, and nonconformity.

8. What is meant by the term *correlation*?

9. List and briefly describe at least five different types of fossils.

10. List two conditions that improve an organism's chances of being preserved as a fossil.

11. Why are fossils such useful tools in correlation?

12. If a radioactive isotope of thorium (atomic number 90, mass number 232) emits six alpha particles and four beta particles during the course of radioactive decay, what are the atomic number and mass number of the stable daughter product?

13. Why is radiometric dating the most reliable method of dating the geologic past?

14. Assume that a hypothetical radioactive isotope has a half-life of 10,000 years. If the ratio of radioactive parent to stable daughter product is 1:3, how old is the rock containing the radioactive material?

15. To make calculations easier, let us round the age of Earth to 5 billion years.

   a. What fraction of geologic time is represented by recorded history (assume 5000 years for the length of recorded history)?

   b. The first abundant fossil evidence does not appear until the beginning of the Cambrian period (542 million years ago). What percentage of geologic time is represented by abundant fossil evidence?

16. What subdivisions make up the geologic time scale? What is the primary basis for differentiating the eras?

17. Briefly describe the difficulties in assigning numerical dates to layers of sedimentary rock.

COMPANION WEBSITE

The *Foundations of Earth Science* Website uses the resources and flexibility of the Internet to aid in your study of the topics in this chapter. Written and developed by the authors and other Earth science instructors, this site will help improve your understanding of Earth science. Visit **www.mygeoscienceplace.com** in order to:

• **Review** key chapter concepts.

• **Read** with links to the ebook and to chapter-specific web resources.

• **Visualize** and comprehend challenging topics using learning activities in *GEODe: Earth Science*.

• **Test** yourself with online quizzes.

GEODe: EARTH SCIENCE

GEODe: Earth Science is a valuable and easy to use learning aid that can be accessed from your chapter's Companion Website: **www.mygeoscienceplace.com**. It is a dynamic instructional tool that promotes understanding and reinforces important concepts by using tutorials, animations, and exercises that actively engage the student.

Earth's Evolution through Geologic Time

From Chapter 12 of *Earth Science*, Twelfth Edition, Edward J. Tarbuck, Frederick K. Lutgens, Dennis Tasa.

Earth's Evolution through Geologic Time

Maroon Bells, part of the Rocky Mountains, Snowmass Colorado. (Photo by Tim Fitzharris/Minden Pictures)

arth has a long and complex history. Time and again, the splitting and colliding of continents has resulted in the formation of new ocean basins and the creation of great mountain ranges. Furthermore, the nature of life on our planet has experienced dramatic changes through time.

Many of the changes on planet Earth occur at a "snail's pace," generally too slow for people to perceive. Thus, human awareness of evolutionary change is fairly recent. Evolution is not confined to life forms, for all Earth's "spheres" have evolved together: the atmosphere, hydrosphere, geosphere, and biosphere (Figure 1). These changes can be observed in the air we breathe, the composition of the world's oceans, the ponderous movements of crustal plates that give rise to mountains, and the evolution of a vast array of life-forms. As each of Earth's spheres has evolved, it has powerfully influenced the others.

Is Earth Unique?

There is only one place in the entire universe, as far as we know, that can support life—a modest-sized planet called Earth that orbits an average-sized star, the Sun. Life on Earth is ubiquitous; it is found in boiling mudpots and hot springs, in the deep abyss of the ocean, and even under the Antarctic ice sheet. However, living space on our planet is greatly limited when we consider the needs of individual organisms, particularly humans. The global ocean covers 71 percent of Earth's surface, but only a few hundred meters below the water's surface pressures are so great that our lungs would begin to collapse. Further, many continental areas are too steep, too high, or too cold for us to inhabit (Figure 2).

FIGURE 1 Earth's spheres have evolved together through the long expanse of geologic time. (Photos by **A.** Momatiuk Eastcott, **B.** Carr Clifton/Minden Pictures, **C.** and **D.** Michael Collier)

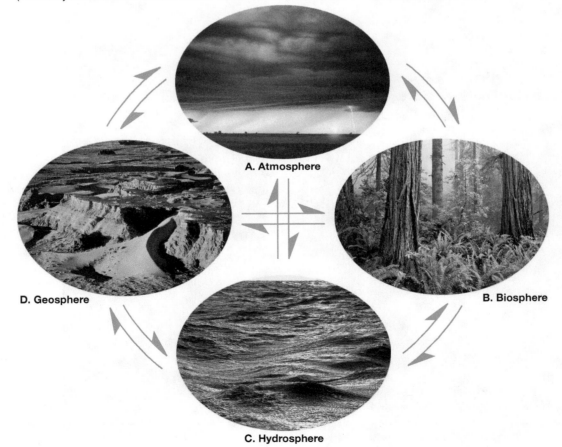

A. Atmosphere

B. Biosphere

C. Hydrosphere

D. Geosphere

FIGURE 2   Climbers near the top of Mount Everest. At this altitude the level of oxygen is only one-third the amount available at sea level. (Photo courtesy of Woodfin Camp and Associates)

Nevertheless, based on what we know about other bodies in the solar system—and the 80 or so planets recently discovered orbiting around other stars—Earth is still, by far, the most accommodating.

What fortuitous events produced a planet so hospitable to living organisms like us? Earth was not always as we find it today. During its formative years, our planet became hot enough to support a magma ocean. It also went through a several-hundred-million-year period of extreme bombardment, to which the heavily cratered lunar surface testifies. Even the oxygen-rich atmosphere that makes higher life forms possible is a relatively recent event, geologically speaking. Nevertheless, Earth seems to be the right planet, in the right location, at the right time.

The Right Planet

What are some of the characteristics that make Earth unique among the planets? Consider the following:

1. If Earth were considerably larger (more massive) the force of gravity would be proportionately greater. Like the giant planets, Earth would have retained a thick, hostile atmosphere consisting of ammonia and methane, and possibly even hydrogen and helium.
2. If Earth were much smaller, oxygen, water vapor and other volatiles would escape into space and be lost for-

ever. Thus, like the Moon and Mercury, which lack an atmosphere, Earth would be void of life.
3. If Earth did not have a rigid lithosphere overlaying a weak asthenosphere, plate tectonics would not operate. Our continental crust (Earth's "highlands") would not have formed without the recycling of plates. Consequently, the entire planet would likely be covered by an ocean a few kilometers deep. As the author Bill Bryson so aptly stated, "There might be life in that lonesome ocean, but there certainly wouldn't be baseball."
4. Most surprisingly, perhaps, is the fact that if our planet did not have a molten metallic core, most of the life forms on Earth would not exist. Although this may seem like a stretch of the imagination, without the flow of iron in the core, Earth could not support a magnetic field. It is the magnetic field which prevents lethal cosmic rays (the solar wind) from showering Earth's surface.

The Right Location

One of the primary factors that determines whether or not a planet is suitable for higher life-forms is its location in the solar system. Earth is in a great location:

1. If Earth were about 10 percent closer to the Sun, like Venus, our atmosphere would consist mainly of the

greenhouse gas, carbon dioxide. As a result, Earth's surface temperature would be too hot to support higher life-forms.

2. If Earth were about 10 percent farther from the Sun, the problem would be the opposite—too cold rather than too hot. The ocean would freeze over and Earth's active water cycle would not exist. Without liquid water most life-forms would perish.

3. Earth is located near a star of modest size. Stars like the Sun have a life span of roughly 10 billion years. During most of this time radiant energy is emitted at a fairly constant level. Giant stars on the other hand consume their nuclear fuel at very high rates and thus "burn out" in a few hundred million years. This is simply not enough time for the evolution of humans, which first appeared on this planet only a few million years ago.

FIGURE 3   Paleontologist excavating a dinosaur (*Protoceratops*) skull at Ukhaa Tolgod in the Gobi Desert, Mongolia. (Photo by Louie Psihoyos/ CORBIS)

The Right Time

The last, but certainly not the least fortuitous factor is timing. The first life-forms to inhabit Earth were extremely primitive and came into existence roughly 3.8 billion years ago. From this point in Earth's history innumerable changes occurred—life-forms came and went along with changes in the physical environment of our planet. Two of many timely, Earth-altering events include:

1. The development of our modern atmosphere. Earth's primitive atmosphere is thought to have been composed mostly of water vapor and carbon dioxide, with small amounts of other gases, but no free oxygen. Fortunately, microorganisms evolved that produced oxygen by the process of *photosynthesis*. By about 2.2 billion years ago an atmosphere with free oxygen came into existence. The result was the evolution of the forbearers of life-forms that occupy Earth today.

2. About 65 million years ago our planet was struck by an asteroid 10 kilometers in diameter. This impact caused a mass extinction during which nearly three-quarters of all plant and animal species died out—including the dinosaurs (Figure 3). Although this may not seem like a fortuitous event, the extinction of the dinosaurs opened new habitats for the small mammals that survived the impact. These habitats, along with evolutionary forces, led to the development of the many large mammals that occupy our modern world. Without this event, mammals might still be small rodentlike creatures that live in burrows.

As various observers have noted, Earth developed under "just right" conditions to support higher life-forms. Astronomers like to refer to this as the *Goldilocks scenario*. As in the classic Goldilocks and the Three Bears fable, Venus is too hot (the papa bear's porridge), Mars is too cold (the mama bear's porridge), but Earth is just right (the baby bear's porridge). Did these "just right" conditions come about purely by chance as some researchers suggest, or as others have argued, might Earth's hospitable environment have developed for the evolution and survival of higher life-forms?

The remainder of this chapter will focus on the origin and evolution of planet Earth—the one place in the Universe we know fosters life. Researchers utilize many tools to interpret the clues about Earth's past. Using these tools, and clues that are contained in the rock record, scientists have been able to unravel many of the complex events of the geologic past. The goal of this chapter is to provide a brief overview of the history of our planet and its life-forms. The journey takes us back about 4.5 billion years to the formation of Earth and its atmosphere. Next we will consider how our physical world assumed its present form and how Earth's inhabitants changed through time. We suggest that you reacquaint yourself with the *geologic time scale* presented in Figure 4 and refer to it as needed throughout the chapter.

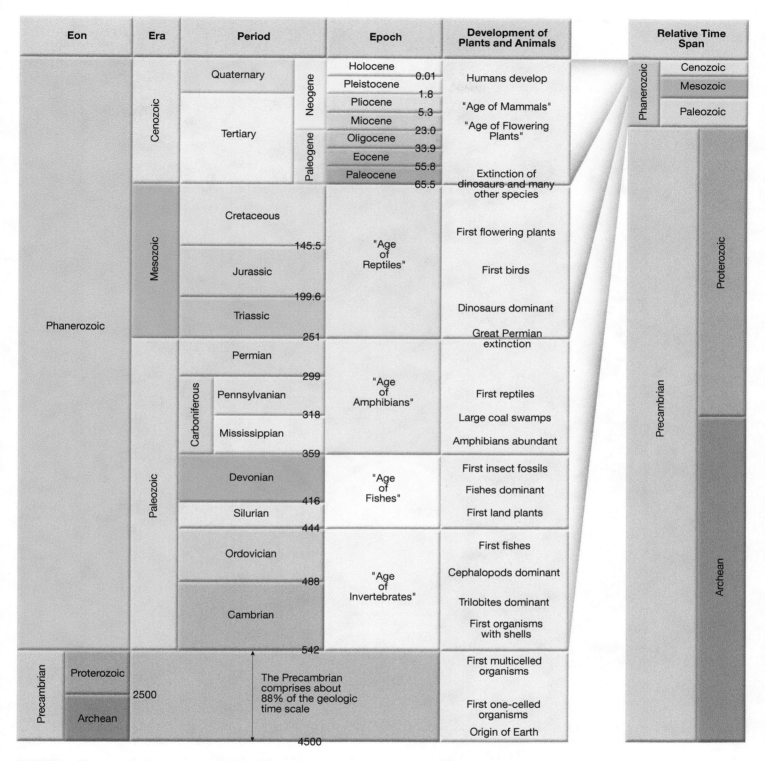

FIGURE 4 The geologic time scale. Numbers represent time in millions of years before the present. These dates were added long after the time scale had been established using relative dating techniques. The Precambrian accounts for about 88 percent of geologic time.

Birth of a Planet

According to the Big Bang theory, the formation of our home planet began about 13.7 billion years ago with a cataclysmic explosion that created all matter and space almost instantaneously (Figure 5). Initially atomic particles (protons, neu-

trons, and electrons) formed, then later as this debris cooled, atoms of hydrogen and helium, the two lightest elements, began to form. Within a few hundred million years, clouds of these gases condensed into stars that compose the galactic systems we now observe fleeing from their birthplace.

FIGURE 5 Major events that led to the formation of early Earth. Ga stands for billions of years ago and Ma for millions of years ago.

As these gases contracted to form the first stars, heating triggered the process of *nuclear fusion*. Within stars' interiors, hydrogen atoms are converted to helium atoms, releasing enormous amounts of energy in the form of radiation (heat, light, cosmic rays). Astronomers have determined that in stars more massive than our Sun, other thermonuclear reactions occur that generate all the elements on the periodic table up to number 26, iron. The heaviest elements (beyond number 26) are only created at extreme temperatures during the explosive death of a star perhaps 10 to 20 times more massive than the Sun. During one of these cataclysmic **supernova** events, an exploding star produces all of the elements heavier than iron and spews them into interstellar space. It is from such debris that our Sun and solar system formed. According to the Big Bang scenario, the atoms in your body were produced billions of years ago in the hot interior of now defunct stars, and the gold in your jewelry was formed during a supernova explosion that occurred trillions of miles away.

From Planetesimals to Protoplanets

Recall that Earth, along with the rest of the solar system, formed about 4.5 billion years ago from the **solar nebula**, a large rotating cloud of interstellar dust and gas. As the solar nebula contracted, most of the matter collected in the center to form the hot *protosun*, while the remainder became a flattened spinning disk. Within this spinning disk, matter gradually formed clumps that collided and stuck together to form asteroid-size objects called **plan-etesimals.** The composition of each planetesimal was governed largely by its distance from the hot protosun.

Near the present day orbit of Mercury only metallic grains condensed from the solar nebula. Further out, near Earth's orbit, metallic as well as rocky substances condensed, and beyond Mars, ices of water, carbon dioxide, methane, and ammonia formed. It was from these clumps of matter that the planetesimals formed and through repeated collisions and accretion (sticking together) grew into eight **protoplanets** and their moons (Figure 5).

At some point in Earth's evolution a giant impact occurred between a Mars-sized planetesimal and a young, semi-molten Earth. This collision ejected huge amounts of debris into space, some of which coalesced (joined together) to form the Moon.

Earth's Early Evolution

As material continued to accumulate, the high-velocity impact of interplanetary debris (planetesimals) and the decay of radioactive elements caused the temperature of our planet to steadily increase. During this period of intense heating, Earth became hot enough that iron and nickel began to melt. Melting produced liquid blobs of heavy metal that sank under their own weight. This process occurred rapidly on the scale of geologic time and produced Earth's dense iron-rich core. The formation of a molten iron core was only the first stage of chemical differentiation, in which Earth was converted from a homogeneous body, with roughly the same stuff at all depths, to a layered planet with material sorted by density (Figure 5).

This early period of heating also resulted in a magma ocean, perhaps several hundred kilometers deep. Within the magma ocean buoyant masses of molten rock rose toward the surface, where they eventually solidified to produce a thin, primitive crust. Earth's first crust was probably basaltic in composition, not unlike modern oceanic crust. Whether or not plate tectonics was active at this time is not known. However, vigorous, fluidlike motions in the hot, upper mantle must have continually recycled the crust over and over again.

This period of chemical differentiation established the three major divisions of Earth's interior—the iron-rich *core*, the thin *primitive crust*, and Earth's largest layer, the *mantle*, which is located between the core and the crust. In addition, the lightest material, including water vapor, carbon dioxide, and other gases, escaped to form a primitive atmosphere and, shortly thereafter, the oceans (Figure 6).

Origin of the Atmosphere and Oceans

Thank goodness for our atmosphere; without it Earth would be nearly 60 degrees Fahrenheit colder. Although not as cold as the surface of Mars, most water bodies on Earth would be frozen over and the hydrological cycle, where water leaves the ocean as a vapor and returns as a liquid, would be meager at best. Recall that the warming effect of certain gases in the atmosphere, mainly carbon dioxide and water vapor, is called the greenhouse effect.

FIGURE 6   Artistic depiction of Earth over 4 billion years ago. This was a time of intense volcanic activity that produced Earth's primitive atmosphere and oceans, while early life forms produced mound-like structures called stromatolites.

Today, the air we breathe is a stable mixture of 78 percent nitrogen, 21 percent oxygen, about 1 percent argon (an inert gas), and small amounts of gases such as carbon dioxide and water vapor. But our planet's original atmosphere 4.5 billion years ago was very different.

Earth's Primitive Atmosphere

When Earth formed, any atmosphere it might have had would have consisted of the gases most common in the early solar system—hydrogen, helium, methane, ammonia, carbon dioxide, and water vapor. The lightest of these gases, hydrogen and helium, would have escaped into space as Earth's gravity is too weak to hold them. Most of the remaining gases were probably blown off by strong *solar winds* (a vast stream of particles) from a young, active Sun. (All stars, including the Sun, apparently experience a highly active stage early in their evolution known as the *T-Tauri phase*, during which their solar winds are very intense.)

Earth's first enduring atmosphere formed by a process called **outgassing,** through which gases trapped in the planet's interior are released. Outgassing continues today from hundreds of active volcanoes worldwide (Figure 7). However, early in Earth's history, when massive heating and fluidlike motion occurred in the mantle, the gas output must have been immense. The composition of the gases emitted then were probably roughly equivalent to those released during volcanism today. Depending on the chemical makeup of the magma, the gaseous components of modern eruptions consist of between 35–90 percent water vapor, 5–30 percent carbon dioxide, 2–30 percent sulfur dioxide, and lesser amounts of nitrogen, chorine, hydrogen, and argon. Thus, Earth's primitive atmosphere probably consisted of mostly water vapor, carbon dioxide, and sulfur dioxide with minor amounts of other gases, but no free oxygen and little nitrogen.

Oxygen in the Atmosphere

As Earth cooled, water vapor condensed to form clouds, and torrential rains began to fill low-lying areas forming the oceans. It was in the oceans nearly 3.5 billion years ago that photosynthesizing bacteria began to release oxygen into the water. During *photosynthesis*, the Sun's energy is used by organisms to produce organic material (energetic molecules of sugar containing hydrogen and carbon) from carbon dioxide (CO_2) and water (H_2O). The first bacteria probably used hydrogen sulfide (H_2S), rather than water, as the source of hydrogen. Nevertheless, one of the earliest types of bacteria, the *cyanobacteria* began to produce oxygen as a by-product of photosynthesis.

Initially, the newly liberated oxygen was readily consumed by chemical reactions with other atoms and molecules in the ocean, especially iron. The source of most iron appears to be submarine volcanism and associated hydrothermal vents (black smokers). Iron has tremendous affinity for oxygen, and these two elements joined to form iron oxide (also known as rust), which accumulated on the seafloor as sediment. These early iron oxide deposits consist of alternating layers of iron-rich rocks and chert, and are called **banded iron formations** (Figure 8). Most banded iron deposits were laid down in the Precambrian between 3.5 and 2 billion years ago, and represent the world's most important reservoir of iron ore.

Once much of the available iron had precipitated and the numbers of oxygen-generating organisms increased, oxygen began to accumulate in the atmosphere. Chemical analysis of rocks suggest that a significant amount of oxygen appeared in the atmosphere as early as 2.2 billion years ago and that the amount increased steadily until it reached a stable level about 1.5 billion years ago. The availability of free oxygen had a major impact on the development of life.

FIGURE 7 Earth's first enduring atmosphere formed by a process called outgassing, which continues today from hundreds of active volcanoes worldwide. Augustine Volcano, Alaska. (Photo by Game McGimsey/CORBIS)

FIGURE 8   These layered iron-rich rocks, called banded iron formations, were deposited during the Precambrian. Much of the oxygen generated as a by-product of photosynthesis was readily consumed by chemical reaction with iron to produce these rocks. (Photo courtesy of Spencer R. Titley)

Another significant benefit of the "oxygen explosion" is that when oxygen (O_2) molecules in the atmosphere are bombarded by ultraviolet radiation they rearrange themselves to form *ozone* (O_3). Today, ozone is concentrated above the surface in a layer called the *stratosphere* where it absorbs much of the ultraviolet radiation that strikes the atmosphere. For the first time, Earth's surface was protected from this form of solar radiation, which is particularly harmful to DNA. Marine organisms had always been shielded from ultraviolet radiation by the oceans, but with the development of the protective ozone layer the continents became a more hospitable place for life to develop.

Evolution of the Oceans

About 4 billion years ago, as much as 90 percent of the current volume of seawater was contained in the ocean basins. Because the primitive atmosphere was rich in carbon dioxide as well as sulfur dioxide and hydrogen sulfide, the earliest rain water was highly acidic—even more so than the acid rain that recently damaged lakes and streams in eastern North America. Consequently, weathering of Earth's rocky surface occurred at an accelerated rate. The products released by chemical weathering included atoms and molecules of various

substances, including sodium, calcium, potassium, and silica, that were carried into the newly formed oceans. Some of these dissolved substances precipitated to form chemical sediment that mantled the ocean floor. Others gradually built up, increasing the salinity of seawater. Today seawater contains an average of 3.5 percent dissolved salts, most of which is common table salt (sodium chloride). Research suggests that the salinity of the oceans increased rapidly at first, but has not changed dramatically in the last few billion years.

Earth's oceans also served as a depository for tremendous volumes of carbon dioxide, a major constituent in the primitive atmosphere—and they still do today. This is significant because carbon dioxide is a greenhouse gas that strongly influences the heating of the atmosphere. Venus, which was once thought to very similar to Earth, has an atmosphere composed of 97 percent carbon dioxide that produced a "runaway" greenhouse effect. The surface of Venus has a temperature of 475°C (900°F)—hot enough to melt lead.

Carbon dioxide is readily soluble in seawater where it often joins with other atoms or molecules to produce various chemical precipitates. By far the most common compound generated by this process is calcium carbonate ($CaCO_3$), which makes up the most abundant chemical sedimentary rock, *limestone*. Later in Earth's history, marine organisms began to remove calcium carbonate from seawater to make their shells and other hard parts. Included were trillions of tiny marine organisms such as foraminifera, that died and were deposited on the seafloor. Today some of these deposits make up the chalk beds exposed along the White Cliffs of Dover, England shown in Figure 9. By locking up carbon dioxide, these limestone deposits prevent this greenhouse gas from easily reentering the atmosphere.

FIGURE 9   This prominent chalk deposit, the White Cliffs of Dover, is found in southern England. Similar deposits are also found in northern France. (Photo by Jon Arnold/Getty Images/Taxi)

Precambrian History: The Formation of Earth's Continents

The first 4 billion years of Earth's history are encompassed in the span of time called the *Precambrian*. Representing nearly 90 percent of Earth's history, the Precambrian is divided into the *Archean eon* ("ancient age") and the succeeding *Proterozoic eon* ("early life"). To get a visual sense of the proportion of time represented by the Precambrian, look at the right side of Figure 4, which shows relative time spans for the Precambrian and the eras of the Phanerozoic eon.

Our knowledge of this ancient time is sketchy, for much of the early rock record has been obscured by the very Earth processes you have been studying, especially plate tectonics, erosion, and deposition. Most Precambrian rocks are devoid of fossils, which hinders correlation of rock units. In addition, rocks of this great age are metamorphosed and deformed, extensively eroded, and sometimes obscured by overlying strata of younger age. Indeed, Precambrian history is written in scattered, speculative episodes, like a long book with many missing chapters.

We are, however, relatively certain that during the early Archean, Earth was covered by a magma ocean. It is from this material that Earth's atmosphere, oceans and first continents arose.

Earth's First Continents

More than 95 percent of Earth's population lives on the continents—not included are people living on volcanic islands such as the Hawaiian Islands and Iceland. These islanders inhabit unusually thick pieces of oceanic crust, thick enough to rise above sea level.

What differentiates continental crust from oceanic crust? Recall that oceanic crust is a comparatively dense ($3.0\ \mathrm{g/cm^3}$), homogeneous layer of basaltic rocks derived from partial melting of the rocky, upper mantle. Furthermore, oceanic crust is thin, averaging only 7 kilometers in thickness. Unusually thick blocks of oceanic crust, such as ocean plateaus, tend to form over mantle plumes (hot spot volcanism). Continental crust, on the other hand, is composed of a variety of rock types, has an average thickness of nearly 40 kilometers, and contains a large percentage of low-density ($2.7\ \mathrm{g/cm^3}$) silica-rich rocks such as granite.

These are very important differences. Oceanic crust, because it is relatively thin and dense, occurs several kilometers below sea level—unless, of course it has been shoved up onto a landmass by tectonic forces. Continental crust, because of its great thickness and lower density, extends well above sea level. Also, recall that oceanic crust of normal thickness will readily subduct, whereas thick, buoyant blocks of continental crust resist being recycled into the mantle.

Making Continental Crust Earth's first crust was probably basalt, like that generated at modern oceanic ridges. But we do not know for sure because none has ever been found. The hot turbulent mantle that existed during the Archean eon probably recycled most of this material back into the mantle. In fact, it may have been recycled over and over again, much like the "crust" that forms on a lava lake is continually being replaced with fresh lava from below (Figure 10).

The oldest preserved continental rocks (greater than 3.5 billion years old) occur as small, highly deformed terranes, which are incorporated within somewhat younger blocks of continental crust (Figure 11). The oldest of these is the 4 billion-year-old Acasta gneiss located in the Slave Province of Canada's Northwest Territories. (A few tiny crystals of zircon, found in the Jack Hills area of Australia have radiometric dates between 3.8 and 4.4 billion years.)

The formation of continental crust is simply a continuation of the gravitational segregation of Earth materials that began during the final stage in the accretion of our planet. After the metallic core and rocky mantle formed, low density, silica-rich minerals were gradually extracted from the mantle to form continental crust. This occurs through a multistage process during which partial melting of ultramafic mantle rocks (peridotite) generates basaltic rocks and remelting of basalts

FIGURE 10 Rift pattern on lava lake. The crust covering this lava lake is continually being replaced with fresh lava from below, much like the Earth's crust was recycled early in its history. (Photo by Juerg Alean/www.stromboli.net)

FIGURE 11 These rocks at Isua, Greenland, some of the world's oldest, have been dated at 3.8 billion years. (Photo courtesy of Corbis/Bettmann)

produces magmas that crystallize to form felsic, quartz-bearing rocks. However, little is known about the details of the mechanisms that operated during the Archean to generate these silica-rich rocks.

Many geologists, but certainly not all, conclude that some type of plate-like motion that included subduction operated early in Earth's history. In addition, hot spot volcanism likely played a role as well. However, because the mantle was hotter in the Archean than it is today, both of these phenomena would have progressed at higher rates than their modern counterparts. Hot spot volcanism is thought to have created immense shield volcanoes as well as oceanic plateaus. At the same time, subduction of oceanic crust generated volcanic island arcs. These relatively small, thin crustal fragments represent the first phase in creating stable, continental-size landmasses.

From Continental Crust to Continents According to one model, the growth of large continental masses was accomplished through the collision and accretion of various types of terranes as illustrated in Figure 12. This type of collision tectonics deformed and metamorphosed the sediments caught between the converging crustal fragments, shortening and thickening the developing crust. Within the deepest regions of these collision zones, partial melting of the thickened crust generated silica-rich magmas that ascended and intruded the rocks above. The result was the formation of large crustal prov-

inces that, in turn, accreted with others to form even larger crustal blocks called **cratons**. (That portion of a modern craton that is exposed at the surface is referred to as a *shield*.) The assembly of a large craton involved several major mountain building episodes such as occurred when the Indian subcontinent collided with Asia. Figure 13 shows the extent of crustal material that was produced during the Archean and Proterozoic eons. This was accomplished by the collision and accretion of many thin and highly mobile terranes into nearly recognizable continental masses.

The Precambrian was a time when much of Earth's continental crust was generated. However, a substantial amount of crustal material was destroyed as well. Crust can be lost in two ways, by weathering and erosion or by direct reincorporation into the mantle through subduction. Evidence suggests that during much of the Archean, thin slabs of continental crust were destroyed mainly by subduction into the mantle. However, by about 3 billion years ago, cratons grew sufficiently large and thick to resist direct reincorporation into the mantle. From this point onward, weathering and erosion took over as the primary processes of crustal destruction. By the end of the Precambrian most of the modern continental crust had formed—perhaps 85 percent.

In summary, terranes are the basic building blocks of continents and terrane collisions are the major means by which continents grow.

The Making of North America

North America provides an excellent example of the development of continental crust and its piecemeal assembly into a continent. Notice in Figure 14 that very little continental crust older that 3.5 billion years still remains. In the late Archean, between 3–2.5 billion years ago, there was a period

FIGURE 12 According to one model, the growth of large continental masses was accomplished through the collision and accretion of various types of terranes, including volcanic island arcs and oceanic plateaus.

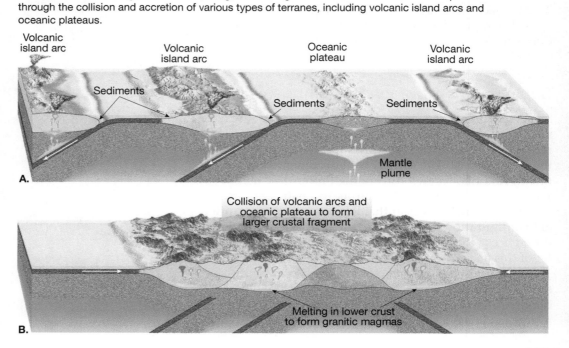

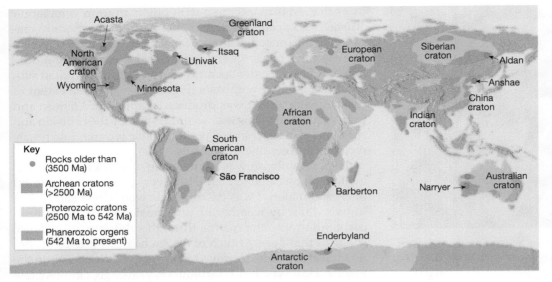

FIGURE 13   Illustration showing the extent of crustal material remaining from the Archean and Proterozoic eons.

Key

- Rocks older than (3500 Ma)
- Archean cratons (>2500 Ma)
- Proterozoic cratons (2500 Ma to 542 Ma)
- Phanerozoic orgens (542 Ma to present)

of major crustal growth. During this time span, the accretion of numerous island arcs and other crustal fragments generated several large crustal provinces. North America contains some of these crustal units, including the Superior and Hearne/Rae cratons shown in Figure 14. The locations of these ancient continental blocks during their formation are not known.

About 1.9 billion years ago these crustal provinces collided to produce the Trans-Hudson mountain belt (Figure 14). (This mountain-building episode was not restricted to North America, because ancient deformed strata of similar age are also found on other continents.) This event built the North America craton, around which several large and numerous small crustal fragments were later added. Examples of these late arrivals include the Blue Ridge and Piedmont provinces of the Appalachians and several terranes that were added to the western margin of North America during the Mesozoic and Cenozoic eras to generate the mountainous North American Cordillera.

Supercontinents of the Precambrian

Supercontinents are large landmasses that contain all, or nearly all, of the existing continents. Pangaea was the most recent but certainly not the only supercontinent to exist in the geologic past. The earliest well-documented supercontinent, Rodinia, formed during the Proterozoic eon about 1.1 billion years ago. Although its reconstruction is still being researched, it is clear that Rodinia had a much different configuration than Pangaea (Figure 15). One obvious difference is that North America was located near the center of this ancient landmass.

Between 800 and 600 million years ago, Rodinia gradually split apart and the pieces dispersed. By the close of the Precambrian, many of the fragments had reassembled to produce a large landmass located in the Southern Hemisphere called

Gondwana. Sometimes considered a supercontinent in its own right, Gondwana was comprised mainly of present-day South America, Africa, India, Australia, and Antarctica (Figure 16). Other continental fragments also formed—North America, Siberia, and northern Europe. We will consider the fate of these Precambrian landmasses later in the chapter.

Supercontinent Cycle The idea that rifting and dispersal of one supercontinent is followed by a long period during which the fragments are gradually reassembled into a new supercontinent having a different configuration is called the **supercontinent cycle**. As indicated earlier the assembly and dispersal of supercontinents had a profound impact on the evolution of Earth's continents. In addition, this phenomenon has greatly

FIGURE 14   Map showing the major geological provinces of North America and their ages in billions of years (Ga). It appears that North America was assembled from crustal blocks that were joined by processes very similar to modern plate tectonics. These ancient collisions produced mountainous belts that include remnant volcanic island arcs trapped by colliding continental fragments.

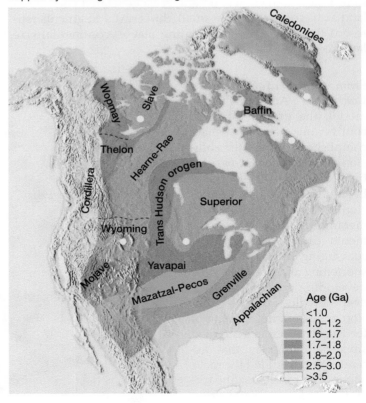

Age (Ga)
- <1.0
- 1.0–1.2
- 1.6–1.7
- 1.7–1.8
- 1.8–2.0
- 2.5–3.0
- >3.5

FIGURE 15 Simplified drawing showing one of several possible configurations of the supercontinent Rodinia. For clarity, the continents are drawn with somewhat modern shapes rather than their actual shapes as they were 1 billion years ago.

influenced global climates as well as contributing to periodic episodes of rising and falling sea level.

Climate and Supercontinents Moving continents change the patterns of ocean currents and affect global wind patterns, resulting in a change in the distribution of temperature and precipitation. One relatively recent example of how the dispersal of a supercontinent influenced climate relates to the formation of the Antarctic ice sheet. Although eastern Antarctica remained over the South Pole for more than 100 million years, it was not glaciated until about 25 million years ago. Prior to this time South America was connected to the Antarctic Peninsula. This arrangement of landmasses helped maintain a circulation pattern in which warm ocean currents reached the coast of Antarctica as shown in Figure 17A. This is similar to how the modern Gulf Stream keeps Iceland mostly ice free—despite its name. However, as South America separated from Antarctica, it moved northward, permitting ocean circulation to flow from west to east around the entire continent of Antarctica (Figure 17B). This current, called the West Wind Drift, effectively cut off the entire Antarctic coast from the warm, poleward-directed currents in the southern oceans. This led to eventual covering of almost the entire Antarctic landmass with glacial ice.

Local and regional climates have also been impacted by large mountain systems that formed through the collision of large cratons. Because of their high elevations, mountains exhibit markedly lower average temperatures than the surrounding lowlands. In addition, when air is forced to rise over these lofty structures, lifting "squeezes" moisture from the air, leaving the region downwind relatively dry. A modern analogy is the wet, heavily forested western slopes of the Sierra Nevada and the dry climate of the Great Basin

desert that lies directly to the east. Furthermore, large mountain systems, depending on their elevation and latitude, may support extensive valley glaciation, as the Himalayas do today.

Because early Precambrian life was very primitive (mostly bacteria) and left few remains, little is known about Earth's climate during this period. However, evidence from the rock record indicates that continental glaciation occurred several times in the geologic past, including the late Precambrian.

Sea Level Changes and Supercontinents Significant sea level changes have been documented numerous times in geologic history and many appear related to the assembly and dispersal of supercontinents. If sea level rises, or the average

FIGURE 16 Reconstruction of Earth as it may have appeared in late Precambrian time, about 600 million years ago. **A.** The southern continents were joined into a single landmass called Gondwana. **B.** Other landmasses that were not part of Gondwana included North America, northwestern Europe, and northern Asia. (After P. Hoffman, J. Rogers, and others)

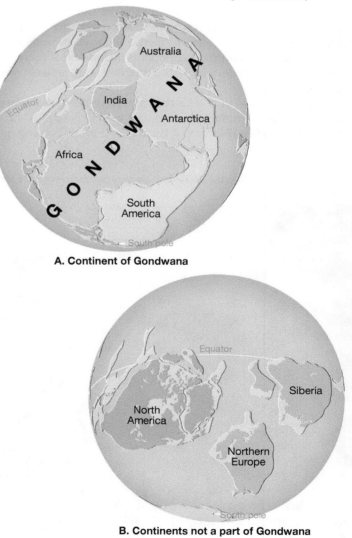

A. Continent of Gondwana

B. Continents not a part of Gondwana

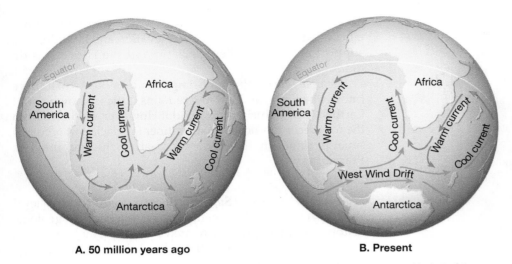

A. 50 million years ago   **B. Present**

FIGURE 17   Comparison of the oceanic circulation pattern 50 million years ago with that of the present. When South America separated from Antarctica the West Wind Drift developed, which effectively isolated the entire Antarctic coast from the warm, poleward-directed currents in the southern oceans. This led to the eventual covering of much of Antarctica with glacial ice.

cial ice will accumulate, sea level will drop, and shallow inland seas will retreat, thereby exposing large areas of the continental margins.

The supercontinent cycle and sea level changes are directly related to the rates of *seafloor spreading*. When the rate of spreading is rapid, as it is along the East Pacific Rise today, the production of warm oceanic crust is also high. Because warm oceanic crust is less dense (takes up more space) than cold crust, fast spreading ridges occupy more volume in the ocean basins than slow spreading centers. (Think of getting into a bathtub full of water.) As a result, when the rates of seafloor spreading increase, sea level rises. This, in turn, causes shallow seas to advance onto the low-lying portions of the continents.

elevation of a landmass is lowered by erosional or tectonic forces, shallow seas advance onto the continents. The result is the deposition of widespread marine sediments, often a few hundred meters thick. Evidence for such periods when the seas advanced onto the continents include thick sequences of ancient sedimentary rocks that blanket large areas of modern landmasses.

Sea level tends to rise during a period of "global warming" that results in melting of glacial ice. (This appears to be happening today.) Naturally, during periods of cooling, gla-

Phanerozoic History: The Formation of Earth's Modern Continents

The time span since the close of the Precambrian, called the *Phanerozoic eon*, encompasses 542 million years and is divided into three eras: Paleozoic, Mesozoic, and Cenozoic. The beginning of the Phanerozoic is marked by the appearance of the first life forms with hard parts such as shells, scales,

FIGURE 18   Trilobite fossil. Trilobites were very common Paleozoic life forms. (Photo courtesy of Peter Arnold, Inc.)

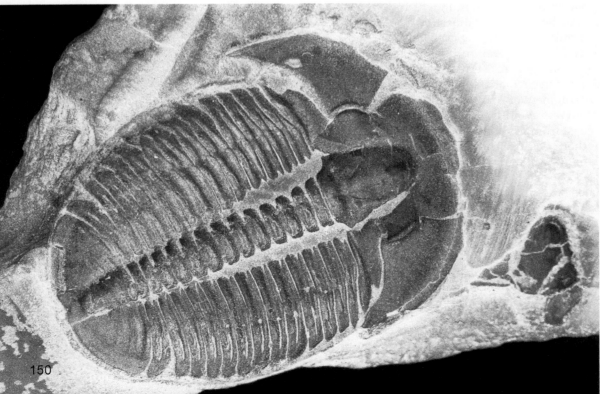

bones, or teeth that greatly enhance the chance of an organism being preserved in the fossil record (Figure 18). Consequently, the study of Phanerozoic crustal history was aided by the availability of fossils, which facilitated much more refined methods for dating geologic events. Moreover, because every organism is associated with its own particular niche, the greatly improved fossil record provided invaluable information for deciphering ancient environments.

Paleozoic History

As the Paleozoic era opened, North America was a land with no living things, either plant or animal. There were no Appalachian or Rocky Mountains; the continent was a largely barren lowland. Several times during the early Paleozoic, shallow seas moved inland and then receded from the interior of the continent. Deposits of clean sandstones mark the shorelines of these shallow seas in the midcontinent. One deposit, the St. Peter sandstone, is mined extensively in Missouri and Illinois for the manufacture of glass, filters, abrasives, and for "tract sand" used in oil and natural gas drilling.

Formation of Pangaea One of the major events of the Paleozoic was the formation of the supercontinent of Pangaea. It began with a series of collisions that gradually joined North America, Europe, Siberia, and other smaller crustal fragments (Figure 19). These events eventually generated a large northern continent called *Laurasia*. This landmass was located in the tropics where warm wet conditions led to the formation of vast swamps that ultimately became the coal which fueled the Industrial Revolution of the 1800s and that we still use in large quantities today. During the early Paleozoic, the vast southern continent of Gondwana encompassed five continents—South America, Africa, Australia, Antarctica, India, and perhaps portions of China. Evidence of an extensive continental glaciation places this landmass near the South Pole! By the end of the Paleozoic, Gondwana had migrated northward to collide with Laurasia, culminating in the formation of the supercontinent of Pangaea.

The accretion of Pangaea spans more than 200 million years and resulted in the formation of several mountain belts. This time period saw the collision of northern Europe (mainly Norway) with Greenland to produce the Caledonian Mountains. At roughly the same time at least two microcontinents collided with and deformed the sediments that had accumulated along the eastern margin of North America. This event was an early phase in the formation of the Appalachian Mountains.

By the late Paleozoic, the joining of northern Asia (Siberia) and Europe created the Ural Mountains. Northern China is also thought to have accreted to Asia by the end of the Paleozoic, whereas southern China may not have become part of Asia until after Pangaea had begun to rift apart. (Recall that India did not accrete to Asia until about 45 million years ago.)

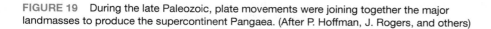

FIGURE 19 During the late Paleozoic, plate movements were joining together the major landmasses to produce the supercontinent Pangaea. (After P. Hoffman, J. Rogers, and others)

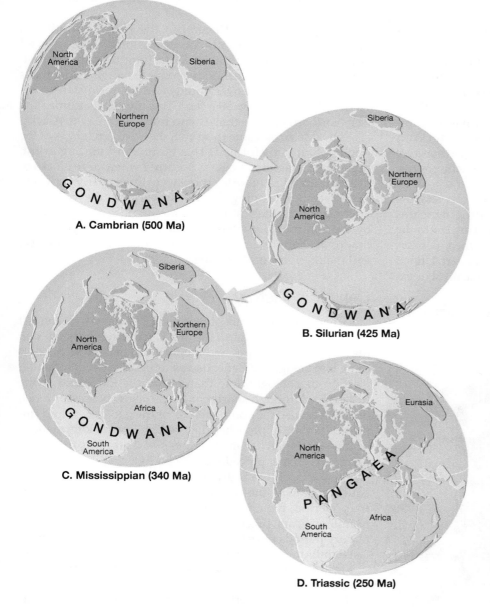

A. Cambrian (500 Ma)

B. Silurian (425 Ma)

C. Mississippian (340 Ma)

D. Triassic (250 Ma)

Pangaea reached its maximum size about 250 million years ago as Africa collided with North America (Figure 19D). This event marked the final episode of growth in the long history of the Appalachian Mountains.

Mesozoic History

Spanning about 186 million years, the Mesozoic era is divided into three periods: the Triassic, Jurassic, and Cretaceous. Major geologic events of the Mesozoic include the breakup of Pangaea and the evolution of our modern ocean basins.

The Mesozoic era began with much of the world's land above sea level. In fact, in North America no period exhibits a more meager sedimentary record than the Triassic period. Of the exposed Triassic strata, most are red sandstones and mudstones that lack marine fossils, features that indicate a terrestrial environment. (The red color in sandstone comes from the oxidation of iron.)

As the Jurassic period opened, the sea invaded western North America. Adjacent to this shallow sea, extensive continental sediments were deposited on what is now the Colorado Plateau. The most prominent is the Navajo Sandstone, windblown, white quartz sandstone that, in places, approaches a thickness of 300 meters (1,000 feet). These remnants of massive dunes indicate that a major desert occupied much of the American Southwest during early Jurassic times (Figure 20). Another well-known Jurassic deposit is the Morrison Formation—the world's richest storehouse of dinosaur fossils. Included are the fossilized bones of huge dinosaurs such as Apatosaurus (formerly Brontosaurus), Brachiosaurus, and Stegosaurus.

As the Jurassic period gave way to the Cretaceous, shallow seas once again invaded much of western North America, as well as the Atlantic and Gulf coastal regions. This led to the formation of great swamps similar to those of the Paleozoic era. Today the Cretaceous coal deposits in the western United States and Canada are very important economically. For ex-

ample, on the Crow Native American reservation in Montana, there are nearly 20 billion tons of high-quality coal of Cretaceous age.

Another major event of the Mesozoic era was the breakup of Pangaea. About 165 million years ago a rift developed between what is now North America and western Africa, marking the birth of the Atlantic Ocean. As Pangaea gradually broke apart, the westward-moving North American plate began to override the Pacific basin. This tectonic event marked the beginning of a continuous wave of deformation that moved inland along the entire western margin of North America. By Jurassic times, subduction of the Farallon plate had begun to produce the chaotic mixture of rocks that exist today in the Coast Ranges of California. Further inland, igneous activity was widespread, and for nearly 60 million years volcanism was rampant as huge masses of magma rose to within a few miles of the surface. The remnants of this activity include the granitic plutons of the Sierra Nevada as well as the Idaho batholith, and British Columbia's Coast Range batholith.

Tectonic activity that began in the Jurassic continued throughout the Cretaceous. Compressional forces moved huge rock units in a shinglelike fashion toward the east. Across much of North America's western margin, older rocks were thrust eastward over younger strata, for distances exceeding 150 kilometers (90 miles). This ultimately formed the vast Northern Rockies that extend from Wyoming to Alaska.

As the Mesozoic came to an end, the southern ranges of the Rocky Mountains formed. This mountain-building event, called the Laramide Orogeny, occurred when large blocks of deeply buried Precambrian rocks were lifted nearly vertically along steeply dipping faults, upwarping the overlying younger sedimentary strata. The mountain ranges produced by the Laramide Orogeny include the Front Range of Colorado, the Sangre de Cristo of New Mexico and Colorado, and the Bighorns of Wyoming.

Cenozoic History

The Cenozoic era, or "era of recent life," encompasses the last 65.5 million years of Earth history. It is during this span that the physical landscapes and life-forms of our modern world came into being. The Cenozoic era represents a much smaller fraction of geologic time than either the Paleozoic or the Mesozoic. Although shorter, it nevertheless possesses a rich history because the completeness of the geologic record improves as time approaches the present. The rock formations of this time span are more widespread and less disturbed than those of any preceding time period.

The Cenozoic era is divided into two periods of very unequal duration—the Tertiary and the Quaternary. The Tertiary period includes five epochs and embraces about 63 million years, practically all of the Cenozoic era. The Quaternary period consists of two epochs that represent only the last 2 million years of geologic time.

Most of North America was above sea level throughout the Cenozoic era. However, the eastern and western margins of the continent experienced markedly contrasting events

FIGURE 20 These massive, cross-bedded sandstone cliffs in Zion National Park, Utah, are the remnants of ancient sand dunes. (Photo by Tim Fitzharris/Minden Pictures)

because of their different relationships with plate boundaries. The Atlantic and Gulf coastal regions, far removed from an active plate boundary, were tectonically stable. By contrast, western North America was the leading edge of the North American plate. As a result, plate interactions during the Cenozoic gave rise to many events of mountain building, volcanism, and earthquakes.

Eastern North America   The stable continental margin of eastern North America was the site of abundant marine sedimentation. The most extensive deposition surrounded the Gulf of Mexico, from the Yucatán Peninsula to Florida. Here, the great buildup of sediment caused the crust to downwrap and produced numerous faults. In many instances, the faults created structures in which oil and natural gas accumulated. Today, these and other petroleum traps are the most economically important resource of the Gulf Coast, as evidenced by the numerous offshore drilling platforms.

By early Cenozoic time, most of the original Appalachians had been eroded to a low plain. Later, isostatic adjustments raised the region once again, rejuvenating its rivers. Streams eroded with renewed vigor, gradually sculpting the surface into its present-day topography. The sediments from this erosion were deposited along the eastern margin of the continent, where they attained a thickness of many kilometers. Today, portions of the strata deposited during the Cenozoic are exposed as the gently sloping Atlantic and Gulf coastal plains. It is here that much of the population of the eastern and southeastern United States resides.

Western North America   In the West, the Laramide Orogeny that built the southern Rocky Mountains was coming to an end. As erosion lowered the mountains, the basins between uplifted ranges filled with sediments. Eastward, a great wedge of sediment from the eroding Rockies was creating the Great Plains.

Beginning in the Miocene epoch about 20 million years ago, a broad region from northern Nevada into Mexico experienced crustal extension that created more than 150 fault-block mountain ranges. Today, they rise abruptly above the adjacent basins, creating the Basin and Range Province.

As the Basin and Range Province was forming, the entire western interior of the continent was gradually uplifted. This event re-elevated the Rockies and rejuvenated many of the West's major rivers. As the rivers became incised, many spectacular gorges were formed, including the Grand Canyon of the Colorado River, the Grand Canyon of the Snake River, and the Black Canyon of the Gunnison River.

Volcanic activity was also common in the West during much of the Cenozoic. Beginning in the Miocene epoch, great volumes of fluid basaltic lava flowed from fissures in portions of present-day Washington, Oregon, and Idaho. These eruptions built the extensive (1.3 million square miles) Columbia Plateau. Immediately west of the Columbia Plateau, volcanic activity was different in character. Here, more viscous magmas with higher silica contents erupted explosively, creating the Cascades, a chain of stratovolcanoes extending from northern California into Canada (Figure 21). Some of these volcanoes are still active.

A final episode of deformation occurred in the West in late Tertiary time, creating the Coast Ranges that stretch along the Pacific Coast. Meanwhile, the Sierra Nevada were faulted and uplifted along their eastern flank, forming the imposing mountain front we know today.

As the Tertiary period drew to a close, the effect of mountain building, volcanic activity, isostatic adjustments, and extensive erosion and sedimentation had created a physical landscape very similar to the configuration of today. All that remained of Cenozoic time was the final 2 million year episode called the Quaternary period. During this most recent (and current) phase of Earth history, in which humans evolved, the action of the glacial ice, wind, and running water added the finishing touches.

FIGURE 21   Mount Hood, Oregon. This volcano is one of several large composite cones that comprise the Cascade Range. (Photo by John M. Roberts/CORBIS/Stock Market)

Earth's First Life

The oldest fossils show that life on Earth was established at least 3.5 billion years ago. Microscopic fossils similar to modern cyanobacteria (formerly known as blue-green algae) have been found in silica-rich chert deposits in locations worldwide. Two notable areas are in southern Africa, where the rocks date to more than 3.1 billion years, and in the Gunflint Chert (named for its use in flintlock rifles) of Lake Superior. Chemical traces of organic matter in even older rocks have led paleontologists to conclude that life may have existed 3.8 billion years ago.

How did life begin? A requirement for life, in addition to a hospitable environment, is the chemical raw materials needed to form life's critical molecules, DNA, RNA, and proteins. One of the building blocks of these substances are organic compounds called *amino acids*. The first amino acids may have been synthesized from methane and ammonia which were plentiful in Earth's primitive atmosphere. The question remains whether these gases could have been easily reorganized into useful organic molecules by ultraviolet light. Or lightning may have been the impetus, as the well-known experiments conducted by Stanley Miller and Harold Urey attempted to demonstrate.

Other researchers suggest that amino acids arrived ready-made, delivered by asteroids or comets that collided with a young Earth. A group of meteorites (debris from asteroids and comets that strike Earth) called *carbonaceous chrondrites* are known to contain amino acidlike organic compounds. Maybe early life had an extraterrestrial beginning.

Yet another hypothesis proposes that the organic material needed for life came from the methane and hydrogen sulfide that spews from deep-sea hydrothermal vents. The study of modern bacteria and other "hyperthermophiles" that live around hydrothermal vents (black smokers) suggests that life may have formed in this extreme environment, where temperatures exceed the boiling point of water.

FIGURE 22 The Grand Prismatic Pool, Yellowstone National Park, Wyoming. This hot-water pool gets its blue color from several species of heat-tolerant cyanobacteria (Photo by George Steinmetz/CORBIS)

Is it possible that life originated near a hydrothermal vent deep on the ocean floor, or within a hot spring similar to those in Yellowstone National Park (Figure 22)? Some origin-of-life researchers think that this scenario is highly improbable as the scalding temperatures would have destroyed any early types of self-replicating molecules. They argue that life's first home would have been along sheltered stretches of ancient beaches, where waves and tides would have brought together various organic materials formed in the Precambrian oceans.

Regardless of where life originated, change was inevitable (Figure 23). The first known organisms were single-cell bacteria that belong to the group called **prokaryotes** which means their genetic material (DNA) is not separated from the rest of the cell by a nucleus. Because oxygen was absent from Earth's early atmosphere and oceans, the first organisms employed anaerobic (without oxygen) metabolism to extract energy from "food." Their food source was likely organic molecules in their surroundings, but the supply of this material was limited. Then a type of bacteria evolved that used solar energy to synthesize organic compounds (sugars). This event was an important turning point in evolution—for the first time organisms had the capability of producing food for themselves as well as for other organisms.

Recall that photosynthesis by ancient cyanobacteria, a type of prokaryote, contributed to the gradual rise in the level of oxygen, first in the ocean and then in the atmosphere. Thus, these early organisms radically transformed our planet. Fossil evidence for the existence of these microscopic bacteria includes distinctively layered mounds of calcium carbonate, called **stromatolites** (Figure 24A). Stromatolites are not actually the remains of organisms, but limestone mats built up by lime-accreting bacteria. Strong evidence for the origin of these ancient fossils is the close similarity they have to modern stromatolites found in Shark Bay, Australia (Figure 24B).

The oldest fossils of more advanced organisms, called **eukaryotes**, are about 2.1 billion years old. Like prokaryotes, the first eukaryotes were microscopic, water-dwelling organisms. Their cellular structure did, however, contain nuclei. It is these primitive organisms that gave rise to essentially all of the multicelled organisms that now inhabit our planet—trees, birds, fishes, reptiles, and even humans.

During much of the Precambrian, life consisted exclusively of single-celled organisms. It wasn't until perhaps 1.5 billion years ago that multicelled eukaryotes evolved. Green algae, one of the first multicelled organisms, contained chloroplasts (used in photosynthesis) and were the forbears of modern plants. The first primitive marine animals did not appear until somewhat later, perhaps 600 million years ago; we just do not know for sure (Figure 25).

Fossil evidence suggests that organic evolution progressed at an excruciatingly slow pace until the end of the Precambrian. At this time, Earth's continents were barren, and the oceans were populated primarily by organisms too small to be seen with the naked eye. Nevertheless, the stage was set for the evolution of larger and more complex plants and animals at the dawn of the Paleozoic.

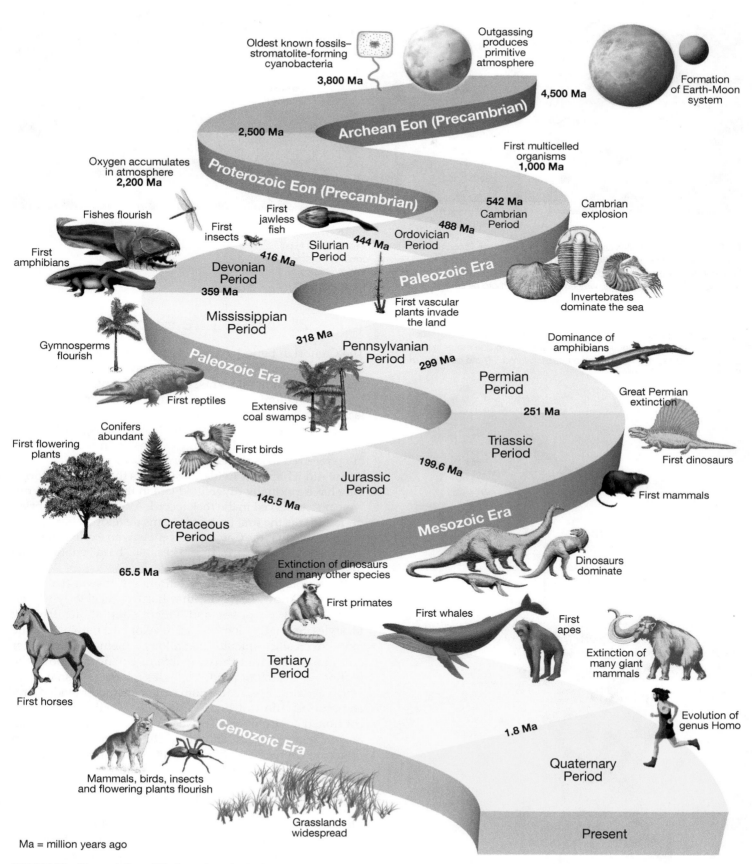

FIGURE 23 The evolution of life through geologic time.

Ma = million years ago

A.

B.

FIGURE 24 Stromatolites are among the most common Precambrian fossils. **A.** Precambrian fossil stromatolites composed of calcium carbonate deposited by algae in the Helena Formation, Glacier National Park, Montana. (Photo by Ken M. Johns/Photo Researchers, Inc.) **B.** Modern stromatolites growing in shallow saline seas, western Australia. (Photo by Bill Bachman/Photo Researchers, Inc.)

FIGURE 25 Ediacaran fossil. The Ediacarans are a group of sea-dwelling animals that may have come into existence about 600 million years ago. These soft-bodied organisms were up to one meter in length and are the oldest animal fossils so far discovered. (Photo courtesy of the South Australian Museum)

Paleozoic Era: Life Explodes

The Cambrian period marks the beginning of the Paleozoic era, about 542 million years ago. This time span saw the emergence of new animal forms, the likes of which have never been seen, before or since. All major invertebrate (animals lacking backbones) groups made their appearance, including jellyfish, sponges, worms, mollusks (clams), and arthropods (insects, crabs). This huge expansion in biodiversity is often referred to as the *Cambrian explosion*.

But did it happen? Evidence suggests that these life forms may have gradually diversified late in the Precambrian, but were not preserved in the rock record. After all, the Cambrian period marks the first time organisms developed hard parts. Is it possible that the Cambrian event was an explosion of animal forms that grew in size and became "hard" enough to be fossilized?

Paleontologists may never definitively answer that question. They know, however, that hard parts clearly served many useful purposes and aided adaptations to new lifestyles. Sponges, for example, developed a network of fine interwoven silica spicules that allowed them to grow larger and more erect, and thus capable of extending above the seafloor in search of food. Mollusks (clams and snails) secreted external shells of calcium carbonate that provided protection and allowed body organs to function in a more controlled environment. The successful trilobites developed an exoskeleton of a protein called chitin (similar to a human fingernail), which permitted them to search for food by burrowing through soft sediment (see Figure 18).

Early Paleozoic Life-Forms

The Cambrian period was the golden age of *trilobites*. More than 600 genera of these mud-burrowing scavengers flourished worldwide. The Ordovician marked the appearance of abundant cephalopods—mobile, highly developed mollusks that became the major predators of their time (Figure 26). The descendants of these cephalopods include the squid, octopus, and

FIGURE 26　During the Ordovician period (488–444 million years ago), the shallow waters of an inland sea over central North America contained an abundance of marine invertebrates. Shown in this reconstruction are straight-shelled cephalopods, trilobites, brachiopods, snails, and corals. (© The Field Museum, Neg. # GEO80820c, Chicago)

chambered nautilus that inhabit our modern oceans. Cephalopods were the first truly large organisms on Earth, one species reaching a length of nearly 10 meters (30 feet).

The early diversification of animals was partly driven by the emergence of predatory lifestyles. The larger mobile cephalopods preyed on trilobites that were mostly smaller than a child's hand. The evolution of efficient movement was often associated with the evolution of greater sensory capabilities and more complex nervous systems. These animals developed sensory devices for detecting light, smells, and touch.

Approximately 400 million years ago, green algae that had adapted to survive at the water's edge, gave rise to the first multicellular land plants. The primary difficulty of sustaining plant life on land was obtaining water and staying upright despite gravity and winds. These earliest land plants were leafless, vertical spikes about the size of your index finger (Figure 27). However, by the end of the Devonian period, 40 million years later, the fossil record indicates the existence of forests with trees tens of meters tall.

In the oceans, fishes perfected a new form of support for the body, an internal skeleton, and were the first creatures to have jaws. Armor-plated fishes that had evolved during the Ordovician continued to adapt. Their armor plates thinned to lightweight scales that permitted increased speed and mobility. Other fishes evolved during

the Devonian, including primitive sharks that had skeletons made of cartilage and bony fishes, the groups to which many modern fishes belong. Fishes, the first large vertebrates, proved to be faster swimmers than invertebrates and possessed more acute senses and larger brains. Hence, they

FIGURE 27　Land plants of the Paleozoic. The Silurian saw the first upright-growing (vascular) plants. Plant fossils became increasingly common from the Devonian onward.

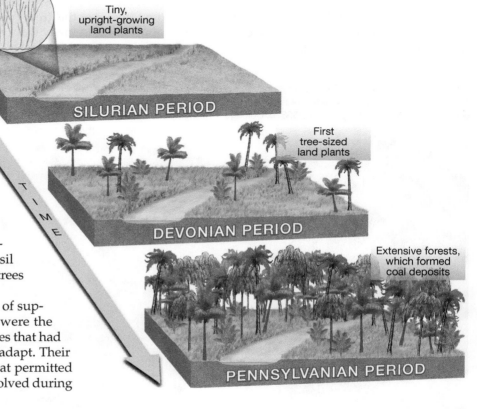

157

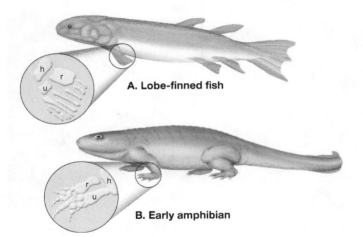

A. Lobe-finned fish

B. Early amphibian

FIGURE 28 Comparison of the anatomical features of the lobe-finned fish and early amphibians. **A.** The fins on the lobed-finned fish contained the same basic elements (*h*, humerus, or upper arm; *r*, radius; and *u*, ulna, or lower arm) as those of the amphibians. **B.** This amphibian is shown with the standard five toes, but early amphibians had as many as eight toes. Eventually the amphibians evolved to have a standard toe count of five.

became the dominant predators of the sea. Because of this, the Devonian period is often referred to as the "Age of the Fishes."

Vertebrates Move to Land

During the Devonian, a group of fishes called the *lobe-finned fish* began to adapt to terrestrial environments (Figure 28). Like their modern relative, these fishes had sacks that could be filled with air to supplement their "breathing" through gills. The first lobe-finned fish probably occupied freshwater tidal flats or small ponds near the ocean. Some began to use their fins to move from one pond to another in search of food, or to evacuate a pond that was drying up. This favored the evolution of a group of animals that could stay out of water longer and move about on land more efficiently. By the late

Devonian, lobe-finned fish had evolved into air-breathing amphibians (Figure 28). Although they had developed strong legs, they retained a fishlike head and tail.

Modern amphibians, such as frogs, toads, and salamanders, are small and occupy limited biological niches. But conditions during the late Paleozoic were ideal for these newcomers to the land. Large tropical swamps extended across North America, Europe and Siberia that were teeming with large insects and millipedes (Figure 29). With no predators to speak of, amphibians diversified rapidly. Some groups took on lifestyles and forms similar to modern reptiles, such as crocodiles.

Despite their success, the early amphibians were not fully adapted to life out of the water. In fact, amphibian means "double life," because these creatures need both the watery world from which they came and the land onto which they moved. Amphibians are born in the water, as exemplified by tadpoles, complete with gills and tails. In time, these features disappear and an air breathing adult with legs emerges.

Near the end of the Paleozoic, Earth's major landmasses were joined to form the supercontinent of Pangaea (see Figure 19). This redistribution of land and water along with changes in the elevations of landmasses brought pronounced changes in world climates. Broad areas of the northern continents became elevated above sea level, and the climate grew drier. These changes apparently resulted in the decline of the amphibians and the diversification of the reptiles. (Figure 30) (see Box 1).

Mesozoic Era: Age of the Dinosaurs

As the Mesozoic era dawned, its life forms were the survivors of the great Permian extinction. These organisms diversified in many ways to fill the biological voids created at the close of the Paleozoic. On land, conditions favored those that could

FIGURE 29 Restoration of a Pennsylvanian-age coal swamp (318–299 million years ago). Shown are the scale trees (left), seed ferns (lower left), and scouring rushes (right). Also note the large dragonfly. (© The Field Museum, Neg. # GEO85637c, Chicago. Photographer: John Weinstein.)

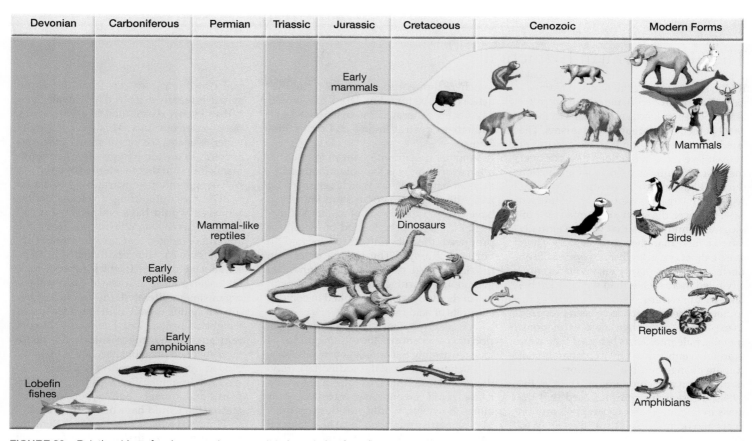

Devonian	Carboniferous	Permian	Triassic	Jurassic	Cretaceous	Cenozoic	Modern Forms

Early mammals

Mammal-like reptiles

Dinosaurs

Early reptiles

Mammals

Early amphibians

Birds

Lobefin fishes

Reptiles

Amphibians

FIGURE 30 Relationships of various vertebrates and their evolution from fish-like ancestors.

adapt to drier climates. Among plants, the gymnosperms were one such group. Unlike the first plants to invade the land, the seed-bearing gymnosperms did not depend on free-standing water for fertilization. Consequently, these plants were not restricted to a life near water's edge.

The gymnosperms quickly became the dominant trees of the Mesozoic. They included the following: cycads that resembled a large pineapple plant; ginkgoes that had fanshaped leaves, much like their modern relatives; and the largest plants, the conifers, whose modern descendants include the pines, firs, and junipers. The best-known fossil occurrence of these ancient trees is in northern Arizona's Petrified Forest National Park. Here, huge petrified logs lie exposed at the surface, having been weathered from rocks of the Triassic Chinle Formation (Figure 31).

Reptiles: The First True Terrestrial Vertebrates

Among the animals, reptiles readily adapted to the drier Mesozoic environment, thereby relegating amphibians to the wetlands where most remain today. Reptiles were the first true terrestrial vertebrates with improved lungs for an active lifestyle and "waterproof" skin that helped prevent the loss of body fluids. Most importantly, reptiles developed shell-covered eggs that can be laid on land. The elimination of a water-dwelling stage (like the tadpole stage in frogs) was an important evolutionary step.

Of interest is the fact that the watery fluid within the reptilian egg closely resembles seawater in chemical composition. Because the reptile embryo develops in this watery environment, the shelled egg has been characterized as a "private aquarium" in which the embryos of these land

FIGURE 31 Petrified logs of Triassic age in Arizona's Petrified Forest National Park. (Photo by David Muench)

BOX 1 ▶ EARTH AS A SYSTEM

The Great Permian Extinction

By the close of the Permian period, a mass extinction destroyed 70 percent of all vertebrate species on land, and perhaps as much as 90 percent of all marine organisms. The late Permian extinction was the greatest of at least five mass extinctions to occur over the past 500 million years. Each extinction wreaked havoc with the existing biosphere, wiping out large numbers of species. In each case, however, the survivors formed new biological communities that were eventually more diverse than their predecessors. Thus, mass extinctions actually invigorated life on Earth, as the few hardy survivors eventually filled more niches than the ones left behind by the victims.

Several mechanisms have been proposed to explain these ancient mass extinctions. Initially, paleontologists believed they were gradual events caused by a combination of climate change and biological forces, such as predation and competition. Then, in the 1980s, a research team proposed that the mass extinction that happened 65 million years ago occurred swiftly as a result of an explosive impact by an asteroid about 10 kilometers in diameter. This event, which caused the extinction of the dinosaurs, is described in Box 2

Was the Permian extinction also caused by a giant impact, like the now-famous dinosaur extinction? For many years, re-searchers thought so. However, scant evidence could be found of debris that would have been generated by an impact large enough to destroy many of Earth's lifeforms.

Another possible mechanism for the Permian extinction was the voluminous eruptions of basaltic lavas which began about 251 million years ago and are known to have covered thousands of square kilometers of the land. (This period of volcanism produced the Siberian Traps located in northern Russia.) The release of carbon dioxide would certainly have enhanced greenhouse warning, and the emissions of sulfur dioxide probably resulted in copious amounts of acid rain.

A recent hypothesis begins with this period of volcanism and the ensuing period of global warming but adds a new twist. These researchers agree that the additional carbon dioxide released into the atmosphere would cause rapid greenhouse warming. This alone, however, would not destroy most plants because they tend to be heat tolerant and consumer CO_2 in photosynthesis. They contend, instead, that the trouble begins in the ocean rather than on land.

Most organisms on Earth use oxygen to metabolize food, as do humans. However, some forms of bacteria employ *anaerobic* (without oxygen) metabolism. Under nor-mal conditions, oxygen from the atmosphere is readily dissolved in seawater, and is then evenly distributed to all depths by deep-water currents. This oxygen "rich" water relegates "oxygen-hating" anaerobic bacteria to anoxic (oxygen free) environments found in deep-water sediments.

The greenhouse warming associated with the vast outpouring of volcanic debris, however, would have warmed the ocean surface, thereby significantly reducing the amount of oxygen that seawater would absorb (Figure A). This condition favors deep-sea anaerobic bacteria, which generate toxic hydrogen sulfide as a waste gas. As these organisms proliferated, the amount of hydrogen sulfide dissolved in seawater would have steadily increased. Eventually, the concentration of hydrogen sulfide reached a threshold and great bubbles of this toxin exploded into the atmosphere (Figure A). On land, hydrogen sulfide was lethal to both plants and animals, but oxygen-breathing marine life would have been hit hardest.

How plausible is this scenario? Remember that the ideas that were just described represent a hypothesis, a tentative explanation regarding a set of observations. Additional research about this and other hypotheses that relate to the Permian extinction continues.

FIGURE A Model for the "Great Permian Extinction." Extensive volcanism released greenhouse gases, which resulted in extreme global warming. This condition reduced the amount of oxygen dissolved by seawater. This, in turn, favored "oxygen-hating" anaerobic bacteria, which generated toxic hydrogen sulfide as a waste gas. Eventually, the concentration of hydrogen sulfide reached a critical threshold and great bubbles of the toxin exploded into the atmosphere, wreaking havoc on organisms on land, but oxygen-breathing marine life was hit the hardest.

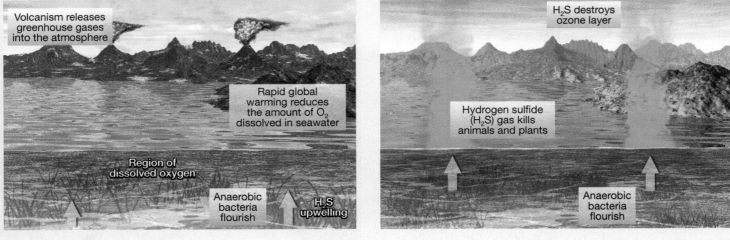

Apatosaurus, which weighed more than 30 tons and measured over 25 meters (80 feet) from head to tail. For nearly 160 million years, dinosaurs reigned supreme.

Some of the largest dinosaurs were carnivorous (*Tyrannosaurus*), whereas others were herbivorous (like ponderous *Apatosaurus*). The extremely long neck of *Apatosaurus* may have been an adaptation for feeding on tall conifer trees. However, not all dinosaurs were large. Some small forms closely resembled modern, fleet-footed lizards.

The reptiles made one of the most spectacular adaptive radiations in all of Earth history. One group, the pterosaurs, took to the air. These "dragons of the sky" possessed huge membranous wings that allowed them rudimentary flight. Another group of reptiles, exemplified by the fossil *Archaeopteryx*, led to more successful flyers: the birds (Figure 32). Whereas some reptiles took to the skies, others returned to the sea, including the fish-eating plesiosaurs and ichthyosaurs (Figure 33). These reptiles became proficient swimmers, but they retained their reptilian teeth and breathed by means of lungs.

At the close of the Mesozoic, many reptile groups became extinct. Only a few types survived to recent times, including the turtles, snakes, crocodiles, and lizards. The huge, land-dwelling dinosaurs, the marine plesiosaurs, and the flying pterosaurs are known only through the fossil record. What caused this great extinction? (See Box 2.)

Cenozoic Era: Age of Mammals

During the Cenozoic, mammals replaced reptiles as the dominant land animals. At nearly the same time, angiosperms (flowering plants with covered seeds) replaced gymnosperms as the dominant plants. The Cenozoic is often called the "Age of the Mammals," but could also appropriately be called the "Age of Flowering Plants," for the angiosperms enjoy a similar status in the plant world.

FIGURE 32   Paleontologists think that flying reptiles similar to *Archaeopteryx* were the ancestors of modern birds. (Photo by Louis Psihoyos/CORBIS)

vertebrates spend their water-dwelling stage of life. With this "sturdy egg," the remaining ties to the oceans were broken, and reptiles moved inland.

The first reptiles were small, but larger forms evolved rapidly, particularly the dinosaurs. One of the largest was

FIGURE 33   Marine reptiles such as this *Ichthyosaur* were the most spectacular of sea animals. (Photo by Chip Clark)

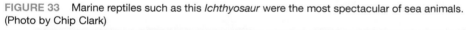

BOX 2 ▶ UNDERSTANDING EARTH

Demise of the Dinosaurs

The boundaries between divisions on the geologic time scale represent times of significant geological and/or biological charge. Of special interest is the boundary between the Mesozoic era ("middle life") and Cenozoic era ("recent life"), about 65 million years ago. Around this time, about three-quarters of all plant and animal species died out in a *mass extinction*. This boundary marks the end of the era in which dinosaurs and other reptiles dominated the landscape and the beginning of the era when mammals become very important (Figure B). Because the last period of the Mesozoic is the Cretaceous (abbreviated K to avoid confusion with other "C" periods), and the first period of the Cenozoic is the Tertiary (abbreviated T), the time of this mass extinction is called the *Cretaceous–Tertiary or KT boundary*.

The extinction of the dinosaurs is generally attributed to this group's inability to adapt to some radical change in environmental conditions. What event could have triggered the rapid extinction of the dinosaurs—one of the most successful groups of land animals ever to have lived?

The most strongly supported hypothesis proposes that about 65 million years ago our planet was struck by a large carbonaceous meteorite, a relic from the formation of the solar system. The errant mass of rock was approximately 10 kilometers in diameter and was travelling at about 90,000 kilometers per hour at impact. It collided with the southern portion of North America in what is now Mexico's Yucatán Peninsula but at the time was a shallow tropical sea (Figure C). The energy released by the impact is estimated to have been equivalent to 100 million megatons (*mega* = million) of high explosives.

For a year or two after the impact, suspended dust greatly reduced the sunlight reaching Earth's surface. This caused global cooling ("impact winter") and inhibited photosynthesis, greatly disrupting food production. Long after the dust settled, carbon dioxide, water vapor, and sulfur oxides that had been added to the atmosphere by the blast remained. If significant quantities of sulfate aerosols formed, their high reflectivity would have helped to perpetuate the cooler surface temperatures for a few more years. Eventually sulfate aerosols leave the atmosphere as acid precipitation. By contrast, carbon dioxide has a much longer residence time in the atmosphere. Carbon dioxide is a *greenhouse gas*, a gas that traps a portion of the radiation emitted by Earth's surface. With the aerosols gone, the enhanced greenhouse effect caused by the carbon dioxide would have led to a long-term rise in average global temperatures. The likely result was that some of the plant and animal life that had survived the initial environmental assault finally fell victim to stresses associated with global cooling, followed by acid precipitation and global warming.

The extinction of the dinosaurs opened up habitats for the small mammals that survived. These new habitats, along with evolutionary forces, led to the development of the large mammals that occupy our modern world.

What evidence points to such a catastrophic collision 65 million years ago? First, a thin layer of sediment nearly 1 centimeter thick has been discovered at the KT boundary, worldwide. This sediment contains a high level of the element *iridium*, rare in Earth's crust but found in high proportions in stony meteorites. Could this layer be the scattered remains of the meteorite that was responsible for the environmental changes that led to the demise of many reptile groups?

Despite growing support, some scientists disagree with the impact hypothesis. They suggest instead that huge volcanic eruptions may have led to a breakdown in the

FIGURE C Chicxulub crater is a giant impact crater that formed about 65 million years ago and has since been filled with sediments. About 180 kilometers in diameter, Chicxulub crater is regarded by some researchers to be the impact site that resulted in the demise of the dinosaurs and many other organisms.

The development of the flowering plants strongly influenced the evolution of both birds and mammals that feed on seeds and fruits. During the middle Tertiary, grasses (angiosperms) developed rapidly and spread over the plains (Figure 34). This fostered the emergence of herbivorous (plant-eating) mammals which, in turn, established the setting for the evolution of the large, predatory mammals.

During the Cenozoic the ocean was teeming with modern fish such as tuna, swordfish and, barracuda. In addition, some mammals, including seals, whales, and walruses, returned to the sea.

From Reptiles to Mammals

The earliest mammals coexisted with dinosaurs for nearly 100 million years but were small rodentlike creatures that gathered food at night when the dinosaurs were less active.

Then, about 65 million years ago, fate intervened when a large asteroid collided with Earth and dealt a crashing blow to the reign of the dinosaurs. This transition, during which one dominant group is replaced by another, is clearly visible in the fossil record.

Mammals are distinct from reptiles in that they give birth to live young (which they suckle on milk) and they are warm-blooded. This latter adaptation allowed mammals to lead more active lives and to occupy more diverse habitats than reptiles because they could survive in cold regions. (Most modern reptiles are dormant during cold weather.) Other mammalian adaptations included the development of insulating body hair and more efficient heart and lungs.

With the demise of the large Mesozoic reptiles, Cenozoic mammals diversified rapidly. The many forms that exist today evolved from small primitive mammals that were characterized by short legs, flat five-toed feet, and small food chain. To support this hypothesis, they cite enormous outpourings of lavas in the Deccan Plateau of northern India about 65 million years ago.

Whatever caused the KT extinction, we now have a greater appreciation of the role of catastrophic events in shaping the history of our planet and the life that occupies it. Could a catastrophic event having similar results occur today? This possibility may explain why an event that occurred 65 million years ago has captured the interest of so many.

FIGURE B Dinosaurs dominated the Mesozoic landscape until their extinction at the close of the Cretaceous period. **A.** Dinosaurs such as *Allosaurus* were fearsome predators. (Image by Joe Tucciarone/Photo Researchers, Inc.) **B.** These dinosaur footprints near Cameron, Arizona, were originally made in mud that eventually became a sedimentary rock. (Photo by Tom Bean/DRK Photo)

brains. Their development and specialization took four principal directions: (1) increase in size, (2) increase in brain capacity, (3) specialization of teeth to better accommodate their diet, and (4) specialization of limbs to better equip the animal for a particular lifestyle or environment.

Marsupial and Placental Mammals   Two groups of mammals, the marsupials and the placentals, evolved and diversified during the Cenozoic. The groups differ principally in their modes of reproduction. Young marsupials are born live but at a very early stage of development. At birth, the tiny and immature young enter the mother's pouch to suckle and complete their development. Today, marsupials are found primarily in Australia, where they underwent a separate evolutionary expansion largely isolated from placental mammals. Modern marsupials include kangaroos, opossums, and koalas (Figure 35).

Placental mammals, conversely, develop within the mother's body for a much longer period, so that birth occurs after the young are comparatively mature. Most modern mammals are placental, including humans.

In South America, primitive marsupials and placentals coexisted in isolation for about 40 million years after the breakup of Pangaea. Evolution and specialization of both groups continued undisturbed until about 3 million years ago when the Panamanian land-bridge connected the two American continents. This event permitted the exchange of fauna between the two continents. Monkeys, armadillos, sloths, and opossums arrived in North America, while various types of horses, bears, rhinos, camels, and wolves migrated southward. Many animals that had been unique to South America disappeared completely after this event, including hoofed mammals, rhino-sized rodents, and a number of carnivorous marsupials. Because this period of extinction

FIGURE 34 Angiosperms, commonly known as flowering plants, are seed-plants that have reproductive structures called flowers and fruits. **A.** The most diverse and widespread of modern plants, many angiosperms display easily recognizable flowers. **B.** Some angiosperms, including grasses, have very tiny flowers. The expansion of the grasslands during the Cenozoic era greatly increased the diversity of grazing mammals and the predators that feed on them. (Photo by **A.** Mike Potts and **B.** Torleif/CORBIS)

coincided with the formation of the Panamanian land-bridge, it was thought that the advanced carnivores from North America were responsible. Recent research, however, suggests that other factors, including climatic changes, may have played a significant role.

Large Mammals and Extinction

As you have seen, mammals diversified rapidly during the Cenozoic era. One tendency was for some groups to become very large. For example, by the Oligocene epoch, a hornless rhinoceros that stood nearly 5 meters (16 feet) high had evolved. It is the largest land mammal known to have existed. As time passed many other mammals evolved to larger sizes—more, in fact, than now exist. Many of these large forms were common as recently as 11,000 years ago. However, a wave of late Pleistocene extinctions rapidly eliminated these animals from the landscape.

In North America, the mastodon and mammoth, both huge relatives of the elephant, became extinct. In addition, sabertoothed cats, giant beavers, large ground sloths, giant bison, and others died out (Figure 36). In Europe, late Pleistocene extinctions included woolly rhinos, large cave bears, and the Irish elk. The reason for this recent wave of extinctions that targeted large animals puzzles scientists. These animals had survived several major glacial advances and interglacial periods, so it is difficult to ascribe these extinctions to climate change. Some scientists hypothesize that early humans hastened the decline of these mammals by selectively hunting large forms (Figure 37).

FIGURE 35 Following the breakup of Pangaea, the Australian marsupials evolved differently than their relatives in the Americas. (Photo by Martin Harvey)

FIGURE 36 Mammoths, related to modern elephants, were among the large mammals that became extinct at the close of the Ice Age. (Image courtesy of Jonathan Blair/Woodfin Camp)

FIGURE 37 Cave painting of animals that early humans encountered about 17,000 years ago. (Photo courtesy of National Geographic)

Summary

- The history of Earth began about 13.7 billion years ago when the first elements were created during the *Big Bang*. It was from this material, plus other elements ejected into interstellar space by now defunct stars, that Earth along with the rest of the solar system formed. As material collected, high velocity impacts of chunks of matter called *planetesimals* and the decay of radioactive elements caused the temperature of our planet to steadily increase. Iron and nickel melted and sank to form the metallic core, while rocky material rose to form the mantle and Earth's initial crust.

- Earth's primitive atmosphere, which consisted mostly of water vapor and carbon dioxide, formed by a process called *outgassing*, which resembles the steam eruptions of modern volcanoes. About 3.5 billion years ago, photosynthesizing bacteria began to release oxygen, first into the oceans and then into the atmosphere. This began the evolution of our modern atmosphere. The oceans, formed early in Earth's history, as water vapor condensed to form clouds, and torrential rains filled low lying areas. The salinity in seawater came from volcanic outgassing and from elements weathered and eroded from Earth's primitive crust.

- The Precambrian, which is divided into the Archean and Proterozoic eons, spans nearly 90 percent of Earth's history, beginning with the formation of Earth about 4.5 billion years ago and ending approximately 542 million years ago. During this time, much of Earth's stable continental crust was created through a multistage process. First, partial melting of the mantle generated magma that rose to form volcanic island arcs and oceanic plateaus. These thin crustal fragments collided and accreted to form larger crustal provinces, which in turn assembled into larger blocks called *cratons*. Cratons, which form the core of modern continents, were created mainly during the Precambrian.

- Supercontinents are large landmasses that consist of all, or nearly all, existing continents. *Pangaea* was the most recent supercontinent, but a massive southern continent called *Gondwana*, and perhaps an even larger one, *Rodinia*, preceded it. The splitting and reassembling of supercontinents have generated most of Earth's major mountain belts. In addition, the movement of these crustal blocks have profoundly affected Earth's climate, and have caused sea level to rise and fall.

- The time span following the close of the Precambrian, called the *Phanerozoic eon*, encompasses 542 million years and is divided into three eras: *Paleozoic, Mesozoic*, and *Cenozoic*. The Paleozoic era was dominated by continental collisions as the supercontinent of Pangaea assembled—forming the Caledonian, Appalachian, and Ural Mountains. Early in the Mesozoic, much of the land was above sea level. However, by the middle Mesozoic, seas invaded western North America. As Pangaea began to break up, the westward-moving North American plate began to override the Pacific plate, causing crustal deformation along the entire western margin of North America. Most of North America was above sea level throughout the Cenozoic. Owing to their different relations with plate boundaries, the eastern and western margins of the continent experienced contrasting events. The stable eastern margin was the site of abundant sedimentation as isostatic adjustment raised the Appalachians, causing streams to erode with renewed vigor and deposit their sediment along the continental margin. In the West, building of the Rocky Mountains (the *Laramide Orogeny*) was coming to an end, the Basin and Range Province was forming, and volcanic activity was extensive.

- The first known organisms were single-celled bacteria, *prokaryotes*, which lack a nucleus. One group of these organisms, called cyanobacteria, that used solar energy to synthesize organic compounds (sugars) evolved. For the first time, organisms had the ability to produce their own food. Fossil evidence for the existence of these bacteria includes layered mounds of calcium carbonate called *stromatolites*.

- The beginning of the Paleozoic is marked by the *appearance of the first life-forms with hard parts* such as shells. Therefore, abundant Paleozoic fossils occur, and a far more detailed record of Paleozoic events can be constructed. Life in the early Paleozoic was restricted to the seas and consisted of several invertebrate groups, including trilobites, cephalopods, sponges and corals. During the Paleozoic, organisms diversified dramatically. Insects and plants moved onto land, and lobe-finned fishes that adapted to land became the first amphibians. By the Pennsylvanian period, large tropical swamps, which became the major coal deposits of today, extended across North America, Europe, and Siberia. At the close of the Paleozoic, a mass extinction destroyed 70 percent of all vertebrate species on land and 90 percent of all marine organisms.

- The Mesozoic era, literally the era of middle life, is often called the *"Age of Reptiles."* Organisms that survived the extinction at the end of the Paleozoic began to diversify in spectacular ways. *Gymnosperms* (cycads, conifers, and ginkgoes) became the dominant trees of the Mesozoic because they could adapt to the drier climates. Reptiles became the dominant land animals. The most awesome of the Mesozoic reptiles were the *dinosaurs*. At the close of the Mesozoic, many large reptiles, including the dinosaurs, became extinct.

- The Cenozoic is often called the *"Age of Mammals"* because these animals replaced the reptiles as the dominant vertebrate life forms on land. Two groups of mammals, the marsupials and the placentals, evolved and expanded during this era. One tendency was for some mammal groups to become very large. However, a wave of late *Pleistocene* extinctions rapidly eliminated these animals from the landscape. Some scientists suggest that early humans hastened their decline by selectively hunting the larger animals. The Cenozoic could also be called the *"Age of Flowering Plants."* As a source of food, flowering plants (angiosperms) strongly influenced the evolution of both birds and herbivorous (plant-eating) mammals throughout the Cenozoic era.

Review Questions

1. Why is Earth's molten, metallic core important to humans living today?

2. What two elements made up most of the very early universe?

3. What is the cataclysmic event called in which an exploding star produces all of the elements heavier than iron?

4. Briefly describe the formation of the planets from the solar nebula.

5. What is meant by outgassing and what modern phenomenon serves that role today?

6. Outgassing produced Earth's early atmosphere, which was rich in what two gases?

7. Why is the evolution of a type of bacteria that employed photosynthesis to produce food important to most modern organisms?

8. What was the source of water for the first oceans?

9. How does the ocean remove carbon dioxide from the atmosphere? What role do tiny marine organisms, such as foraminifera, play?

10. Explain why Precambrian history is more difficult to decipher than more recent geological history.

11. Briefly describe how cratons come into being.

12. What is the supercontinent cycle?

13. How can the movement of continents trigger climate change?

14. Match the following words and phrases to the most appropriate time span. Select from the following: *Precambrian, Paleozoic, Mesozoic, Cenozoic.*

   a. Pangaea came into existence.

   b. First trace fossils.

   c. The era that encompasses the least amount of time.

   d. Earth's major cratons formed.

   e. "Age of Dinosaurs."

   f. Formation of the Rocky Mountains.

   g. Formation of the Appalachian Mountains.

   h. Coal swamps extended across North America, Europe, and Siberia.

   i. Gulf Coast oil deposits formed.

   j. Formation of most of the world's major iron-ore deposits.

   k. Massive sand dunes covered a large portion of the Colorado Plateau region.

   l. The "Age of the Fishes" occurred during this span.

   m. Pangaea began to break apart and disperse.

   n. "Age of Mammals."

o. Animals with hard parts first appeared in abundance.

p. Gymnosperms were the dominant trees.

q. Stromatolites were abundant.

r. Fault-block mountains formed in the Basin and Range region.

15. Contrast the eastern and western margins of North America during the Cenozoic era in terms of their relationships to plate boundaries.

16. What did plants have to overcome to move onto land?

17. What group of animals is thought to have left the ocean to become the first amphibians?

18. Why are amphibians not considered "true" land animals?

19. What major development allowed reptiles to move inland?

20. What event is thought to have ended the reign of the dinosaurs?

Key Terms

banded iron formations	planetesimals	stromatolites	supercontinent cycle
cratons	prokaryotes	supercontinent	supernova
eukaryotes	protoplanets		
outgassing	solar nebula		

Examining the Earth System

1. The Earth system has been responsible for both the conditions that favored the evolution of life on this planet and for the mass extinctions that have occurred throughout geologic time. Describe the role of the biosphere, hydrosphere, and solid Earth in forming the current level of atmospheric oxygen. How did Earth's nearspace environment interact with the atmosphere and biosphere to contribute to the great mass extinction that marked the end of the dinosaurs?

2. Most of the vast North American coal resources located from Pennsylvania to Illinois began forming during the Pennsylvanian and Mississippian periods of Earth history. (This time period is also referred to as the Carboniferous period.) Using Figure 29, a restoration of a Pennsylvania period coal swamp, describe the climatic and biological conditions associated with this unique environment. Next, examine Figure 19B,C. The maps show the formation of the supercontinent of Pangaea and illustrate the geographic position of North America during the period of coal formation. Where, relative to the equator, was North America located during the time of coal formation? What role did plate tectonics play in determining the conditions that eventually produced North America's eastern coal reserves? Why is it unlikely that the coal-forming environment will repeat itself in North America in the near future? (You may find it helpful to visit the Illinois State Museum Mazon Creek Fossils exhibit at **http://www.museum.state.il.us/exhibits/mazon_ creek**, and/or the University of California Time Machine Exhibit at **http://www.ucmp.berkeley.edu/carboniferous/ carboniferous.html**.)

Online Study Guide

The *Earth Science* Website uses the resources and flexibility of the Internet to aid in your study of the topics in this chapter. Written and developed by Earth science instructors, this site will help improve your understanding of Earth science. Visit **www.mygeoscienceplace.com** and click on the cover of *Earth Science 12e* to find:

- Online review quizzes
- Critical thinking exercises
- Links to chapter-specific Web resources
- Internet-wide key term searches

168

Plate Tectonics and the Ocean Floor

From Chapter 3 of *Introduction to Oceanography*, Tenth Edition, Harold V. Thurman, Alan P. Trujillo.

Plate Tectonics and the Ocean Floor

APT photo

Tall mountains created by tectonic uplift. Tall coastal mountains such as these in Glacier Bay National Park in southeast Alaska have been uplifted by plate tectonic processes, creating a large amount of relief. Some of the uplifted rocks here have come from distant areas and include parts of the sea floor.

- What evidence did Alfred Wegener use to formulate his idea of continental drift?
- How did the early idea of continental drift differ from the more modern version of plate tectonics?
- What are the lines of evidence that support the theory of plate tectonics?
- How do structure, composition, and physical properties vary within the deep Earth?
- What types of features are found at the three main types of plate boundaries?
- How do mantle plumes and hotspots fit into the plate tectonic model?
- How have the features on Earth looked in the past and how will they look in the future?

The answers to these questions (and much more) can be found in the highlighted concept statements within this chapter.

"It is just as if we were to refit the torn pieces of a newspaper by matching their edges and then check whether the lines of print run smoothly across. If they do, there is nothing left but to conclude that the pieces were in fact joined in this way."

—Alfred Wegener, *The Origin of Continents and Oceans* (1929)

Several thousand earthquakes and dozens of volcanic eruptions occur on land and under the oceans each year, indicating that our planet is very dynamic. These events have occurred throughout history, constantly changing the surface of our planet, yet only a few decades ago most scientists believed the continents were stationary over geologic time. Since then, however, a bold new theory has been advanced that helps explain, for the first time, the following surface features and phenomena on Earth:

- The worldwide locations of volcanoes, faults, earthquakes, and mountain building
- Why mountains on Earth haven't been eroded away
- The origin of most landforms and ocean floor features
- How the continents and ocean floor formed, and why they are different
- The continuing development of Earth's surface
- The distribution of past and present life on Earth

This revolutionary new theory is called **plate tectonics** (*plate* = plates of the **lithosphere**; *tekton* = to build), or "the new global geology." According to the theory of plate tectonics, the outermost portion of Earth is composed of a patchwork of thin, rigid plates[1] that move hor-

izontally with respect to one another, like icebergs floating on water. The interaction of these plates as they move builds features of Earth's crust (such as volcanoes, mountain belts, and ocean basins). As a result, the continents are mobile and move about on Earth's surface, controlled by forces deep within Earth.

In this chapter, we examine the early ideas about the movement of plates, the evidence for those ideas, and how they led to the theory of plate tectonics. Then we look at Earth structure, plate boundaries, and some applications of plate tectonics, including what our planet may look like in the future.

Evidence for Continental Drift

Alfred Wegener (Figure 1), a German meteorologist and geophysicist, was the first to advance the idea of mobile continents in 1912. He envisioned that the continents were slowly drifting across the globe and called his idea **continental drift**. Let's examine the evidence that Wegener compiled that led him to formulate the idea of drifting continents.

Fit of the Continents

The idea that continents—particularly South America and Africa—fit together like pieces of a jigsaw puzzle originated with the development of reasonably accurate world maps.

---

[1]These thin, rigid plates are pieces of the lithosphere (*lithos* = rock, *sphere* = ball) that comprise Earth's outermost portion.

Figure 1 Alfred Wegener, circa 1912–1913.

As far back as 1620, Sir Francis Bacon wrote about how the continents appeared to fit together. However, little significance was given to this idea until 1912, when Wegener used the shapes of matching shorelines on different continents as a supporting piece of evidence for continental drift.

Wegener suggested that during the geologic past, the continents collided to form a large landmass, which he named **Pangaea** (*pan* = all, *gaea* = Earth) (Figure 2). Further, a huge ocean surrounded Pangaea, called **Panthalassa** (*pan* = all, *thalassa* = sea). Panthalassa, the ancient precursor of the Pacific Ocean, included several smaller seas, including the **Tethys** (*Tethys* = a Greek seagoddess) **Sea**. Wegener's evidence indicated that about 200 million years ago, Pangaea began to split apart, and the various continental masses started to drift toward their present geographic positions.

Wegener's attempt at matching shorelines revealed considerable areas of crustal overlap and large gaps. Some of the differences could be explained by material deposited by rivers or eroded from coastlines. What Wegener didn't know was the shallow parts of the ocean floor close to shore are closely related to the continents. In the early 1960s, Sir Edward Bullard and two associates used a computer to fit the continents together (Figure 3). Instead of using the shorelines of the continents as Wegener had done, Bullard achieved the best fit (i.e., with minimal overlaps or gaps) by using a depth of 2000 meters (6560 feet) below sea level. This depth corresponds to halfway between the shoreline and the deep ocean basins and represents the true edge of the continents. By using this depth, the overall fit of the continents was even better than expected.

Matching Sequences of Rocks and Mountain Chains

If the continents were once together as Wegener had hypothesized, then evidence should appear in rock sequences that were originally continuous but now separated by large distances. To test the idea of drifting continents, geologists began comparing the rocks along the edges of continents with rocks found in adjacent positions on matching continents. They wanted to see if the

After Dietz, R. S., and Holden, J. C. 1970. Reconstruction of Pangaea: Breakup and dispersion of continents, Permian to present. *Journal of Geophysical Research* 75:26, 4939–4956

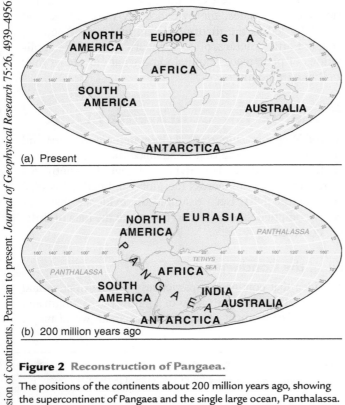

Figure 2 Reconstruction of Pangaea.

The positions of the continents about 200 million years ago, showing the supercontinent of Pangaea and the single large ocean, Panthalassa.

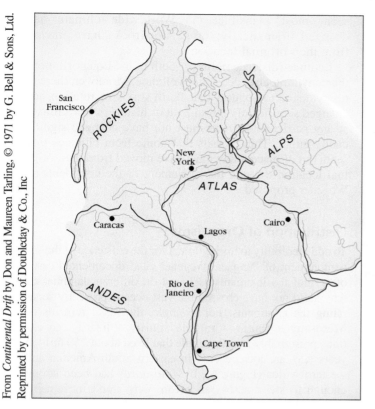

Figure 3 Computer fit of the continents.

In 1965, Sir Edward Bullard used a depth of 2000 meters (6560 feet) for a best-fit match of the continents, which shows few gaps and minimal overlap.

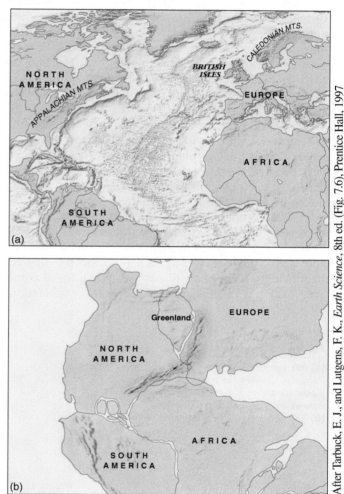

Figure 4 Matching mountain ranges across the North Atlantic Ocean.

(a) Present-day positions of continents and mountain ranges.
(b) Positions of the continents about 300 million years ago, showing how mountain ranges with similar age, type, and structure form one continuous belt.

rocks had similar types, ages, and structural styles (the type and degree of deformation). In some areas younger rocks had been deposited during the millions of years since the continents separated, covering the rocks that held the key to the past history of the continents. In other areas, the rocks had been eroded away. Nevertheless, in many other areas the key rocks were present.

These studies showed that many rock sequences from one continent matched up with identical rock sequences on a matching continent—although the two were separated by an ocean. In addition, mountain ranges that terminated abruptly at the edge of a continent continued on another continent across an ocean basin, with identical rock sequences, ages, and structural styles. Figure 4 shows, for example, how similar rocks from the Appalachian Mountains in North America match up with identical rocks from the British Isles and the Caledonian Mountains in Europe.

Wegener noted the similarities in rock sequences on both sides of the Atlantic and used the information as a supporting piece of evidence for continental drift. He suggested that mountains such as those seen on opposite sides of the Atlantic formed during the collision when Pangaea was formed. Later, when the continents split apart, once-continuous mountain ranges were separated. Confirmation of this idea exists in a similar match with mountains extending from South America through Antarctica and across Australia.

Glacial Ages and Other Climate Evidence

Wegener also noticed the occurrence of past glacial activity in areas now tropical and suggested that it, too,

provided supporting evidence for drifting continents. Currently, the only places in the world where thick continental *ice sheets* occur are in the polar regions of Greenland and Antarctica. However, evidence of ancient glaciation is found in the lower latitude regions of South America, Africa, India, and Australia.

These deposits, which have been dated at 300 million years old, indicate one of two possibilities: (1) There was a worldwide **ice age** and even tropical areas were covered by thick ice, or (2) some continents that are now in tropical areas were once located much closer to one of the poles. It is unlikely that the entire world was covered by ice 300 million years ago because coal deposits from the same geologic age now present in North America and Europe originated as vast semitropical swamps. Thus, a reasonable conclusion is that some of the continents must have been closer to the poles than they are today.

There is another type of glacial evidence that indicates certain continents have moved from more polar regions during the last 300 million years. When glaciers flow, they move and abrade the underlying rocks, leaving grooves that indicate the direction of flow. The blue arrows in Figure 5a show how the glaciers would have flowed away from the South Pole on Pangaea 300 million years ago. The direction of flow is consistent with the grooves found on many continents today (Figure 5b), providing additional evidence for drifting continents.

Many examples of plant and animal fossils indicate very different climates than today. Two such examples are fossil palm trees in Arctic Spitsbergen and coal deposits in Antarctica. Earth's past environments can be interpreted from these rocks because plants and animals need specific environmental conditions in which to live. Corals, for example, generally need seawater above 18 degrees Centigrade (°C) or 64 degrees Fahrenheit (°F) in order to survive. When fossil corals are found in areas that are cold today, two explanations

seem most plausible: (1) Worldwide climate has changed dramatically; or (2) the rocks have moved from their original location.

Latitude (distance north or south of the Equator), more than anything else, determines climate. Moreover, there is no evidence to suggest that Earth's axis of rotation has changed significantly throughout its history, so the climate at any particular latitude must not have changed significantly either. Thus, fossils that come from climates that seem out of place today must have moved from their original location through the movement of the continents as Wegener proposed.

Distribution of Organisms

To add credibility to his argument for the existence of the supercontinent of Pangaea, Wegener cited documented cases of several fossil organisms found on different landmasses that could not have crossed the vast oceans presently separating the continents. For example, the fossil remains of **Mesosaurus** (*meso* = middle, *saurus* = lizard), an extinct, presumably aquatic reptile that lived about 250 million years ago, are located only in eastern South America and western Africa (Figure 6). If *Mesosaurus* had been strong enough to swim across an ocean, why aren't its remains more widely distributed?

Figure 5 Ice age on Pangaea.

(a) Reconstruction of the supercontinent Pangaea, showing the area covered by glacial ice about 300 million years ago. Arrows indicate direction of ice flow.
(b) The positions of the continents today.

After Tarbuck, E. J., and Lutgens, F. K., *Earth Science*, 8th ed. (Fig. 7.7), Prentice Hall, 1997

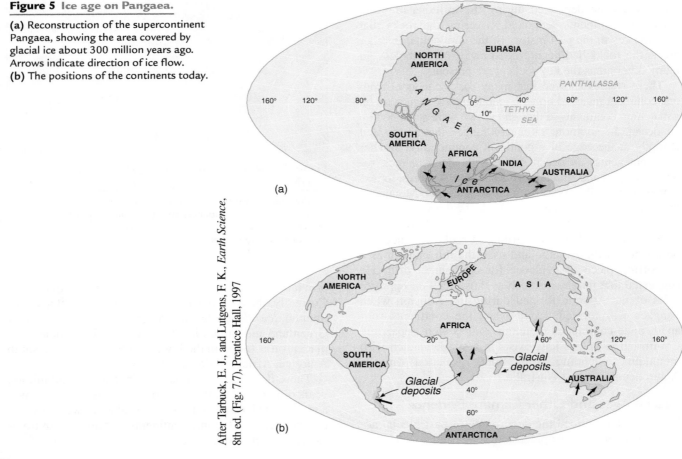

Wegener's idea of continental drift provided an elegant solution to this problem. He suggested that the continents were closer together in the geologic past, so *Mesosaurus* didn't have to be a good swimmer to leave remains on two different continents. Later, after *Mesosaurus* became extinct, the continents moved to their present-day positions, and a large ocean now separates the once-connected landmasses. Other examples of similar fossils on different continents include those of plants, which would have had a difficult time traversing a large ocean.

Before continental drift, several ideas were proposed to help explain the curious pattern of these fossils, such as the existence of island stepping stones or a land bridge. It was even suggested that at least one pair of land-dwelling *Mesosaurus* survived the arduous journey across several thousand kilometers of open ocean by rafting on floating logs. However, there is no evidence to support the idea of island stepping stones or a land bridge and the idea of *Mesosaurus* rafting across an ocean seems implausible.

Wegener also cited the distribution of present-day organisms as evidence to support the concept of drifting continents. For example, modern organisms with similar ancestries clearly had to evolve in isolation during the last few million years. Most obvious of these are the Australian marsupials (such as the kangaroos, koalas, and wombats), which have a distinct similarity to the marsupial opossums found in the Americas.

Objections to the Continental Drift Model

In 1915, Wegener published his ideas in *The Origins of Continents and Oceans*, but the book did not attract much attention until it was translated into English, French, Spanish, and Russian in 1924. From that point until his death in 1930,[2] his drift hypothesis received much hostile criticism—and sometimes open ridicule—from the scientific community because of the mechanism he proposed

for the movement of the continents. Wegener suggested the continents plowed through the ocean basins to reach their present day positions and that the leading edges of the continents deformed into mountain ridges because of the drag imposed by ocean rocks. Further, the driving mechanism he proposed was a combination of the gravitational attraction of Earth's equatorial bulge and tidal forces from the Sun and Moon.

Scientists rejected the idea as too fantastic and contrary to the laws of physics. Material strength calculations showed that ocean rock was too strong for continental rock to plow through it and analysis of gravitational and tidal forces indicated that they were too small to move the great continental landmasses. Even without an acceptable mechanism, many geologists who studied rocks in South America and Africa accepted continental drift. North American geologists—most of whom were unfamiliar with these Southern Hemisphere rock sequences—remained highly skeptical.

As compelling as Wegener's evidence may seem today, he was unable to convince the scientific community as a whole of the validity of his ideas. Although his hypothesis was correct in principle, it contained several incorrect details, such as the driving mechanism for continental motion and how continents move across ocean basins. In order for any scientific viewpoint to gain wide acceptance, it must explain all available observations and have supporting evidence from a wide variety of scientific fields. This supporting evidence would not come until more details of the nature of the ocean floor were revealed, which, along with new technology that enabled scientists to determine the original positions of rocks on Earth, provided additional observations in support of drifting continents.

---

[2]Wegener perished in 1930 during an expedition in Greenland while collecting data to help support his idea of continental drift.

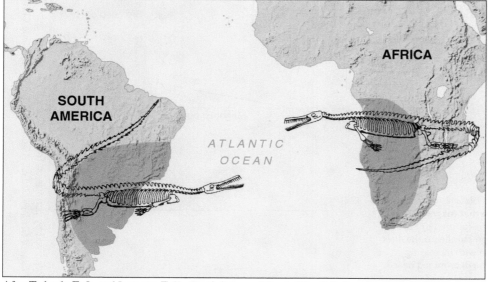

Figure 6 Fossils of *Mesosaurus.*

Mesosaurus fossils are found only in South America and Africa and appear to link these two continents.

After Tarbuck, E. J., and Lutgens, F. K., *Earth Science*, 8th ed. (Fig. 7.4), Prentice Hall, 1997

Alfred Wegener used a variety of interdisciplinary information from land to support continental drift. However, he did not have a suitable mechanism or any information about the sea floor.

Evidence for Plate Tectonics

Very little new information about Wegener's continental drift hypothesis was introduced between the time of Wegener's death in 1930 and the early 1950s. However, bathymetric studies of the sea floor using sonar that were initiated during World War II and continued after the war provided critical evidence in support of drifting continents. In addition, technology unavailable in Wegener's time enabled scientists to begin analyzing the way rocks retained the signature of Earth's **magnetic field**. These developments caused scientists to reexamine continental drift and advance it into the more encompassing theory of plate tectonics.

Earth's Magnetic Field and Paleomagnetism

Earth's magnetic field is shown in Figure 7. The invisible lines of magnetic force that originate within Earth and travel out into space resemble the magnetic field produced by a large bar magnet.[3] Similar to Earth's magnetic field, the ends of a bar magnet have opposite polarities (labeled either $+$ and $-$ or N for north and S for south)

that cause magnetic objects to align parallel to its magnetic field. In addition, notice in Figure 7b that Earth's geographic north pole (the rotational axis) and Earth's magnetic north pole (magnetic north) do not coincide.

S T U D E N T S   S O M E T I M E S   A S K . . .
What causes Earth's magnetic field?

Studies of Earth's magnetic field and research in the field of *magnetodynamics* suggest that convective movement of fluids in Earth's liquid iron-nickel outer core is the cause of Earth's magnetic field. The most widely accepted view is that the core behaves like a self-sustaining *dynamo*, which converts the energy in convective motion into magnetic energy. Interestingly, most other planets (and even some planet's moons) have magnetic fields. The Sun has a strong magnetic field, which reverses its orientation about every 22 years and is closely tied to the Sun's 11-year sunspot cycle.

---

[3]The properties of a magnetic field can be explored easily enough with a bar magnet and some iron particles. Place the iron particles on a table and place a bar magnet nearby. Depending on the strength of the magnet, you should get a pattern resembling Figure 7a.

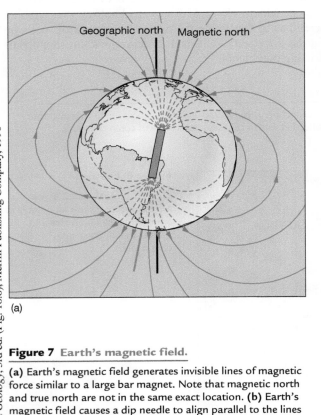

(a)

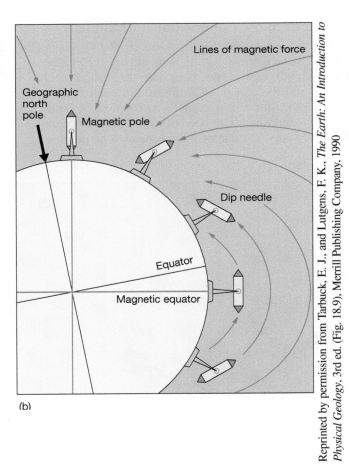

(b)

Figure 7 Earth's magnetic field.

(a) Earth's magnetic field generates invisible lines of magnetic force similar to a large bar magnet. Note that magnetic north and true north are not in the same exact location. **(b)** Earth's magnetic field causes a dip needle to align parallel to the lines of magnetic force and change orientation with increasing latitude. Consequently, the latitude can be determined based on the dip angle.

Rocks Affected by Earth's Magnetic Field *Igneous* (*igne* = fire, *ous* = full of) *rocks* solidify from molten *magma* (*magma* = a mass) either underground or after volcanic eruptions at the surface, which produce *lava* (*lava* = to wash). Nearly all igneous rocks contain **magnetite**, a naturally magnetic iron mineral. Particles of magnetite in magma align themselves with Earth's magnetic field because magma and lava are fluid. Volcanic lavas such as basalt are high in magnetite and solidify from molten material at temperatures in excess of 1000°C (1832°F); however, the magnetic signatures are not set until the rock cools below 600°C (1112°F), the temperature called the **Curie point** after Pierre Curie, a French physical chemist known for his work, with his wife Marie, on radioactivity.

At the Curie point, magnetite particles in igneous rocks become fixed in the direction of Earth's magnetic field and record the angle of Earth's magnetic field at that place and time. In essence, grains of magnetite serve as tiny compass needles that record the strength and orientation of Earth's magnetic field. Unless the rock is again heated to the Currie point, which would allow magnetite grains to be mobile, these magnetite grains contain information about the magnetic field where the rock originated regardless of where the rock subsequently moves.

Magnetite is also deposited in sediments. As long as the sediment is surrounded by water, the magnetite particles can align themselves with Earth's magnetic field. Sediment can be buried and solidified into *sedimentary* (*sedimentum* = settling) rock. As this occurs, the particles are no longer able to realign themselves if they are subsequently moved. Thus, magnetite grains in sedimentary rocks also contain information about the magnetic field where the rock originated. Although other rock types have been successfully used to reveal information about Earth's ancient magnetic field, the most reliable ones are igneous rocks that have high concentrations of magnetite such as basalt.

Paleomagnetism The study of Earth's ancient magnetic field is called **paleomagnetism** (*paleo* = ancient). The scientists who study paleomagnetism analyze magnetite particles in rocks to determine not only their north–south direction but also their angle relative to Earth's surface. The degree to which a magnetite particle points into Earth is called its **magnetic dip**, or **magnetic inclination**.

Magnetic dip is directly related to latitude. Figure 7b shows that a dip needle does not dip at all at Earth's magnetic equator. Instead, the needle lies horizontal to Earth's surface. At Earth's magnetic north pole, however, a dip needle points straight into the surface. A dip needle at Earth's south magnetic pole is also vertical to the surface, but it points out instead of in. Thus, magnetic dip increases with increasing latitude, from 0 degrees at the magnetic equator to 90 degrees at the magnetic poles. Because magnetic dip is retained in magnetically oriented rocks, measuring the dip angle reveals the latitude at which the rock initially formed. For instance, rocks found today near the Equator in southern India with a high magnetic dip angle suggest that they were not formed at that location but at a higher latitude. Done with care, paleomagnetism is an extremely powerful tool for interpreting where rocks first formed. Based on paleomagnetic studies, convincing arguments could finally be made that the continents had drifted relative to one another.

Apparent Polar Wandering When magnetic dip data for rocks on the continents were used to determine the apparent position of the magnetic north pole over time, it appeared that the magnetic pole was wandering. Figure 8a, for example, shows the **polar wandering curves** for North America and Eurasia. Both curves have a similar shape but, for all

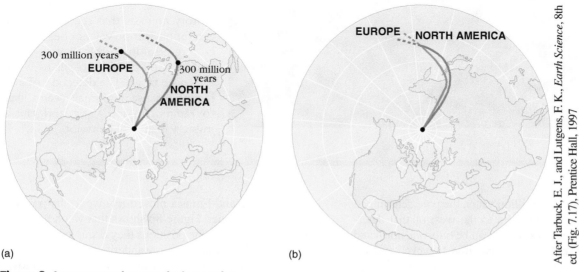

After Tarbuck, E. J., and Lutgens, F. K., *Earth Science*, 8th ed. (Fig. 7.17), Prentice Hall, 1997

(a) (b)

Figure 8 Apparent polar wandering paths.

(a) Apparent polar wandering paths for North America and Eurasia resulted in a dilemma because they were not in alignment. **(b)** The positions of the polar wandering paths when the landmasses are assembled.

BOX 1   Research Methods in Oceanography

DO SEA TURTLES (AND OTHER ANIMALS) USE EARTH'S MAGNETIC FIELD FOR NAVIGATION?

Sea turtles travel great distances across the open ocean so they can lay their eggs on the island where they themselves were hatched. How do they know where the island is located and how do they navigate at sea during their long voyage? Studies have indicated that during their migration, green sea turtles (*Chelonia mydas*) often travel in an essentially straight-line path to reach their destination. One hypothesis suggests that, like the Polynesian navigators, the sea turtles use wave direction to help them steer. However, sea turtles have been radio-tagged and tracked by satellites, which reveals that they continue along their straight-line path independent of wave direction.

Research in *magnetoreception*, the study of an animal's ability to sense magnetic fields, suggests that sea turtles use Earth's magnetic field for navigation. For instance, turtles can distinguish between different magnetic inclination angles, which in effect would allow them to sense latitude. Sea turtles can also distinguish magnetic field intensity, a rough indication of longitude. By sensing these two magnetic field properties, a sea turtle could determine its position at sea and relocate a tiny island thousands of kilometers away. Like any good navigator, sea turtles may also use other tools, such as olfactory (scent) clues, Sun angles, local landmarks, and oceanographic phenomena.

Other animals may also use magnetic properties to navigate. For example, some whales and dolphins may detect and follow the magnetic stripes on the sea floor during their movements, which may help to explain why whales sometimes beach themselves. In addition, certain bacteria use the magnetic mineral magnetite to align themselves parallel to Earth's magnetic field. Subsequently, magnetite has been found in many other organisms that have a "homing" ability, including tuna, salmon, honeybees, pigeons, turtles, and even humans. What has been unclear is how these animals detect—and potentially use—Earth's magnetic field. Recent findings by a research team studying rainbow trout (close relatives of salmon) have traced magnetically receptive fibers of nerves back to the brain, more closely linking a magnetic sense with an organism's sensory system.

Do humans have an innate ability to use Earth's magnetic field for navigation? Studies conducted on humans indicate that the majority of people can identify north after being blindfolded and disoriented. Interestingly, many people point *south* instead of north, but this direction is along the lines of magnetic force. Similarly, migratory animals that rely on magnetism for navigation will not be confused by a reversal in Earth's magnetic field and will still be able to get to where they need to go. The detection of a directional sense in animals seems likely to remain an intriguing and elusive mystery in animal behavior.

Green sea turtle.

rocks older than about 70 million years, the pole determined from North American rocks lies to the west of that determined from Eurasian rocks. There can be only one north and one south magnetic pole at any given time, however, and it is unlikely that their positions change with time. This discrepancy implies that magnetic poles remained stationary while North America and Eurasia moved relative to the pole and relative to each other. Figure 8b shows that when the continents are moved into the positions they occupied when they were part of Pangaea, the two wandering curves match up, providing strong evidence that the continents have moved throughout geologic time.

Magnetic Polarity Reversals Magnetic compasses on Earth today follow lines of magnetic force and point toward magnetic north. It turns out, however, that the **polarity** (the directional orientation of the magnetic field) has reversed itself periodically throughout geologic time. Thus, the north magnetic pole has become the south magnetic pole and vice versa. Figure 9 shows how rocks have recorded the switching of Earth's magnetic polarity through time.

The time during which a particular paleomagnetic condition existed ("normal" or "reversed") can be determined by radiometric dating. Over the last 76 million years, magnetic polarity has switched irregularly at the rate of about once or twice each million years. It takes a few thousand years for a change in polarity to occur and is identified in rock sequences by a gradual decrease in the intensity of the magnetic field of one polarity, followed by a gradual increase in the intensity of the magnetic field of opposite polarity. Earth's present magnetic field has been weakening during the past 150 years, which suggests Earth's current "normal" polarity might reverse itself within the next 2000 years.

Paleomagnetism and the Ocean Floor Paleomagnetism had certainly proved its usefulness on land, but, up until the mid-1950s, it had only been conducted on continental rocks. Would the ocean floor also show variations in magnetic polarity? To test this idea, the United States Coast and Geodetic Survey in conjunction with scientists from Scripps Institution of Oceanography undertook an extensive deep-water mapping program off Oregon and Washington in 1955. Using a sensitive instrument called a *magnetometer* (*magneto* = magnetism, *meter* = measure), which is towed behind a research ship, the scientists spent several weeks at sea moving back and forth in a regularly spaced pattern, measuring Earth's magnetic field and how it was affected by the magnetic properties of rocks on the ocean floor.

When the scientists analyzed their data, it revealed that the entire surveyed area had a pattern of north–south stripes in a surprisingly regular and alternating pattern of above-average and below-average magnetism. What was even more surprising was that the pattern appeared to be symmetrical with respect to a long mountain range that was fortuitously in the middle of their survey area.

Detailed paleomagnetism studies of this and other areas of the sea floor confirmed that a similar pattern of alternating stripes of above-average and below-average magnetism. These stripes are called **magnetic anomalies** (*a* = without, *nomo* = law; an anomaly is a departure from normal conditions). The ocean floor had embedded in it a regular pattern of alternating magnetic stripes unlike anywhere on land. Researchers had a difficult time explaining why the ocean floor had such a regular pattern of magnetic anomalies. Nor could they explain how the sequence on one side of the underwater mountain range matched the sequence on the opposite side—in essence, they were a mirror image of each other. To understand how this pattern could have formed, more information about ocean floor features and their origin was needed.

Figure 9 Paleomagnetism preserved in rocks.

The switching of Earth's magnetic polarity through time is preserved in rocks like these lava flows.

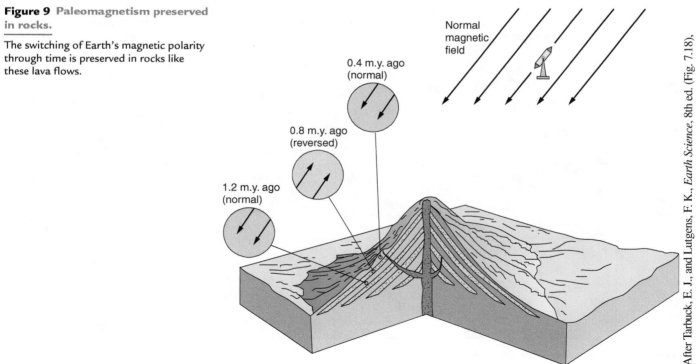

0.4 m.y. ago
(normal)

0.8 m.y. ago
(reversed)

1.2 m.y. ago
(normal)

Normal
magnetic
field

After Tarbuck, E. J., and Lutgens, F. K., *Earth Science*, 8th ed. (Fig. 7.18), Prentice Hall, 1997

Sea Floor Spreading and Features of the Ocean Basins

Geologist *Harry Hess* (1906–1969), when he was a U.S. Navy captain in World War II, developed the habit of leaving his depth recorder on at all times while his ship was traveling at sea. After the war, compilation of these and many other depth records showed extensive mountain ridges near the centers of ocean basins and extremely deep, narrow trenches at the edges of ocean basins. In 1960, Hess published the idea of **sea floor spreading** with **convection** (*con* = with, *vect* = carried) **cells** as the driving mechanism (Figure 10). He suggested that new ocean crust was created at the ridges, split apart, moved away from the ridges, and later disappeared back into the deep Earth at trenches. Mindful of the resistance of North American scientists to the idea of continental drift, Hess referred to his own work as "geopoetry."

As it turns out, Hess's initial ideas about sea floor spreading have been confirmed. The **mid-ocean ridge** (Figure 10) is a continuous underwater mountain range that winds through every ocean basin in the world and resembles the seam on a baseball. It is entirely volcanic in origin, wraps one-and-a-half times around the globe, and rises over 2.5 kilometers (1.5 miles) above the surrounding deep ocean floor. It even rises above sea level in places such as Iceland. New ocean floor forms at the crest, or axis, of the mid-ocean ridge. By the process of sea-floor spreading, new ocean floor is split in two and carried away from the axis, replaced by the upwelling of volcanic material that fills the void with new strips of sea floor. Sea floor spreading occurs along the axis of the mid-ocean ridge, which is

referred to as a **spreading center**. One way to think of the mid-ocean ridge is as a zipper that is being pulled apart. Thus, Earth's zipper (the mid-ocean ridge) is becoming unzipped!

At the same time, ocean floor is being destroyed at **ocean trenches**. Trenches are the deepest parts of the ocean floor and resemble a narrow crease or trough (Figure 10). Some of the largest earthquakes in the world occur near these trenches, caused by a lithospheric plate that bends downward and slowly plunges back into Earth's interior. This process is called **subduction** (*sub* = under, *duct* = lead), and the sloping area from the trench along the downward plate is called a **subduction zone**.

In 1963, geologists **Fredrick Vine** and **Drummond Matthews** of Cambridge University combined the seemingly unrelated pattern of magnetic sea floor stripes with the process of sea floor spreading to explain the perplexing pattern of alternating and symmetric stripes on the sea floor (Figure 11). They proposed that the above-average magnetic stripes represented "normal" polarity sea floor rocks that enhanced Earth's current normal magnetic polarity and the below-average magnetic stripes represented the presence of "reverse" polarity sea floor rocks that subtracted from Earth's current polarity. The pattern could be created when newly formed rocks at the mid-ocean ridge are magnetized with whichever polarity exists on Earth during their formation. As those rocks are slowly moved away from the crest of the mid-ocean ridge, the periodic switches of Earth's magnetic polarity are recorded in subsequent rock. The result is an alternating pattern of magnetic polarity stripes that are symmetric with respect to the mid-ocean ridge.

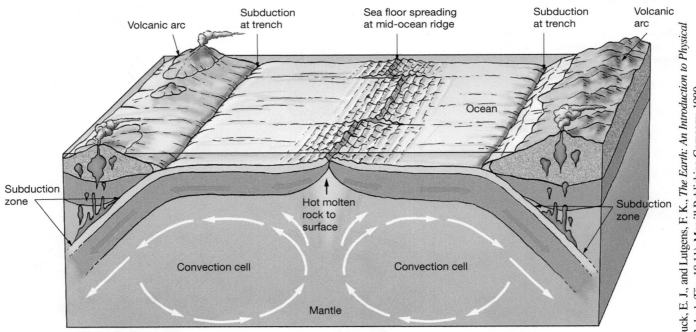

Figure 10 Processes of plate tectonics.

Hot molten rock comes to the surface at the mid-ocean ridge and moves outward by the process of sea floor spreading. Eventually, sea floor is destroyed at the trenches, where the process of subduction occurs. Convection of material in the mantle produces convection cells.

After Tarbuck, E. J., and Lutgens, F. K., *The Earth: An Introduction to Physical Geology*, 3rd ed. (Fig. 18.11), Merrill Publishing Company, 1990

The pattern of alternating reversals of Earth's magnetic field as recorded in the sea floor was the most convincing piece of evidence set forth to support the concept of sea floor spreading—and, as a result, continental drift. However, the continents weren't plowing through the ocean basins as Wegener had envisioned. Instead, the ocean floor was a conveyer belt that was being continuously formed at the mid-ocean ridge and destroyed at the trenches, with the continents just passively riding along on the conveyer. By the late 1960s, most geologists had changed their stand on continental drift in light of this new evidence.

> The plate tectonic model states that new sea floor is created at the mid-ocean ridge where it moves outward by the process of sea floor spreading and is destroyed by subduction into ocean trenches.

Other Evidence from the Ocean Basins

Even though the tide of scientific opinion had indeed switched to favor a mobile Earth, additional evidence from the ocean floor would further support the ideas of continental drift and sea floor spreading.

Age of the Ocean Floor In the late 1960s, an ambitious deep-sea drilling program was initiated to test the existence of sea floor spreading. One of the program's primary missions was to drill into and collect ocean floor rocks for radiometric age dating. If sea floor spreading does indeed occur, then the youngest sea floor rocks would be atop the mid-ocean ridge and the ages of rocks would increase on either side of the ridge in a symmetric pattern.

The map in Figure 12, showing the age of the ocean floor beneath deep-sea deposits, is based on the pattern of magnetic stripes verified with thousands of radiometrically age dated samples. It shows the ocean floor is youngest along the mid-ocean ridge, where new ocean floor is created, and the age of rocks increases with increasing distance in either direction away from the axis of the ridge. The symmetric pattern of ocean floor ages confirms that the process of sea floor spreading must indeed be occurring.

The Atlantic Ocean has the simplest and most symmetric pattern of age distribution in Figure 12. The pattern results from the newly formed Mid-Atlantic Ridge that rifted Pangaea apart. The Pacific Ocean has the least symmetric pattern because many subduction zones sur-

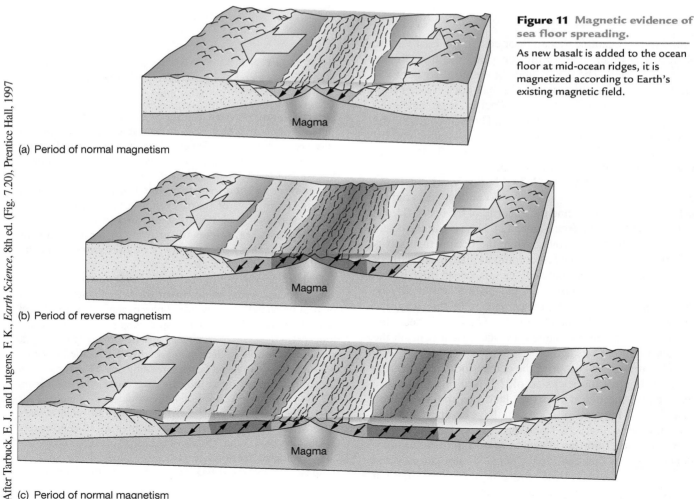

Figure 11 Magnetic evidence of sea floor spreading.

As new basalt is added to the ocean floor at mid-ocean ridges, it is magnetized according to Earth's existing magnetic field.

(a) Period of normal magnetism

(b) Period of reverse magnetism

(c) Period of normal magnetism

After Tarbuck, E. J., and Lutgens, F. K., *Earth Science*, 8th ed. (Fig. 7.20), Prentice Hall, 1997

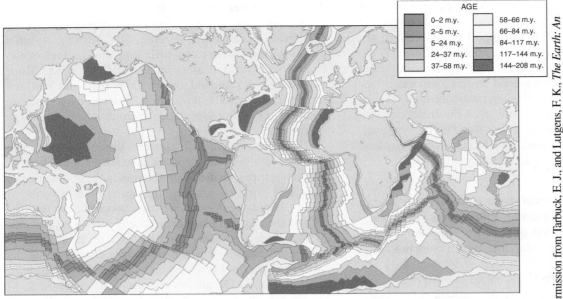

Figure 12 Age of the ocean crust beneath deep-sea deposits.

The youngest rocks (*bright red areas*) are found along the mid-ocean ridge. Farther away from the mid-ocean ridge, the rocks increase linearly in age in either direction. Age shown in millions of years before present.

Reprinted by permission from Tarbuck, E. J., and Lutgens, F. K., *The Earth: An Introduction to Physical Geology*, 3rd ed. (Fig. 19.16), Merrill Publishing Company, 1990. After *The Bedrock Geology of the World*, by R. L. Larson et al., Copyright © 1985 by W. H. Freeman

round it. For example, ocean floor east of the East Pacific Rise that is older than 40 million years old has already been subducted. The ocean floor in the northwestern Pacific, about 180 million years old, has not yet been subducted. A portion of the East Pacific Rise has even disappeared under North America. The age bands in the Pacific Ocean are wider than those in the Atlantic and Indian Oceans, which suggests the rate of sea floor spreading is greatest in the Pacific Ocean.

Recall that the ocean is at least 4 billion years old. However, the oldest ocean floor is only 180 million years old (or 0.18 billion years old), and the majority of the ocean floor is not even half that old (see Figure 12). How could the ocean floor be so incredibly young while the oceans themselves are so phenomenally old? According to plate tectonic theory, new ocean floor is created at the mid-ocean ridge by sea floor spreading and moves off the ridge to eventually be subducted and remelted in the mantle. In this way, the ocean floor keeps regenerating itself. The floor beneath the oceans today is not the same one that existed beneath the oceans 4 billion years ago.

If the rocks that comprise the ocean floor are so young, why are continental rocks so old? Based on radiometric age dating, the oldest rocks on land are about 4 billion years old. Many other continental rocks approach this age, implying that the same processes that constantly renew the sea floor do not operate on land. Rather, evidence suggests that continental rocks do not get recycled by the process of sea floor spreading and thus remain at Earth's surface for long periods of time.

STUDENTS SOMETIMES ASK...
How fast do plates move, and have they always moved at the same rate?

Currently, plates move an average of 2 to 12 centimeters (1 to 5 inches) per year, which is about as fast as a person's fingernails grow. A person's fingernail growth is dependent on many factors, including heredity, gender, diet, and amount of exercise, but averages about 8 centimeters (3 inches) per year. This may not sound very fast, but the plates have been moving for millions of years. Even an object moving slowly will eventually travel a great distance over a very long time. For instance, fingernails growing at a rate of 8 centimeters (3 inches) per year for 1 million years would be 80 kilometers (50 miles) long!

Evidence shows the plates were moving faster millions of years ago. Geologists can determine the rate of plate motion in the past by analyzing the width of new oceanic crust produced by sea floor spreading since fast spreading produces more sea floor rock. (Using this relationship and by looking at Figure 12, you should be able to determine whether the Pacific Ocean or the Atlantic Ocean has a faster spreading rate.) Recent studies using this same technique indicate that about 50 million years ago, India attained a speed of 19 centimeters (7.5 inches) per year. Other research indicates that about 530 million years ago, plate motions may have been as high as 30 centimeters (1 foot) per year! What caused these rapid bursts of plate motion? Geologists are not sure why plates moved more rapidly in the past, but increased heat release from Earth's interior is a likely mechanism.

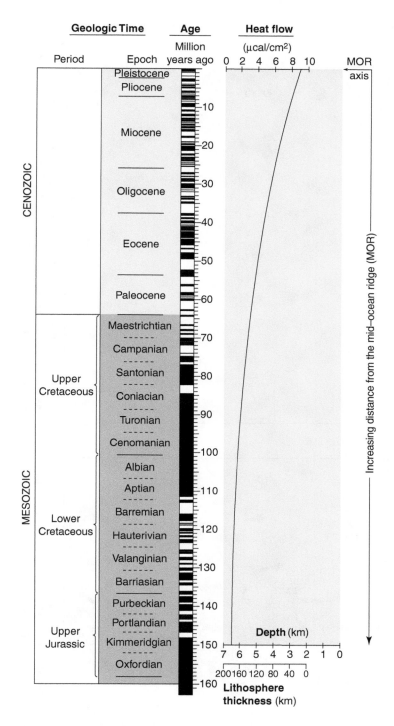

Geologic Time | Age | Heat flow

Period | Epoch | Million years ago | (μcal/cm²)

Figure 13 Relationships relative to the mid-ocean ridge.

From left, geologic time scale; magnetic polarity reversal scale (*black bands* = normal polarity; *white bands* = reversed polarity); geologic age in millions of years before present; and graph showing decreasing heat flow, increasing ocean depth, and increasing lithosphere thickness with increasing distance from the mid-ocean ridge.

as little as one-tenth the average. Increased heat flow at the mid-ocean ridge and decreased heat flow at subduction zones is what would be expected based on thin crust at the mid-ocean ridge and a double thickness of crust at the trenches (see Figure 10).

A summary of various physical relationships relative to the mid-ocean ridge is shown in Table 1. Moreover, many of these relationships exist because as sea floor spreading brings new crustal material to the surface along the mid-ocean ridge, it cools; as it cools, it contracts, and as it contracts, it subsides. Figure 13 is a graphical representation of many of these same relationships but also shows specific geologic ages and the pattern of magnetic polarity reversals through time.

Worldwide Earthquakes

Earthquakes are sudden releases of energy caused by fault movement or volcanic eruptions. The map in Figure 14a shows that most large earthquakes occur along ocean trenches, reflecting the energy released during subduction. Other earthquakes occur along the mid-ocean ridge, reflecting the energy released during sea floor spreading. Still others occur along major faults in the sea floor and on land, reflecting the energy released when moving plates contact other plates along their edges. The two maps in Figure 14 show that the distribution of worldwide earthquakes closely matches the locations of plate boundaries.

Heat Flow   The heat from Earth's interior is released to the surface as **heat flow**. Current models indicate this heat moves to the surface with magma in convective motion. Most of the heat is carried to regions of the mid-ocean ridge spreading centers (see Figure 10). Cooler portions of the mantle descend in deep-sea trenches to complete each circular-moving convection cell.

Heat flow measurements show the amount of heat flowing to the surface along the mid-ocean ridge can be up to eight times greater than the average amount flowing to other parts of Earth's crust. Additionally, heat flow at deep-sea trenches, where ocean floor is subducted, can be

183

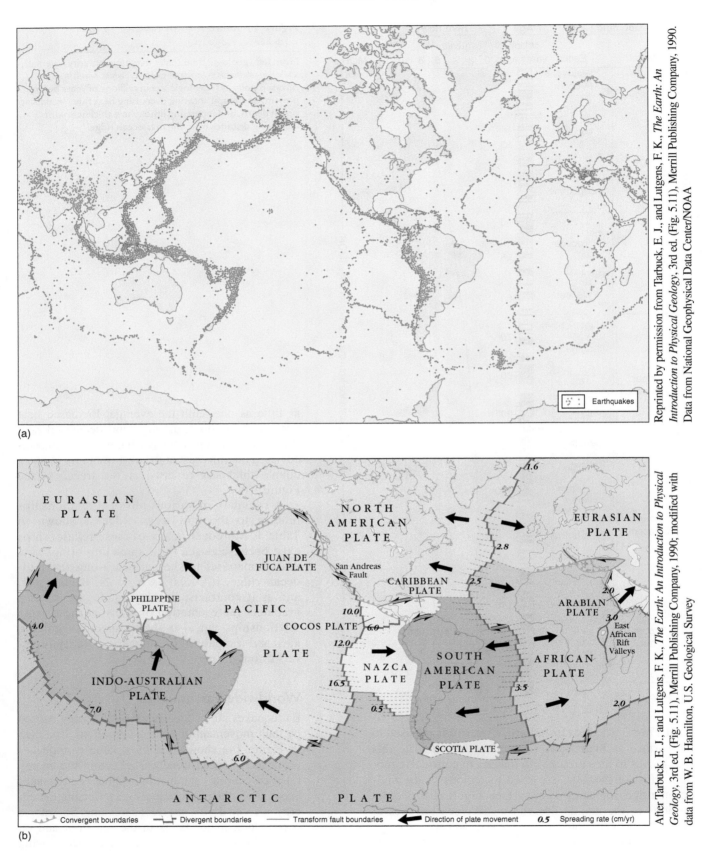

(a)

Reprinted by permission from Tarbuck, E. J., and Lutgens, F. K., *The Earth: An Introduction to Physical Geology*, 3rd ed. (Fig. 5.11), Merrill Publishing Company, 1990. Data from National Geophysical Data Center/NOAA

EURASIAN PLATE

NORTH AMERICAN PLATE

EURASIAN PLATE

JUAN DE FUCA PLATE

San Andreas Fault

CARIBBEAN PLATE

ARABIAN PLATE

PHILIPPINE PLATE

PACIFIC PLATE

COCOS PLATE

East African Rift Valleys

INDO-AUSTRALIAN PLATE

NAZCA PLATE

SOUTH AMERICAN PLATE

AFRICAN PLATE

SCOTIA PLATE

ANTARCTIC PLATE

1.6 *2.8* *2.5* *2.0* *3.0* *10.0* *6.0* *12.0* *16.5* *0.5* *3.5* *2.0* *4.0* *7.0* *6.0*

⤳ Convergent boundaries   ⊥ Divergent boundaries   Transform fault boundaries   ← Direction of plate movement   *0.5* Spreading rate (cm/yr)

(b)

After Tarbuck, E. J., and Lutgens, F. K., *The Earth: An Introduction to Physical Geology*, 3rd ed. (Fig. 5.11), Merrill Publishing Company, 1990; modified with data from W. B. Hamilton, U.S. Geological Survey

Figure 14 Earthquakes and lithospheric plates.

(a) Distribution of earthquakes with magnitudes equal to or greater than $M_w = 5.0$ for the period 1980–1990. **(b)** Plate boundaries define the major lithospheric plates (*shaded*), with arrows indicating the direction of motion and numbers representing the rate of motion in centimeters per year. Notice how closely the pattern of major earthquakes follows plate boundaries.

TABLE 1 **Relationships relative to increasing distance in either direction from the axis of a mid-ocean ridge.**

Relationship	Reason
1. Volcanic activity decreases	Magma chambers are concentrated only along the crest of the mid-ocean ridge
2. The age of ocean crust increases	New ocean floor is created at the mid-ocean ridge
3. The thickness of sea floor deposits increases	Older ocean floor has more time to accumulate a thicker deposit of debris due to settling
4. The thickness of the lithospheric plate increases	As plates move away from the spreading center, they are cooler and gain thickness as material beneath the lithosphere attaches to the bottom of the plate
5. Heat flow decreases	As the thickness of the lithospheric plate increases (see Relationship 3), less heat can escape because conduction heat transfer through the lithosphere is poor
6. Water depth increases	The mid-ocean ridge is a topographically high feature, and as plates move away from there, they move into deeper water because plates undergo thermal contraction and isostatic adjustment downward

Evidence for plate tectonics includes many types of information from land and the sea floor, including the symmetric pattern of magnetic stripes relative to the mid-ocean ridge.

The Acceptance of a Theory

The accumulation of these and many other lines of evidence in support of moving continents has convinced scientists of the validity of continental drift. Since the late 1960s, the concepts of continental drift and sea floor spreading have been united into a much more encompassing theory known as plate tectonics, which describes the movement of the outermost portion of Earth and the resulting creating of continental and sea floor features.

Although several mechanisms have been proposed for the force or forces responsible for driving this motion, none of them are able to explain all aspects of plate motion. Nevertheless, it is clear that the unequal distribution of heat within Earth is the underlying driving force for this movement. The various properties of Earth's internal layers can help account for the movement of plates.

Earth Structure

Earth's internal structure consists of a series of nested spheres (similar to the layers of an onion) that differ in density. Let's examine these layers and discover their importance to plate tectonic processes.

Chemical Composition versus Physical Properties

Earth is a layered sphere based on density, with the highest-density material found near the center of Earth and the lowest-density material located near the surface. The cross-sectional view of Earth in Figure 15 shows that Earth's inner structure can be subdivided according to its chemical composition (the chemical makeup of Earth materials) or its physical properties (how the rocks respond to increased temperature and pressure at depth).

Chemical Composition Based on chemical composition, Earth consists of three layers: the **core**, the **mantle**, and the **crust** (Figure 15). If Earth were an apple, then the crust would be its thin skin. It extends from the surface to an average depth of 30 kilometers (20 miles). The crust is composed of relatively low-density rock, consisting mostly of various *silicate minerals* (common rock-forming minerals with silicon and oxygen that form silicate tetrahedra). There are two types of crust, oceanic and continental, which will be discussed in the next section.

Immediately below the crust is the mantle. It occupies the largest volume of the three layers and extends to a depth of 2900 kilometers (1800 miles). The mantle is composed of relatively high-density iron and magnesium silicate rock.

Beneath the mantle is the core. It forms a large mass from a depth of 2900 kilometers (1800 miles) to the center of Earth at 6370 kilometers (3960 miles). The core is composed of even higher-density metal (mostly iron and nickel).

Physical Properties Based on physical properties, Earth is composed of five layers: the **inner core**, the **outer core**, the **mesosphere** (*mesos* = middle, *sphere* = ball), the **asthenosphere** (*asthenos* = weak, *sphere* = ball), and, as previously mentioned, the lithosphere (Figure 15). The lithosphere is Earth's cool, rigid, outermost layer. It extends from the surface to an average depth of about 100 kilometers (62 miles) and includes the crust plus the topmost portion of the mantle. The lithosphere is *brittle* (*brytten* = to shatter), meaning that it will fracture when force is applied to it. The plates involved in plate tectonic motion are the plates of the lithosphere.

Figure 15 Comparison of Earth's chemical composition and physical properties.

A cross-sectional view of Earth with Earth's layers classified by chemical composition shown along the left side of the diagram. For comparison, Earth's layers classified by physical properties are shown along the right side of the diagram.

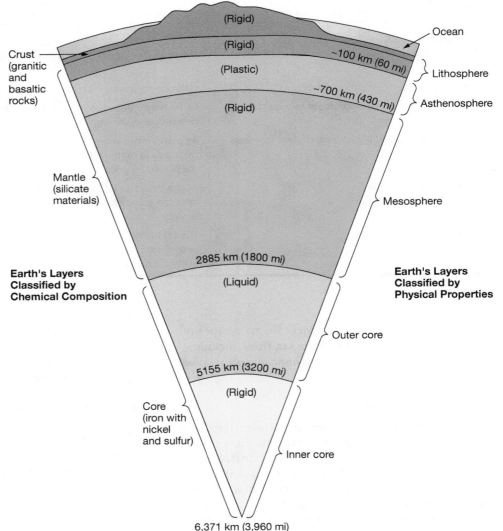

Crust (granitic and basaltic rocks)

Mantle (silicate materials)

Core (iron with nickel and sulfur)

Earth's Layers Classified by Chemical Composition

(Rigid)

(Rigid)

(Plastic)

(Rigid)

~100 km (60 mi)

~700 km (430 mi)

2885 km (1800 mi)

(Liquid)

5155 km (3200 mi)

(Rigid)

6,371 km (3,960 mi)

Ocean

Lithosphere

Asthenosphere

Mesosphere

Outer core

Inner core

Earth's Layers Classified by Physical Properties

Beneath the lithosphere is the asthenosphere. The asthenosphere is *plastic* (*plasticus* = to mold), meaning it will flow when a gradual force is applied to it. It extends from about 100 kilometers (62 miles) to 700 kilometers (430 miles) below the surface, which is the base of the upper mantle. At these depths, it is hot enough to partially melt portions of most rocks.

Beneath the asthenosphere is the mesosphere. The mesosphere extends to a depth of 2900 kilometers (1800 miles), which corresponds to the middle and lower mantle. Although the asthenosphere deforms plastically, the meso-sphere is rigid due to increased pressure at these depths.

Beneath the mesosphere is the core. The core consists of the outer core, which is liquid and capable of flowing; and the inner core, which is rigid and does not flow. Again, the increased pressure at the center of Earth keeps the inner core from flowing.

Knowledge of Earth's Inner Structure How have scientists determined the inner structure of Earth? Remarkably, the deepest well in the world, which was drilled in the Kola Peninsula of Russia, reached a depth of 12,266 meters (40,478 feet, or nearly 8 miles) in 1992 but still never came close to penetrating the crust. Instead of directly sampling the deep Earth, Earth scientists have had to rely on *indirect* methods to understand what lies deep below the surface. For example, determining the gravitational attraction that Earth exerts on other bodies of the solar system gives scientists information about the density of deep Earth layers.

Another powerful indirect sampling method is used by *seismologists* (*seismo* = earthquake, *ologist* = one who studies), who analyze the pattern of seismic waves bouncing around within Earth (similar to listening through a doctor's stethoscope) to decipher the chemical composition and physical properties of Earth's internal layers. All earthquakes generate low-frequency *seismic waves*, which travel at different speeds dependant on the density of the materials they pass through. After an earthquake is generated, a host of waves travels outward from the earthquake's source at different speeds. Two of the most important of these waves for determining Earth structure are the P and S waves.

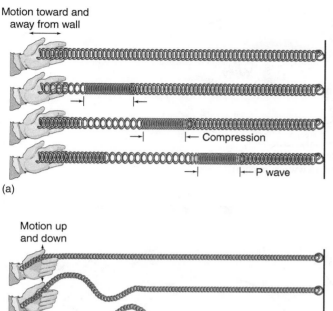

Motion toward and
away from wall

← Compression

→| |← P wave

(a)

Motion up
and down

S wave

(b)

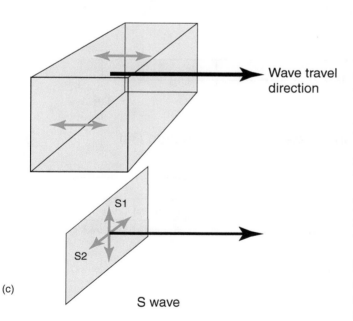

P wave

Wave travel
direction

S1

S2

(c)

S wave

Figure 16 P and S waves.

(a) P waves are created when a spring is compressed or stretched, causing back-and-forth compression and extension along the length of the spring. (b) S waves are created when a spring is shaken up and down (S1) [or back and forth (S2)], causing side-to-side shearing of the spring. (c) Taken together, P, S1, and S2 waves record motion of materials in three dimensions.

The *P* (primary) *wave* is a compressional wave that compresses and extends the material through which it travels. A spring attached to a wall, for example, exhibits this type of phenomenon when you pull it, which causes extension, or push it, which causes compression (Figure 16a). The *S* (secondary) *wave* is a shear wave that creates transverse motions like those created by moving the end of the spring up and down or back and forth (Figure 16b). In fact, there are two S waves, called S1 and S2, that move at right angles to each other. At seismic listening stations, speedy P waves arrive first, followed by more slowly moving S waves (which is how they received their names). Together, P and S waves create motion in three dimensions (Figure 16c).

Solid rocks transmit P and S waves, but liquids transmit only P waves because liquids cannot be sheared. The patterns of S wave arrivals at Earth's surface are a major line of evidence that helps Earth scientists determine that the outer core of Earth must be liquid (see Figure 15).

The wealth of seismic information has recently allowed seismologists to create three-dimensional maps of Earth that can be viewed as vertical slices (similar to CAT-scan images used in medical applications). This technique is called *seismic tomography tomos =* (section, *graphy* = the name of a descriptive science). Based on small variations in seismic shear wave velocities, the slices display temperature differences within Earth's mantle (Figure 17). These images show hot plumes of magma rising to the surface as well as the colder slabs of lithosphere descending during subduction, adding to the evidence in support of mantle convection.

Near the Surface

The top portion of Figure 18 shows an enlargement of Earth's layers closest to the surface.

Lithosphere The lithosphere is a relatively cool, rigid shell that includes all of the crust and the topmost part of the mantle. In essence, the topmost part of the mantle is attached to the crust and the two act as a single unit, approximately 100 kilometers (62 miles) thick. The expanded view in Figure 18 shows that the crust portion of the lithosphere is further subdivided into oceanic crust and continental crust, which are compared in Table 2.

Oceanic crust is composed of the igneous rock **basalt**, which is dark-colored and has a relatively high density of about 3.0 grams per cubic centimeter.[4] The average thickness of the oceanic crust is only about 8 kilometers (5 miles). Basalt originates as molten magma beneath Earth's crust. This magma comes to the surface mostly along the mid-ocean ridge, where it cools and hardens to form new oceanic crust.

---

[4]As a comparison, water has a density of 1.0 grams per cubic centimeter. Thus, basalt, which has a density of 3.0 grams per cubic centimeter, is three times the density of water.

Figure 17 Shear wave tomography reveals mantle structure.

(a) View of Earth's mantle at 1500 kilometers (932 miles) depth showing hot, low-velocity (*red*) and cold, high-velocity (*blue*) regions. (b) Views of two slices of the mantle beneath the eastern (*upper*) and western (*lower*) Pacific Ocean, with various features labeled.

Courtesy of Bunge, H. Reprinted with permission from *Nature* 397:571b, 203 © 1999, Macmillan Magazines Ltd. (www.nature.com)

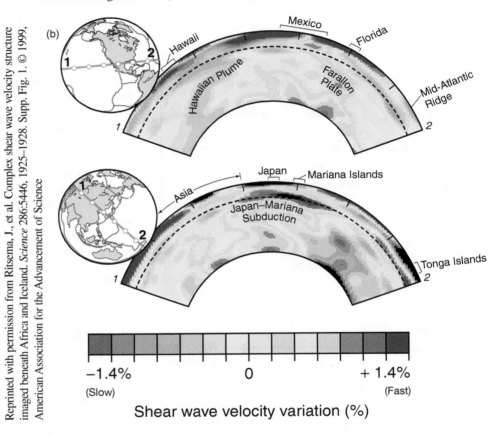

Reprinted with permission from Ritsema, J., et al. Complex shear wave velocity structure imaged beneath Africa and Iceland. *Science* 286:5446, 1925–1928. Supp. Fig. 1. © 1999, American Association for the Advancement of Science

−1.4%
(Slow)

0

+ 1.4%
(Fast)

Shear wave velocity variation (%)

TABLE 2 **Comparing oceanic and continental crust.**

	Oceanic Crust	Continental Crust
Main rock type	Basalt (dark-colored igneous rock)	Granite (light-colored igneous rock)
Density (grams per cubic centimeter)	3.0	2.7
Average thickness	8 kilometers (5 miles)	35 kilometers (22 miles)

Continental crust is composed mostly of a lower-density and lighter-colored igneous rock **granite**.[5] It has a density of about 2.7 grams per cubic centimeter. The average thickness of the continental crust is about 35 kilometers (22 miles) but may reach a maximum of 60 kilometers (37 miles) beneath the highest mountain ranges. Most granite originates beneath the surface as molten magma that cools and hardens within Earth's crust. No matter which type of crust is at the surface, it is all part of the lithosphere.

---

[5]At the surface, continental crust is often covered by a relatively thin layer of surface sediments. Below these, granite can be found.

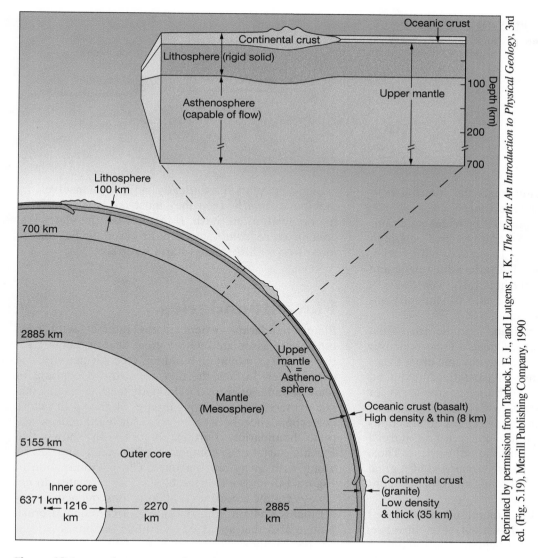

Figure 18 Internal structure of Earth.

Enlargement (*top*) shows that the rigid lithosphere includes the crust (either continental or oceanic) plus the topmost part of the mantle to about 100 kilometers (60 miles) depth. Beneath the lithosphere, the plastic asthenosphere extends to a depth of 700 kilometers (430 miles).

Asthenosphere The asthenosphere is a relatively hot, plastic region beneath the lithosphere. It extends from the base of the lithosphere to a depth of about 700 kilometers (430 miles) and is entirely contained within the upper mantle. The asthenosphere can deform without fracturing if a force is applied slowly. It has the ability to flow but has high **viscosity** (*viscos* = sticky). Viscosity is a measure of a substance's resistance to flow.[6] Studies indicate that the high-viscosity asthenosphere is flowing slowly through time, which has important implications in plate tectonic processes.

> Earth has differences in composition and physical properties that create layers such as the brittle lithosphere and the plastic asthenosphere, which is capable of flowing slowly over time.

Isostatic Adjustment

Isostatic (*iso* = equal, *stasis* = standing) **adjustment**— the vertical movement of crust—is the result of the buoyancy of Earth's lithosphere as it floats on the denser, plastic-like asthenosphere below. Isostatic adjustment of Earth's crust accounts for the difference in heights

---

[6]Substances that have high viscosity (a high resistance to flow) include toothpaste, honey, tar, and silly putty; a common substance that has low viscosity is water. A substance's viscosity often changes with temperature. For instance, as honey is heated, it flows more easily.

Figure 19 A container ship experiences isostatic adjustment.

A ship will ride higher in water when it is empty and will ride lower in water when it is loaded with cargo, illustrating the principle of isostatic adjustment.

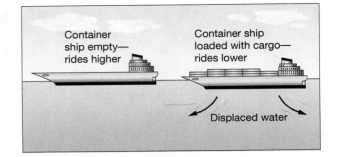

of the continental and oceanic crusts and contributes to the mechanism of global plate tectonics.

The container ship in Figure 19 provides an example of isostatic adjustment. An empty ship floats high in the water. Once the ship is loaded with cargo, though, the ship undergoes isostatic adjustment and floats lower in the water (but hopefully won't sink!). When the cargo is unloaded, the ship isostatically adjusts itself and floats higher again.

Similarly, both continental and oceanic crust float on the denser mantle beneath. Oceanic crust is denser than continental crust, however, so oceanic crust floats lower in the mantle because of isostatic adjustment. Oceanic crust is also thin, which creates low areas for the oceans to occupy. Areas where the continental crust is thickest (in large mountain ranges on the continents) float higher than continental crust of normal thickness, also because of isostatic adjustment. Thus, tall mountain ranges on Earth are composed of a great thickness of crustal material that in essence keeps them buoyed up.

Areas that are exposed to an increased or decreased load experience isostatic adjustment. For instance, during the most recent Ice Age (which occurred during the Pleistocene Epoch between 2 million and 10,000 years ago), massive ice sheets covered far northern regions such as Scandinavia and northern Canada. The additional weight of ice several kilometers thick caused these areas to isostatically adjust themselves lower in the mantle. Since the end of the Ice Age, the reduced load on these areas caused by the melting of ice caused these areas to rise and experience **isostatic rebound**, which continues today. The rate at which isostatic rebound occurs gives scientists important information about the properties of the upper mantle.

Isostatic adjustment also affects some areas of Earth that have higher elevations than would normally be expected, such as eastern Africa and the Colorado Plateau of the southwestern United States. In these locations, hot, low-density mantle material provides additional buoyancy that is usually associated with deep roots of continental crust and causes them to rise to anomalously high levels.

Further, isostatic adjustment provides additional evidence for the movement of Earth's tectonic plates. Because continents isostatically adjust themselves by moving *vertically*, then they must not be firmly fixed in one position on Earth. If this is true, the plates that contain these continents should certainly be able to move *horizontally* across Earth's surface.

Plate Boundaries

Plate boundaries—where plates interact with each other—are associated with a great deal of tectonic activity, such as mountain building, volcanic activity, and earthquakes. In fact, the first clues to the locations of plate boundaries were the dramatic tectonic events that occur there. For example, Figure 14 shows the close correspondence between worldwide earthquakes and plate boundaries. Further, Figure 14b shows that Earth's surface is composed of seven major plates along with many smaller ones. Close examination of Figure 14b shows that the boundaries of plates do not always follow coastlines and, as a consequence, nearly all plates contain both oceanic and continental crust. Notice also that about 90% of plate boundaries occur on the sea floor.

There are three types of plate boundaries, as shown in Figure 20. **Divergent** (*di* = apart, *vergere* = to incline) **boundaries** are found along oceanic ridges where new lithosphere is being added. **Convergent** (*con* = together, *vergere* = to incline) **boundaries** are found where plates are moving together and one plate subducts beneath the other. **Transform** (*trans* = across, *form* = shape) **boundaries** are found where lithospheric plates slowly grind past one another. Table 3 summarizes characteristics, tectonic processes, and examples of these plate boundaries.

Divergent Boundaries

Divergent plate boundaries occur where two plates move apart, such as along the crest of the mid-ocean ridge where sea floor spreading creates new oceanic lithosphere (Figure 21). A common feature along the mid-ocean ridge is a central downdropped linear **rift valley** (Figure 22). Pull-apart faults located along the central rift valley show that the plates are being *continuously*

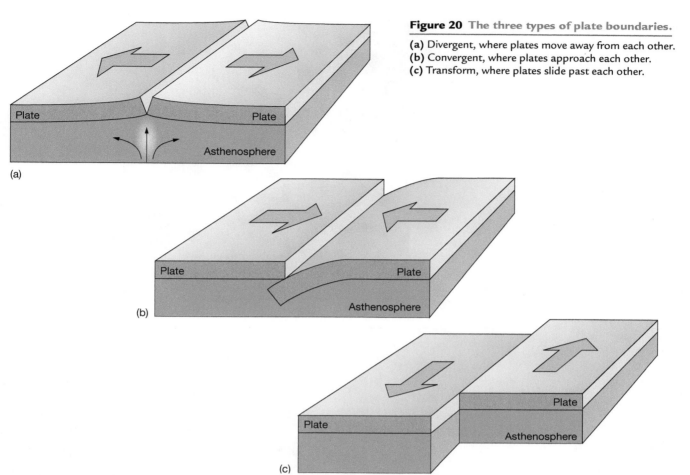

Figure 20 The three types of plate boundaries.

(a) Divergent, where plates move away from each other.
(b) Convergent, where plates approach each other.
(c) Transform, where plates slide past each other.

Reprinted by permission from Tarbuck, E. J., and Lutgens, F. K., *The Earth: An Introduction to Physical Geology*, 3rd ed. (Fig. 6.7), Merrill Publishing Company, 1990

TABLE 3 **Characteristics, tectonic processes, and examples of plate boundaries.**

Plate boundary	Plate movement	Crust type(s)	Sea floor created or destroyed?	Tectonic process	Geographic examples
Divergent plate boundaries	Apart ← →	Ocean–ocean	New sea floor created	Sea floor spreading	Mid-Atlantic Ridge, East Pacific Rise
		Continent–continent	As continent splits apart, new sea floor created	Continental rifting	East Africa Rift Valleys, Red Sea, Gulf of California
Convergent plate boundaries	Together → ←	Ocean–continent	Old sea floor destroyed	Subduction	Andes Mountains, Cascade Mountains
		Ocean–ocean	Old sea floor destroyed	Subduction	Aleutian Islands, Mariana Islands
		Continent–continent	N/A	Collision	Himalaya Mountains, Alps
Transform plate boundaries	Past each other → ←	Oceanic	Sea floor neither created nor destroyed	Transform faulting	Mendocino fault, Eltanin fault (between mid-ocean ridges)
		Continental	Sea floor neither created nor destroyed	Transform faulting	San Andreas fault, Alpine fault (New Zealand)

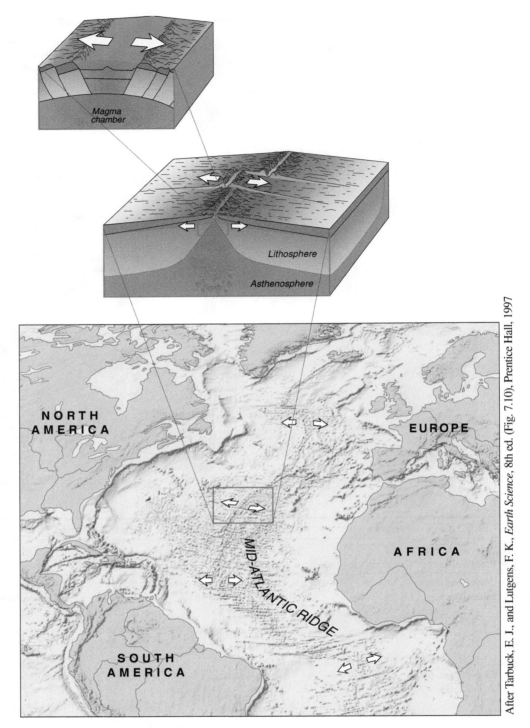

Figure 21 Divergent boundary at the Mid-Atlantic Ridge.

Most divergent plate boundaries occur along the crest of the mid-ocean ridge, where sea floor spreading creates new oceanic lithosphere.

After Tarbuck, E. J., and Lutgens, F. K., *Earth Science*, 8th ed. (Fig. 7.10), Prentice Hall, 1997

pulled apart rather than being pushed apart by the upwelling of material beneath the mid-ocean ridge. Upwelling of magma beneath the mid-ocean ridge is simply filling in the void left by the separating plates of lithosphere. In the process, sea floor spreading produces about 20 cubic kilometers (4.8 cubic miles) of new ocean crust worldwide each year.

Studies of the geometry of *magma chambers* along mid-ocean ridges indicate that magma rises to the surface in discrete blobs at intervals along the mid-ocean ridge

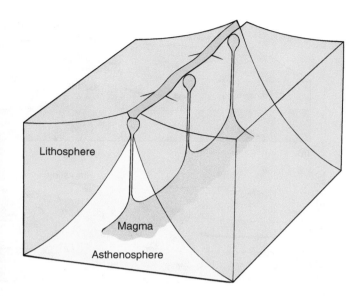

Figure 23 Segmentation of magma chambers along the mid-ocean ridge.

Beneath the mid-ocean ridge, heat-bearing asthenosphere (*yellow*) rises between separating lithospheric plates (*green*). A zone of partially molten asthenosphere (*orange*) supplies blobs of low-density magma as shallow magma chambers along the ridge axis.

Courtesy of Patricia Deen, Palomar College

Figure 22 Rift valley on Iceland.

View along a rift valley looking south from Laki volcano in Iceland, which sits atop the Mid-Atlantic Ridge. Note bus to the left of the rift valley in the middle of the picture for scale.

axis (Figure 23). These shallow magma chambers supply molten material to the central rift valley as sea-floor spreading occurs.

Figure 24 shows how the development of a mid-ocean ridge creates an ocean basin. Initially, molten material rises to the surface, causing upwarping and thinning of the crust. Volcanic activity produces vast quantities of high-density basaltic rock. As the plates begin to move apart, a linear rift valley is formed and volcanism continues. Further **rifting** of the land and more spreading cause the area to drop below sea level. When this occurs, the rift valley eventually floods with seawater and a young linear sea is formed. After millions of years of sea floor spreading, a full-fledged ocean basin is created with a mid-ocean ridge in the middle.

Two different stages of ocean basin development are shown in the map of East Africa in Figure 25. First, the rift valleys are actively pulled apart and are at the rift valley stage of formation. Second, the Red Sea is at the linear sea stage. It has rifted apart so far that the land has dropped below sea level. The Gulf of California in Mexico is another linear sea. The Gulf of California and the Red Sea are two of the youngest seas in the world, having been created only a few million years ago. If plate motions continue rifting the plates apart in these areas, they will eventually become large oceans.

The rate at which the sea floor spreads apart varies along the mid-ocean ridge and dramatically affects its appearance. Faster spreading, for instance, produces broader and less rugged segments of the global mid-ocean ridge system. This is because fast-spreading segments of the mid-ocean ridge produce vast amounts of rock, which move away from the spreading center at a rapid rate and consequently undergo less thermal contraction and subsidence than slower spreading segments do. In addition, central rift valleys on slow-spreading segments tend to be larger and better developed.

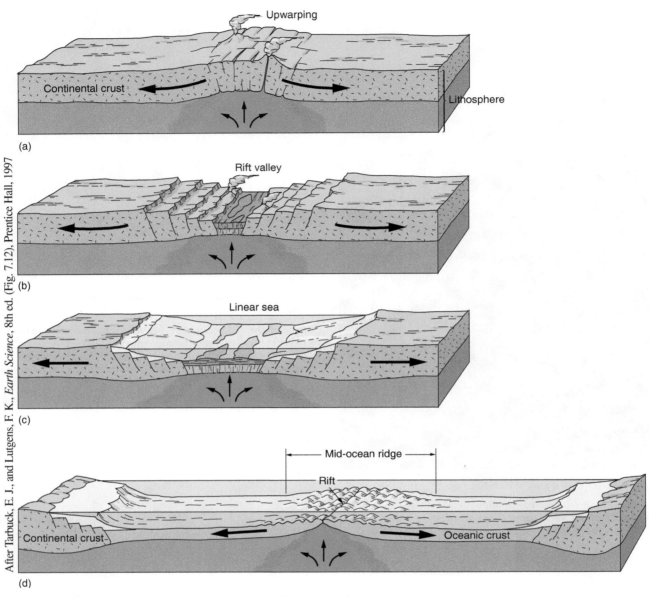

Figure 24 Formation of an ocean basin by sea floor spreading.

Sequence of events in the formation of an ocean basin. **(a)** A shallow heat source develops under a continent, causing initial upwarping and volcanic activity. **(b)** Movement apart creates a rift valley. **(c)** With increased spreading, a linear sea is formed. **(d)** After millions of years, a full-fledged ocean basin is created, separating continental pieces that were once connected.

The gently sloping and fast-spreading parts of the mid-ocean ridge are called **oceanic rises**. For example, the **East Pacific Rise** (Figure 26, *bottom*) between the Pacific and Nazca Plates is a broad, low, gentle swelling of the sea floor with a small central rift valley and has a spreading rate as high as 16.5 centimeters (6.5 inches) per year.[7] Conversely, steeper-sloping and slower-spreading areas of the mid-ocean ridge are called **oceanic ridges**. The **Mid-Atlantic Ridge** (Figure 26, *top*) between the South American and African Plates is an example of a tall,

steep, rugged oceanic ridge with a prominent rift valley and has a spreading rate of only 2 to 3 centimeters (0.8 to 1.2 inches) per year.

The amount of energy released by earthquakes along the divergent plate boundaries is closely related to the spreading rate. The faster the sea floor spreads, the less energy released in each earthquake. Earthquake intensity

---

[7]The spreading rate is the total widening rate of an ocean basin resulting from motion of both plates away from a spreading center.

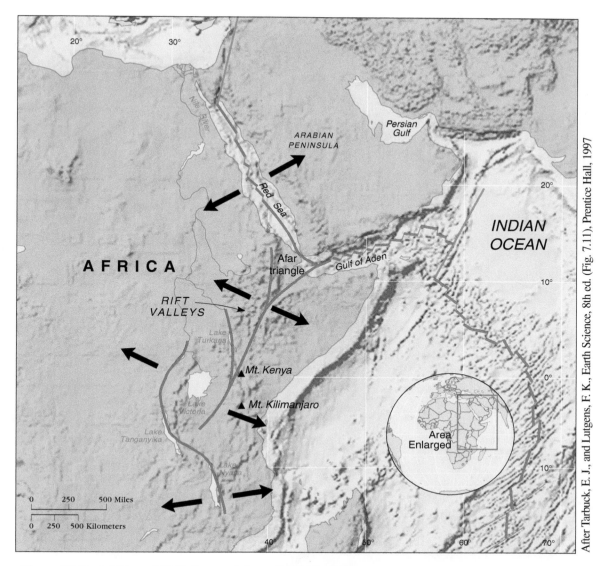

Figure 25 East African Rift Valleys and Associated Features

Parts of east Africa are splitting apart (*arrows*), creating a series of linear downdropped rift valleys (*red lines*) along with prominent volcanoes (*triangles*). Similarly, the Red Sea and Gulf of Aden have split apart so far they are now below sea level. The mid-ocean ridge in the Indian Ocean has experienced similar stages of development.

After Tarbuck, E. J., and Lutgens, F. K., Earth Science, 8th ed. (Fig. 7.11), Prentice Hall, 1997

is usually measured on a scale called the **seismic moment magnitude**, which reflects the energy released to create very long-period seismic waves. Because it more adequately represents larger magnitude earthquakes, the moment magnitude scale is increasingly used instead of the well-known Richter scale and is represented by the symbol M_w. Earthquakes in the rift valley of the slow-spreading Mid-Atlantic Ridge reach a maximum magnitude of about $M_w = 6.0$, whereas those occurring along the axis of the fast-spreading East Pacific Rise seldom exceed $M_w = 4.5$.[8]

Convergent Boundaries

Convergent boundaries—where two plates move together and collide—result in the destruction of ocean crust as one plate plunges below the other and is remelted in the mantle. The physiographic ocean floor feature associated with a convergent plate boundary is a deep-ocean trench. Trenches are deep linear scars where subduction occurs. Melting in the subduction

[8]Note that each one-unit increase of earthquake magnitude represents an increase of energy release of about 30 times.

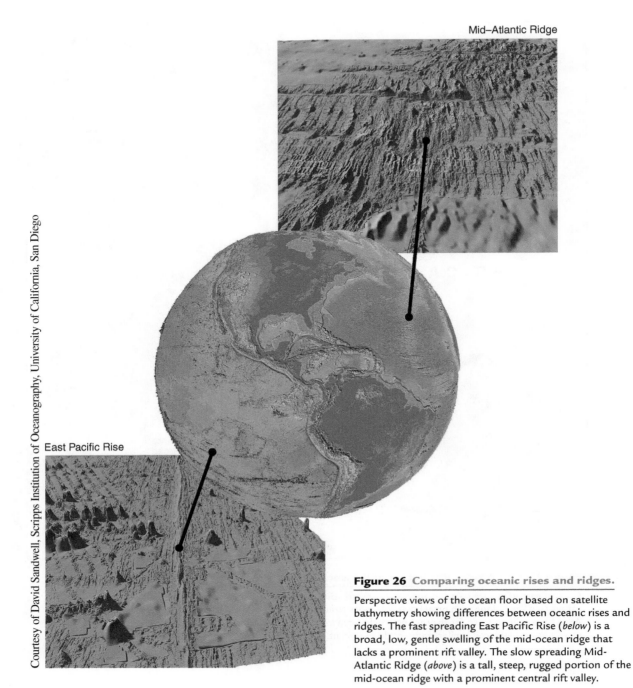

Mid–Atlantic Ridge

East Pacific Rise

Courtesy of David Sandwell, Scripps Institution of Oceanography, University of California, San Diego

Figure 26 Comparing oceanic rises and ridges.

Perspective views of the ocean floor based on satellite bathymetry showing differences between oceanic rises and ridges. The fast spreading East Pacific Rise (*below*) is a broad, low, gentle swelling of the mid-ocean ridge that lacks a prominent rift valley. The slow spreading Mid-Atlantic Ridge (*above*) is a tall, steep, rugged portion of the mid-ocean ridge with a prominent central rift valley.

zone causes an arc-shaped row of highly active and explosively erupting volcanoes that parallel the trench called a **volcanic arc**.

Figure 27 shows the three subtypes of convergent boundaries that result from interactions between two different types of crust (oceanic and continental).

Oceanic–Continental Convergence When an oceanic and a continental plate converge, the denser oceanic plate is subducted (Figure 27a). The oceanic plate becomes heated as it is subducted into the asthenosphere and some of the basaltic rock is melted. This molten rock mixes with superheated gases (mostly water and other volatiles) and begins to rise to the surface through the overriding continental plate. The rising basalt-rich magma mixes with the granite of the continental crust, producing lava in volcanic eruptions at the surface that is intermediate in composition between basalt and granite. One type of vol-

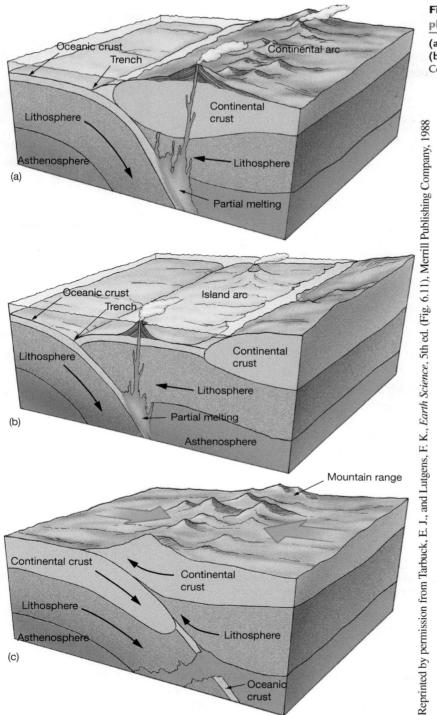

Reprinted by permission from Tarbuck, E. J., and Lutgens, F. K., *Earth Science*, 5th ed. (Fig. 6.11), Merrill Publishing Company, 1988

Figure 27 Three sub-types of convergent plate boundaries.

(a) Oceanic–continental convergence.
(b) Oceanic–oceanic convergence. (c) Continental–continental convergence.

canic rock with this composition is called **andesite**, named after the Andes Mountains of South America because it is so common there. Andesitic volcanic eruptions are usually quite explosive and have historically been very destructive because andesite contains high silica content and is quite viscous. The result of this volcanic activity on the continent above the subduction zone produces a type of volcanic arc called a **continental arc**, which occurs along the edge of a continent. Continental arcs are created by andesitic volcanic eruptions and by the folding and uplifting associated with plate collision.

If the spreading center producing the subducting plate is far enough from the subduction zone, an oceanic trench becomes well developed along the margin of the continent. The Peru-Chile Trench is an example, and the Andes Mountains are the associated continental arc produced by melting of the subducting plate. If the spreading center producing the subducting plate is close to the subduction zone,

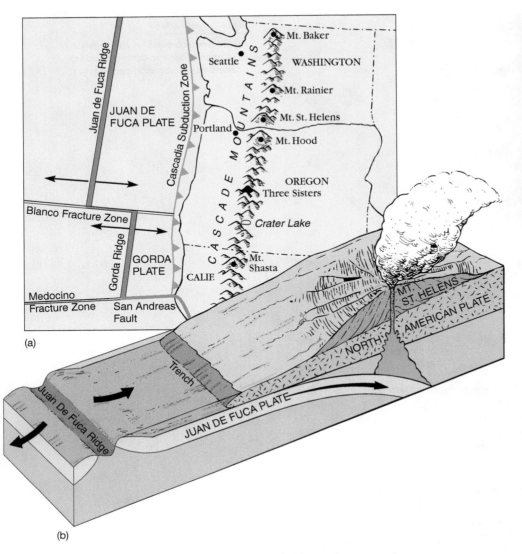

(a)

(b)

(c)

Figure 28 Convergent tectonic activity produces the Cascade Mountains.

(a) Tectonic features of the Cascade Mountain Range and vicinity. **(b)** The volcanoes of the Cascade Mountains are created by the subduction of the Juan de Fuca Plate beneath the North American Plate. **(c)** The eruption of Mount St. Helens in 1980.

however, the trench is not nearly as well developed. This is the case where the Juan de Fuca Plate subducts beneath the North American Plate off the coasts of Washington and Oregon to produce the Cascade Mountains continental arc (Figure 28). Here, the Juan de Fuca Ridge is so close to the North American Plate that the subducting lithosphere is less than 10 million years old and has not cooled enough to become very deep. In addition, the large amount of sediment carried to the ocean by the Columbia River has filled most of the trench with sediment. Many of the Cascade volcanoes of this continental arc have been active within the last 100 years. Most recently, Mount St. Helens erupted in May 1980, killing 62 people.

Oceanic–Oceanic Convergence When two oceanic plates converge, the denser oceanic plate is subducted (Figure 27b). Typically, the older oceanic plate is denser because it has had more time to cool and contract. This type of convergence produces the deepest trenches in the world, such as the Mariana Trench in the western Pacific Ocean. The subducting oceanic plate becomes heated and melts in the asthenosphere. Similar to oceanic–continental convergence, molten material mixes with super-heated gases and rises to the surface to produce volcanoes. The molten material is mostly basaltic because there is no mixing with granitic rocks from the continents. Basalt contains less silica and is less viscous than andesite—thus the eruptions are not nearly as destructive. The result of this volcanic activity is a type of volcanic arc called an **island arc**, which usually is separated from the nearest continent by a marginal sea. Examples of island arc/trench systems are the West Indies' Leeward and Windward Islands/Puerto Rico Trench in the Caribbean Sea and the Aleutian Islands/Aleutian Trench in the North Pacific Ocean.

Continental–Continental Convergence When two continental plates converge, which one is subducted? You might expect the older of the two (which is probably the denser one) will be subducted. Continental lithosphere forms differently than oceanic lithosphere, however, and old continental lithosphere is no denser than young continental lithosphere. It turns out that neither subducts because both are too low in density to be pulled very far down into the mantle. Instead, a tall uplifted mountain range is created by the collision of the two

plates (Figure 27c). These mountains are composed of folded and deformed sedimentary rocks originally deposited on the sea floor that previously separated the two continental plates. The oceanic crust itself may subduct beneath such mountains. A prime example of continental–continental convergence is the collision of India with Asia (Figure 29). It began 45 million years ago and has created the Himalaya Mountains, presently the tallest mountains on Earth.

Earthquakes Associated with Convergent Boundaries
Both spreading centers and trench systems are characterized by earthquakes, but in different ways. Spreading centers have shallow earthquakes, usually less than 10 kilometers (6 miles) deep. Earthquakes associated with trenches, on the other hand, vary from near the surface down to 670 kilometers (415 miles) deep, which are the deepest earthquakes in the world. These earthquakes are clustered in a band about 20 kilometers (12.5 miles)

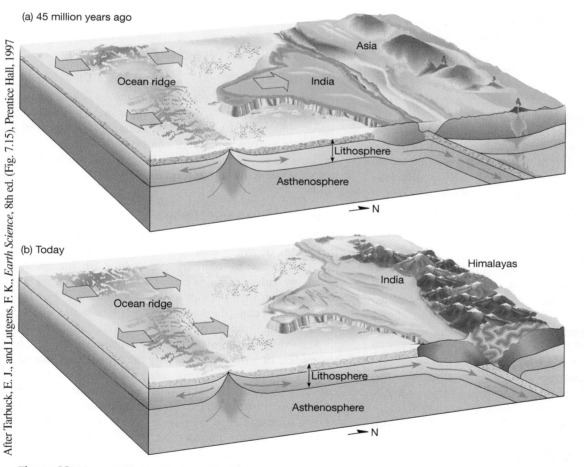

After Tarbuck, E. J., and Lutgens, F. K., *Earth Science*, 8th ed. (Fig. 7.15), Prentice Hall, 1997

Figure 29 The collision of India with Asia.

(a) Sea floor spreading along the mid-ocean ridge south of India caused the collision of India with Asia, which began about 45 million years ago. **(b)** The collision closed the shallow sea between India and Asia, crumpled the two continents together, and is responsible for the continued uplift of the Himalaya Mountains.

thick of successively deeper earthquakes extending from the trench that dips at an angle of approximately 45 degrees, becoming steeper with depth. This band is called a *Wadati-Benioff seismic zone*, which represents a subducting plate in a convergent plate boundary.

Many factors combine to produce large earthquakes at convergent boundaries. The forces involved in convergent-plate boundary collisions are enormous. Huge lithospheric slabs of rock are relentlessly pushing against each other, and the subducting plate must actually bend as it dives below the surface. In addition, thick crust associated with convergent boundaries tends to store more energy than the thinner crust at divergent boundaries. Also, mineral structure changes occur at the higher pressures encountered deep below the surface, which are thought to produce changes in volume that lead to some of the most powerful earthquakes in the world. In fact, the largest earthquake ever recorded was the 1960 Chilean earthquake near the Peru-Chile Trench, which had a magnitude of $M_w = 9.5$!

Transform Boundaries

A global sea floor map shows that the mid-ocean ridge is offset by many large features oriented perpendicular (at right angles) to the crest of the ridge. What causes these offsets? They occur because spreading at a mid-ocean ridge only occurs perpendicular to the axis of a ridge and all parts of a plate must move together. As a result, offsets are oriented perpendicular to the ridge and parallel to each other to accommodate spreading of a linear ridge system on a spherical Earth. In addition, the offsets allow different segments of the mid-ocean ridge to spread apart at different rates. These offsets—called **transform faults**—give the mid-ocean ridge a zigzag appearance. There are thousands of these transform faults, some large and some small, which dissect the global mid-ocean ridge.

There are two types of transform faults. The first and most common type occurs wholly on the ocean floor and is called an **oceanic transform fault**. The second type cuts across a continent and is called a **continental transform fault**. Regardless of type, though, transform faults *always* occur between two segments of a mid-ocean ridge, as shown in Figure 30.

The movement of one plate past another—a process called **transform faulting**—produces shallow but often strong earthquakes in the lithosphere. Magnitudes of $M_w = 7.0$ have been recorded along some oceanic transform faults. One of the best studied faults in the world is California's **San Andreas Fault**, a continental transform fault that runs from the Gulf of California past San Francisco and beyond into northern California. Because the San Andreas Fault cuts through continental crust, which is much thicker than oceanic crust, earthquakes are considerably larger than those produced by oceanic transform faults, sometimes up to $M_w = 8.5$.

Because California experiences large periodic earthquakes, many people are mistakenly concerned that it will "fall off into the ocean" during a large earthquake along the San Andreas Fault. These earthquakes occur as the Pacific Plate continues to move to the northwest past the North American Plate at a rate of about 5 centimeters (2 inches) a year. At this rate, Los Angeles (on the Pacific Plate) will be adjacent to San Francisco (on the North American Plate) in about 18.5 million years—a length of time for about 1 million generations of people to live their lives. Although California will never fall into the ocean, people living near this fault should be very aware they are likely to experience a large earthquake within their lifetime.

> The three main types of plate boundaries are divergent (plates moving apart such as at the mid-ocean ridge), convergent (plates moving together such as at an ocean trench), and transform (plates sliding past each other such as at a transform fault).

Testing the Model: Some Applications of Plate Tectonics

One of the strengths of plate tectonic theory is how it unifies so many seemingly separate events into a single consistent model. Let's look at a few examples that illustrate how plate tectonic processes can be used to explain the origin of features that, up until the acceptance of plate tectonics, were difficult to explain.

Mantle Plumes and Hotspots

Although the theory of plate tectonics helped explain the origin of many features near plate boundaries, it did not seem to explain the origin of *intraplate* (*intra* = within, *plate* = plate of the lithosphere) *features* that are far from any plate boundary. For instance, how can plate tectonics explain volcanic islands near the middle of a plate?

According to the plate tectonic model, volcanism in the middle of a plate is caused by the presence of mantle plumes that are most likely related to the positions of convection cells in the mantle. **Mantle plumes** (*pluma* = a soft feather) are columnar areas of hot molten rock that arise from deep within the mantle. The areas where mantle plumes come to the surface are called **hotspots** and are marked by an abundance of volcanic activity. For example, the continuing volcanism in Yellowstone National Park and Hawaii is caused by hotspots.

Note that hotspots are different from either a volcanic arc or a mid-ocean ridge, even though all three are marked by a high degree of volcanic activity. Rela-

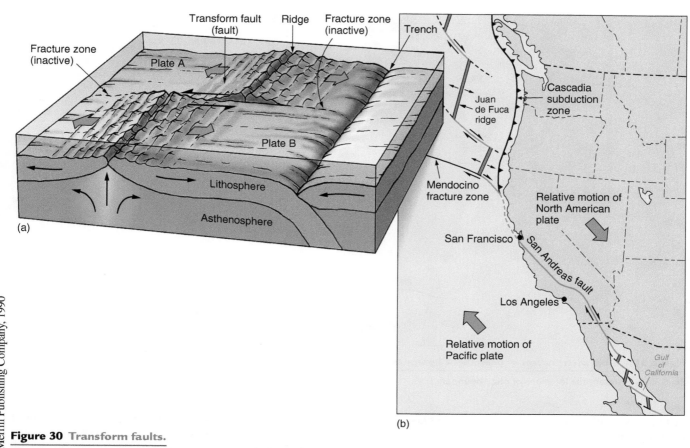

After Tarbuck, E. J., and Lutgens, F. K., *The Earth: An Introduction to Physical Geology*, 3rd ed. (Figs. 18.22, 18.23), Merrill Publishing Company, 1990

Figure 30 Transform faults.

The Juan de Fuca Ridge is offset by several oceanic transform faults. Also shown is the San Andreas Fault, a continental transform fault connecting the Juan de Fuca Ridge and the spreading center in the Gulf of California.

tive to basalts typical of hotspots, those produced at the mid-ocean ridge are chemically different, containing reduced concentrations of the elements potassium, rubidium, cesium, uranium, and thorium. Based on this difference, Earth scientists have suggested that mid-ocean ridge basalt is probably derived from the upper mantle, whereas hotspot basalt is likely from the lower mantle, perhaps as deep as the core-mantle boundary. If this is true, it implies that mantle plumes may have a very deep Earth source.

Worldwide, more than 100 hotspots have been active within the last 10 million years and several dozen remain active today. Figure 31 shows the global distribution of prominent hotspots. In general, hotspots do not coincide with plate boundaries. Notable exceptions are those that are near divergent boundaries where the lithosphere is thin, such as at the Galápagos Islands and Iceland. Not only does Iceland straddle the Mid-Atlantic Ridge (a divergent plate boundary), it also sits directly over a 150-kilometer (93-mile)-wide

mantle plume, which accounts for its remarkable amount of volcanic activity. In fact, the volume of volcanic rock generated at Iceland is so large that it has caused Iceland to be one of the few places along the global mid-ocean ridge that rises high above sea level.

Throughout the Pacific Plate, many island chains are oriented in a northwestward–southeastward direction. The most intensely studied of these is the **Hawaiian Islands–Emperor Seamount Chain** in the northern Pacific Ocean (Figure 32). What created this chain of over 100 intraplate volcanoes that stretch over 5800 kilometers (3000 miles)? Further, what caused the prominent bend in the overall direction that occurs in the middle of the chain?

To help answer these questions, look at the ages of the volcanoes in the chain. Every volcano in the chain has long since become extinct, except the volcano Kilauea on the island of Hawaii, which is the southeasternmost island of the chain. The age of volcanoes progressively increases northwestward from Hawaii (Figure 32). To the northwest, the volcanoes increase

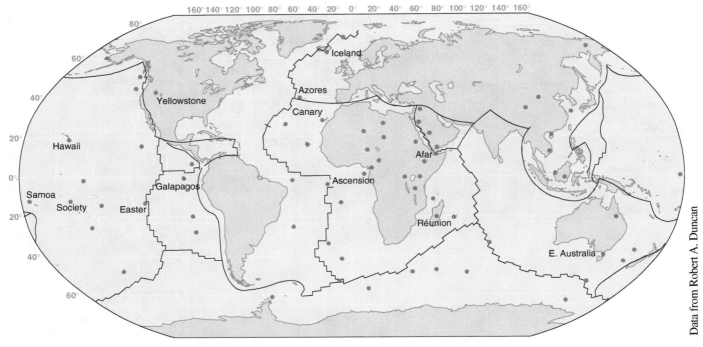

Figure 31 Global distribution of prominent hotspots.

Black lines represent the locations of plate boundaries.

in age past Suiko Seamount (65 million years old) to Detroit Seamount (81 million years old) near the Aleutian Trench.

These age relationships suggest that the Pacific Plate has moved steadily northwestward while the underlying mantle plume remained relatively stationary. The resulting Hawaiian hotspot created each of the volcanoes in the chain. As the plate moved, it carried the active volcano off the hotspot and a new volcano began forming, younger in age than the previous one. A chain of extinct volcanoes that is progressively older as one travels away from a hotspot is called a **nematath** (*nema* = thread, *tath* = dung or manure). Evidence suggests that about 40 million years ago, the Pacific Plate shifted from a northerly to a northwesterly direction with a rearrangement of plate boundaries along western North America. This change in plate motion accounts for the bend in Figure 32 about halfway through the chain, separating the Hawaiian Islands from the Emperor Seamounts. Alternatively, recent research suggests that the change in direction of the chain seen in Figure 32 could be related to movement of the Hawaiian hotspot itself.

If Hawaii is directly above the hotspot now, what will become of it in the future? It will be carried to the northwest off the hotspot, become inactive, and eventually be subducted into the Aleutian Trench like all the rest of the volcanoes in the chain to the north of it. In turn, other volcanoes will build up over the hotspot. In fact, a 3500-meter (11,500-foot) volcano already exists 32 kilometers (20 miles) southeast of Hawaii, named **Loihi**. Still 1 kilometer (0.6 mile) below sea level, Loihi is volcanically active and should reach the surface sometime between 30,000 and 100,000 years from now at its current rate of activity. As it builds above sea level, it will become the newest island in the long chain of volcanoes created by the Hawaiian hotspot.

> Mantle plumes create hotspots at the surface, which produce volcanic chains called nemataths that record the motion of plates.

Seamounts and Tablemounts

Many areas of the ocean floor (most notably on the Pacific Plate) contain tall volcanic peaks that are called **seamounts** if conical on top, and **tablemounts**—or **guyots**, after Princeton University's first geology professor Arnold Guyot[9]—if flat on top. Until the theory of plate tectonics, how seamounts and tablemounts formed was unclear. The theory explained why tablemounts were flat on top and why the tops of some tablemounts had shallow-water deposits despite being located in very deep water.

The origin of many seamounts and tablemounts is related to the volcanic activity occurring at hotspots; others are related to processes occurring at the mid-ocean ridge (Figure 33). Because of sea floor spreading, active volcanoes (seamounts) occur along the crest of the mid-ocean ridge. Some may be built up so high they rise above sea level and become islands, at which point wave erosion becomes

---

[9]Guyot is pronounced "GEE-oh" with a hard g as in "give."

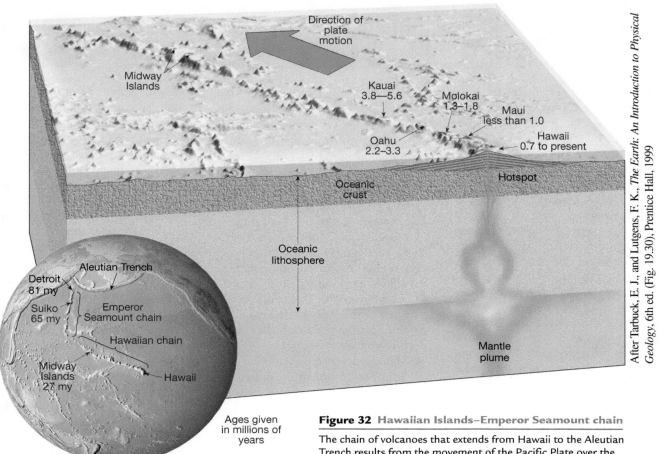

After Tarbuck, E. J., and Lutgens, F. K., *The Earth: An Introduction to Physical Geology*, 6th ed. (Fig. 19.30), Prentice Hall, 1999

Figure 32 Hawaiian Islands–Emperor Seamount chain

The chain of volcanoes that extends from Hawaii to the Aleutian Trench results from the movement of the Pacific Plate over the relatively stationary Hawaiian hot spot. Numbers represent radiometric age dates in millions of years before present.

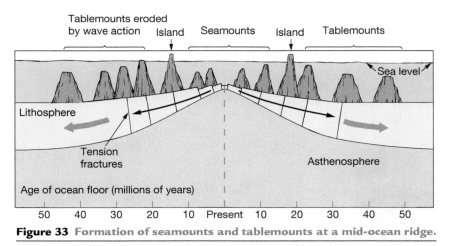

Figure 33 Formation of seamounts and tablemounts at a mid-ocean ridge.

Seamounts are formed along a mid-ocean ridge. If they are tall enough to reach the surface, their tops get eroded flat by wave activity and become tablemounts. Through sea floor spreading, seamounts and tablemounts are transported into deeper water, sometime carrying with them evidence of their tops reaching shallower water.

important. When sea floor spreading has moved the seamount off its source of magma (whether it is a mid-ocean ridge or a hot spot), the top of the seamount can be flattened by waves in just a few million years. This flattened seamount—now a tablemount—continues to be carried away from its source and, after millions of years, is submerged deeper into the ocean. Frequently, tops of tablemounts contain evidence of shallow-water conditions (such as ancient coral reef deposits) that were carried with it into deeper water.

BOX 2   Historical Feature

OPHIOLITES: A GIFT FROM THE SEA FLOOR TO THE BRONZE AGE

As a result of plate tectonic processes, most oceanic lithosphere that is created at spreading centers is ultimately subducted and returned to the underlying mantle. However, a very small amount—only about 0.001%—of oceanic lithosphere does not get subducted; instead, it is uplifted onto the edge of a continent in a process called *obduction* (*ob* = against, *duct* = lead). Fragments of the sea floor that are hoisted onto land are composed of a unique sequence of rocks called *ophiolites* (*ophis* = snake, *lite* = stone), which have long, slender, curvy shapes. Ophiolite sequences on land have long been recognized but only recently have they been connected to their environment of formation on the sea floor.

Idealized ophiolite sequence, which contains the following rock types vertically from top to bottom:

1. Layered *marine sediments*, which get progressively older with depth.

2. *Pillow basalts*, which indicate the lava flows that produced them flowed out on the ocean floor and cooled quickly during contact with water.

3. *Vertical basalt dikes*, which form by being injected into cracks in oceanic crust as lithospheric plates pull apart and move away from the spreading center. Because they are essentially thin planar features, they are often called *sheet dikes*.

4. *Massive gabbro*, a rock similar to basalt in composition but of a coarser texture due to slower cooling. This gabbro may represent the cooling of magma near the roof of the magma chamber that was the source of the overlying basalts.

5. *Layered gabbro* that may have crystallized within the upper region of the magma chamber.

6. *Layered peridotite*, a mantle rock composed mostly of iron- and magnesium-rich minerals called pyroxene and olivine. The boundary between the peridotite and the overlying gabbro is thought to represent the contact between ocean crust and the underlying mantle.

The main features of an idealized ophiolite sequence can also be observed in cores drilled into the sea floor near mid-ocean ridges. Such is the case for cores recovered from the Deep Sea Drilling Project (DSDP) Drill Hole No. 504B, which is located on the southern flank of the Costa Rica Rift. The hole was drilled to a depth of 1350 meters (4429 feet) beneath the ocean floor, making it the deepest hole ever drilled in ocean crust. Although it did not penetrate

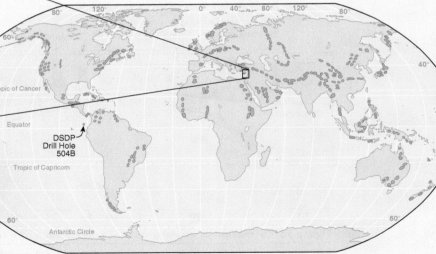

Worldwide ophiolite distribution.

Ophiolites found near the margins of continents where subduction occurs are generally younger (less than 200 million years old) than those embedded deep within continents, some of which are as much as 1.2 billion years old. The location of DSDP Drill Hole No. 504B—the deepest hole drilled through ocean crust—is also shown. Inset shows location of the Troodos Massif ophiolite on the island of Cyprus in the eastern Mediterranean Sea. Photo shows mining of the Troodos Massif sulfide ore, which is the dark material in the bottom of the pit.

through the complete ophiolite sequence, the rocks it did penetrate show how well this sequence resembles those observed in ophiolites studied on land.

Many ophiolites contain rich metallic ores with patterns of enrichment similar to those occurring in the sediments and oceanic crust near deep-sea hydrothermal vents on the sea floor. However, there is increasing evidence that many ophiolites may have formed at back-arc spreading centers associated with subduction zones rather than at oceanic ridges and rises.

One of the best-studied ophiolite sequences is the Troodos Massif on the island of Cyprus in the eastern Mediterranean Sea. Troodos Massif is also one of the oldest known ore deposits, having been mined for copper[11] since the time of the Phoenicians. In fact, this copper deposit was largely responsible for helping civilization advance from the Stone Age to the Bronze Age. Archeological evidence indicates in about 2760 B.C., people living on Cyprus discovered that copper could be hardened with the addition of tin during smelting. The smelted

Continued...

---

[11]"Cyprus" means copper; even today, it is unclear if the island is named for the metal, or vice versa.

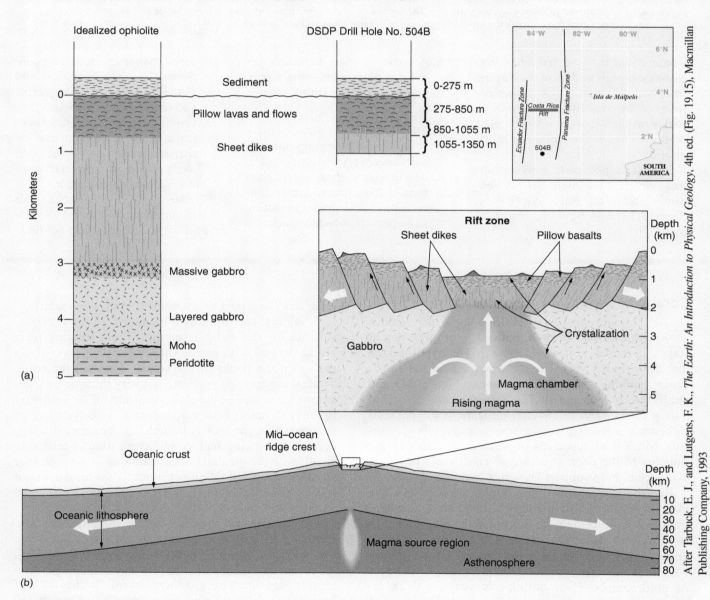

After Tarbuck, E. J., and Lutgens, F. K., The Earth: An Introduction to Physical Geology, 4th ed. (Fig. 19.15), Macmillan Publishing Company, 1993

Ophiolite rock types.

(a) The column at left shows an idealized sequence of rock types found in ophiolite complexes such as the Troodos Massif of Cyprus. On the right is the sequence of rocks encountered in Deep Sea Drilling Project (DSDP) Drill Hole No. 504B, which closely resembles those in the upper idealized ophiolite complex. **(b)** Diagram showing the environment of formation for pillow basalts, sheet dikes, and gabbros of an ophiolite complex.

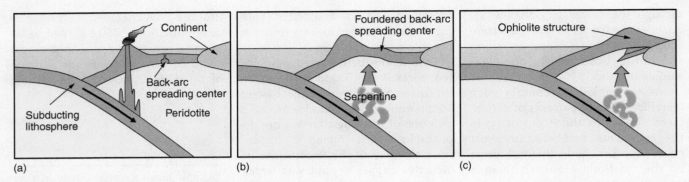

The obduction of ophiolites onto a continent.

(a) Subducting lithosphere contains water-bearing minerals. (b) Water-bearing minerals are heated and hot water is released into the peridotite, which is altered to lower-density serpentine. The expansion of the serpentine lifts the overlying mantle and oceanic crust. (c) Continued compressional forces break the uplifted segments of oceanic crust and wedge them onto the margin of a continent where they remain as ophiolites.

bronze could then be fashioned into various weapons and tools that, at the time, had no equal. If the copper deposits of Troodos Massif were not so readily available, humankind might have remained in the Stone Age much longer!

Still, it is not clear how ophiolites—which have high density—become obducted onto continents. Figure 3D shows how this might be accomplished:

a. An oceanic plate subducts beneath a plate containing a continent and a section of oceanic lithosphere.

b. The subducting oceanic plate contains water-bearing minerals such as zeolites and amphiboles, which release their water when heated. This heated water converts the mantle rock, peridotite, to serpentine, which is much less

dense than the surrounding peridotite. The serpentine rises and pushes up the overlying crust and mantle above sea level.

c. Continued compressional forces cause the oceanic crust and associated serpentine to break into wedges that are obducted onto the margin of a continent.

Further study is needed to answer questions that remain about the origin and emplacement of ophiolites.

Coral Reef Development

On his voyage aboard the HMS *Beagle*, the famous naturalist **Charles Darwin** noticed a progression of stages in **coral reef** development. He hypothesized that the origin of coral reefs depended on the subsidence (sinking) of volcanic islands (Figure 34) and published the concept in *The Structure and Distribution of Coral Reefs* in 1842. What Darwin's hypothesis lacked was a mechanism for how volcanic islands subside. Much later, advances in plate tectonic theory and samples of the deep structure of coral reefs provided evidence to help support Darwin's hypothesis.

Reef-building corals are colonial animals that live in shallow, warm, tropical seawater and produce a hard skeleton of limestone. Once corals are established in an area that has the conditions necessary for their growth, they continue to grow upward layer by layer with each new generation attached to the skeletons of its predecessors. Over millions of years, a thick sequence of coral reef deposits may develop if the conditions remain favorable.

The three stages of development in coral reefs are called fringing, barrier, and atoll. **Fringing reefs** (Figure 34a) initially develop along the margin of a

landmass (an island or a continent) where the temperature, salinity, and turbidity (cloudiness) of the water are suitable for reef-building corals. Often, fringing reefs are associated with active volcanoes whose lava flows run down the flanks of the volcano and kill the coral. Thus, these fringing reefs are not very thick or well developed. Because of the close proximity of the landmass to the reef, runoff from the landmass can carry so much sediment that the reef is buried. The amount of living coral in a fringing reef at any given time is relatively small, with the greatest concentration in areas protected from sediment and salinity changes. If sea level does not rise or the land does not subside, the process stops at the fringing reef stage.

The **barrier reef** stage follows the fringing reef stage. Barrier reefs are linear or circular reefs separated from the landmass by a well-developed lagoon (Figure 34b). As the landmass subsides, the reef maintains its position close to sea level by growing upward. Studies of reef growth rates indicate most have grown 3 to 5 meters (10 to 16 feet) per 1000 years during the recent geologic past. Evidence suggests that some fast-growing reefs in the Caribbean have grown more than 10 meters (33 feet) per 1000 years. Note that if the landmass subsides at a rate

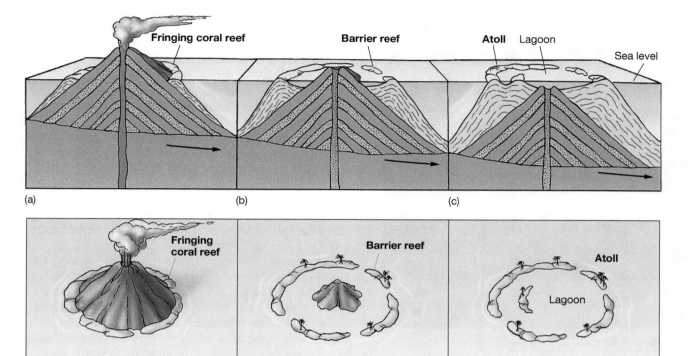

Figure 34 Stages of development in coral reefs.

Cross-sectional view (*above*) and map view (*below*) of **(a)** fringing reef, **(b)** barrier reef, and **(c)** atoll. With the right conditions for coral growth, coral reefs change through time from fringing reef to barrier reef to atoll.

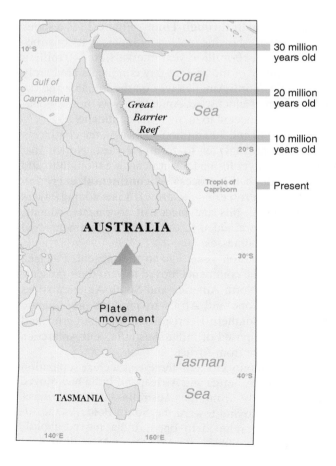

Figure 35 Australia's Great Barrier Reef records plate movement.

About 30 million years ago, the Great Barrier Reef began to develop as northern Australia moved into tropical waters that allowed coral growth.

faster than coral can grow upward, the coral reef will be submerged in water too deep for it to live.

The largest reef system in the world is Australia's **Great Barrier Reef**, a series of over 3000 individual reefs collectively in the barrier reef stage of development, home to hundreds of coral species and thousands of other reef-dwelling organisms. The Great Barrier Reef lies 40 kilometers (25 miles) or more offshore, averages 150 kilometers (90 miles) in width, and extends for more than 2000 kilometers (1200 miles) along Australia's shallow northeastern coast. The effects of the Indian-Australian plate moving north toward the Equator from colder Antarctic waters are clearly visible in the age and structure of the Great Barrier Reef (Figure 35). It is oldest (around 25 million years old) and thickest at its northern end because the northern part of Australia reached water warm enough to grow coral before the southern parts did. In other areas of the Pacific, Indian, and Atlantic Oceans, smaller barrier reefs are found around the tall volcanic peaks that form tropical islands.

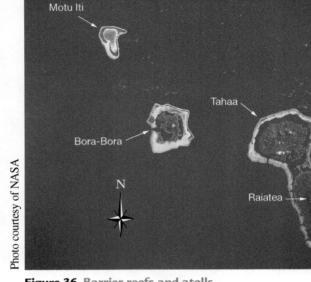

Figure 36 Barrier reefs and atolls.

A portion of the Society Islands in the Pacific Ocean as photographed from the space shuttle. From lower right, the islands of Raiatea, Tahaa, and Bora-Bora are in the barrier reef stage of development, while Motu Iti is an atoll.

The **atoll** (*atar* = to be crowded together) stage (Figure 34c) comes after the barrier reef stage. As a barrier reef around a volcano continues to subside, coral builds up toward the surface. After millions of years, the volcano becomes completely submerged, but the coral reef continues to grow. If the rate of subsidence is slow enough for the coral to keep up, a circular reef called an atoll is formed. The atoll encloses a lagoon usually not more than 30 to 50 meters (100 to 165 feet) deep. The reef generally has many channels that allow circulation between the lagoon and the open ocean. Buildups of crushed-coral debris often form narrow islands that encircle the central lagoon (Figure 36) and are large enough to allow human habitation.

Detecting Plate Motion with Satellites

Since the late 1970s, orbiting satellites allow the accurate positioning of locations on Earth (this technique is also used for navigation by ships at sea). If the plates are moving, satellite positioning should show this movement over time. The map in Figure 37 shows locations that have been measured in this manner over a 20-year period. It demonstrates that locations on Earth are moving in good agreement with the direction and rate of motion predicted by plate tectonics. Successful prediction that locations on Earth are moving with respect to one another very strongly supports plate tectonic theory.

The Past: Paleoceanography

The study of historical changes of continental shapes and positions is called **paleogeography** (*paleo* = ancient, *geo* = earth, *graphy* = the name of a descriptive science). **Paleoceanography** (*paleo* = ancient, *ocean* = the marine environment, *graphy* = the name of a descriptive science) is the study of changes in the physical shape, composition, and character of the oceans brought about by paleogeographical changes.

An important point to remember when considering past locations of features is that nothing is permanently fixed in place on Earth's surface. During the passage of geologic time, continents have moved all around the globe and ocean basins open and close with regularity. Even the mid-ocean ridge moves relative to the continents, which sometimes causes segments of the mid-ocean ridge to be subducted! In addition, the mid-ocean ridge is moving relative to a fixed location outside Earth. This means that an observer orbiting Earth would notice, after only a few million years, that most continental and sea floor features—even plate boundaries—are moving. Hotspots, however, are the exception. They seem to be relatively stationary and can be used to determine the relative motions of other features.

Changes on Earth through Time Figure 38 is a series of world maps showing paleogeographical reconstructions of Earth at 60-million-year intervals. At 540 million years ago, many of the present-day continents are barely recognizable. North America was on the Equator and rotated 90 degrees clockwise. Antarctica was on the Equator and was connected to many other continents.

Between 540 and 300 million years ago, the continents began to come together to form Pangaea. Notice that Alaska had not yet formed. Continents are thought to add material through the process of **continental accretion** (*ad* = toward, *crescere* = to grow). Like adding layers onto a snowball, bits and pieces of continents, islands, and volcanoes are added to the edges of continents and create larger landmasses.

From 180 million years ago to the present, Pangaea separated and the continents moved toward their present-day positions. North America and South America rifted away from Europe and Africa to produce the Atlantic Ocean. In the Southern Hemisphere, South America and a continent composed of India, Australia, and Antarctica begin to separate from Africa.

By 120 million years ago, there was a clear separation between South America and Africa, and India had moved northward, away from the Australia-Antarctica mass, which began moving toward the South Pole. As the Atlantic Ocean continued to open, India moved rapidly northward and collided with Asia about 45 million years

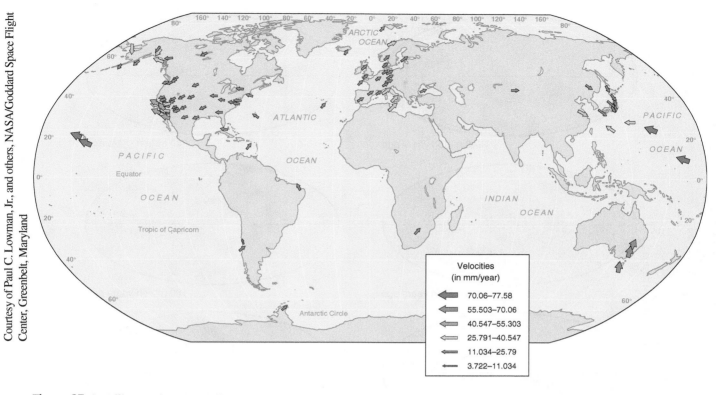

Courtesy of Paul C. Lowman, Jr. and others, NASA/Goddard Space Flight Center, Greenbelt, Maryland

Figure 37 Satellite positioning of locations on Earth.

Arrows show direction of motion based on satellite measurement of positions on Earth during the period 1979–1997. Rate of plate motion in millimeters per year is indicated with different colored arrows (*see legend*).

ago. Australia had also begun a rapid journey to the north since separating from Antarctica.

Studies of plate motion suggest that rates of spreading have historically been higher at lower latitudes. This is apparent in the pattern of formation of the North Atlantic Ocean: Europe and North America have separated at a much lower rate than have Africa and North America. Further, North America and South America were not fully connected by the Isthmus of Panama until about 5 million years ago, which had a marked effect on ocean circulation patterns and the distribution of marine life.

One major result of global plate tectonic events over the past 180 million years has been the creation of the Atlantic Ocean, which continues to grow as sea floor spreads along the Mid-Atlantic Ridge. At the same time, the Pacific Ocean continues to shrink due to subduction along the many trenches that surround it and continental plates that bear in from both the east and west.

Laurasia and Gondwanaland Figure 39 is a series of detailed paleogeographic maps showing Earth before the time of Pangaea to the present, including the distribution of coral and other fossils. The present-day pattern of these fossils can be explained using paleogeographic re-

constructions. For example, Figure 39a (*red stripes*) shows that the exact same species of fossilized coral are found in a band of 350 million-year-old rocks in western Europe and eastern North America, as well as throughout the Alps and Himalayas. This pattern implies that these areas must have been in geographic proximity at that time, even though they are widely separated today (Figure 39c).

Additionally, several lines of evidence suggest that from 350 to 250 million years ago the shallow Tethys Sea separated the supercontinent **Laurasia** (composed of what are now North America, Europe, and Asia) from the supercontinent **Gondwanaland** (composed of what are now South America, Africa, India, Australia, and Antarctica). In time, these two supercontinents bridged parts of the Tethys Sea and combined to form the giant landmass of Pangaea about 200 million years ago (Figure 39b).

Fossils from sediments that were laid down on land aid in determining the latitudinal positions of the two supercontinents. From about 350 to 280 million years ago, there were two distinct floral (*flora* = flower) assemblages, one on each supercontinent. The *Laurasian floral assemblage* (Figure 39, *green shading*) included many

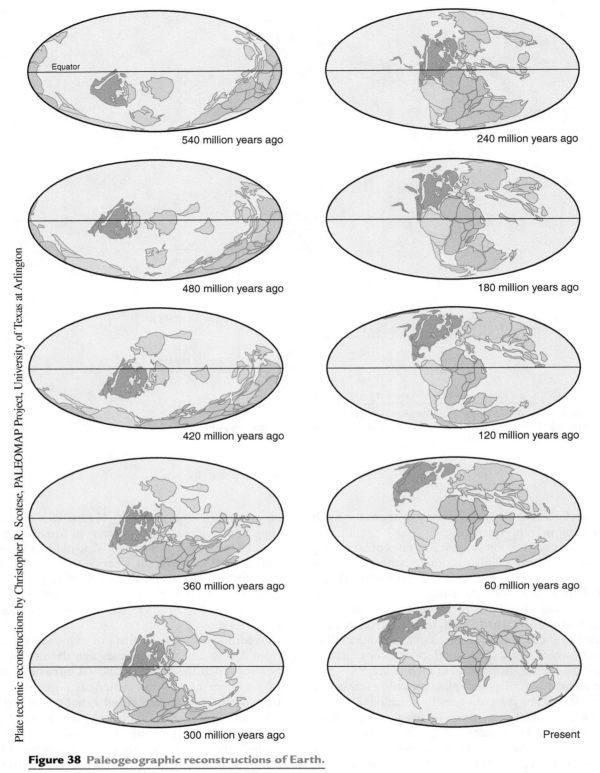

540 million years ago

240 million years ago

480 million years ago

180 million years ago

420 million years ago

120 million years ago

360 million years ago

60 million years ago

300 million years ago

Present

Equator

Plate tectonic reconstructions by Christopher R. Scotese, PALEOMAP Project, University of Texas at Arlington

Figure 38 Paleogeographic reconstructions of Earth.

The positions of the continents at 60-million-year intervals.

species of tropical plants that were incorporated into the sediment that formed the extensive coal beds mined throughout the eastern United States and Europe. These tropical plants indicate that Lau-rasia occupied low latitudes during that time. The *Gondwanaland floral assemblage* (Figure 39, *green dots*) is represented by a few species of plants thought to have grown in cold climates, presumably at a high southern latitude. Supporting evidence for this includes the occurrence of glacial deposits in South America, Africa, India, and Australia, all of which at that time must have been very near the southern polar region. As the plates moved, the landmasses

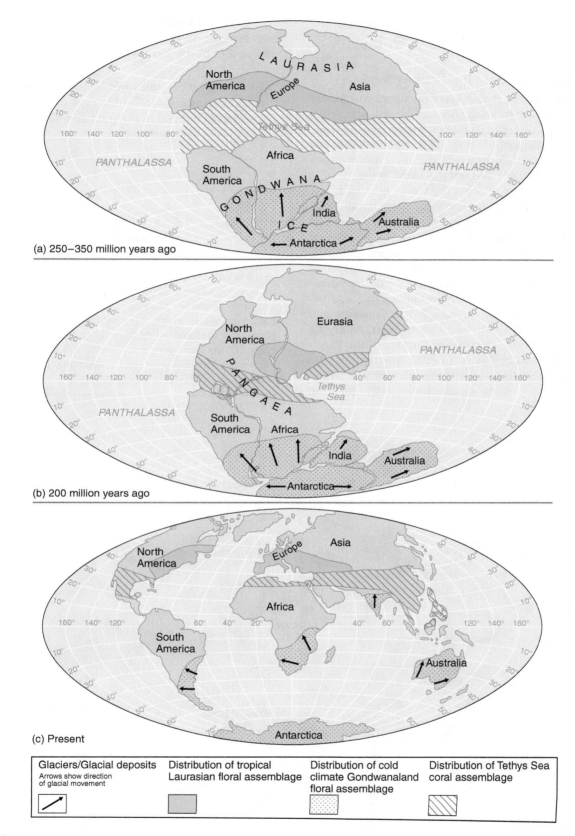

Figure 39 Laurasia and Gondwanaland.

Paleogeographic maps showing the distribution of the tropical Laurasian floral assemblage (*green shading*), the cold-climate Gondwanaland floral assemblage (*green dots*), and the shallow-water Tethys Sea coral assemblage (*red stripes*). Arrows show the direction of ancient glacial flow from the south polar region. **(a)** The distribution of continents 250–350 million years ago. **(b)** By 200 million years ago, Laurasia and Gondwanaland combined to produce the single large continent Pangaea. **(c)** The present-day configuration of the continents.

carried this ancient evidence of past climates to their present geographic positions (Figure 39c).

The Future: Some Bold Predictions

Using plate tectonics, a prediction of the future positions of features on Earth can be made based on the assumption that the rate and direction of plate motion will remain the same. Although these assumptions may not be entirely valid, they do provide a framework for the prediction of the positions of continents and other Earth features in the future.

Figure 40 is a map of what the world may look like 50 million years from now, showing many notable differences as compared to today. For instance, the east African rift valleys may enlarge to form a new linear sea and the Red Sea may be greatly enlarged from rifting there. India may continue to plow into Asia, further uplifting the Himalaya Mountains. As Australia moves north toward Asia, it may use New Guinea like a snowplow to accrete various islands. North America and South America may continue to move west, enlarging the Atlantic Ocean but decreasing the size of the Pacific Ocean. The land bridge of Central America may no longer connect North and South America, which would dramatically alter ocean circulation. Lastly, the thin sliver of land that lies west of the San Andreas Fault may become an island in the North Pacific, soon to be accreted onto southern Alaska.

> The geographic positions of the continents and ocean basins are not fixed in time or place. Rather, they have changed in the past and will continue to change in the future.

STUDENTS SOMETIMES ASK...
Will the continents come back together and form a single landmass anytime soon?

Yes, it is very likely that the continents will come back together, but not anytime soon. Since all of the continents are on the same planetary body, a continent can travel only so far before it collides with other continents. Recent research suggests that the continents may form a supercontinent once every 500 million years or so. Since it has been 200 million years since Pangaea split up, we have only about 300 million years to establish world peace!

After Dietz, R. S., and Holden, J. C. 1970. The breakup of Pangaea, *Scientific American* 223:4, 30–41

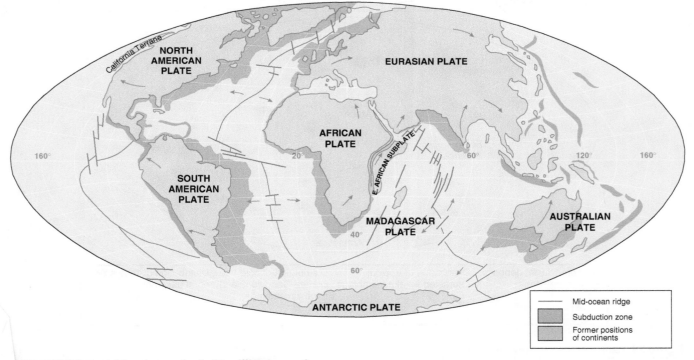

Figure 40 The world as it may look 50 million years from now.

Dark blue shadows indicate the present-day positions of continents and tan shading indicates positions of the continents in 50 million years. Arrows indicate direction of plate motion.

Plate Tectonics ... To Be Continued

Since its inception by Alfred Wegener nearly 100 years ago, plate tectonics has been supported by a wealth of scientific evidence (some of which has been presented in this chapter). Although there are still details to be worked out (such as the exact driving mechanism), it has been universally accepted by Earth scientists today because it helps explain so many observations about our planet. Further, it has led to predictive models that have been used to successfully understand Earth behavior. One such example is the **Wilson cycle** (Figure 41), named in

honor of *John Tuzo Wilson* for his contribution to the early ideas of plate tectonics. The Wilson cycle uses plate tectonic processes to show the distinctive life cycle of ocean basins during their formation, growth, and destruction.

Not only is plate tectonic activity primarily responsible for the creation of landforms, it also plays a prominent role in the development of ocean floor features. Armed with the knowledge of plate tectonic processes you've gained from this chapter, understanding the history and development of ocean floor features in various marine provinces will be a much simpler task.

STAGE	MOTION	PHYSIOGRAPHY	EXAMPLE
EMBRYONIC 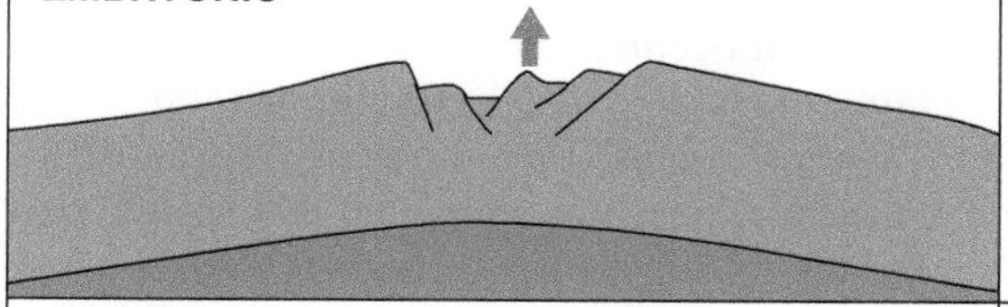	Uplift	Complex system of linear rift valleys on continent	East African rift valleys
JUVENILE 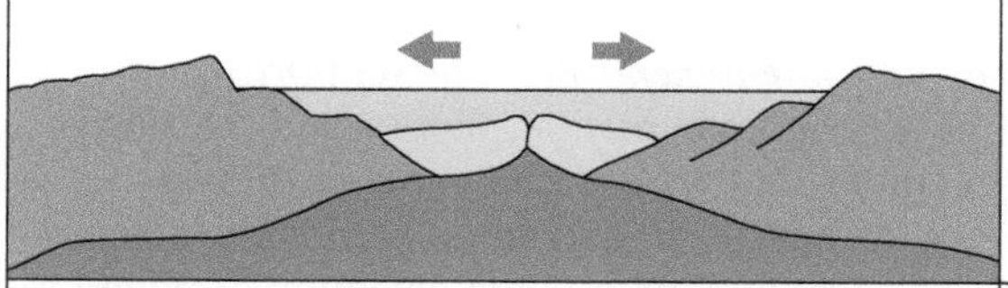	Divergence (spreading)	Narrow seas with matching coasts	Red Sea
MATURE 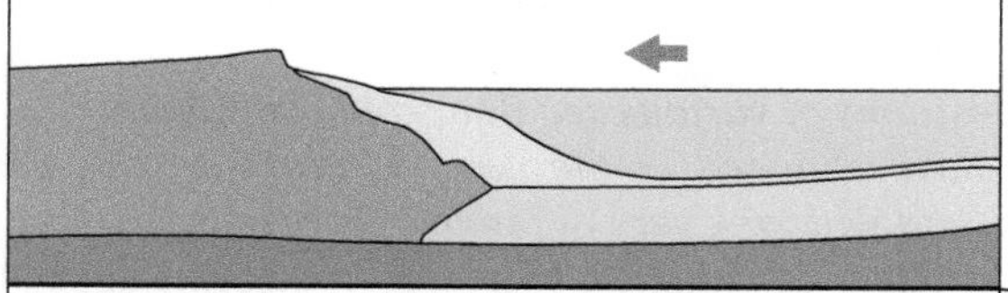	Divergence (spreading)	Ocean basin with continental margins	Atlantic and Arctic Oceans
DECLINING 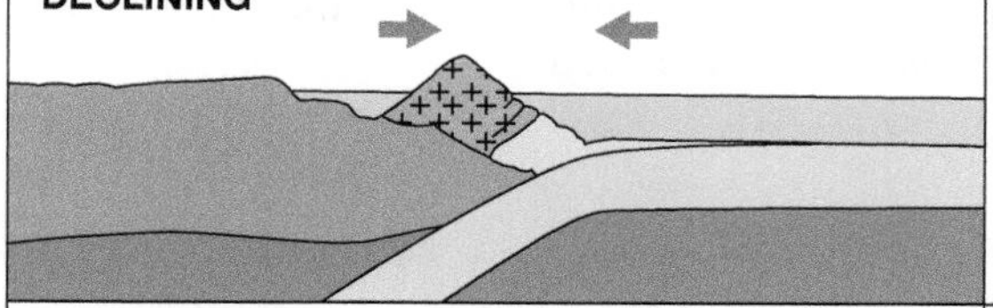	Convergence (subduction)	Island arcs and trenches around basin edge	Pacific Ocean
TERMINAL 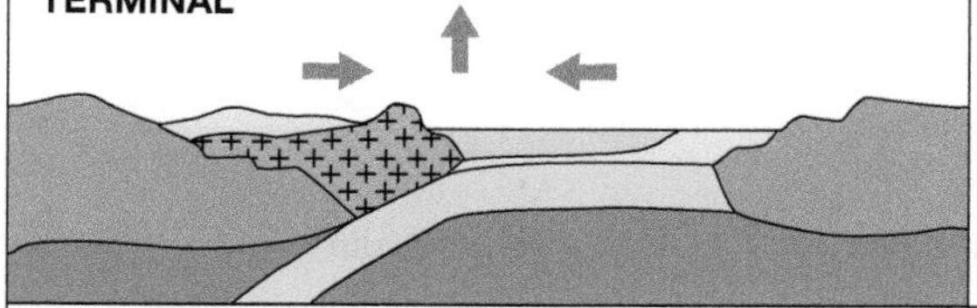	Convergence (collision) and uplift	Narrow, irregular seas with young mountains	Mediterranean Sea
SUTURING 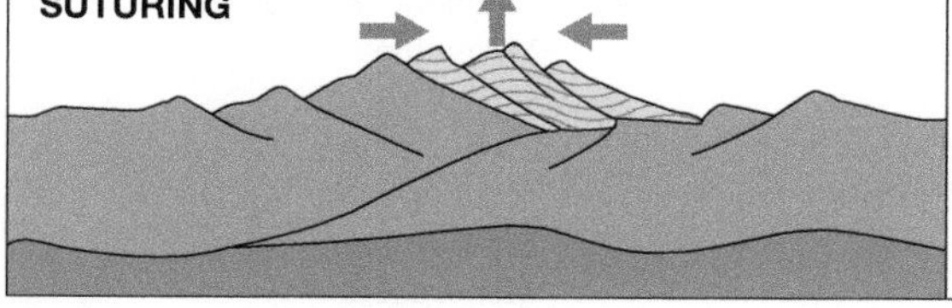	Convergence and uplift	Young to mature mountain belts	Himalaya Mountains

Adapted from Wilson, J. T., *American Philosophical Society Proceedings* 112, 309–320, 1968; Jacobs, J. A., Russell, R. D., and Wilson, J. T., *Physics and Geology*, McGraw–Hill, New York, 1971

Figure 41 The Wilson cycle of ocean basin evolution.

The Wilson cycle depicts the stages of ocean basin development, from the initial embryonic stage of formation to the destruction of the basin as continental masses collide and undergo suturing.

Chapter in Review

- According to the theory of plate tectonics, *the outermost portion of Earth is composed of a patchwork of thin, rigid lithospheric plates that move horizontally* with respect to one another. The idea began as a hypothesis called continental drift proposed by *Alfred Wegener* at the start of the 20th century. He suggested that *about 200 million years ago, all the continents were combined* into one large continent (*Pangaea*) surrounded by a single large ocean (*Panthalassa*).

- *Many lines of evidence were used to support the idea of continental drift*, including the similar shape of nearby continents, matching sequences of rocks and mountain chains, glacial ages and other climate evidence, and the distribution of fossil and present-day organisms. Although this evidence suggested that continents have drifted, other incorrect assumptions about the mechanism involved caused many geologists and geophysicists to discount this hypothesis throughout the first half of the twentieth century.

- *More convincing evidence for drifting continents was introduced in the 1960s when paleomagnetism*—the study of Earth's ancient magnetic field—*was developed* and the significance of features of the ocean floor became better known. The paleomagnetism of the ocean floor is permanently recorded in oceanic crust and reveals stripes of normal and reverse magnetic polarity in a symmetric pattern relative to the mid-ocean ridge.

- *Harry Hess advanced the idea of sea floor spreading.* New *sea floor is created at the crest of the mid-ocean ridge* and moves apart in opposite directions and is *eventually destroyed by subduction into an ocean trench*. This helps explain the pattern of magnetic stripes on the sea floor and why sea floor rocks increase linearly in age in either direction from the axis of the mid-ocean ridge. Other supporting evidence for plate tectonics includes oceanic heat flow measurements and the pattern of worldwide earthquakes. The combination of evidence *convinced geologists* of Earth's dynamic nature and helped advance the idea of continental drift into the more encompassing plate tectonic theory.

- *Studies of Earth structure indicate that Earth is a layered sphere*, with the brittle plates of the *lithosphere* riding on a plastic, high-viscosity *asthenosphere*. Near the surface, the lithosphere is composed of continental and oceanic crust. Continental crust consists mostly of granite, but oceanic crust consists mostly of basalt. Continental crust is lower in density, lighter in color, and thicker than oceanic crust. Both types float isostatically on the denser mantle below.

- *As new crust is added to the lithosphere at the mid-ocean ridge* (*divergent boundaries* where plates move apart), the opposite ends of the *plates are subducted into the mantle at ocean trenches* or beneath continental mountain ranges such as the Himalayas (*convergent boundaries* where plates come together). Additionally, oceanic ridges and rises are offset and plates slide past one another along transform faults (*transform boundaries* where plates slowly grind past one another).

- *Tests of the plate tectonic model indicate that many features and phenomena provide support for shifting plates*. These include mantle plumes and their associated hotspots that record the motion of plates past them, the origin of flat-topped tablemounts, stages of coral reef development, and the detection of plate motion by accurate positioning of locations on Earth using satellites.

- *The positions of various sea floor and continental features have changed in the past, continue to change today, and will look very different in the future*. Before the formation of Pangaea, two large continents appear to have existed, *Laurasia* in the north and *Gondwanaland* to the south.

Key Terms

Andesite	Coral reef	Hawaiian Islands–Emperor Seamount Chain	Magnetic anomaly
Asthenosphere	Core		Magnetic dip
Atoll	Crust	Heat flow	Magnetic field
Barrier reef	Curie point	Hess, Harry	Magnetic inclination
Basalt	Darwin, Charles	Hot spot	Magnetite
Continental accretion	Divergent boundary	Ice age	Mantle
Continental arc	East Pacific Rise	Inner core	Mantle plume
Continental crust	Fringing reef	Isostatic adjustment	Matthews, Drummond
Continental drift	Gondwanaland	Isostatic rebound	Mesosaurus
Continental transform fault	Granite	Laurasia	Mesosphere
Convection cell	Great Barrier Reef	Lithosphere	Mid-Atlantic Ridge
Convergent boundary	Guyot	Loihi	Mid-ocean ridge

Nematath
Ocean trench
Oceanic crust
Oceanic ridge
Oceanic rise
Oceanic transform fault
Outer core
Paleoceanography
Paleogeography

Paleomagnetism
Pangaea
Panthalassa
Plate tectonics
Polar wandering curve
Polarity
Rift valley
Rifting
San Andreas Fault

Sea floor spreading
Seamount
Seismic moment magnitude
(M_w)
Spreading center
Subduction
Subduction zone
Tablemount
Tethys Sea

Transform boundary
Transform faulting
Transform fault
Vine, Frederick
Viscosity
Volcanic arc
Wegener, Alfred
Wilson cycle

Questions and Exercises

1. Cite the lines of evidence Alfred Wagener used to support his idea of continental drift. Why did scientists doubt that continents drifted?

2. If you could travel back in time with three figures (illustrations) from this chapter to help Alfred Wegener convince the scientists of his day that continental drift does exist, what would they be and why?

3. How does the dip of magnetic particles found in igneous rocks tell us at what latitude they were formed?

4. Why was the pattern of alternating reversals of Earth's magnetic field as recorded in the sea-floor rocks such an important piece of evidence for advancing plate tectonics?

5. Describe sea floor spreading and why it was an important piece of evidence in support of plate tectonics.

6. Describe the general relationships that exist among distance from the spreading centers, heat flow, age of the ocean crustal rock, and ocean depth.

7. Why does a map of worldwide earthquakes closely match the locations of worldwide plate boundaries?

8. Discuss how the chemical composition of Earth's interior differs from its physical properties. Include specific examples.

9. What are differences between the lithosphere and the asthenosphere?

10. Describe differences between granite and basalt. Which property is responsible for making the granitic crust "float" higher in the mantle?

11. List and describe the three types of plate boundaries. Include in your discussion any sea floor features that are related to these plate boundaries, and include a real-world example of each. Construct a map view and cross section showing each of the three boundary types and direction of plate movement.

12. Most lithospheric plates contain both oceanic- and continental-type crust. Use plate boundaries to explain why this is true.

13. Describe the differences between oceanic ridges and oceanic rises. Include in your answer why these differences exist.

14. Convergent boundaries can be divided into three types based on the type of crust contained on the two colliding plates. Compare and contrast the different types of convergent boundaries that result from these collisions.

15. Describe the difference in earthquake magnitudes that occur between the three types of plate boundaries, and include why these differences occur.

16. How can plate tectonics be used to help explain the difference between a seamount and a tablemount?

17. How is the age distribution pattern of the Hawaiian Islands–Emperor Seamount Chain explained by the position of the Hawaiian hotspot? What could have caused the curious bend in the chain?

18. Describe the differences in origin between the Aleutian Islands and the Hawaiian Islands. Provide evidence to support your explanation.

19. What are differences between a mid-ocean ridge and a hotspot?

20. Using the paleogeographic reconstructions shown in Figure 38, determine when the following events first appear in the geologic record:
a. North America lies on the Equator.
b. The continents come together as Pangaea.
c. The North Atlantic Ocean opens.
d. India separates from Antarctica.

Marine Provinces

From Chapter 4 of *Introduction to Oceanography*, Tenth Edition, Harold V. Thurman, Alan P. Trujillo.

Marine Provinces

Courtesy of Walter H. Fl Smith and David T. Sandwell, Science, 1997/National Geophysical Data Center/NOAA. "Primary Funding from National Science Foundation"

North Atlantic sea floor. The sea floor has many interesting features, some of which are completely different from those on land. Recent improvements in technology have aided exploration of the sea floor and given scientists the ability to create high-resolution maps like this one.

Key Questions

- How do scientists collect information about the depth and shape of the sea floor?
- What is the difference between a passive and an active continental margin?
- How are submarine canyons formed?
- Where are the deepest areas of the ocean?
- What kinds of features are found at the mid-ocean ridge?
- What are differences between transform faults and fracture zones?

The answers to these questions (and much more) can be found in the highlighted concept statements within this chapter.

"Could the waters of the Atlantic be drawn off so as to expose to view this great sea-gash which separates the continents, and extends from the Arctic to the Antarctic, it would present a scene most rugged, grand, and imposing."

—Matthew Fontaine Maury (1854), commenting about the Mid-Atlantic Ridge

What does the ocean floor look like? Over a century and a half ago, most scientists believed that the ocean floor was completely flat and carpeted with a thick layer of muddy sediment containing little of scientific interest. Further, it was believed that the deepest parts were somewhere in the middle of the ocean basins. However, as more and more vessels crisscrossed the seas to map the ocean floor and to lay transoceanic cables, scientists found the terrain of the sea floor was highly varied and included deep troughs, ancient volcanoes, submarine canyons, and great mountain chains. It was unlike anything on land and, as it turns out, some of the deepest parts of the oceans are actually close to land!

As marine geologists and oceanographers began to analyze the features of the ocean floor, they realized that certain features had profound implications not only for the history of the ocean floor, but also for the history of Earth. How could all these remarkable features have formed, and how can their origin be explained? Over long periods of time, the shape of the ocean basins has changed as continents have ponderously migrated across Earth's surface in response to forces within Earth's interior. The ocean basins as they presently exist reflect the processes of plate tectonics, which help explain the origin of sea floor features.

Bathymetry

Bathymetry (*bathos* = depth, *metry* = measurement) is the measurement of ocean depths and the charting of the shape or topography (*topos* = place, *graphy* = discription of) the ocean floor. Determining bathymetry involves measuring the vertical distance from the ocean surface down to the mountains, valleys, and plains of the sea floor.

Bathymetric Techniques

The first recorded attempt to measure the ocean's depth was conducted in the Mediterranean Sea in about 85 B.C. by a Greek named Posidonius. His mission was to answer an age-old question: How deep is the ocean? Posidonius's crew made a **sounding** by letting out nearly 2 kilometers (1.2 miles) of line before the heavy weight on the end of the line touched bottom. Sounding lines were used for the next 2000 years by voyagers who used them to probe the ocean's depths. The standard unit of ocean depth is the **fathom** (*fathme* = outstretched arms[1]) and is equal to 1.8 meters (6 feet).

The first systematic bathymetric measurements of the oceans were made in 1872 aboard the HMS *Challenger* during its historic three-and-a-half-year voyage. Every so often, *Challenger's* crew stopped and measured the depth, along with many other ocean properties. These measurements indicated that the deep ocean floor was not flat but had significant *relief* (variations in elevation), just as dry land does. However, determining bathymetry by making occasional soundings rarely gives a complete picture of the ocean floor. For instance, imagine trying to determine what the surface features on land look like while flying in a blimp at an altitude of several kilometers on a foggy night using only a long weighted rope to determine your height above the surface. This is analogous to how bathymetric measurements were collected from ships using sounding lines.

It wasn't until the early 1900s that ships began to use **echo sounders** to more clearly delineate ocean floor features. An echo sounder sends a sound signal (called a *ping*) into the ocean to produce echoes when the sound bounces off any density difference, such as marine organisms or the ocean floor (Figure 1). Water is a good transmitter of sound, so the time it takes for the echoes to return[2] is used to determine the depth and corresponding shape of the ocean floor. Recall that the German vessel *Meteor* used echo soundings in 1925 to identify a mountain range running through the center of the South Atlantic Ocean.

---

[1]This term is derived from how depth sounding lines were brought back on board a vessel by hand. While hauling in the line, the workers counted the number of arm-lengths collected. By measuring the length of the person's outstretched arms, the amount of line taken in could be calculated. Much later, the distance of 1 fathom was standardized to equal exactly 6 feet.)

---

[2]This technique uses the speed of sound in seawater, which is 1507 meters (4945 feet) per second.

Figure 1 An echo sounder record.

An echo sounder record from the east coast U.S. shows the provinces of the sea floor. Vertical exaggeration (the amount of expansion of the vertical scale) is 12 times. The scattering layer probably represents a concentration of marine organisms.

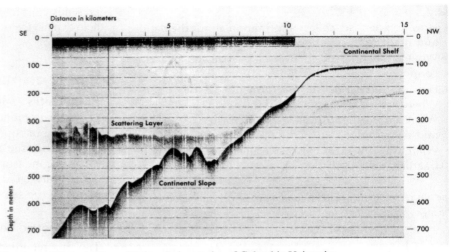

Courtesy of Peter A. Rona, Hudson Laboratories of Columbia University

Echo sounding, however, lacks detail and often gives an inaccurate view of the relief of the sea floor. For instance, the sound beam emitted from a ship 4000 meters (13,100 feet) above the ocean floor widens to a diameter of about 4600 meters (15,000 feet) at the bottom. Consequently, the first echoes to return from the bottom are usually from the closest (highest) peak within this broad area. Nonetheless, most of our knowledge of ocean bathymetry has been provided by the echo sounder.

During and after World War II, there was great improvement in sonar technology. For example, the **precision depth recorder (PDR)**, which was developed in the 1950s, uses a focused high-frequency sound beam to measure depths to a resolution of about 1 meter (3.3 feet). Throughout the 1960s, PDRs were used extensively and provided a reasonably good representation of the ocean floor. From thousands of research vessel tracks, the first reliable global maps of sea floor bathymetry were produced. These maps helped confirm the ideas of sea floor spreading and plate tectonics.

Today, *multibeam echo sounders* (which use multiple frequencies of sound simultaneously) and side-scan **sonar** (an acronym for *s*ound *n*avigation *a*nd *r*anging) give oceanographers a more precise picture of the ocean floor. **SeaBeam**—the first multibeam echo sounder—made it possible for a survey ship to map the features of the ocean floor along a strip up to 60 kilometers (37 miles) wide. The system uses sound emitters directed away from both sides of the ship, with receivers permanently mounted on the hull of the ship. Side-scan sonar systems such as **Sea MARC** (*Sea M*apping *a*nd *R*emote *C*haracterization) and **GLORIA** (*G*eological *L*ong-*R*ange *I*nclined *A*coustical instrument) can be towed behind a survey ship to produce a strip map of ocean floor bathymetry (Figure 2).

To make a more detailed picture of the ocean floor, a side-scan instrument can be towed behind a ship on a cable so that it "flies" just above the ocean floor. One newly developed deep-tow system combines a side-scan sonar instrument with a sub-bottom imaging package (Figure 3). This allows a simultaneous view of the surface of the ocean floor and a cross-section of the sediment below at water depths to 6500 meters (21,325 feet).

STUDENTS SOMETIMES ASK...

All this sea floor mapping is interesting, but haven't we found everything on the sea floor already?

Certainly not! The world's ocean floor—equal in area to almost two moons plus two Mars-sized planets—is one of the most poorly mapped surfaces in the solar system. Recent satellite missions to other planets and their moons have produced stunning high-resolution images of these worlds. In contrast, the ocean floor image produced from sea surface height data shown in Figure 4C is still an order of magnitude lower in resolution that the optic images obtained from a satellite flyby of Mercury in the early 1970s!

Despite satellites that monitor ocean surface conditions and recent advances in mapping technology, only 5% of the ocean floor has been mapped as precisely as the surface of the Moon. In fact, there are areas of the ocean floor as large as the state of Kansas where no ship soundings have been made, and even well-surveyed areas are based on widely separated ship tracks. The great depth of the oceans along with seawater's opaque character has hindered mapping efforts, leaving room for major discoveries in the future (such as new sea floor features, shipwrecks, and mineral deposits).

Although multibeam and side-scan sonar produce fairly detailed bathymetric maps, mapping the sea floor by ship is a time-consuming process. A research vessel must tediously travel back and forth throughout an area (called "mowing the lawn") to produce an accurate map of bathymetric features. A satellite, on the other hand, can observe large areas of the ocean at one time. Consequently, satellites are increasingly

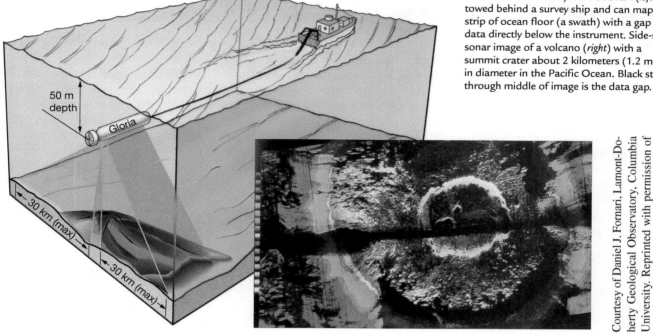

Courtesy of Daniel J. Fornari, Lamont-Doherty Geological Observatory, Columbia University. Reprinted with permission of the American Geophysical Union

Figure 2 Side-scanning sonar.

The side-scan sonar system GLORIA (*left*) is towed behind a survey ship and can map a strip of ocean floor (a swath) with a gap in data directly below the instrument. Side-scan sonar image of a volcano (*right*) with a summit crater about 2 kilometers (1.2 miles) in diameter in the Pacific Ocean. Black stripe through middle of image is the data gap.

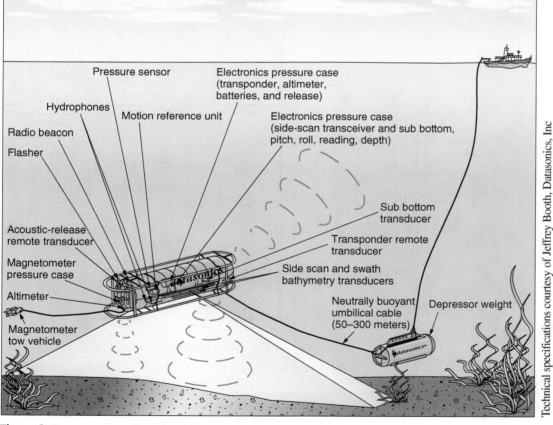

Technical specifications courtesy of Jeffrey Booth, Datasonics, Inc

Figure 3 Deep-tow sea floor imaging system.

Deep-tow side-scan sonar systems are towed close to the ocean floor and provide detailed sonar maps of the ocean floor as well as a profile view of the sediment below.

Recently, satellite measurements of the ocean surface have been used to make maps of the sea floor. How does a satellite—which orbits at a great distance above the planet and can only view the ocean's *surface*—obtain a picture of the sea *floor*?

The answer lies in the fact that sea floor features directly influence Earth's gravitational field. Deep areas such as trenches correspond to a lower gravitational attraction, and large undersea objects such as seamounts exert an extra gravitational pull. These differences affect sea level, causing the ocean surface to bulge outward and sink inward mimicking the relief of the ocean floor. A 2000-meter (6500-foot)-high seamount, for example, exerts a small but measurable gravitational pull on the water around it, creating a bulge 2 meters (7 feet) high on the ocean surface. These irregularities are easily detectable by satellites, which use microwave beams to measure sea level to within 4 centimeters (1.5 inches) accuracy. After corrections are made for waves, tides, currents, and atmospheric effects, the resulting pattern of lumps and bulges at the ocean surface can be used to indirectly reveal ocean floor bathymetry. For example, compares two different maps of the same area: one based on bathymetric data from ships (*top*) and the other based on satellite measurements (*bottom*), which shows much higher resolution of sea floor features.

Data from the European Space Agency's ERS-1 satellite and from Geosat, a U.S. Navy satellite, were

After Gross, M. G., *Oceanography*, 6th ed. (Fig. 16.10), Prentice Hall, 1993

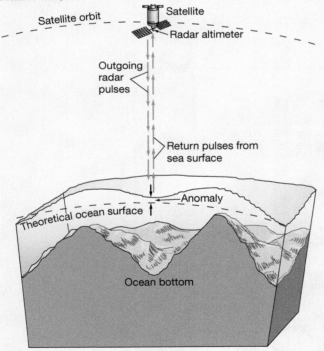

Satellite measurements of the ocean surface.

A satellite measures the variation of ocean surface elevation, which is caused by gravitational attraction and mimics the shape of the sea floor. The sea surface *anomaly* is the difference between the measured and theoretical ocean surface.

Courtesy of David Sandwell, Scripps Institution of Oceanography, University of California, San Diego

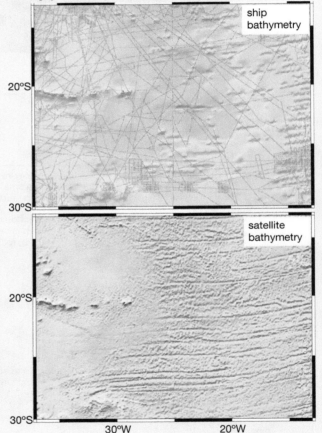

Comparing bathymetric maps of the sea floor.

Both bathymetric maps show the same portion of the Brazil Basin in the South Atlantic Ocean. *Top:* A map made using conventional echo sounder records from ships (ship tracks shown by thin lines). *Bottom:* A map from satellite data made using measurements of the ocean surface.

collected during the 1980s. When this information was recently declassified, Walter Smith of the National Oceanic and Atmospheric Administration and David Sandwell of Scripps Institution of Oceanography began producing sea floor maps based on the shape of the sea surface. What is unique about these re- searchers' maps is that they provide a view of Earth similar to being able to drain the oceans and view the ocean floor directly. Their map of ocean surface gravity uses depth soundings to calibrate the gravity measurements. Although gravity is not exactly bathymetry, this new map of the ocean floor clearly delin- eates many ocean floor features, such as the mid-ocean ridge, trenches, seamounts, and nemataths (island chains). In addition, this new mapping technique has revealed sea floor bathymetry in areas where research vessels have not conducted surveys.

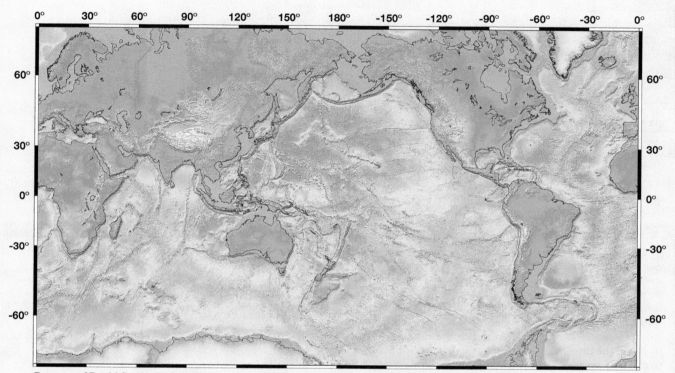

Courtesy of David Sandwell, Scripps Institution of Oceanography, University of California, San Diego

Global sea surface elevation map from satellite data.

Map showing the satellite-derived global gravity field, which, when adjusted using measured depths, closely corresponds to ocean depth. Purple indicates deep water; the mid-ocean ridge (intermediate water depths) is mostly light green and yellow; brown indicates shallowest water. Map also shows land surface elevations, with dark green color indicating low elevations and white color indicating high elevations.

used to determine ocean properties. Remarkably, satellite measurements allow the ocean floor to be mapped from space (Box 1).

Oceanographers who want to know about ocean structure beneath the sea floor use strong low-frequency sounds produced by explosions or air guns, as shown in Figure 4. These sounds penetrate beneath the sea floor and reflect off the boundaries between different rock or sediment layers, producing **seismic reflec- tion profiles**, which have applications in mineral and petroleum exploration.

Sending pings of sound into the ocean (echo sounding) is commonly used to determine ocean bathymetry. More recently, satellites have also been used to map sea floor features.

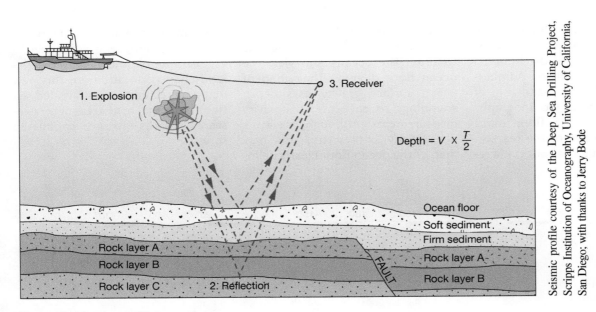

Depth $= V \times \dfrac{T}{2}$

Seismic profile courtesy of the Deep Sea Drilling Project, Scripps Institution of Oceanography, University of California, San Diego; with thanks to Jerry Bode

Figure 4 Seismic profiling.

An air-gun explosion emits low frequency sounds (1) that can penetrate bottom sediments and rock layers. The sound reflects off the boundaries between these layers (2) and returns to the receiver (3).

EXAMPLE 1

Using the equation shown in Figure 4-4, how deep is the water in an area where it takes a ping of sound 10 seconds to reach the bottom and return?

If we know the time it takes for sound to be transmitted, we can use the equation in Figure 4-4 to determine the water depth (the speed of sound in seawater is a constant value, given in footnote 2). Remember, the reason we need to divide the time by 2 is to account for the sound traveling to the bottom *and back to the surface*! The general equation is

$$Depth = Velocity \times \frac{Time}{2}$$

Since the velocity of sound in seawater is 1507 meters per second and the time is 10 seconds, this gives

$$Depth = 1507 \text{ meters per second} \times \frac{10 \text{ seconds}}{2}$$

So, the water depth is 7535 meters (24,700 feet), which is quite deep!

The Hypsographic Curve

Figure 5 illustrates Earth's **hypsographic** (*hypsos* = height, *graphic* = drawn) **curve**, which shows the relationship between the height of the land and the depth of the oceans. The bar graph (Figure 5, *left*) gives the percentage of Earth's surface area at various ranges of elevation and depth. The cumulative curve (Figure 5, *right*) gives the percentage of surface area from the highest peaks to the deepest depths of the oceans. Together, they show that 70.8% of Earth's surface is covered by oceans and that the average depth of the ocean is 3729 meters (12,234 feet) while the average height of the land is only 840 meters (2756 feet). The difference results from the greater density and lesser thickness of oceanic crust as compared to continental crust.

The cumulative hypsographic curve (Figure 5, *right*) shows five differently sloped segments. On land, the first steep segment of the curve represents tall mountains while the gentle slope represents low coastal plains (and continues just offshore, representing the shallow parts of the continental margin). The first slope below sea level represents steep areas of the continental margins and also includes the mountainous mid-ocean ridge. Further offshore, the longest, flattest part of the whole curve represents the deep-ocean basins, followed by the last steep part, which represents ocean trenches.

The shape of the hypsographic curve can be used to support the existence of plate tectonics on Earth. Specifically, the two flat areas and three sloped areas of the curve show that there is a very uneven distribution of area at different depths and elevations. If there were no active mechanism involved in creating such features on

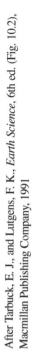

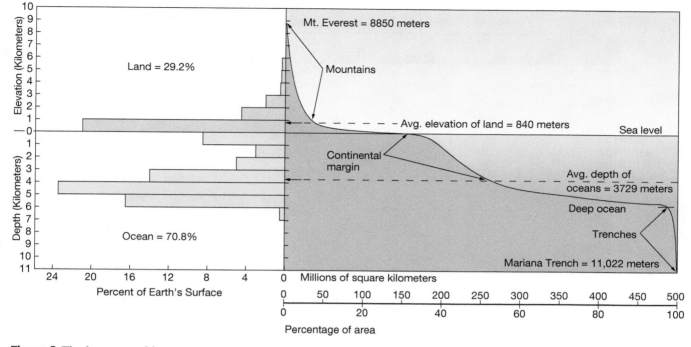

Figure 5 The hypsographic curve.

The bar graph (*left*) gives the percentage of Earth's surface area at various ranges of elevation and depth. The cumulative hypsographic curve (*right*) gives the percentage of surface area from the highest peaks to the deepest depths of the oceans. Also shown is the average ocean depth and land elevation.

Earth, the bar graph portions would all be about the same length and the cumulative curve would be a straight line. Instead, the variations in the curve suggest that plate tectonics is actively working to modify Earth's surface. The flat portions of the curve represent various intraplate elevations both on land and underwater while the slopes of the curve represent mountains, continental slopes, the mid-ocean ridge, and deep-ocean trenches, all of which are created by plate tectonic processes. Interestingly, hypsographic curves constructed for other planets and moons using satellite data have been used to determine if plate tectonics is actively modifying the surface of these worlds.

Provinces of the Ocean Floor

The ocean floor can be divided into three major provinces (Figure 6): (1) **continental margins**, which are shallow-water areas close to continents; (2) **deep-ocean basins**, which are deep-water areas farther from land; and (3) the **mid-ocean ridge**, which is comprised of shallower areas near the middle of an ocean. Plate tectonic processes are integral to the formation of these provinces: Through the process of sea floor spreading, mid-ocean ridges and deep-ocean basins are created; elsewhere, as a continent is split apart, new continental margins are formed.

Features of Continental Margins

Passive and Active Continental Margins   Continental margins can be classified as either passive or active depending on their proximity to plate boundaries. **Passive margins** (Figure 7, *left*) are imbedded within the interior of lithospheric plates and are therefore not in close proximity to any plate boundary. Thus, passive margins usually lack major tectonic activity (large earthquakes, eruptive volcanoes, and mountain building).

The east coast of the United States, where there is no plate boundary, is an example of a passive continental margin. Passive margins are usually produced by rifting of continental landmasses and continued sea floor spreading over geologic time. Features of passive continental margins include the continental shelf, the continental slope, and the continental rise that extends toward the deep-ocean basins (Figures 7 and 8).

Active margins (Figure 7, *right*) are associated with lithospheric plate boundaries and are marked by a high degree of tectonic activity. Two types of active margins exist. **Convergent active margins** are associated with oceanic–continental convergent plate boundaries. Features include a continental arc onshore, a narrow shelf, a steep slope, and an offshore trench that delineates the plate boundary. Western South America, where the Nazca Plate is being subducted beneath the South American Plate, is an example of a convergent active margin. **Transform active margins** are less

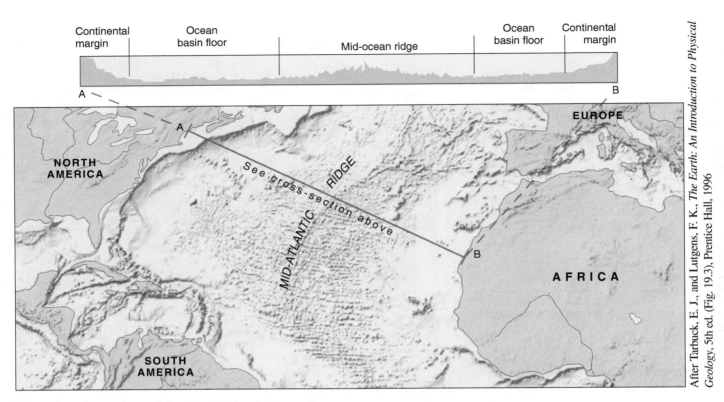

Figure 6 Major regions of the North Atlantic Ocean floor.

Map view below and profile view above, showing that the ocean floor can be divided into three major provinces: continental margins, deep ocean basins, and mid-ocean ridge.

common and are associated with transform plate boundaries. At these locations, faults that parallel the transform plate boundary create linear islands, banks (shallowly submerged areas), and deep basins close to shore. Coastal California along the San Andreas Fault is an example of a transform active margin.

> Passive continental margins lack a plate boundary and have different features than active continental margins, which include a plate boundary (either convergent or transform).

Continental Shelf The **continental shelf** is defined as a generally flat zone extending from the shore beneath the ocean surface to a point at which a marked increase in slope angle occurs, called the **shelf break** (Figure 8). It is usually flat and relatively featureless because of marine sediment deposits but can contain coastal islands, reefs, and raised banks. The underlying rock is granitic continental crust, so the continental shelf is geologically part of the continent. The general bathymetry of the continental shelf can usually be predicted by examining the topography of the adjacent coastal region. With few exceptions, the coastal topography extends beyond the shore and onto the continental shelf.

The average width of the continental shelf is about 70 kilometers (43 miles), but it varies from a few tens of meters to 1500 kilometers (930 miles). The broadest shelves occur off the northern coasts of Siberia and North America in the Arctic Ocean. The average depth at which the shelf break occurs is about 135 meters (443 feet). Around the continent of Antarctica, however, the shelf break occurs at 350 meters (2200 feet). The average slope of the continental shelf is only about a tenth of a degree, similar to the slope given to a large parking lot for drainage purposes.

Sea level has fluctuated over the history of Earth, causing the shoreline to migrate back and forth across the continental shelf. When colder climates prevailed during the Ice Age, for example, more of Earth's water was frozen as glaciers on land, so sea level was lower than it is today. During this time, more of the continental shelf was exposed.

The type of continental margin will determine the shape and features associated with the continental shelf. For example, the east coast of South America has a broader continental shelf than its west coast. The east coast is a passive margin, which typically has a wider shelf. In contrast, the convergent active margin present along the west coast of South America is characterized by a narrow continental shelf and a shelf break close to shore. For transform active margins such as along California, the presence of offshore faults produces a continental shelf that is not flat. Rather, it is marked by a high degree of relief (islands, shallow banks, and deep basins) called a **continental borderland**.

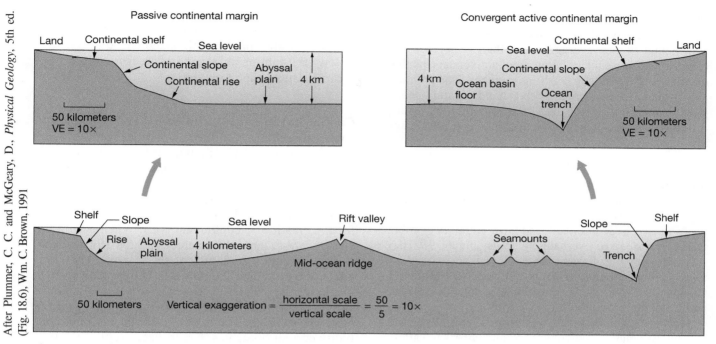

After Plummer, C. C. and McGeary, D., *Physical Geology*, 5th ed. (Fig. 18.6), Wm. C. Brown, 1991

Figure 7 Passive and active continental margins.

Cross-sectional view (*below*) of typical features across an ocean basin, including a passive continental margin (*left enlargement*) and a convergent active continental margin (*right enlargement*). Vertical exaggeration is 50 times.

After Tarbuck, E. J., and Lutgens, F. K., *The Earth: An Introduction to Physical Geology*, 5th ed. (Fig. 19.4), Prentice Hall, 1996

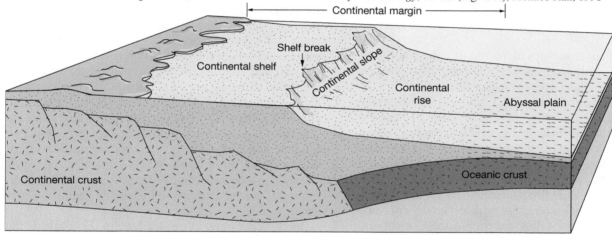

Figure 8 Features of a passive continental margin.

Schematic view showing the main features of a passive continental margin.

Continental Slope   The **continental slope**, which lies beyond the shelf break, is where the deep-ocean basins begin. Total relief in this region is similar to that found in mountain ranges on the continents. The break at the top of the slope may be from 1 to 5 kilometers (0.6 to 3 miles) above the deep-ocean basin at its base. Along convergent active margins where the slope descends into submarine trenches, even greater vertical relief is measured. Off the west coast of South America, for in-stance, the total relief from the top of the Andes Mountains to the bottom of the Peru-Chile Trench is about 15 kilometers (9.3 miles).

Worldwide, the slope of the continental slopes averages about 4 degrees, but varies from 1 to 25 degrees.[3] A study that compared the average of five different continental

[3]For comparison, the windshield of an aerodynamically designed car has a slope of about 25 degrees.

slopes in the United States revealed that it is just over 2 degrees. Around the margin of the Pacific Ocean, the continental slopes average more than 5 degrees because of the presence of convergent active margins that drop directly into deep offshore trenches. The Atlantic and Indian Oceans, on the other hand, contain many passive margins, which lack plate boundaries. Thus, the amount of relief is lower and slopes in these oceans average about 3 degrees.

Submarine Canyons and Turbidity Currents The continental slope—and, to a lesser extent, the continental shelf—exhibit **submarine canyons**. Submarine canyons are V-shaped in profile view and have branches or tributaries with steep to overhanging walls (Figure 9). They resemble canyons formed on land that are carved by rivers and can be quite large. In fact, the Monterey Canyon off California is comparable in depth, steepness, and length to Arizona's Grand Canyon.

How are submarine canyons formed? Initially it was thought submarine canyons were ancient river valleys created by the erosive power of rivers when sea level was lower and the continental shelf was exposed. Although some canyons are directly offshore from where rivers enter the sea, the majority of them are not. Many, in fact, are confined exclusively to the continental slope. Additionally, submarine canyons continue to the base of the continental slope, which averages some 3500 meters (11,500 feet) below sea level. There is no evidence, however, that sea level has ever been lowered by that much.

Side-scan sonar surveys along the Atlantic coast indicate that the continental slope is dominated by submarine canyons from Hudson Canyon near New York City to Baltimore Canyon in Maryland. Canyons confined to the continental slope are straighter and have steeper canyon floor gradients than those that extend into the continental shelf. These characteristics suggest the canyons are created on the continental slope by some marine process and enlarge into the continental shelf through time.

Both indirect and direct observation of the erosive power of **turbidity** (*turbidus* = disordered) **currents** (Box 2) has suggested they are responsible for carving submarine canyons. Turbidity currents are underwater avalanches of muddy water mixed with rocks and other debris. When sediment moves across the continental shelf into the head of the canyon and accumulates there, turbidity currents may result from shaking by an earthquake, the oversteepening of sediment that accumulates on the shelf, hurricanes passing over the area, or the rapid input of sediment from flood waters. The mass moves down the slope under the force of gravity when set in motion, carving the canyon as it goes, analogous to a flash flood on land. Turbidity currents are strong enough to carry large rocks down submarine canyons and do a considerable amount of erosion over time.

> Turbidity currents are underwater avalanches of muddy water mixed with sediment that move down the continental slope and are responsible for carving submarine canyons.

Continental Rise The **continental rise** is a transition zone between the continental margin and the deep-ocean floor comprised of a huge submerged pile of debris. Where did all this debris come from, and how did it get there?

The existence of turbidity currents suggests that the material transported by these currents is responsible for the creation of continental rises. When a turbidity current moves through and erodes a submarine canyon, it exits through the mouth of the canyon. The slope angle decreases and the turbidity current slows, causing suspended material to settle out in a distinctive type of layering called **graded bedding** that *grades in size upward* (Figure 9a, *inset*). As the energy of the turbidity current dissipates, larger pieces settle first, then progressively smaller pieces settle, and eventually even very fine pieces settle out, which may occur weeks or months later.

An individual turbidity current deposits one graded bedding sequence. The next turbidity current may partially erode the previous deposit and then deposit another graded bedding sequence on top of the previous one. After some time, a thick sequence of graded bedding deposits can develop one on top of another. These stacks of graded bedding are called **turbidite deposits**, of which the continental rise is composed.

As viewed from above, the deposits at the mouths of submarine canyons are fan-, lobate-, or apron-shaped (Figures 9a and 9c). Consequently, these deposits are called **deep-sea fans** or **submarine fans**. These deep-sea fans create the continental rise when they merge together along the base of the continental slope. Along convergent active margins, however, the steep continental slope leads directly into a deep-ocean trench. Sediment from turbidity currents accumulates in the trench and there is no continental rise.

One of the largest deep-sea fans in the world is the Indus Fan, a passive margin fan that extends 1800 kilometers (1100 miles) south of Pakistan (Figure 9c). The Indus River carries extensive amounts of sediment from the Himalaya Mountains to the coast. This sediment eventually makes its way down the submarine canyon and builds the fan, which, in some areas, has sediment that is more than 10 kilometers (6.2 miles) thick. The Indus Fan has a main submarine canyon channel extending seaward onto the fan but soon divides into several branching distributary channels. These distributary channels are similar to those found on deltas, which form at the mouths of streams. On the lower fan, the surface has a very low slope and the flow is no longer con-

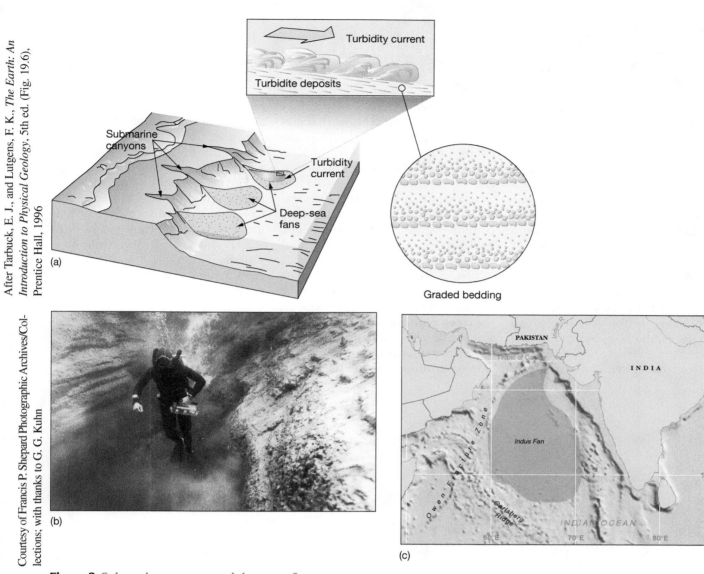

After Tarbuck, E. J., and Lutgens, F. K., *The Earth: An Introduction to Physical Geology*, 5th ed. (Fig. 19.6), Prentice Hall, 1996

Courtesy of Francis P. Shepard Photographic Archives/Collections; with thanks to G. G. Kuhn

Turbidity current

Turbidite deposits

Submarine canyons

Turbidity current

Deep-sea fans

Graded bedding

(a)

(b)

(c)

Figure 9 Submarine canyons and deep-sea fans.

(a) Turbidity currents move downslope, eroding the continental margin to enlarge submarine canyons. Deep-sea fans are created by turbidite deposits, which consist of sequences of graded bedding (*inset*). **(b)** A diver descends into La Jolla Submarine Canyon, offshore California. **(c)** Map of the Indus Fan, a large but otherwise typical example of a passive margin fan.

fined to channels, so it spreads out and forms layers of fine sediment across the fan surface. The Indus Fan has so much sediment, in fact, that it partially buries an active mid-ocean ridge, the Carlsberg Ridge!

Features of the Deep-Ocean Basin

The deep-ocean floor lies beyond the continental margin province (the shelf, slope, and the rise).

Abyssal Plains Extending from the base of the continental rise into the deep-ocean basins are flat depositional surfaces with slopes that average a small fraction of a degree and cover extensive portions of the deep-ocean basins.

These **abyssal** (*a* = without, *byssus* = bottom) **plains** average between 4500 meters (15,000 feet) and 6000 meters (20,000 feet) deep. They are not literally bottomless, but they are some of the deepest (and flattest) regions on Earth.

Abyssal plains are formed by fine particles of sediment slowly drifting onto the deep-ocean floor. Over millions of years, a thick blanket of sediment is produced by **suspension settling**, where fine particles (analogous to "marine dust") accumulate on the ocean floor. With enough time, these deposits cover most irregularities of the deep ocean, as shown in Figure 10. In addition, sediment traveling in turbidity currents from land adds to the sediment load.

BOX 2   Research Methods in Oceanography

A GRAND "BREAK": EVIDENCE FOR TURBIDITY CURRENTS

How do earthquakes and telephone cables help explain how turbidity currents move across the ocean floor and carve submarine canyons? In 1929, the Grand Banks earthquake in the North Atlantic Ocean severed some of the trans-Atlantic telephone and telegraph cables that lay across the sea floor south of Newfoundland near the earthquake epicenter. At first, it was assumed that sea floor movement caused all these breaks. However, analysis of the data revealed that the cables closest to the earthquake broke simultaneously with the earthquake, but cables that crossed progressively further downslope from the epicenter were snapped

one after another like a string of firecrackers. It seemed unusual that certain cables were affected by the failure of the slope due to ground shaking, but others were broken several minutes later.

Reanalysis of the pattern several years later suggested that a turbidity current moving down the slope could account for the pattern of cable breaks. Based on the sequence of breaks, the turbidity current must have reached speeds approaching 80 kilometers (50 miles) per hour on the steep portions of the continental slope, and about 24 kilometers (15 miles) per hour on the more gently sloping continental rise. Thus, tur-

bidity currents reach high speeds and are strong enough to break underwater cables, suggesting that they must be powerful enough to erode submarine canyons.

Further evidence of turbidity currents comes from several studies that have documented turbidity currents using sonar. For instance, a study of Rupert Inlet in British Columbia, Canada, monitored turbidity currents moving through an underwater channel. These studies indicate that submarine canyons are carved by turbidity currents over long periods of time, just as canyons on land are carved by running water.

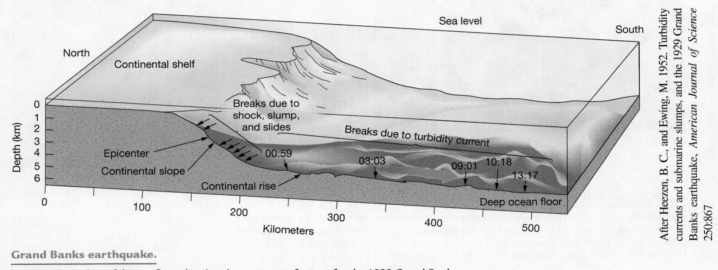

After Heezen, B. C., and Ewing, M. 1952. Turbidity currents and submarine slumps, and the 1929 Grand Banks earthquake, *American Journal of Science* 250:867

Grand Banks earthquake.

Diagrammatic view of the sea floor showing the sequence of events for the 1929 Grand Banks Earthquake. The epicenter is the point on Earth's surface directly above the earthquake.

The type of continental margin determines the distribution of abyssal plains. For instance, few abyssal plains are located in the Pacific Ocean; instead, most occur in the Atlantic and Indian Oceans. The deep-ocean trenches found on the convergent active margins of the Pacific Ocean prevent sediment from moving past the continental slope. In essence, the trenches act like a gutter that traps sediment transported off the land by turbidity currents. On the passive margins of the Atlantic and Indian Oceans, however, turbidity currents travel directly down the continental margin and deposit sediment on the abyssal plains. In addition, the great distance from the

continental margin to the floor of the deep-ocean basins in the Pacific Ocean is so great that most of the suspended sediment settles out before it reaches these distant regions. Conversely, the smaller size of the Atlantic and Indian Oceans does not prevent suspended sediment from reaching their deep-ocean basins.

Volcanic Peaks of the Abyssal Plains   Poking through the sediment cover of the abyssal plains are a variety of volcanic peaks, which extend to various elevations above the ocean floor (see Figure 2). Some even extend above sea level to form islands. Those that are below sea level

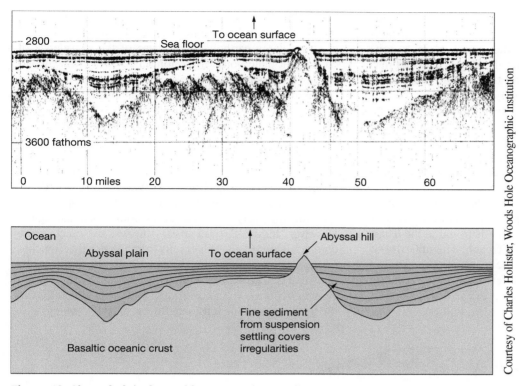

Figure 10 **Abyssal plain formed by suspension settling.**

Seismic cross-section (*above*) and matching drawing (*below*) across part of the deep Madeira abyssal plain in the eastern Atlantic Ocean showing irregular volcanic terrain buried by sediments.

but rise more than 1 kilometer (0.6 mile) above the deep-ocean floor are called *seamounts*. Analysis of satellite bathymetry data suggests there may be as many as 100,000 seamounts on the ocean floor. If seamounts have flattened tops, they are called *tablemounts*, or *guyots*.

Volcanic features on the ocean floor that are less than 1000 meters (0.6 mile) tall—the minimum height of a seamount—are called **abyssal hills** or **seaknolls**. Abyssal hills are one of the most abundant features on the planet (several hundred thousand have been identified) and cover a large percentage of the entire ocean basin floor. Many are gently rounded in shape and they have an average height of about 200 meters (650 feet). Many abyssal hills are found buried beneath the sediments of the abyssal plains of the Atlantic and Indian Oceans. In the Pacific Ocean, the abundance of active margins means the rate of sediment deposition is lower. Consequently, extensive regions dominated by abyssal hills have resulted, which are called **abyssal hill provinces**. The evidence of volcanic activity on the bottom of the Pacific Ocean is particularly widespread—more than 20,000 volcanic peaks exist there.

Flood Basalts Some marine volcanic activity produces widespread, generally flat surfaces where large volumes of lava flowed out in broad sheets and solidified. Such features commonly surround volcanic islands but sometimes are large enough to form elevated plateaus called *large igneous provinces*.

When found on the continents, such volcanic accumulations are called **continental flood basalts**. They are formed where a mantle plume reaches the bottom of the lithosphere and forms a broad rounded head that may range from 1000 to 2000 kilometers (620 to 1240 miles) in diameter. The temperature within this head is hotter than the surrounding mantle and produces a wide uplifted dome at Earth's surface from thermal expansion of the rock below. If the continental crust above thins either from erosion of the uplifted dome or from the early stages of continental rifting, hot magma of basaltic composition escapes and floods out at the surface. The Colombia River and Snake River flood basalts in Washington, Oregon, and Idaho were formed in this manner.

The volume of lava released during the formation of flood basalts is impressive. Continental flood basalts, for example, typically contain up to 2 million cubic kilometers (480,000 cubic miles) of lava and erupt at rates of about 1 cubic kilometer (0.24 cubic mile) per year over a relatively short interval of about 1 or 2 million years. However, the 120-million-year-old Ontong Java Plateau in the equatorial western Pacific contains about 65 million cubic kilometers (15.6 million cubic miles) of lava—more than 30 times the volume of most continental flood basalts. Remarkably, this large volume was produced over a period of no more than 3 million years, which must have required an average eruption rate of about 22 cubic kilometers (5.3 cubic miles) per year.

Ocean Trenches Along passive margins, the continental rise commonly occurs at the base of the continental slope and merges smoothly into the abyssal plain. In convergent active margins, however, the slope descends into a long, narrow, steep-sided **ocean trench**. Ocean trenches are deep linear scars in the ocean floor, caused by the collision of two plates along convergent plate margins. The landward side of the trench rises as a **volcanic arc** that may produce islands (such as the islands of Japan, an **island arc**) or a volcanic mountain range along the margin of a continent (such as the Andes Mountains, a **continental arc**).

The deepest portions of the world's oceans are found in these trenches. In fact, the deepest point on Earth's surface—11,022 meters (36,161 feet)—is found in the Challenger Deep area of the Mariana Trench. The majority of ocean trenches are found along the margins of the Pacific Ocean (Figure 11) while only a few exist in the Atlantic and Indian Oceans. Table 1 compares the dimensions of selected trenches.

The **Pacific Ring of Fire** occurs along the margins of the Pacific Ocean. It has the majority of Earth's active volcanoes and large earthquakes because of the prevalence of convergent plate boundaries along the Pacific Rim. A part of the Pacific Ring of Fire is South America's western coast, including the Andes Mountains and the associated Peru-Chile Trench. Figure 12 shows a cross-sectional view of this area, illustrating the tremendous amount of relief at convergent plate boundaries where deep-ocean trenches are associated with tall volcanic arcs.

Back-Arc Spreading Centers When plates collide at subduction zones, you might suspect that compressional (pressing together) stresses would be dominant in the region. However, tensional (pull-apart) stresses are much more commonly observed. This results from the fact that trenches are not stationary; rather, they move in the direction of the plate that will be subducted in a process called *seaward migration*. As a result, the overriding plate gets pulled toward the trench, producing tensional forces, crustal thinning, and,

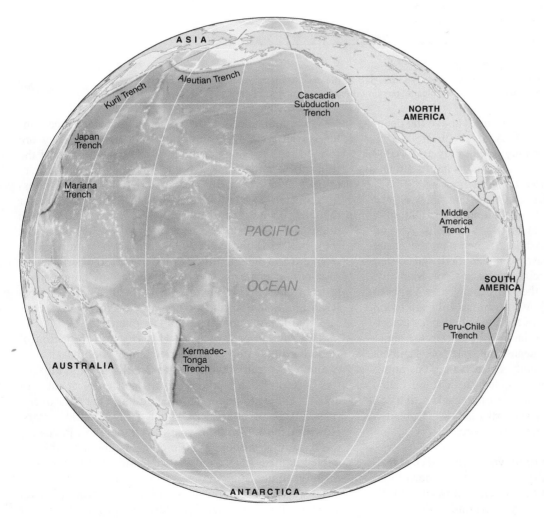

Figure 11 Location of ocean trenches.

The majority of ocean trenches are along the margins of the Pacific Ocean where plates are being subducted.
Most of the world's large earthquakes (due to subduction) and active volcanoes (as volcanic arcs) occur
around the Pacific Rim, which is why the area is also called the Pacific Ring of Fire.

TABLE 1 Dimensions of selected trenches.

Trench	Ocean	Depth (kilometers)	Average width (kilometers)	Length (kilometers)
Middle America	Pacific	6.7	40	2800
Java	Indian	7.5	80	4500
Aleutian	Pacific	7.7	50	3700
Peru-Chile	Pacific	8.0	100	5900
South Sandwich	Atlantic	8.4	90	1450
Japan	Pacific	8.4	100	800
Puerto Rico	Atlantic	8.4	120	1550
Kermadec-Tonga	Pacific	10.0	50	2900
Philippine	Pacific	10.5	60	1400
Kuril	Pacific	10.5	120	2200
Mariana	Pacific	11.0	70	2550

in some cases, a spreading center behind (landward of) the volcanic arc called a **back-arc spreading center**. A back-arc spreading center has all the features of a full mid-ocean ridge, which will be discussed in the next section.

Figure 13 shows a cross-sectional view of a well-developed back-arc spreading center created by the Mariana Trench/Island Arc subduction system. The Pacific Plate is being subducted beneath the Philippine Plate, creating tensional stresses and the back-arc spreading center. An ancient *remnant arc* called the West Mariana Ridge exists about 200 kilometers (124 miles) to the west of the back-arc spreading center and indicates a former location of back-arc spreading.

Unusual seamounts composed of serpentine[4] are sometimes associated with a subduction zone's *fore-arc* region (the portion of the overriding plate that lies seaward of the volcanic arc) (Figure 13). It is thought that

the serpentine formed when seawater either entered the mantle through fractures in the fore-arc crust or was available from dewatering of subducted sediments. Because of its low density, the serpentine flowed up to the surface of the fore-arc, carrying with it blocks of peridotite (mantle rock) and basalt (possibly from subducting ocean crust) to produce volcano-like seamounts near the seaward front of the fore-arc structure.

> Deep-ocean trenches and volcanic arcs are a result of the collision of two plates at convergent plate boundaries and mostly occur along the margins of the Pacific Ocean (Pacific Ring of Fire).

Features of the Mid-Ocean Ridge

The global mid-ocean ridge is a continuous, fractured-looking mountain ridge that extends through all the ocean basins. The portion of the mid-ocean ridge found in the North Atlantic Ocean is called the Mid-Atlantic

---

[4]Recall that serpentine is a mineral that forms when water reacts with *peridotite*, which is rock from Earth's mantle.

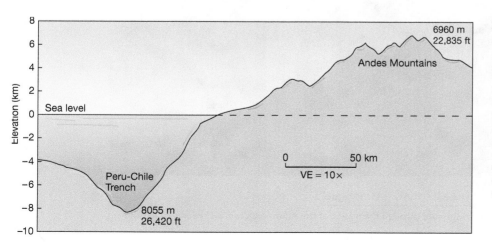

Figure 12 Profile across the Peru-Chile Trench and the Andes Mountains.

Over a distance of 200 kilometers (125 miles), there is a change in elevation of more than 14,900 meters (49,000 feet) from the Peru-Chile Trench to the Andes Mountains. This dramatic relief is a result of plate interactions at a convergent active margin, producing a deep-ocean trench and associated continental volcanic arc. Vertical scale is exaggerated 10 times.

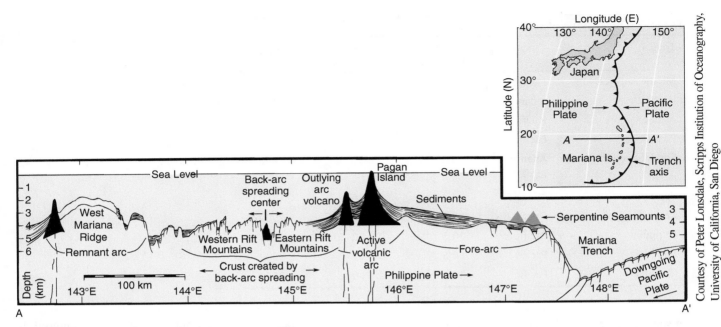

Courtesy of Peter Lonsdale, Scripps Institution of Oceanography, University of California, San Diego

Figure 13 Mariana Trench and back-arc spreading.

Cross-sectional view of features created by the Mariana island arc subduction system. From left to right: the West Mariana Ridge is an ancient remnant arc; back-arc spreading occurs as the trench migrates seaward, creating tensional stresses; Pagan Island is part of the active volcanic arc; rare serpentine seamounts occur on the leading edge of the fore-arc; the Mariana Trench is a result of subduction of the Pacific Plate beneath the Philippine Plate. Vertical exaggeration is 14 times.

Courtesy of Aluminum Company of America (Alcoa)

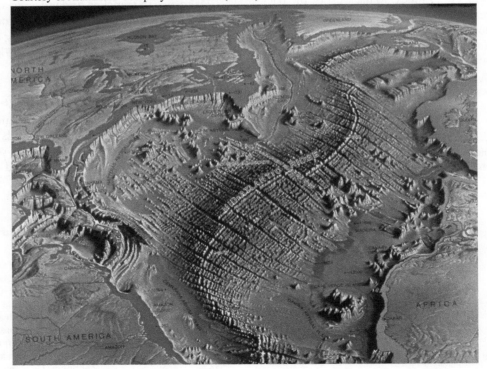

Figure 14 Floor of the North Atlantic Ocean.

The global mid-ocean ridge cuts through the center of the Atlantic Ocean, where it is called the Mid-Atlantic Ridge.

Ridge and is shown in Figure 14. The mid-ocean ridge results from sea floor spreading along divergent plate boundaries. The mid-ocean ridge forms Earth's longest mountain chain, extending across some 75,000 kilometers (46,600 miles) of the deep-ocean basin. The width of the mid-ocean ridge varies along its length but averages about 1000 kilometers (620 miles). The mid-ocean ridge is a topographically high feature, extending an average of 2.5 kilometers (1.5 miles) above the surrounding sea floor. In some areas, such as in Iceland, the mid-ocean ridge even extends above sea level. Remarkably, the mid-ocean ridge covers 23% of Earth's surface.

The mid-ocean ridge is entirely volcanic and is composed of basaltic lavas characteristic of the oceanic crust. Along its crest is a central downdropped **rift valley** (Figure 15) created by sea floor spreading (rifting) where two plates diverge. Cracks called *fissures* (*fissus* = split) and faults are commonly observed in the central rift valley. Swarms of small earthquakes occur along the central rift valley caused by underground movement of magma or rifting along faults.

Volcanic features include volcanoes (seamounts[5]; Figure 16a) and recent underwater lava flows. When hot basaltic lava spills onto the sea floor, it is exposed to cold seawater that chills the margins of the lava. This creates **pillow lavas** or **pillow basalts**, which are smooth, rounded lobes of rock that resemble a stack of bed pillows (Figure 16b). Although most people are not usually aware of it, frequent volcanic activity is common along the mid-ocean ridge. In fact, every year about 12 cubic kilometers (3 cubic miles) of molten rock erupts underwater—enough to fill 20 Olympic-sized swimming pools every minute. Bathymetric studies along the Juan de Fuca Ridge off Washington and Oregon, for example, revealed that 50 million cubic meters (1800 million cubic feet) of new lava was released sometime between 1981 and 1987. Subsequent surveys of the area indicated many changes along the mid-ocean ridge, including new volcanic features, recent lava flows, and depth changes of up to 37 meters (121 feet).

---

[5]In a number of cases, researchers have discovered seamounts that initially formed along the crest of the mid-ocean ridge and have been split in two as the plates spread apart.

Figure 15 Rift valley fissures.

A large fissure in the rift valley of Iceland (*above*). A smaller fissure in the rift valley of the Mid-Atlantic Ridge (*below*), which was photographed by researchers in the submersible *Alvin*.

Courtesy of Br. Robert McDermott, S. J

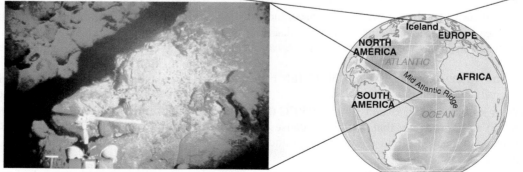

Courtesy of Woods Hole Oceanographic Institution

Map produced by S. P. Miller; provided courtesy of K. C. McDonald, University of California, Santa Barbara

(a)

Courtesy of A. E. J. Engel and Scripps Geological Collections, Scripps Institution of Oceanography, University of California, San Diego

(b)

Figure 16 East Pacific Rise volcanoes and pillow lava.

(a) False-color perspective view based on sonar mapping of a portion of the East Pacific Rise (*center*) showing volcanic seamount (*left*). Depth in meters indicated by the color scale along the left margin; vertical exaggeration is six times. **(b)** Recently formed pillow lava along the East Pacific Rise. Photo shows an area of the sea floor about 3 meters (10 feet) across that also displays ripple marks from deep ocean currents.

S ? STUDENTS SOMETIMES ASK ...
Has anyone ever seen pillow lava forming?

Amazingly, yes! In the 1960s, an underwater film crew ventured to Hawaii during an eruption of the volcano Kilauea where lava spilled into the sea. They braved high water temperatures and risked being burned on the red-hot lava, but filmed some incredible footage. Underwater, the formation of pillow lava occurs where a tube emits molten lava directly into the ocean. When hot lava comes into contact with cold seawater, it forms the characteristic smooth and rounded margins of pillow basalt. The divers also experimented with a hammer on newly formed pillows and were able to initiate new lava outpourings.

Other features in the central rift valley include hot springs called **hydrothermal** (*hydro* = water, *thermo* = heat) **vents**. Seawater seeps along fractures in the ocean crust and is heated when it comes in contact with underlying magma (Figure 17). It then rises back toward the surface and exits through the sea floor. The temperature of the water that rushes out of a particular hydrothermal vent determines its appearance:

- **Warm-water vents** are below 30°C (86°F) and generally emit water clear in color.
- **White smokers** are between 30° and 350°C (86° to 662°F) and emit water that is white because of the presence of various light-colored compounds, including barium sulfide.
- **Black smokers** are above 350°C (662°F) and emit water that is black because of the presence of dark-

colored **metal sulfides**, including lead, iron, nickel, copper, zinc, and chromium. Black smokers were named for their resemblance to factory smoke-stacks belching clouds of smoke.

S ? STUDENTS SOMETIMES ASK ...
If black smokers are so hot, why isn't there steam coming out of them instead of hot water?

Indeed, black smokers emit water that can be up to three and a half times the boiling point of water at the surface. However, the depth where black smokers are found results in much higher pressure than at the surface. At these higher pressures, water has a higher boiling point. Thus, water from hydrothermal vents remains in the liquid state instead of turning into water vapor (steam).

Chemical studies of seawater indicate that the entire volume of ocean water is cycled through hydrothermal circulation systems about every 3 million years. As a result, chemical exchange between ocean water and basaltic crust has a significant influence on the chemical composition of seawater.

Many black smokers spew out of chimneylike structures (Figure 17b) that can be up to 60 meters (200 feet) high. The dissolved metal particles often come out of solution, or **precipitates**[6] when the hot water mixes with cold seawater,

---

[6]A chemical precipitate is formed whenever dissolved materials change from existing in the dissolved state to existing in the solid state.

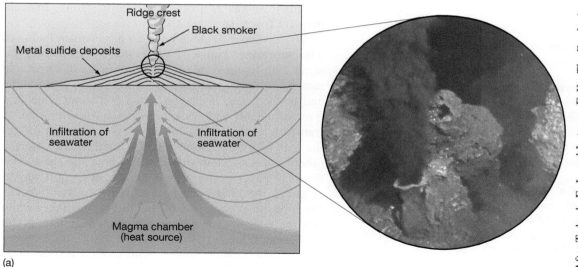

(a)

After Tarbuck, E. J., and Lutgens, F. K., *The Earth: An Introduction to Physical Geology*, 5th ed. (Fig. 21.23), Prentice Hall, 1996. Inset photo by Fred N. Spiess, Scripps Institution of Oceanography, University of California, San Diego

(b)

Photo Ifremer, from Manaute Cruise, courtesy of Jean-Marie Auzende

Figure 17 Hydrothermal vents.

(a) Diagram showing hydrothermal circulation along the mid-ocean ridge and the creation of black smokers. Photo (*inset*) shows a close-up view of a black smoker along the East Pacific Rise. **(b)** Black smoker chimney and fissure at Susu north active site, Manus Basin, western Pacific Ocean. Chimney is about 3 meters (10 feet) tall.

creating coatings of mineral deposits on nearby rocks. Chemical analyses of these deposits reveal that they are composed of various metal sulfides and sometimes even silver and gold. Mining these modern sea floor deposits is neither economically nor politically feasible at present but has often been considered. However, many deposits of these metals that are mined on land today probably originated as hydrothermal deposits at ancient mid-ocean ridges. One such example is the copper deposits that have been mined since antiquity in Cyprus.

In addition, most hydrothermal vents support unusual biological communities, including large clams, mussels, tubeworms, and many other organisms—most of which were new to science when they were first encountered. These organisms are able to survive in the absence of sunlight because the vents discharge hydrogen sulfide gas. Archaeons[7] and bacteria oxidize the hydrogen sulfide gas to provide a food source for other organisms in the community.

Segments of the mid-ocean ridge called **oceanic ridges** have a prominent rift valley and steep, rugged slopes while **oceanic rises** have slopes that are gentler and less rugged. The differences in overall shape are caused by the fact that oceanic ridges (such as the Mid-Atlantic Ridge) spread more slowly than oceanic rises (such as the East Pacific Rise).

---

[7] Archaeons are microscopic bacteria-like organisms—a newly discovered domain of life.

What effect does all this volcanic activity along the mid-ocean ridge have at the ocean's surface?

Sometimes the underwater volcanic eruption is large enough to create what is called a *"megaplume"* of warm, mineral-rich water that is lower in density than the surrounding seawater and thus rises to the surface. Remarkably, a few research vessels have reported experiencing the effects of a megaplume at the surface while directly above an erupting sea floor volcano! Researchers on board describe bubbles of gas and steam at the surface, a marked increase in water temperature, and the presence of enough volcanic material to turn the water cloudy. In terms of warming the ocean, the heat released into the ocean at mid-ocean ridges is probably not very significant, mostly because the ocean is so good at absorbing and redistributing heat.

The mid-ocean ridge is created by plate divergence and typically includes a central rift valley, faults and fissures, seamounts, pillow basalts, hydrothermal vents, and metal sulfide deposits.

Fracture Zones and Transform Faults The mid-ocean ridge is cut by a number of **transform faults**, which offset the spreading zones. Oriented perpendicular to the spreading zones, transform faults give the mid-ocean ridge the zigzag appearance seen in Figure 14. Transform faults occur to accommodate spreading of a linear ridge system on a spherical Earth and because different segments of the mid-ocean ridge spread apart at different rates.

In the Pacific Ocean, where scars are less rapidly covered by sediment than in other ocean basins, transform faults can be seen to extend for thousands of kilometers away from the mid-ocean ridge and have widths of up to 200 kilometers (120 miles). These ex-

tensions, however, are not transform faults. Instead, they are **fracture zones**.

What is the difference between a transform fault and a fracture zone? Figure 18 shows that both run along the same long linear zone of weakness in Earth's crust. In fact, by following the same zone of weakness from one end to the other, it changes from a fracture zone to a transform fault and back again to a fracture zone. A transform fault is a seismically active area that offsets the axis of a mid-ocean ridge. A fracture zone, on the other hand, is a seismically inactive area that shows evidence of past transform fault activity. A helpful way to visualize the difference is that transform faults occur *between* offset segments of the mid-ocean ridge, while fracture zones occur *beyond* the offset segments of the mid-ocean ridge.

The relative direction of plate motion across transform faults and fracture zones further differentiates these two features. Across a transform fault, two lithospheric plates are moving in opposite directions. Across a fracture zone (which occurs entirely within a plate), there is no relative motion because the parts of the lithospheric plate cut by a fracture zone are moving in the same direction (Figure 18). Transform faults are actual plate boundaries, whereas fracture zones are not. Rather, fracture zones are ancient, inactive fault scars embedded in a plate.

In addition, earthquake activity is different in transform faults and fracture zones. Earthquakes shallower than 10 kilometers (6 miles) are common when plates move in opposite directions along transform faults. Along fracture zones, where plate motion is in the same direction, seismic activity is almost completely absent. Table 2 summarizes the differences between transform faults and fracture zones.

Many fracture zones exhibit dramatic relief. For example, the Mendocino Fracture Zone in the North Pacific Ocean (see map inside the front cover) is more than 1000 meters (3300 feet) deeper on the south side than on the north side, creating the *Mendocino Escarpment*. The Owen Fracture Zone in the Indian Ocean (Figure 19) has

Figure 18 Transform faults and fracture zones.

Transform faults are active transform plate boundaries that occur *between* the segments of the mid-ocean ridge. Fracture zones are inactive intraplate features that occur *beyond* the segments of the mid-ocean ridge.

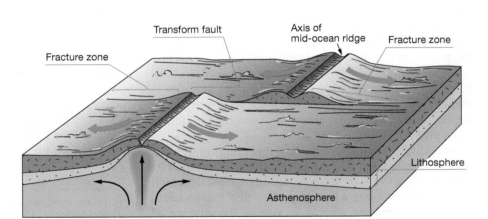

TABLE 2 **Comparison between transform faults and fracture zones.**

	Transform faults	Fracture zones
Plate boundary?	Yes—a transform plate boundary	No—an intraplate feature
Relative movement across feature	Movement in opposite directions	Movement in the same direction
	←	←
	——	——
	→	←
Earthquakes?	Many	Few
Relationship to mid-ocean ridge	Occur *between* offset mid-ocean ridge segments	Occur *beyond* offset mid-ocean ridge segments
Geographic examples	San Andreas Fault, Alpine Fault, Dead Sea Fault	Mendocino Fracture Zone, Molokai Fracture Zone

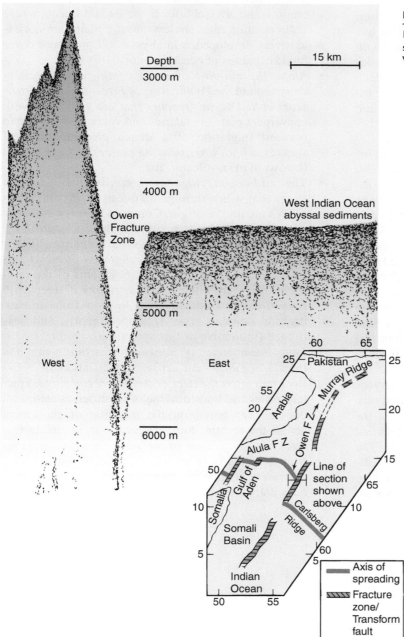

Figure 19 Owen Fracture Zone.

Interpreted seismic profile of the Owen Fracture Zone showing high relief, which is typical of many fracture zones. Vertical exaggeration is 25 times.

Courtesy of Enrico Bonatti, Lamont–Doherty Geological Observatory of Columbia University

relief of over 2000 meters (6600 feet). Much of this difference in elevation is attributable to the vast age difference of the ocean floor on either side of a fracture zone: The older ocean floor undergoes much more thermal contraction and subsequent deepening than the younger ocean floor adjacent to it.

Transform faults are plate boundaries that occur *between* offset segments of the mid-ocean ridge while fracture zones are intraplate features that occur *beyond* the offset segments of the mid-ocean ridge.

Chapter in Review

- *Bathymetry is the measurement of ocean depths and the charting of ocean floor topography.* The varied bathymetry of the ocean floor was first determined using *soundings* to measure water depth. Later, the development of the *echo sounder* gave ocean scientists a more detailed representation of the sea floor. Today, much of our knowledge of the ocean floor has been obtained using various *multibeam echo sounders* or *side-scan sonar instruments* (to make detailed bathymetric maps of a small area of the ocean floor), *satellite measurement* of the ocean surface (to produce maps of the world ocean floor), and *seismic reflection profiles* (to examine ocean structure beneath the sea floor).

- *Earth's hypsographic curve* shows the amount of Earth's surface area at different elevations and depths. The *distribution of area is uneven* with respect to height above or below sea level. The shape of the curve also *reflects the existence of plate tectonic processes*.

- *Continental margins can be either passive* (not associated with any plate boundaries) *or active* (associated with convergent or transform plate boundaries). Extending from the shoreline is the generally shallow, low relief, and gently sloping *continental shelf* that can contain various features such as coastal islands, reefs, and banks. The boundary between the continental slope and the *continental shelf* is marked by an increase in slope that occurs at the *shelf break*. Cutting deep into the slopes are *submarine canyons*, which resemble canyons on land but are created by erosive turbidity currents. *Turbidity currents* deposit their sediment load at the base of the continental slope, creating deep-sea fans that merge to produce a gently sloping continental rise. The deposits from turbidity currents (called *turbidite deposits*) have characteristic sequences of graded bedding. Active margins have similar features, although they are modified by their associated plate boundary.

- The *continental rises* gradually become flat, extensive, deep-ocean *abyssal plains*, which form by *suspension settling* of fine sediment. Poking through the sediment cover of the abyssal plains are numerous *volcanic peaks*, including volcanic islands, seamounts, tablemounts, and abyssal hills. In the Pacific Ocean, where sedimentation rates are low, abyssal plains are not extensively developed, and abyssal hill provinces cover broad expanses of ocean floor.

- *Along the margins of many continents*—especially those around the *Pacific Ring of Fire*—are deep linear scars called ocean trenches that are associated with convergent plate boundaries and volcanic arcs. Due to seaward migration of a trench creating tensional stresses, a *back-arc spreading center* can form behind (landward of) a volcanic arc.

- The *mid-ocean ridge is a continuous mountain range* that winds through all ocean basins and is entirely volcanic in origin. Common features associated with the mid-ocean ridge include a *central rift valley, faults* and *fissures, seamounts, pillow basalts, hydrothermal vents, deposits of metal sulfides*, and *unusual life forms*. Segments of the mid-ocean ridge are either *oceanic ridges* if steep with rugged slopes (indicative of slow sea floor spreading) or *oceanic rises* if sloped gently and less rugged (indicative of fast spreading).

- *Long linear zones of weakness—fracture zones and transform faults*—cut across vast distances of ocean floor and *offset the axes of the mid-ocean ridge*. Fracture zones and transform faults are differentiated from one another based on the direction of movement across the feature. *Fracture zones* (an intraplate feature) *have movement in the same direction*, whereas *transform faults* (a transform plate boundary) *have movement in opposite directions*. Many fracture zones have dramatic relief.

Key Terms

Abyssal hill	Convergent active margin	Oceanic ridge	Shelf break
Abyssal hill province	Deep-ocean basin	Oceanic rise	Sonar
Abyssal plain	Deep-sea fan	Pacific Ring of Fire	Sounding
Active margin	Echo sounder	Passive margin	Submarine canyon
Back-arc spreading center	Fathom	Pillow basalt	Submarine fan
Bathymetry	Fracture zone	Pillow lava	Suspension settling
Black smoker	GLORIA	Precipitate	Transform active margin
Continental arc	Graded bedding	Precision depth recorder	Transform fault
Continental borderland	Hydrothermal vent	(PDR)	Turbidite deposit
Continental flood basalt	Hypsographic curve	Rift valley	Turbidity current
Continental margin	Island arc	SeaBeam	Volcanic arc
Continental rise	Metal sulfides	Seaknoll	Warm-water vent
Continental shelf	Mid-ocean ridge	Sea MARC	White smoker
Continental slope	Ocean trench	Seismic reflection profile	

Questions and Exercises

1. What is bathymetry?

2. Discuss the development of bathymetric techniques, indicating significant advancements in technology.

3. Describe what is shown by a hypsographic curve and explain why its shape reflects the presence of active tectonic processes on Earth.

4. Describe the differences between passive and active continental margins. Be sure to include how these features relate to plate tectonics, and include an example of each type of margin.

5. Describe the major features of a passive continental margin: continental shelf, continental slope, continental rise, submarine canyon, and deep-sea fans.

6. Explain how submarine canyons are created.

7. What are differences between a submarine canyon and an ocean trench?

8. Explain what graded bedding is and how it forms.

9. Describe the process by which abyssal plains are created.

10. Discuss the origin of the various volcanic peaks of the abyssal plains: seamounts, tablemounts, and abyssal hills.

11. In which ocean basin are most ocean trenches found? Use plate tectonic processes to help explain why.

12. Describe characteristics and features of the mid-ocean ridge, including the difference between oceanic ridges and oceanic rises.

13. List and describe the different types of hydrothermal vents.

14. What kinds of unusual life can be found associated with hydrothermal vents? How do these organisms survive?

15. Use pictures and words to describe differences between fracture zones and transform faults.

Ocean Circulation

Patterns of ocean currents seen from space. This composite satellite view of
Earth during the austral summer highlights ocean circulation patterns near southern
Africa, where the Agulhas Retroflection occurs. As the Agulhas Current flows south
past the east coast of Africa, it meets the strong eastward-flowing Antarctic Circumpo-
lar Current, which makes it turn abruptly and creates the wavy current pattern between
Africa and Antarctica.

From Chapter 8 of *Introduction to Oceanography*, Tenth Edition, Harold V. Thurman, Alan P. Trujillo.
Copyright © 2004 by Pearson Education, Inc. Published by Pearson Prentice Hall. All rights reserved.

- How are ocean currents measured?
- How are surface currents organized in each ocean basin?
- What is western intensification?
- Why is upwelling associated with abundant marine life?
- What environmental effects do El Niños and La Niñas produce?
- What is thermohaline circulation?

The answers to these questions (and much more) can be found in the highlighted concept statements within this chapter.

"The general circulation of the world's oceans is a matter of great interest not only from various practical points of view—climate, fishing, dumping of radioactive wastes and so forth— but primarily from the standpoint of understanding the dynamics and history of the planet on which we live."

—Physical Oceanographer Henry Stommel (1955)

Ocean currents are masses of ocean water that flow from one place to another. The amount of water can be large or small, currents can be at the surface or deep below, and the phenomena that create them can be simple or quite complex. Simply put, currents are *water masses in motion.*

Huge current systems dominate the surfaces of the major oceans. These currents transfer heat from warmer to cooler areas on Earth, just as the major wind belts of the world do. Wind belts transfer about two-thirds of the total amount of heat from the tropics to the poles; ocean surface currents transfer the other third. Ultimately, energy from the Sun drives surface currents and they closely follow the pattern of the world's major wind belts.

More locally, surface currents affect the climates of coastal continental regions. Cold currents flowing toward the Equator on the western sides of continents produce arid conditions. Conversely, warm currents flowing poleward on the eastern sides of continents produce warm, humid conditions. Additionally, ocean currents contribute to the mild climate of northern Europe and Iceland, whereas conditions at similar latitudes along the Atlantic coast of North America (such as Labrador) are much colder.

Currents profoundly affect ocean life, especially those organisms in the deep sea, where currents provide a continuing supply of oxygen. This oxygen is carried there by cold, dense water that sinks in polar regions and spreads across the deep-ocean floor. Ocean currents influence the abundance of life in surface waters by affecting the growth of microscopic algae, which is the basis of most oceanic food chains. Currents have also aided the travel of prehistoric peoples from Europe and Africa to the New World and throughout the Pacific Ocean islands.

Measuring Ocean Currents

Ocean currents are either *wind driven* or *density driven.* Moving air masses—particularly the major wind belts of the world—set wind-driven currents in motion. This motion is parallel to the surface (horizontal) and occurs primarily in the ocean's surface waters, so these currents are called **surface currents**. Density-driven circulation, on the other hand, moves vertically and accounts for the thorough mixing of the deep masses of ocean water. Temperature and salinity conditions at the surface that produce high-density water initiate density-driven circulation. The dense water sinks and spreads slowly beneath the surface, so these currents are called **deep currents**.

Surface currents rarely flow in the same direction and at the same rate for very long, so measuring average flow rates can be difficult. Some consistency, however, exists in the *overall* surface current pattern worldwide. Surface currents can be measured directly or indirectly.

Two main methods are used to *directly* measure currents. In one, a floating device is released into the current and tracked through time. Typically, radio-transmitting float bottles or other devices are used (Figure 1a), but other accidentally released items also make good drift meters (Box 1). The other method is done from a fixed position (such as a pier) where a current-measuring device, such as the propeller flow meter shown in Figure 1b, is lowered into the water. Propeller devices can also be towed behind ships, and the ship's speed is then subtracted to determine a current's true flow rate.

Three different methods can be used to *indirectly* measure surface currents. Water flows parallel to a pressure gradient, so one method is to determine the internal distribution of density and the corresponding pressure gradient across an area of the ocean. A second method uses radar altimeters, such as the one launched aboard the TOPEX/Poseidon satellite in 1992, to determine the lumps and bulges at the ocean surface, which are a result of the shape of the underlying sea floor and current flow. From these data, *dynamic topography* maps can be produced that show the speed and direction of surface currents (Figure 2). A third method uses a *Doppler flow meter* to transmit low-frequency sound signals through the water. The flow meter measures the shift in frequency between the sound waves emitted and those backscattered by particles in the water to determine current movement.

The location of deep currents far below the surface makes them even more difficult to measure. Often, they are mapped using devices that are carried with the current or by tracking telltale chemical tracers. Some tracers are

(a)

Figure 1 Current-measuring devices.

(a) Drift current meter. Depth of metal vanes is 1 meter (3.3 feet).
(b) Propeller-type flow meter. Length of instrument is 0.6 meter (2 feet).

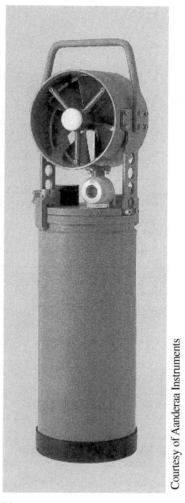

(b)

BOX 1 Research Methods in Oceanography
RUNNING SHOES AS DRIFT METERS: JUST DO IT

Any floating object can serve as a makeshift drift meter, as long as it is known where the object entered the ocean and where it was retrieved. The path of the object can then be inferred, providing information about the movement of surface currents. If the time of release and retrieval are known, the speed of currents can also be determined. Oceanographers have long used *drift bottles* (a floating "message in a bottle" or a radio-transmitting device set adrift in the ocean) to track the movement of currents.

Many objects have inadvertently become drift meters when ships have lost some (or all) of their cargo at sea. In this way, Nike athletic shoes and colorful floating bathtub toys have advanced the understanding of current movement in the North Pacific Ocean.

In May 1990, the container vessel *Hansa Carrier* was en route from Korea to Seattle, Washington, when it encountered a severe North Pacific storm. The ship was transporting 12.2-meter (40-foot)-long rectangular metal shipping containers, many of which were lashed to the ship's deck for the voyage. During the storm, the ship lost 21 deck containers overboard, including five that held Nike athletic shoes. The shoes floated, so those that were released from their containers were carried east by the North Pacific Current. Within six months, thousands of the shoes began to wash up along the beaches of Alaska, Canada, Washington, and Oregon, over 2400 kilometers (1500 miles) from the site of the spill. A few shoes were found on beaches in northern California, and over two years later shoes from the spill were even recovered from the north end of the Big Island of Hawaii!

Even though the shoes had spent considerable time drifting in the ocean, they were in good shape and wearable (after barnacles and oil were removed). Because the shoes were not tied together, many beachcombers found individual shoes or pairs that did not match. Many of the shoes retailed for around $100,

Continued...
245

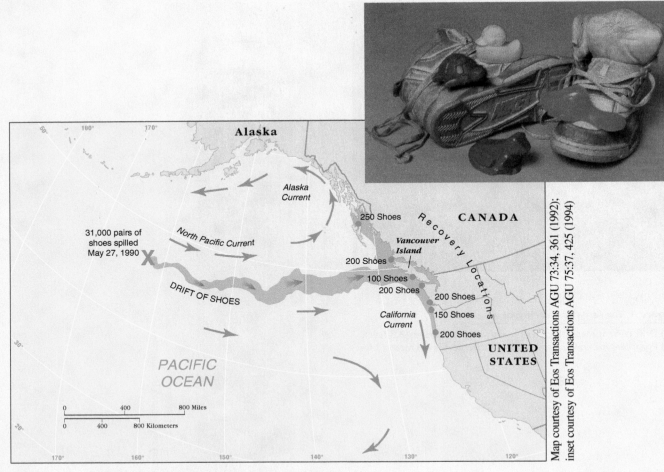

Path of drifting shoes and recovery locations from the 1990 spill; recovered shoes and plastic bathtub toys (*inset*).

Map courtesy of Eos Transactions AGU 73:34, 361 (1992); inset courtesy of Eos Transactions AGU 75:37, 425 (1994)

so people interested in finding matching pairs placed ads in newspapers or attended local swapmeets.

With help from the beachcombing public (as well as lighthouse operators), information on the location and number of shoes collected was compiled during the months following the spill. Serial numbers inside the shoes were traced to individual containers, and they indicated that only four of the five containers had released their shoes; evidently, one entire container sank without opening. Thus, a maximum of 30,910 pairs of shoes (61,820 individual shoes) were released. The almost instantaneous release of such a large number of drift items helped oceanographers refine computer models of North Pacific circulation. Before the shoe spill, the largest number of drift bottles purposefully released at one time by

oceanographers was about 30,000. Although only 2.6% of the shoes were recovered, this compares favorably with the 2.4% recovery rate of drift bottles released by oceanographers conducting research.

In January 1992, another cargo ship lost 12 containers during a storm to the north of where the shoes had previously spilled. One of these containers held 29,000 packages of small, floatable, colorful plastic bathtub toys in the shapes of blue turtles, yellow ducks, red beavers, and green frogs. Even though the toys were housed in plastic packaging glued to a cardboard backing, studies showed that after 24 hours in seawater, the glue deteriorated and over 100,000 of the toys were released.

The floating bathtub toys began to come ashore in southeast Alaska

10 months later, verifying the computer models. The models indicate that many of the bathtub toys will continue to be carried by the Alaska Current, eventually dispersing throughout the North Pacific Ocean. Some may find their way into the Arctic Ocean, where they could spend time within the Arctic Ocean ice pack. From there, the toys may drift into the North Atlantic, eventually washing up on beaches in northern Europe, thousands of kilometers from where they were accidentally released into the ocean.

Since 1992, oceanographers have continued to study ocean currents by tracking other floating items spilled from cargo ships, including 34,000 hockey gloves, 5 million plastic Lego pieces, at least 3000 computer monitors, and an unidentified number of small plastic doll parts.

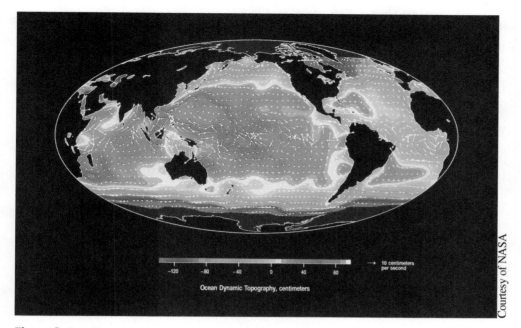

Figure 2 Satellite view of ocean dynamic topography.

Map showing TOPEX/Poseidon radar altimeter data in centimeters from September 1992 to September 1993. Red colors are areas that have higher than normal sea level; blue colors are areas that are lower than normal. White arrows indicate the flow direction of currents, with longer arrows indicating faster flow rates.

naturally absorbed into seawater, while others are intentionally added. Some useful tracers that have inadvertently been added to seawater include tritium (a radioactive isotope of hydrogen produced by nuclear bomb tests in the 1950s and early 1960s) and chlorofluorocarbons (freons and other gases now thought to be depleting the ozone layer). Other techniques used to identify deep currents include measuring the distinctive temperature and salinity characteristics of a deep-water mass.

Wind-induced surface currents are measured with floating objects, by satellites, or by other techniques. Density-induced deep currents are measured using tracers or other devices.

Surface Currents

Surface currents develop from friction between the ocean and the wind that blows across its surface. Only about 2% of the wind's energy is transferred to the ocean surface, so a 50-knot[1] wind will create a 1-knot current. You can simulate this on a tiny scale simply by blowing gently and steadily across a cup of coffee.

If there were no continents on Earth, the surface currents would simply follow the major wind belts of the world. In each hemisphere, therefore, a current would

---

[1]A *knot* is one nautical mile per hour. A nautical mile is defined as the distance of one minute of latitude and is equivalent to 1.15 statute (land) miles or 1.85 kilometers.

flow between 0 and 30 degrees latitude due to the trade winds, a second would flow between 30 and 60 degrees latitude due to the prevailing westerlies, and a third would flow between 60 and 90 degrees latitude due to the polar easterlies.

However, the distribution of continents on Earth influences the nature and the direction of flow of surface currents. For example, Figure 3 shows how the trade winds and prevailing westerlies create large circular-moving loops of water in the Atlantic Ocean. Other ocean basins show a similar pattern, and surface currents are also influenced by gravity, friction, and the Coriolis effect.

Surface currents occur within and above the *pycnocline* (layer of rapidly changing density) to a depth of about 1 kilometer (0.6 mile) and affect only about 10% of the world's ocean water.

Equatorial Currents, Boundary Currents, and Gyres

The trade winds, which blow from the southeast in the Southern Hemisphere and from the northeast in the Northern Hemisphere, set in motion the water masses between the tropics. The resulting currents are called **equatorial currents**, which travel westward along the Equator (Figure 4). They are called north or south equatorial currents, depending on their position relative to the Equator.

When equatorial currents reach the western portion of an ocean basin, they must turn because they cannot cross land. The Coriolis effect deflects these currents away from the Equator as **western boundary currents**. The

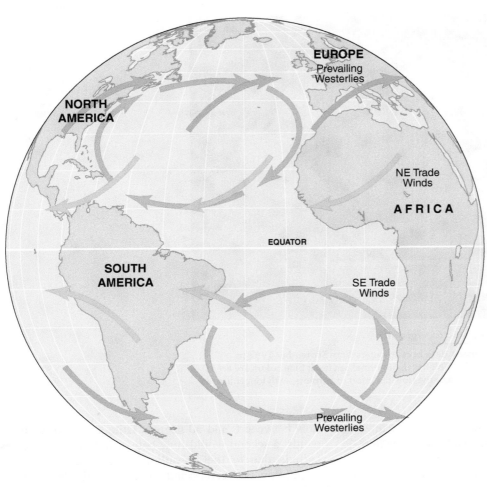

Figure 3 Atlantic Ocean surface circulation pattern.

The trade winds (*blue arrows*) in conjunction with the prevailing westerlies (*green arrows*) create circular-moving loops of water (*underlying purple arrows*) at the surface in both parts of the Atlantic Ocean basin. If there were no continents, the ocean's surface circulation pattern would closely match the major wind belts of the world.

name means they are currents traveling along the western boundary of their ocean basin.[2] The Gulf Stream and the Brazil Current, which are shown in Figure 4, are western boundary currents. They come from equatorial regions, where water temperatures are warm, so they carry warm water to higher latitudes. Figure 4 shows warm currents as red arrows.

Between 30 and 60 degrees latitude, the prevailing westerlies blow from the northwest in the Southern Hemisphere and from the southwest in the Northern Hemisphere. These winds direct ocean surface water in an easterly direction across the ocean basin, as shown in Figure 4 by the North Atlantic Current and the West Wind Drift.

When currents flow back across the ocean basin, the Coriolis effect and continental barriers turn them toward the Equator, creating **eastern boundary currents** along

the eastern boundary of the ocean basins. The Canary Current and the Benguela Current, which are shown in Figure 4, are eastern boundary currents.[3] They come from high-latitude regions where water temperatures are cool, so they carry cool water to lower latitudes. Figure 4 shows cold currents as blue arrows.

The equatorial, western boundary, prevailing westerly, and eastern boundary currents combine to create a circular flow within an ocean basin called a **gyre** (*gyros* = a circle). Figure 4 shows the world's five **subtropical gyres**: (1) the *North Atlantic Gyre*, (2) the *South Atlantic Gyre*, (3) the *North Pacific Gyre*, (4) the *South Pacific Gyre*, and (5) the *Indian Ocean Gyre* (which is mostly within the Southern Hemisphere). The center of each subtropical gyre coincides with the subtropics at 30 degrees north or south latitude. As shown in

---

[2]Notice that the western boundary currents are off the *eastern* coasts of continents. This sounds confusing but is a result of the fact that we have a land-based perspective. From an oceanic perspective, the western side of the ocean basin is where the western boundary current resides.

[3]Currents are sometimes named for a prominent geographic location near where they pass. For instance, the Canary Current passes the Canary Islands; the Benguela Current is named for the Benguela Province in Angola, Africa.

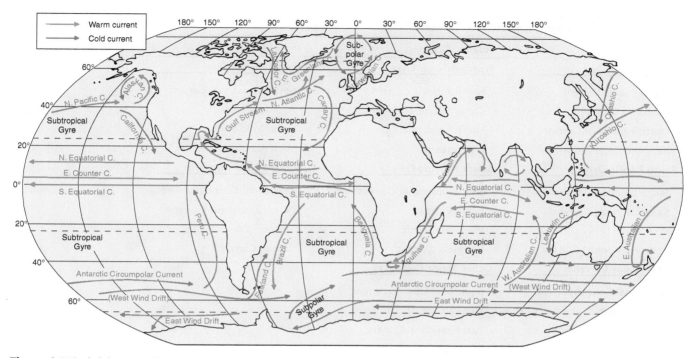

Figure 4 Wind-driven surface currents.

Major wind-driven surface currents of the world's oceans during February–March. The five major subtropical gyres are the North and South Pacific Ocean Gyres, the North and South Atlantic Ocean Gyres, and the Indian Ocean Gyre. The smaller subpolar gyres rotate in the reverse direction of the adjacent subtropical gyres.

Figures 3 and 4, subtropical gyres rotate clockwise in the Northern Hemisphere and counterclockwise in the Southern Hemisphere.

Generally, each subtropical gyre is composed of four main currents that flow progressively into one another (Table 1). The North Atlantic Gyre, for instance, is composed of the North Equatorial Current, the Gulf Stream, the North Atlantic Current, and the Canary Current (Figure 4).

Surface currents moving eastward as a result of the prevailing westerlies approach subpolar latitudes (about 60 degrees north or south latitude). Here, they are driven in a westerly direction by the polar easterlies, producing **subpolar gyres** that rotate opposite the adjacent subtropical gyres. Subpolar gyres are smaller and fewer than subtropical gyres and are best developed in the Atlantic Ocean between Greenland and Europe and the Weddell Sea off Antarctica (Figure 4).

> The principal ocean surface current pattern consists of subtropical and subpolar gyres that are large circular-moving loops of water powered by the major wind belts of the world.

Ekman Spiral and Ekman Transport

During the voyage of the *Fram*, Norwegian explorer Fridtjof Nansen observed that Arctic Ocean ice moved 20 to 40 degrees to the *right* of the wind blowing across its surface (Figure 5). Surface water in the Northern Hemi-

sphere behaves similarly and, in the Southern Hemisphere, surface currents move to the left of the wind direction. Why does surface water move in a direction different than the wind? *V. Walfrid Ekman* (1874–1954), a Swedish physicist, developed a circulation model called the **Ekman spiral** (Figure 6) that explains Nansen's observations in accordance with the Coriolis effect.

The Ekman spiral describes the speed and direction of flow of surface waters at various depths. It is caused by wind blowing across the surface and is modified by the Coriolis effect. Ekman's model assumes that a uniform column of water is set in motion by wind blowing across its surface. Because of the Coriolis effect, the immediate surface water moves in a direction 45 degrees to the right of the wind (in the Northern Hemisphere). The surface water moves as a thin "layer" on top of deeper layers of water. As the surface layer moves, it also sets in motion other layers beneath it, thus passing the energy of the wind down through the water column.

Current speed decreases with increasing depth, however, and the Coriolis effect increases curvature to the right (like a spiral). Thus, each successive layer of water is set in motion at a progressively slower velocity, and in a direction progressively to the right of the one above it. At some depth, a layer of water may move in a direction *exactly opposite to the wind direction that initiated it*! If the water is deep enough, friction will consume the energy imparted by the wind and no motion will occur below that depth. Although it depends on wind speed

TABLE 1 **Subtropical gyres and surface currents.**

Pacific Ocean	Atlantic Ocean	Indian Ocean
North Pacific Gyre	**North Atlantic Gyre**	**Indian Ocean Gyre**
North Pacific Current	North Atlantic Current	South Equatorial Current
California Current[a]	Canary Current[a]	Agulhas Current[b]
North Equatorial Current	North Equatorial Current	West Wind Drift
Kuroshio (Japan) Current[b]	Gulf Stream[b]	West Australian Current[a]
South Pacific Gyre	**South Atlantic Gyre**	**Other Major Currents**
South Equatorial Current	South Equatorial Current	Equatorial Countercurrent
East Australian Current[b]	Brazil Current[b]	North Equatorial Current
West Wind Drift	West Wind Drift	Leeuwin Current
Peru (Humboldt) Current[a]	Benguela Current[a]	Somali Current
Other Major Currents	**Other Major Currents**	
Equatorial Countercurrent	Equatorial Countercurrent	
Alaskan Current	Florida Current	
Oyashio Current	East Greenland Current	
	Labrador Current	
	Falkland Current	

[a]Denotes an eastern boundary current of a gyre, which is relatively *slow, wide,* and *shallow* (and is also a *cold-water* current).
[b]Denotes a western boundary current of a gyre, which is relatively *fast, narrow,* and *deep* (and is also a *warm-water* current).

Figure 5 Transport of floating objects.

Fridtjof Nansen first noticed that floating objects, such as icebergs and ships, were carried to the right of the wind direction in the Northern Hemisphere.

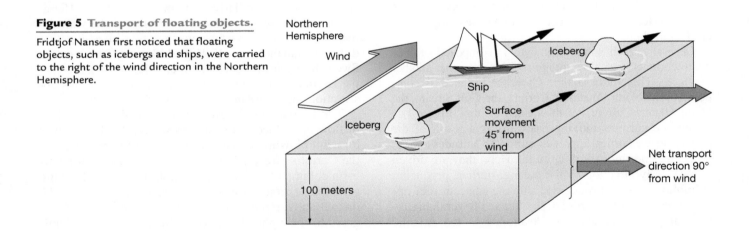

and latitude, this stillness normally occurs at a depth of about 100 meters (330 feet).

Figure 6 shows the spiral nature of this movement with increasing depth from the ocean's surface. The length of each arrow in Figure 6 is proportional to the velocity of the individual layer, and the direction of each arrow indicates the direction it moves.[4] Under ideal conditions, therefore, the surface layer should move at an angle of 45 degrees from the direction of the wind. All the layers combine, however, to create a net water movement that is 90 degrees from the direction of the wind. This average movement, called **Ekman transport,** is 90 degrees to the *right* in the Northern Hemisphere and 90 degrees to the *left* in the Southern Hemisphere.

"Ideal" conditions rarely exist in the ocean, so the actual movement of surface currents deviates slightly from the angles shown in Figure 6. Generally, surface currents move at an angle somewhat less than 45 degrees from the direction of the wind and Ekman transport in the open ocean is typically about 70 degrees from the wind direction. In shallow coastal waters, Ekman transport may be very nearly the same direction as the wind.

---

[4]The name Ekman *spiral* refers to the spiral observed by connecting the tips of the arrows shown in Figure 6.

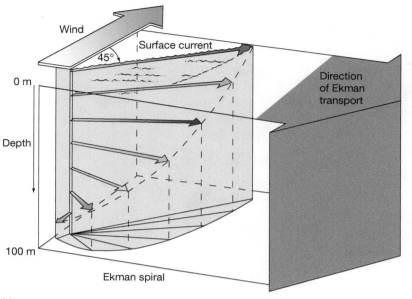

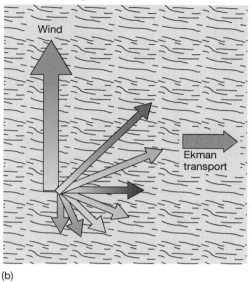

Looking down on ocean surface

Figure 6 Ekman spiral.

Perspective view **(a)** and top view **(b)** of Ekman spiral and Ekman transport. Wind drives surface water in a direction 45 degrees to the right of the wind in the Northern Hemisphere. Deeper water continues to deflect to the right and moves at a slower speed with increased depth, causing the Ekman spiral. Ekman transport, which is the net water movement, is at a right angle (90 degrees) to the wind direction.

STUDENTS SOMETIMES ASK...

What does an Ekman spiral look like at the surface? Is it strong enough to disturb ships?

The Ekman spiral creates different layers of surface water that move in slightly different directions at slightly different speeds. It is too weak to create eddies or whirlpools (vortexes) at the surface and so presents no danger to ships. In fact, the Ekman spiral is unnoticeable at the surface. It can be observed, however, by lowering oceanographic equipment over the side of a vessel. At various depths, the equipment can be observed to drift at various angles from the wind direction according to the Ekman spiral.

Geostrophic Currents

Ekman transport deflects surface water to the right in the Northern Hemisphere, so a clockwise rotation develops within an ocean basin and produces a **subtropical convergence** of water in the middle of the gyre, causing water literally to pile up in the center of the subtropical gyre. Thus, there is a hill of water within all subtropical gyres that is as much as 2 meters (6.6 feet) high.

Surface water in a subtropical convergence tends to flow downhill in response to gravity. The Coriolis effect opposes gravity, however, deflecting the water to the right in a curved path (Figure 7a) into the hill again. When these two factors balance, the net effect is a **geostrophic** (*geo* = earth, *strophio* = turn) **current** that moves in a circular path around the hill.[5] In Figure 7a it is labeled as

the *path of ideal geostrophic flow*. Friction between water molecules, however, causes the water to move gradually down the slope of the hill as it flows around it. This is the *path of actual geostrophic flow* labeled in Figure 7a.

Western Intensification

Figure 7a shows that the apex (top) of the hill formed within a rotating gyre is closer to the western boundary than the center of the gyre. As a result, the western boundary currents of the subtropical gyres are faster, narrower, and deeper than their eastern boundary current counterparts. For example, the Kuroshio Current (a western boundary current) of the North Pacific Subtropical Gyre is up to 15 times faster, 20 times narrower, and five times as deep as the California Current (an eastern boundary current). This phenomenon is called **western intensification**, and currents affected by this phenomenon are said to be western intensified. *The western boundary currents of all subtropical gyres are western intensified, even in the Southern Hemisphere.*

A number of factors cause western intensification, including the Coriolis effect. The Coriolis effect increases toward the poles, so eastward-flowing high-latitude water turns toward the Equator more strongly than westward-flowing equatorial water turns toward higher latitudes. This causes a wide, slow, and shallow

[5]The term *geostrophic* for these currents is appropriate, since the currents behave as they do because of Earth's rotation.

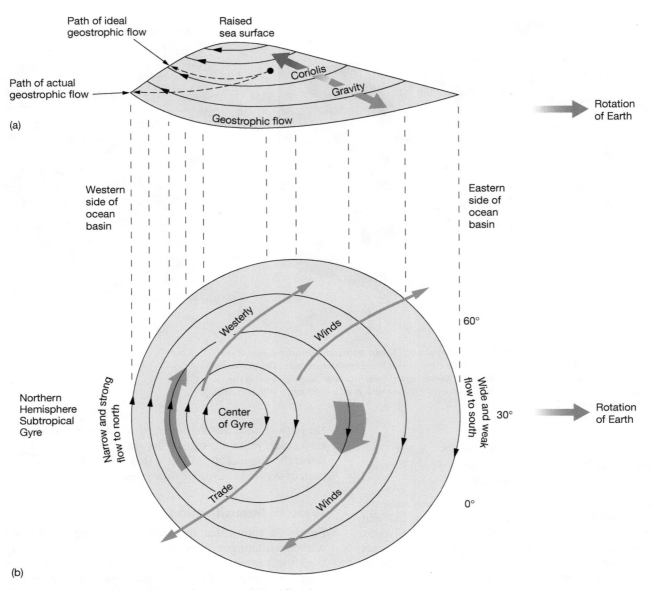

Figure 7 Geostrophic current and western intensification.

(a) A cross-sectional view of a subtropical gyre showing how water literally piles up in the center, forming a hill up to 2 meters (6.6 feet) high. Gravity and the Coriolis effect balance to create an ideal geostrophic current that flows in equilibrium around the hill. However, friction makes the current gradually run downslope (*actual geostrophic flow*). (b) A map view of the same subtropical gyre, showing that the flow pattern is restricted (lines are closer together) on the western side of the gyre, resulting in western intensification.

flow of water toward the Equator across most of each subtropical gyre, leaving only a narrow band through which the poleward flow can occur along the western margin of the ocean basin. If a constant volume of water rotates around the apex of the hill in Figure 7b, then the velocity of the water along the western margin will be much greater than the velocity around the eastern side.[6] In Figure 7b, the lines are close together along the western margin, indicating the faster flow. The end result is a high-speed western boundary current that flows along the hill's steeper westward slope and a slow drift of water toward the Equator along the more gradual eastern slope. Table 2 summarizes the

differences between western and eastern boundary currents of subtropical gyres.

> Western intensification is a result of Earth's rotation and causes the western boundary current of all subtropical gyres to be fast, narrow, and deep.

[6]A good analogy for this phenomenon is a funnel: In the narrow end of a funnel, the flow rates are speeded up (such as in western intensified currents); in the wide end, the flow rates are sluggish (such as in eastern boundary currents).

TABLE 2 **Characteristics of western and eastern boundary currents of subtropical gyres.**

Current type (examples)	Width	Depth	Speed	Transport volume (millions of cubic meters per second [a])	Comments
Western boundary currents (Gulf Stream, Brazil Current, Kuroshio Current)	*Narrow*: usually less than 100 kilometers (60 miles)	*Deep*: to depths of 2 kilometers (1.2 miles)	*Fast*: hundreds of kilometers per day	*Large*: as much as 100 Sv[a]	Waters derived from low latitudes and are warm; little or no upwelling
Eastern boundary currents (Canary Current, Benguela Current, California Current)	*Wide*: up to 1000 kilometers (600 miles)	*Shallow*: to depths of 0.5 kilometer (0.3 mile)	*Slow*: tens of kilometers per day	*Small*: typically 10 to 15 Sv[a]	Waters derived from mid-latitudes and are cool; coastal upwelling common

[a]One million cubic meters per second is a flow rate equal to one Sverdrup (Sv).

Equatorial Countercurrents

A large volume of water is driven westward due to the north and south equatorial currents. The Coriolis effect is minimal near the Equator, so much of the water is not turned toward higher latitudes. Instead, it piles up at the western margins of the ocean basins, which causes average sea level on the western side of the basin to be as much as 2 meters (6.6 feet) higher than on the eastern side. The water on the western margins then flows downhill under the influence of gravity, creating narrow **equatorial countercurrents** that flow to the east *counter to* and *between* the adjoining equatorial currents.

Figure 4 shows that an equatorial countercurrent is particularly apparent in the western Pacific Ocean, where a dome of equatorial water is trapped in the island-filled embayment between Australia and Asia. This dome of water with very weak current flow has the highest year-round ocean surface temperatures found anywhere in the world ocean, as shown in Figure 8. Continual influx of water from equatorial currents builds the dome and creates an eastward countercurrent that stretches across the Pacific toward South America.

If you reexamine the satellite image of sea surface elevation in Figure 2, you'll see that the hills of water within the subtropical gyres of the Atlantic Ocean are clearly visible. The hill in the North Pacific is visible as well, but the elevation of the equatorial Pacific is not as low as expected because the map shows conditions during a moderate El Niño event,[7] so there is a well-developed warm and anomalously high equatorial countercurrent. Figure 2 also shows very little distinction between the North and South Pacific gyres. Moreover, the South Pacific subtropical gyre is less intense than other gyres, mostly because it covers such a large

area, it lacks confinement by continental barriers along its western margin, and it has numerous islands (really the tops of tall sea floor mountains). The South Indian Ocean hill is rather well developed in the figure, although its northeastern boundary stands high because of the influx of warm Pacific Ocean water through the East Indies islands.

Ocean Currents and Climate

Ocean surface currents directly influence the climate of adjoining landmasses. For instance, warm ocean currents warm the nearby air. This warm air can hold more water vapor, which puts more moisture (high humidity) in the atmosphere. When this warm, moist air travels over a continent, it releases its water vapor in the form of precipitation. Continental margins that have warm ocean currents offshore (Figure 8, *red arrows*) typically have a humid climate. The presence of a warm current off the east coast of the United States helps explain why the area experiences such high humidity, especially in the summer.

Conversely, cold ocean currents cool the nearby air, which cannot hold as much water vapor. When the cool, dry air travels over a continent, it results in very little precipitation. Continental margins that have cool ocean currents offshore (Figure 8, *blue arrows*) typically have a dry climate. The presence of a cold current off California is part of the reason why it has such an arid climate.

Upwelling and Downwelling

Upwelling is the vertical movement of cold, deep, nutrient-rich water to the surface; **downwelling** is the vertical movement of surface water to deeper parts of the ocean. Upwelling hoists chilled water to the surface. This cold water, rich in nutrients, creates high **productivity** (an abundance of microscopic algae), which establishes the base of the food web and, in turn, supports incredible numbers of

---

[7]El Niño events are discussed later in this chapter under "Pacific Ocean Circulation."

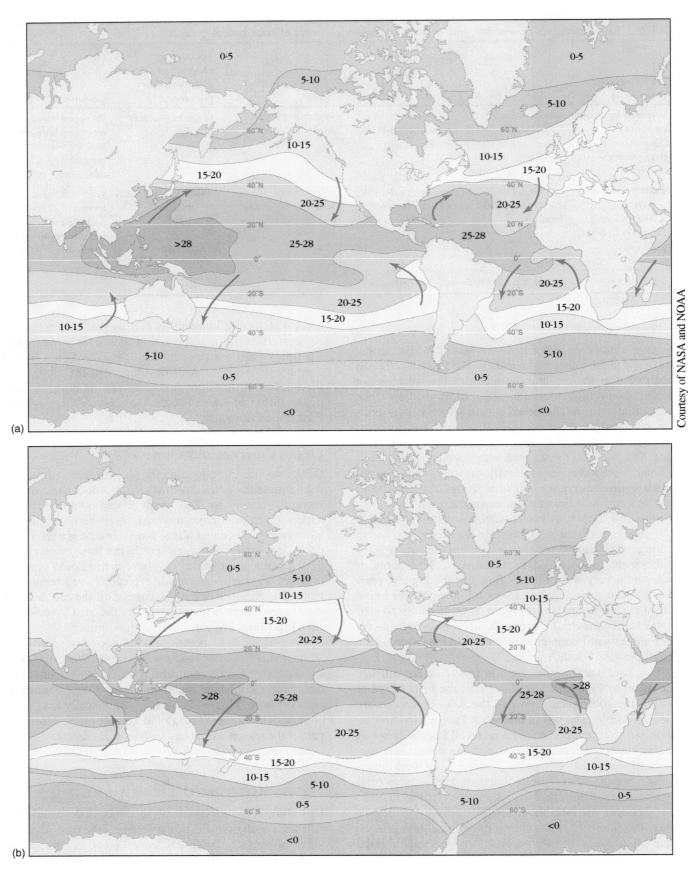

Figure 8 Surface temperature of the world ocean.

Average sea surface temperature distribution in degrees centigrade for August **(a)** and for February **(b)**. Note that temperatures migrate north–south with the seasons. Red arrows indicate warm surface currents; blue arrows indicate cool surface currents.

larger marine life like fish and whales. Downwelling, on the other hand, is associated with much lower amounts of surface productivity but carries necessary dissolved oxygen to those organisms living on the deep-sea floor.

Upwelling and downwelling provide important mixing mechanisms between surface and deep waters and are accomplished by a variety of methods.

Diverging Surface Water

Current divergence occurs when surface waters move *away from* an area on the ocean's surface, such as along the Equator. As shown in Figure 9, the South Equatorial Current occupies the area along the *geographical Equator* (most notably in the Pacific Ocean; see Figure 4), while the *meteorological Equator* (where the doldrums exist) typically occurs a few degrees of latitude to the north. As the southeast trade winds blow across this region, Ekman transport causes surface water north of the Equator to veer to the right (northward) and water south of the Equator to veer to the left (southward). The net result is a divergence of surface currents along the geographical Equator, which causes upwelling of cold, nutrient-rich water. Since this type of upwelling is com-

mon along the Equator—especially in the Pacific—it is called **equatorial upwelling** and creates areas of high productivity that are some of the most prolific fishing grounds in the world.

Converging Surface Water

Current convergence occurs when surface waters move *toward* each other. In the North Atlantic Ocean, for instance, the Gulf Stream, the Labrador Current, and the East Greenland Current all come together in the same vicinity. When currents converge, water stacks up and has no place to go but downward. The surface water slowly sinks in a process called downwelling (Figure 10). Unlike upwelling, areas of downwelling are not associated with prolific marine life because the necessary nutrients are not continuously replenished from the cold, deep, nutrient-rich water below the surface. Consequently, downwelling areas have low productivity.

Coastal Upwelling and Downwelling

Coastal winds can cause upwelling or downwelling due to Ekman transport. Figure 11 shows a coastal region along the west coast of a continent in the Southern

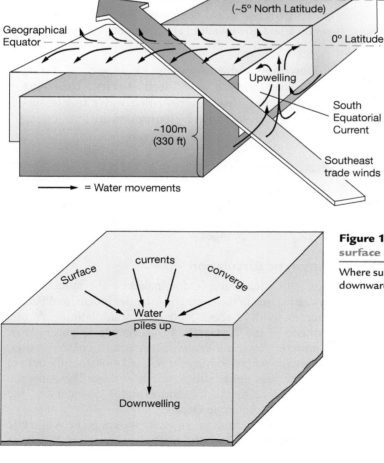

Figure 9 Equatorial upwelling.

As the southeast trade winds pass over the geographical Equator to the meteorological Equator, they cause water within the South Equatorial Current north of the Equator to veer to the right (northward) and water south of the Equator to veer to the left (southward). Thus, surface water diverges, which causes equatorial upwelling.

Figure 10 Downwelling caused by convergence of surface currents.

Where surface currents converge, water piles up and slowly sinks downward, creating downwelling.

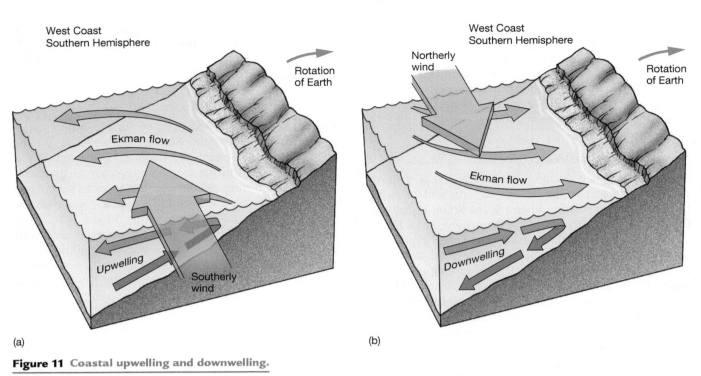

Figure 11 Coastal upwelling and downwelling.

(a) Where southerly coastal winds blow parallel to a west coast in the Southern Hemisphere, Ekman transport carries surface water away from the continent. Upwelling of deeper water occurs to replace the surface water that has moved away from the coast. **(b)** A reversal of the direction of the winds that cause upwelling causes water to pile up against the shore and causes downwelling.

Hemisphere with winds moving parallel to the coast. If the winds are from the south (Figure 11a), Ekman transport moves the coastal water to the left of the wind direction, causing the water to flow *away from* the shoreline. Water rises from below to replace the water moving away from shore in a process called **coastal upwelling**. Areas where coastal upwelling occurs, such as the West Coast of the United States, are characterized by high concentrations of nutrients, resulting in high biological productivity and rich marine life. This coastal upwelling also creates low water temperatures in areas such as San Francisco that provide a natural form of air conditioning (and much cool weather and fog) in the summer.

If the winds are from the north, Figure 11b shows that Ekman transport still moves the coastal water to the left of the wind direction but, in this case, the water flows *toward* the shoreline. This causes the water to stack up along the shoreline, where it has nowhere to go but down, in a process called **coastal downwelling**. Areas where coastal downwelling occurs have low productivity. Coastal downwelling can occur in areas that typically experience coastal upwelling when the winds reverse.

Other Upwelling

Figure 12 shows how upwelling can be created by offshore winds, sea floor obstructions, or a sharp bend in a coastline. Upwelling also occurs in high-latitude regions, where there is no pycnocline (a layer of rapidly changing density). The absence of a pycnocline allows significant vertical mixing between high-density cold surface water and high-density cold deep water below. Thus, both upwelling and downwelling are common in high latitudes.

> Upwelling and downwelling cause vertical mixing between surface and deep waters. Upwelling brings cold, deep, nutrient-rich water to the surface, which results in high productivity.

Surface Currents of the Oceans

The pattern of surface currents varies from ocean to ocean depending upon the geometry of the ocean basin, the pattern of major wind belts, seasonal factors, and other periodic changes.

Antarctic Circulation

Antarctic circulation is dominated by the movement of water masses in the southern Atlantic, Indian, and Pacific Oceans south of about 50 degrees south latitude. At this latitude is the **Antarctic Convergence** (Figure 13) or *Antarctic Polar Front*, which is where colder, denser, Antarctic waters converge with (and sink sharply below) warmer, less dense sub-Antarctic waters. The Antarctic Convergence marks the northernmost boundary of the Southern or Antarctic Ocean.

The main current in Antarctic waters is the **Antarctic Circumpolar Current**, which is also called the **West**

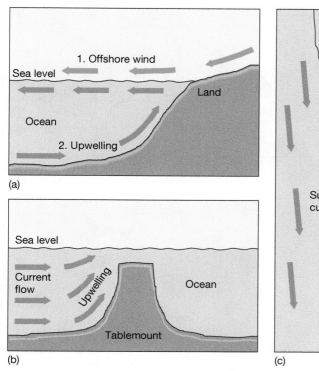

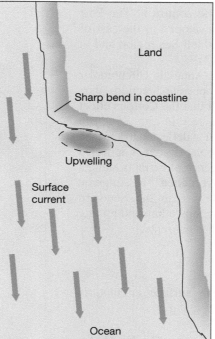

Figure 12 Other types of upwelling.

Upwelling can be caused by **(a)** offshore winds; **(b)** a sea floor obstruction: in this case, a tablemount; **(c)** a sharp bend in coastal geometry.

Wind Drift. It encircles Antarctica and flows from west to east at approximately 50 degrees south latitude but varies between 40 and 65 degrees south latitude. At about 40 degrees south latitude is the Subtropical Convergence (Figure 13), which forms the northernmost boundary of the Antarctic Circumpolar Current. The Antarctic Circumpolar Current is driven by the powerful prevailing westerly wind belt, which creates winds so strong that these Southern Hemisphere latitudes have been called the "Roaring Forties," "Furious Fifties," and "Screaming Sixties."

The Antarctic Circumpolar Current is the only current that completely circumscribes Earth and is allowed to do so because of the lack of land at high southern latitudes. It meets its greatest restriction as it passes through the Drake Passage (named for explorer Sir Francis Drake) between the Antarctic Peninsula and the southern islands of South America, which is about 1000 kilometers (600 miles) wide. Although the current is not speedy [its maximum surface velocity is about 2.75 kilometers (1.65 miles) per hour], it transports more water (an average of about 130 million cubic meters per second[8] than any other surface current.

The **East Wind Drift**, a surface current propelled by the polar easterlies, moves from an easterly direction

[8]One million cubic meters per second is a useful flow rate for describing ocean currents, so it has become a standard unit, named the **Sverdrup (Sv)** after Norwegian explorer Otto Sverdrup.

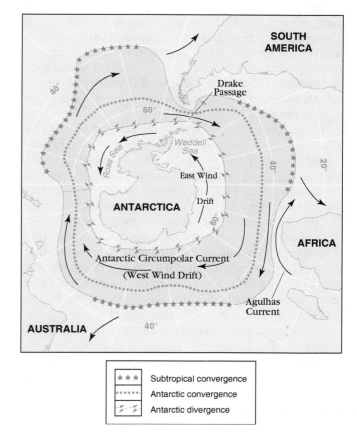

Figure 13 Antarctic surface circulation.

The East Wind Drift is driven by the polar easterlies and flows around Antarctica from the east. The Antarctic Circumpolar Current (West Wind Drift) flows around Antarctica from the west but is further from the continent and is a result of the strong prevailing westerlies. Antarctic Convergence and Divergence is caused by interactions at the boundaries of these two currents.

around the margin of the Antarctic continent. The East Wind Drift is most extensively developed to the east of the Antarctic Peninsula in the Weddell Sea region and in the area of the Ross Sea (Figure 13).

As the East Wind Drift and the Antarctic Circumpolar Current flow around Antarctica in opposite directions, they create a surface divergence. Recall that the Coriolis effect deflects moving masses to the left in the Southern Hemisphere, so the East Wind Drift is deflected toward the continent and the Antarctic Circumpolar Current is deflected away from it. This creates a divergence of currents along a boundary called the **Antarctic Divergence**. The Antarctic Divergence has abundant marine life in the Southern Hemisphere summer because of the upwelling and mixing of these two currents, which supplies nutrients.

Atlantic Ocean Circulation

Figure 14 shows Atlantic Ocean surface circulation, which consists of two large subtropical gyres.

The North and South Atlantic Gyres   The **North Atlantic Gyre** rotates clockwise and the **South Atlantic Gyre** rotates counterclockwise, due to the combined effects of the trade winds, the prevailing westerlies, and the Coriolis effect. Figure 14 shows that each gyre consists of a poleward-moving warm current (*red*) and an equatorward-moving cold "return" current (*blue*). The two gyres are partially offset by the shapes of the surrounding continents and the *Atlantic Equatorial Countercurrent* moves in between them.

In the South Atlantic Gyre, the **South Equatorial Current** reaches its greatest strength just below the Equator, where it encounters the coast of Brazil and splits in two. Part of the South Equatorial Current moves off along the northeastern coast of South America toward the Caribbean Sea and the North Atlantic. The rest is turned southward as the Brazil Current, which ultimately merges with the West Wind Drift and moves eastward across the South Atlantic. The **Brazil Current** is much smaller than its Northern Hemisphere counterpart, the Gulf Stream, due to the splitting of the South Equatorial Current. The **Benguela Current**, slow-moving and cold, flows toward the Equator along Africa's western coast, completing the gyre.

Outside the gyre, the *Falkland Current* (Figure 14), which is also called the *Malvinas Current*, moves a significant amount of cold water along the coast of Argentina as far north as 25 to 30 degrees south latitude, wedging its way between the continent and the south-bound Brazil Current.

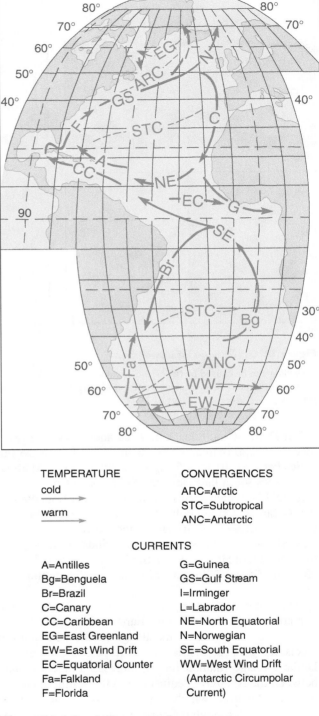

TEMPERATURE
cold ———▶
warm ———▶

CONVERGENCES
ARC=Arctic
STC=Subtropical
ANC=Antarctic

CURRENTS

A=Antilles
Bg=Benguela
Br=Brazil
C=Canary
CC=Caribbean
EG=East Greenland
EW=East Wind Drift
EC=Equatorial Counter
Fa=Falkland
F=Florida

G=Guinea
GS=Gulf Stream
I=Irminger
L=Labrador
NE=North Equatorial
N=Norwegian
SE=South Equatorial
WW=West Wind Drift
   (Antarctic Circumpolar
   Current)

Figure 14 Atlantic Ocean surface currents.

Atlantic Ocean surface circulation is composed primarily of two subtropical gyres.

The Gulf Stream   The **Gulf Stream** is the best studied of all ocean currents. It moves northward along the East Coast of the United States, warming coastal states and moderating winters in these and northern European regions.

Figure 15 shows the network of currents in the North Atlantic Ocean that contribute to the flow of the Gulf Stream. The **North Equatorial Current** moves parallel to the Equator in the Northern Hemisphere, where it is joined by the portion of the South Equatorial Current that turned northward along the South American coast. This flow then splits into the *Antilles Current*, which passes along the Atlantic side of the West Indies, and the *Caribbean Current*,

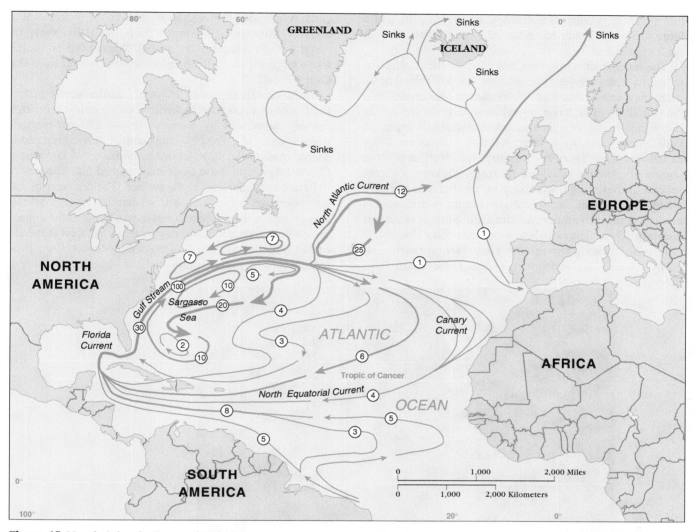

Figure 15 North Atlantic Ocean circulation.

The North Atlantic Gyre, showing average flow rates in Sverdrups (1 Sverdrup = 1 million cubic meters per second). The four major currents include the western intensified Gulf Stream, the North Atlantic Current, the Canary Current, and the North Equatorial Current. Some water splits off in the North Atlantic, where it becomes cold and dense, so it sinks. The Sargasso Sea occupies the stagnant eddy in the middle of the subtropical gyre.

which passes through the Yucatán Channel into the Gulf of Mexico. These masses reconverge as the *Florida Current*.

The Florida Current flows close to shore over the continental shelf at a rate that at times exceeds 35 Sverdrups. As it moves off North Carolina's Cape Hatteras and flows across the deep ocean in a northeasterly direction, it is called the Gulf Stream. The Gulf Stream is a western boundary current, so it is subject to western intensification. Thus, it is only 50 to 75 kilometers (31 to 47 miles) wide, but it reaches depths of 1.5 kilometers (1 mile) and speeds from 3 to 10 kilometers (2 to 6 miles) per hour, making it the fastest current in the world ocean.

The western boundary of the Gulf Stream is usually abrupt, but it periodically migrates closer to and farther away from the shore. Its eastern boundary is very difficult to identify because it is usually masked by meandering water masses that change their position continuously.

The Gulf Stream gradually merges eastward with the water of the **Sargasso Sea**. The Sargasso Sea is the water that circulates around the rotation center of the North Atlantic gyre. The Sargasso Sea, therefore, is the stagnant eddy of the North Atlantic Gyre. Its name is derived from a type of floating marine alga called *Sargassum* (*sargassum* = grapes) that abounds on its surface.

The transport rate of the Gulf Stream off Chesapeake Bay is about 100 Sverdrups,[9] which suggests that a large volume of water from the Sargasso Sea has combined with the Florida Current to produce the Gulf Stream. By the time the Gulf Stream nears Newoundland, however, the

---

[9]The Gulf Stream's flow of 100 Sverdrups equates to a volume of about 100 major league football stadiums passing by the southeast U.S. coast *each second* and is more than 100 times greater than the combined flow of *all* the world's rivers!

transport rate is only 40 Sverdrups, which suggests that a large volume of water has returned to the diffuse flow of the Sargasso Sea.

The mechanisms involved that produce such a dramatic loss of water are yet to be determined. Meanders, however, may cause much of it. *Meanders* (*Menderes* = a river in Turkey that has a very sinuous course) are snake-like bends in the current that often disconnect from the Gulf Stream and form large rotating masses of water called *vortexes* (*vertere* = to turn), which are more commonly known as *eddies* or *rings*. Figure 16 shows several of these rings, which are noticeable near the center of each image. The figure also shows that meanders along the north boundary of the Gulf Stream pinch off and trap warm Sargasso Sea water in eddies that rotate clockwise, creating **warm-core rings** (*yellow*) surrounded by cooler (*blue* and *green*) water. These warm rings

contain shallow, bowl-shaped masses of warm water about 1 kilometer (0.6 mile) deep, with diameters of about 100 kilometers (60 miles). Warm-core rings remove large volumes of water as they disconnect from the Gulf Stream.

Cold nearshore water spins off to the south of the Gulf Stream as counterclockwise-rotating **cold-core rings** (*green*) surrounded by warmer (*yellow* and *red-orange*) water (Figure 16). The cold rings consist of spinning cone-shaped masses of cold water that extend over 3.5 kilometers (2.2 miles) deep. These rings may exceed 500 kilometers (310 miles) in diameter at the surface. The diameter of the cone increases with depth and sometimes reaches all the way to the sea floor, where cones have a tremendous impact on sea floor sediment. Cold rings move southwest at speeds of 3 to 7 kilometers (2 to 4 miles) per day toward Cape Hatteras, where they often rejoin the Gulf Stream.

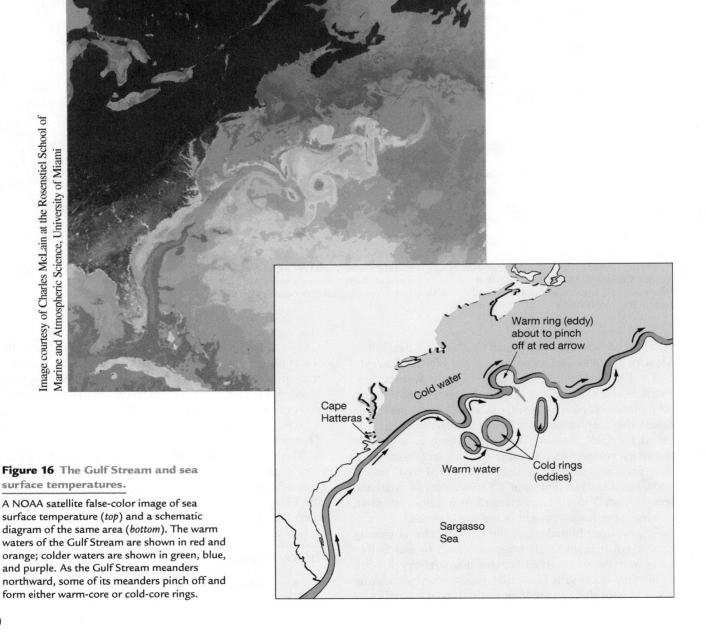

Image courtesy of Charles McLain at the Rosenstiel School of Marine and Atmospheric Science, University of Miami

Figure 16 The Gulf Stream and sea surface temperatures.

A NOAA satellite false-color image of sea surface temperature (*top*) and a schematic diagram of the same area (*bottom*). The warm waters of the Gulf Stream are shown in red and orange; colder waters are shown in green, blue, and purple. As the Gulf Stream meanders northward, some of its meanders pinch off and form either warm-core or cold-core rings.

Both warm- and cold-core rings maintain not only unique temperature characteristics but also unique biological populations. Studies of rings have found they are isolated habitats for either warm-water organisms in a cold ocean or, conversely, cold-water organisms in a warmer ocean. The organisms can survive as long as the ring does; in some cases, rings have been documented to last as long as two years.

STUDENTS SOMETIMES ASK...
Is the Gulf Stream rich in life?

The Gulf Stream *itself* isn't, but its *boundaries* often are. The oceanic areas that have abundant marine life are typically associated with cool water—either in high-latitude regions, or in any region where upwelling occurs. These areas are constantly resupplied with oxygen- and nutrient-rich water, which results in high productivity. Warm-water areas develop a prominent thermocline that isolates the surface water from colder, nutrient-rich water below. Nutrients used up in warm waters tend not to be resupplied. The Gulf Stream, therefore, which is a western intensified, warm-water current, is associated with low productivity and an absence of marine life. The reason New England fishers knew about the Gulf Stream was because they sought their catch along the *sides* of the current, where mixing and upwelling occur.

Actually, all western intensified currents are warm and are associated with low productivities. The Kuroshio Current in the North Pacific Ocean, for example, is named for its conspicuous absence of marine life. In Japanese, *Kuroshio* means "black current," in reference to its clear, lifeless waters.

Southeast of Newfoundland, the Gulf Stream continues in an easterly direction across the North Atlantic (Figure 15). Here the Gulf Stream breaks into numerous branches, many of which become cold and dense enough to sink beneath the surface. As shown in Figure 14, one major branch combines the cold water of the *Labrador Current* with the warm Gulf Stream, producing abundant fog in the North Atlantic. This branch eventually breaks into the *Irminger Current*, which flows along Iceland's west coast, and the *Norwegian Current*, which moves northward along Norway's coast. The other major branch crosses the North Atlantic as the **North Atlantic Current** (also called the *North Atlantic Drift*, emphasizing its sluggish nature) and turns southward to become the cool Canary Current. The **Canary Current** is a broad, diffuse southward flow that eventually joins the North Equatorial Current, thus completing the gyre.

Climatic Effects of North Atlantic Currents The warming effects of the Gulf Stream are far ranging. It not only moderates temperatures along the East Coast of the United States, but also in Northern Europe (in conjunction with heat transferred by the atmosphere). Thus, the temperatures across the Atlantic at different latitudes are much higher in Europe than in North America because of the effects of heat transfer from the Gulf Stream to Europe. For example, Spain and Portugal have warm climates yet they are at the same latitude as the New England states, which are known for severe winters. The warming that Northern Europe experiences because of the Gulf Stream is as much as 9°C (20°F), which is enough to keep high-latitude Baltic ports ice free throughout the year.

The warming effects of western boundary currents in the North Atlantic Ocean can be seen on the average sea surface temperature map for February shown in Figure 8b. Off the east coast of North America from latitudes 20 degrees north (the latitude of Cuba) to 40 degrees north (the latitude of Philadelphia), for example, there is a 20°C (36°F) difference in sea surface temperatures. On the eastern side of the North Atlantic, on the other hand, there is only a 5°C (9°F) difference in temperature between the same latitudes, indicating the moderating effect of the Gulf Stream.

The average sea surface temperature map for August (see Figure 8a) also shows how the North Atlantic and Norwegian Currents (branches of the Gulf Stream) warm northwestern Europe compared with the same latitudes along the North American coast. On the western side of the North Atlantic, the southward-flowing Labrador Current—which is cold and often contains icebergs from western Greenland—keeps Canadian coastal waters much cooler. During the Northern Hemisphere winter (Figure 8b), North Africa's coastal waters are cooled by the southward-flowing Canary Current and are much cooler than waters near Florida and the Gulf of Mexico.

Pacific Ocean Circulation

Two large subtropical gyres dominate the circulation pattern in the Pacific Ocean, resulting in surface water movement and climatic effects similar to those found in the Atlantic. However, the Equatorial Countercurrent is much better developed in the Pacific Ocean than in the Atlantic (Figure 17), because the Pacific Ocean basin is larger and more unobstructed than the Atlantic Ocean basin.

Normal Conditions Figure 17 shows the **North Pacific Gyre**, which consists in part of the North Equatorial Current, which flows westward into the western intensified **Kuroshio Current**[10] near Asia. Because of its proximity to Japan, the Kuroshio Current is also called the *Japan Current*. Its warm waters make Japan's climate warmer than would be expected for its latitude. The

---

[10]Kuroshio is pronounced "kuhr-ROH-shee-oh."

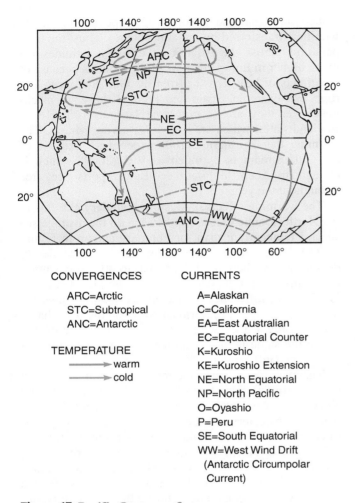

CONVERGENCES

ARC=Arctic
STC=Subtropical
ANC=Antarctic

TEMPERATURE

→ warm
→ cold

CURRENTS

A=Alaskan
C=California
EA=East Australian
EC=Equatorial Counter
K=Kuroshio
KE=Kuroshio Extension
NE=North Equatorial
NP=North Pacific
O=Oyashio
P=Peru
SE=South Equatorial
WW=West Wind Drift
(Antarctic Circumpolar
Current)

Figure 17 Pacific Ocean surface currents.

Similar to the Atlantic Ocean, the Pacific contains two large subtropical gyres. However, the equatorial countercurrent is more strongly developed here than in smaller ocean basins.

northern part of the Kuroshio Current is called the *Kuroshio Extension*, which flows to about 170 degrees east longitude. This current flows into the **North Pacific Current**, which connects to the cool-water **California Current**. The California Current flows south along the coast of California to complete the loop. Some North Pacific Current water also flows to the north and merges into the **Alaskan Current** in the Gulf of Alaska.

Figure 17 also shows the **South Pacific Gyre**, which consists in part of the South Equatorial Current, which flows westward into the western intensified **East Australian Current**.[11] From there, it joins the Antarctic Circumpolar Current (West Wind Drift) and completes the gyre as the **Peru Current** (also called the *Humboldt Current*, after German naturalist Friedrich Heinrich Alexander von Humboldt). Flowing underneath the South Equatorial Current of this gyre is a thin, ribbonlike **Equatorial Un-**

[11]Note that the western intensified East Australian Current was named because it lies off the *East Coast* of Australia, even though it occupies a position along the *western* margin of the Pacific Ocean basin.

dercurrent that flows in an easterly direction along the Equator and extends for more than 6000 kilometers (3700 miles) across the Pacific at depths of up to 200 meters (656 feet). Although it is only 0.2 kilometer (0.12 mile) deep and about 300 kilometers (186 miles) wide, it has a volume transport of approximately 40 Sverdrups.

The cool water of the Peru Current has historically been one of Earth's richest fishing grounds. What conditions produce such an abundance of fish? Figure 18a shows that along the west coast of South America, coastal winds create Ekman transport that moves water away from shore, causing upwelling of cool, nutrient-rich water. This upwelling increases productivity and results in an abundance of marine life, including small silver-colored fish called *anchovetas* (anchovies) that become particularly plentiful near Peru and Ecuador. Anchovies provide a food source for many larger marine organisms and also supply Peru's commercial fishing industry, which was established in the 1950s. Anchovies are so abundant in the waters off South America that by 1970, Peru was the largest producer of fish from the sea in the world, with a peak production of 12.3 million metric tons (13.5 million short tons), accounting for about one-quarter of *all* fish from the sea worldwide.

STUDENTS SOMETIMES ASK...

The amount of anchovies produced by Peru is impressive! Besides a topping for pizza, what are some other uses of anchovies?

Anchovies are an ingredient in certain dishes, hors d'oeuvres, sauces, and salad dressing, and they are also used as bait by fishers. Historically, however, most of the *anchoveta* caught in Peruvian waters were exported and used as fishmeal (consisting of ground anchovies). The fishmeal, in turn, was used largely in pet food and as a high-protein chicken feed. As unbelievable as it may seem, El Niños affected the price of eggs! Prior to the collapse of the Peruvian *anchoveta* fishing industry in 1972–1973, El Niño events significantly reduced the availability of *anchoveta*. This drastically cut the export of anchovies from Peru, causing U.S. farmers to pursue more expensive options for chicken feed. Thus, egg prices typically increased.

The collapse of the *anchoveta* fishing industry in Peru was triggered by the 1972–1973 El Niño event but was caused by chronic overfishing in prior years. Interestingly, the shortage of fishmeal after 1972–1973 led to an increased demand for soyameal, an alternative source of high-quality protein. Increased demand for soyameal increased the price of soy commodities, thereby encouraging U.S. farmers to plant soybeans instead of wheat. Reduced production of wheat, in turn, caused a major global food crisis—all triggered by an El Niño event.

Figure 18a shows that high pressure and sinking air dominates the coastal region of South America, resulting in clear, fair, and dry weather. On the other side of the Pacific, a low-pressure region and rising air creates cloudy

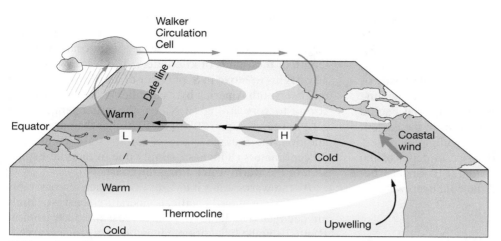

(a) Normal conditions

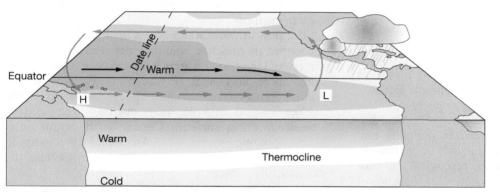

(b) El Niño conditions

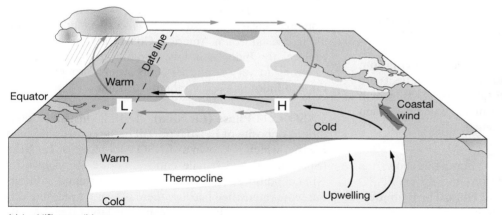

(c) La Niña conditions

Figure 18 Normal, El Niño, and La Niña conditions.

(a) Normal oceanic and atmospheric conditions in the equatorial Pacific. (b) El Niño (ENSO warm phase) conditions. (c) La Niña (ENSO cool phase) conditions.

conditions with plentiful precipitation in Indonesia, New Guinea, and northern Australia. This pressure difference causes the strong southeast trade winds to blow across the equatorial South Pacific. The resulting atmospheric circulation cell in the equatorial South Pacific Ocean is named the **Walker Circulation Cell** (*green arrows*) after Sir Gilbert T. Walker, the British meteorologist who first described the effect in the 1920s.

The southeast trade winds set ocean water in motion, which also moves across the Pacific toward the west. The water warms as it flows in the equatorial region and creates a wedge of warm water on the western side of the Pacific Ocean, called the **Pacific warm pool** (see Figure 8). Due to the movement of equatorial currents to the west, the Pacific warm pool is thicker along the western side of the Pacific than along the eastern side. The thermocline beneath the warm pool in the western equatorial Pacific occurs below 100 meters (330 feet) depth. In the eastern Pacific, however, the *thermocline* is within 30 meters (100 feet) of the surface. The difference in depth of the thermocline can be seen by the sloping boundary between the warm surface water and the cold deep water in Figure 18a.

El Niño–Southern Oscillation (ENSO) Conditions

Historically, Peru's residents knew that every few years, a current of warm water reduced the population of anchovies in coastal waters. The decrease in anchovies caused a dramatic decline not only in the fishing industry, but also in marine life such as sea birds and seals that depended on anchovies for food. The warm current also brought about changes in the weather—usually intense rainfall—and even brought such interesting items as floating coconuts from tropical islands near the Equator. At first, these events were called *años de abundancia* (years of abundance) because the additional rainfall dramatically increased plant growth on the normally arid land. What was once thought of as a joyous event, however, soon became associated with the ecological and economic disaster that is now a well-known consequence of the phenomenon.

This warm-water current usually occurred around Christmas and thus was given the name **El Niño**, Spanish for "the child," in reference to baby Jesus. In the 1920s, Walker was the first to recognize that an east–west atmospheric pressure seesaw accompanied the warm current and called the phenomenon the **Southern Oscillation**. Today, the combined oceanic and atmospheric effects are called **El Niño–Southern Oscillation (ENSO)**, which periodically alternate between warm and cold phases and cause dramatic environmental changes.

ENSO Warm Phase (El Niño)

Figure 18b shows the atmospheric and oceanic conditions during an ENSO warm phase, which is known as El Niño. The high pressure along the coast of South America weakens, reducing the difference between the high- and low-pressure regions of the Walker Circulation Cell. This, in turn, causes the southeast trade winds to diminish. In very strong El Niño events, the trade winds actually blow in the *reverse* direction.

Without the trade winds, the Pacific warm pool that has built up on the western side of the Pacific begins to flow back across the ocean toward South America. Aided by an increase in the flow of the Equatorial Countercurrent, the Pacific warm pool creates a band of warm water that stretches across the equatorial Pacific Ocean (Figure 19a). It travels across the Pacific as a large wave called a *Kelvin wave*, which has a wavelength of thousands of kilometers. The warm water usually begins to move in September of an El Niño year and reaches South America by December or January. During strong to very strong El Niños, the water temperature off Peru can be up to 10°C (18°F) higher than normal. In addition, the average sea level can increase as much as 20 centimeters (8 inches), simply due to thermal expansion of the warm water along the coast.

As the warm water increases sea surface temperatures across the equatorial Pacific, temperature-sensitive corals are decimated in Tahiti, the Galápagos, and other tropical Pacific islands. In addition, many other organisms are affected by the warm water (Box 2). Once the warm water reaches South America, it moves north and south along the west coast of the Americas, increasing average sea level and the number of tropical hurricanes formed in the eastern Pacific.

The flow of warm water across the Pacific also causes the sloped thermocline boundary between warm surface waters and the cooler waters below to flatten out and become more horizontal (Figure 19b). Near Peru, upwelling brings warmer, nutrient-depleted water to the surface instead of cold, nutrient-rich water. In fact, *downwelling* can sometimes occur as the warm water stacks up along coastal South America. Productivity diminishes and most types of marine life in the area are dramatically reduced.

As the warm water moves to the east across the Pacific, the low-pressure zone also migrates. In a strong to very strong El Niño event, the low pressure can move entirely across the Pacific and remain over South America. The low pressure substantially increases precipitation along coastal South America. Conversely, high pressure replaces the Indonesian low, bringing dry conditions or, in strong to very strong El Niño events, drought conditions to Indonesia and northern Australia.

ENSO Cool Phase (La Niña)

In some instances, conditions opposite of El Niño prevail in the equatorial South Pacific, which is known as ENSO cool phase or **La Niña** (Spanish for "the female child"). Figure 19c shows La Niña conditions, which are similar to normal conditions but more intensified because there is a larger pressure difference across the Pacific Ocean. This larger pressure difference creates stronger Walker Circulation and stronger trade winds, which in turn causes more upwelling, a shallower thermocline in the eastern Pacific, and a band of cooler than normal water that stretches across the equatorial South Pacific (Figure 19b).

La Niña conditions commonly occur following an El Niño. For instance, the 1997–1998 El Niño was followed by several years of persistent La Niña conditions. The alternating pattern of El Niño–La Niña conditions since 1950 is shown by the multivariate **ENSO index** (Figure 20),

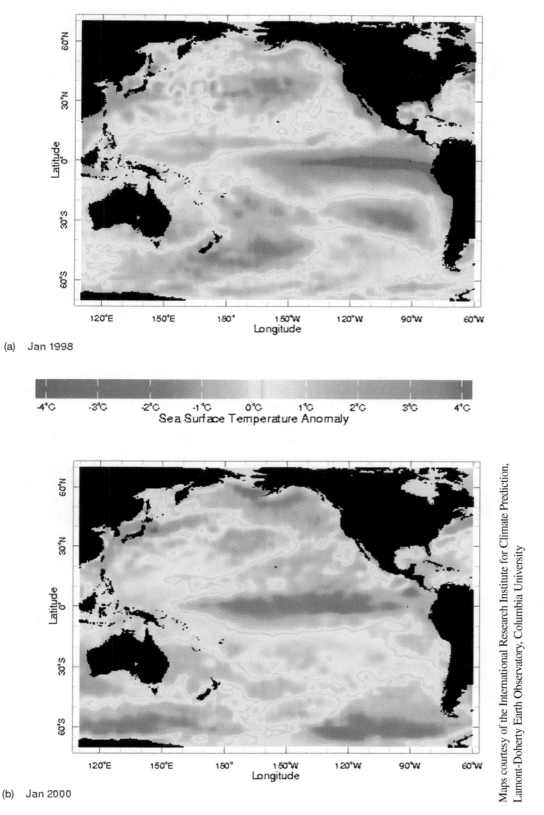

(a) Jan 1998

(b) Jan 2000

Maps courtesy of the International Research Institute for Climate Prediction,
Lamont-Doherty Earth Observatory, Columbia University

Figure 19 Sea surface temperature anomaly maps.

Maps showing sea surface temperature anomalies, which represent departures from normal conditions. Red colors indicate water warmer than normal and blue colors represent water cooler than normal. **(a)** Map of the Pacific Ocean in January 1998, showing the anomalous warming during the 1997–1998 El Niño. **(b)** Map of the same area in January 2000, showing cooling in the equatorial Pacific related to La Niña.

BOX 2 Research Methods in Oceanography

EL NIÑO AND THE INCREDIBLE SHRINKING MARINE IGUANAS OF THE GALÁPAGOS ISLANDS

The world's only marine lizards are the marine iguanas (*Amblyrhynchus cristatus*) of Ecuador's Galápagos Islands. The iguanas are vegetarians that eat only marine algae and have adaptations that enable them to spend long periods foraging for food in the ocean. The islands they inhabit are severely affected by El Niño events, which cause periodic food shortages for the iguanas.

When El Niño conditions occur, warm water from the Pacific warm pool moves to the east along the Equator. This change, accompanied by a decrease in upwelling along the eastern Pacific, causes ocean surface temperatures to rise by as much as 10°C (18°F). In the Galápagos Islands, these conditions cause severe hardship for species that like cooler water temperatures, such as green and red algae that are the iguana's preferred food. Instead, these types of algae are replaced by brown algae, which are harder for the iguanas to digest. Unlike many marine animals that can migrate to other areas where food

supplies are plentiful, the iguanas are confined to the islands where food supplies become limited. During a severe El Niño, up to 90% of the iguana population can die of starvation.

Two studies covering 8 and 18 years reveal that the iguana's main adaptation for this lack of food is to shrink in size, allowing iguanas to utilize meager food supplies more efficiently. During the 1997–1998 El Niño, for example, Galápagos marine iguanas shrank by as much as 20%, with larger animals shrinking the most. Also, females shrank more than similar-sized males, probably because of the additional energy females expended producing eggs the previous year.

About half of the shrinkage can be attributed to decreases in the mass of

cartilage and connective tissue, while bone absorption may account for the remainder. In addition, the iguanas don't forage for food and thus get little exercise during El Niño events, which may result in additional shrinkage (similar to the decrease in weight associated with inactivity experienced by astronauts that spend long periods in weightlessness).

Following El Niño conditions, upwelling is reestablished, which creates cooler surface water temperatures. As a result, the iguana's preferred food supply again becomes abundant and the iguanas grow back to normal size. Remarkably, the marine iguanas of the Galápagos Islands repeatedly shrink and regrow in response to El Niño-induced changes in the environment.

Photo courtesy of Martin Wikelski, University of Illinois

Marine iguana and location maps of the Galápagos Islands.

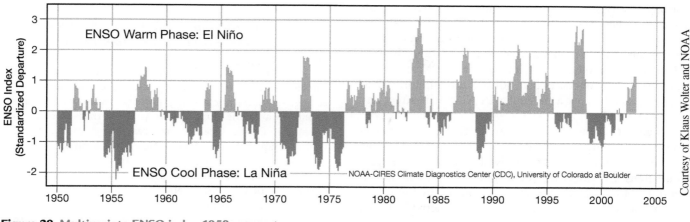

Figure 20 Multivariate ENSO index 1950–present.

The multivariate ENSO index is calculated using a variety of atmospheric and oceanic factors. ENSO index values greater than zero (*red areas*) indicate El Niño conditions while ENSO index values less than zero (*blue areas*) indicate La Niña conditions. The greater the value is from zero, the stronger the corresponding El Niño or La Niña.

which is calculated using a weighted average of atmospheric and oceanic factors including atmospheric pressure, winds, and sea surface temperatures. Positive ENSO index numbers indicate El Niño conditions whereas negative numbers reflect La Niña conditions. Normal conditions are indicated by a value near zero, and the greater the index value differs from zero (either negative or positive), the stronger the respective condition.

How Often Do El Niño Events Occur? Records of sea surface temperatures over the past 100 years reveal that throughout the twentieth century, El Niño conditions occur on average about every 2 to 10 years, but in a highly irregular pattern. In some decades, for instance, there has been an El Niño event every few years, while in others there may have been only one. Figure 20 shows the pattern since 1950, revealing that the equatorial Pacific fluctuates between El Niño and La Niña conditions, with only a few years that could be considered "normal" conditions (represented by an ENSO index value close to zero). Typically, El Niño events last for 12 to 18 months and are followed by La

Niña conditions that exist for a similar length of time. However, some El Niño or La Niña conditions can last for several years.

El Niño events—especially severe ones—may occur more frequently as a result of increased global warming. For instance, the two most severe El Niño events in the 20th century occurred in 1982–1983 and 1997–1998. Presumably, increased ocean temperatures could trigger more frequent and more severe El Niños. However, this pattern could also be a part of a long-term natural climate cycle. Recently, oceanographers have recognized a phenomenon called the **Pacific Decadal Oscillation (PDO)**, which lasts 20 to 30 years and appears to influence Pacific sea surface temperatures. Analysis of TOPEX/Poseidon satellite data suggests that the Pacific Ocean has been in the warm phase of the PDO from 1977 to 1999 and that it has just entered the cool phase, which may suppress the initiation of El Niño events.

Effects of El Niños and La Niñas Mild El Niño events influence only the equatorial South Pacific Ocean while

TABLE 3 **El Niño–Southern Oscillation: A summary.**

- El Niño (ENSO warm phase) is the name of a warm water current that occurs periodically around Christmastime in the equatorial Pacific Ocean; Southern Oscillation describes the switching of atmospheric pressure that accompanies El Niño.

- El Niño events are characterized by warmer than normal water and a deepened thermocline in the east Pacific, a rise in sea level along the Equator, a decrease or reversal of the southeast trade winds, and reduced upwelling and less abundant marine life in waters near Peru and Ecuador.

- El Niños of various strengths occur every 2 to 10 years, but in a highly irregular pattern.

- Strong El Niño events produce unusual weather worldwide.

- La Niña conditions (ENSO cool phase) are characterized by conditions opposite of El Niño; the Pacific Ocean experiences alternating El Niño and La Niña events.

strong to very strong El Niño events can influence world-wide weather. Typically, stronger El Niños alter the atmospheric jet steam and produce unusual weather in most parts of the globe. Sometimes the weather is drier than normal; at other times, it is wetter. The weather may also be warmer or cooler than normal. It is still difficult to predict exactly how a particular El Niño will affect any region's weather.

Figure 21 shows how very strong El Niño events can result in flooding, erosion, droughts, fires, tropical storms, and effects on marine life worldwide. These weather perturbations also affect the production of corn, cotton, and coffee. More locally, the satellite images in Figure 22 show that sea surface temperatures off southern California are significantly higher during an El Niño year.

Even though severe El Niños are typically associated with vast amounts of destruction, they can be beneficial in some areas. Tropical hurricane formation, for instance, is generally suppressed in the Atlantic Ocean, some desert regions receive much-needed rain, and organisms adapted to warm-water conditions thrive in the Pacific.

La Niña events are associated with sea surface temperatures and weather phenomena opposite to those of El Niño. Indian Ocean monsoons, for instance, are typically drier than usual in El Niño years but wetter than usual in La Niña years.

S T U D E N T S   S O M E T I M E S   A S K ...
Do El Niño events occur in other ocean basins?

Yes, the Atlantic and Indian Oceans both experience events similar to the Pacific's El Niño. These events are not nearly as strong, however; nor do they influence worldwide weather phenomena to the same extent as those that occur in the equatorial Pacific Ocean. The great width of the Pacific Ocean in equatorial latitudes is the main reason that El Niño events occur more strongly in the Pacific.

In the Atlantic Ocean, this phenomenon is related to the North Atlantic Oscillation (NAO), which is a periodic change in atmospheric pressure between Iceland and the Azores Islands. This pressure difference determines the strength of the prevailing westerlies in the North Atlantic, which in turn affects ocean surface currents there. The Atlantic Ocean periodically experiences NAO events, which sometimes cause intense cold in the northeast U.S., unusual weather in Europe, and heavy rainfall along the normally arid coast of southwest Africa.

Examples from Recent El Niños   Recent El Niños provide an indication of the variability of the effects of El Niño events. For instance, in the winter of 1976, a moderate

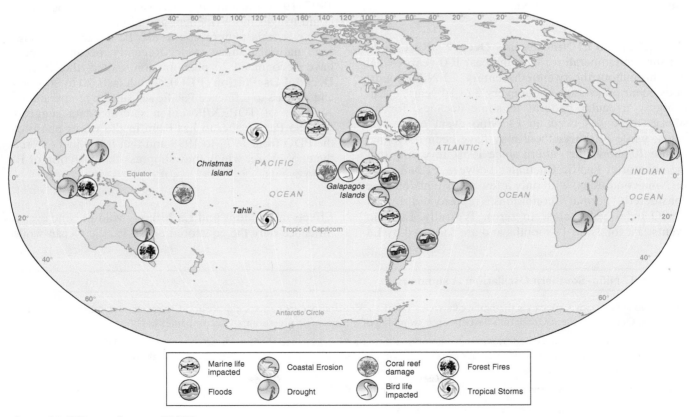

Figure 21 Effects of severe El Niños.

Flooding, erosion, droughts, fires, tropical storms, and effects on marine life are all associated with severe El Niño events.

(a) Normal　　　　　　　　　　　　(b) El Niño

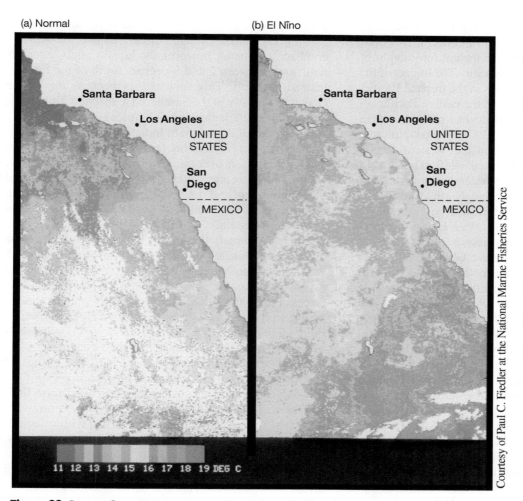

11 12 13 14 15 16 17 18 19 DEG C

Courtesy of Paul C. Fiedler at the National Marine Fisheries Service

Figure 22 Sea surface temperatures off southern California.

Sea surface temperature maps (in °C) for southern California from data collected by the satellite-mounted Advanced Very High Resolution Radiometer. Blue is cold water; red is warm water. **(a)** Water temperatures in January 1982, a non–El Niño year. **(b)** Water temperatures a year later, during an El Niño event.

El Niño event coincided with northern California's worst drought of the last century, showing that El Niño events don't always bring torrential rains to the western United States. During that same winter, the eastern United States experienced record cold temperatures.

The 1982–1983 El Niño is the strongest ever recorded, causing far-ranging effects across the globe. Not only was there anomalous warming in the tropical Pacific, but the warm water spread along the coast of North America, influencing sea surface temperatures from California (Figure 22) to Alaska. Sea level was higher than normal (due to thermal expansion of the water), which, when high surf was experienced, caused damage to coastal structures and increased coastal erosion. In addition, the jet stream swung much farther south than normal across the United States, bringing a series of powerful storms that resulted in three times normal rainfall across the southwestern United States. The increased rainfall caused severe flooding and landslides as well as higher than normal snowfall in the Rocky Mountains. Alaska and western Canada had a relatively warm winter, and the eastern United States had its mildest winter in 25 years.

The full strength of El Niño was experienced in western South America. Normally arid Peru was drenched with more than 3 meters (10 feet) of rain, causing extreme flooding and landslides. Sea surface temperatures were so high for so long that temperature-sensitive coral reefs across the equatorial Pacific were decimated. Marine mammals and sea birds, which depend on the food normally available in the highly productive waters along the west coast of South America, went elsewhere or died. In the Galápagos Islands, for example, over half of the island's seals and sea lions died of starvation during the 1982–1983 El Niño.

French Polynesia had not experienced a hurricane in 75 years; in 1983, it endured six. The Hawaiian Island of Kauai also experienced a rare hurricane. Meanwhile, in Europe, severe cold weather prevailed. Worldwide, droughts occurred in Australia, Indonesia, China, India, Africa, and Central America. In all, over 2000 deaths and at least $10 billion in property damage ($2.5 billion in the United States) were attributed to the 1982–1983 El Niño event.

The 1997–1998 El Niño event began several months earlier than normal and peaked in January 1998. The amount of Southern Oscillation and sea surface warming in the equatorial Pacific was initially as strong as the 1982–1983 El Niño, which caused a great deal of concern. However, the 1997–1998 El Niño weakened in the last few months of 1997 before reintensifying in early 1998. The impact of the 1997–1998 El Niño was felt mostly in the tropical Pacific, where surface water temperatures in the eastern Pacific averaged more than 4°C (7°F) warmer than normal, and, in some locations, reached up to 9°C (16°F) above normal (see Figure 19a). High pressure in the western Pacific brought drought conditions that caused wildfires to burn out of control in Indonesia. Also, the warmer than normal water along the west coast of Central and North America increased the number of hurricanes off Mexico.

In the United States, the 1997–1998 El Niño caused killer tornadoes in the southeast, massive blizzards in the upper Midwest, and flooding in the Ohio River Valley. Most of California received twice the normal rainfall, which caused flooding and landslides in many parts of the state. The lower Midwest, the Pacific Northwest, and the eastern seaboard, on the other hand, had relatively mild weather. In all, the 1997–1998 El Niño caused 2100 deaths and $33 billion in property damage worldwide.

Predicting El Niño Events   The 1982–1983 El Niño event was not predicted; nor was it recognized until it was near its peak. Because it affected weather worldwide and caused such extensive damage, the **Tropical Ocean–Global Atmosphere (TOGA)** program was initiated in 1985 to study how El Niño events developed. The goal of the TOGA program was to monitor the equatorial South Pacific Ocean during El Niño events to enable scientists to model and predict future El Niño events. The 10-year program studied the ocean from research vessels, analyzed surface and subsurface data from radio-transmitting sensor buoys, monitored oceanic phenomena by satellite, and developed computer models.

These models made it possible to predict El Niño events since 1987 as much as one year in advance. After the completion of TOGA, the **Tropical Atmosphere and Ocean (TAO)** project (sponsored by the United States, Canada, Australia, and Japan) has continued to monitor the equatorial Pacific Ocean with a series of 70 moored buoys, providing real-time information about the conditions of the tropical Pacific that is available on the Internet. Although monitoring has improved, the causes of El Niño events are still not fully understood.

El Niño is a combined oceanic–atmospheric phenomenon that occurs periodically in the tropical Pacific Ocean, bringing warm water to the east. La Niña describes conditions opposite of El Niño.

Indian Ocean Circulation

From November to March, equatorial circulation in the Indian Ocean is similar to that in the other oceans, with two westward-flowing equatorial currents (North and South Equatorial Currents) separated by an eastward-flowing Equatorial Countercurrent. Unlike the Atlantic and Pacific systems, however, the Equatorial Countercurrent flows between 2 and 8 degrees south of the Equator instead of north. This flow occurs because the Indian Ocean lies mostly in the Southern Hemisphere (it extends only to about 20 degrees north latitude).

The winds of the northern Indian Ocean have a seasonal pattern called **monsoon** (*mausim* = season) winds. During winter, air over the Asian mainland rapidly cools, creating high pressure, which forces atmospheric masses off the continent and out over the ocean (*green arrows* in Figure 23a). These northeast trade winds are called the *northeast monsoon*.

During summer, the winds reverse. Because of the lower heat capacity of rocks and soil compared with water, the Asian mainland warms faster than the adjacent ocean, creating low pressure over the continent. This forces air over the Indian Ocean onto the Asian landmass, giving rise to the *southwest monsoon* (*green arrows* in Figure 23b), which may be thought of as a continuation of the southeast trade winds across the Equator.

The North Equatorial Current disappears during the summer and is replaced by the *Southwest Monsoon Current*, which flows from west to east across the North Indian Ocean. The **Somali Current**, which flows northward from the Equator along the coast of Africa with velocities approaching 4 kilometers (2.5 miles) per hour, feeds the Southwest Monsoon Current. In September or October, the northeast trade winds are reestablished, and the North Equatorial Current reappears (Figure 23a).

Surface circulation in the southern Indian Ocean (the **Indian Ocean Gyre**) is similar to subtropical gyres observed in other southern oceans. When the northeast trade winds blow, the South Equatorial Current provides water for the Equatorial Countercurrent and the **Agulhas Current**, which flows southward along Africa's east coast and joins the Antarctic Circumpolar Current (West Wind Drift). The *Agulhas Retroflection* is created when the Agulhas Current makes an abrupt turn as it meets the strong Antarctic Circumpolar Current. Turning northward out of the Antarctic Circumpolar Current is the **West Australian Current**, an eastern boundary current that merges with the South Equatorial Current, completing the gyre.

Eastern boundary currents in other subtropical gyres are cold drifts toward the Equator that produce arid coastal climates [that is, they receive less than 25 centimeters (10 inches) of rain per year]. In the southern Indian Ocean, however, the *Leeuwin Current* displaces the West Australian Current offshore. The Leeuwin Current is driven southward along the Australian coast from the warm-water dome piled up in the East Indies by the Pacific equatorial currents.

The Leeuwin Current produces a mild climate in southwestern Australia, which receives about 125 centimeters (50 inches) of rain per year. During El Niño events, however, the Leeuwin Current weakens, so the cold Western Australian Current brings drought instead.

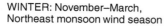

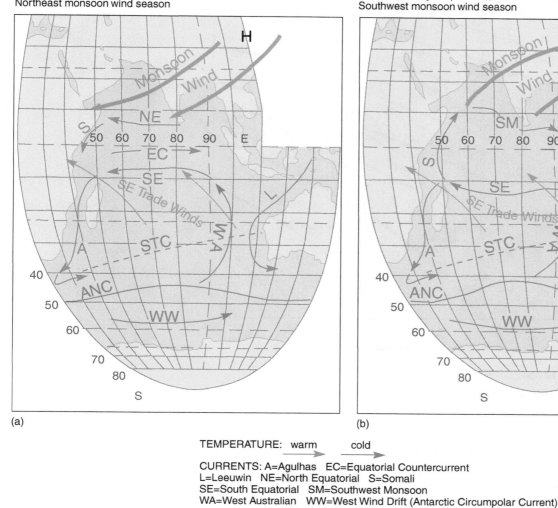

WINTER: November–March,
Northeast monsoon wind season

SUMMER: May–September,
Southwest monsoon wind season

(a)

(b)

TEMPERATURE: warm   cold

CURRENTS: A=Agulhas   EC=Equatorial Countercurrent
L=Leeuwin   NE=North Equatorial   S=Somali
SE=South Equatorial   SM=Southwest Monsoon
WA=West Australian   WW=West Wind Drift (Antarctic Circumpolar Current)

CONVERGENCES: STC=Subtropical   ANC=Antarctic

Figure 23 Indian Ocean surface currents.

Surface currents in the Indian Ocean are influenced by the seasonal monsoons. **(a)** Northeast monsoon, which occurs during winter. **(b)** Southwest monsoon, which occurs during summer.

Deep Currents

Deep currents occur in the deep zone below the pycnocline, so they influence about 90% of all ocean water. Density differences create deep currents. Although these density differences are usually small, they are large enough to cause denser waters to sink. Because the density variations that cause deep ocean circulation are caused by differences in temperature and salinity, deep ocean circulation is also referred to as **thermohaline** (*thermo* = heat, *haline* = salt) **circulation**.

Origin of Thermohaline Circulation

Recall that an increase in seawater density can be caused by a *decrease* in temperature or an *increase* in salinity. Temperature, though, has the greater influence on density. Density changes due to salinity are important only in

very high latitudes, where water temperature remains low and relatively constant.

Most water involved in deep-ocean currents (thermohaline circulation) begins in high latitudes *at the surface*. In these regions, surface water becomes cold and its salinity increases as sea ice forms. When this surface water becomes dense enough, it sinks, initiating deep-ocean currents. Once this water sinks, it is removed from the physical processes that increased its density in the first place, and so its temperature and salinity don't change very much during the time it spends in the deep ocean. Thus, a **temperature–salinity (T–S) diagram** can be used to identify deep-water masses based on their characteristic temperature, salinity, and resulting density. Figure 24 shows a T–S diagram for the North Atlantic Ocean.

As these surface-water masses become dense and are sinking (downwelling) in high-latitude areas, deep-water

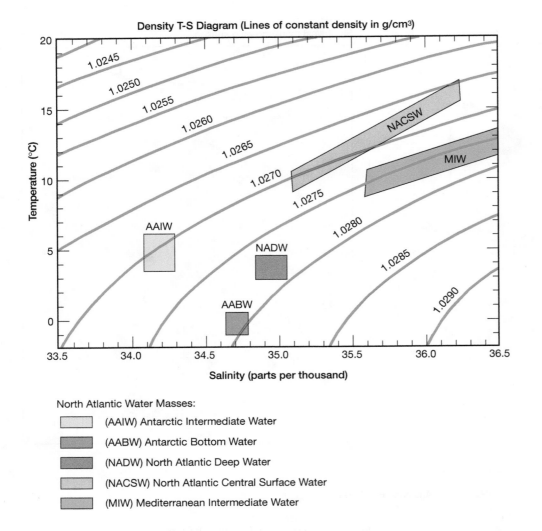

Density T-S Diagram (Lines of constant density in g/cm³)

North Atlantic Water Masses:

- (AAIW) Antarctic Intermediate Water
- (AABW) Antarctic Bottom Water
- (NADW) North Atlantic Deep Water
- (NACSW) North Atlantic Central Surface Water
- (MIW) Mediterranean Intermediate Water

Figure 24 Temperature–salinity (T–S) diagram.

A density T–S diagram for the North Atlantic Ocean. Lines of constant density are in grams per cubic centimeter (g/cm³). After various deep-water masses sink below the surface, they can be identified based on their characteristic temperature, salinity, and resulting density.

masses are also rising to the surface (upwelling). Because the water temperature in high latitude regions is the same at the surface as it is down below, the water column is isothermal, there is no thermocline or associated pycnocline, and upwelling and downwelling can easily be accomplished.

Deep-water currents move larger volumes of water and are much slower than surface currents. Typical speeds of deep currents range from 10 to 20 kilometers (6 to 12 miles) per year. Thus, it takes a deep current *an entire year* to travel the same distance that a western intensified surface current can move in *one hour*.

Sources of Deep Water

In southern subpolar latitudes, huge masses of deep water form beneath sea ice along the margins of the Antarctic continent. Here, rapid winter freezing produces very cold, high-density water that sinks down the continental slope of Antarctica and becomes **Antarctic Bottom Water**, the densest water in the open ocean (Figure 25). Antarctic Bottom Water slowly sinks beneath the surface and spreads into all the world's ocean basins, eventually returning to the surface perhaps 1000 years later.

In the northern subpolar latitudes, large masses of deep water form in the Norwegian Sea. From there, it flows as a subsurface current into the North Atlantic, where it becomes part of the **North Atlantic Deep Water**. North Atlantic Deep Water also comes from the margins of the Irminger Sea off southeastern Greenland, the Labrador Sea, and the dense, salty Mediterranean Sea. Like Antarctic Bottom Water, North Atlantic Deep Water spreads throughout the ocean basins. It is less dense, however, so it layers on top of the Antarctic Bottom Water (Figure 25).

Surface-water masses converge within the subtropical gyres and in the Arctic and Antarctic. Subtropical convergences do not produce deep water, however, because the

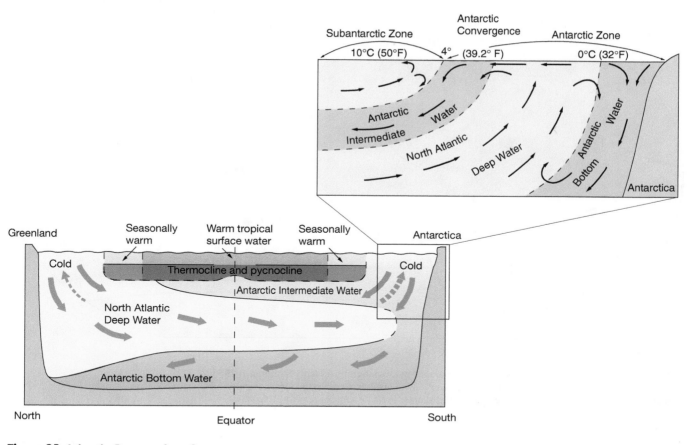

Figure 25 Atlantic Ocean subsurface water masses.

Schematic diagram of the various water masses in the Atlantic Ocean. Similar but less distinct layering based on density occurs in the Pacific and Indian Oceans as well. Upwelling and downwelling occurs in the North Atlantic and near Antarctica (*inset*), creating deep-water masses.

density of warm surface waters is too low for them to sink. Major sinking does occur, however, along the **Arctic Convergence** and Antarctic Convergence (Figure 25, *inset*). The deep-water mass formed from sinking at the Antarctic convergence is called the **Antarctic Intermediate Water** mass (Figure 25). Scientists have not yet thoroughly studied Antarctic Intermediate Water, so it remains a true frontier of knowledge, awaiting further exploration.

Figure 25 also shows that the highest-density water is found along the ocean bottom, with less-dense water above. In low-latitude regions, the boundary between the warm surface water and the deeper cold water is marked by a prominent thermocline and corresponding pycnocline that prevent vertical mixing. There is no pycnocline in high-latitude regions, so substantial vertical mixing (upwelling and downwelling) occurs.

This same general pattern of layering based on density occurs in the Pacific and Indian Oceans as well. They have no source of Northern Hemisphere deep water, however, so they lack a deep-water mass. In the northern Pacific Ocean, the low salinity of surface waters prevents it from sinking into the deep ocean. In the northern Indian Ocean, surface waters are too warm to sink. **Oceanic Common Water,** which is created when Antarctic Bottom Water and North Atlantic Deep Water mix, lines the bottoms of these basins.

Worldwide Deep-Water Circulation

For every liter of water that sinks from the surface into the deep ocean, a liter of deep water must return to the surface somewhere else. It is difficult to identify specifically where this vertical flow to the surface is occurring. It is generally believed that it occurs as a gradual, uniform upwelling throughout the ocean basins. It may be somewhat greater in low-latitude regions, where surface temperatures are higher.

Figure 26 shows a general deep-water circulation model of the world ocean. The most intense deep-water flow in each ocean basin is along the western side, due to the Coriolis effect and bathymetric features along the sea floor (such as the mid-ocean ridge).

Conveyer-Belt Circulation An integrated model combining deep thermohaline circulation and surface currents is shown in Figure 27. Because the overall circulation pattern resembles a large conveyer belt, the model is called **conveyer-belt circulation**. Beginning in the North Atlantic, surface water carries heat to high latitudes via the Gulf Stream. During the cold winter months, this heat is transferred to the overlying atmosphere, warming northern Europe.

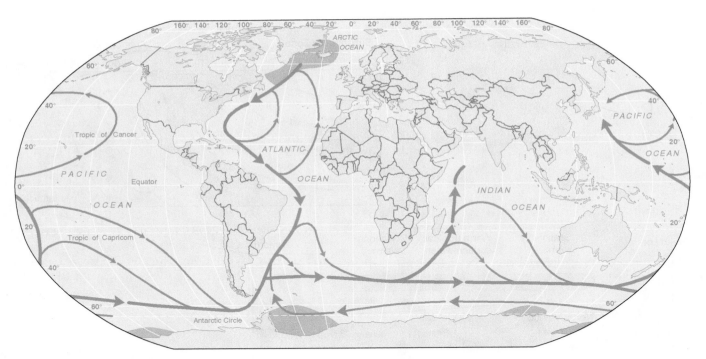

Figure 26 Deep-water circulation model.

Schematic model of deep-water circulation first developed by oceanographer Henry Stommel in 1958. Heavy lines mark the major western boundary currents, which result from the same forces that produce western intensified surface currents. The purple shaded areas indicate source areas for deep water.

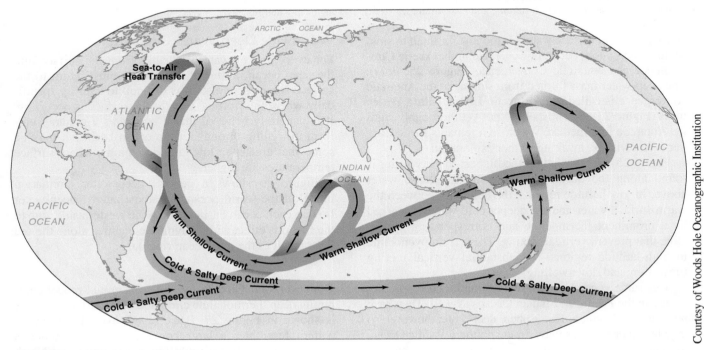

Figure 27 Conveyer-belt circulation.

Conveyer-belt circulation is initiated in the North Atlantic Ocean, where warm water cools and sinks below the surface. This water moves southward as a subsurface flow and joins water near Antarctica. This deep water spreads into the Indian and Pacific Oceans, where it slowly rises and completes the conveyer as it travels along the surface into the North Atlantic Ocean.

Cooling in the North Atlantic increases the density of this surface water to the point where it sinks to the bottom and flows southward, initiating the lower limb of the "conveyor." Here, seawater flows downward at a rate equal to 100 Amazon Rivers and begins its long journey into the deep basins of all of the world's oceans. This limb extends all the way to the southern tip of Africa, where it joins the deep water that encircles Antarctica. The deep water that encircles Antarctica includes deep water that descends along the margins of the Antarctic continent. This mixture of deep waters flows northward into the deep Pacific and Indian Ocean basins, where it eventually surfaces and completes the conveyer belt by flowing west and then north again into the North Atlantic Ocean.

Dissolved Oxygen in Deep Water Cold water can dissolve more oxygen than warm water. Thus, deep-water circulation brings dense, cold, oxygen-enriched water from the surface to the deep ocean. During its time in the deep ocean, deep water becomes enriched in nutrients, as well, due to decomposition of dead organisms and the lack of organisms using nutrients there.

At various times in the geologic past, warmer water probably constituted a larger proportion of deep oceanic waters. As a result, the oceans had a lower oxygen concentration than today because warm water cannot hold as much oxygen. In essence, the oxygen content of the oceans has probably fluctuated widely throughout time.

If high-latitude surface waters did not sink and eventually return from the deep sea to the surface, the distribution of life in the sea would be considerably different. There would be no life in the deep ocean, for instance, because there would be no oxygen for organisms to breathe. Life in surface waters would be significantly reduced and confined to the extreme margins of the oceans, where the only source of oxygen and nutrients would be runoff from streams.

Thermohaline Circulation and Climate Change
Evidence from deep-sea sediments and recently developed computer models indicate that changes in the global deep-water circulation pattern can dramatically and abruptly change climate. If surface waters stopped sinking, for instance, the oceans would absorb and redistribute heat from solar radiation less efficiently. This might cause much warmer surface water temperatures and much higher land temperatures than we have now.

Alternatively, the buildup of greenhouse gases in the atmosphere may change ocean circulation. Warmer temperatures, for example, may increase the rate at which glaciers in Greenland melt, forming a pool of fresh, low-density surface water in the North Atlantic Ocean. This fresh water could inhibit the downwelling that generates North Atlantic Deep Water, altering global deep-water circulation patterns and causing a corresponding change in climate. Because changes such as these can occur rapidly, it would be difficult for plant and animal life to adapt successfully to the new conditions on the planet.

Based on historical oceanic observations during the past 50 years, global surface water temperatures have been increasing. In fact, the top 3000 meters (9840 feet) of ocean water has warmed by an average of 0.06°C (0.11°F). Although this doesn't seem like much, it represents an enormous amount of energy absorbed by the oceans because of water's tremendous ability to absorb large quantities of heat. What is the cause of this warming? Although it is tempting to point to global warming as the cause, it could just as easily be due to natural variations or—more likely—a combination of the two. Only continued monitoring of ocean properties will help determine its cause as well as its potential effect on ocean circulation.

> Thermohaline circulation describes the movement of deep currents, which are created at the surface in high latitudes where they become cold and dense, so they sink.

Chapter in Review

- *Ocean currents are masses of water that flow* from one place to another and can be divided into *surface currents that are wind driven* or *deep currents that are density driven*. Currents can be measured directly or indirectly.

- *Surface currents occur within and above the pycnocline*. They consist of circular-moving loops of water called *gyres*, set in motion by the major wind belts of the world. They are modified by the positions of the continents, the Coriolis effect, and other factors. There are *five major subtropical gyres* in the world, which rotate *clockwise in the Northern Hemisphere* and *counterclockwise in the Southern Hemisphere*. Water is pushed toward the center of the gyres, forming low "hills" of water.

- The *Ekman spiral* influences shallow surface water and is *caused by winds and the Coriolis effect*. The average net flow of water affected by the Ekman spiral causes the water to move at *90-degree angles to the wind direction*. At the center of a gyre, the Coriolis effect deflects the water so that it tends to move into the hill, whereas gravity moves the water down the hill. When gravity and the Coriolis effect balance, a *geostrophic current* flowing parallel to the contours of the hill is established.

- *The apex (top) of the hill is located to the west of the geographical center of the gyre* due to Earth's rotation. A phenomenon called *western intensification* occurs in which western boundary currents of subtropical gyres are faster, narrower, and deeper than their eastern boundary counterparts.

- *Upwelling and downwelling help vertically mix deep and surface waters.* Upwelling—the movement of cold, deep, nutrient-rich water to the surface—stimulates biologic productivity and creates large amounts of marine life. Upwelling and downwelling can occur in a variety of ways.

- *Antarctic circulation is dominated by a single large current, the Antarctic Circumpolar Current* (West Wind Drift), which flows in a clockwise direction around Antarctica and is driven by the Southern Hemisphere's prevailing westerly winds. Between the Antarctic Circumpolar Current and the Antarctic continent is a current called the East Wind Drift, which is powered by the polar easterly winds. The two currents flow in opposite directions, so the Coriolis effect deflects them away from each other, creating the Antarctic Divergence, an area of abundant marine life due to upwelling and current mixing.

- *The North Atlantic Gyre and the South Atlantic Gyre dominate circulation in the Atlantic Ocean.* A poorly developed equatorial countercurrent separates these two subtropical gyres. The highest-velocity and best-studied ocean current is the Gulf Stream, which carries warm water along the southeastern U.S. Atlantic coast. Meanders of the Gulf Stream produce warm- and cold-core rings. The warming effects of the Gulf Stream extend along its route and reach as far away as Northern Europe.

- *Circulation in the Pacific Ocean consists of two subtropical gyres: the North Pacific Gyre and the South Pacific Gyre*, which are separated by a well-developed equatorial countercurrent.

- *A periodic disruption of normal sea surface and atmospheric circulation patterns in the Pacific Ocean is called El Niño–Southern Oscillation (ENSO).* The *warm phase of ENSO (El Niño)* is associated with the eastward movement of the Pacific warm pool, halting or reversal of the trade winds, a rise in sea level along the Equator, a decrease in productivity along the west coast of South America, and, in very strong El Niños, worldwide changes in weather. El Niños fluctuate with the *cool phase of ENSO (La Niña conditions)*, which are associated with cooler than normal water in the eastern tropical Pacific.

- *The Indian Ocean consists of one gyre, the Indian Ocean Gyre,* which exists mostly in the Southern Hemisphere. The *monsoon wind system*, which changes direction with the seasons, dominates circulation in the Indian Ocean. The monsoons blow from the northeast in the winter and from the southwest in the summer.

- *Deep currents occur below the pycnocline.* They affect much larger amounts of ocean water and move much more slowly than surface currents. Changes in temperature and/or salinity at the surface create slight increases in density, which set deep currents in motion. Deep currents, therefore, are called *thermohaline circulation*.

- *The deep ocean is layered based on density.* Antarctic Bottom Water, the densest deep-water mass in the oceans, forms near Antarctica and sinks along the continental shelf into the South Atlantic Ocean. Farther north, at the Antarctic Convergence, the low-salinity *Antarctic Intermediate Water* sinks to an intermediate depth dictated by its density. Sandwiched between these two masses is the *North Atlantic Deep Water*, rich in algal nutrients after hundreds of years in the deep ocean. Layering in the Pacific and Indian oceans is similar, except there is no source of Northern Hemisphere deep water.

- *Worldwide circulation models that include both surface and deep currents resemble a conveyer belt.* Deep currents carry oxygen into the deep ocean, which is extremely important for life on the planet. Recent investigations indicate that *worldwide deep-water circulation is closely linked to global climate change*.

Key Terms

Agulhas Current	Conveyer-belt circulation	Equatorial upwelling	Oceanic Common Water
Alaskan Current	Deep current	Geostrophic current	Pacific Decadal Oscillation (PDO)
Antarctic Bottom Water	Downwelling	Gulf Stream	Pacific warm pool
Antarctic Circumpolar Current	East Australian Current	Gyre	Peru Current
Antarctic Convergence	East Wind Drift	Indian Ocean Gyre	Productivity
Antarctic Divergence	Eastern boundary current	Kuroshio Current	Sargasso Sea
Antarctic Intermediate Water	Ekman spiral	La Niña	Somali Current
Arctic Convergence	Ekman transport	Monsoon	South Atlantic Gyre
Benguela Current	El Niño	North Atlantic Current	South Equatorial Current
Brazil Current	El Niño–Southern Oscillation (ENSO)	North Atlantic Deep Water	South Pacific Gyre
California Current	ENSO index	North Atlantic Gyre	Southern Oscillation
Canary Current	Equatorial countercurrent	North Equatorial Current	Subpolar gyre
Coastal downwelling	Equatorial current	North Pacific Current	Subtropical convergence
Coastal upwelling	Equatorial Undercurrent	North Pacific Gyre	Subtropical gyre
Cold-core ring		Ocean current	

Surface current
Sverdrup (Sv)
Temperature–salinity (T–S)
  diagram
Thermohaline circulation

Tropical Atmosphere and Ocean
  (TAO)
Tropical Ocean–Global
  Atmosphere (TOGA)
Upwelling

Warm-core ring
Walker Circulation Cell
West Australian Current
West Wind Drift

Western boundary current
Western intensification

Questions and Exercises

1. Compare the forces that are directly responsible for creating horizontal and deep vertical circulation in the oceans. What is the ultimate source of energy that drives both circulation systems?

2. Describe the different ways in which currents are measured.

3. What would the pattern of ocean surface currents look like if there were no continents on Earth?

4. On a base map of the world, plot and label the major currents involved in the surface circulation gyres of the oceans. Use colors to represent warm versus cool currents and indicate which currents are western intensified. On an overlay, superimpose the major wind belts of the world on the gyres and describe the relationship between wind belts and currents.

5. What atmospheric pressure is associated with the centers of subtropical gyres? With subpolar gyres? Explain why the subtropical gyres in the Northern Hemisphere move in a clockwise fashion while the subpolar gyres rotate in a counterclockwise pattern.

6. Diagram and discuss how Ekman transport produces the "hill" of water within subtropical gyres that causes geostrophic current flow. As a starting place on the diagram, use the wind belts (the trade winds and the prevailing westerlies).

7. What causes the apex of the geostrophic "hills" to be offset to the west of the center of the ocean gyre systems?

8. Draw or describe several different oceanographic conditions that produce upwelling.

9. During flood stage, the largest river in the world—the mighty Amazon River—dumps 200,000 cubic meters of water into the Atlantic Ocean each second. Compare its flow rate with the volume of water transported by the West Wind Drift and the Gulf Stream. How many times larger than the Amazon is each of these two ocean currents?

10. Observing the flow of Atlantic Ocean currents in Figure 14, offer an explanation as to why the Brazil Current has a much lower velocity and volume transport than the Gulf Stream.

11. Explain why Gulf Stream eddies that develop northeast of the Gulf Stream rotate clockwise and have warm-water cores, whereas those that develop to the southwest rotate counterclockwise and have cold-water cores.

12. Describe changes in oceanographic phenomena, including Walker Circulation, the Pacific warm pool, trade winds, equatorial countercurrent flow, upwelling/downwelling, and abundance of marine life, that occur during an El Niño event. What are some global effects of El Niño?

13. How often do El Niño events occur? Using Figure 20, determine how many years since 1950 have been El Niño years. Has the pattern of El Niño events occurred at regular intervals?

14. How is La Niña different from El Niño? Describe the pattern of La Niña events in relation to El Niños since 1950 (see Figure 20).

15. Describe the relationship between atmospheric pressure, winds, and surface currents during the monsoons of the Indian Ocean.

16. Discuss the origin of thermohaline vertical circulation. Why do deep currents form only in high-latitude regions?

17. Name the two major deep-water masses and give the locations of their formation at the ocean's surface.

18. The Antarctic Intermediate Water can be identified throughout much of the South Atlantic based on its temperature, salinity, and dissolved oxygen content. Why is it colder and less salty—and contain more oxygen—than the surface-water mass above it and the North Atlantic Deep Water below it?

Waves and Water Dynamics

From Chapter 9 of *Introduction to Oceanography*, Tenth Edition, Harold V. Thurman, Alan P. Trujillo.

Waves and Water Dynamics

Wipeout at Maverick's. On December 19, 1994, 16-year old Jay Moriarity, one of surfing's bright young stars, caught this wave at Maverick's in central California. At the beginning of his takeoff, he slipped off his board and fell down the 60-foot (18-meter) face of the wave, creating what would be called the most spectacular wipeout ever caught on film. Fortunately, Moriarity survived the tumble. A combination of oceanographic factors produces waves so large here that only the most accomplished surfers even attempt to wade into the surf zone. In fact, professional surfer Mark Foo was killed here only four days after Moriarity's dramatic wipeout. (©*Bob Barbour*)

The answers to these questions (and much more) can be found in the highlighted concept statements within this chapter.

"There's no time to put on survival suits or grab a life vest; the boat's moving through the most extreme motion of her life and there isn't even time to shout. The refrigerator comes out of the wall and crashes across the galley. Dirty dishes cascade out of the sink. The TV, the washing machine, the VCR tapes, the men, all go flying. And, seconds later, the water moves in."

—Sebastian Junger, *The Perfect Storm* (1997)

What combination of oceanographic factors cause waves to reach extreme heights at places such as Maverick's? This site, which is rated as the world's premier big wave surf spot, is located 0.5 kilometer (0.3 mile) offshore of Pillar Point in Half Moon Bay along the central California coast. One factor is that Maverick's is located offshore of a prominent point of land, which, as will be explained in this chapter, tends to concentrate wave energy due to *wave refraction*. Another factor is that the point juts directly into the North Pacific Ocean, which is known for its wintertime storms and giant waves. Still another factor is that the shoreline abruptly rises from deep depths to a shallowly submerged rock reef, which causes waves to build up to extreme heights in a very short distance. These factors combined with cold ocean temperatures, unforgiving boulders just below the surface, and the presence of large sharks make the site challenging to even the most skilled surfers. Still, surfing competitions are held every year at Maverick's for those brave enough to catch some of the world's most extreme waves.

Most waves are driven by the wind and are relatively small, so release their energy gently, although ocean storms can build up waves to extreme heights. When these waves come ashore, they often produce devastating effects—or, in the case at Maverick's, a wild ride. Waves are *moving energy* traveling along the interface between ocean and atmosphere, often transferring energy from a storm far out at sea over distances of several thousand kilometers. That's why even on calm days, the ocean is in continual motion as waves travel across its surface.

What Causes Waves?

All waves begin as *disturbances*; the energy that causes ocean waves to form is called a **disturbing force**. A rock thrown into a still pond creates waves that radiate out in all directions. Releases of energy, similar to the rock hitting the water, are the cause of all waves.

Wind blowing across the surface of the ocean generates most ocean waves. The waves radiate out in all directions, just as when the rock is thrown into the pond, but on a much larger scale.

The movement of fluids with different densities can also create waves. These waves travel along the interface (boundary) between the two different fluids. Both the air and the ocean are fluids, so waves can be created along interfaces *between* and *within* these fluids as follows:

- Along an *air–water interface*, the movement of air across the ocean surface creates **ocean waves** (simply called *waves*).

- Along an *air–air interface*, the movement of different air masses creates **atmospheric waves**, which are often represented by ripplelike clouds in the sky. Atmospheric waves are especially common when cold fronts (high-density air) invade an area.

- Along a *water–water interface*, the movement of water of different densities creates **internal waves**, as shown in Figure 1a. Because these waves travel along the boundary between waters of different density, they are associated with a *pycnocline*.[1] Internal waves can be much larger than surface waves, with heights exceeding 100 meters (330 feet), but they are not as energetic. Tidal movement, turbidity currents, wind stress, or even passing ships at the surface create internal waves, which can sometimes be observed from space (Figure 1b). Internal waves can even be a hazard for submarines: If submarines are caught in an internal wave while testing their depth limits, the submarines can inadvertently be carried to depths exceeding their designed pressure strength. At the surface, parallel slicks caused by a film of surface debris may indicate the presence of internal waves below. On a smaller scale, internal waves are prominently featured sloshing back and forth in "desktop oceans," which contain two fluids that do not mix.

---

[1]A *pycnocline* is a layer of rapidly changing density.

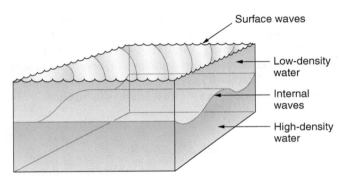

Surface waves

Low-density water

Internal waves

High-density water

(a)

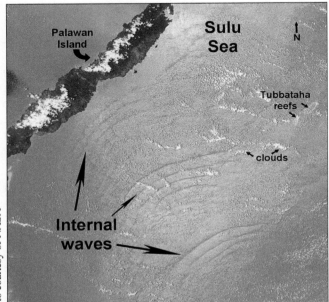

Palawan Island

Sulu Sea

N

Tubbataha reefs

clouds

Internal waves

Photo courtesy of NASA

(b) Internal waves, Sulu Sea

Figure 1 Internal wave.

(a) An internal wave moving along the density interface (*pycnocline*) below the ocean surface. **(b)** Internal waves in the Sulu Sea between the Philippines and Malaysia. Image taken April 8, 2003 by the Moderate Resolution Imaging Spectroradiometer (MODIS) instrument aboard the Aqua satellite.

STUDENTS SOMETIMES ASK ...
Can internal waves break?

Internal waves do not break in the way that surface waves break in the surf zone because the density difference across an interface at depth is much smaller than that between the atmosphere and the surface. When internal waves approach the edges of continents, however, they do undergo similar physical changes as waves in the surf zone. This causes the waves to build up and expend their energy with much turbulent motion, in essence "breaking" against the continent.

Mass movement into the ocean, such as coastal landslides and calving icebergs, also creates waves. These waves are commonly called *splash waves* (see Box 2 for a description of a large splash wave).

Sea floor movement, which changes the shape of the ocean floor and can release large amounts of energy to the entire water column (compared to wind-driven waves, which affect only surface water), can create very large waves. Examples include underwater avalanches (turbidity currents), volcanic eruptions, and fault slippage. The resulting waves are called *seismic sea waves* or *tsunami*. Fortunately, tsunami occur infrequently. When they do, however, they can flood coastal areas and cause large amounts of destruction.

The gravitational pull of the Moon and the Sun tug on every part of Earth's oceans and create vast, low, highly predictable waves called *tides*.

Human activities also cause ocean waves. When ships travel across the ocean, they leave behind a wake, which is a wave. In fact, smaller boats are often carried along in the wake of larger ships, and marine mammals sometimes play there. Also, the detonation of nuclear devices at or near sea level releases huge amounts of energy that creates waves.

In all cases, though, some type of energy release creates waves. Figure 2 shows the distribution of energy in waves, indicating that most ocean waves are wind-generated.

Most ocean waves are caused by wind, but many other types of waves are created by releases of energy in the ocean, including internal waves, splash waves, tsunami, tides, and human-induced waves.

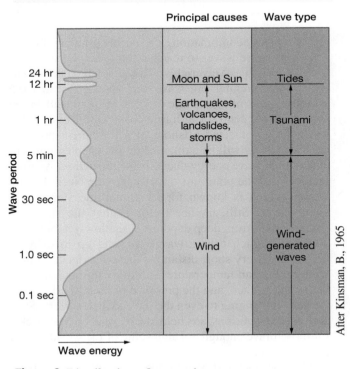

Principal causes | Wave type

24 hr
12 hr — Moon and Sun — Tides

Earthquakes, volcanoes, landslides, storms

1 hr — Tsunami

5 min

30 sec

Wave period

1.0 sec — Wind — Wind-generated waves

0.1 sec

Wave energy →

After Kinsman, B., 1965

Figure 2 Distribution of energy in ocean waves.

Most of the energy possessed by ocean waves exists as wind-generated waves while other peaks of wave energy represent tsunami and ocean tides.

How Waves Move

Waves are energy in motion. Waves transmit energy by means of cyclic movement through matter. The medium itself (solid, liquid, or gas) does not actually travel in the direction of the energy that is passing through it. The particles in the medium simply oscillate, or cycle, back and forth, up and down, or around and around, transmitting energy from one particle to another. If you thump your fist on a table, for example, the energy travels through the table as waves that someone sitting at the other end can feel, but the table itself does not move.

Waves move in different ways. Simple *progressive waves* (Figure 3a) are waves that oscillate uniformly and *progress* or travel without breaking. Progressive waves may be *longitudinal, transverse*, or a combination of the two motions, called *orbital*.

In **longitudinal waves** (also known as push-pull waves), the particles that vibrate "push and pull" in the same direction that the energy is traveling, like a spring whose coils are alternately compressed and expanded. The shape of the wave (called a *waveform*) moves through the medium by compressing and decompressing as it goes. Sound, for instance, travels as longitudinal waves. Clapping your hands initiates a percussion that compresses and decompresses the air as the sound moves through a room. Energy can be transmitted through all states of matter—gaseous, liquid, or solid—by this longitudinal movement of particles.

In **transverse waves** (also known as side-to-side waves), energy travels at right angles to the direction of the vibrating particles. If one end of a rope is tied to a doorknob while the other end is moved up and down (or side to side) by hand, for example, a waveform progresses along the rope and energy is transmitted from the motion of the hand to the doorknob. The waveform moves up and down (or side to side) with the hand, but the motion is at right angles to the direction in which energy is transmitted (from the hand to the doorknob). Generally, transverse waves transmit energy only through solids, because the particles in solids are bound to one another strongly enough to transmit this kind of motion.

Longitudinal and transverse waves are called *body waves* because they transfer energy through a body of matter. Ocean waves are body waves, too, because they transmit energy through the upper part of the ocean near the interface between the atmosphere and the ocean. The

LONGITUDINAL WAVE
Particles (color) move back and forth in direction of energy transmission. These waves transmit energy through all states of matter.

TRANSVERSE WAVE
Particles (color) move back and forth at right angles to direction of energy transmission. These waves transmit energy only through solids.

ORBITAL WAVE
Particles (color) move in orbital path. These waves transmit energy along interface between two fluids of different density (liquids and/or gases).

(a) Types of progressive waves

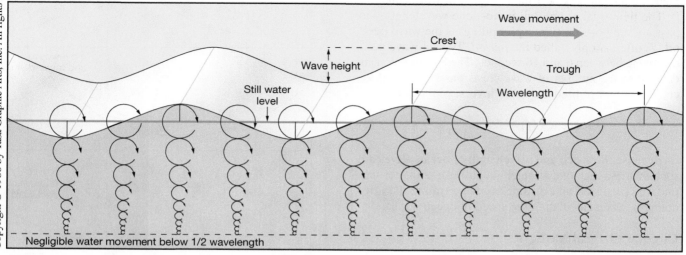

(b) Wave characteristics

Figure 3 Types and characteristics of progressive waves.

(a) Types of progressive waves. **(b)** A diagrammatic view of an idealized ocean wave showing its characteristics.

movement of particles in ocean waves involves components of *both* longitudinal and transverse waves, so particles move in circular orbits. Thus, waves at the ocean surface are **orbital waves** (also called *interface waves*).

Wave Characteristics

Figure 3b shows the characteristics of an idealized ocean wave. The simple, uniform, moving waveform transmits energy from a single source and travels along the ocean–atmosphere interface. These waves are also called *sine waves* because their uniform shape resembles the oscillating pattern expressed by a sine curve. Even though idealized waveforms do not exist in nature (actual waves have sharper crests and elongated troughs), they help us understand wave characteristics.

As the idealized wave passes a permanent marker, such as a pier piling, a succession of high parts of the waves, called **crests**, alternate with low parts, called **troughs**. Halfway between the crests and the troughs is the **still water level**, or *zero energy level*. This is the level of the water if there were no waves. The **wave height**, designated by the symbol H, is the vertical distance between a crest and a trough.

The horizontal distance between any two corresponding points on successive waveforms, such as from crest to crest or from trough to trough, is the **wavelength**, L. **Wave steepness** is the ratio of wave height to wavelength:

$$\text{Wave steepness} = \frac{\text{wave height } (H)}{\text{wavelength } (L)} \qquad (1)$$

If the wave steepness exceeds $\frac{1}{7}$, the wave *breaks* (spills forward) because the wave is too steep to support itself. A wave can break anytime the 1:7 ratio is exceeded, either along the shoreline or out at sea. This ratio also dictates the maximum height of a wave. For example, a wave 7 meters long can only be 1 meter high or it will break.

The time it takes one full wave—one wavelength—to pass a fixed position (like a pier piling) is the **wave period**, T, often simply called the *period*. Typical wave periods range between 6 and 16 seconds. The **frequency** (f) is defined as the number of wave crests passing a fixed location per unit of time and is the inverse of the period:

$$\text{Frequency } (f) = \frac{1}{\text{period } (T)} \qquad (2)$$

Because the speed and wavelength of ocean waves are such that less than one wavelength passes a point per second, the preferred unit of time is period (rather than frequency), when calculating the speed of ocean waves.

Circular Orbital Motion

Waves can travel great distances across ocean basins. In one study, waves generated near Antarctica were tracked as they traveled through the Pacific Ocean basin. After more than 10,000 kilometers (over 6000 miles), the

---

EXAMPLE 1

What is the frequency of waves with a period of 12 seconds?
Since the frequency is the inverse of the period, we can use Equation (2).

$$\text{Frequency } (f) = \frac{1}{\text{period } (T)}$$

$$= \frac{1}{12 \text{ secs}} = 0.083 \text{ waves per second}$$

Since there are 60 seconds in 1 minute, 0.083 waves per second can be multiplied by 60, which equals 5 waves per minute.

---

waves finally expended their energy a week later along the shoreline of the Aleutian Islands of Alaska. The water itself doesn't travel the entire distance, but the waveform does. As the wave travels, the water passes the energy along by moving in a circle. This movement is called **circular orbital motion**.

Observation of an object floating in the waves reveals that it moves not only up and down, but also slightly forward and backward with each successive wave. Figure 4 shows that a floating object moves up and backward as the crest approaches, up and forward as the crest passes, down

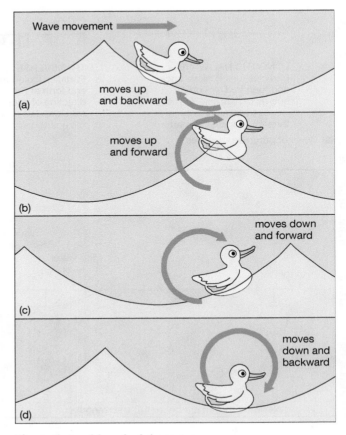

Wave movement

(a) moves up and backward

(b) moves up and forward

(c) moves down and forward

(d) moves down and backward

Figure 4 A rubber duck in water.

As waves pass, the motion of a floating rubber duck resembles that of a circular orbit.

and forward after the crest, down and backward as the trough approaches, and rises and moves backward again as the next crest advances. When the movement of the rubber duck shown in Figure 4 is traced as a wave passes, it can be seen that the duck moves in a circle and returns close to its original position.[2] This motion allows a wave-form (the wave's shape) to move forward through the water while the individual water particles that transmit the wave move around in a circle and return to essentially the same place. Wind moving across a field of wheat causes a similar phenomenon: The wheat itself doesn't travel across the field, but the waves do.

The circular orbits of an object floating at the surface have a diameter equal to the wave height (Figure 3b). Figure 5 shows that circular orbital motion dies out quickly below the surface. At some depth below the surface, the circular orbits become so small that movement is negligible. This depth is called the **wave base**, and it is equal to one-half the wavelength ($L/2$) *measured from still water level*. Thus, only wavelength controls the depth of the wave base such that the longer the wave, the deeper the wave base.

The decrease of orbital motion with depth has many practical applications. For instance, submarines can avoid large ocean waves simply by submerging below the wave base. Even the largest storm waves will go unnoticed if a submarine submerges to only 150 meters (500 feet). Floating bridges and floating oil rigs are constructed so that most of their mass is below wave base, so that they will be unaffected by wave motion. In fact, offshore float-ing airport runways have been designed using similar principles. Additionally, seasick scuba divers find relief when they submerge into the calm, motionless water below wave base. Finally, as you walk from the beach into the ocean, you reach a point where it is easier to dive under an incoming wave than to jump over it. That is, it is easier to swim through the smaller orbital motion below the surface than to fight the large waves at the surface.

---

[2]Actually, the circular orbit does not quite return the floating object to its original position because the half of the orbit accomplished in the trough is slower than the crest half of the orbit. This slight forward movement (net mass transport) is called *wave drift*.

The ocean transmits wave energy by circular or-bital motion, where the water particles move in circular orbits and return to approximately the same location.

Deep-Water Waves

If the water depth (d) is greater than the wave base ($L/2$), the waves are called **deep-water waves** (Figure 6a). Deep-water waves have no interference with the ocean bottom, so they include all wind-generated waves in the open ocean, where water depths far exceed wave base.

Wave speed (S) is defined as

$$\text{Wave speed } (S) = \frac{\text{wavelength } (L)}{\text{period } (T)} \qquad (3)$$

Wave speed is more correctly known as *celerity* (C). Celerity is different from the traditional concept of speed in that it is used only in relation to waves where no mass is in motion, just the wave form.

EXAMPLE 2

If a wave has a wavelength of 156 meters and a period of 10 seconds, what is its speed?

Since we have wavelength and period, we can use Equation (3):

$$\text{Wave speed } (S) = \frac{\text{wavelength } (L)}{\text{period } (T)} = \frac{156 \text{ meters}}{10 \text{ seconds}}$$

$$= 15.6 \text{ meters per second}$$

According to the equations that govern the movement of progressive waves, the speed of deep-water waves is dependent upon (1) wavelength and (2) several other vari-ables (such as gravitational attraction) that remain con-stant on Earth. So, by filling in the constants with numbers, the equation for wave speed of deep-water waves varies only with wavelength and becomes (in me-ters per second)

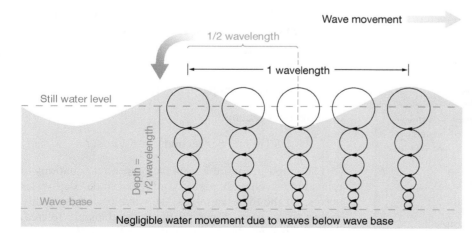

Wave movement

Figure 5 Orbital motion in waves.

The orbital motion of water particles in waves extends to a depth of one-half the wavelength, measured from still water level, which is the wave base.

1/2 wavelength

1 wavelength

Still water level

Depth = 1/2 wavelength

Wave base

Negligible water movement due to waves below wave base

Figure 6 Characteristics of deep-water, shallow-water, and transitional waves.

(a) Deep-water waves, showing the diminishing size of the circular orbits with increasing depth. (b) Shallow-water waves, where the ocean floor interferes with circular orbital motion, causing the orbits to become more flattened. (c) Transitional waves, which are intermediate between deep-water and shallow-water waves. All diagrams are not to scale.

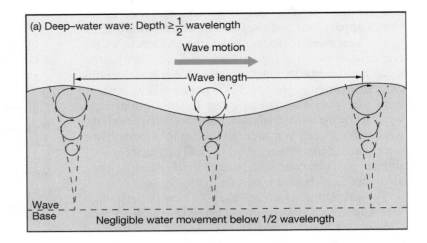

(a) Deep–water wave: Depth $\geq \frac{1}{2}$ wavelength

Wave motion

Wave length

Wave Base

Negligible water movement below 1/2 wavelength

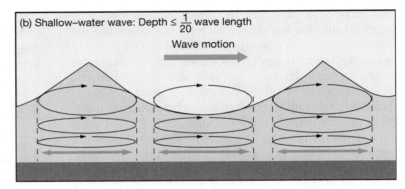

(b) Shallow–water wave: Depth $\leq \frac{1}{20}$ wave length

Wave motion

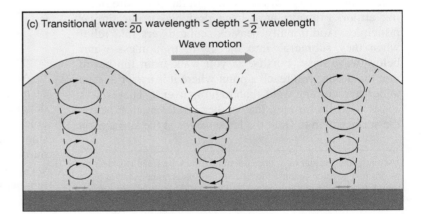

(c) Transitional wave: $\frac{1}{20}$ wavelength $\leq$ depth $\leq \frac{1}{2}$ wavelength

Wave motion

$$S \text{ (in meters per second)} = 1.25\sqrt{L \text{ (in meters)}} \quad (4)$$

or, in feet per second,

$$S \text{ (in feet per second)} = 2.26\sqrt{L \text{ (in feet)}} \quad (5)$$

EXAMPLE 3

If a wave has a wavelength of 156 meters, what is its speed?
Since wave speed varies as a function of wavelength and we have wavelength known in meters, we can use Equation (4):

Wave speed $(S) = 1.25\sqrt{L \text{ (in meters)}}$
$1.25\sqrt{156 \text{ meters}} = 15.6$ meters per second

Note that this is the same answer as in Example 2.

We can also determine wave speed knowing only the period (T) because wave speed (S) is defined in Equation (3) as L/T. Doing this and filling in the known variables with numbers gives (in meters per second)

$$S \text{ (in meters per second)} = 1.56 \times T \quad (6)$$

or, in feet per second,

$$S \text{ (in feet per second)} = 5.12 \times T \quad (7)$$

The graph in Figure 7 uses the preceding equations to relate the wavelength, period, and speed of de 0ep-water waves. Of the three variables, the wave period is usually easiest to measure. Since all three variables are related, the other two can be determined using Figure 7.

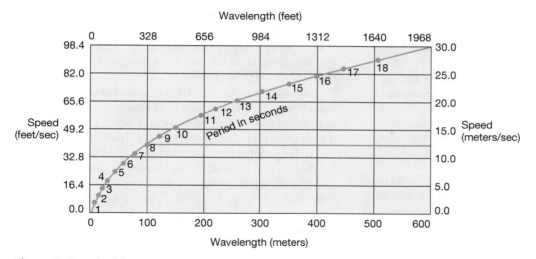

Figure 7 Speed of deep-water waves.

Ideal relations among wavelength, period (*blue line*), and wave speed for deep-water waves. Red lines show an example wave with a wavelength of 100 meters, a period of 8 seconds, and a speed of 12.5 meters per second.

EXAMPLE 4

Using Figure 7, what is the wave speed for a wave with a wavelength of 100 meters and a period of 8 seconds?

The vertical red line on Figure 7 shows a wave with a wavelength of 100 meters, which has a period of 8 seconds (where the vertical red line intersects the blue line). Thus, the speed of the wave is shown by the horizontal red line on the graph, which is 12.5 meters per second.

Note that we can also use Equation (3) to calculate the answer:

$$\text{Speed }(S) = \frac{L}{T} = \frac{100 \text{ meters}}{8 \text{ seconds}}$$

$$= 12.5 \text{ meters per second}$$

The general relationship shown by Equations (3) through (7) (and shown in Figure 7) for deep-water waves is *the longer the wavelength, the faster the wave travels*. A fast wave does not necessarily have a large wave height, however, because wave speed depends *only* on wavelength.

Shallow-Water Waves

Waves in which depth (d) is less than $\frac{1}{20}$ of the wavelength ($L/20$) are called **shallow-water waves**, or *long waves* (Figure 6b). Shallow-water waves are said to *touch bottom* or *feel bottom* because the ocean floor interferes with their orbital motion.

The speed of shallow-water waves is influenced only by gravitational acceleration and the water depth (d). Since gravitational acceleration remains constant on

Earth, the equation for wave speed becomes (in meters per second)

$$S \text{ (in meters per second)} = 3.13\sqrt{d \text{ (in meters)}} \quad (8)$$

or, in feet per second,

$$S \text{ (in feet per second)} = 5.67\sqrt{d \text{ (in feet)}} \quad (9)$$

These equations show that wave speed in shallow-water waves is determined *only* by water depth, where *the deeper the water, the faster the wave travels*.

Shallow-water waves include wind-generated waves that have moved into shallow nearshore areas; *tsunami* (seismic sea waves), generated by earthquakes in the ocean floor; and the *tides*, which are a type of wave generated by the gravitational attraction of the Moon and the Sun. Tsunami and tides are very long-wavelength waves, which far exceed even the deepest ocean water depths.

Particle motion in shallow-water waves is in a very flat elliptical orbit that approaches horizontal (back-and-forth) oscillation. The vertical component of particle motion decreases with increasing depth, causing the orbits to become even more flattened.

Transitional Waves

Waves that have some characteristics of shallow-water waves and some of deep-water waves are called **transitional waves** or *intermediate waves*. The wavelengths of transitional waves are between two times and 20 times the water depth (Figure 6c). Recall that the wave speed of shallow-water waves is a function of water depth; for deep-water waves, wave speed is a function of wavelength. Because transitional waves are intermediate between the two, their wave speed depends partially on water depth and partially on wavelength.

Deep-water waves exist in water that is deeper than wave base and move at speeds controlled by wavelength; shallow-water waves exist in water in which depth is less than $\frac{1}{20}$ the wavelength and at speeds controlled by water depth; transitional waves are intermediate between the two.

Wind-Generated Waves

The life history of a wind-generated wave includes its origin in a windy region of the ocean, its movement across great expanses of open water without subsequent aid of wind, and its termination when it breaks and releases its energy, either in the open ocean or against the shore.

"Sea"

As the wind blows over the ocean surface, it creates pressure and stress. These factors deform the ocean surface into small, rounded waves with V-shaped troughs and wavelengths less than 1.74 centimeters (0.7 inch). Commonly called *ripples*, oceanographers call them **capillary** (*cappilaris* = hair) **waves** (Figure 8, *left*). The name comes from *capillarity*, a property that results from the surface tension of water. Capillarity is the dominant **restoring force** that works to destroy these tiny waves, restoring the smooth ocean surface once again.

As capillary wave development increases, the sea surface takes on a rougher appearance. The water "catches" more of the wind, allowing the wind and ocean surface to interact more efficiently. As more energy is transferred to the ocean, **gravity waves** develop, which are symmetric waves that have wavelengths exceeding 1.74 centimeters (0.7 inch) (Figure 8, *middle*). Because they reach greater height at this stage, gravity replaces capillarity as the dominant restoring force, giving these waves their name.

The length of gravity waves is generally 15 to 35 times their height. As additional energy is gained, wave height increases more rapidly than wavelength. The crests become pointed and the troughs are rounded, resulting in a *trochoidal* (*trokhos* = wheel) waveform (Figure 8, *right*).

Energy imparted by the wind increases the height, length, and speed of the wave. When wave speed equals wind speed, neither wave height nor length can change because there is no net energy exchange and the wave has reached its maximum size.

The area where wind-driven waves are generated is called **"sea"** or the *sea area*. It is characterized by choppiness and waves moving in many directions. The waves have a variety of periods and wavelengths (most of them short) due to frequently changing wind speed and direction.

Factors that determine the amount of energy in waves are (1) the *wind speed*, (2) the *duration*—the length of time during which the wind blows in one direction, and (3) the *fetch*—the distance over which the wind blows in one direction, as shown in Figure 9.

Wave height is directly related to the energy in a wave. Wave heights in a sea area are usually less than 2 meters (6.6 feet), but waves with heights of 10 meters (33 feet) and periods of 12 seconds are not uncommon. As "sea" waves gain energy, their steepness increases. When steepness reaches a critical value of $\frac{1}{7}$, open ocean breakers—called *whitecaps*—form. The appearance of a sea surface as it changes from calm to the condition that results from hurricane-force winds is described in Table 1.

Figure 10 is a map based on satellite data of average wave heights during October 3–12, 1992. The waves in the Southern Hemisphere are particularly large because the prevailing westerlies between 40 and 60 degrees south latitude reach the highest average wind speeds on Earth, creating the latitudes called the "Roaring Forties," "Furious Fifties," and "Screaming Sixties."

How high can waves be? According to a U.S. Navy Hydrographic Office bulletin published in the early 1900s, the theoretical maximum height of wind-generated waves should be no higher than 18.3 meters (60 feet), which became known as the "60-foot rule." Although there were some isolated eyewitness accounts of larger waves, the U.S. Navy considered any sightings of waves over 60 feet to be exaggerations. Certainly, embellishment of reported wave height under conditions of extremely heavy seas would be understandable. For many years, the "60-foot rule" was accepted as fact.

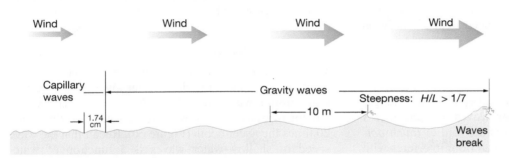

Figure 8 Wind creates capillary and gravity waves.

As wind increases (*left to right*), the height and wavelength of waves increases, beginning as capillary waves and progressing to gravity waves. When the wave steepness (*H/L*) exceeds a 1:7 ratio, the waves become unstable and break. Not to scale.

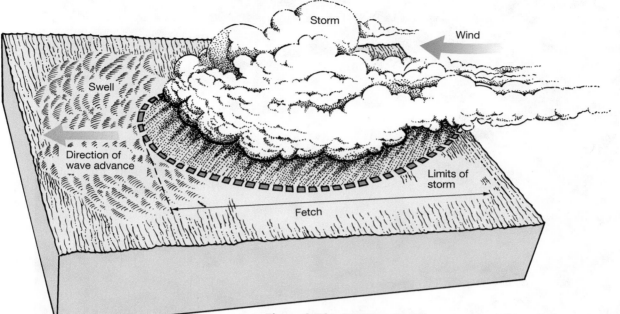

Figure 9 The "sea" and swell.

As wind blows across the "sea" (*red dash*), wave size increases with increasing wind speed, duration, and fetch. As waves advance beyond their area of origination, they advance across the ocean surface and become sorted into uniform, symmetric swell.

TABLE 1 **Beaufort Wind Scale and the state of the sea.**

Beaufort number	Descriptive term	Wind speed (km/h)	(mi/h)	Appearance of the sea
0	Calm	<1	<1	Like a mirror
1	Light air	1–5	1–3	Ripples with the appearance of scales, no foam crests
2	Light breeze	6–11	4–7	Small wavelets; crests of glassy appearance, no breaking
3	Gentle breeze	12–19	8–12	Large wavelets; crests begin to break, scattered whitecaps
4	Moderate breeze	20–28	13–18	Small waves, becoming longer; numerous whitecaps
5	Fresh breeze	238	124	Moderate waves, taking longer form; many whitecaps, some spray
6	Strong breeze	349	25–31	Large waves begin to form, whitecaps everywhere, more spray
7	Near gale	50–61	32–38	Sea heaps up and white foam from breaking waves begins to be blown in streaks
8	Gale	62–74	346	Moderately high waves of greater length, edges of crests begin to break into spindrift, foam is blown in well-marked streaks
9	Strong gale	75–88	47–54	High waves, dense streaks of foam and sea begins to roll, spray may affect visibility
10	Storm	8102	55–63	Very high waves with overhanging crests; foam is blown in dense white streaks, causing the sea to appear white; the rolling of the sea becomes heavy; visibility reduced
11	Violent storm	103–117	64–72	Exceptionally high waves (small and medium-sized ships might for a time be lost from view behind the waves), the sea is covered with white patches of foam, everywhere the edges of the wave crests are blown into froth, visibility further reduced
12	Hurricane	118+	73+	The air is filled with foam and spray, sea completely white with driving spray, visibility greatly reduced

Source: After Bowditch, N. 1958

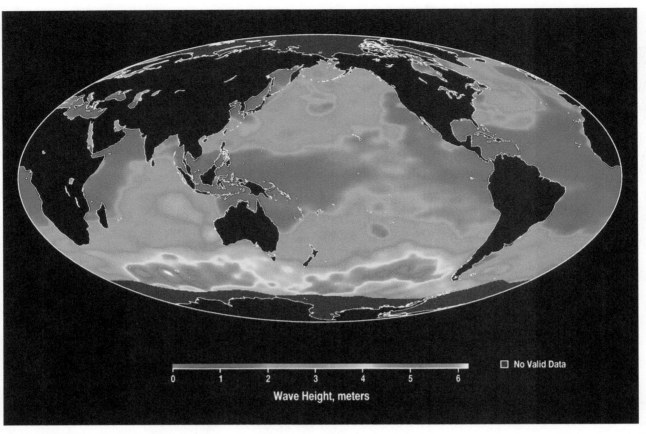

Courtesy of Jet Propulsion Laboratory, NASA

Figure 10 TOPEX/Poseidon wave height, October 3–12, 1992.

The TOPEX/Poseidon satellite receives a return of stronger signals from calm seas and weaker signals from seas with large waves. Based on these data, a map of wave height can be produced. The largest average wave heights (*red areas*) are in the prevailing westerly wind belt in the Southern Hemisphere. Scale in meters.

However, careful observations made aboard the 152-meter (500-foot)-long U.S. Navy tanker USS *Ramapo* in 1935 proved otherwise. The ship was caught in a typhoon in the western Pacific Ocean and encountered 108-kilometer (67-mile)-per-hour winds en route from the Philippines to San Diego. The resulting waves were symmetrical, uniform, and had a period of 14.8 seconds. Because the *Ramapo* was traveling with the waves, the vessel's officers were able to measure the waves accurately. The officers used the dimensions of the ship, including the *eye height* of an observer on the ship's bridge (Figure 11). Geometric relationships revealed that the waves were 34 meters (112 feet) high, which

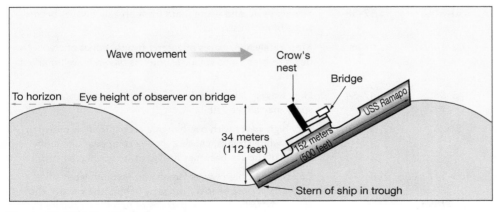

Figure 11 USS *Ramapo* in heavy seas.

Bridge officers aboard the USS *Ramapo* in 1935 measured the largest authentically recorded wave by sighting from the bridge across the crow's nest to the horizon while the ship's stern was directly in the trough of a large wave. A wave height of 34 meters (112 feet) was calculated based on geometric relationships of the vessel and the waves.

made them taller than an 11-story building! These waves proved to be a record that still stands today for the largest authentically recorded wind-generated waves, shattering the "60-foot rule." Although the *Ramapo* was largely undamaged, other ships traveling in heavy seas aren't always so lucky (Figure 12).

For a given wind speed, Table 2 lists the minimum fetch and duration of wind beyond which the waves cannot grow. Waves cannot grow because an equilibrium condition, called a **fully developed sea**, has been achieved. Waves can grow no further in a fully developed sea because they lose as much energy breaking as whitecaps under the force of gravity as they receive from the wind. Table 2 also lists the average characteristics of waves resulting from a fully developed sea, including the height of the highest 10% of the waves.

EXAMPLE 5

Based on the period of the giant waves the USS Ramapo *experienced, what were the waves' speed and wavelength?*

Since the waves the USS *Ramapo* experienced were in the open ocean, they must have been deep-water waves. Knowing that the period (T) = 14.8 seconds, we can use Equation (6) to determine wave speed (S):

$$S = 1.56T = 1.56 \times 14.8 \text{ seconds}$$
$$= 23.1 \text{ meters per second}$$

Note that 23.1 meters per second = 83.1 kilometers (51.6 miles) per hour.

Now that wave speed is known, wavelength (L) can be determined using Equation (3):

$$S = \frac{L}{T}, \text{ so } L = S \times T$$

$$L = 23.1 \text{ meters per second} \times 14.8 \text{ seconds}$$
$$= 342 \text{ meters (1121 feet)}$$

Figure 12 Wave damage on the aircraft carrier *Bennington.*

The *Bennington* returns from heavy seas encountered in a typhoon off Okinawa in 1945 with part of its reinforced steel flight deck bent down over the bow. Damage to the flight deck, which is 16.5 meters (54 feet) above still water level, was caused by large waves.

Official photograph U.S. Navy

TABLE 2 **Conditions necessary to produce a fully developed sea at various wind speeds and the characteristics of the resulting waves.**

Wind speed in km/h (mi/h)	Fetch in km (mi)	Duration in hours	Average height in m (ft)	Average wavelength in m (ft)	Average period in seconds	Highest 10% of waves in m (ft)
20 (12)	24 (15)	2.8	0.3 (1.0)	10.6 (34.8)	3.2	0.8 (2.5)
30 (19)	77 (48)	7.0	0.9 (2.9)	22.2 (72.8)	4.6	2.1 (6.9)
40 (25)	176 (109)	11.5	1.8 (5.9)	39.7 (130.2)	6.2	3.9 (12.8)
50 (31)	380 (236)	18.5	3.2 (10.5)	61.8 (202.7)	7.7	6.8 (22.3)
60 (37)	660 (409)	27.5	5.1 (16.7)	89.2 (292.6)	9.1	10.5 (34.4)
70 (43)	1093 (678)	37.5	7.4 (24.3)	121.4 (398.2)	10.8	15.3 (50.2)
80 (50)	1682 (1043)	50.0	10.3 (33.8)	158.6 (520.2)	12.4	21.4 (70.2)
90 (56)	2446 (1517)	65.2	13.9 (45.6)	201.6 (661.2)	13.9	28.4 (93.2)

Swell

As waves generated in a sea area move toward its margins, wind speeds diminish and the waves eventually move faster than the wind. When this occurs, wave steepness decreases, and waves become long-crested waves called **swells** (*swellan* = swollen). Swells are uniform, symmetrical waves that have traveled out of the area where they originated. Swells move with little loss of energy over large stretches of the ocean surface, transporting energy away from one sea area and depositing it in another. Thus, there can be waves at distant shorelines where there is no wind.

STUDENTS SOMETIMES ASK ...

I know that swell is what surfers hope for. Is swell always big?

Not necessarily. Swell is defined as waves that have moved out of their area of origination, so these waves do not have to be a certain wave height to be classified as swell. It is true, however, that the uniform and symmetrical shape of most swell delights surfers.

Waves with longer wavelengths travel faster, and thus leave the sea area first. They are followed by slower, shorter **wave trains**, or groups of waves. The progression from long, fast waves to short, slow waves illustrates the principle of **wave dispersion** (*dis* = apart, *spargere* = to scatter)—the sorting of waves by their wavelength.

Waves of many wavelengths are present in the generating area. Wave speed depends on wavelength in deep water (see Figure 7), however, so the longer waves "outrun" the shorter ones. The distance over which waves change from a choppy "sea" to uniform swell is called the **decay distance**, which can be up to several hundred kilometers.

As a group of waves leaves a sea area and becomes a swell *wave train*, the leading wave keeps disappearing. However, the same number of waves always remains in the group because as the leading wave disappears, a new wave replaces it at the back of the group (Figure 13). For example, if four waves are generated, the lead wave keeps dying out as the wave train travels, but one is created in the back, so the wave train stays four waves. Because of the progressive dying out and creation of new waves, the group moves across the ocean surface at only *half* the velocity of an individual wave in the group.

Interference Patterns When swells from different storms run together, the waves clash, or interfere with one another, giving rise to **interference patterns**. An interference pattern produced when two or more wave systems collide is the sum of the disturbance that each wave would have produced individually. Figure 14 shows that the result may be a larger or smaller trough or crest, depending on conditions.

When swells from two storm areas collide, the interference pattern may be constructive or destructive, but it is more likely to be mixed. **Constructive interference**

Figure 13

Movement of a wave train.

As energy in the leading waves (**a**, *waves 1 and 2*) is transferred into circular orbital motion, the waves in front die out and are replaced by new waves from behind (**b**). Even though new waves take up the lead (**c** and **d**), the length of the wave train and the total number of waves remain the same. This causes the group speed to be one-half that of the individual wave.

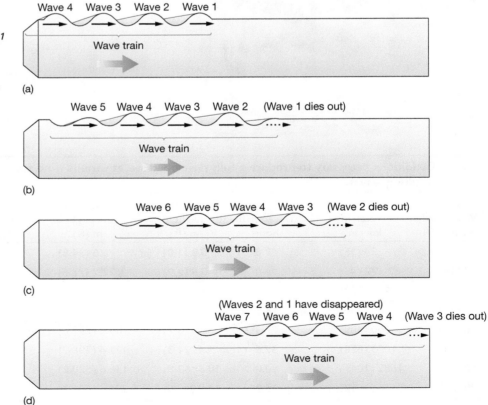

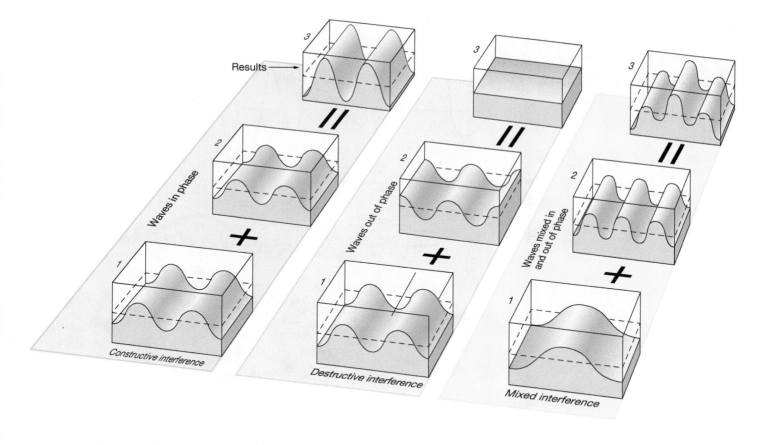

Figure 14 Constructive, destructive, and mixed interference patterns.

Constructive interference (*left*) occurs when waves of the same wavelength come together in phase (crest to crest and trough to trough), producing waves of greater height. Destructive interference (*center*) occurs when overlapping waves have identical characteristics but come together out of phase, resulting in a canceling effect. More commonly, waves of different lengths and heights encounter one another and produce a complex, mixed interference pattern (*right*).

occurs when wave trains having the same wavelength come together *in phase*, meaning crest to crest and trough to trough. If the displacements from each wave are added together, the interference pattern results in a wave with the same wavelength as the two overlapping wave systems, but with a wave height equal to the sum of the individual wave heights (Figure 14, *left*).

Destructive interference occurs when wave trains having the same wavelength come together *out of phase*, meaning the crest from one wave coincides with the trough from a second wave. If the waves have identical heights, the sum of the crest of one and the trough of another is zero, so the energies of these waves cancel each other (Figure 14, *center*).

It is more likely, however, that the two swells consist of waves of various heights and lengths that come together with a mixture of constructive and destructive interference. Thus, a more complex **mixed interference** pattern develops (Figure 14, *right*), which explains the varied sequence of high and lower waves (called *surf beat*) and other irregular wave patterns that occur when swell approaches the shore. In the open ocean, several swell systems often interact, creating complex wave patterns (Figure 15).

Constructive interference results from in phase overlapping of waves and creates larger waves, while destructive interference results from waves overlapping out of phase, reducing wave height.

Free and Forced Waves   Swell is an example of a **free wave**, which is a wave moving with the momentum and energy imparted to it in the sea area but it is not experiencing a maintaining force that keeps it in motion. A **forced wave** is one that is maintained by a force that has a periodicity coinciding with the period of the wave. For most ocean waves, this force is the wind. Because of the high variability of wind in a storm, many wave systems in the sea area alternate between forced and free waves. Another example of a forced wave is the tides, which are always maintained by the gravitational attraction of the Moon and the Sun.

Figure 15

Mixed interference pattern.

The observed wave pattern in the ocean (*above*) is often the result of mixed interference of many different overlapping wave sets (*below*).

After Gross, M. G., *Oceanography*, 6th ed. (Fig. 8-4), Prentice Hall, 1993

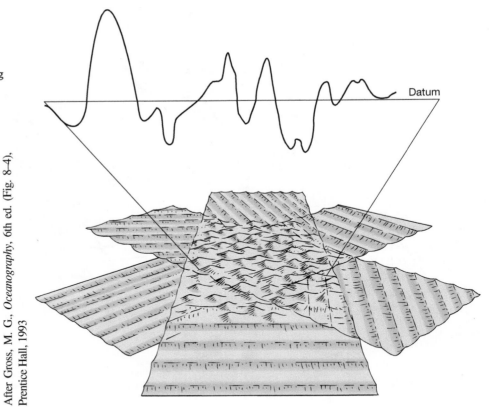

Datum

Rogue Waves

Rogue waves are massive, solitary waves that can reach enormous height and often occur at times when normal ocean waves are not unusually large. In a sea of 2-meter (6.5-foot) waves, for example, a 20-meter (65-foot) rogue wave may suddenly appear. *Rogue* means "unusual" and, in this case, the waves are unusually large. Rogue waves—sometimes called *superwaves*—can be quite destructive and have been popularized in literature and movies such as *The Perfect Storm*.

In the open ocean, one wave in 23 will be over twice the height of the wave average, one in 1175 will be three times as high, and one in 300,000 will be four times as high. The chances of a truly monstrous wave, therefore, are only one in several billion. Nevertheless, rogue waves do occur, though no one knows specifically when or where they will arise. For instance, the 17-meter (56-foot) NOAA research vessel R/V *Ballena* was flipped and sunk in November 2000 by a 15-foot (4.6-meter) rogue wave off the California coast while conducting a survey in shallow, calm water. Fortunately, the three people on board survived the incident.

Even with satellites that can measure average wave size and forecast storms, about 10 large ships each year are reported missing without a trace. Worldwide, the total number of vessels lost of all sizes may reach 1000 per year, some of which are the victims of rogue waves. Recent satellites designed to observe the ocean have provided a wealth of data about ocean waves but still don't allow the prediction of rogue waves.

The main cause of rogue waves is theorized to be an extraordinary case of constructive wave interference where multiple waves overlap in phase to produce an extremely large wave (Box 1). Rogue waves also tend to occur more frequently downwind from islands or shoals. In addition, rogue waves can occur when storm-driven waves move against strong ocean currents, causing the waves to steepen, shorten, and become larger. These conditions exist along the "Wild Coast" off the southeast coast of Africa, where the Agulhas Current flows directly against large Antarctic storm waves, creating rogue waves that can crash onto the bow of a ship, overcome its structural capacity, and cause the ship to sink (Figure 16). This stretch of water is probably responsible for sinking more ships than any other place on Earth.

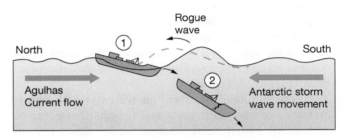

Figure 16 Rogue waves along Africa's "Wild Coast."

Rogue waves can be formed where the Algulhas Current flows directly against large Antarctic Storm waves along Africa's "Wild Coast." These large and steep rogue waves can crash onto the bow of a ship, causing it to sink.

BOX 1   People and Ocean Environment

YACHTING IN MONSTER SEAS: THE SYDNEY TO HOBART AND FASTNET RACING DISASTERS

"The 1998 Sydney to Hobart took us beyond sport, beyond the drive to compete. We found ourselves at the edge of life-and-death survival."

—Ed Psaltsis, winning skipper of the 1998 Sydney to Hobart Yacht Race

The world championship of yacht racing is determined each year by standings in the five Admiral's Cup Series races. Two of these races are the Sydney to Hobart Race off Australia and the Fastnet Race off England. Recently, both of these challenging yachting events proved fatal because of high winds (created by low pressure) and rogue waves (created by overlapping seas).

On December 26, 1998, 115 boats sailed out of Sydney Harbor at the start of the 1180-kilometer (735-mile)-long Sydney to Hobart Race. Ranked as one of the most treacherous races in the world, its course takes sailors along the east coast of Australia, across Bass Strait, and down the length of Tasmania. Prior to the race, the Australian Bureau of Meteorology issued a warning for winds of 90 kilometers (56 miles) per hour in Bass Strait, later upping the severity of the storm and describing the conditions as "atrocious," which proved to be an understatement.

The first storm hit the fleet around midnight, causing many boats to turn and sail for home. By midafternoon on December 27, three massive low-pressure weather systems collided in Bass Strait, producing a killer sea. Over the next 24 hours, mammoth waves of 20 meters (66 feet) and winds of 161 kilometers (100 miles) per hour battered the remaining boats. Eyewitnesses reported waves tall enough to send 25-ton yachts "spearing into midair," then "plunging down into the trough... like repeatedly launching a truck off a 30-foot ramp and awaiting the

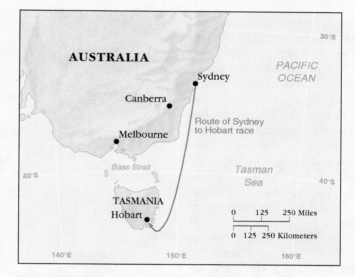

Route of the Sydney to Hobart Race off Australia.

Image courtesy of NASA's Earth Observatory and Jacques Descloitres, MODIS Land Rapid Response Team at NASA GSFC

Rescue in extreme conditions at sea.

A helicopter rescues the crew of a stricken yacht in Bass Strait during the 1998 Sydney to Hobart Race.

crash." Survivors' testimony indicates that large rogue waves dismasted, capsized, rolled and sank several vessels. By the end of the day on December 29, five boats had been sunk, 24 boats were abandoned, 55 sailors had been rescued under near-impossible circumstances, and six lives were lost.

Even more people lost their lives in the 1979 Fastnet Race. The 1000-kilometer (620-mile) race starts from the Isle of Wight off the south coast

of England and requires rounding Fastnet Rock off the southern tip of Ireland with a return to Plymouth, England. On August 12, the second day of that year's Fastnet race, a low-pressure system approached the British Isles, but the storm's winds were not excessive and it did not appear to pose a threat to the race at the time.

By August 13, however, the storm intensified and its pressure dropped rapidly. As atmospheric pressure

Continued...

Route of the Fastnet Race off England.

In the Fastnet Race, yachts sail from the Isle of Wight, around Fastnet Rock just off Ireland, and back to Plymouth, England. The track of the 1979 storm is also shown.

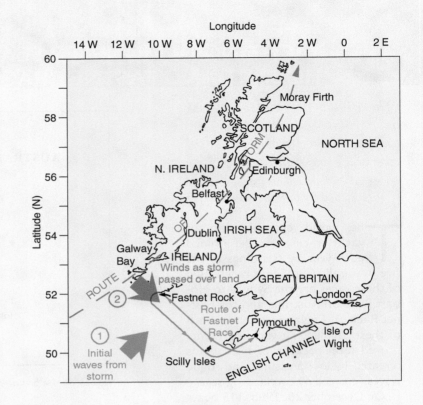

drops, winds increase because the lower the pressure, the greater the pressure gradient force, which drives winds. With increased wind speed, waves become larger, too. Although the yachts in the lead had already rounded Fastnet Rock and now had the wind at their backs, most of the fleet was struggling into west-south-west winds and rising seas.

On August 14, the storm center arrived in Galway Bay in central-western Ireland and the pressure decreased even further. As the trough of the storm hit the fleet, the winds shifted from west-southwest to northwest, producing wind gusts approaching 145 kilometers (90 miles) per hour and waves as high as 15 meters (49 feet). Soon thereafter, the storm center moved to Moray Firth in northeastern Scotland, and the seas subsided dramatically.

Analysis of the oceanographic conditions present during the race revealed that the right-angle change in the winds as the storm crossed over the British Isles was a major factor in the tragedy. As the crests of incoming waves from the northwest merged with the crests of waves created by west-southwest winds, *constructive interference* produced very short, steep rogue waves. These compact waves caused many of the yachts to be rolled on their sides so far that their masts tipped into the water—an extremely vulnerable position. As the next wave struck the ship's keel, the yacht would have a tendency to roll upside down in the water and even continue through for a complete roll! Many of the yachts rolled in this way, and some yachts reported being rolled a number of times. Eyewitnesses recalled how some of the yachts crashed into others as they were tossed and rolled in the large waves.

During the 1979 Fastnet Race, only 85 out of the 303 yachts made it back to the finish line. In all, 23 yachts were sunk or abandoned, 114 people were rescued, and 15 died, making the 1979 Fastnet Race the worst disaster in the history of yachting. Although weather forecasters were criticized for not giving sufficient warning to allow the yachts to seek safety, they did not have adequate advance knowledge that conditions would become so severe. Even with adequate warnings, it is unlikely that many yacht captains would have chosen to withdraw from the race considering the competitive nature of yachting enthusiasts. In fact, Allan Green of the Royal Ocean Racing Club, which organized the event, said, "The lessons of the Fastnet [disaster] should be studied carefully and applied sensibly but in the knowledge that they can never expel the danger from yachting ... it will be a sad and bad day when the seafaring people declines the challenge of the ocean."

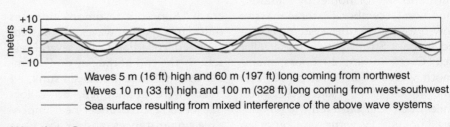

Waves 5 m (16 ft) high and 60 m (197 ft) long coming from northwest
Waves 10 m (33 ft) high and 100 m (328 ft) long coming from west-southwest
Sea surface resulting from mixed interference of the above wave systems

Wave interference creates monster waves.

The large waves created during the 1979 Fastnet Race were caused by mixed interference between west-southwest waves (*black line*) and northwest waves (*red line*), both of which were produced by a storm that swept through the area. The maximum amount of constructive interference produced 15-meter (49.2-foot) waves (*blue line*).

Surf

Most waves generated in the sea area by storm winds move across the ocean as swell. These waves then release their energy along the margins of continents in the **surf zone**, which is the zone of breaking waves. Breaking waves exemplify power and persistence, and sometimes they have the ability to move objects weighing several tons. In doing so, energy from a distant storm can travel thousands of kilometers until it is finally expended along a distant shoreline in a few wild moments.

As deep-water waves of swell move toward continental margins over gradually **shoaling** (*shold* = shallow) water, they eventually encounter water depths that are less than one-half of their wavelength (Figure 17) and become transitional waves. Actually, any shallowly submerged obstacle (such as a coral reef, sunken wreck, or sand bar) will cause waves to release some energy. Navigators have long known that breaking waves indicate dangerously shallow water.

Many physical changes occur to a wave as it encounters shallow water, becomes a shallow-water wave, and breaks. The shoaling depths interfere with water particle movement at the base of the wave, so the *wave speed decreases*. As one wave slows, the following waveform, which is still moving at its original speed, moves closer to the wave that is being slowed, causing a *decrease in wavelength*. Although some wave energy is lost due to friction, the wave energy that remains must go somewhere, so *wave height increases*. This increase in wave height combined with the decrease in wavelength causes an *increase in wave steepness* (H/L). When the wave steepness reaches the 1:7 ratio, the waves break as surf (Figure 17).

If the surf is swell that has traveled from distant storms, breakers will develop relatively near shore in shallow water. The horizontal motion characteristic of shallow-water waves moves water alternately toward and away from the shore as an oscillation. The surf will be characterized by parallel lines of relatively uniform breakers.

If the surf consists of waves generated by local winds, the waves may not have been sorted into swell. The surf may be mostly unstable, deep-water, high-energy waves with steepness already near the 1:7 ratio. In this case, the waves will break shortly after feeling bottom some distance from shore, and the surf will be rough, choppy, and irregular.

When the water depth is about one and one-third times the wave height, the crest of the wave breaks, producing surf.[3] When the water depth becomes less than $\frac{1}{20}$ the wavelength, waves in the surf zone begin to behave as shallow-water waves (see Figure 6). Particle motion is greatly impeded by the bottom, and a significant transport of water toward the shoreline occurs (Figure 17).

Waves break in the surf zone because particle motion near the bottom of the wave is severely restricted, slowing the waveform. At the surface, however, individual orbiting water particles have not yet been slowed because they have no contact with the bottom. In addition, the wave height increases in shallow water. The difference in speed between the top and bottom parts of the wave cause the top part of the wave to overrun the lower part, which results in the wave toppling over and breaking. Breaking waves are analogous to a person who leans too far forward. If you don't catch yourself, you may also "break" something when you fall.

---

[3]This is a handy way of estimating water depth in the surf zone: The depth of the water where waves are breaking is one and one-third times the breaker height.

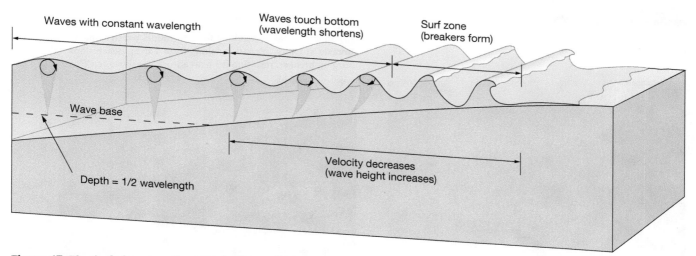

Figure 17 Physical changes of a wave in the surf zone.

As waves approach the shore and encounter water depths of less than one-half wavelength, the waves "feel bottom." The *wave speed decreases* and waves stack up against the shore, causing the *wavelength to decrease*. This results in an *increase in wave height* to the point where the *wave steepness is increased* beyond the 1:7 ratio, causing the wave to pitch forward and break in the surf zone.

As waves come into shallow water and feel bottom, their speed and wavelength decrease while their wave height and wave steepness increase, causing the wave to break.

Breakers and Surfing   Figure 18a shows a **spilling breaker**. Spilling breakers result from a gently sloped ocean bottom, which extracts energy from the wave more gradually, producing a turbulent mass of air and water that runs down the front slope of the wave instead of producing a spectacular cresting curl. Spilling breakers have a longer life span and give surfers a long—but somewhat less exciting—ride than other breakers.

Figure 18b shows a **plunging breaker**, which has a curling crest that moves over an air pocket. The curling crest occurs because the particles in the crest literally outrun the wave, and there is nothing beneath them to support their motion. Plunging breakers form on moderately steep beach slopes, and are the best waves for surfing.

(a)

STUDENTS SOMETIMES ASK ...

Why is surfing so much better along the west coast of the United States than along the east coast?

There are three main reasons why the west coast has better surfing conditions:

- The waves are generally bigger in the Pacific. The Pacific is larger than the Atlantic, so the fetch is larger, allowing bigger waves to develop in the Pacific.
- The beach slopes are generally steeper along the west coast. Along the east coast, the gentle slopes often create spilling breakers, which are not as favorable for surfing. The steeper beach slopes along the west coast cause plunging breakers, which are better for surfing.
- The wind is more favorable. Most of the United States is influenced by the prevailing westerlies, which blow toward shore and enhance waves along the west coast. Along the east coast, the wind blows away from shore.

When the ocean bottom has an abrupt slope, the wave energy is compressed into a shorter distance and the wave will surge forward, creating a **surging breaker** (Figure 18c). These waves build up and break right at the shoreline, so board surfers tend to avoid them. For body surfers, however, these waves present the greatest challenge.

Surfing is analogous to riding a gravity-operated water sled by balancing the forces of gravity and buoyancy. The particle motion of ocean waves (see Figure 3b) shows that water particles move up into the front of the crest. This force, along with the buoyancy of the surfboard, helps maintain a surfer's position in front of a

Figure 18   Types of breakers.

(a) Spilling breaker, resulting from a gradual beach slope. **(b)** Plunging breaker at Oahu, Hawaii, resulting from a steep beach slope. **(c)** Surging breaker, resulting from an abrupt beach slope.

(b)
Vince Cavataio/Allsport/ Agency Vandystadt/Photo Researchers, Inc.

(c)

breaking wave. The trick is to perfectly balance the force of gravity (directed downward) with the buoyant force (directed perpendicular to the wave face) to enable a surfer to be propelled forward by the wave's energy. A skillful surfer, by positioning the board properly on the wave front, can regulate the degree to which the propelling gravitational forces exceed the buoyancy forces, and speeds up to 40 kilometers (25 miles) per hour can be obtained while moving along the face of a breaking wave. When the wave passes over water that is too shallow to allow the upward movement of water particles to continue, the ride is over.

Wave Refraction

Waves seldom approach a shore at a perfect rig (90 degrees). Therefore, as a wave approaches at angle to the shore, some segment of the wave wi bottom" first and will slow before the rest of the This results in **wave refraction** (*refringere* = to up) or the *bending* of each wave crest (also called a front) as the waves approach the shore.

Figure 19a shows how waves coming toward a stra shoreline are refracted and tend to align themsel *nearly* parallel to the shore. This explains why all wav

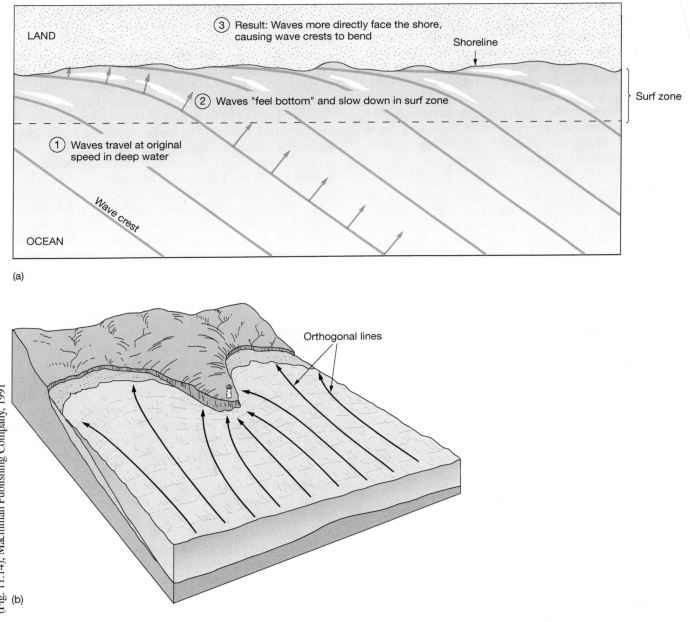

(a)

Adapted from Tarbuck, E. J., and Lutgens, F. K., *Earth Science*, 6th ed. (Fig. 11.14), Macmillan Publishing Company, 1991

(b)

Figure 19 Wave refraction.

(a) Wave refraction along a straight shoreline. Waves approaching the shore at an angle first "feel bottom" close to shore. This causes the segment of the wave in shallow water to slow, causing the crest of the wave to refract or bend so that the waves arrive at the shore nearly parallel to the shoreline. Red arrows represent direction and speed of the wave. (b) Wave refraction along an irregular shoreline. As waves first "feel bottom" in the shallows off the headlands, they are slowed, causing the waves to refract and align nearly parallel to the shoreline. Evenly spaced orthogonal lines (*black arrows*) show that wave energy is concentrated on headlands (causing erosion) and dispersed in bays (resulting in deposition).

come almost straight in toward a beach, no matter what their original orientation was.

Figure 19b shows how waves coming toward an irregular shoreline refract so that they, too, nearly align with the shore. However, the refraction of waves along an irregular shoreline distributes wave energy unevenly along the shore.

The long black arrows in Figure 19b are called **orthogonal** (*ortho* = straight, *gonia* = angle) **lines** or *wave rays*. Orthogonal lines are drawn perpendicular to the wave fronts (so they indicate the direction that waves travel) and are spaced so that the energy between lines is equal at all times. They help show how energy is distributed along the shoreline by breaking waves.

The orthogonals in Figure 19b are equally spaced far from shore. As they approach the shore, however, the orthogonals *converge* on headlands that jut into the ocean, and *diverge* in bays. This means that wave energy is concentrated against the headlands, but dispersed in bays. The result is heavy erosion of headlands and deposition of sediment in bays. The greater energy of waves breaking on headlands is reflected in an increased wave height.[4] Conversely, the smaller waves in bays provide areas for good boat anchorages.

Wave Diffraction

Wave diffraction (*dis* = apart, *frangere* = to break) results from wave energy being transferred around or behind barriers that impede the wave's forward motion. Diffraction occurs because any point on a wave front is a source from which energy can propagate in all directions. For example, as waves move past a barrier at the entrance to a harbor, wave diffraction causes some wave energy to move laterally along the wave crest, thereby producing diffracted waves that move into the harbor (Figure 20). In

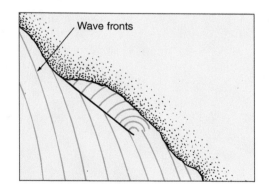

Figure 20 Wave diffraction in a harbor.

As waves move past a barrier such as a harbor breakwater, wave diffraction causes wave energy to be transferred behind the barrier. By diffraction, wave energy can spread to even the most protected areas within a harbor.

---

[4]Sailors have long known that "the points draw the waves." Surfers also know how wave refraction causes good "point breaks."

this way, at least some wave energy can spread to even the most protected areas within a harbor.

Wave Reflection

Not all wave energy is expended as waves rush onto the shore. A vertical barrier, such as a seawall or a rock ledge, can reflect waves back into the ocean with little loss of energy—a process called **wave reflection** (*reflecten* = to bend back), which is similar to how a mirror reflects (bounces) back light. If the incoming wave strikes the barrier at a right (90-degree) angle, the wave energy is reflected back parallel to the incoming wave, often interfering with the next incoming wave and creating unusual waveforms. More commonly, waves approach the shore at an angle, causing wave energy to be reflected at an angle equal to the angle at which the wave approached the barrier.

An outstanding example of wave reflection occurs in an area called "The Wedge," which develops west of the jetty that protects the harbor entrance at Newport Harbor, California (Figure 21). The jetty is a solid human-made object that extends into the ocean 400 meters (1300 feet) and has a near-vertical side facing the waves. As incoming waves strike the vertical side of the jetty at an angle, they are reflected at an equivalent angle. Because the original waves and the reflected waves have the same wavelength, a constructive interference pattern develops, creating plunging breakers that may exceed 8 meters (26 feet) in height (Figure 21, *inset*). Too dangerous for board surfers, these waves present a fierce challenge to the most experienced body surfers. The Wedge has crippled or even killed many who have come to try it.

Standing waves (or *stationary waves*) can be produced when waves are reflected at right angles to a barrier. Standing waves are the sum of two waves with the same wavelength moving in opposite directions, resulting in no net movement. Although the water particles continue to move vertically and horizontally, there is none of the circular motion that is characteristic of a progressive wave.

Figure 22 shows the movement of water during the wave cycle of a standing wave. Lines along which there is no vertical movement are called *nodes* (*node* = knot), or nodal lines. *Antinodes*, crests that alternately become troughs, are the points of greatest vertical movement within a standing wave.

There is no particle motion when an antinode is at its greatest vertical displacement, and the maximum particle movement occurs when the water surface is level. At this time, the maximum movement of the water is in a horizontal direction directly beneath the nodal lines. The movement of water particles beneath the antinodes is entirely vertical.

Under certain conditions, the development of standing waves significantly affects the tidal character of coastal regions.

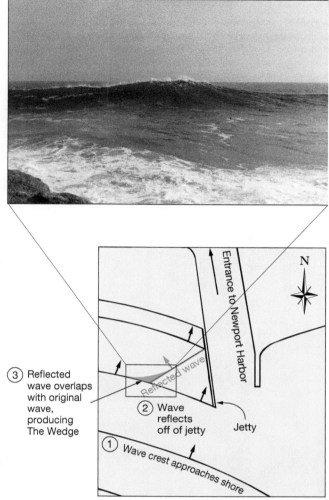

Photo by Hal Thurman.

Figure 21 **Wave reflection at The Wedge, Newport Harbor, California.**

As waves approach the shore (1), some of the wave energy is reflected off the long jetty at the entrance to the harbor (2). The reflected wave overlaps and constructively interferes with the original wave (3), resulting in a wedge-shaped wave (*dark blue triangle*) that may reach heights exceeding 8 meters (26 feet). Photo of The Wedge (*inset*) shows three dots in front of the wave that are the heads of body surfers.

Wave refraction is the bending of waves c. when waves slow in shallow water; wave refle. is the bouncing back of wave energy caused v waves strike a hard barrier.

Tsunami

The Japanese term for the large, sometimes destruct waves that occasionally roll into their harbors is **tsuna** (*tsu* = harbor, *nami* = wave). Tsunami originate fro. sudden changes in the topography of the sea floor cause. by slippage along underwater faults, underwater avalanch-es, or underwater volcanic eruptions. Many people mis-takenly call them "tidal waves," but tsunami are unrelated to the tides. The mechanisms that trigger tsunami are typ-ically seismic events, so tsunami are *seismic sea waves*.

The majority of tsunami are caused by *fault movement*. Underwater fault movement displaces Earth's crust, gen-erates earthquakes, and, if it ruptures the sea floor, pro-duces a sudden change in water level at the ocean surface (Figure 23a). Faults that produce *vertical* displacements (the uplift or downdropping of ocean floor) change the volume of the ocean basin, which affects the entire water column and generates tsunami. Conversely, faults that produce *horizontal* displacements (such as the lateral movement associated with transform faulting) generally do not generate tsunami because the side-to-side move-ment of these faults does not change the volume of the ocean basin. Much less common events, such as underwa-ter avalanches triggered by shaking, meteorite impacts, or underwater volcanic eruptions—which create the largest waves—also produce tsunami.

The wavelength of a typical tsunami exceeds 200 kilo-meters (125 miles). In the open ocean, tsunami move at well over 700 kilometers (435 miles) per hour—they could easily keep pace with a jet airplane—and have heights of only about 0.5 meter (1.6 feet). Even though they are fast, tsunami are small in the open ocean and pass unnoticed in deep water until they reach shore, where they slow in the shallow water, and the water begins to pile up.

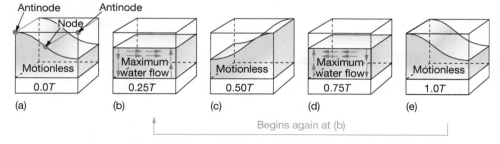

Figure 22 **Sequence of motion in a standing wave.**

In a standing wave, water is motionless when antinodes reach maximum displacement (*a*, *c*, and *e*; *a* and *e* are identical). Water movement is at a maximum (*blue arrows*) when the water is horizontal (*b* and *d*). Movement is vertical beneath the antinodes, and maximum horizontal movement occurs beneath the node. After *e*, cycle begins again at *b*.

Figure 23 Origin of a tsunami.

(a) Abrupt vertical movement along a fault on the sea floor raises or drops the ocean water column above a fault, creating a tsunami that travels from deep to shallow water where it is experienced as alternating surges and withdrawals of water at the shore. **(b)** Sequence of photos of a 1983 tsunami in northern Japan that surges toward fleeing spectators in a harbor. Red arrow shows stationary motorcycle.

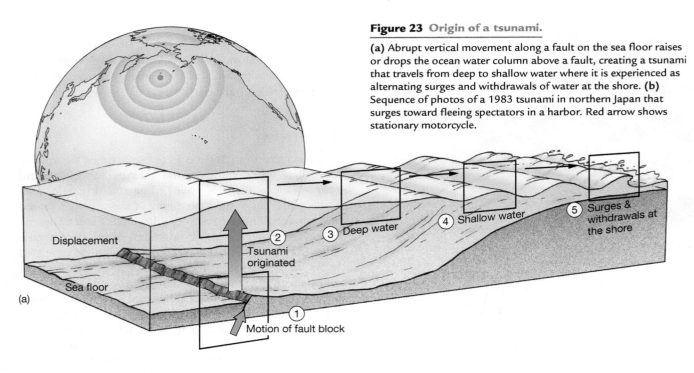

Photos courtesy Kyodo News Agency, Japan

EXAMPLE 6

Given the typical wavelength of a tsunami is 200 kilometers (125 miles) and the deepest depth of the oceans is 11 kilometers (7 miles), can a tsunami ever be a deep-water wave?

Recall that the depth of the wave base is one-half a wave's wavelength. For a tsunami with a wavelength of 200 kilometers, its wave base would be $200 \div 2 = 100$ kilometers (62 miles), which is deeper than even the deepest ocean trenches. Remarkably, tsunami are shallow-water waves everywhere in the ocean! Because they are shallow-water waves, remember that a tsunami's speed is determined *only* by water depth.

Coastal Effects

A tsunami does not form a huge breaking wave at the shoreline. Instead, it is a strong flood or surge of water that causes the ocean to advance (or, in certain cases, retreat) dramatically. In fact, a tsunami resembles a sudden, *extremely* high tide, which is why they are misnamed "tidal waves." It takes several minutes for the tsunami to express itself fully, during which time sea level can rise up to 40 meters (131 feet) above normal, with normal waves superimposed on top of the higher sea level. The strong surge of water can rush into low-lying areas with destructive results (Figure 23b).

As the trough of the tsunami arrives at the shore, the water will rapidly drain off the land. In coastal areas, it will look like a sudden and *extremely* low tide, where sea level is many meters lower than even the lowest low tide. Because tsunami are typically a series of waves, there are often an alternating series of dramatic surges and withdrawals of water, separated by only a few minutes. The first surge may not always be the largest; the third, fourth, or even seventh surge may be, instead.

In some cases, the trough of a tsunami arrives at the coast first, exposing parts of the lowermost shoreline that are rarely seen. For people at the shoreline, the temptation is to explore these newly exposed areas and catch stranded fish. Within a few minutes, however, a strong surge of water (the crest of the tsunami) is due to arrive.

The alternating surges and retreats of water by tsunami can severely damage coastal structures. Tsunami can be deadly as well. The speed of the advance—up to 4 meters (13 feet) per second—is faster than a person can run. Those who are trapped by tsunami are often drowned or crushed by floating debris (Figure 24).

Historic Tsunami

Many small tsunami are created each year, and go largely unnoticed. On average, 57 tsunami occur every decade, with a large tsunami occurring somewhere in the world every two to three years and an extremely large and damaging one occurring every 15 to 20 years. About 86% of all great waves are generated in the Pacific Ocean because large-magnitude earthquakes occur along the series of trenches that ring its ocean basin where oceanic plates are subducted along convergent plate boundaries. Volcanic activity is also common along the Pacific "Ring of Fire," and the large earthquakes that occur along its margin are capable of producing extremely large tsunami.

One of the most destructive tsunami ever generated came from the eruption of the volcanic island of Krakatau[5] on August 27, 1883. Approximately the size of a small Hawaiian Island in what is now Indonesia, Krakatau exploded with the greatest release of energy from Earth's interior observed in historic times. The island was nearly obliterated and the sound of the explosion was heard up to 4800 kilometers (2980 miles) away. Dust from the explosion ascended into the atmosphere and circled Earth on high-altitude winds, producing unusual and beautiful sunsets for nearly a year.

Not many were killed by the outright explosion of the volcano because the island was uninhabited. However, the displacement of water from the energy released during the explosion was enormous, creating a tsunami that exceeded 35 meters (116 feet)—as high as a 12-story building. It devastated the coastal region of the Sunda Strait between the nearby islands of

---

[5]The volcanic island Krakatau (which is *west* of Java) is also called Krakatoa.

Figure 24 Tsunami damage in Hilo, Hawaii.

Flattened parking meters in Hilo, Hawaii, caused by the 1946 tsunami that resulted in more than $25 million in damage and 159 deaths.

CORBIS.

Sumatra and Java, drowning over 1000 villages and taking more than 36,000 lives. The energy carried by this wave reached every ocean basin and was detected by tide recording stations as far away as London and San Francisco.

Several ships were along the coast of Java during the eruption of Krakatau, containing eyewitnesses to the tsunami and its destruction. N. van Sandick, an engineer aboard the Dutch vessel *Loudon*, gave the following account:

> Suddenly we saw a gigantic wave of prodigious height advancing from the sea-shore with considerable speed. Immediately the crew set to under considerable pressure and managed after a fashion to set sail in face of the imminent danger; the ship had just enough time to meet with the wave from the front. After a moment, full of anguish, we were lifted up with a dizzy rapidity. The ship made a formidable leap, and immediately afterwards we felt as though we had plunged into the abyss. But the ship's blade went higher and we were safe. Like a high mountain, the monstrous wave precipitated its journey towards the land. Immediately afterwards another three waves of colossal size appeared. And before our eyes this terrifying upheaval of the sea, in a sweeping transit, consumed in one instant the ruin of the town; the lighthouse fell in one piece, and all the houses of the town were swept away in one blow like a castle of cards. All was finished. There, where a few moments ago lived the town of Telok Betong, was nothing but the open sea.

Another strong tsunami was experienced in the port of Hilo, Hawaii, on April 1, 1946. The tsunami was from a magnitude $M_w = 7.3$ earthquake in the Aleutian Trench off the island of Unimak, Alaska, over 3000 kilometers (1850 miles) away. The bathymetry in horseshoe-shaped Hilo Bay tends to focus a tsunami's energy directly toward town, building up waves to tremendous heights. In this case, the tsunami expressed

BOX 2   Historical Feature
THE BIGGEST WAVE IN RECORDED HISTORY: LITUYA BAY, ALASKA (1958)

L ituya Bay is located in southeast Alaska about 200 kilometers (125 miles) west of Juneau, Alaska's capital. It is a deep, T-shaped, 11-kilometer (7-mile)-long bay with a sand bar named La Chaussee Spit that separates it from the Pacific Ocean. The largest wave ever authentically recorded occurred in Lituya Bay. Remarkably, the wave was witnessed by six people on board three small fishing boats that were near the bay's entrance.

Lituya Bay, Alaska, with aerial view before the 1958 splash wave (*top*) and after (*bottom*).

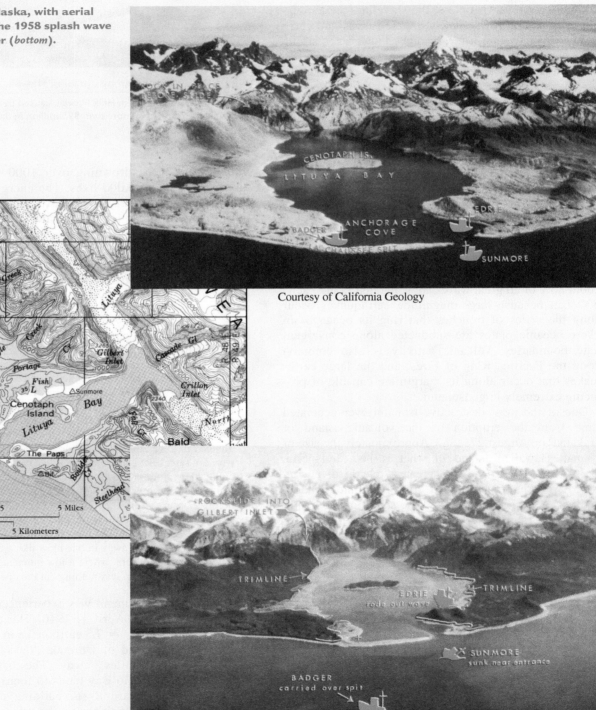

Courtesy of California Geology

At about 10:00 P.M. on July 9, 1958, an earthquake of magnitude $M_w = 7.9$* occurred along the Fairweather Fault, which runs along the top of the "T" portion of the bay. The earthquake didn't produce the wave directly, but it triggered an enormous rockslide that dumped at least 90 million tons of rock—some of it from as high as 914 meters (3000 feet) above sea level—into the upper part of the bay. The rockslide created a huge **splash wave** (a long-wavelength wave produced when an object splashes into water) that swept over the ridge facing the rockslide area and uprooted, debarked, or snapped off trees up to 530 meters (1740 feet) above the water level of the bay—a full 87 meters (285 feet) *higher* than the world's tallest building, the Sears Tower in Chicago. As the giant wave raced down the bay toward the boats at a speed of over 160 kilometers (100 miles) per hour, it continued to snap off trees and completely overtopped the island in the middle of the bay.

During the summer in Alaska, it was still light enough at 10:00 P.M. for the people on board the boats

---

*The symbol M_w indicates the *moment magnitude* of an earthquake.

to see the rockslide occur—and the giant wave bearing down on them. The *Badger*, a 13.4-meter (44-foot) fishing vessel, had its anchor chain snapped and was lifted up bow-first into the oncoming wave. Amazingly, the vessel surfed the wave over the sand bar! The two people on board reported looking down from a height of 24 meters (80 feet) above the tops of the trees on the sand bar, in an area where trees reach heights of 30 meters (100 feet). The *Badger* plunged into the Pacific Ocean on the other side of the sand bar stern-first, where it foundered and eventually sank. The people on board were able to launch a small skiff before the *Badger* sank and were rescued a few hours later, shaken but alive.

The *Edrie* was at anchor in the bay when the wave arrived. Its anchor chain snapped, and the vessel (including two people on board) was washed onto land. After the wave passed, the withdrawal of water washed it back into the bay, leaving the vessel largely undamaged. The two people on board the *Sunmore* were not nearly so lucky. The wave hit their vessel broadside, which capsized and sank the *Sunmore*, killing both people on board. The wave spread out into the Pacific and was even detected over six hours later at

a tide-recording station in Hawaii, where the wave was only 10 centimeters (4 inches) tall.

The most noticeable damage to the shoreline of the bay included a trimline of trees that extended around the bay and across the island. The wave also knocked down all the trees on the sand bar and killed most of the shellfish living near the water's edge. Additionally, floating logs from the destruction filled Lituya Bay for many years.

Older knocked-down trees suggest that Lituya Bay periodically experiences rockslides that generate giant splash waves. For instance, there is evidence of a 120-meter (395-foot) wave in 1853, a 61-meter (200-foot) wave in 1899, and a 150-meter (490-foot) wave on October 27, 1936. Even though other events may have produced larger waves (such as the 914-meter (3000-foot) wave created by a meteorite impact in the Gulf of Mexico about 65 million years ago), the 1958 splash wave in Lituya Bay stands as the largest wave in recorded history.

---

itself as a strong recession followed by a surge of water nearly 17 meters (55 feet) above normal high tide, causing more than $25 million in damage and killing 159 people. Remarkably, it stands as Hawaii's worst natural disaster (Figure 24).

Closer to the source of the earthquake, the tsunami was considerably larger. The tsunami struck Scotch Cap, Alaska, on Unimak Island, where a two-story reinforced concrete lighthouse stood 14 meters (46 feet) above sea level at its base. The lighthouse was destroyed by a wave that is estimated to have reached 36 meters (118 feet), killing all five people inside the lighthouse at the time. Vehicles on a nearby mesa 31 meters (103 feet) above water level were also moved by the onrush of water.

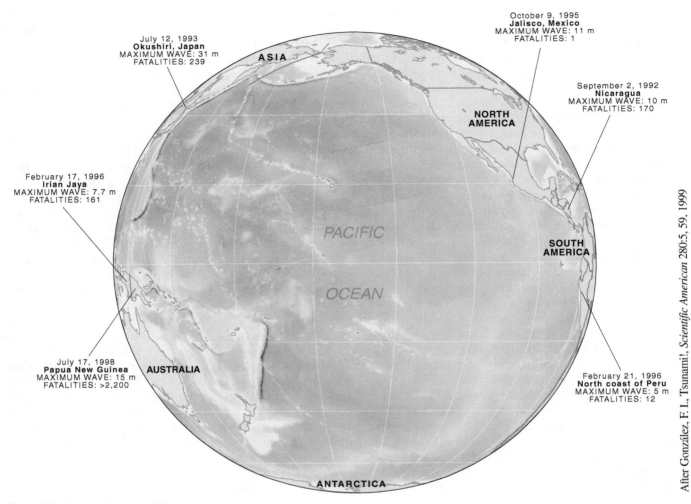

October 9, 1995
Jalisco, Mexico
MAXIMUM WAVE: 11 m
FATALITIES: 1

July 12, 1993
Okushiri, Japan
MAXIMUM WAVE: 31 m
FATALITIES: 239

September 2, 1992
Nicaragua
MAXIMUM WAVE: 10 m
FATALITIES: 170

February 17, 1996
Irian Jaya
MAXIMUM WAVE: 7.7 m
FATALITIES: 161

July 17, 1998
Papua New Guinea
MAXIMUM WAVE: 15 m
FATALITIES: >2,200

February 21, 1996
North coast of Peru
MAXIMUM WAVE: 5 m
FATALITIES: 12

ASIA

NORTH AMERICA

SOUTH AMERICA

PACIFIC

OCEAN

AUSTRALIA

ANTARCTICA

After González, F. I., Tsunami!, *Scientific American* 280:5, 59, 1999

Figure 25 Tsunami since 1990.

Ten destructive tsunami have claimed more than 4000 lives since 1990. These killer waves are most often generated by earthquakes along colliding tectonic plates of the Pacific Rim, although the deadly 1998 Papua New Guinea tsunami that killed more than 2200 was generated by an underwater landslide.

Figure 25 shows that since 1990, ten destructive tsunami along the Pacific Ring of Fire have claimed more than 4000 lives. Of these tsunami, the one that caused the greatest number of casualties occurred in Papua New Guinea in July 1998. An offshore magnitude $M_w = 7.1$ earthquake was followed shortly thereafter by a 15-meter (49-foot) tsunami, which was up to five times larger than expected for a quake that size. The tsunami completely overtopped a heavily populated low-lying sand bar, destroying three entire villages and resulting in at least 2200 deaths. Researchers who mapped the sea floor after the tsunami discovered the remains of a huge underwater landslide, which was apparently triggered by the shaking and generated the deadliest tsunami in 65 years.

Pacific Ocean. It led to what is now the **Pacific Tsunami Warning Center (PTWC)**, which coordinates information from 25 Pacific Rim countries and is headquartered in Ewa Beach (near Honolulu), Hawaii. In the open ocean, tsunami have small wave heights and are difficult to detect, so the tsunami warning system uses seismic waves—some of which travel through Earth at speeds 15 times faster than tsunami—to forecast destructive tsunami.[6] When a seismic disturbance occurs beneath the ocean surface that is large enough to be tsunamigenic (capable of producing a tsunami), a *tsunami watch* is issued. At this point, a tsunami may or may not have been generated, but the potential for one exists.

The PTWC is linked to over 50 tide-measuring stations throughout the Pacific, so the recording station

Tsunami Warning System

In response to the tsunami that struck Hawaii in 1946, a tsunami warning system was established throughout the

---

[6]A new method of tracking tsunami that is currently being tested uses a series of sensitive pressure sensors on the ocean floor that can detect the passage of tsunami in the open ocean.

nearest the earthquake is closely monitored for any indication of unusual wave activity. If unusual wave activity is verified, the tsunami watch is upgraded to a *tsunami warning*. Generally, earthquakes smaller than magnitude $M_w = 6.5$ are not tsunamigenic because they lack the duration of ground shaking necessary to initiate a tsunami. Additionally, transform faults do not usually produce tsunami because lateral movement does not offset the ocean floor and impart energy to the water column in the same way that vertical fault movements do.

STUDENTS SOMETIMES ASK ...

If there is a tsunami warning issued, what is the best thing to do?

The *smartest* thing to do is to stay out of coastal areas, but people often want to see the tsunami firsthand. For instance, when an earthquake of magnitude $M_w = 7.7$ occurred offshore of Alaska in May 1986, a tsunami warning was issued for the west coast of the United States. In southern California, people flocked to the beach to observe the phenomenon. Fortunately, the tsunami was only a few centimeters high by the time it reached southern California, so it went unnoticed.

If you must go to the beach to observe a tsunami, expect crowds, road closings, and general mayhem. It would be a good idea to stay at least 30 meters (100 feet) above sea level. If you happen to be at a remote beach where the water suddenly withdraws, evacuate immediately to higher ground (Figure 26). And, if you happen to be at a beach where an earthquake occurs and shakes the ground so hard that you can't stand up, then *RUN*—don't walk—for high ground as soon as you *can* stand up!

After the first surge of the tsunami, stay out of low-lying coastal areas for several hours because several more surges (and withdrawals) can be expected. There are many documented cases where curious people have been killed when they are trapped by the third or fourth surge of a tsunami.

Once a tsunami is detected, warnings are sent to all the coastal regions that might encounter the destructive wave, along with its estimated time of arrival. This warning, usually just a few hours in advance of the tsunami, makes it possible to evacuate people from low-lying areas and remove ships from harbors before the waves arrive. If the disturbance is nearby, however, there is not enough time to issue a warning because a tsunami travels so rapidly. Unlike hurricanes, whose high winds and waves threaten ships at sea and send them to the protection of a coastal harbor, a tsunami washes ships from their coastal moorings into the open ocean or onto shore. Thus, the best strategy during a tsunami warning is to move ships out of coastal harbors and into deep water, where tsunami are not easily felt.

Since the PTWC was established in 1948, it has effectively prevented loss of life due to tsunami when people have heeded the evacuation warnings. Property damage, however, has increased as more buildings have been constructed close to shore. To combat the damage caused by tsunami, countries that are especially prone to tsunami like Japan have invested in shoreline barriers, seawalls, and other coastal fortifications.

Perhaps one of the best strategies to limit tsunami damage and loss of life is to restrict construction projects in low-lying coastal regions where tsunami have frequently struck in the past. However, the long time interval between large tsunami can lead people to forget past disasters.

> Most tsunami are generated by underwater fault movement, which transfers energy to the entire water column. When these fast and long waves surge ashore, they can do considerable damage.

Figure 26 Tsunami warning sign.

This tsunami warning sign in Oregon advises residents to evacuate low-lying areas during a tsunami.

Courtesy of Oregon Department of Geology

Chapter in Review

- *All ocean waves begin as disturbances caused by releases of energy.* The releases of energy include wind, the movement of fluids of different densities (which create internal waves), mass movement into the ocean, underwater sea floor movements, the gravitational pull of the Moon and the Sun on Earth, and human activities in the ocean.

- Once initiated, *waves transmit energy through matter by oscillatory motion* in the particles that make up the matter. Progressive waves are longitudinal, transverse, or orbital, depending on the pattern of particle oscillation. Particles in ocean waves move primarily in orbital paths.

- *Waves are described according to their wavelength (L), wave height (H), wave steepness (H/L), wave period (T), frequency (f), and wave speed (S).* As a wave travels, the water passes the energy along by moving in a circle, called *circular orbital motion*. This motion advances the waveform, not the water particles themselves. Circular orbital motion decreases with depth, ceasing entirely at wave base, which is equal to one-half the wavelength measured from still water level.

- If water depth is greater than one-half the wavelength, a progressive wave travels as a *deep-water wave with a speed that is directly proportional to wavelength.* If water depth is less than $\frac{1}{20}$ wavelength (L/20), the wave moves as a *shallow-water wave with a speed that is directly proportional to water depth.* Transitional waves have wavelengths between deep- and shallow-water waves, with speeds that depend on both wavelength and water depth.

- As wind-generated waves form in a sea area, *capillary waves* with rounded crests and wavelengths less than 1.74 centimeters (0.7 inch) *form first. As the energy of the waves increases, gravity waves form*, with increased wave speed, wavelength, and wave height. Factors that influence the size of wind-generated waves include wind speed, duration (time), and fetch (distance). An equilibrium condition called a *fully developed sea* is reached when the maximum wave height is achieved for a particular wind speed, duration, and fetch.

- *Energy is transmitted from the sea area across the ocean by uniform, symmetrical waves called swell.*

Different wave trains of swell can create either constructive, destructive, or mixed interference patterns. Constructive interference produces unusually large waves called rogue waves or superwaves.

- *As waves approach shoaling water near shore, they undergo many physical changes.* Waves release their energy in the surf zone when their steepness exceeds a 1:7 ratio and break. If waves break on a relatively flat surface, they produce spilling breakers. The curling crests of plunging breakers, which are the best for surfing, form on steep slopes and abrupt beach slopes create surging breakers.

- When swell approaches the shore, *segments of the waves that first encounter shallow water are slowed*, whereas other parts unaffected by shallow water move ahead, *causing the wave to refract, or bend.* Refraction concentrates wave energy on headlands, whereas low-energy breakers are characteristically found in bays.

- *Reflection of waves off seawalls or other barriers* can cause an interference pattern called a standing wave. The crests of standing waves do not move laterally as in progressive waves but alternate with troughs at antinodes. Between the antinodes are nodes, where there is no vertical movement of the water.

- *Sudden changes in the elevation of the sea floor, such as from fault movement or volcanic eruptions, generate tsunami, or seismic sea waves.* These waves often have lengths exceeding 200 kilometers (125 miles) and travel across the open ocean with undetectable heights of about 0.5 meter (1.6 feet) at speeds in excess of 700 kilometers (435 miles) per hour. Upon approaching shore, a tsunami produces a series of rapid withdrawals and surges, some of which may increase the height of sea level by 40 meters (131 feet) or more. Most tsunami occur in the Pacific Ocean, where they have caused millions of dollars of coastal damage and taken tens of thousands of lives. The Pacific Tsunami Warning Center (PTWC) has dramatically reduced fatalities by successfully predicting tsunami using real-time seismic information.

Key Terms

Atmospheric wave	Gravity wave	Sea	Tsunami
Capillary wave	Interference pattern	Shallow-water wave	Wave base
Circular orbital motion	Internal wave	Shoaling	Wave diffraction
Constructive interference	Longitudinal wave	Splash wave	Wave dispersion
Crest	Mixed interference	Spilling breaker	Wave height
Decay distance	Ocean wave	Standing wave	Wave period
Deep-water wave	Orbital wave	Still water level	Wave reflection
Destructive interference	Orthogonal line	Surf zone	Wave refraction
Disturbing force	Pacific Tsunami Warning	Surging breaker	Wave speed
Free wave	Center (PTWC)	Swell	Wave steepness
Forced wave	Plunging breaker	Transitional wave	Wave train
Frequency	Restoring force	Transverse wave	Wavelength
Fully developed sea	Rogue wave	Trough	

Questions and Exercises

1. Discuss several different ways in which waves form. How are most ocean waves generated?

2. Why is the development of internal waves likely within the pycnocline?

3. Discuss longitudinal, transverse, and orbital wave phenomena, including the states of matter in which each can transmit energy.

4. Draw a diagram of a simple progressive wave. From memory, label the crest, trough, wavelength, wave height, and still water level.

5. Can a wave with a wavelength of 14 meters ever be more than 2 meters high? Why or why not?

6. What physical feature of a wave is related to the depth of the wave base? On the diagram that you drew for Question 4, add the wave base. What is the difference between the wave base and still water level?

7. Explain why the following statements for deep-water waves are either true or false:
   a. The longer the wave, the deeper the wave base.
   b. The greater the wave height, the deeper the wave base.
   c. The longer the wave, the faster the wave travels.
   d. The greater the wave height, the faster the wave travels.
   e. The faster the wave, the greater the wave height.

8. Calculate the speed (S) in meters per second for deep-water waves with the following characteristics:

   a. $L = 351$ meters, $T = 15$ seconds
   b. $T = 12$ seconds
   c. $f = 0.125$ wave per second

9. Define *swell*. Does swell necessarily imply a particular wave size? Why or why not?

10. Waves from separate sea areas move away as swell and produce an interference pattern when they come together. If Sea A has wave heights of 1.5 meters (5 feet) and Sea B has wave heights of 3.5 meters (11.5 feet), what would be the height of

waves resulting from constructive interference and destructive interference? Illustrate your answer (see Figure 14).

11. Describe the physical changes that occur to a wave's wave speed (S), wavelength (L), height (H), and wave steepness (H/L) as a wave moves across shoaling water to break on the shore.

12. Describe the three different types of breakers and indicate the slope of the beach that produces the three types. How is the energy of the wave distributed differently within the surf zone by the three types of breakers?

13. Using examples, explain how wave refraction is different from wave reflection.

14. Using orthogonal lines, illustrate how wave energy is distributed along a shoreline with headlands and bays. Identify areas of high and low energy release.

15. Define the terms *node* and *antinode* as they relate to standing waves.

16. Why is it more likely that a tsunami will be generated by faults beneath the ocean along which vertical rather than horizontal movement has occurred?

17. While shopping in a surf shop, you overhear some surfing enthusiasts mention that they would really like to ride the curling wave of a tidal wave at least once in their life, because it is a single breaking wave of enormous height. What would you say to these surfers?

18. Explain what it would look like at the shoreline if the trough of a tsunami arrives there first. What is the impending danger?

19. What ocean depth would be required for a tsunami with a wavelength of 220 kilometers (136 miles) to travel as a deep-water wave? Is it possible that such a wave could become a deep-water wave any place in the world ocean? Explain.

20. Explain how the tsunami warning system in the Pacific Ocean works. Why must the tsunami be verified at the closest tide recording station?

Tides

From Chapter 10 of *Introduction to Oceanography*, Tenth Edition, Harold V. Thurman, Alan P. Trujillo.

Tides

Courtesy of Tides Photography, photographic artist Dick Killam;
website address: *www.tidesinhallsharbour.com*

Extreme tidal variation. High and low tides at Hall's
Harbor in Nova Scotia, Canada, demonstrate the dra-
matic change of sea level experienced daily in the Bay of
Fundy, which has the world's largest tidal range.

Generating Tides

Fundamentally, tides are generated by forces imposed on Earth that are generated by a combination of *gravity* and *motion* among Earth, the Moon, and the Sun.

Tide-Generating Forces

Newton's work on quantifying the forces involved in the Earth–Moon–Sun system led to the first understanding of why tides behave as they do. It is well known that gravity tethers the Sun, its planets, and their moons together. Most of us are taught that "the Moon orbits Earth," but it is not quite that simple. The two bodies actually rotate around a common center of mass called the **barycenter** (*barus* = heavy, *center* = center), which is located 1600 kilometers (1000 miles) beneath Earth's surface (Figure 1a). This can be visualized by imagining Earth and its Moon as ends of a sledgehammer, flung into space, tumbling slowly end over end about its balance point, which is closest to the hammer. The barycenter follows a smooth orbit around the Sun, while Earth and the Moon themselves follow wavy paths (Figure 2). Moreover, the Earth–Moon system is involved in a mutual orbit held together by gravity and motion, which prevents the Moon and Earth from colliding. In this way, orbits are established that keep objects at more-or-less fixed distances. Gravity also tugs every particle of water on Earth toward the Moon and the Sun, thus creating tides on Earth.

Gravitational and Centripetal Forces in the Earth–Moon System To understand how *tide-generating forces* influence the oceans, let's examine how *gravitational forces* and *centripetal forces* affect objects on Earth within the Earth–Moon system. (We'll ignore the influence of the Sun for the moment.)

The **gravitational force** is derived from Newton's law of universal gravitation, which states that *every particle of mass in the universe attracts every other particle of mass*. Mathematically, gravitational force is expressed as

$$\text{Gravitational force} = \frac{Gm_1m_2}{r^2} \qquad (1)$$

where G is the universal gravitational constant, m_1 and m_2 are two masses, and r is the distance between the two masses. Note that for spherical bodies, all of the mass can be considered to exist at the center of the sphere, and thus r will always be the distance between the centers of bodies being considered.

Equation (1) has several implications. For example, it explains why objects with a large mass (such as the Sun) produce a large gravitational force. This is because as mass increases, the gravitational force increases. Also, it shows that gravitational force varies with the square of distance, so even a small *increase* in the distance between two objects significantly *decreases* the gravitational force between them. Thus, the *greater* the mass of the objects

Key Questions

The answers to these questions (and much more) can be found in the highlighted concept statements within this chapter

"I derive from the celestial phenomena the forces of gravity with which bodies tend to the sun and several planets. Then from these forces, by other propositions which are also mathematical, I deduce the motions of the planets, the comets, the moon, and the sea."

—Sir Isaac Newton, *Philosophiae Naturalis Principia Mathematica (Philosophy of Natural Mathematical Principles)* (1686)

Tides are the periodic raising and lowering of average sea level that occurs throughout the oceans of the world. As sea level rises and falls, the edge of the sea slowly shifts landward and seaward daily, often destroying sand castles built during low tide. Knowledge of tides is important in many coastal activities, including tide pooling, shell collecting, surfing, fishing, navigation, and preparing for storms. Tides are so important that accurate records have been kept at nearly every port for several centuries and there are many examples of the term *tide* in everyday vocabulary (for instance, "to tide someone over," "to go against the tide," or to wish someone "good tidings").

People have undoubtedly observed the tides for as long as they have inhabited coastal regions. However, no written record of tides exists before Herodotus' observations of the Mediterranean Sea in about 450 B.C. Even the earliest sailors knew the Moon had some connection with the tides because both followed a similar cyclic pattern. However, it wasn't until **Isaac Newton** (1642–1727) developed the *universal law of gravitation* that the tides could be adequately explained.

Although the study of the tides can be complex, tides are fundamentally very long and regular shallow-water waves. Their wavelengths are measured in thousands of kilometers and their heights range to more than 15 meters (50 feet). The gravitational attraction of the Sun and Moon generate ocean tides, thereby affecting every particle of water from the surface to the deepest ocean basin.

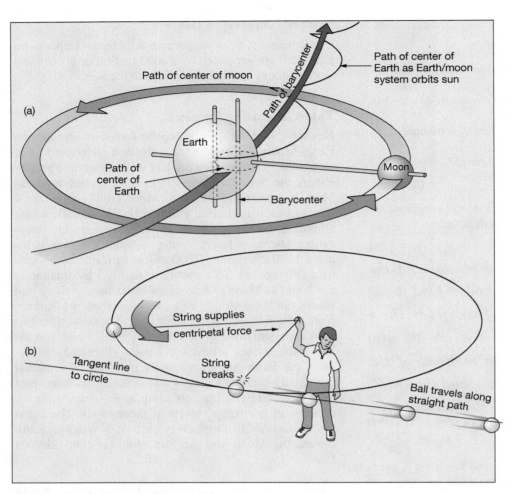

Figure 1 Earth–Moon system rotation.

(a) The center of mass (barycenter) of the Earth–Moon system moves in a nearly circular orbit around the Sun. **(b)** If a ball with a string attached is swung overhead, it stays in a circular orbit because the string exerts a centripetal (center-seeking) force on the ball. If the string breaks, the ball will fly off along a straight path along a tangent to the circle.

and the *closer* they are together, the greater their gravitational attraction.

Figure 3 shows how gravitational forces for points on Earth (caused by the Moon) vary depending on their distances from the Moon. The greatest gravitational attraction (the longest arrow) is at Z, the *zenith* (*zenith* = a path over the head), which is the point closest to the Moon. The gravitational attraction is weakest at *N*, the *nadir* (*nadir* = opposite the zenith), which is the point farthest from the Moon. The direction of the gravitational attraction between most particles and the center of the Moon is at an angle relative to a line connecting the center of Earth and the Moon (Figure 3). This angle causes the force of gravitational attraction between each particle and the Moon to be slightly different.

The **centripetal** (*centri* = the center, *pet* = seeking) **force**[1] required to keep planets in their orbits is provided by the gravitational attraction between each of them and the Sun. Centripetal force "tethers" an orbiting body to its parent, pulling the object *inward* toward the parent, "seek-

ing the center" of its orbit. For example, if you tie a string to a ball and swing the tethered ball around your head (Figure 1b), the string pulls the ball toward your hand. The string provides a *centripetal force* on the ball, forcing the ball to *seek the center* of its orbit. If the string should break, the force is gone and the ball can no longer maintain its circular orbit. The ball flies off in a *straight* line,[2] *tangent* (*tangent* = touching) to the circle (Figure 1b).

The Earth and Moon are tethered, too, not by strings but by gravity. Gravity provides the centripetal force that holds the Moon and Earth in a mutual orbit. If all gravity in the solar system could be shut off, centripetal force

---

[1]This is not to be confused with the so-called *centrifugal* (*centri* = the center, *fug* = flee) *force*, an apparent force that is oriented outward.

[2]At the moment that the string breaks, the ball will continue along a straight-line path, obeying Newton's first law of motion (the law of inertia), which states that moving objects follow straight-line paths until they are compelled to change that path by other forces.

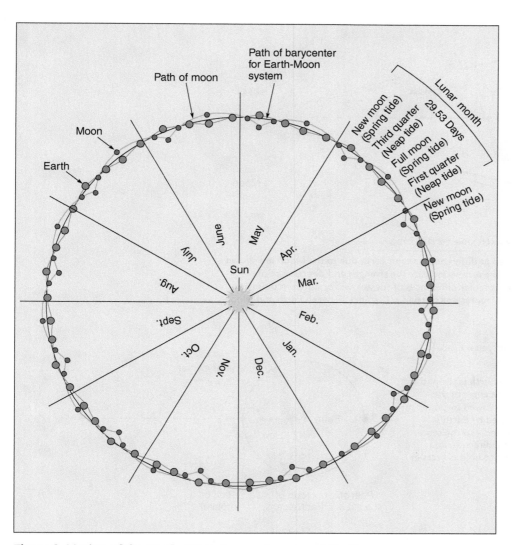

Figure 2 Motion of the Earth–Moon barycenter around the Sun.

As the barycenter (center of mass) of the Earth–Moon system orbits the Sun in a nearly circular path (*black line*), both the Moon (*green line*) and Earth (*red line*) follow separate wavy paths as they rotate about the barycenter, which is located 1600 kilometers (1000 miles) beneath Earth's surface. The phases of the Moon and the resulting tidal conditions are explained later in this chapter.

would vanish, and the momentum of the celestial bodies would send them flying off into space along straight-line paths, tangent to their orbits.

As the Earth and Moon rotate around their common barycenter, all particles that make up Earth follow circles of equal radii (Figure 4a). If Earth is divided into a great number of particles of equal mass, the centripetal force required to keep each particle of Earth following an identical orbit is the same (Figure 4b). The required centripetal force for each particle is supplied by its gravitational attraction to the Moon. In essence, the centripetal force required for all particles is identical and is directed toward the center of each particle's orbit (Figure 5).

Resultant and Tide-Generating Forces Gravitational attraction between the particle and the Moon supplies the centripetal force, but the *supplied* force is different than the *required* force (because gravitational attraction varies with distance from the Moon) except at the center of Earth. This difference creates tiny **resultant forces**, which are the mathematical difference between the two sets of arrows shown in Figures 3 and 5.

Figure 6 combines Figures 3 and 5 to show that resultant forces are produced by the difference between the required centripetal (C) and supplied gravitational (G) forces. However, do not think that both of these forces are being applied to the points, because (C) is a force that would be required to keep the particles in a perfectly circular path, while (G) is the force actually provided for this purpose by gravitational attraction between the particles and the Moon. The resultant forces (*blue arrows*) are established by constructing an arrow from the tip of the centripetal (*red*) arrow to the tip of the gravity (*black*) arrow and located where the red and black arrows begin.

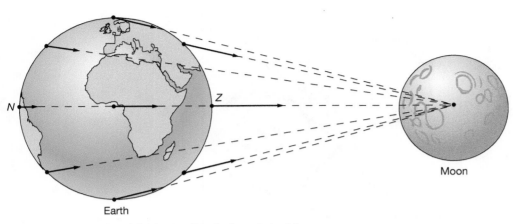

Figure 3 Gravitational forces on Earth due to the Moon.

The gravitational forces on objects located at different places on Earth due to the Moon are shown by arrows. The length and orientation of the arrows indicate the strength and direction of the gravitational force. Notice the length and angular differences of the arrows for different points on Earth. The letter *Z* represents the zenith; *N* represents the nadir. Distance between Earth and Moon not shown to scale.

Figure 4 Earth–Moon rotation and centripetal (center-seeking) forces.

(a) The dashed line through the center of Earth is the path of Earth's center as it moves around the barycenter of the Earth–Moon system. The circular paths followed by points *a* and *b* have the same radius as that followed by Earth's center. **(b)** Arrows from points *a, b, c, d,* and *e* to the center of their circular orbits show that the same direction and magnitude of centripetal force is required to hold objects in their orbital paths.

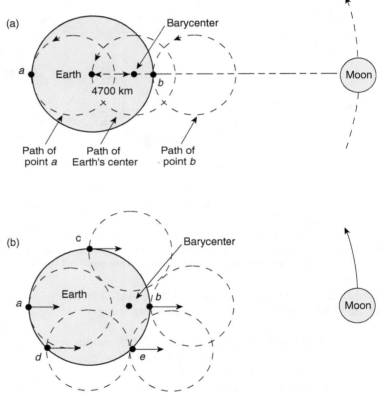

Resultant forces are small, averaging about one-millionth the magnitude of Earth's gravity. If the resultant force is vertical to Earth's surface, as it is at the zenith and nadir (oriented upward) and along an "equator" connecting all points halfway between the zenith and nadir (oriented downward), it has no tide-generating effect (Figure 7). However, if the resultant force has a significant *horizontal component*—that is, tangent to Earth's surface—it produces tidal bulges on Earth, creating what are known as the **tide-generating forces**. These tide-gen-

erating forces are quite small but reach their maximum value at points on Earth's surface at a "latitude" of 45 degrees relative to the "equator" between the zenith and nadir (Figure 7).

The tide-generating force is the difference between the gravitational force of the tide-generating object acting on a mass at the Earth's surface and at the Earth's center. Although the tide-generating force is derived from the gravitational force [Equation (1)], it is not linearly proportional to it. The tide-generating force can be written as

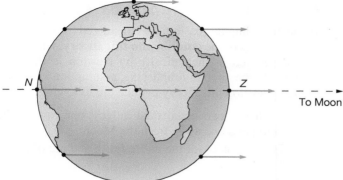

Figure 5 Required centripetal (center-seeking) forces.

Centripetal forces required to keep identical-sized particles in identical-sized orbits as a result of the rotation of the Earth–Moon system around its barycenter. As in Figure 4, notice that the arrows are all the same length, and are oriented in the same direction for all points on Earth. Z = zenith; N = nadir.

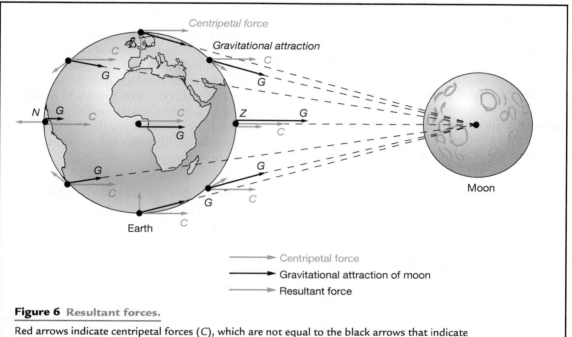

Figure 6 Resultant forces.

Red arrows indicate centripetal forces (C), which are not equal to the black arrows that indicate gravitational attraction (G). The small blue arrows show resultant forces, which are established by constructing an arrow from the tip of the centripetal (*red*) arrow to the tip of the gravity (*black*) arrow and located where the red and black arrows begin. Z = zenith; N = nadir. Distance between Earth and Moon not shown to scale.

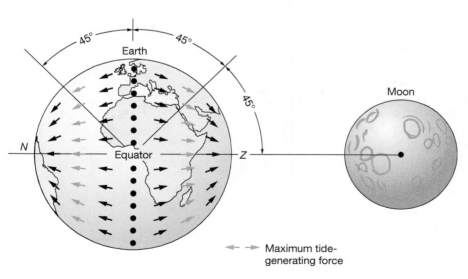

Figure 7 Tide-generating forces.

Where the resultant force acts vertically relative to Earth's surface, the tide-generating force is zero. This occurs at the zenith (Z) and nadir (N), and along an "equator" connecting all points halfway between the zenith and nadir (*black dots*). However, where the resultant force has a significant *horizontal component*, it produces a tide-generating force on Earth. These tide-generating forces reach their maximum value at points on Earth's surface at a "latitude" of 45 degrees relative to the "equator" mentioned here (*blue arrows*). Distance between Earth and Moon not shown to scale.

$$\text{Tide-generating force} \propto \frac{m_1 m_2}{r^3} \qquad (2)$$

where the $\propto$ symbol means "proportional to." Equation (2) shows that the tide-generating force varies inversely as the *cube* of the distance from the center of Earth to the center of the tide-generating object (instead of varying inversely as the *square* of the distance as does the gravitational force). In the tide-generating equation, therefore, distance is a more highly weighted variable. So, the greater the distance from Earth the tide-generating body (Moon or Sun) is, the smaller the tide-generating force will be. This is why the Moon influences tides far more than the Sun (even though the Sun is much more massive).

The tide-generating forces push water into two bulges: one on the side of Earth directed *toward* the Moon (the zenith) and the other on the side directed *away from* the Moon (the nadir) (Figure 8). On the side directly facing the Moon, the bulge is created because the gravitational force is greater than the required centripetal force. Conversely, on the side facing away from the Moon, the bulge is created because the required centripetal force is greater than the gravitational force. Although the forces are oriented in opposite directions on the two sides of Earth, the resultant forces are equal in magnitude, so the bulges are equal, too.

STUDENTS SOMETIMES ASK...

Are there also tides in other objects, such as lakes and swimming pools?

The Moon and the Sun act on all objects that have the ability to flow, so there are tides in lakes, wells, and swimming pools. In fact, there are even extremely tiny tidal bulges in a glass of water! However, the tides in the atmosphere and the "solid" Earth have greater significance. Tides in the atmosphere—called *atmospheric tides*—can be miles high. The tides inside Earth's interior—called *Earth tides*—cause a slight but measurable stretching of Earth's crust, typically only a few centimeters high.

The tides are caused by an imbalance between the required centripetal and the provided gravitational forces acting on Earth. This difference produces residual forces, the horizontal component of which pushes ocean water into two equal tidal bulges on opposite sides of Earth.

Figure 8 Idealized equilibrium tidal bulges.

In an idealized case, the Moon creates two bulges in the ocean surface: One that extends *toward* the Moon and the other *away from* the Moon. As Earth rotates, it carries various locations into and out of the two tidal bulges so that all points on its surface (except the poles) experience two high tides daily.

Equilibrium Theory of Tides

In the preceding discussion, we considered the forces that form the basis of the **equilibrium tide theory**, which was first developed mathematically by Newton in the 17th century. Some of the simplifying assumptions Newton made to develop this theory include the following:

1. Earth has two equal tidal bulges, one toward the Moon and one away from the Moon.
2. The oceans cover the entire Earth and are of a uniform depth.
3. There is no friction between ocean water and the sea floor.
4. The continents have no influence.

Because the equilibrium tide theory ignores some of the complexities of real tides, it cannot be used to accurately predict the tides at specific locations on Earth. However, it does provide an adequate model of basic tidal phenomena and, as such, it can be used to predict the general behavior of tides in the world's oceans. Later in this chapter, we will consider the *dynamic tide theory*, which addresses the variables not accounted for by the equilibrium tide theory.

Tidal Bulges: The Moon's Effect

In the equilibrium tide theory, the ideal Earth has two tidal bulges, one toward the Moon and one away from the Moon (called the **lunar bulges**) as shown in Figure 8. If the Moon is stationary and aligned with the ideal Earth's Equator, the maximum bulge will occur on the Equator on opposite sides of Earth. If you were standing on the Equator, you would experience two high tides each day. The time between high tides, the **tidal period**, would be 12 hours. If you moved to any latitude north or south of the Equator, you would experience the same tidal period, but the high tides would be less high, because you would be at a lower point on the bulge.

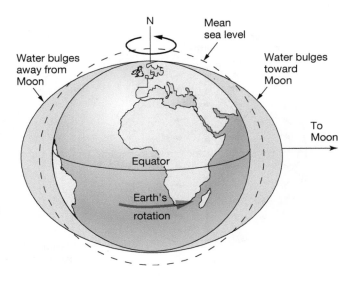

In most places on Earth, however, high tides occur every 12 hours 25 minutes because tides depend on the lunar day, not the solar day. The **lunar day** (also called a *tidal day*) is measured from the time the Moon is on the meridian of an observer—that is, directly overhead—to the next time the Moon is on that meridian, and is 24 hours 50 minutes.[3] The **solar day** is measured from the time the Sun is on the meridian of an observer to the next time the Sun is on that meridian, and is 24 hours. Why is the lunar day 50 minutes longer than the solar day? During the 24 hours it takes Earth to make a full rotation, the Moon has continued moving another 12.2 degrees to the east in its orbit around Earth (Figure 9). Thus, Earth must rotate an additional 50 minutes to "catch up" to the Moon so that the Moon is again on the meridian (directly overhead) of our observer.

The difference between a solar day and a lunar day can be seen in some of the natural phenomena related to the tides. For example, alternating high tides are normally 50

minutes *later* each successive day and the Moon rises 50 minutes *later* each successive night.

> A solar day (24 hours) is shorter than a lunar day (24 hours and 50 minutes). The extra 50 minutes is caused by the Moon's movement in its orbit around Earth.

Tidal Bulges: The Sun's Effect

The Sun affects the tides, too. Like the Moon, the Sun produces tidal bulges on opposite sides of Earth, one oriented toward the Sun and one oriented away from the Sun.

Even though the Sun is 27 million times more massive than the Moon, its tide-generating force is not 27 million times greater than the Moon's. This is because the Sun is 390 times farther from Earth than the Moon (Figure 10). Recall from Equation (2) that tide-generating forces vary inversely as the *cube* of the distance between objects. Thus, the tide-generating force is reduced by the cube of 390, or about 59 million times compared

[3]A lunar day is exactly 24 hours, 50 minutes, 28 seconds long.

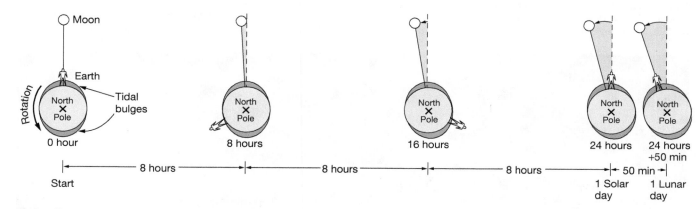

Figure 9 The lunar day.

A lunar day is the time that elapses between when the Moon is directly overhead and the next time the Moon is directly overhead. During one complete rotation of Earth (the 24-hour solar day), the Moon moves eastward 12.2 degrees, and Earth must rotate an additional 50 minutes to place the Moon in the exact same position overhead. Thus, a lunar day is 24 hours 50 minutes long.

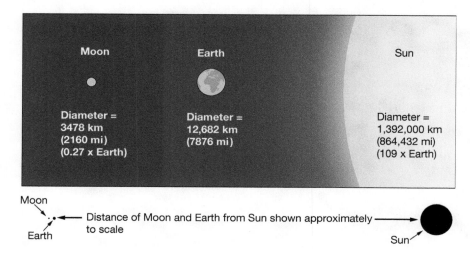

Figure 10 Relative sizes and distances of the Moon, Earth, and Sun.

Top: The relative sizes of the Moon, Earth, and Sun, showing the diameter of the Moon is roughly one-fourth that of Earth, while the diameter of the Sun is 109 times the diameter of Earth. *Bottom*: The relative distances of the Moon, Earth, and Sun are shown to scale.

with that of the Moon. These conditions result in the Sun's tide-generating force being $\frac{27}{59}$ that of the Moon, or 46% (about one-half). As a result, the **solar bulges** are only 46% the size of the lunar bulges.

Earth's Rotation

The tides appear to move water in toward shore (the **flood tide**) and to move water away from shore (the **ebb tide**). However, according to the nature of the idealized tides presented so far, *Earth's rotation carries various locations into and out of the tidal bulges*, which are in fixed positions relative to the Moon and the Sun. In essence, alternating high and low tides are created as Earth constantly rotates inside fluid bulges that are supported by the Moon and the Sun.

Figure 11 Earth–Moon–Sun positions and the tides.

Top: When the Moon is in the new or full position, the tidal bulges created by the Sun and Moon are aligned, there is a large tidal range on Earth, and spring tides are experienced. *Bottom*: When the Moon is in the first- or third-quarter position, the tidal bulges produced by the Moon are at right angles to the bulges created by the Sun. Tidal ranges are smaller and neap tides are experienced

The lunar bulges are about twice the size of the solar bulges. In an idealized case, the rise and fall of the tides are caused by Earth's rotation carrying various locations into and out of the tidal bulges.

The Monthly Tidal Cycle

The monthly tidal cycle is $29\frac{1}{2}$ days because that's how long it takes the Moon to complete an orbit around Earth.[4] During this time, the phase of the Moon changes dramatically. When the Moon is between Earth and the Sun, it cannot be seen at night, and it is called the **new moon**. When the Moon is on the side of Earth opposite the Sun, its entire disk is brightly visible, and it is called a **full moon**. A **quarter moon**—a moon that is half lit and half dark as viewed from Earth—occurs when the Moon is at right angles to the Sun relative to Earth.

Figure 11 shows the positions of the Earth, Moon, and Sun at various points during the $29\frac{1}{2}$-day lunar cycle

---

[4]The $29\frac{1}{2}$-day monthly tidal cycle is also called a *lunar cycle*, a *lunar month*, or a *synodic* (*synodos* = meeting) *month*.

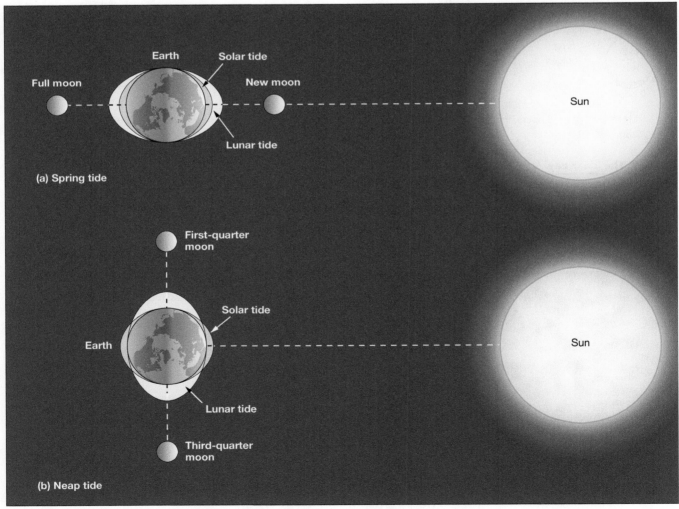

(a) Spring tide

(b) Neap tide

(see also Figure 2). When the Sun and Moon are aligned, either with the Moon between Earth and the Sun (new moon; Moon in *conjunction*) or with the Moon on the side opposite the Sun (full moon; Moon in *opposition*), the tide-generating forces of the Sun and Moon combine (Figure 11, *top*). At this time, the **tidal range** (the vertical difference between high and low tides) is large (very *high* high tides and quite *low* low tides) because there is *constructive interference*[5] between the lunar and solar tidal bulges (Figure 12a).The maximum tidal range is called a **spring** (*springen* = to rise up) **tide**,[6] because the tide is extremely large or "springs forth." When the Earth–Moon–Sun system is aligned, the Moon is said to be in **syzygy** (*syzygia* = union).

When the Moon is in either the first- or third-quarter[7] phase (Figure 11, *bottom*), the tide-generating force of the Sun is working at right angles to the tide-generating force of the Moon. The tidal range is small (*lower* high tides and *higher* low tides) because there is destructive interference[8] between the lunar and solar tidal bulges (Figure 12b). This is called a **neap** (*nep* =

scarcely or barely touching) **tide**,[9] and the Moon is said to be in **quadrature** (*quadra* = four).

The time between successive spring tides (full moon and new moon) or neap tides (first quarter and third quarter) is one-half the monthly lunar cycle, which is about two weeks. The time between a spring tide and a successive neap tide is one-quarter the monthly lunar cycle, which is about one week.

---

[5]Constructive interference occurs when two waves (or, in this case, two tidal bulges) overlap crest to crest and trough to trough.

[6]Spring tides have no connection with the spring season; they occur twice a month during the time when the Earth–Moon–Sun system is aligned.

[7]The third-quarter moon is often called the last-quarter moon, which is not to be confused with certain sports that have a fourth quarter.

[8]Destructive interference occurs when two waves (or, in this case, two tidal bulges) match up crest to trough and trough to crest.

[9]To help you remember a *neap* tide, think of it as one that has been "*nipped* in the bud," indicating a small tidal range.

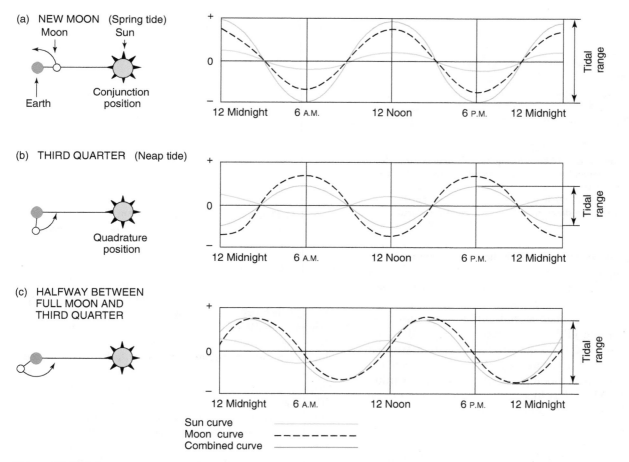

Sun curve
Moon curve
Combined curve

Figure 12 Tidal curves.

Tides experienced during various positions of the Earth–Moon–Sun system. Tidal curve graphs show a combined curve (*blue line*), which is produced by constructive and destructive interference between the Sun curve (*yellow line*) and the Moon curve (*black dashed line*). **(a)** New moon (spring tide) shows a maximum tidal range. **(b)** Third-quarter moon (neap tide) shows a minimum tidal range. **(c)** Halfway between full moon and third quarter (waning gibbous phase) shows a tidal range halfway between that of spring and neap tides.

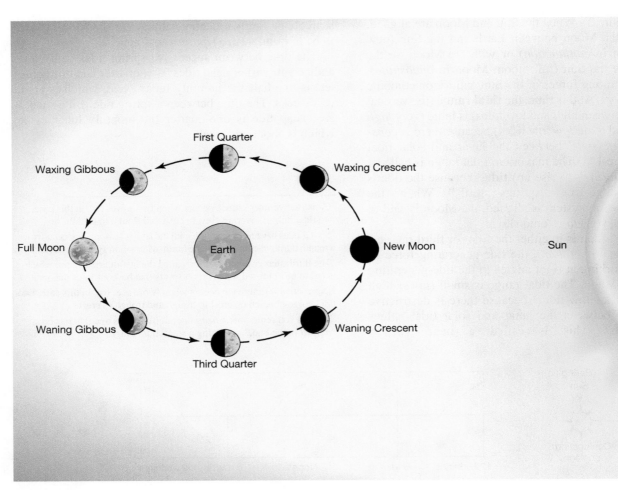

Figure 13 Phases of the Moon.

As the Moon moves around Earth during its 29$\frac{1}{2}$-day lunar cycle, its phase changes depending on its position relative to the Sun and Earth. During a new moon, the dark side of the Moon faces Earth while during a full moon, the lit side of the Moon faces Earth. Moon phases are shown diagrammatically as seen from Earth.

Figure 13 shows the pattern that the Moon experiences as it moves through its monthly cycle. As the Moon progresses from new moon to first-quarter phase, the Moon is a **waxing crescent** (*waxen* = to increase; *crescere* = to grow). In between the first-quarter and full moon phase, the Moon is a **waxing gibbous** (*gibbus* = hump). Between the Moon's full and third-quarter phase, it is a **waning gibbous** (*wanen* = to decrease). And, in between the third-quarter and new moon phase, the Moon is a **waning crescent**. The Moon has identical periods of rotation on its axis and revolution around Earth (a property called *synchronous rotation*). As a result, the same side of the Moon always faces Earth.

Figure 12c shows the tide conditions on Earth during a waning gibbous moon but is also representative of any situation where the Moon is halfway between sygygy and quadrature. The resulting mixed interference pattern shows that the tidal range is less than that of spring tides but greater than that of neap tides.

STUDENTS SOMETIMES ASK...
I've heard of a blue moon. Is the Moon really blue then?

No. "Once in a blue moon" is just a phrase that has gained popularity and is synonymous with a rather unlikely occurrence. A blue moon is the second full moon of any calendar month, which occurs when the 29$\frac{1}{2}$-day lunar cycle falls entirely within a 30- or 31-day month. Because the divisions between our calendar months were determined arbitrarily, a blue moon has no special significance, other than it occurs only once every 2.72 years (about 33 months). At that rate, it's certainly less common than a month of Sundays!

The origin of the term *blue moon* is not exactly known, but it probably has nothing to do with color (although large forest fires or volcanic eruptions can put enough pollution in the atmosphere to cause the Moon to appear blue). One likely explanation involves the Old English word *belewe*, meaning "to betray." Thus, the Moon is *belewe* because it betrays the usual perception of one full moon per month. Another explanation links the term to the *Farmer's Almanac*, which was first published in color in 1938 and included a calendar designating the first full moon of each month in red color and the second full moon in blue.

Spring tides occur during the full and new moon when the lunar and solar tidal bulges constructively interfere, producing a large tidal range. Neap tides occur during the quarter moon phases when the lunar and solar tidal bulges destructively interfere, producing a small tidal range.

Declination of the Moon and Sun

Up to this point, we have assumed that the Moon and Sun have remained directly overhead at the Equator, but this is not usually the case. Most of the year, in fact, they are either north or south of the Equator. The angular distance of the Sun or Moon above or below Earth's equatorial plane is called **declination** (*declinare* = to turn away).

Earth revolves around the Sun along an invisible ellipse in space. The imaginary plane that contains this ellipse is called the **ecliptic** (*ekleipein* = to fail to appear) (Figure 14, *yellow plane*). Earth's axis of rotation is tilted 23.5 degrees with respect to the ecliptic and that this tilt causes Earth's seasons. It also means the maximum declination of the Sun relative to Earth's Equator is 23.5 de-

grees (Figure 14a). Because of this tilt, the Sun's declination varies between 23.5 degrees north and 23.5 degrees south of the Equator on a yearly cycle.

To complicate matters further, the plane of the Moon's orbit is tilted 5 degrees with respect to the ecliptic (Figure 14a). Thus, the maximum declination of the Moon's orbit relative to Earth's Equator is 28.5 degrees (5 degrees plus the 23.5 degrees of Earth's tilt). In addition, the plane of the Moon's orbit also *precesses*, or rotates, while maintaining this 5 degree angle. This **precession** (*praecedere* = to go before) completes a cycle every 18.6 years. Figure 14 shows the relationship of the ecliptic, the plane of the Moon's orbit, and the plane of Earth's Equator through one-half a precession (9.3 years).

Meanwhile, the Moon's declination changes from 28.5 degrees south to 28.5 degrees north and back to 28.5 degrees south of the Equator during the multiple lunar cycles within one year. As a result, tidal bulges are rarely aligned with the Equator. Instead, they occur mostly north and south of the Equator. The Moon affects Earth's tides more than the Sun, so tidal bulges follow the Moon, ranging from a maximum of 28.5 degrees north to a maximum of 28.5 degrees south of the Equator (Figure 15).

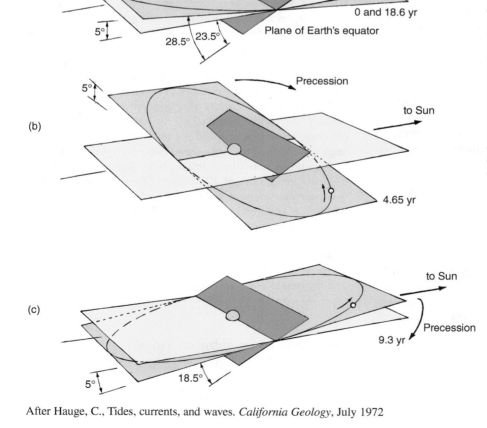

Figure 14 The precession of the Moon's declination.

Diagrammatic views of the Moon's orbit (*gray plane*), the plane of the ecliptic (*yellow plane*), and Earth's equatorial plane (*blue plane*). (a) The Moon's declination reaches a maximum of 28.5 degrees: 23.5 degrees (the angle of tilt of Earth's equatorial plane relative to the plane of the ecliptic) plus 5 degrees (the angle between the plane of the Moon's orbit and the ecliptic). (b) Positions of the planes 4.65 years later when the Moon has achieved one-fourth of its 18.6-year precessional rotation. (c) Positions of the planes after 9.3 years or one-half of the Moon's precession. Note that the maximum declination of the Moon relative to Earth's equatorial plane is now 18.5 degrees (23.5 degrees less 5 degrees).

After Hauge, C., Tides, currents, and waves. *California Geology*, July 1972

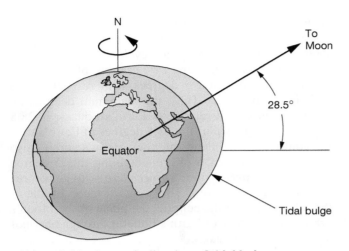

Figure 15 Maximum declination of tidal bulges from the Equator.

The center of the tidal bulges may lie at any latitude from the Equator to a maximum of 28.5 degrees on either side of the Equator, depending on the season of the year (solar angle) and the Moon's position.

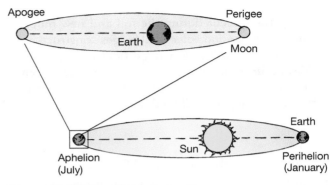

Figure 16 Effects of elliptical orbits.

Top: The Moon moves from its most distant point (*apogee*) to its closest point to Earth (*perigee*), which causes greater tidal ranges every $27\frac{1}{2}$ days. *Bottom:* The Earth also moves from its most distant point (*aphelion*) to its closest point (*perihelion*), which causes greater tidal ranges every year in January. Diagram is not to scale.

Effects of Elliptical Orbits

Earth revolves around the Sun in an elliptical orbit (Figure 16) such that Earth is 148.5 million kilometers (92.2 million miles) from the Sun during the Northern Hemisphere winter and 152.2 million kilometers (94.5 million miles) from the Sun during summer. Thus, the distance between Earth and the Sun varies by 2.5% over the course of a year. Tidal ranges are largest when Earth is near its closest point, called **perihelion** (*peri* = near, *helios* = Sun) and smallest near its most distant point, called **aphelion** (*apo* = away from, *helios* = Sun). Thus, the greatest tidal ranges typically occur in January each year.

The Moon revolves around Earth in an elliptical orbit, too. The Earth–Moon distance varies by 8% [between 375,000 kilometers (233,000 miles) and 405,800 kilometers (252,000 miles)]. Tidal ranges are largest when the Moon is closest to Earth, called **perigee** (*peri* = near, *geo* = Earth), and smallest when most distant, called **apogee** (*apo* =away from, *geo* = Earth) (Figure 16, *top*). The Moon cycles between perigee, apogee, and back to perigee every $27\frac{1}{2}$ days. When spring tides coincide with perigee, the tides—called **proxigean** (*proximus* = nearest, *geo* = Earth) or "closest of the close moon" tides—are especially large, which often result in the flooding of low-lying coastal areas during high tide. If a storm occurs during this time, damage can be extreme. For example, the most damaging winter storm along the U.S. east coast (the Ash Wednesday storm of March 5–8, 1962) occurred during a proxigean tide.

The elliptical orbits of Earth around the Sun and the Moon around Earth change the distances between Earth, the Moon, and the Sun, thus affecting Earth's tides. The net result is that spring tides have greater ranges during the North-

ern Hemisphere winter than in the summer, and spring tides have greater ranges when they coincide with perigee.

? STUDENTS SOMETIMES ASK...
How often are conditions right to produce the maximum tide-generating force?

Maximum tides occur when Earth is closest to the Sun (at perihelion), the Moon is closest to Earth (at perigee), and the Earth–Moon–Sun system is aligned (at syzygy) with both the Sun and Moon at zero declination. This rare condition—which creates an absolute *maximum* spring tidal range—occurs once every 1600 years. Fortunately, the next occurrence is predicted for the year 3300.

However, there are other times when conditions produce large tide-generating forces. During early 1983, for example, large, slow-moving low-pressure cells developed in the North Pacific Ocean that caused strong northwest winds. In late January, the winds produced a near fully developed 3-meter (10-foot) swell that affected the west coast from Oregon to Baja California. The large waves would have been trouble enough under normal conditions, but there were also unusually high spring tides of 2.25 meters (7.4 feet) because Earth was near perihelion at the same time that the Moon was at perigee. In addition, a strong El Niño had raised sea level by as much as 20 centimeters (8 inches). When the waves hit the coast during these unusual conditions, they caused over $100 million in damages, including the destruction of 25 homes, damage to 3500 others, the collapse of several commercial and municipal piers, and at least a dozen deaths.

Prediction of Equilibrium Tides

In the equilibrium tide model, the declination of the Moon determines the position of the tidal bulges. The example illustrated in Figure 17 shows that the Moon is di-

rectly overhead at 28 degrees north latitude when its declination is 28 degrees north of the Equator. If you stand at
this latitude when the Moon is directly overhead, it will
be high tide (Figure 17a). Low tide occurs six lunar hours
later (6 hours 12$\frac{1}{2}$ minutes solar time) (Figure 17b). Another high tide, but one much lower than the first, occurs
six lunar hours later (Figure 17c). Another low tide occurs six lunar hours later (Figure 17d). Six lunar hours
later, at the end of a 24-lunar-hour period (24 hours 50
minutes solar time), you will have passed through a
complete lunar-day cycle of two high tides and two low
tides.

The graphs in Figure 17e show the heights of the tides
observed during the same lunar day at 28 degrees north
latitude, the Equator, and 28 degrees south latitude when
the declination of the Moon is 28 degrees north of the
Equator. Tide curves for 28 degrees north and 28 degrees
south latitude have identically timed highs and lows, but
the *higher* high tides and *lower* low tides occur 12 hours
later. The reason that they occur out of phase by 12 hours

is because the bulges in the two hemispheres are on opposite sides of Earth in relation to the Moon. Table 1 summarizes the characteristics of equilibrium tides on the
idealized Earth.

STUDENTS SOMETIMES ASK...
What are tropical tides?

Differences between successive high tides and successive low
tides occur each lunar day (see, for example, Figure 17e). Because these differences occur within a period of one day, they
are called diurnal (daily) inequalities. These inequalities are at
their greatest when the Moon is at its maximum declination,
and such tides are called *tropical tides* because the Moon is
over one of Earth's tropics. When the Moon is over the Equator (*equatorial tides*), the difference between successive high
tides and low tides is minimal.

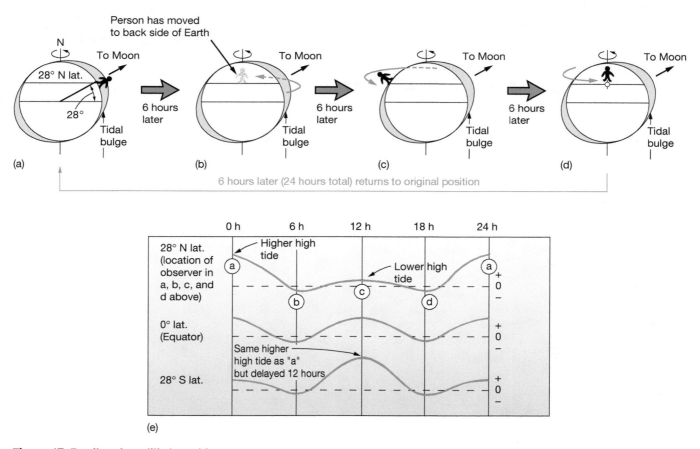

(e)

Figure 17 Predicted equilibrium tides.

(a)–(d) Sequence showing the tide experienced every 6 lunar hours at 28 degrees north latitude when
the declination of the Moon is 28 degrees north. **(e)** Tide curves for 28 degrees north, 0 degrees, and
28 degrees south latitudes during the lunar day shown in the sequence above. The tide curves for 28
degrees north and 28 degrees south latitude show that the higher high tides occur 12 hours later.

TABLE 1 **Summary of characteristics of equilibrium tides on the idealized Earth.**

- Any location (except the poles) will have two high tides and two low tides per lunar day.
- Neither the two high tides nor the two low tides are of the same height because of the declination of the Moon and the Sun (except for the rare occasions when the Moon and Sun are simultaneously above the Equator).
- Monthly and yearly cycles of tidal range are related to the changing distances of the Moon and Sun from Earth.
- Each week, there would be alternating spring and neap tides. Thus, in a lunar month, there are two spring tides and two neap tides.

Dynamic Theory of Tides

The equilibrium tide theory uses the model of tidal bulges to explain the tides. Tides in the ocean, however, behave in much more complex ways than predicted by this simplistic model. The **dynamic tide theory** takes into account the factors ignored by the equilibrium tide theory and does a better job of approximating real ocean tides.

For example, if equilibrium tidal bulges are truly wave crests separated by a distance of one-half Earth's circumference—about 20,000 kilometers (12,420 miles)—one would expect the bulges to move across Earth at about 1600 kilometers (1000 miles) per hour. Tides, however, are an extreme example of shallow-water waves, so their speed is proportional to the water depth. For a tide wave to travel at 1600 kilometers (1000 miles) per hour, the ocean would have to be 22 kilometers (13.7 miles) deep! Instead, the average depth of the ocean is only 3.7 kilometers (2.3 miles), so tidal bulges move as *forced waves*, with their speed determined by ocean depth.

Based on the average ocean depth, the average speed at which tide waves can travel across the open ocean is only about 700 kilometers (435 miles) per hour. Thus, the idealized bulges that are oriented toward and away from a tide-generating body cannot exist because they cannot keep up with the rotational speed of Earth. Instead, ocean tides break up into distinct units called *cells*.

Amphidromic Points and Cotidal Lines

In the open ocean, the crests and troughs of the tide wave rotate around an **amphidromic** (*amphi* = around, *dromus* = running) **point** near the center of each cell. There is essentially no tidal range here, but radiating from this point are **cotidal** (*co* = with, *tidal* = tide) **lines**, which connect points where high tide occurs simultaneously. The labels on the cotidal lines in Figure 18 indicate the time of high tide in hours after the Moon crosses the Greenwich Meridian.

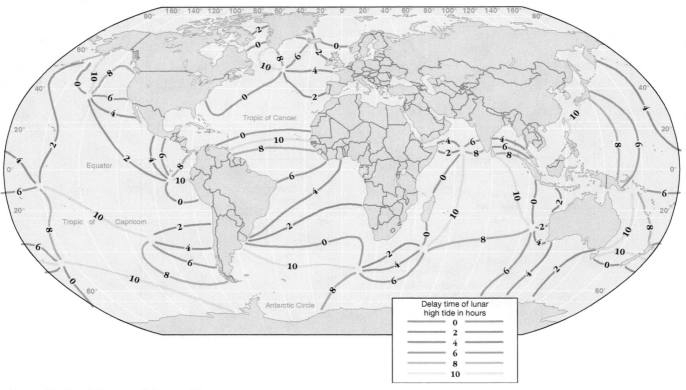

Figure 18 Cotidal map of the world.

Cotidal lines indicate times of the main lunar daily high tide in lunar hours after the Moon has crossed the Greenwich Meridian (0 degrees longitude). Tidal ranges generally increase with increasing distance along cotidal lines away from the amphidromic points. Where cotidal lines terminate at both ends in amphidromic points, maximum tidal range will be near the midpoints of the lines.

After von Arx, W. S., 1962; original by H. Poincaré 1910, Leçons de Mécanique Céleste, a Gauther-Crofts, Vol. 3

The times in Figure 18 indicate that the tide wave rotates counterclockwise in the Northern Hemisphere and clockwise in the Southern Hemisphere. The wave must complete one rotation during the tidal period (usually 12 lunar hours), so this limits the size of the cells.

Low tide occurs six hours after high tide in an amphidromic cell. If high tide is occurring along the cotidal line labeled "10," for example, then low tide is occurring along the cotidal line labeled "4."

Effect of the Continents

The continents affect tides, too, because they interrupt the free movement of the tidal bulges across the ocean surface. The ocean basins between continents have free standing waves set up within them. The positions and shapes of the continents modify the forced astronomical tide waves that develop within an ocean basin.

Other Considerations

Over 150 different factors affect the tides at a particular coast, which are far more than can be adequately addressed here. One of the results of these factors, however, is that high tide rarely occurs when the Moon is at its highest point in the sky. Instead, the time between the Moon crossing the meridian and a corresponding high tide varies from place to place.

Because of the complexity of the tides, a completely mathematical model of the tides is beyond the limits of marine science. Instead, a combination of mathematical analysis and observation is required to adequately model the tides.

Just as the sea is composed of multiple wave systems, the tides are also composed of multiple tide waves called **partial tides**. A mathematical approach useful in studying tides is called *harmonic analysis*, which takes into account the numerous tide-generating variables that possess a periodicity (cyclic pattern). Moreover, the actual tide observed at any given location is the combined effect of all the partial tides at that point.

Remarkably, a reasonably accurate model of actual tides can be computed considering only the seven major partial tides that affect a coastal area (Figure 19a). Combining the periods of each of the partial tides with the amplitudes and phases that can be obtained from observation results in a relatively accurate prediction of the tides (Figure 19b). To make the predictions as accurate as possible, the observations must be made throughout a period of at least 18.6 years, which is the period of the precession of the plane of the Moon's orbit through the ecliptic.

Tidal Patterns

In theory, most areas on Earth should experience two high tides and two low tides of unequal heights during a lunar day. In practice, however, the various depths, sizes, and shapes of ocean basins modify tides so they exhibit three different patterns in different parts of the world. The three tidal patterns, which are illustrated in Figure 20, are *diurn-*

al (*diurnal* = daily), *semidiurnal* (*semi* = twice, *diurnal* = daily), and *mixed*.[10]

A **diurnal tidal pattern** has a single high and low tide each lunar day. These tides are common in shallow inland seas such as the Gulf of Mexico and along the coast of Southeast Asia. Diurnal tides have a tidal period of 24 hours 50 minutes.

---

[10]Sometimes a *mixed* tidal pattern is referred to as *mixed semidiurnal*.

	Symbol	Period in solar hours	Amplitude $M_2 = 100$	Description
Semidiurnal tides	M_2	12.42	100.00	Main lunar (semidiurnal) constituent
	S_2	12.00	46.6	Main solar (semidiurnal) constituent
	N	12.66	19.1	Lunar constituent due to monthly variation in moon's distance
	K_2	11.97	12.7	Soli-lunar constituent due to changes in declination of sun and moon throughout their orbital cycle
Diurnal tides	K_1	23.93	58.4	Soli-lunar constituent
	O	25.82	41.5	Main lunar (diurnal) constituent
	P	24.07	19.3	Main solar (diurnal) constituent

(a) The seven most important partial tides

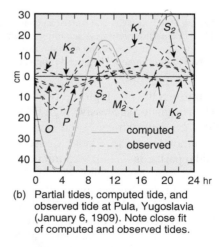

(b) Partial tides, computed tide, and observed tide at Pula, Yugoslavia (January 6, 1909). Note close fit of computed and observed tides.

Figure 19 Partial tides.

(a) Table showing the seven most important partial tides and their characteristics. (b) Tidal curves for January 6, 1909 at Pula, Yugoslavia, showing the partial tides described in part *a* along with the computed (*solid red line*) and observed tides (*dashed red line*). Note the close match of the two red lines.

From Defant, A., *Ebb and flow*. The University of Michigan Press, Ann Arbor, 1958

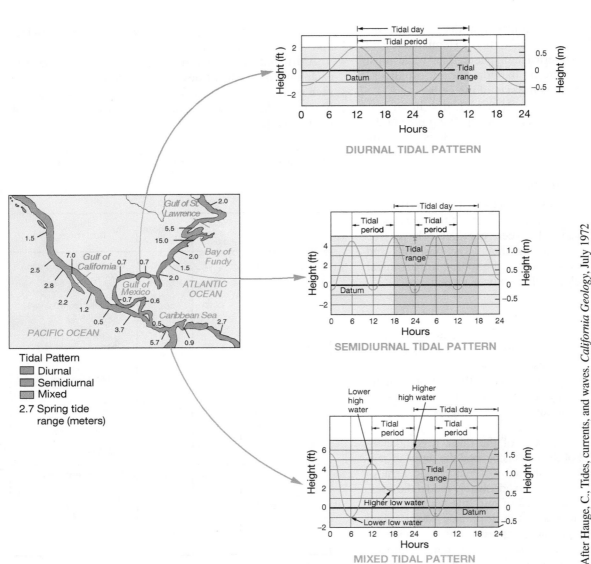

Figure 20 Tidal patterns.

Tidal patterns experienced along North and Central American coasts. A diurnal tidal pattern (*top graph*) shows one high and low tide each lunar day. A semidiurnal pattern (*middle graph*) shows two highs and lows of approximately equal heights during each lunar day. A mixed tidal pattern (*bottom graph*) shows two highs and two lows of unequal heights during each lunar day.

After Hauge, C., Tides, currents, and waves. *California Geology*, July 1972

A **semidiurnal tidal pattern** has two high and two low tides each lunar day. The heights of successive high tides and successive low tides are approximately the same.[11] Semidiurnal tides are common along the Atlantic Coast of the United States. The tidal period is 12 hours 25 minutes.

A **mixed tidal pattern** may have characteristics of both diurnal and semidiurnal tides. Successive high tides and/or low tides will have significantly different heights, called *diurnal inequalities*. Mixed tides commonly have a tidal period of 12 hours 25 minutes, but they may also have diurnal periods. Mixed tides are the most common type in the world, including along the Pacific Coast of North America.

---

[11]Since tides are always growing higher or lower at any location due to the spring-neap tide sequence, successive high tides and successive low tides can never be *exactly* the same at any location.

STUDENTS SOMETIMES ASK ...

Figure 20 shows negative tides. How can there ever be a negative tide?

Negative tides occur because the *datum* (starting point or reference point from which tides are measured) is an average of the tides over many years. Along the west coast of the United States, for instance, the datum is Mean Lower Low Water (MLLW), which is the average of the *lower* of the two low tides that occur daily in a mixed tidal pattern. Because the datum is an average, there will be some days when the tide is less than the average (similar to the distribution of exam scores, some of which will be below the average). These lower-than-average tides are given negative values, occur only during spring tides, and are often the best times to visit local tide pool areas.

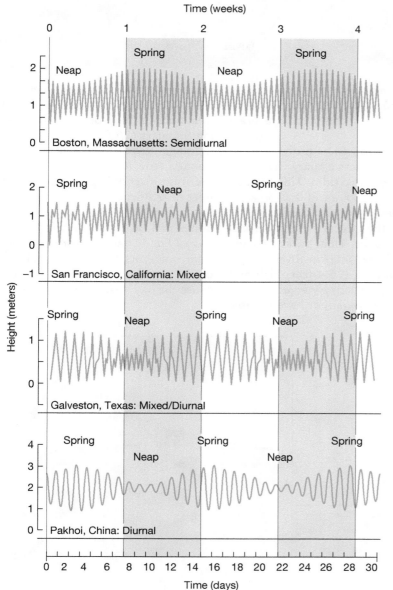

Time (weeks)

Time (days)

Height (meters)

Figure 21 Monthly tidal curves.

Top: Boston, Massachusetts, showing semidiurnal tidal pattern. *Upper middle*: San Francisco, California, showing mixed tidal pattern. *Lower middle*: Galveston, Texas, showing mixed tidal pattern with strong diurnal tendencies. *Bottom*: Pakhoi, China, showing diurnal tidal pattern.

Figure 21 shows examples of monthly tidal curves for various coastal locations. Even though a tide at any particular location follows a single tidal pattern, it still may pass through stages of one or both of the other tidal patterns. Typically, however, the tidal pattern for a location remains the same throughout the year. Also, the tidal curves in Figure 21 clearly show the weekly switching of the spring tide–neap tide cycle.

A diurnal tidal pattern exhibits one high and low tide each lunar day; a semidiurnal tidal pattern exhibits two high and low tides daily of about the same height; a mixed tidal pattern usually has two high and low tides daily of different heights but may also exhibit diurnal qualities.

Tidal Phenomena

Remember that the tides are fundamentally a wave. When tide waves enter coastal waters, they are subject to reflection and amplification similar to what wind-generated waves experience. In certain locations, reflected wave energy causes water to slosh around in a bay, producing *standing waves*. As a result, interesting tidal phenomena are sometimes experienced in coastal waters.

Large lakes and coastal rivers experience tidal phenomena, too. In some low-lying rivers, for instance, a *tidal bore* is produced by an incoming high tide (Box 1). Further, the tides profoundly affect the behavior of certain marine organisms (Box 2).

BOX 1   People and Ocean Environment

TIDAL BORES: BORING WAVES THESE ARE NOT!

A tidal bore (*bore*=crest or wave) is a wall of water that moves up certain low-lying rivers due to an incoming tide. Because it is a wave created by the tides, it is a *true* tidal wave. When an incoming tide rushes up a river, it develops a steep forward slope because the flow of the river resists the advance of the tide. This creates a tidal bore, which may reach heights of 5 meters (16.4 feet) or more and move at speeds up to 22 kilometers (14 miles) per hour.

Tidal bores develop where there is a large tidal range and a low-lying coastal river. Although tidal bores do not attain the size of some waves in the surf zone, tidal bores have been successfully surfed. They can give a surfer a very long ride because the bore travels many kilometers upriver. If you miss the bore, though, you have to wait about half a day before the next one comes along because the incoming high tide occurs only twice a day. In some locations, tidal bore rafting is promoted as a draw for tourists.

The Amazon River probably possesses the longest estuary that is affected by oceanic tides. Tides can be measured as far as 800 kilometers (500 miles) from the river's mouth, although the effects are quite small at this distance. Tidal bores near the mouth of the Amazon River can be up to 5 meters (16.4 feet) high and are locally called *pororocas* (waterfalls). Other rivers that have notable tidal bores include the Chientang River in China [which has the largest tidal bores in the world, often reaching 8 meters (26 feet) high]; the Petitcodiac River in New Brunswick, Canada; the River Seine in France; the Trent River in England; and Cook Inlet near Anchorage, Alaska (where the largest tidal bore in the United States can be found). Although the Bay of Fundy has the world's largest tidal range, its tidal bore rarely exceeds 1 meter (3.3 feet), mostly because the bay is so wide.

Photo courtesy of New Brunswick Department of Tourism

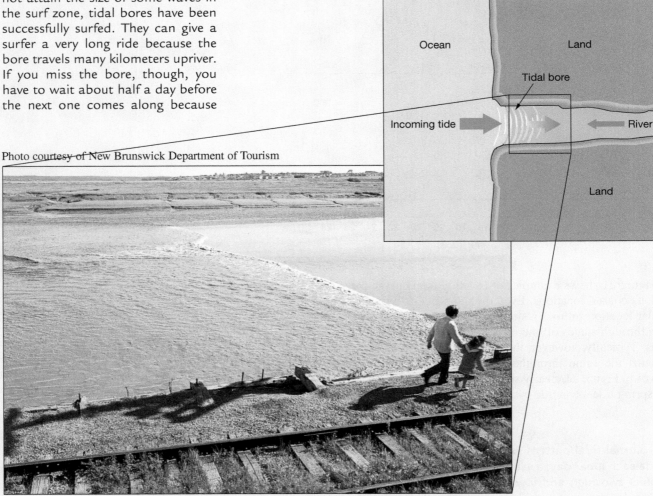

A tidal bore moving quickly upriver in Chignecto Bay, New Brunswick, Canada.

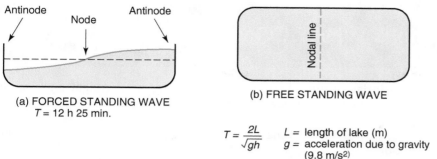

(a) FORCED STANDING WAVE
T = 12 h 25 min.

(b) FREE STANDING WAVE

$$T = \frac{2L}{\sqrt{gh}}$$

L = length of lake (m)
g = acceleration due to gravity (9.8 m/s²)
h = depth of lake (m)

Figure 22 Tides in lakes.

(a) A forced standing wave generated by tide-generating forces, which has a period of 12 hours 25 minutes. (b) A single nodal free standing wave (*seiche*), which has a period determined by the size and shape of the basin of the lake (*equations below figure*). If the period of the seiche is approximately equal to (or a multiple of) the forced tide-generated wave, resonance occurs, producing greater displacements at the antinodes.

Tides in Lakes

Although most lake basins are too small to have noticeable tidal effects, tides may be significant in large lakes especially when the long axis of the basin extends in an east-west direction. In any such basin, very small standing waves may be generated with a period equal to that of the tide-generating force, producing a *forced standing wave* (Figure 22a).

Of much greater importance is the *free standing wave* (Figure 22b) that is initiated by strong winds at the surface (or, less commonly, by a seismic disturbance). The period of a free standing wave is determined by the length and depth of the basin, and is termed the *characteristic period* for the basin. If the characteristic period of the free wave is very near that (or a multiple) of the period of a forced wave resulting from tide-generating forces, the oscillations may reinforce one another and produce a *resonance tide*. Lake Ontario, for example, displays such tides.

Free standing waves of the type described above were first noticed in Lake Geneva in Switzerland and are called **seiches**[12] (*seiche* = exposed lake bottom) because of the way the sloshing water exposed parts of the lake bottom. For seiches that have a single nodal line, the formula for the period in Figure 22b gives a close approximation of the period that actually develops. For rectangular basins with two and three nodal lines, the periods would be approximately one-half and one-third those of a single nodal seiche, respectively.

Tides in Narrow Basins Connected to the Ocean

Even under conditions of resonance between free and forced oscillations in lakes, the tides still do not get very large (they only rarely exceed a few centimeters). However, in similarly sized seas, bays, and gulfs that are relatively narrow but open at one end to the ocean, the tides may become much larger. What causes this difference?

To help answer this question, consider a rectangular narrow bay with one end open to the ocean (Figure 23). Although one end of the basin is open, the bay still develops free standing waves that are reflected from the open end around the basin. At the open end of the bay, the water must

always be at the same level as the ocean at that location. Therefore, the tidal range is of greater magnitude than it is in closed basins. If the free standing wave (which is caused by wave energy reflected from the closed end of the basin) is in resonance with the forced wave produced by tidal forces, the energy of these two waves produces a standing wave with increased amplitude within the basin.

An Example of Tidal Extremes: The Bay of Fundy

As we have seen, standing waves that have a period near that of the forced tide wave result in constructive interference that produces significant increases in tidal range. Nova Scotia's **Bay of Fundy** is one such place where this occurs, and it is here that the largest tidal range in the world is found. With a length of 258 kilometers (160 miles), the Bay of Fundy has a wide opening into the Atlantic Ocean. At its northern end, however, it splits into two narrow basins, Chignecto Bay and Minas Basin (Figure 24). The

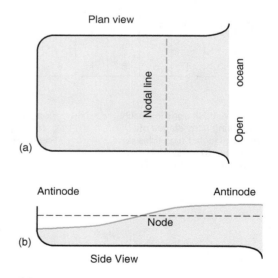

Figure 23 Tides in narrow seas, bays, and gulfs.

Top view (a) and side view (b) of a narrow body of water such as a sea, bay, or gulf. In these bodies, forced standing waves have a greater height than those that develop in lakes because the height of the tide at the open end of the basin must be the same as the open ocean. Therefore, the development of a resonant condition between the free and forced standing waves in such basins produce much greater displacements at the antinodes.

[12]Seiche is pronounced "*saysh*."

BOX 2   Research Methods in Oceanography

GRUNIONS: DOING WHAT COMES NATURALLY ON THE BEACH

From March through September, shortly after the maximum spring tide has occurred, the grunion (*Leuresthes tenuis*) come ashore along the beaches of southern California and Baja California to bury their fertilized eggs in the sand. Grunion—slender, silvery, and 12 to 15 centimeters (4.7 to 6 inches) long—are the only marine fish in the world that come completely out of water to spawn. The name **grunion** comes from the Spanish *gruñón*, which means "grunter" and refers to the faint noise they make during spawning.

A mixed tidal pattern occurs along southern California and Baja California beaches. On most lunar days (24 hours and 50 minutes), there are two high and two low tides. There is usually a significant difference in the heights of the two high tides that

occur each day. During the summer months, the higher high tide occurs at night. The night high tide becomes higher each night as the maximum spring-tide range is approached, causing sand to be eroded from the beach. After the maximum spring tide has occurred, the night high tide diminishes each night. As neap tide is approached, sand is deposited on the beach.

Grunion spawn only after each night's higher high tide has peaked on the three or four nights following the night of the highest spring high tide. This assures that their eggs will be covered deeply in sand deposited by the receding higher high tides each succeeding night. The fertilized eggs buried in the sand are ready to hatch nine days after spawning. By this time, another spring tide is ap-

proaching, so the night high tide is getting progressively higher each night again. The beach sand is eroding again, too, which exposes the eggs to the waves that break ever higher on the beach. The eggs hatch about three minutes after being freed in the water. Tests done in laboratories have shown that the grunion eggs will not hatch until agitated in a manner that simulates that of the eroding waves.

The spawning begins as the grunion come ashore immediately following an appropriate high tide, and it may last from one to three hours. Spawning usually peaks about an hour after it starts and may last an additional 30 minutes to an hour. Thousands of fish may be on the beach at this time. During a run, the females, which are larger than the males, move high on the

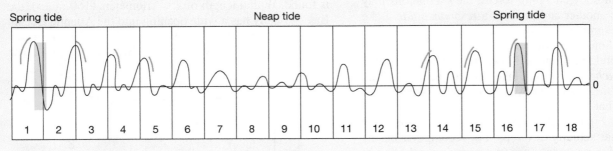

Spring tide   Neap tide   Spring tide

Days

⋀ Grunion deposit eggs in beach sand during early stages of the ebb of higher high tides on the three or four days following maximum spring tidal range.

⋀ Flood tides erode sand and free grunion eggs during higher high tide as maximum spring tidal range is approached.

▮ Maximum spring tidal range

The tidal cycle and spawning grunion.

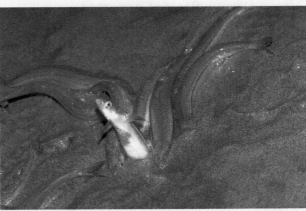

Photo by Eda Rogers

beach. If no males are near, a female may return to the water without depositing her eggs. In the presence of males, she drills her tail into the semifluid sand until only her head is visible. The female continues to twist, depositing her eggs 5 to 7 centimeters (2 to 3 inches) below the surface.

The male curls around the female's body and deposits his milt against it. The milt runs down the body of the female to fertilize the eggs. When the spawning is completed, both fish return to the water with the next wave.

Larger females are capable of producing up to 3000 eggs for each series of spawning runs, which are separated by the two-week period between spring tides. As soon as the eggs are deposited, another group of eggs begins to form within the female. They will be deposited during the next spring tide run. Early in the season, only older fish spawn. By May, however, even the one-year-old females are in spawning condition.

Young grunion grow rapidly and are about 12 centimeters (5 inches) long when they are a year old and ready for their first spawning. They usually live two or three years, but four-year-olds have been recovered. The age of a grunion can be determined by the scales. After growing rapidly during the first year, they grow very slowly thereafter. There is no growth at all during the 6-month spawning season, which causes marks to form on each scale that can be used to identify the grunion's age.

It is not known how grunion are able to time their spawning behavior so precisely with the tides. Some investigators believe the grunion are able to sense very small changes in the hydrostatic pressure caused by the changing level of the water associated with rising and falling sea level due to the tides. Certainly, a very dependable detection mechanism keeps the grunion accurately informed of the tidal conditions, because their survival depends on a spawning behavior precisely tuned to tidal motions.

The Bay of Fundy, site of the world's largest tidal range.

Even though the maximum spring tidal range at the mouth of the Bay of Fundy is only 2 meters (6.6 feet), amplification of tidal energy causes a maximum tidal range at the northern end of Minas Basin of 17 meters (56 feet), often stranding ships (*insets*).

Photos courtesy of Nova Scotia Department of Tourism

period of free oscillation in the bay—the oscillation that occurs when a body is displaced and then released—is very nearly that of the tidal period. The resulting constructive interference—along with the narrowing and shoaling of the bay to the north—causes a buildup of tidal energy in the northern end of the bay. In addition, the bay curves to the right, so the Coriolis effect in the Northern Hemisphere adds to the extreme tidal range.

During maximum spring tide conditions, the tidal range at the mouth of the bay (where it opens to the ocean) is only about 2 meters (6.6 feet). However, the tidal range increases progressively from the mouth of the bay northward. In the northern end of Minas Basin, the maximum spring tidal range is 17 meters (56 feet), which leaves boats high and dry during low tide (Figure 24, *insets*).

> The world's largest tides occur in the upper end of the Bay of Fundy, where reflection and amplification produce a maximum spring tidal range of 17 meters (56 feet).

Coastal Tidal Currents

The current that accompanies the slowly turning tide crest in a Northern Hemisphere basin rotates counterclockwise, producing a **rotary current** in the open portion of the basin. Friction increases in nearshore shoaling waters, so the rotary current changes to an alternating or **reversing current** that moves into and out of restricted passages along a coast.

The velocity of rotary currents in the open ocean is usually well below 1 kilometer (0.6 mile) per hour. Reversing currents, however, can reach velocities up to 44 kilometers (28 miles) per hour in restricted channels such as between islands of coastal waters.

Reversing currents also exist in the mouths of bays (and some rivers) due to the daily flow of tides. Figure 25 shows that a **flood current** is produced when water rushes into a bay (or river) with an incoming high tide. Conversely, an **ebb current** is produced when water drains out of a bay (or river) because a low tide is approaching. No currents occur for several minutes during either **high slack water** (which occurs at the peak of each high tide) or during **low slack water** (at the peak of each low tide).

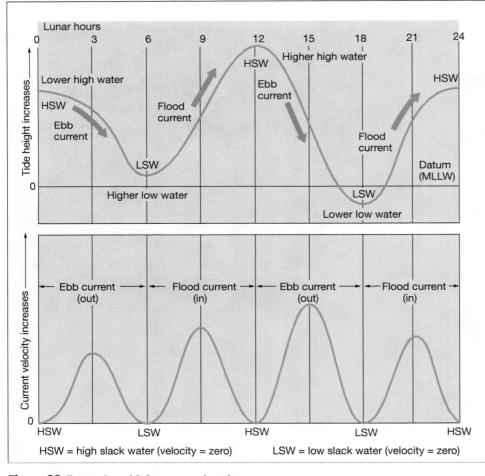

Figure 25 Reversing tidal currents in a bay.

Top: Tidal curve for a bay, showing ebb currents are created by an outgoing low tide and flood currents are created by an incoming high tide. No currents occur during either high slack water (*HSW*) or low slack water (*LSW*). The datum of MLLW means mean lower low water, which is the average of the lower of the two low tides that occur daily in a mixed tidal pattern. *Bottom*: Corresponding chart showing velocity of ebb and flood currents.

Reversing currents in bays can sometimes reach speeds of 40 kilometers (25 miles) per hour, creating a navigation hazard for ships. On the other hand, the daily flow of these currents often keeps sediment from closing off the bay and resupplies the bay with new seawater and ocean nutrients.

Tidal currents can be significant even in deep ocean waters. For example, tidal currents were encountered shortly after the discovery of the remains of the *Titanic* at a depth of 3795 meters (12,448 feet) on the continental slope south of Newfoundland's Grand Banks in 1985.

These tidal currents were so strong that they forced researchers to abandon the use of the camera-equipped tethered remotely operated vehicle, *Jason Jr.*

Rotary tidal currents occur in the deep ocean while reversing tidal currents occur close to shore—most notably in bays and rivers—due to the change in the tides.

Chapter in Review

- *Gravitational attraction of the Moon and Sun create Earth's tides*, which are fundamentally long-wavelength waves. According to the simplified *equilibrium theory of tides*, which assumes an ocean of uniform depth and ignores the effects of friction, small horizontal forces (the tide-generating forces, which vary as the cube of distance) tend to push water into *two bulges on opposite sides of Earth*. One bulge is directly facing the tide-generating body (the Moon and the Sun), and the other is directly opposite.

- Despite its vastly smaller size, *the Moon has about twice the tide-generating effect of the Sun* because the Moon is so much closer to Earth. The tidal bulges due to the Moon's gravity (the lunar bulges) dominate, so lunar motions dominate the periods of Earth's tides. However, the changing position of the solar bulges relative to the lunar bulges modifies tides. According to the simplified equilibrium tide theory, *Earth's rotation carries locations on Earth into and out of the various tidal bulges*.

- For most places on Earth, *the time between successive high tides would be 12 hours 25 minutes (half a lunar day). The $29\frac{1}{2}$-day monthly tidal cycle* would consist of tides with maximum tidal range (spring tides) and minimum tidal range (neap tides). *Spring tides would occur each new moon and full moon, and neap tides would occur each first- and third-quarter phases of the Moon.*

- The *declination of the Moon* varies between 28.5 degrees north or south of the Equator during the lunar month, and the *declination of the Sun* varies between 23.5 degrees north or south of the Equator during the year, so *the location of tidal bulges usually creates two high tides and two low tides of unequal height per lunar day*. Tidal ranges are greatest when Earth is nearest the Sun and Moon.

- *Friction and the true shape of ocean basins are considered in the dynamic theory of tides*, which is more complex but does a better job of approximating real ocean tides. Moreover, the two bulges on opposite sides of Earth cannot exist because they cannot keep up with the rotational speed of Earth. Instead, the bulges are broken up into *several tidal cells that rotate around an amphidromic point*—a point of zero tidal range. Rotation is counterclockwise in the Northern Hemisphere and clockwise in the Southern Hemisphere. *Many other factors influence tides on Earth*, too, such as the placement of the continents and the shapes of the coasts. The seven major partial tides approximate real tidal conditions.

- The *three types of tidal patterns* observed on Earth are *diurnal* (a single high and low tide each lunar day), *semidiurnal* (two high and two low tides each lunar day), and *mixed* (characteristics of both). Mixed tidal patterns usually consist of semidiurnal periods with significant diurnal inequality. Mixed tidal patterns are the most common type in the world.

- *Tidal phenomena include tides in lakes and coastal water bodies*, both of which are influenced by basin size and water depth. All basins have a characteristic *free standing wave*, or *seiche*. It is usually not very large for small basins, but if it is in phase with the *forced standing wave created by tide-generating bodies*, its height can be significant.

- The effects of constructive interference and the shoaling and narrowing of coastal bays creates the *largest tidal range in the world—17 meters (56 feet)—at the northern end of Nova Scotia's Bay of Fundy*. Tidal currents follow a *rotary pattern* in open-ocean basins but are converted to *reversing currents* along continental margins. The maximum velocity of reversing currents occurs during flood and ebb currents when the water is halfway between high and low slack waters. *Tidal bores are true tidal waves* (a wave produced by the tides) that occur in certain rivers and bays due to an incoming high tide.

- *The tides are important to many marine organisms.* For instance, *grunion*—small silvery fish that inhabit waters along the west coast of North America—time their spawning cycle to match the pattern of the tides.

Key Terms

Amphidromic point
Aphelion
Apogee
Barycenter
Bay of Fundy
Centripetal force
Cotidal line
Declination
Diurnal tidal pattern
Dynamic tide theory
Ebb current
Ebb tide
Ecliptic
Equilibrium tide theory

Flood current
Flood tide
Full moon
Gravitational force
Grunion (*Leuresthes tenuis*)

High slack water
Low slack water
Lunar bulge
Lunar day
Mixed tidal pattern
Neap tide
New moon
Newton, Isaac

Partial tide
Perigee
Perihelion
Precession
Proxigean
Quadrature
Quarter moon
Resultant force
Reversing current
Rotary current
Seiche
Semidiurnal tidal pattern
Solar bulge
Solar day

Spring tide
Syzygy
Tidal bore
Tidal period
Tidal range
Tide-generating force
Tides
Waning crescent
Waning gibbous
Waxing crescent
Waxing gibbous

Questions and Exercises

1. Explain why the Sun's influence on Earth's tides is only 46% that of the Moon's, even though the Sun is so much more massive than the Moon.

2. Why is a lunar day 24 hours 50 minutes long, while a solar day is 24 hours long?

3. Which is more technically correct: The tide comes in and goes out; or Earth rotates into and out of the tidal bulges? Why?

4. From memory, draw the positions of the Earth–Moon–Sun system during a complete monthly tidal cycle. Indicate the tide conditions experienced on Earth, the phases of the Moon, the time between those phases, and syzygy and quadrature.

5. Explain why the maximum tidal range (spring tide) occurs during new and full moon phases and the minimum tidal range (neap tide) at first-quarter and third-quarter moons.

6. If Earth did not have the Moon orbiting it, would there still be tides? Why or why not?

7. Assume that there are two moons in orbit around Earth that are on the same orbital plane but always on opposite sides of Earth and that each moon is the same size and mass of our Moon. How would this affect the tidal range during spring and neap tide conditions?

8. What is declination? Discuss the degree of declination of the Moon and Sun relative to Earth's Equator. What are the effects of declination of the Moon and Sun on the tides?

9. Diagram the Earth–Moon system's orbit about the Sun. Label the positions on the orbit at which the Moon and Sun are clos-

est to and farthest from Earth, stating the terms used to identify them. Discuss the effects of the Moon's and Earth's positions on Earth's tides.

10. Are tides considered deep-water waves anywhere in the ocean? Why or why not?

11. Describe the number of high and low tides in a lunar day, the period, and any inequality of the following tidal patterns: diurnal, semidiurnal, and mixed.

12. What forces produce forced and free standing waves in lakes and narrow ocean embayments?

13. Discuss factors that help produce the world's greatest tidal range in the Bay of Fundy.

14. Discuss the difference between rotary and reversing tidal currents.

15. Of flood current, ebb current, high slack water, and low slack water, when is the best time to enter a bay by boat? When is the best time to navigate in a shallow, rocky harbor? Explain.

16. Describe the spawning cycle of grunion, indicating the relationship between tidal phenomena, where grunion lay their eggs, and the movement of sand on the beach.

17. Observe the Moon from a reference location every night at about the same time for two weeks. Keep track of your observations about the shape (phase) of the Moon and its position in the sky. Then compare these to the reported tides in your area. How do the two compare?

Marine Sediments

From Chapter 5 of *Introduction to Oceanography*, Tenth Edition, Harold V. Thurman, Alan P. Trujillo.

Marine Sediments

Courtesy of Alfred Wegener Institute

Arranged diatoms. The objects in this photomicrograph are diatoms, which are microscopic sea creatures that exist in incredible abundance in the ocean. This image was made by carefully arranging various diatoms under a microscope.

Key Questions

- How are marine sediments collected?
- What do marine sediments indicate about past environmental conditions on Earth?
- How are the four main types of marine sediment formed?
- Where can each of the four main types of marine sediment be found?
- Which types of marine sediment comprise coastal and deep-sea deposits?

The answers to these questions (and much more) can be found in the highlighted concept statements within this chapter.

"When I think of the floor of the deep sea, the single, overwhelming fact that possesses my imagination is the accumulation of sediments. I see always the steady, unremitting, downward drift of materials from above, flake upon flake, layer upon layer. . . . For the sediments are the materials of the most stupendous snowfall the Earth has ever seen."

—Rachel Carson, *The Sea Around Us* (1956)

Why are **sediments** (*sedimentum* = settling) interesting to oceanographers? Although ocean sediments are little more than eroded particles and fragments of dirt, dust, and other debris that have settled out of the water and accumulated on the ocean floor (Figure 1), they reveal much about Earth's history. For example, sediments provide clues to past climates, movements of the ocean floor, ocean circulation patterns, and nutrient supplies for marine organisms. By examining **cores** of sediment retrieved from ocean drilling (Figure 2) and interpreting them, oceanographers can ascertain the timing of major extinctions, global climate change, and the movement of plates. In fact, most of what is known of Earth's past geology, climate, and biology has been learned through studying ancient marine sediments.

Over time, sediments can become *lithified* (*lithos* = stone, *fic* = making)—turned to rock—and form *sedimentary rock*. More than half of the rocks exposed on the continents are sedimentary rocks deposited in ancient ocean environments and uplifted onto land by plate tectonic processes. Even in the tallest mountains on the continents, far from any ocean, telltale marine fossils indicate that these rocks originated on the ocean floor in the geologic past.

Particles of sediment come from worn pieces of rocks, as well as living organisms, minerals dissolved in water, and outer space. Table 1 show a classification of marine sediments according to type, composition, sources, and main locations found. Clues to sediment origin are found in its mineral composition and its **texture** (the size and shape of its particles).

> Marine sediments accumulate on the ocean floor and contain a record of recent Earth history including past environmental conditions. Most sediment cores are obtained by rotary drilling.

Lithogenous Sediment

Lithogenous (*lithos* = stone, *generare* = to produce) **sediment** is derived from preexisting rock material. Because most lithogenous sediment comes from the landmasses, it is also called **terrigenous** (*terra* = land, *generare* = to produce) **sediment**. Volcanic islands in the open ocean are also important sources of lithogenous sediment.

Figure 1 Oceanic sediment.

View of the deep-ocean floor from a submersible. Most of the deep-ocean floor is covered with particles of material that have settled out through the water.

BOX 1   Research Methods in Oceanography

COLLECTING THE HISTORICAL RECORD OF THE DEEP-OCEAN FLOOR

During early exploration of the oceans, a bucketlike device called a *dredge* was used to scoop up sediment from the deep-ocean floor for analysis. This technique, however, was limited to gathering samples from the *surface* of the ocean floor. Later, the *gravity corer*—a hollow steel tube with a heavy weight on top—was thrust into the sea floor to collect the first **cores** (cylinders of sediment and rock). Although the gravity corer could sample below the surface, its depth of penetration was limited.

In 1963, the National Science Foundation of the United States funded a program that borrowed drilling technology from the offshore oil industry to obtain long sections of core from deep below the surface of the ocean floor. The program united four leading oceanographic institutions (Scripps Institution of Oceanography in California; Rosenstiel School of Atmospheric and Oceanic Studies at the University of Miami, Florida; Lamont-Doherty Earth Observatory of Columbia University in New York; and the Woods Hole Oceanographic Institution in Massachusetts) to form the *Joint Oceanographic Institutions for Deep Earth Sampling (JOIDES)*. JOIDES was later joined by the oceanography departments of several other leading universities.

The first phase of the **Deep Sea Drilling Project (DSDP)** was initiated in 1968 when the specially designed drill ship *Glomar Challenger* was launched. It had a tall drilling rig resembling a steel tower. Cores could be collected by drilling into the ocean floor in water up to 6000 meters (3.7 miles) deep. From the initial cores collected, scientists confirmed the existence of sea floor spreading by documenting that (1) the age of the ocean floor increased progressively with distance from the mid-ocean ridge; (2) sediment thickness increased progressively with distance from the mid-ocean ridge; and (3) Earth's magnetic field polarity reversals were recorded in ocean floor rocks.

Although the oceanographic research program was initially financed by the U.S. government, it became international in 1975 when West Germany, France, Japan, the United Kingdom, and the Soviet Union also provided financial and scientific support. In 1983, the Deep Sea Drilling Project became the **Ocean Drilling Program (ODP)** with 20 participating countries under the supervision of Texas A&M University and a broader objective of drilling the thick sediment layers near the continental margins.

In 1985, the *Glomar Challenger* was decommissioned and replaced by the drill ship *JOIDES Resolution*. The new ship also has a tall metal drilling rig to conduct **rotary drilling**. The drill pipe is in individual sections of 9.5 meters (31 feet) and sections can be screwed together to make a single string of pipe up to 8200 meters (27,000 feet) long. The drill bit, located at the end of the pipe string, rotates as it is pressed against the ocean bottom and can drill up to 2100 meters (6900 feet) below the sea floor. Like twirling a soda straw into a layer cake, the drilling operation crushes the rock around the outside and retains a cylinder of rock (a core sample) on the inside of the hollow pipe, which can then be raised on board the ship. Cores are retrieved from inside the pipe and analyzed with state-of-the-art laboratory facilities on board the *Resolution*. Worldwide, more than 2000 holes have been drilled into the sea floor using this method, allowing the collection of cores that provide scientists with valuable information about Earth history as recorded in sea floor sediments.

The ODP was replaced in 2003 by the **Integrated Ocean Drilling Program (IODP)**, which is led by the United States and Japan. The program features two new drill ships: one for drilling shallow high-resolution cores, and one with advanced technology that can drill up to 7000 meters (23,000 feet) below the sea floor. The primary objective of the new program is to collect cores that will allow scientists to better understand Earth history and Earth system processes, including

Origin

Lithogenous sediment begins as rocks on continents or islands. Over time, **weathering** agents such as water, temperature extremes, and chemical effects break rocks into smaller pieces, as shown in Figure 3. When rocks are in smaller pieces, they can be more easily **eroded** (picked up) and transported. This eroded material is the basic component of which all lithogenous sediment is composed.

Eroded material from the continents is carried to the oceans by streams, wind, glaciers, and gravity (Figure 4). Each year, streamflow alone carries about 20 billion metric tons (22 billion short tons) of sediment to Earth's continental margins; almost 80% is provided by runoff from Asia.

Figure 5, is a map of the oceans' major sources of river-, wind-, and glacial-borne sediments. The figure shows that the source of stream-transported sediment occurs in regions on land with high rainfall and resulting large runoff. In particular, several major rivers carry large volumes of sediment from the Asian continent. The figure also shows that wind-blown sediment is largely derived from the world's arid regions and that the source of glacial sediment is in high latitude regions associated with large continental ice sheets.

The drill ship *JOIDES Resolution.*

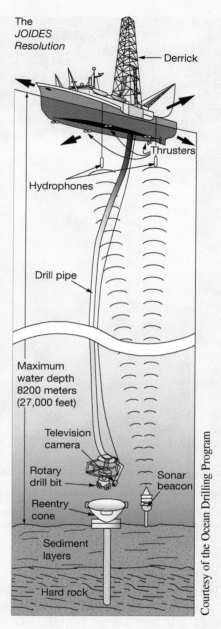

The
*JOIDES
Resolution*

Derrick

Thrusters

Hydrophones

Drill pipe

Maximum
water depth
8200 meters
(27,000 feet)

Television
camera

Rotary
drill bit

Sonar
beacon

Reentry
cone

Sediment
layers

Hard rock

Rotary drilling from the *JOIDES Resolution.*

the properties of the deep crust, climate change patterns, earthquake mechanisms, and the microbiology of the deep ocean floor.

Transported sediment can be deposited in many environments, including bays or lagoons near the ocean, as deltas at the mouths of rivers, along beaches at the shoreline, or further offshore across the continental margin. It can also be carried beyond the continental margin to the deep-ocean basin by turbidity currents.

The greatest quantity of lithogenous material by far is found around the margins of the continents, where it is constantly moved by high-energy currents along the shoreline and in deeper turbidity currents. Lower-energy currents distribute finer components that settle out onto the deep-ocean basins. Microscopic particles from wind-blown dust or volcanic eruptions can even be carried far out over the open ocean by prevailing winds. These particles either settle into fine layers as the velocity of the wind decreases or disperse into the ocean when they serve as nuclei around which raindrops and snowflakes form.

ocean floor and the strong prevailing winds in the desert regions of Africa, Asia, and Australia. Satellite observations of dust storms (Figure 7, *inset*) confirm this relationship.

Sediment Texture

One of the most important properties of lithogenous sediment is its texture, including its **grain[1] size**. The **Wentworth scale of grain size** (Table 2) indicates that particles can be classified as boulders (largest), cobbles, pebbles, granules, sand, silt, or clay (smallest). Grain size is proportional to the energy needed to lay down a deposit.

Figure 8 is a graph showing the relationship between grain size and horizontal current velocities, which results in erosion, transportation, or deposition of sediment (colored fields on the graph).[2] The deposition curve (the line between the tan and blue fields on Figure 8) shows that at high current velocities, only larger particles settle out (the smaller particles are carried along in the current). Thus, deposits laid down where current action is strong (areas of high energy) are composed primarily of larger particles. The deposition curve also shows that small particles can be transported until current velocities are quite low. As a result, fine-grained particles are deposited where the energy level is low and the current speed is minimal.

APT photo; with thanks to Steve Prinz and Warren Smith

Figure 2 Examining deep-ocean sediment cores.
Long cylinders of sediment and rock called cores are cut in half and examined, revealing interesting aspects of Earth history.

Composition

The composition of lithogenous sediment reflects the material from which it was derived. Rocks are composed of discrete crystals of naturally occurring compounds called *minerals*. One of the most abundant, chemically stable, and durable minerals in Earth's crust is **quartz** (SiO_2), which is composed of silicon and oxygen tetrahedran and has the same composition as ordinary glass. Quartz is the major component of nearly all rocks. Because quartz is resistant to abrasion, it can be transported long distances and deposited far from its source area. The majority of lithogenous deposits—such as beach sands—are composed primarily of quartz (Figure 6).

A large percentage of lithogenous particles that find their way into deep-ocean sediments far from continents are transported by prevailing winds that remove small particles from the continents' subtropical desert regions. The map in Figure 7, shows a close relationship between the location of microscopic fragments of lithogenous quartz in the surface sediments of the

---

[1]Sediment grains are also known as particles, fragments, or clasts.

[2]Note that both the horizontal and vertical scales on the graph are logarithmic—meaning that they increase by powers of ten—so the graph is said to have a *log-log scale*.

TABLE 1 **Classification of marine sediments.**

Type	Composition			Sources		Main locations found
Lithogenous	Continental Margin	Rock fragments		Rivers; coastal erosion; landslides		Continental shelf
		Quartz sand		Glaciers		Continental shelf in high latitudes
		Quartz silt		Turbidity currents		Continental slope and rise; ocean basin margins
		Clay				
	Oceanic	Quartz silt		Wind-blown dust; rivers		Deep-ocean basins
		Clay				
		Volcanic ash		Volcanic eruptions		
Biogenous	Calcium carbonate (CaCO₃)	Calcareous ooze (microscopic)		Warm surface water	Coccolithophores (algae); Foraminifers (protozoans)	Low-latitude regions; sea floor above CCD; along mid-ocean ridges & the tops of volcanic peaks
		Shell/coral fragments (macroscopic)			Macroscopic shell-producing organisms	Continental shelf; beaches
					Coral reefs	Shallow low-latitude regions
	Silica (SiO₂·nH₂O)	Siliceous ooze		Cold surface water	Diatoms (algae); Radiolarians (protozoans)	High-latitude regions; sea floor below CCD; surface current divergence near the Equator
Hydrogenous	Manganese nodules (manganese, iron, copper, nickel, cobalt)			Precipitation of dissolved materials directly from seawater due to chemical reactions		Abyssal plain
	Phosphorite (phosphorous)					Continental shelf
	Oolites (CaCO₃)					Shallow shelf in low-latitude regions
	Metal sulfides (iron, nickel, copper, zinc, silver)					Hydrothermal vents at mid-ocean ridges
	Evaporites (gypsum, halite, other salts)					Shallow restricted basins where evaporation is high in low-latitude regions
Cosmogenous	Iron-nickel spherules			Space dust		In very small proportions mixed with all types of sediment and in all marine environments
	Tektites (silica glass)					
	Iron-nickel meteorites			Meteors		Localized near meteor impact structures
	Silicate chondrites					

After Patricia Deen, Palomar College

$\text{Silica} = SiO_2 \cdot nH_2O$

Figure 8 also shows the energy needed to erode various sizes of sediment. The erosion curve (the diffuse line between the blue and purple fields on Figure 8) shows that the velocity required to erode sediment is much higher than for deposition. Generally, the larger the grain size, the higher the velocity is required to erode it. Surprisingly, erosion of finer clay-sized particles requires higher velocities than larger sand-sized particles. This is because clay-sized particles—many of which are flat—tend to stick together by cohesive forces. Consequently, higher-energy conditions than what would be expected based on grain size alone are required to erode and transport clays.

The texture of lithogenous sediment also depends on its **sorting**. Sorting is a measure of the uniformity of

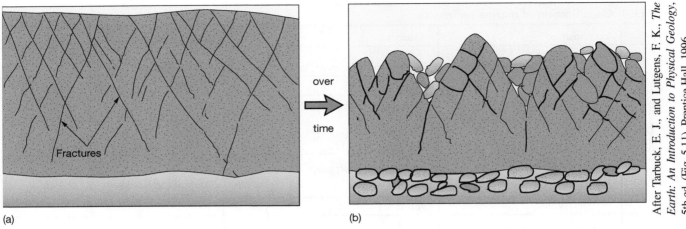

After Tarbuck, E. J., and Lutgens, F. K., *The Earth: An Introduction to Physical Geology,* 5th ed. (Fig. 5.11), Prentice Hall, 1996

(a)   (b)

Figure 3 Weathering.

Weathering often occurs along fractures in rock, breaking the rocks into smaller fragments over time.

grain sizes and indicates the selectivity of the transportation process. For example, sediments composed of particles that are primarily the same size are well sorted—such as in coastal sand dunes, where winds can only pick up a certain size particle. Poorly sorted deposits, on the other hand, contain a variety of different sized particles and indicate a transportation process capable of picking up clay- to boulder-sized particles. An example of poorly sorted sediment is that which is carried by a glacier and left behind when the glacier melts.

The texture of lithogenous sediment also depends on its **maturity**. Sediment maturity increases as (1) clay content decreases; (2) sorting increases; (3) non-quartz minerals decrease; and (4) grains within the deposit become more rounded. Particles increase in maturity as they are carried from the source to their point of deposition because more time is available during transportation to (1) remove clays (which are carried in suspension and washed out to sea); (2) sort the sediment; (3) eliminate non-quartz minerals (which lack durability); and (4) round particles through abrasion.

A poorly sorted glacial deposit, which contains relatively large quantities of clay-sized particles and poorly rounded larger particles, is immature. Well-sorted beach sand, on the other hand, which contains well-rounded particles and very little clay, is a mature sedimentary deposit. Figure 9, illustrates the difference between mature and immature sediments.

Distribution

Marine sedimentary deposits can be categorized as neritic or pelagic. **Neritic** (*neritos* = of the coast) **deposits** are found along continental margins and near islands, and **pelagic** (*pelagios* = of the sea) **deposits** are found in the deep-ocean basins. Lithogenous sediment in the ocean is ubiquitous: At least a small percentage of lithogenous sediment is found nearly everywhere on the ocean floor.

Neritic Deposits Lithogenous sediment dominates most neritic deposits. Lithogenous sediment is derived from rocks on nearby landmasses, consists of coarse-grained deposits, and accumulates rapidly on the continental shelf, slope, and rise. Examples of lithogenous neritic deposits include beach deposits, continental shelf deposits, turbidite deposits, and glacial deposits.

Beach Deposits Beaches are made of whatever materials are locally available. Beach materials are composed mostly of quartz-rich sand that is washed down to the coast by rivers but can also be composed of a wide variety of sizes and compositions. This material is transported by waves that crash against the shoreline, especially during storms.

Continental Shelf Deposits At the end of the last Ice Age (about 18,000 years ago), glaciers melted and sea level rose. As a result, many rivers of the world today deposit their sediment in drowned river mouths rather than carry it onto the continental shelf as they did during the geologic past. In many areas, the sediments that cover the continental shelf—called *relict* (*relict* = left behind) *sediments*—were deposited from 3000 to 7000 years ago and have not yet been covered by more recent deposits. These sediments presently cover about 70% of the world's continental shelves. In other areas, deposits of sand ridges on the continental shelves appear to have been formed more recently than the Ice Age and at present water depths.

Turbidite Deposits **Turbidity currents** are underwater avalanches that periodically move down the continental slopes and carve submarine canyons. Turbidity currents

Figure 4 Sediment transporting media.

Sediment transporting media include: **(a)** Streams. **(b)** Wind. **(c)** Glaciers. **(d)** Gravity, which creates landslides.

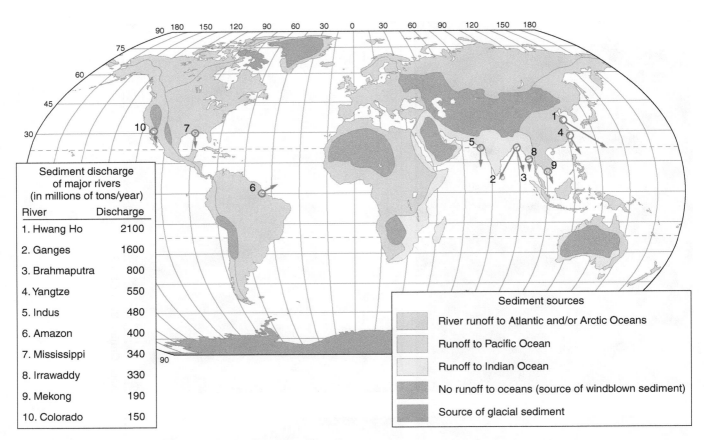

Figure 5 Major sources of lithogenous sediment.
Map showing the global distribution of major sources of lithogenous sediment. Blue circles with arrows indicate mouths of selected rivers; length of arrow is proportional to the average yearly amount of sediment discharged.

Sediment discharge of major rivers (in millions of tons/year)	
River	Discharge
1. Hwang Ho	2100
2. Ganges	1600
3. Brahmaputra	800
4. Yangtze	550
5. Indus	480
6. Amazon	400
7. Mississippi	340
8. Irrawaddy	330
9. Mekong	190
10. Colorado	150

Sediment sources	
	River runoff to Atlantic and/or Arctic Oceans
	Runoff to Pacific Ocean
	Runoff to Indian Ocean
	No runoff to oceans (source of windblown sediment)
	Source of glacial sediment

Courtesy of Walter N. Mack, Michigan State University

Figure 6 Lithogenous beach sand.
Lithogenous beach sand is composed mostly of particles of white quartz, plus small amounts of other minerals. This sand is from North Beach, Hampton, New Hampshire and is magnified approximately 23 times.

also carry vast amounts of neritic material. This material spreads out as deep-sea fans, comprises the continental rise, and gradually thins toward the abyssal plains. These deposits are called **turbidite deposits** and are composed of characteristic layering called *graded bedding*.

Glacial Deposits Poorly sorted deposits containing particles ranging from boulders to clays may be found in the high-latitude[3] portions of the continental shelf. These **glacial deposits** were laid down after the Ice Age when glaciers that covered the continental shelf eventually melted. Glacial deposits are currently forming around the continent of Antarctica and around Greenland by **ice rafting**. In this process, rock particles trapped in glacial ice are carried out to sea by icebergs that break away from coastal glaciers. As the icebergs melt, lithogenous particles of many sizes are released and settle onto the ocean floor.

___
[3]High-latitude regions are those far from the Equator (either north or south); low latitudes are areas close to the Equator.

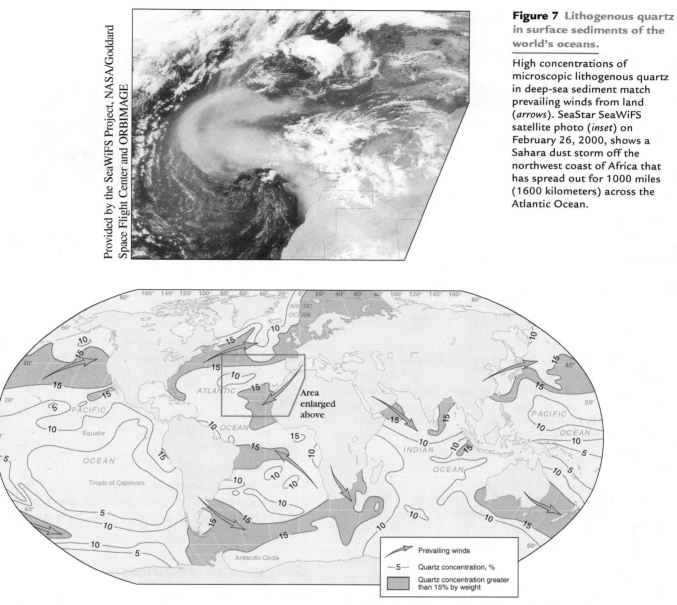

After Leinen, M. et al., 1986, Distribution of biogenic silica and quartz in recent deep-sea sediments. *Geology* 14:3, 199–203.

Provided by the SeaWiFS Project, NASA/Goddard Space Flight Center and ORBIMAGE

Figure 7 Lithogenous quartz in surface sediments of the world's oceans.

High concentrations of microscopic lithogenous quartz in deep-sea sediment match prevailing winds from land (*arrows*). SeaStar SeaWiFS satellite photo (*inset*) on February 26, 2000, shows a Sahara dust storm off the northwest coast of Africa that has spread out for 1000 miles (1600 kilometers) across the Atlantic Ocean.

TABLE 2 **Wentworth scale of grain size for sediments**

Size range (millimeters)	Particle name		Grain size	Example	Energy conditions
Above 256	Boulder		Coarse-grained	Coarse material found in	High energy
64 to 256	Cobble	Gravel		stream beds near the source	
4 to 64	Pebble			areas of rivers	
2 to 4	Granule				
$^1/_{16}$ to 2	Sand			Beach sand	
$^1/_{256}$ to $^1/_{16}$	Silt			Feels gritty in teeth	
$^1/_{4096}$ to $^1/_{256}$	Clay		Fine-grained	Microscopic; feels sticky	Low energy

Source: Wentworth, 1922; After Udden, 1898

Scale in millimeters
0 10 20 30 40 50 60

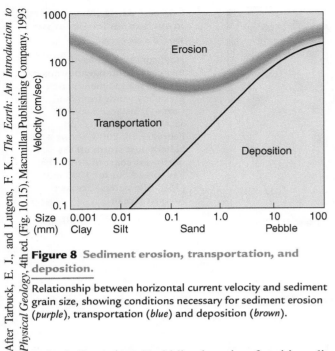

After Tarbuck, E. J., and Lutgens, F. K., *The Earth: An Introduction to Physical Geology*, 4th ed. (Fig. 10.15), Macmillan Publishing Company, 1993

Figure 8 Sediment erosion, transportation, and deposition.

Relationship between horizontal current velocity and sediment grain size, showing conditions necessary for sediment erosion (*purple*), transportation (*blue*) and deposition (*brown*).

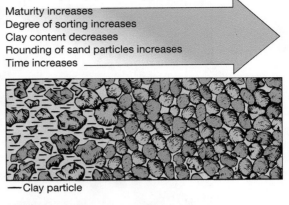

—Clay particle

Figure 9 Sediment maturity.

As sediment maturity increases with time (*left to right*), the degree of sorting and rounding of particles increases, whereas clay content decreases.

Pelagic Deposits Turbidite deposits of neritic sediment on the continental rise can spill over into the deep-ocean basin. However, most pelagic deposits are composed of fine-grained material that accumulates slowly on the deep-ocean floor. Pelagic lithogenous sediment includes particles that have come from volcanic eruptions, wind-blown dust, and fine material that is carried by deep ocean currents.

Abyssal Clay **Abyssal clay** is composed of at least 70% (by weight) fine clay-sized particles from the continents. Even though they are far from land, deep abyssal plains contain thick sequences of abyssal clay deposits composed of particles transported great distances by winds or ocean currents and deposited on the deep ocean floor. Because abyssal clays contain oxidized iron, they are commonly red-brown or buff in color and are sometimes referred to as **red clays**. The predominance of abyssal clay on abyssal plains is caused not by an abundance of clay settling on the ocean floor but by the absence of other material that would otherwise dilute it.

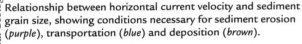

STUDENTS SOMETIMES ASK...

Are there any areas of the ocean floor where no sediment is being deposited?

Various types of sediment accumulate on nearly all areas of the ocean floor in the same way dust accumulates in all parts of your home (which is why marine sediment is often referred to as "marine dust"). Even the deep-ocean floor far from land receives small amounts of wind-blown material, microscopic biogenous particles, and space dust.

There are a few places in the ocean, however, where very little sediment accumulates. One such place is along the con-

tinental slope, where there is active erosion by turbidity and other deep-ocean currents. Another place where very little sediment can be found is along the mid-ocean ridge. Here, the sea floor along the crest of the mid-ocean ridge is so young (because of sea floor spreading) and the rates of sediment accumulation far from land are so slow there hasn't been enough time for sediments to form.

> Lithogenous sediment is produced from preexisting rock material, is found on most parts of the ocean floor, and can occur as thick deposits close to land.

Biogenous Sediment

Biogenous (*bio* = life, *generare* = to produce) **sediment** is derived from the remains of hard parts of once-living organisms.

Origin

Biogenous sediment begins as the hard parts (shells, bones, and teeth) of living organisms ranging from minute algae and protozoans to fish and whales. When organisms that produce hard parts die, their remains settle onto the ocean floor and can accumulate as biogenous sediment.

Biogenous sediment can be classified as either macroscopic or microscopic. **Macroscopic biogenous sediment** is large enough to be seen without the aid of a microscope and includes shells, bones, and teeth of large organisms. Except in certain tropical beach localities where shells and coral fragments are numerous, this type of sediment is relatively rare in the marine environment, especially in deep water where fewer organisms live. Much more abundant is **microscopic biogenous sediment**, which contains particles so small they can only be seen well through a microscope.

Microscopic organisms produce tiny shells called **tests** (*testa* = shell) that begin to sink after the organisms die and continually rain down in great numbers onto the ocean floor. These microscopic tests can accumulate on the deep-ocean floor and form deposits called **ooze**(*wose* = juice). As its name implies, ooze resembles very fine-grained mushy material.[4] Technically, biogenous ooze must contain at least 30% biogenous test material by weight. What comprises the other part—up to 70% of an ooze? Commonly, it is fine-grained lithogenous clay that is deposited along with biogenous tests in the deep ocean. By volume, much more microscopic ooze than macroscopic biogenous sediment exists on the ocean floor.

The organisms that contribute to biogenous sediment are chiefly **algae** (*alga* = seaweed) and **protozoans** (*proto* = first, *zoa* = animal). Algae are primarily aquatic, eukaryotic,[5] photosynthetic organisms, ranging in size from microscopic single cells to large organisms like giant kelp. Protozoans are any of a large group of single-celled, eukaryotic, usually microscopic organisms that are generally not photosynthetic.

Composition

The two most common chemical compounds in biogenous sediment are **calcium carbonate** ($CaCO_3$, which forms the mineral **calcite**) and **silica** (SiO_2). Often, the silica is chemically combined with water to produce $SiO_2 \cdot nH_2O$, the hydrated form of silica, which is called *opal*.

Silica Most of the silica in biogenous ooze comes from microscopic algae called **diatoms** (*diatoma* = cut in half) and protozoans called **radiolarians** (*radio* = a spoke or ray).

Because diatoms photosynthesize, they need strong sunlight and are found only within the upper sunlit surface waters of the ocean. Most diatoms are free-floating or **planktonic** (*planktos* = wandering). The living organism builds a glass greenhouse out of silica as a protective covering and lives inside. Most species have two parts to their test that fit together like a petri dish or pillbox (Figure 10a). The tiny tests are perforated with small holes in intricate patterns to allow nutrients to pass in and waste products to pass out. Where diatoms are abundant at the ocean surface, thick deposits of diatom-rich ooze can accumulate below on the ocean floor. When this ooze lithifies, it becomes **diatomaceous earth**,[6] a lightweight white rock composed of diatom tests and clay that has many uses (Box 2).

Radiolarians are microscopic single-celled protozoans, most of which are also planktonic. As their name implies, they often have long spikes or rays of silica protruding from their siliceous shell (Figure 10b). They do not photosynthesize but rely on external food sources such as bacteria and other plankton. Radiolarians typically display well-developed symmetry, which is why they have been described as living snowflakes of the sea.

The accumulation of siliceous tests of diatoms, radiolarians, and other silica-secreting organisms produces **siliceous ooze** (Figure 10c).

Calcium Carbonate Two significant sources of calcium carbonate biogenous ooze are the **foraminifers** (*foramen* = an opening)—close relatives of radiolarians—and microscopic algae called **coccolithophores** (*coccus* = berry; *lithos* = stone; *phorid* = carrying).

Coccolithophores are single-celled algae, most of which are planktonic. Coccolithophores produce thin plates or shields made of calcium carbonate, 20 or 30 of which overlap to produce a spherical test (Figure 11a). Like diatoms, coccolithophores photosynthesize, so they need sunlight to live. Coccolithophores are about 10 to 100 times smaller than most diatoms (Figure 11b), which is why coccolithophores are often called **nannoplankton** (*nanno* = dwarf, *planktos* = wandering).

When the organism dies, the individual plates (called **coccoliths**) disaggregate and can accumulate on the ocean floor as coccolith-rich ooze. When this ooze lithifies over time, it forms a white deposit called **chalk**, which is used for a variety of purposes (including writing on chalkboards). The White Cliffs of southern England are composed of hardened coccolith-rich calcium carbonate ooze, which was deposited on the ocean floor and has been uplifted onto land (Figure 12). Deposits of chalk the same age as the White Cliffs are so common throughout Europe, North America, Australia, and the Middle East that the geologic period in which these deposits formed is named the Cretaceous (*creta* = chalk) Period.

Foraminifers are single-celled protozoans, many of which are planktonic, ranging in size from microscopic to macroscopic. They do not photosynthesize, so they must ingest other organisms for food. Foraminifers produce a hard calcium carbonate test in which the organism lives (Figure 11c,). Most foraminifers produce a segmented or chambered test, and all tests have a prominent opening in one end. Although very small in size, the tests of foraminifers resemble the large shells that one might find at a beach.

Deposits comprised primarily of tests of foraminifers, coccoliths, and other calcareous-secreting organisms are called **calcareous ooze** (Figure 11d).

Distribution

Biogenous sediment is commonly found in pelagic deposits but only rarely found as neritic deposits. The distribution of biogenous sediment on the ocean floor depends on three fundamental processes: productivity, destruction, and dilution.

---

[4]Ooze has the consistency of toothpaste mixed about half and half with water. To help you remember this term, imagine walking barefoot across the deep-ocean floor and how the sediment would *ooze* between your toes.

[5]Eukaryotic (*eu* = good, *karyo* = thenucleus) cells contain a distinct membrane-bound nucleus.

[6]Diatomaceous earth is also called diatomite, tripolite, or kieselguhr.

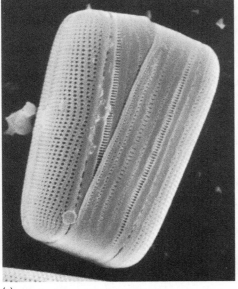

(a)

Figure 10 Microscopic siliceous tests.

Scanning electron micrographs: **(a)** Diatom (length = 30 micrometers, equal to 30 millionths of a meter), showing how the two parts of the diatom's test fit together. **(b)** Radiolarian (length = 100 micrometers). **(c)** Siliceous ooze, showing mostly fragments of diatom tests (magnified 250 times).

Reprinted by permission from Hallegraeff, G. M., *Plankton: A Microscopic World*, 1988 (p. 46). Courtesy of E. J. Brill, Inc.

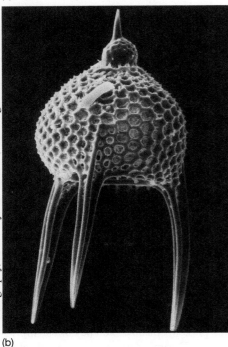

Courtesy of Warren Smith, Scripps Institution of Oceanography, University of California, San Diego

(b)

Photo courtesy of World Minerals, Inc., Lompoc, California (sample from Celite Corporations Diatomite Mine in Lompoc, California).

(c)

Productivity is the number of organisms present in the surface water above the ocean floor. Surface waters with high biologic productivity contain many living and reproducing organisms—conditions that are likely to produce biogenous sediments. Conversely, surface waters with low biologic productivity contain too few organisms to produce biogenous oozes on the ocean floor. *Destruction* occurs when skeletal remains (tests) dissolve in seawater at depth.

Dilution occurs when other sediments are prevalent enough to keep the amount of biogenous test material below 30%. Dilution occurs most often because of the abundance of coarse-grained lithogenous material in ner-

itic environments, so biogenous oozes are uncommon along continental margins.

Neritic Deposits Although neritic deposits are dominated by lithogenous sediment, both microscopic and macroscopic biogenous material may be incorporated into lithogenous sediment in neritic deposits. In addition, biogenous carbonate deposits are common in some areas.

Carbonate Deposits **Carbonate** minerals are those that contains CO_3 in its chemical formula—such as calcium carbonate, $CaCO_3$. Rocks from the marine environment

BOX 2   People and Ocean Environment

DIATOMS: THE MOST IMPORTANT THINGS YOU HAVE (PROBABLY) NEVER HEARD OF

"Few objects are more beautiful than the minute siliceous cases of the diatomaceae: were these created that they might be examined and admired under the higher powers of the microscope?"

—Charles Darwin (1872)

Although most people are scarcely aware of it, diatoms are incredibly important to life on Earth. They are also used to produce a variety of common products. What exactly are diatoms?

Diatoms are microscopic single-celled photosynthetic organisms. Each one lives inside a protective silica test, most of which contain two halves that fit together like a shoebox and its lid. First described with the aid of a microscope in 1702, their tests are exquisitely ornamented with holes, ribs, and radiating spines unique to individual species. The fossil record indicates that diatoms have been on Earth since the Jurassic Period (180 million years ago) and at least 70,000 species of diatoms have been identified.

Diatoms live for a few days to as much as a week, can reproduce sexually or asexually, and occur individually or linked together into long communities. They are found in great abundance floating in the ocean and in certain freshwater lakes but can also be found in many diverse environments, such as on the undersides of polar ice, on the skins of whales, in soil, in thermal springs, and even on brick walls.

Continued...

Photo courtesy of World Minerals, Inc., Lompoc, California

Reprinted by permission from Hallegraeff, G. M., *Plankton: A Microscopic World*, 1988 (p. 20). Courtesy of E. J. Brill, Inc.

Products containing or produced using diatomaceous earth (diatom *Thalassiosira eccentrica*, inset).

When marine diatoms die, their tests rain down and accumulate on the sea floor as siliceous ooze. Hardened deposits of siliceous ooze, called diatomaceous earth, can be as much as 900 meters (3000 feet) thick. Diatomaceous earth consists of billions of minute silica tests and has many unusual properties: It is lightweight, has an inert chemical composition, is resistant to high temperatures, and has excellent filtering properties. Diatomaceous earth is used to produce a variety of common products. The main uses of diatomaceous earth include

- filters (for refining sugar, separating impurities from wine, straining yeast from beer, and filtering swimming pool water)
- mild abrasives (in toothpaste, facial scrubs, matches, and household cleaning and polishing compounds)
- absorbents (for chemical spills and pest control)
- chemical carriers (in pharmaceuticals, paint, and dynamite)

Other products from diatomaceous earth include optical-quality glass (because of the pure silica content of diatoms), space shuttle tiles (because they are lightweight and provide good insulation), an additive in concrete, a filler in tires, an anti-caking agent, and even building stone for constructing houses.

Further, the vast majority of oxygen that all animals breathe is a byproduct of photosynthesis by diatoms. In addition, each living diatom contains a tiny droplet of oil. When diatoms die, their tests containing droplets of oil accumulate on the sea floor and are the beginnings of petroleum deposits, such as those found offshore California.

Given their many practical applications, it is difficult to imagine how different our lives would be without diatoms!

Reprinted by permission from Hallegraeff, G. M., *Plankton: A Microscopic World*, 1988 (p. 8). Courtesy of E. J. Brill, Inc.

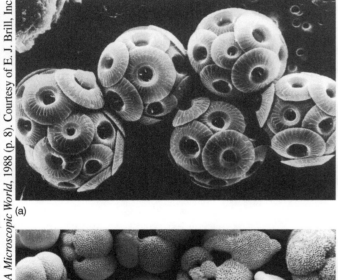

(a)

Reprinted by permission from Hallegraeff, G. M., *Plankton: A Microscopic World*, 1988 (p. 16). Courtesy of E. J. Brill, Inc.

(b)

(c)

Radiolarians

Foraminifers

(d)

Courtesy of the Deep Sea Drilling Project, Scripps Institution of Oceanography, University of California, San Diego

Figure 11 Microscopic calcareous tests.

Scanning electron micrographs: **(a)** Coccolithophores (diameter of individual coccolithophores = 20 micrometers, equal to 20 millionths of a meter). **(b)** Diatom (siliceous) and coccoliths (diameter of diatom = 70 micrometers). **(c)** Foraminifers (most species 400 micrometers in diameter). **(d)** Calcareous ooze, which also includes some siliceous radiolarian tests (magnified 160 times).

Courtesy of Memorie Yasuda, Scripps Institution of Oceanography, University of California, San Diego

Figure 12 The White Cliffs of southern England.

The White Cliffs near Dover in southern England are composed of hardened coccolith-rich calcareous ooze (chalk).

APT photo

composed primarily of calcium carbonate are called **limestones**. Most limestones contain fossil marine shells, suggesting a biogenous origin, while others appear to have formed directly from seawater without the help of any marine organism. Modern environments where calcium carbonate is currently forming (such as in the Bahama Banks, Australia's Great Barrier Reef, and the Persian Gulf) suggest that these carbonate deposits occurred in shallow, warm-water shelves and around tropical islands as coral reefs and beaches.

Ancient marine carbonate deposits constitute 2% of Earth's crust and 25% of all sedimentary rocks on Earth. These limestone deposits form the bedrock underlying Florida and many Midwestern states from Kentucky to Michigan and from Pennsylvania to Colorado. Percolation of groundwater through these deposits has dissolved the limestone to produce sinkholes and spectacular caverns.

Stromatolites (*stromat* = covering, *ite* = stone) are lobate structures consisting of fine layers of carbonate that form in specific warm, shallow-water environments such as the high salinity tidal pools in Shark Bay, western Australia, and the shifting carbonate sand shoals on Eleuthera Bank in the Bahamas (Figure 13). Cyanobacteria[7] produce these deposits by trapping fine sediment in mucous mats. Other types of algae produce long filaments that bind the particles together. As layer upon layer of these algae colonize the surface, a bulbous structure is formed. In the geologic past—particularly from about 1 to 3 billion years ago—conditions were ideal for stromatolites, so stromatolitic structures hundreds of meters high are common in rocks from these ages.

Pelagic Deposits Microscopic biogenous sediment (ooze) is common on the deep-ocean floor because there is so little

lithogenous sediment deposited at great distances from the continents that could dilute the biogenous material.

Siliceous Ooze Siliceous ooze contains at least 30% (by weight) of the hard remains of silica-secreting organisms. When the siliceous ooze consists mostly of diatoms, it is called *diatomaceous ooze*. When it consists mostly of radiolarians, it is called *radiolarian ooze*. When it consists mostly of single-celled silicoflagellates—another type of alga—it is called *silicoflagellate ooze*.

The ocean is undersaturated with silica at all depths, so seawater slowly but continually dissolves silica. In addition, bacterial decomposition of the protective protein coating on diatom tests also aids the dissolution process. How can siliceous ooze accumulate on the ocean floor if it is being dissolved? One way is to accumulate the siliceous tests faster than seawater can dissolve them. For instance, many tests sinking at the same time will create a deposit of siliceous ooze on the sea floor below (Figure 14).[8] Once buried beneath other siliceous tests, they are no longer exposed to the dissolving effects of seawater. Thus, siliceous ooze is commonly found in areas below surface waters with high biologic productivity of silica-secreting organisms, such as in equatorial and high-latitude regions (Figure 15).

Calcareous ooze Calcareous ooze contains at least 30% (by weight) of the hard remains of calcareous-secreting organisms. When it consists mostly of coccolithophores, it is called *coccolith ooze*. When it consists mostly of foraminifers, it is called *foraminifer ooze*. One of the most common types of foraminifer ooze is *Globigerina ooze*,

---

[7]Cyanobacteria (*kuanos* = dark blue) are descendants of the first photosynthetic organisms.

[8]An analogy to this is trying to get a layer of sugar to form on the bottom of a cup of hot coffee. If a few grains of sugar are slowly dropped into the cup, a layer of sugar won't accumulate. However, if a whole bowl full of sugar is dumped into the coffee, a thick layer of sugar will form on the bottom of the cup.

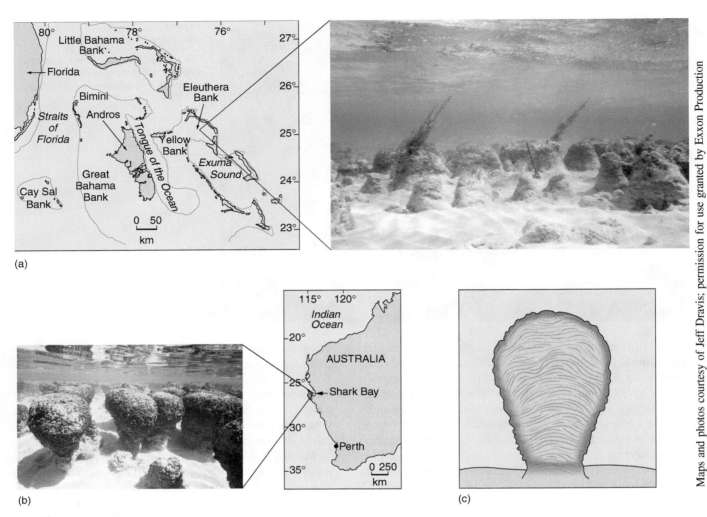

(a)

(b)

(c)

Maps and photos courtesy of Jeff Dravis; permission for use granted by Exxon Production Research Company and American Association for the Advancement of Science

Figure 13 Stromatolites.

(a) Subtidal oolitic stromatolites on the crest of an oolitic tidal bar on Eleuthera Bank, Bahamas. Most reach a maximum height of about 1 meter (3.3 feet). **(b)** Shark Bay stromatolites, which form in high salinity tidal pools and also reach a maximum height of about 1 meter (3.3 feet). **(c)** Cross-section through a stromatolite, showing internal fine layering.

Figure 14 Accumulation of siliceous ooze.

Siliceous ooze accumulates on the ocean floor beneath areas of high productivity, where the rate of accumulation of siliceous tests is greater than the rate at which silica is being dissolved.

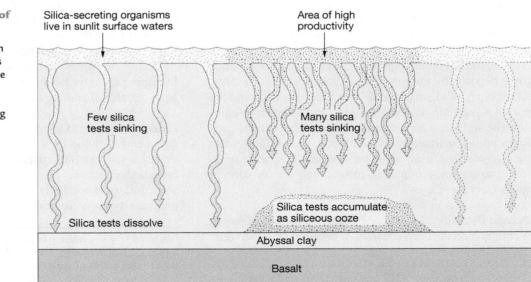

Silica-secreting organisms live in sunlit surface waters

Area of high productivity

Few silica tests sinking

Many silica tests sinking

Silica tests dissolve

Silica tests accumulate as siliceous ooze

Abyssal clay

Basalt

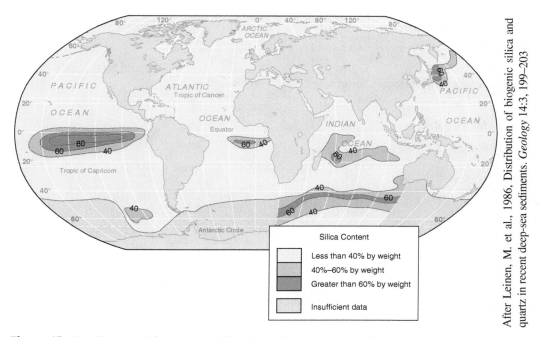

After Leinen, M. et al., 1986, Distribution of biogenic silica and quartz in recent deep-sea sediments. *Geology* 14:3, 199–203

Figure 15 Distribution of biogenous silica in modern surface sediments.

The distribution of biogenous silica ($SiO_2 \cdot nH_2O$, which is opal) in modern surface sediments shows maximum concentrations associated with areas of highest biological productivity. In equatorial regions, high silica content in sediment is produced predominantly by radiolarians in surface waters above; in high latitudes, high silica content in sediment is the result of high surface water concentrations of diatoms.

named for a foraminifer that is especially widespread in the Atlantic and South Pacific Oceans. Other calcareous oozes include *pteropod oozes* and *ostracod oozes*.

The destruction (solubility) of calcium carbonate (calcite) varies with depth. At the warmer surface and in the shallow parts of the ocean, seawater is generally saturated with calcium carbonate, so calcite does not dissolve. In the deep ocean, however, the colder water contains greater amounts of carbon dioxide, which forms carbonic acid and causes calcareous material to dissolve. The higher pressure at depth also helps speed the dissolution of calcium carbonate.

The depth in the ocean at which the pressure is high enough and the amount of carbon dioxide in deep-ocean waters is great enough to begin dissolving calcium carbonate is called the **lysocline** (*lusis* = a loosening, *cline* = slope). Below the lysocline, calcium carbonate dissolves at an increasing rate with increasing depth until the **calcite compensation depth (CCD)**[9] is reached. At the CCD and greater depths, sediment does not usually contain much calcite because it readily dissolves—even the thick tests of foraminifers dissolve within a day or two. The CCD, on average, is 4500 meters (15,000 feet) below sea level, but, depending on the chemistry of the deep ocean, may be as deep as 6000 meters (20,000 feet)

in portions of the Atlantic Ocean, or as shallow as 3500 meters (11,500 feet) in the Pacific Ocean. The depth of the lysocline also varies from ocean to ocean but averages about 4000 meters (13,100 feet).

Because of the CCD, modern carbonate oozes are generally rare below 5000 meters (16,400 feet). Still, buried deposits of ancient calcareous ooze are found beneath the CCD. How can calcareous ooze exist below the CCD? The necessary conditions are shown in Figure 16. The mid-ocean ridge is a topographically high feature that rises above the sea floor. It often pokes up above the CCD, even though the surrounding deep-ocean floor is below the CCD. Thus, calcareous ooze deposited on top of the mid-ocean ridge will not be dissolved. Sea floor spreading causes the newly created sea floor and the calcareous sediment on top of it to move into deeper water away from the ridge, eventually being transported below the CCD. This calcareous sediment will dissolve below the CCD, unless it is covered by a deposit that is unaffected by the CCD (such as siliceous ooze or abyssal clay).

The map in Figure 17 shows the percentage (by weight) of calcium carbonate in the modern surface sediments of the ocean basins. High concentrations of calcareous particles (sometimes exceeding 80%) are found along segments of the mid-ocean ridge, but little is found in deep-ocean basins below the CCD. For example, in the northern Pacific Ocean—one of the deepest parts of the world ocean—there is very little calcium carbonate in the

[9]Because the mineral calcite is composed of calcium carbonate, the calcite compensation depth is also known as the calcium carbonate compensation depth, or the carbonate compensation depth. All go by the handy abbreviation of CCD.

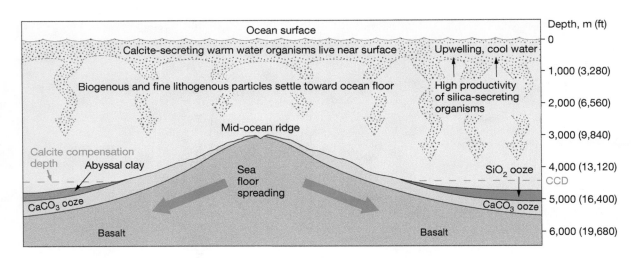

Figure 16 Sea floor spreading and sediment accumulation.

Relationships among carbonate compensation depth, the mid-ocean ridge, sea floor spreading, productivity, and destruction that allow calcareous ooze to be preserved below the CCD.

Figure 17 Distribution of calcium carbonate in modern surface sediments.

The distribution of calcium carbonate (CaCO₃) in modern surface sediments shows that high percentages of calcareous ooze closely follow the mid-ocean ridge, which is above the CCD.

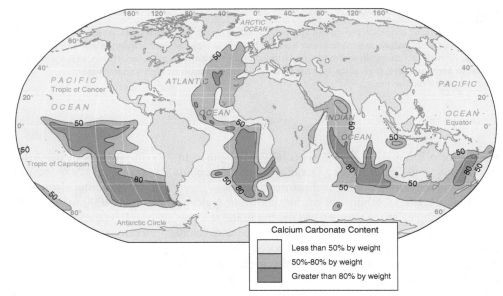

After Biscaye, P. E. et al., 1976; Berger, W. H. et al., 1976; and Kolla V. and Biscaye, P. E., 1976

TABLE 3 **Comparison of environments interpreted from deposits of siliceous and calcareous ooze in surface sediments.**

	Siliceous ooze	Calcareous ooze
Surface water temperature above sea floor deposits	Cool	Warm
Main location found	Sea floor beneath cool surface water in high latitudes	Sea floor beneath warm surface water in low latitudes
Other factors	Upwelling brings deep, cold, nutrient-rich water to the surface	Calcareous ooze dissolves below the CCD
Other locations found	Sea floor beneath areas of upwelling, including along the Equator	Sea floor beneath warm surface water in low latitudes along the mid-ocean ridge

sediment. Calcium carbonate is also rare in sediments accumulating beneath cold, high-latitude waters where calcareous-secreting organisms are relatively uncommon.

Table 3 compares the environmental differences that can be inferred from siliceous and calcareous oozes. It shows that siliceous ooze typically forms below cool surface water regions, including areas of **upwelling** where deep ocean water comes to the surface and supplies nutrients that stimulate high rates of biological productivity. Calcareous ooze, on the other hand, is found on the shallower areas of the ocean floor beneath warmer surface water.

> Biogenous sediment is produced from the hard remains of once-living organisms. Microscopic biogenous sediment is especially widespread and forms deposits of ooze on the ocean floor.

Hydrogenous Sediment

Hydrogenous (*hydro* = water, *generare* = to produce) **sediment** is derived from the dissolved material in water.

Origin

Seawater contains many dissolved materials. Chemical reactions within seawater cause certain minerals to come out of solution or **precipitate** (change from the dissolved

to the solid state). Precipitation usually occurs when there is a *change in conditions*, such as a change in temperature or pressure or the addition of chemically active fluids. To make rock candy, for instance, a pan of water is heated and sugar is added. When the water is hot and the sugar dissolved, the pan is removed from the heat and the sugar water is allowed to cool. The *change in temperature* causes the sugar to become oversaturated, which causes it to precipitate. As the water cools, the sugar precipitates on anything that is put in the pan, such as pieces of string or kitchen utensils.

Composition and Distribution

Although hydrogenous sediments represent a relatively small portion of the overall sediment in the ocean, they have many different compositions and are distributed in diverse environments of deposition. Several types of hydrogenous deposits have economic potential.

Manganese Nodules **Manganese nodules** are rounded, hard lumps of manganese, iron, and other metals typically 5 centimeters (2 inches) in diameter up to a maximum of about 20 centimeters (8 inches). When cut in half, they often reveal a layered structure formed by precipitation around a central nucleation object (Figure 18a). The nucleation

Figure 18 Manganese nodules.

(a) Manganese nodules cut in half, revealing their central nucleation object and layered internal structure. (b) A portion of the South Pacific Ocean floor about 4 meters (13 feet) across showing an abundance of manganese nodules.

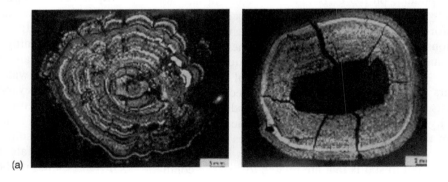

(a)

Courtesy of Scripps Institution of Oceanography, University of California, San Diego

(b)

object may be a piece of lithogenous sediment, coral, volcanic rock, a fish bone, or a shark's tooth. Manganese nodules are found on the deep-ocean floor at concentrations of about 100 nodules per square meter (square yard). In some areas, they occur in even greater abundance (Figure 18b), resembling a scattered field of baseball-sized nodules. The formation of manganese nodules requires extremely low rates of lithogenous or biogenous input so that these sediments do not bury them.

The major components of these nodules are manganese dioxide (around 30% by weight) and iron oxide (around 20%). The element manganese is important for making high-strength steel alloys. Other accessory metals present in manganese nodules include copper (used in electrical wiring, pipe, and in making brass and bronze), nickel (used to make stainless steel), and cobalt (used as an alloy with iron to make strong magnets and steel tools). Although the concentration of these accessory metals is usually less than 1%, they can exceed 2% by weight, which may make them attractive exploration targets in the future.

The origin of manganese nodules has puzzled oceanographers since manganese nodules were first discovered in 1872 during the voyage of HMS *Challenger*. If manganese nodules are truly hydrogenous and precipitate from seawater, then how can they have such high concentrations of manganese (which occurs in seawater at concentrations often too small to measure accurately)? Furthermore, why are the nodules on *top* of ocean floor sediment and not buried by the constant rain of sedimentary particles?

Unfortunately, nobody has definitive answers to these questions. Perhaps the creation of manganese nodules is the result of one of the slowest chemical reactions known—on average, they grow at a rate of about 5 millimeters (0.2 inch) per *million years*. Recent research suggests the formation of manganese nodules may be aided by bacteria and an as-yet-unidentified marine organism that intermittently lifts and rotates them. Other studies reveal that the nodules don't form continuously over time but in spurts that are related to specific conditions such as a low sedimentation rate of lithogenous clay and strong deep-water currents. Interestingly, the larger the nodules are, the faster they grow. The origin of manganese nodules is widely considered the most interesting unresolved problem in marine chemistry.

Phosphates Phosphorus-bearing compounds (**phosphates**) occur abundantly as coatings on rocks and as nodules on the continental shelf and on banks at depths shallower than 1000 meters (3300 feet). Concentrations of phosphates in such deposits commonly reach 30% by weight and indicate abundant biological activity in surface water above where they accumulate. Phosphates are valuable as fertilizers, and ancient marine deposits on land are extensively mined to supply agricultural needs.

Carbonates The two most important carbonate minerals in marine sediment are **aragonite** and calcite. Both are composed of calcium carbonate ($CaCO_3$), but aragonite has a different crystalline structure that is less stable and changes into calcite over time.

As previously discussed, most carbonate deposits are of biogenous origin. However, hydrogenous carbonate deposits can precipitate directly from seawater in tropical climates to form aragonite crystals less than 2 millimeters (0.08 inch) long. Additionally, **oolites** (*oo* = egg, *ite* = stone) are small calcite spheres 2 millimeters (0.08 inch) in diameter or less that have layers like an onion and form in some shallow tropical waters where concentrations of $CaCO_3$ are high. Oolites are thought to precipitate around a nucleus and grow larger as they roll back and forth on beaches by wave action, but some evidence suggests that a type of algae may aid their formation.

Metal Sulfides Deposits of **metal sulfides** are associated with hydrothermal vents and black smokers along the mid-ocean ridge. These deposits contain iron, nickel, copper, zinc, silver, and other metals in varying proportions. Transported away from the mid-ocean ridge by sea floor spreading, these deposits can be found throughout the ocean floor and can even be uplifted onto continents.

Evaporites **Evaporite minerals** form where there is restricted open ocean circulation and where evaporation rates are high. As water evaporates from these areas, the remaining seawater becomes saturated with dissolved minerals, which then begin to precipitate. Heavier than seawater, they sink to the bottom or form a white crust of evaporite minerals around the edges of these areas (Figure 19). Collectively termed "salts," some evaporite minerals taste salty, such as *halite* (common table salt, NaCl), and some do not, such as the calcium sulfate minerals *anhydrite* ($CaSO_4$) and *gypsum* ($CaSO_4 \cdot 2H_2O$).

STUDENTS SOMETIMES ASK...

I've been to Hawaii and seen a black sand beach. Because it forms by lava flowing into the ocean that is broken up by waves, is it hydrogenous sediment?

No. Many active volcanoes in the world have black sand beaches that are created when waves break apart dark-colored volcanic rock. The material that produces the black sand is derived from a continent or an island, so it is considered lithogenous sediment. Even though molten lava sometimes flows into the ocean, the resulting black sand could never be considered hydrogenous sediment because the lava was never *dissolved* in water.

APT photo

Figure 19 Evaporite salts.

Due to a high evaporation rate, salts (white material) precipitate onto the floor of Death Valley, California.

Hydrogenous sediment is produced when dissolved materials precipitate out of solution and includes a variety of materials found in local concentrations on the ocean floor.

Cosmogenous Sediment

Cosmogenous (*cosmos* = universe, *generare* = to produce) **sediment** is derived from extraterrestrial sources.

Origin, Composition, and Distribution

Forming an insignificant portion of the overall sediment on the ocean floor, cosmogenous sediment consists of two main types: microscopic **spherules**, and macroscopic **meteor** debris.

Microscopic spherules are small globular masses. Some spherules are composed of silicate rock material and show evidence of being formed by extraterrestrial impact events on Earth or other planets that eject small molten pieces of crust into space. These **tektites** (*tektos* = molten) then rain down on Earth and can form *tektite fields*. Other spherules are composed mostly of iron and nickel (Figure 20) that form in the asteroid belt between the orbits of Mars and Jupiter and are produced when asteroids collide. This material constantly rains down on Earth as a general component of *space dust* or *micrometeorites* that float harmlessly through the atmosphere. Although about 90% of micrometeorites are destroyed by frictional heating as they enter the atmosphere, it has been estimated that as much as 300,000 metric tons (331,000 short tons) of space dust reach Earth's surface each year. The iron-rich space dust that lands in the oceans often dissolves in seawater. Glassy tektites, however, do not dissolve as easily and sometimes comprise minute proportions of various marine sediments.

Macroscopic meteor debris is rare on Earth but can be found associated with meteor impact sites. Evidence suggests that throughout time, meteors have collided with Earth at great speeds and that some larger ones have released energy equivalent to the explosion of multiple large nuclear bombs (Box 3). The debris from meteors—called **meteorite** material—settles out around the impact site and is either composed of silicate rock material (called *chondrites*) or iron and nickel (called *irons*).

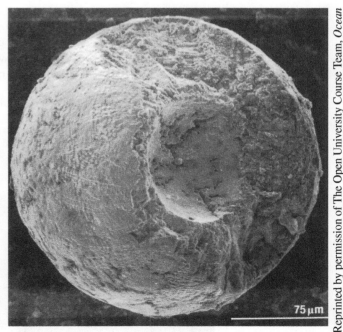

Reprinted by permission of The Open University Course Team, *Ocean Chemistry and Deep-Sea Sediments*, Butterworth-Heinemann, 1989

75 μm

Figure 20 Microscopic cosmogenous spherule.

Scanning electron micrograph of an iron-rich spherule of cosmic dust. Bar scale of 75 micrometers is equal to 75 millionths of a meter.

BOX 3   Research Methods in Oceanography

WHEN THE DINOSAURS DIED: THE CRETACEOUS–TERTIARY (K–T) EVENT

The extinction of the dinosaurs—and two-thirds of all plant and animal species on Earth (including many marine species)—occurred 65 million years ago. This extinction marks the boundary between the Cretaceous (K) and Tertiary (T) Periods of geologic time and is known as the "**K–T event**." Did slow climate change lead to the extinction of these organisms, or was it a catastrophic event? Was their demise related to disease, diet, predation, or volcanic activity? Earth scientists have long sought clues to this mystery.

In 1980, geologist Walter Alvarez, his father, Nobel physics laureate Luis Alvarez, and two nuclear chemists, Frank Asaro and Helen Michel, reported that deposits collected in northern Italy from the K–T boundary contained a clay layer with high proportions of the metallic element iridium (Ir). Iridium is rare in rocks from Earth but occurs in greater concentration in meteorites. Therefore, layers of sediment that contain unusually high concentrations of iridium suggest that the material may be of extraterrestrial origin. Additionally, the clay layer contained shocked quartz grains, which indicate that an event occurred with enough force to fracture and partially melt pieces of quartz. Other deposits from the K–T boundary revealed similar features, supporting the idea that Earth experienced an extraterrestrial impact at the same time that the dinosaurs died.

One problem with the impact hypothesis, however, was that volcanic eruptions on Earth could create similar clay deposits enriched in iridium and containing shocked quartz. In fact, large outpourings of basaltic volcanic rock in India (called the Deccan Traps) and other locations had occurred at about the same time as the dinosaur extinction. Also, if there was a catastrophic meteor impact, where was the crater?

In the early 1990s the *Chicxulub* (pronounced "SCHICK-sue-lube") *Crater* off the Yucatán coast in the Gulf of Mexico was identified as a likely candidate because of its structure, age, and size. Its structure is comparable to other impact craters in the solar system, and its age matches the K–T event. At 190 kilometers (120 miles) in diameter, it is the largest impact crater on Earth. To create a crater this large, a 10-kilometer (6-mile)-wide meteoroid composed of rock and/or ice traveling at speeds up to 72,000 kilometers (45,000 miles) per hour must have slammed into Earth. The impact probably bared the sea floor in the area and created huge waves—estimated to be up to 914 meters (3000 feet) high—that traveled throughout the oceans. This impact is thought to have kicked up so much dust that it blocked sunlight, chilled Earth's surface, and brought about the extinction of dinosaurs and other species. In addition, acid rains and global fires may have added to the environmental disaster.

Supporting evidence for the meteor impact hypothesis was provided in 1997 by the Ocean Drilling Program (ODP). Previous drilling close to the impact site did not reveal any K–T deposits. Evidently, the impact and resulting huge waves had stripped the ocean floor of its sediment. However, at 1600 kilometers (1000 miles) from the impact site, some of the telltale sediments were preserved on the sea floor. Drilling into the continental margin off Florida into an underwater peninsula called the Blake Nose, the ODP scientific party recovered cores from the K–T boundary that contain a complete record of the impact.

The cores reveal that before the impact, the layers of Cretaceous age

The K–T meteorite impact event.

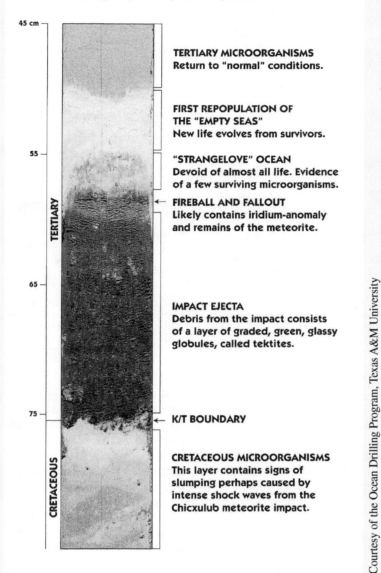

45 cm

TERTIARY MICROORGANISMS
Return to "normal" conditions.

FIRST REPOPULATION OF THE "EMPTY SEAS"
New life evolves from survivors.

55

"STRANGELOVE" OCEAN
Devoid of almost all life. Evidence of a few surviving microorganisms.

← **FIREBALL AND FALLOUT**
Likely contains iridium-anomaly and remains of the meteorite.

65

IMPACT EJECTA
Debris from the impact consists of a layer of graded, green, glassy globules, called tektites.

75

← **K/T BOUNDARY**

CRETACEOUS MICROORGANISMS
This layer contains signs of slumping perhaps caused by intense shock waves from the Chicxulub meteorite impact.

TERTIARY

CRETACEOUS

Courtesy of the Ocean Drilling Program, Texas A&M University

K–T boundary meteorite impact core.

sediment are filled with abundant fossils of calcareous coccoliths and foraminifers and show signs of underwater landslide activity—perhaps the effect of an impact-triggered earthquake. Above this calcareous ooze is a 20-centimeter (8-inch) thick layer of rubble containing evidence of an impact: spherules, tektites, shocked quartz from hard-hit terrestrial rock—even a 2-centimeter (1-inch) piece of reef rock from the Yucatán peninsula! This layer is also rich in iridium, just like other K–T boundary sequences. Atop this layer is a thick gray clay deposit containing meteor debris and severely reduced numbers of coccoliths and foraminifers. Life in the ocean apparently recovered slowly, taking at least 5000 years before sediment teeming with new, Tertiary-age microorganisms began to be deposited.

Convincing evidence of the K–T impact from this and other cores along with the observation of Comet Shoemaker-Levy's 1994 spectacular collision with Jupiter suggests that Earth has experienced many such extraterrestrial impacts over geologic time. In fact, nearly 200 impact craters have been identified on Earth so far. Statistics show that an impact the size of the K–T event should occur on Earth about once every 100 million years. Each impact would severely affect life on Earth as it did for the dinosaurs. Nevertheless, their extinction made it possible for mammals to eventually rise to the position of dominance they hold on Earth today.

Cosmogenous sediment is produced from materials originating in outer space and includes microscopic space dust and macroscopic meteor debris.

Mixtures

Lithogenous and biogenous sediment rarely occur as an absolutely pure deposit that does not contain other types of sediment. For instance,

- Most calcareous oozes contain some siliceous material, and vice versa (see, for example, Figure 11d).
- The abundance of clay-sized lithogenous particles throughout the world and the ease with which they are

transported by winds and currents means that these particles are incorporated into every sediment type.

- The composition of biogenous ooze includes up to 70% fine-grained lithogenous clays.
- Most lithogenous sediment contains small percentages of biogenous particles.
- Other types of sediment can be incorporated into hydrogenous sediment.
- For many types of hydrogenous sediment, evidence suggests they may be formed with the aid of certain marine organisms instead of by purely chemical processes.
- Tiny amounts of cosmogenous sediment are mixed in with all other sediment types.

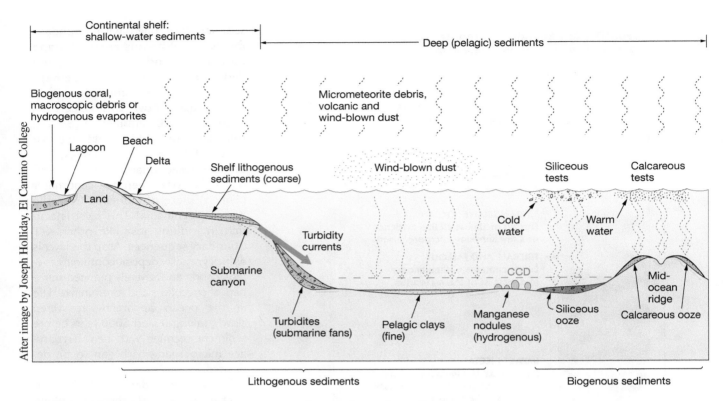

Continental shelf:
shallow-water sediments

Deep (pelagic) sediments

Biogenous coral,
macroscopic debris or
hydrogenous evaporites

Micrometeorite debris,
volcanic and
wind-blown dust

After image by Joseph Holliday, El Camino College

Lagoon Beach

Delta

Shelf lithogenous
sediments (coarse)

Wind-blown dust

Siliceous
tests

Calcareous
tests

Land

Cold
water

Warm
water

Turbidity
currents

Submarine
canyon

CCD

Mid-
ocean
ridge

Turbidites
(submarine fans)

Pelagic clays
(fine)

Manganese
nodules
(hydrogenous)

Siliceous
ooze

Calcareous ooze

Lithogenous sediments

Biogenous sediments

Figure 21 Distribution of sediment across a passive continental margin.

Each deposit is a mixture of different sediment types. Figure 21 shows the distribution of sediment across a passive continental margin and illustrates how mixtures can occur. Typically, however, one type of sediment dominates, which allows the deposit to be classified as primarily lithogenous, biogenous, hydrogenous, or cosmogenous.

Distribution of Neritic and Pelagic Deposits: A Summary

Neritic (nearshore) deposits cover about one-quarter of the ocean floor while pelagic (deep-ocean basin) deposits cover the other three-quarters.

Neritic Deposits

Neritic deposits are composed of materials that are strongly influenced by latitude. Figure 22 shows the distribution of neritic sediment types at various latitudes. The figure indicates that silt and clay are most abundant in equatorial and tropical latitudes, accounting for about 50% of the total sediment at the Equator, about 20% in the tropics, and about 15% at higher latitudes. Sand particles are most abundant at mid-latitudes, accounting for about 60% of the sediment, decreasing to about 30% at the Equator and to about 35% at high latitudes. Coarse, poorly sorted deposits (rock and gravel) are found primarily at high latitudes where they are deposited by glaciers and icebergs. Remarkably, about 6 to 7% of neritic sediment at all latitudes is composed of shell fragments.

Figure 22 also shows that coral reef debris is significant only at low latitudes, which is a result of the fact that corals cannot survive in the cooler waters of higher latitudes. Although some tropical locations near reefs contain sediment that is composed entirely of reef debris, coral debris accounts for only about 20% of the total sediment in tropical regions because these amounts are averaged with other sediments found at low latitudes.

The map in Figure 23 shows the distribution of neritic and pelagic deposits in the world's oceans. Coarse-grained lithogenous neritic deposits dominate continental margin areas (*dark brown shading*). Although neritic deposits usually contain biogenous, hydrogenous, and cosmogenous particles, these constitute only a minor percentage of the total sediment mass.

Pelagic Deposits

Figure 23 shows that pelagic deposits are dominated by biogenous calcareous oozes (*blue shading*), which are found on the relatively shallow deep-ocean areas along the mid-ocean ridge. Biogenous siliceous oozes are found beneath areas of unusually high biologic productivity such as the North Pacific, Antarctic (*light green shading*, where diatomaceous ooze occurs), and the equatorial Pacific (*dark green shading*, where radiolarian ooze occurs). Fine lithogenous pelagic deposits of abyssal clays (*light brown shading*) are common in deeper areas of the ocean basins. Hydrogenous and cosmogenous sediment comprise only a small proportion of pelagic deposits in the ocean.

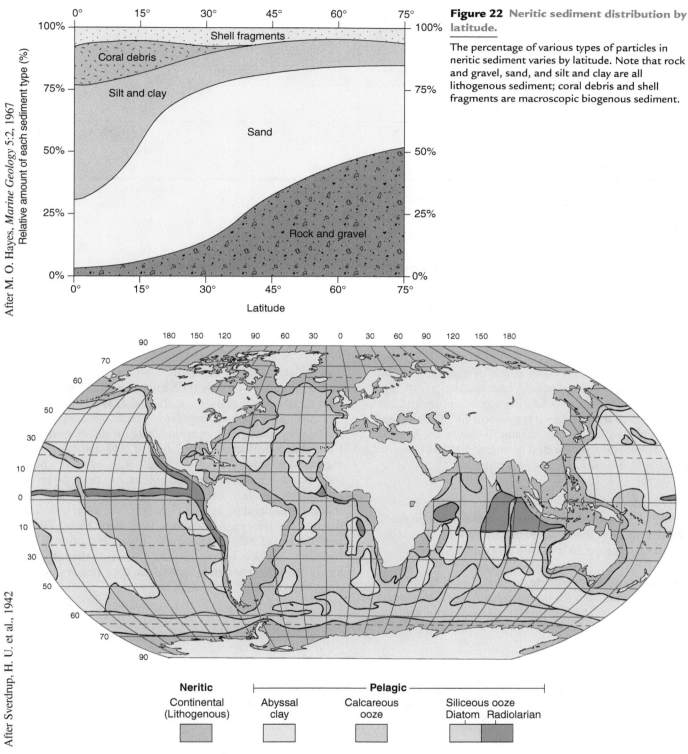

After M. O. Hayes, *Marine Geology* 5:2, 1967

Figure 22 Neritic sediment distribution by latitude.

The percentage of various types of particles in neritic sediment varies by latitude. Note that rock and gravel, sand, and silt and clay are all lithogenous sediment; coral debris and shell fragments are macroscopic biogenous sediment.

After Sverdrup, H. U. et al., 1942

Neritic	**Pelagic**		
Continental (Lithogenous)	Abyssal clay	Calcareous ooze	Siliceous ooze Diatom Radiolarian

Figure 23 Distribution of neritic and pelagic sediments.

The bar graph in Figure 24 shows the proportion of each ocean floor that is covered by pelagic calcareous ooze, siliceous ooze, or abyssal clay. Calcareous oozes predominate, covering almost 48% of the world's deep-ocean floor. Abyssal clay covers 38% and siliceous oozes 14% of the world ocean floor area. The graph also shows that the amount of ocean basin floor covered by calcareous ooze decreases in deeper basins because they generally lie beneath the CCD. The dominant oceanic sediment in the deepest basin—the Pacific—is abyssal clay (see also Figure 23). Calcareous ooze is the most widely deposited sediment in the shallower Atlantic and Indian

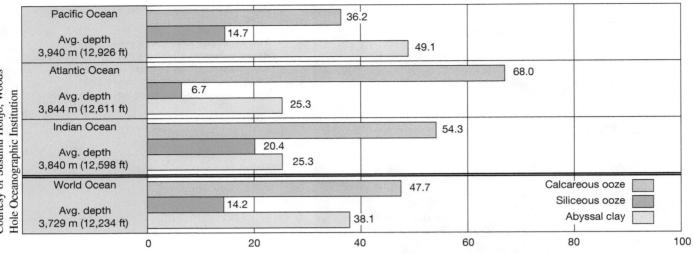

Figure 24 Percentage of pelagic sediment types within each ocean.

Distribution of pelagic calcareous ooze, siliceous ooze, and abyssal clay in each ocean, and for the world ocean. The average depths shown exclude shallow adjacent seas, where little pelagic sediment accumulates.

Oceans. Siliceous oozes cover a smaller percentage of the ocean bottom in all the oceans because regions of high productivity of siliceous-secreting organisms are generally restricted to the equatorial region (for radiolarians) and high latitudes (for diatoms). Table 4 shows the average rates of deposition of selected marine sediments in neritic and pelagic deposits.

> Neritic deposits occur close to shore and are dominated by coarse lithogenous material. Pelagic deposits occur in the deep ocean and are dominated by biogenous oozes and fine lithogenous clay.

Microscopic biogenous tests should take from 10 to 50 years to sink from the ocean surface where the organisms lived to the abyssal depths where biogenous ooze accumulates. During this time, even a sluggish horizontal ocean current of only 0.05 kilometer (0.03 mile) per hour could carry tests as much as 22,000 kilometers (13,700 miles) before they settled onto the deep-ocean floor. Why, then, do biogenous tests on the deep-ocean floor closely reflect the population of organisms living in the surface water directly above? Remarkably, about 99% of the particles that fall to the ocean floor do so as part of *fecal pellets*, which are produced by tiny animals that eat algae and protozoans living in the water column, digest their tissues, and excrete their hard parts. These pellets are full of the remains of algae and protozoans from the surface waters (Figure 25) and, though still small, are large enough to sink to the deep ocean floor in only 10 to 15 days.

TABLE 4 **Average rates of deposition of selected marine sediments.**

Type of sediment/deposit	Average rate of deposition (per 1000 years)	Thickness of deposit after 1000 years equivalent to ...
Coarse lithogenous sediment, neritic deposit	1 meter (3.3 feet)	A meter stick
Biogenous ooze, pelagic deposit	1 centimeter (0.4 inch)	The diameter of a dime
Abyssal clay, pelagic deposit	1 millimeter (0.04 inch)	The thickness of a dime
Manganese nodule, pelagic deposit	0.001 millimeter (0.00004 inch)	A microscopic dust particle

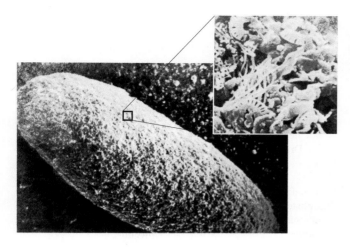

Figure 25 Fecal pellet.

A 200-micrometer (0.008 inch)-long fecal pellet, which is large enough to sink rapidly from the surface to the ocean floor. Close-up of the surface of a fecal pellet (*inset*) shows the remains of coccoliths and other debris.

Chapter in Review

- The existence of *sea floor spreading was confirmed when the* Glomar Challenger *began the Deep Sea Drilling Project* to sample ocean sediments and the underlying crust, which was continued by the *Ocean Drilling Program's* JOIDES Resolution. Today, the *Integrated Ocean Drilling Program* continues the important work of retrieving sediments from the ocean floor. Analysis and interpretation of marine sediments reveal that *Earth has had an interesting and complex history* including mass extinctions, global climate change, and movement of plates.

- Sediments that accumulate on the ocean floor are *classified by origin as lithogenous* (derived from rock), *biogenous* (derived from organisms), *hydrogenous* (derived from water), or *cosmogenous* (derived from outer space).

- *Lithogenous sediments reflect the composition of the rock from which they were derived.* Sediment *texture*—determined in part by the size, sorting, and rounding of particles—is affected greatly by how the particles were transported (by water, wind, ice, or gravity) and the energy conditions under which they were deposited. Coarse lithogenous material dominates neritic deposits that accumulate rapidly along the margins of continents while fine abyssal clays are found in pelagic deposits.

- *Biogenous sediment consists of the hard remains* (shells, bones, and teeth) *of organisms.* These are composed of either *silica* (SiO_2) from diatoms and radiolarians or *calcium carbonate* ($CaCO_3$) from foraminifers and coccolithophores. *Accumulations of microscopic shells* (tests) of organisms must comprise at least 30% of the deposit for it to be classified as *biogenic ooze.* Biogenous oozes are the most common type of pelagic deposits. The rate of biological productivity relative to the rates of destruction and dilution of biogenous sediment determines whether abyssal clay or oozes will form on the ocean floor. *Siliceous ooze* will only form below areas of high biologic productivity of silica-secreting organisms at the surface. *Calcareous ooze* will only form above the *calcite compensation depth (CCD)*—the depth where seawater dissolves calcium carbonate—although it can be covered and transported into deeper water through sea floor spreading.

- *Hydrogenous sediment* includes manganese nodules, phosphates, carbonates, metal sulfides, and evaporites that *precipitate directly from water* or are formed by the interaction of substances dissolved in water with materials on the ocean floor. Hydrogenous sediments represent a relatively small proportion of marine sediment and are distributed in many diverse environments.

- *Cosmogenous sediment is composed of either macroscopic meteor debris* (such as that produced during the K–T impact event) *or microscopic iron-nickel and silicate spherules* that result from asteroid collisions or extraterrestrial impacts. Minute amounts of cosmogenous sediment are mixed into most other types of ocean sediment.

- Although *most ocean sediment is a mixture of various sediment types*, it is usually dominated by lithogenous, biogenous, hydrogenous, or cosmogenous material.

- *The distribution of neritic and pelagic sediment is influenced by many factors*, including proximity to sources of lithogenous sediment, productivity of microscopic marine organisms, depth of the ocean floor, and the distribution of various sea floor features. *Fecal pellets* rapidly transport biogenous particles to the deep-ocean floor and cause the composition of sea floor deposits to match the organisms living in surface waters immediately above them.

Key Terms

Abyssal clay
Algae
Aragonite
Biogenous sediment
Calcareous ooze
Calcite
Calcite compensation depth
 (CCD)
Calcium carbonate
Carbonate
Chalk
Coccolith
Coccolithophore
Core
Cosmogenous sediment
Deep Sea Drilling Project
 (DSDP)
Diatom
Diatomaceous earth

Eroded
Evaporite mineral
Foraminifer
Glacial deposit
Glomar Challenger
Grain size
Hydrogenous sediment
Ice rafting
Integrated Ocean Drilling
 Program (IODP)
JOIDES Resolution
K–T event
Limestone
Lithogenous sediment
Lysocline
Macroscopic biogenous
 sediment
Manganese nodule
Maturity

Metal sulfide
Meteor
Meteorite
Microscopic biogenous
 sediment
Nannoplankton
Neritic deposit
Ocean Drilling Program (ODP)
Oolite
Ooze
Pelagic deposit
Phosphate
Planktonic
Precipitate
Protozoan
Quartz
Radiolarian
Red clay

Rotary drilling
Sediment
Silica
Siliceous ooze
Sorting
Spherule
Stromatolite
Tektite
Terrigenous sediment
Test
Texture
Turbidite deposit
Turbidity current
Upwelling
Weathering
Wentworth scale of grain size

Questions and Exercises

1. Describe the process of how a drilling ship like the *JOIDES Resolution* obtains core samples from the deep-ocean floor.

2. What kind of information can be obtained by examining and analyzing core samples?

3. List and describe the characteristics of the four basic types of marine sediment.

4. How does lithogenous sediment originate?

5. Why is most lithogenous sediment composed of quartz grains? What is the chemical composition of quartz?

6. If a deposit has a coarse grain size, what does this indicate about the energy of the transporting medium? Give several examples of various transporting media that would produce such a deposit.

7. What characteristics of marine sediment indicate increasing maturity? Give an example of a mature and immature sediment.

8. List the two major chemical compounds of which most biogenous sediment is composed and the organisms that produce them. Sketch these organisms.

9. What are several reasons why diatoms are so remarkable? List products that contain or are produced using diatomaceous earth.

10. If siliceous ooze is slowly but constantly dissolving in seawater, how can deposits of siliceous ooze accumulate on the ocean floor?

11. How do oozes differ from abyssal clay? Discuss how productivity, destruction, and dilution combine to determine whether an ooze or abyssal clay will form on the deep-ocean floor.

12. Describe the environmental conditions (e.g., surface water temperature, productivity, dissolution, etc.) that influence the distribution of siliceous and calcareous ooze.

13. Explain the stages of progression that result in calcareous ooze existing below the CCD.

14. Describe manganese nodules, including what is currently known about how they form.

15. Describe the most common types of cosmogenous sediment and give the probable source of these particles.

16. Describe the K–T event, including evidence for it and its effect on the environment.

17. Why is lithogenous sediment the most common neritic deposit? Why are biogenous oozes the most common pelagic deposits?

18. How do fecal pellets help explain why the particles found in the ocean surface waters are closely reflected in the particle composition of the sediment directly beneath? Why would one not expect this?

The Coast: Beaches and Shoreline Processes

House falling into the sea at North Carolina's Outer Banks. When coastal structures are built too close to the sea, they could collapse into it, as did this house in Nags Head, North Carolina in 2000. Understanding coastal dynamics and shoreline processes can help prevent damage such as this.

From Chapter 11 of *Introduction to Oceanography*, Tenth Edition, Harold V. Thurman, Alan P. Trujillo.

The answers to these questions (and much more) can be found in the highlighted concept statements within this chapter.

"The waves which dash upon the shore are, one by one, broken, but the ocean conquers nevertheless. It overwhelms the Armada, it wears out the rock."

—Lord Byron (1821)

Humans have always been attracted to the coastal regions of the world for their moderate climate, seafood, transportation, recreational opportunities, and commercial benefits. In the United States, for example, 80% of the population now lives within easy access of the Atlantic, Pacific, and Gulf Coasts, increasing the stress on these important national resources.

The coastal region is constantly changing because waves crash along most shorelines more than 10,000 times a day, releasing their energy from distant storms. Waves cause erosion in some areas and deposition in others, resulting in changes that occur hourly, daily, weekly, monthly, seasonally, and yearly.

In this chapter, we'll examine the major features of the seacoast and shore and the processes that modify them. We'll also discuss ways people interfere with these processes, creating hazards to themselves and to the environment.

The Coastal Region

The **shore** is a zone that lies between the lowest tide level (low tide) and the highest elevation on land that is affected by storm waves. The **coast** extends inland from the shore as far as ocean-related features can be found (Figure 1). The width of the shore varies between a few meters and hundreds of meters. The width of the coast may vary from less than a kilometer (0.6 mile) to many tens of kilometers. The **coastline** marks the boundary between the shore and the coast. It is the landward limit of the effect of the highest storm waves on the shore.

Beach Terminology

The beach profile in Figure 1 shows features characteristic of a cliffed shoreline. The shore is divided into the **backshore** and the **foreshore**.[1] The backshore is above the high-tide shoreline and is covered with water only during storms. The foreshore is the portion exposed at low tide and submerged at high tide. The **shoreline** migrates back and forth with the tide and is the water's edge. The **nearshore** extends seaward from the low-tide

---

[1] The foreshore is often referred to as the *intertidal* or *littoral* (*litoralis* = the shore) zone.

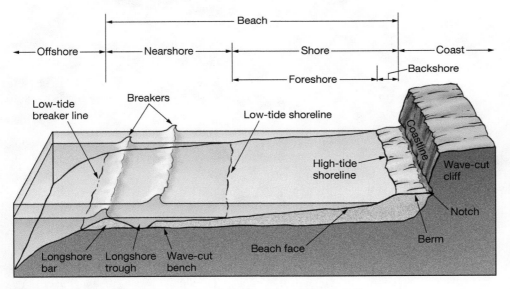

Figure 1 Landforms and terminology of coastal regions.

The beach is the entire active area affected by waves that extends from the low tide breaker line to the base of the coastal cliffs.

shoreline to the low-tide breaker line. It is never exposed to the atmosphere, but it is affected by waves that touch bottom. Beyond the low-tide breakers is the **offshore** zone, which is deep enough that waves rarely affect the bottom.

A **beach** is a deposit of the shore area. It consists of wave-worked sediment that moves along the **wave-cut bench** (a flat, wave-eroded surface). A beach may continue from the coastline across the nearshore region to the line of breakers. Thus, the beach is the entire active area of a coast that experiences changes due to breaking waves. The area of the beach above the shoreline is often called the *recreational beach*.

The **berm** is the dry, gently sloping region at the foot of the coastal cliffs or dunes. The berm is often composed of sand, making it a favorite place of beachgoers. The **beach face** is the wet, sloping surface that extends from the berm to the shoreline. It is more fully exposed during low tide, and is also known as the *low tide terrace*. The beach face is a favorite place for runners because the sand is wet and hard packed. Offshore beyond the beach face is one or more **longshore bars**—sand bars that parallel the coast. A longshore bar may not always be present throughout the year, but when one is, it may be exposed during extremely low tides. Longshore bars can "trip" waves as they approach shore and cause them to begin breaking. Separating the longshore bar from the beach face is a **longshore trough**.

The beach is the coastal area affected by breaking waves and includes the berm, beach face, longshore trough, and longshore bar.

Beach Composition and Slope

Beaches are composed of whatever material is locally available. When this material—sediment—comes from the erosion of beach cliffs or nearby coastal mountains, beaches are composed of mineral particles from these rocks and may be relatively coarse in texture. When the sediment comes primarily from rivers that drain lowland areas, beaches are finer in texture. Often, mud flats develop along the shore because only tiny clay-sized and silt-sized particles are emptied into the ocean. Such is the case for muddy coastlines such as along the coast of Suriname in South America and the Kerala coast of southwest India.

Other beaches have a significant biologic component. For example, in low-relief, low-latitude areas such as southern Florida, where there are no mountains or other sources of rock-forming minerals nearby, most beaches are composed of shell fragments and the remains of organisms that live in coastal waters. Many beaches on volcanic islands in the open ocean are composed of black or green fragments of the basaltic lava that comprise the islands, or of coarse debris from coral reefs that develop around islands in low latitudes.

Regardless of the composition, though, the material that comprises the beach does not stay in one place. Instead, the waves that crash along the shoreline are constantly moving it. Thus, beaches can be thought of as *material in transit along the shoreline.*

Measurements of beach slopes reveal that coarser beach materials have steeper beach slopes (Table 1). This relationship is caused by waves that wash up onto the beach, which transport sand up the beach, too. If most of the water from a wave percolates into the beach, the sediment it carries remains on the beach and increases the beach slope. As a result, beaches composed of coarse, loosely packed materials have steeper beach slopes. Conversely, a beach composed of fine-grained sand that does not allow water to soak in will have a more gently sloping (and firmer) surface. This is because most of the water from breaking waves runs back toward ocean and has enough energy to carry sand back down the beach face. In this way, an equilibrium is reached and a gentle beach slope is produced.

TABLE 1 Relationship between particle size and beach slope.

Wentworth particle name	Maximum size (mm)	Average beach slope
Cobble	64	24°
Pebble	4	17°
Granule	2	11°
Very coarse sand	1	9°
Coarse sand	0.5	7°
Medium sand	0.25	5°
Fine sand	0.125	3°
Very fine sand	0.063	1°

Source: After Shephard, F. P., *Submarine geology,* 3rd ed. (Table 9, P. 127, "Average beach face slopes compared to sediment diameters"), Harper & Row Publishers, Inc., 1973

Movement of Sand on the Beach

The movement of sand on the beach occurs both perpendicular to the shoreline (*toward* and *away from* shore) and parallel to the shoreline (often referred to as *up-coast* and *down-coast*).

Movement Perpendicular to Shoreline Breaking waves move sand perpendicular to the shoreline. As each wave breaks, water rushes up the beach face toward the berm. Some of this **swash** soaks into the beach and eventually returns to the ocean. However, most of the water drains away from shore as backwash, though usually not before the next wave breaks and sends its swash over the top of the previous wave's **backwash**.

While standing in ankle-deep water at the shoreline, you can see that swash and backwash transports sediment up and down the beach face perpendicular to the shoreline. Whether swash or backwash dominates determines whether sand is deposited or eroded from the berm.

In *light wave activity* (characterized by less energetic waves), much of the swash soaks into the beach, so backwash is reduced. The swash dominates the transport system, therefore, causing a net movement of the sand up the beach face toward the berm, making it wide and well developed.

In *heavy wave activity* (characterized by high-energy waves), the beach is saturated with water from previous waves, so very little of the swash soaks into the beach. Backwash dominates the transport system, therefore, causing a net movement of sand down the beach face, which erodes the berm. When a wave breaks, moreover, the incoming swash comes *on top of* the previous wave's backwash, effectively protecting the beach from the swash and adding to the eroding effect of the backwash.

During heavy wave activity, where does the sand from the berm go? The orbital motion in waves is too shallow to move the sand very far offshore. Thus, the sand accumulates just beyond where the waves break and forms one or more offshore sand bars (the longshore bars).

Light and heavy wave activity alternate seasonally at most beaches, so the characteristics of the beaches change, too (Table 2). Light wave activity produces a wide sandy berm and an overall steep beach face—a **summertime beach**—at the expense of the longshore bar (Figure 2a). Conversely, heavy wave activity produces a narrow rocky berm and an overall flattened beach face—a **wintertime beach**—and builds prominent longshore bars (Figure 2b). A wide berm that takes several months to build can be destroyed in just a few hours by high-energy wintertime storm waves.

> Smaller, low-energy waves move sand up the beach face toward the berm and create a summertime beach while larger, high-energy waves scour sand from the berm and create a wintertime beach.

Movement Parallel to Shoreline   At the same time that movement occurs perpendicular to shore, movement parallel to shoreline also occurs. Recall that waves refract (bend) and line up *nearly* parallel to the shore. With each breaking wave, the swash moves up onto the exposed beach at a slight angle, then gravity pulls the backwash straight down the beach face. As a result, water moves in a zigzag fashion along the shore, creating a movement of water within the surf zone called a **longshore current** (Figure 3).

Longshore currents have speeds up to 4 kilometers (2.5 miles) per hour. Speeds increase as beach slope increases, as the angle at which breakers arrive at the beach increases, as wave height increases, and as wave frequency increases.

Swimmers can be inadvertently carried by longshore currents and find themselves carried far from where they initially entered the water. This demonstrates that longshore currents are strong enough to move people as well as a vast amount of sand in a zigzag fashion along the shore.

Longshore drift or **longshore transport** is the movement of *sediment* in a zigzag fashion caused by the longshore current (Figure 3b). Because a longshore current affects the entire surf zone, the resulting longshore drift works within the entire surf zone as well.

The amount of longshore drift in any coastal region depends on the equilibrium between erosional and depositional forces. Any interference with the movement of sediment along the shore disrupts the equilibrium, forming a new erosional and depositional pattern. Nevertheless, longshore drift moves millions of tons of sediment along coastal regions every year.

Both rivers and coastal zones move water *and* sediment from one area (*upstream*) to another (*downstream*). As a result, the beach has often been referred to as a "river of sand." A longshore current moves in a zigzag fashion, however, and rivers flow mostly in a turbulent, swirling fashion. Additionally, the direction of flow of longshore currents along a shoreline can change, whereas rivers always flow in the same direction (downhill). The longshore current changes direction because the direction with which waves approach the beach changes seasonally. Nevertheless, the longshore current generally flows *southward along both the Atlantic and Pacific shores of the United States.*

STUDENTS SOMETIMES ASK...
What is the difference between a rip current and a rip tide? Are they the same thing as an undertow?

Like tidal waves (tsunami), rip tides are a misnomer and have nothing to do with the tides. Rip tides are more correctly called rip currents. Perhaps rip currents have incorrectly been called rip tides because they occur suddenly (like an incoming tide).

An undertow, similar to a rip current, is a flow of water away from shore. An undertow is much wider, however, and is usually more concentrated along the ocean floor. An undertow is really a continuation of backwash that flows down the beach face and is strongest during heavy wave activity. Undertows can be strong enough to knock people off their feet, but they are confined to the immediate floor of the ocean and only within the surf zone.

> Longshore currents are produced by waves approaching the beach at an angle and create longshore drift, which transports sand along the coast in a zigzag fashion.

BOX 1   People and Ocean Environment

WARNING: RIP CURRENTS ... DO YOU KNOW WHAT TO DO?

The backwash from breaking waves usually returns to the open ocean as a flow of water across the ocean bottom, so it is commonly referred to as "sheet flow." Some of this water, however, flows back in surface **rip currents**. Rip currents typically flow perpendicular to the beach and move away from the shore.

Rip currents are between 15 and 45 meters (15 and 150 feet) wide and can attain velocities of 7 to 8 kilometers (4 to 5 miles) per hour—faster than most people can swim for any length of time. In fact, it is useless to swim for long against a current stronger than about 2 kilometers (1.2 miles) per hour. Rip currents can travel hundreds of meters from shore before they break up. If a light-to-moderate swell is breaking, numerous rip currents may develop, which are moderate in size and velocity. A heavy swell usually produces fewer, more concentrated, and stronger rips. They can often be recognized by the way they interfere with incoming waves, by their characteristic brown color caused by suspended sediment, or by their foamy and choppy surface.

The rip currents that occur during heavy swell are a significant hazard to coastal swimmers. In fact, 80% of rescues at beaches by lifeguards involve people who are trapped in rip currents. Swimmers caught in a rip current can escape by swimming parallel to the shore for a short distance (simply swimming out of the narrow rip current) and then riding the waves in toward the beach. However, even excellent swimmers who panic or try to fight the current by swimming directly into it are eventually overcome by exhaustion and may drown. Even though most beaches have warnings posted and are frequently patrolled by lifeguards, many people lose their lives each year because of rip currents.

Rip currents.

A rip current, which extends outward from shore near the middle of the photo and interferes with incoming waves, and warning sign (*inset*).

Photo courtesy of Drew Wilson, Virginian–Pilot © 1999

APT photos

TABLE 2 **Characteristics of beaches affected by light and heavy wave activity.**

	Light wave activity	Heavy wave activity
Berm/longshore bars	Berm is built at the expense of the longshore bars	Longshore bars are built at the expense of the berm
Wave energy	Low wave energy (non-storm conditions)	High wave energy (storm conditions)
Time span	Long time span (weeks or months)	Short time span (hours or days)
Characteristics	Creates summertime beach: sandy, wide berm, steep beach face	Creates wintertime beach: rocky, narrow berm, flattened beach face

Figure 2 Summertime and wintertime beach conditions.

Dramatic differences occur between (**a**) summertime and (**b**) wintertime beach conditions at Boomer Beach in La Jolla, California.

APT photos

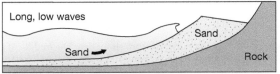

(a) Summertime beach (fair weather)

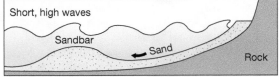

(b) Wintertime beach (storm)

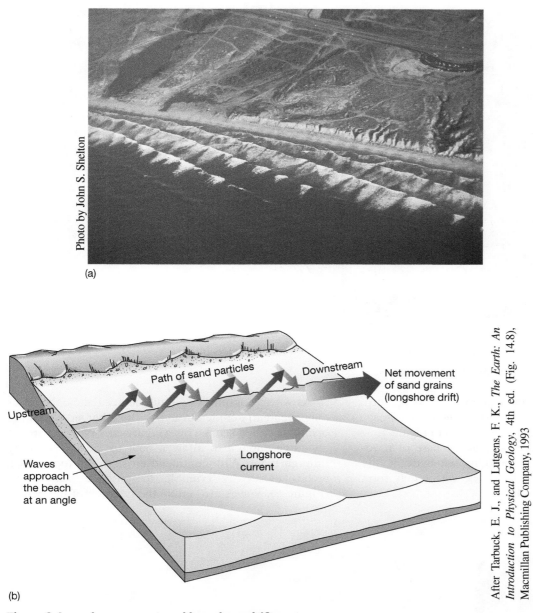

Photo by John S. Shelton

(a)

Upstream

Waves approach the beach at an angle

Path of sand particles

Downstream

Net movement of sand grains (longshore drift)

Longshore current

(b)

After Tarbuck, E. J., and Lutgens, F. K., *The Earth: An Introduction to Physical Geology*, 4th ed. (Fig. 14.8), Macmillan Publishing Company, 1993

Figure 3 Longshore current and longshore drift.

(a) Waves approaching the beach at a slight angle near Oceanside, California, producing a longshore current moving toward the right of the photo. (b) A longshore current, caused by refracting waves, moves water in a zigzag fashion along the shoreline. This causes a net movement of sand grains (longshore drift) from upstream to downstream ends.

Erosional- and Depositional-Type Shores

Sediment eroded from the beach is transported along the shore and deposited in areas where wave energy is low. Even though all shores experience some degree of both erosion and deposition, shores can often be identified primarily as one type or the other. **Erosional-type shores** typically have well-developed cliffs and are in areas where tectonic uplift of the coast occurs, such as along the U.S. Pacific Coast.

The U.S. southeastern Atlantic Coast and the Gulf Coast, on the other hand, are primarily **depositional-type shores**. Sand deposits and offshore barrier islands are common there because the shore is gradually subsiding. Erosion can still be a major problem on depositional shores, especially when human development interferes with natural coastal processes.

Features of Erosional-Type Shores

Because of wave refraction, wave energy is concentrated on any **headlands** that jut out from the continent, while the

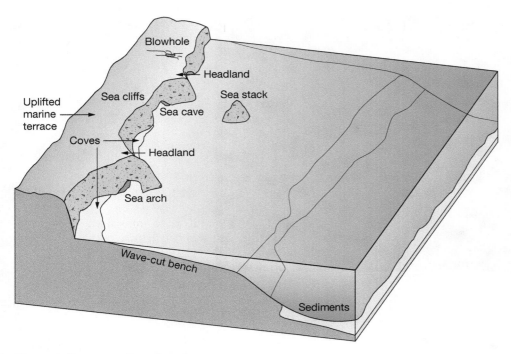

Figure 4 Features of erosional coasts.

Diagrammatic view of features characteristic of erosional coasts.

amount of energy reaching the shore in bays is reduced. Headlands, therefore, are eroded and the shoreline retreats. Some of these erosional features are shown in Figure 4.

Waves pound relentlessly away at the base of head-lands, undermining the upper portions, which eventually collapse to form **wave-cut cliffs**. The waves may form **sea caves** at the base of the cliffs.

As waves continue to pound the headlands, the caves may eventually erode through to the other side, forming openings called **sea arches** (Figure 5). Some sea arches are large enough to allow a boat to maneuver safely through them. With continued erosion, the tops of sea arches eventually crumble to produce **sea stacks** (Figure 5). Waves also erode the bedrock of the bench.

Figure 5 Sea arch and sea stack along the coast of Iceland.

When the roof of a sea arch (*left*) collapses, a sea stack (*right*) is formed.

Uplift of the wave-cut bench creates a gently sloping **marine terrace** above sea level (Figure 6).

Rates of coastal erosion are influenced by the degree of exposure to waves, the amount of tidal range, and the composition of the coastal bedrock. Regardless of the erosion rate, all coastal regions follow the same developmental path. As long as there is no change in the elevation of the landmass relative to the ocean surface, the cliffs will continue to erode and retreat until the beaches widen sufficiently to prevent waves from reaching them. The eroded material is carried from high-energy areas and deposited in low-energy areas.

Features of Depositional-Type Shores

Coastal erosion of sea cliffs produces large amounts of sediment. Additional sediment, which is carried to the shore by rivers, comes from the erosion of inland rocks. Waves then distribute all of this sediment along the continental margin.

Figure 6 Wave-cut bench and marine terrace.

A wave-cut bench is exposed at low tide along the California coast at Bolinas Point near San Francisco. An elevated wave-cut bench, called a marine terrace, is shown at right.

Figure 7 shows some of the features of depositional coasts. These features are primarily deposits of sand moved by longshore drift but are also modified by other coastal processes. Some are partially or wholly separated from the shore.

A **spit** (*spit* = spine) is a linear ridge of sediment that extends in the direction of longshore drift from land into the deeper water near the mouth of a bay. The end of the spit normally curves into the bay due to the movement of currents.

Tidal currents or currents from river runoff are usually strong enough to keep the mouth of the bay open. If not, the spit may eventually extend across the bay and connect to the mainland, forming a **bay barrier** or **bay-mouth bar** (Figure 8a), which cuts off the bay from the open ocean. Although bay barriers are a buildup of sand usually less than 1 meter (3.3 feet) above sea level, permanent buildings are often constructed on them.

A **tombolo** (*tombolo* = mound) is a sand ridge that connects an island or sea stack to the mainland (Figure 8b). Tombolos can also connect two adjacent islands. Formed in the wave-energy shadow of an island, tombolos are usually perpendicular to the average direction from which waves approach.

Barrier Islands Extremely long offshore deposits of sand lying parallel to the coast are called **barrier islands** (Figure 9). They form a first line of defense against storm waves that otherwise would severely assault the shore. Their origin is complex, but many barrier islands seem to have developed during the worldwide rise in sea level that began with the melting of the most recent major glaciers some 18,000 years ago.

At least 280 barrier islands ring the Atlantic and Gulf Coasts of the United States. They are nearly con-

Figure 7 Features of depositional coasts.

Diagrammatic view of features characteristic of depositional coasts.

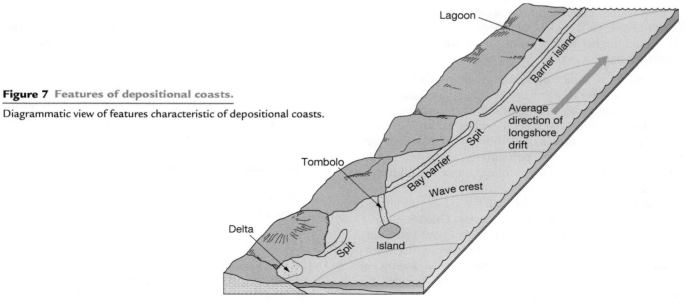

Figure 8 Coastal depositional features.

(a) Barrier coast, spit, and bay barrier along the coast of Martha's Vineyard, Massachusetts. (b) Tombolo at Goat Rock Beach, California.

tinuous from Massachusetts to Florida and continue through the Gulf of Mexico, where they exist well south of the Mexican border. Barrier islands may exceed 100 kilometers (60 miles) in length, have widths of several kilometers, and are separated from the mainland by a lagoon. Notable barrier islands include Fire Island off the New York coast, North Carolina's Outer Banks, and Padre Island off the coast of Texas.

A typical barrier island has the physiographic features shown in Figure 10a. From the ocean landward, they are (1) ocean beach, (2) dunes, (3) barrier flat, (4) high salt marsh, (5) low salt marsh, and (6) lagoon between the barrier island and the mainland.

During the summer, gentle waves carry sand to the *ocean beach*, so it widens and becomes steeper. During the winter, higher-energy waves carry sand offshore and produce a narrow, gently sloping beach.

Winds blow sand inland during dry periods to produce coastal *dunes*, which are stabilized by dune grasses. These plants can withstand salt spray and burial by sand. Dunes protect the lagoon against excessive flooding during storm-driven high tides. Numerous passes exist through the dunes, particularly along the southeastern Atlantic Coast, where dunes are less well developed than to the north.

The *barrier flat* forms behind the dunes from sand driven through the passes during storms. Grasses quickly colonize these flats and seawater washes over them during storms. If storms wash over the barrier flat infrequently enough, the plants undergo natural biological succession, with the grasses successively replaced by thickets, woodlands, and eventually forests.

Salt marshes typically lie inland of the barrier flat. They are divided into the *low marsh*, which extends from about mean sea level to the high neap-tide line, and the *high marsh*, which extends to the highest spring-tide line. The low marsh is by far the most biologically productive part of the salt marsh.

New marshland is formed as overwash carries sediment into the lagoon, filling portions so they become intermittently exposed by the tides. Marshes may be poorly developed on parts of the island that are far from flood-tide inlets. Their development is greatly restricted on barrier islands, where people perform artificial dune enhancement and fill inlets, which are activities that prevent overwashing and flooding.

The gradual sea level rise experienced along the eastern North American coast is causing barrier islands to migrate landward. The movement of the barrier island is similar to a slowly moving tractor tread, with the entire island rolling over itself, impacting structures built on these islands. *Peat deposits*, which are formed by the accumulation of organic matter in marsh environments, provide further evidence of barrier island migration (Figure 10b). As the island slowly rolls over itself and migrates toward land, it buries ancient peat deposits. These peat deposits can be found beneath the island and may even be exposed on the ocean beach when the barrier island has moved far enough.

Deltas Some rivers carry more sediment to the ocean than longshore currents can distribute. These rivers develop a **delta** (*delta* = triangular) deposit at their

Photo by USDA-ASCS

Photo © 2003 Andrew Alden; geology.about.com

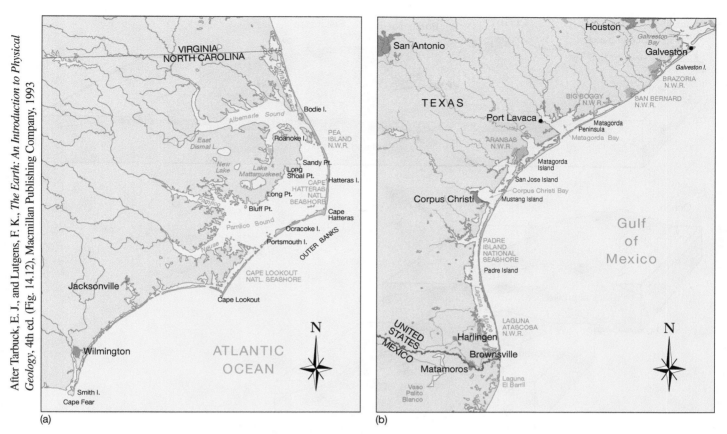

After Tarbuck, E. J., and Lutgens, F. K., *The Earth: An Introduction to Physical Geology*, 4th ed. (Fig. 14.12), Macmillan Publishing Company, 1993

Photo by USDA-ASCS

(c)

Figure 9 Barrier islands.

(a) Barrier islands along North Carolina's Outer Banks. (b) Barrier islands along the south Texas coast. (c) A portion of a heavily developed barrier island near Tom's River, New Jersey.

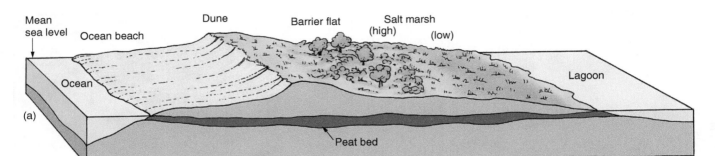

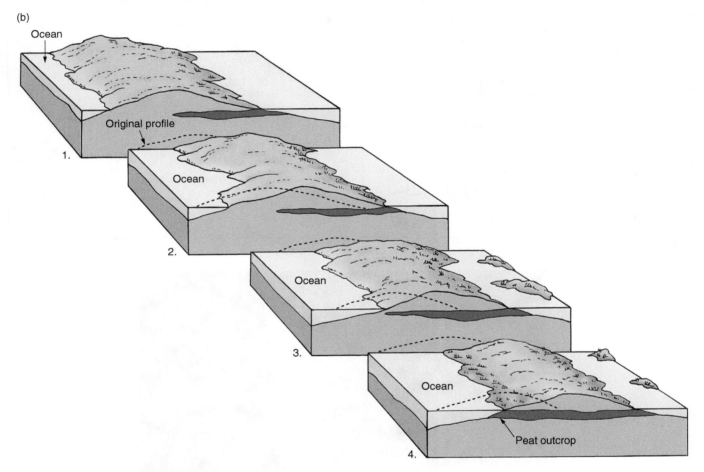

Figure 10 Formation of barrier islands.

(a) Diagrammatic view showing the major physiographic zones of a barrier island. The peat bed represents ancient marsh environments. (b) Sequence (1–4) showing how a barrier island migrates and exposes peat deposits that have been covered by the island as it migrates toward the mainland in response to rising sea level.

mouths. The Mississippi River, which empties into the Gulf of Mexico (Figure 11a), forms one of the largest deltas on Earth. Deltas are fertile, flat, low-lying areas that are subject to periodic flooding.

Delta formation begins when a river has filled its mouth with sediment. The delta then grows through the formation of *distributaries*, which are branching channels that deposit sediment as they radiate out over the delta in fingerlike extensions (Figure 11a). When the fingers get too long, they become choked with sediment. At this point, a flood may easily shift the distrib-

utary's course and provide sediment to low-lying areas between the fingers. When depositional processes exceed coastal erosion and transportation processes, a branching "bird's foot" Mississippi-type delta results.

When erosion and transportation processes exceed deposition, on the other hand, a delta shoreline is smoothed to a gentle curve, like that of the Nile River Delta in Egypt (Figure 11b). The Nile Delta is presently eroding because sediment is trapped behind the Aswan High Dam. Prior to completion of the dam in 1964, the Nile carried huge volumes of sediment into the Mediterranean Sea.

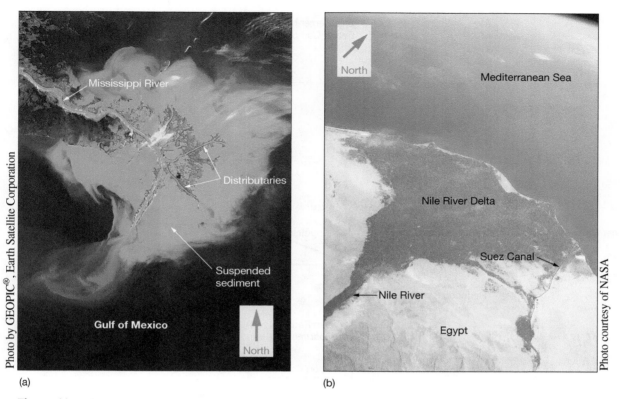

(a)

(b)

Figure 11 Deltas.

(a) False-color infrared image of the branching "bird's foot" structure of the Mississippi River Delta. Red color is vegetation on land; light blue color is suspended sediment within the water. **(b)** Photograph from the space shuttle of Egypt's Nile River Delta, which has a smooth, curved shoreline as it extends into the Mediterranean Sea.

Beach Compartments **Beach compartments** consist of three components: a series of rivers that supply sand to a beach; the beach itself where sand is moving due to longshore transport; and offshore submarine canyons where sand is drained away from the beach. The map in Figure 12 shows that the coast of southern California contains four separate beach compartments.

Primarily rivers, but also coastal erosion, supply sand to the beach within an individual beach compartment (Figure 12, *inset*). The sand moves south with the longshore current, so beaches are wider near the southern (*downstream*) end of each beach compartment. Although some sand is washed offshore along the way, most eventually moves near a head of a submarine canyon, where it is diverted away from the beach and onto the ocean floor. When the sand is removed from the coastal environment, it is lost from the beach forever. To the south of this beach compartment, the beaches will be thin and rocky, without much sand. The process begins all over again at the next beach compartment, where rivers add their sediment. Farther downstream, the beach widens and has an abundance of sand until that sand is also moved down a submarine canyon.

STUDENTS SOMETIMES ASK...
Can submarine canyons fill with sediment?

Yes. In many beach compartments, the submarine canyons that drain sand from the beach empty into deep basins offshore. However, given several million years and tons of sediments per year sliding down the submarine canyons, the offshore basins begin to fill up and can eventually be exposed above sea level. In fact, the Los Angeles basin in California was filled in by sediment derived from local mountains in this manner during the geologic past.

Human activities have altered the natural system of beach compartments. When a dam is built along one of the rivers that feed into the beach compartment, it deprives the beach of sand. Lining rivers with concrete for flood control further reduces the sediment load delivered to coastal regions. Longshore transport continues to sweep the shoreline's sand into the submarine canyons, so the beaches

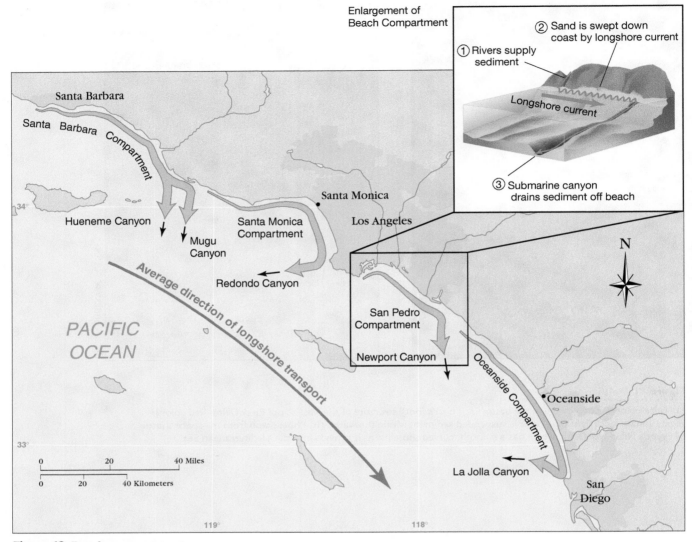

Figure 12 Beach compartments.

Southern California has several beach compartments, which include rivers that bring sediment to the beach, the beach that experiences longshore transport, and the submarine canyons that remove sand from the beaches. Average longshore transport is toward the south.

become narrower and experience **beach starvation**. If all the rivers are blocked, the beaches may nearly disappear.

What can be done to prevent beach starvation in beach compartments? One obvious solution is to eliminate the dams, which would allow rivers to supply sand to the beach and return beach compartments to a natural balance. However, most dams are built for flood protection, water storage, and the generation of hydropower, so it is unlikely that many will be removed.

Another option is **beach replenishment** (also called **beach nourishment**), in which sand is added to the beach to replace the sediment held back by dams. Beach replenishment is expensive, however, because huge volumes of sand must be continually supplied to the beach. When dams are built, their effect on beaches far downstream is rarely considered. It's not until beach starvation occurs that the rivers are seen as parts of much larger systems that operate along the coast.

The cost of beach replenishment depends on the type and quantity of material placed on the beach, how far the material must be transported, and how it is to be distributed on the beach. Most sand used for replenishment comes from offshore areas, but sand that is dredged from nearby rivers, drained dams, harbors, and lagoons is also used.

The average cost of sand used to replenish beaches is between $5 and $10 per 0.76 cubic meter (1 cubic yard). For comparison, a typical top-loading trash dumpster holds about 2.3 cubic meters (3 cubic yards) of material, and a typical dump truck holds about 45 cubic meters (60 cubic yards) of material. The problem with replenishment projects is that a huge volume of sand is needed, and new sand must be supplied continuously. For example, a small beach replenishment project of several hundred cubic meters can cost around

$10,000 per year. Larger projects—several thousand cubic meters of sand—cost several million dollars per year.

Recycled glass that is ground to sand size and spread on the beach has been proposed as a less expensive source for beach replenishment, but the health and safety risks have not been fully explored.

Erosional-type shores are characterized by erosional features such as cliffs, sea arches, sea stacks, and marine terraces. Depositional-type shores are characterized by depositional features such as spits, tombolos, barrier islands, deltas, and beach compartments.

Classification of Coasts

Francis Shepard (1897–1985) was one of the first to study coastal processes and, because of his pioneering work, is considered the "father of marine geology." Among his many accomplishments, he developed a classification of coasts that divided all coasts into one of two types: (1) **primary coasts**, which are younger coasts that have been formed by nonmarine processes; or (2) **secondary coasts**, which have aged to the point where physical and/or biological marine processes dominate the character of the coast. These two main coastal types and various subtypes are shown in Table 3.

Primary coasts are controlled by nonmarine processes. For example, *land erosion coasts* include drowned rivers (such as Chesapeake Bay) and drowned glacial-erosion

TABLE 3 Shepard's classification of coasts.

Coasts Shaped by Nonmarine Processes (*Primary Coasts*)			Coasts Shaped by Marine Processes or Marine Organisms (*Secondary Coasts*)		
Land erosion coasts	Drowned rivers		**Wave erosion**	Straightened coasts	
	Drowned glacial-erosion coasts	Fjord (narrow)		Irregular coasts	
		Trough (wide)	**Marine deposition coasts (prograded by waves, currents)**	Barrier coasts	Sand beaches (single ridge)
Subaerial deposition coasts	River deposition coasts	Deltas			Sand islands (multiple ridges, dunes)
		Alluvial plains			Sand spits (connected to mainland)
	Glacial-deposition coasts	Moraines			Bay barriers
		Drumlins		Cuspate forelands (large projecting points)	
	Wind deposition coasts	Dunes		Beach plains	
	Landslide coasts	Sand flats		Mud flats, salt marshes (no breaking waves)	
Volcanic coasts	Lava flow coasts		**Coasts formed by biological activity**	Coral reef, algae (in the tropics)	
	Tephra coasts			Oyster reefs	
	Coasts formed by volcanic collapse or explosion			Mangrove coasts	
Coasts shaped by Earth movements	Faults			Marsh grass	
	Folds			Serpulid reefs (small reefs constructed of serpulid worm tubes)	
	Sedimentary extrusions	Mud lumps			
		Salt domes			
Ice coasts					

Source: After Shephard, F. P., Coastal classification and changing coastlines, in *Geoscience and Man*, 14, 53–64, 1976.

Figure 13 Examples of primary and secondary coasts.

Primary coasts: **(a)** Drowned glacial-erosion coast: fjord. Fjord and Marjorie Glacier, Glacier Bay, Alaska.
(b) Wind deposition coast: dune. Baja California, Mexico. **(c)** Volcanic coast: lava flow. Kilauea, Hawaii.
Secondary coasts: **(d)** Wave erosion coast: straightened. Leucadia, California. **(e)** Barrier coast: sand beach.
Barrier island, North Carolina. **(f)** Coast formed by biological activity: mangrove. Galápagos Islands, Ecuador.

coasts (such as Puget Sound). These coasts were formed by a relative rise in sea level that accompanied the melting of glaciers at the end of the most recent Ice Age. Other types of coasts that have formed recently by non-marine geologic processes include *subaerial deposition coasts, volcanic coasts, coasts shaped by Earth movements*, and *ice coasts* (Figure 13).

With time, exposure of primary coasts to the action of ocean waves or biological processes destroys all evidence of the nonmarine process that produced them, thereby converting them to secondary coasts. For instance, a primary coast initially formed by Earth movements may be eroded sufficiently by wave action to produce a secondary *wave erosion coast*. Further, if the underlying bedrock is of uniform strength, a straightened coast will be produced (Figure 13); if the resistance of the bedrock varies along the coast, an irregular coast is produced. In fact, the majority of the Pacific Coast of the United States is classified as a wave erosion coast. Alternatively, most of the Atlantic Coast—especially from Massachusetts south—is classified as a *marine deposition coast*. *Coasts formed by biological activity* include coral reef coasts and mangrove coasts (Figure 13), both of which are quite restricted along U.S. shorelines and occur only in low-latitude areas.

Emerging and Submerging Shorelines

Shorelines can also be classified based on their position relative to sea level. *Sea level, however, has changed throughout time.* It can change because the level of the land changes, the level of the sea changes, or a combination of the two. Shorelines that are rising above sea level are called **emerging shorelines** and those sinking below sea level are called **submerging shorelines**.

Marine terraces (Figures 6, 14, and 19) are one feature characteristic of emerging shorelines. Marine terraces are flat platforms backed by cliffs, which form when a wave-cut bench is exposed above sea level. **Stranded beach deposits** and other evidence of marine processes may exist many meters above the present shoreline, indicating that the former shoreline has risen above sea level.

Features characteristic of submerging shorelines include **drowned beaches** (Figure 14), **submerged dune topography**, and **drowned river valleys** along the present shoreline.

What causes the changes in sea level that produce submerging and emerging shorelines? One main cause is tectonic and isostatic movements, which raise or lower the land surface relative to sea level. Another is worldwide changes in sea level, which affect the sea itself.

Tectonic and Isostatic Movements of Earth's Crust

The most dramatic changes in sea level during the past 3000 years have been caused by *tectonic processes*

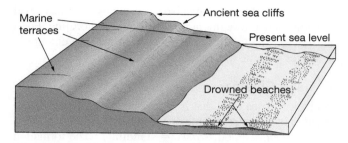

Figure 14 Evidence of ancient shorelines.

Marine terraces result from exposure of ancient sea cliffs and wave-cut benches above present sea level. Below sea level, drowned beaches indicate the sea level has risen relative to the land.

(movement of the land). These changes include uplift or subsidence of major portions of continents or ocean basins, as well as localized folding, faulting, or tilting of the continental crust.

Earth's crust also undergoes *isostatic adjustment*. It sinks under the accumulation of heavy loads of ice, vast piles of sediment, or outpourings of lava, and it rises when heavy loads are removed.

Most of the U.S. Pacific Coast is an emerging shoreline because continental margins where plate collisions occur are tectonically active, producing earthquakes, volcanoes, and mountain chains paralleling the coast. Most of the U.S. Atlantic Coast, on the other hand, is a submerging shoreline. When a continent moves away from a spreading center (such as the Mid-Atlantic Ridge), its trailing edge subsides because of cooling and the additional weight of accumulating sediment. Passive margins experience only a low level of tectonic deformation, earthquakes, and volcanism, making the Atlantic Coast far more quiet and stable than the Pacific Coast.

At least four major accumulations of glacial ice—and dozens of smaller ones—have occurred in high-latitude regions during the last 2.5 to 3 million years. Although Antarctica is still covered by a very large, thick ice cap, much of the ice that once covered much of northern Asia, Europe, and North America has melted.

The weight of ice sheets as much as 3 kilometers (2 miles) thick caused the crust beneath to sink. Today, these areas are still slowly rebounding, 18,000 years after the ice began to melt. The floor of Hudson Bay, for example, which is now about 150 meters (500 feet) deep, will be close to or above sea level by the time it stops isostatically rebounding. Another example is the Gulf of Bothnia (between Sweden and Finland), which has isostatically rebounded 275 meters (900 feet) during the last 18,000 years.

---

[2]The term *eustatic* refers to a highly idealized situation in which all of the continents remain static (in *good standing*), while only the sea rises or falls.

Generally, tectonic and isostatic changes in sea level are confined to a segment of a continent's shoreline. For a *worldwide* change in sea level, there must be a change in seawater volume or ocean basin capacity.

Eustatic Changes in Sea Level

A change in sea level that is experienced worldwide due to changes in seawater volume or ocean basin capacity is called **eustatic** (*eu* = good, *stasis* = standing).[2] The formation or destruction of large inland lakes, for example, causes small eustatic changes in sea level. When lakes form, they trap water that would otherwise run off the land into the ocean, so sea level is lowered worldwide. When lakes are drained and release their water back to the ocean, sea level rises.

Changes in sea floor spreading rates can change the capacity of the ocean basin, resulting in eustatic sea level changes. Fast spreading produces larger rises, such as the East Pacific Rise, which displace more water than slow-spreading ridges such as the Mid-Atlantic Ridge. Thus, fast spreading raises sea level, whereas slower spreading lowers sea level worldwide. Significant changes in sea level due to changes in spreading rate typically take hundreds of thousands to millions of years and may have changed sea level by 1000 meters (3300 feet) or more.

Ice ages cause eustatic sea level changes, too. As glaciers form, they tie up vast volumes of water on land, eustatically lowering sea level. An analogy to this effect is a sink of water representing an ocean basin. To simulate an ice age, some of the water from the sink is removed and frozen, causing the water level of the sink to be lower. In a similar fashion, worldwide sea level is lower during an ice age. During interglacial stages (such as the one we are in at present), the glaciers melt and release great volumes of water that drain to the sea, eustatically raising sea level. This would be analogous to putting the frozen chunk of ice on the counter near the sink and letting the ice melt, causing the water to drain into the sink and raise "sink level."

Glaciers during the Pleistocene Epoch[3] advanced and retreated many times on land near the poles, causing sea level to fluctuate considerably. The thermal contraction and expansion of the ocean as its temperature decreased and increased, respectively, affected sea level too. The thermal contraction and expansion of seawater works much like a mercury thermometer: as the mercury inside the thermometer warms, it expands and rises into the thermometer; as it cools, it contracts. Similarly, cooler seawater contracts and occupies less volume, thereby eustatically *lowering* sea level. Warmer seawater expands, eustatically *raising* sea level.

For every 1°C (1.8°F) change in the average temperature of ocean surface waters, sea level changes about 2 meters (6.6 feet). Microfossils in Pleistocene ocean sediments suggest that ocean surface waters may have been as much as 5°C (9°F) lower than at present. Therefore, thermal contraction of the ocean water may have lowered sea level by about 10 meters (33 feet).

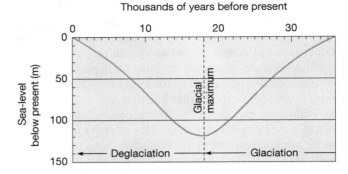

Figure 15 Sea level change during the most recent advance and retreat of Pleistocene glaciers.

Sea level dropped worldwide by about 120 meters (400 feet) as the last glacial advance removed water from the oceans and transferred it to continental glaciers. About 18,000 years ago, sea level began to rise as the glaciers melted and water was returned to the oceans.

Although it is difficult to state definitely the range of shoreline fluctuation during the Pleistocene, evidence suggests that it was at least 120 meters (400 feet) below the present shoreline (Figure 15). It is also estimated that if *all* the remaining glacial ice on Earth were to melt, sea level would rise another 60 meters (200 feet). Thus, the *minimum* sea level change during the Pleistocene is on the order of 180 meters (600 feet), most of which was due to the capture and release of Earth's water by land-based glaciers. In fact, melting of just the West Antarctic ice sheet, which has lost about two-thirds of its mass over the past 20,000 years, has resulted in an meter (36-foot) increase in worldwide sea level.

The combination of tectonic and eustatic changes in sea level is very complex, so it is difficult to classify coastal regions as purely emergent or submergent. In fact, most coastal areas show evidence of *both* submergence and emergence in the recent past. Evidence suggests, however, that until recently sea level has experienced only minor changes as a result of melting glacial ice during the last 3000 years.

Sea Level and the Greenhouse Effect

Carbon dioxide in the atmosphere has increased 30% over the last 200 years and there has been an increase in global temperature of at least 0.6°C (1.1°F) over the last 130 years. Analysis of worldwide tide records indicates that there has also been a eustatic rise in sea level of between 10 and 25 centimeters (4 and 10 inches) over the last 100 years. At certain tide recording stations where data goes back well into the 19th century, there has been an increase in relative sea level of 40 centimeters (16 inches) over the last 150 years (Figure 16). In addition, satellite altimeter data since 1993 indicates a global increase in sea level of 2.5 millimeters (0.1 inch) per year.

Clearly, sea level is rising. Is this rise the result of increased global warming because of the greenhouse effect or is it part of a long-term natural cycle? At this point, the answer cannot be easily determined, but evidence suggests that humans are altering the environment on a global scale with emissions that enhance Earth's greenhouse effect. The rise in sea level most likely represents the combined effect of an

---

[3]The Pleistocene Epoch of geologic time (also called the "Ice Age") is from 1.6 million to 10 thousand years ago.

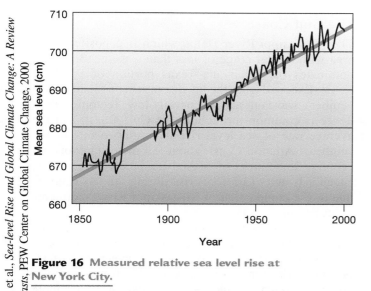

After Neumann, J. E., et al., *Sea-level Rise and Global Climate Change: A Review of Impacts to U.S. Coasts*, PEW Center on Global Climate Change, 2000

Figure 16 Measured relative sea level rise at New York City.

Tide-gauge data from New York City shows an increase in sea level of 40 centimeters (16 inches) since 1850. While some of this rise is due to local effects, the majority is likely caused by thermal expansion of warmer ocean water and the retreat of small ice caps and glaciers.

increase in ocean volume due to thermal expansion and the observed retreat of small ice caps and glaciers that are adding water to the ocean.

According to some estimates, the rate of sea level rise will increase with increased global warming, which may result in as much as a 1-meter (3.3-foot) rise in sea level by

2100. The recent increase in coastal development puts more homes in danger's path and compounds the problem. The great lesson for humankind in all this is that we cannot dominate nature. Rather, we must learn to live within it.

> Sea level is affected by the movement of land and changes in seawater volume or ocean basin capacity. Sea level has changed dramatically in the past because of changes in Earth's climate.

Characteristics of U.S. Coasts

Whether the dominant process along a coast is erosion or deposition depends on the combined effect of many variables, such as composition of coastal bedrock, the degree of exposure to ocean waves, tidal range, tectonic subsidence or emergence, isostatic subsidence or emergence, and eustatic sea level change.

Although many factors contribute to shoreline retreat, sea level rise is the main factor driving worldwide coastal land loss. In fact, more than 70% of the world's sandy beaches are currently eroding, and the percentage increases to nearly 90% for well-studied U.S. sandy coasts. Studies supported by the U.S. Geological Survey produced the rates of shoreline change presented in Figure 17, where erosion rates are shown as *negative* values and deposition rates are shown as *positive* values.

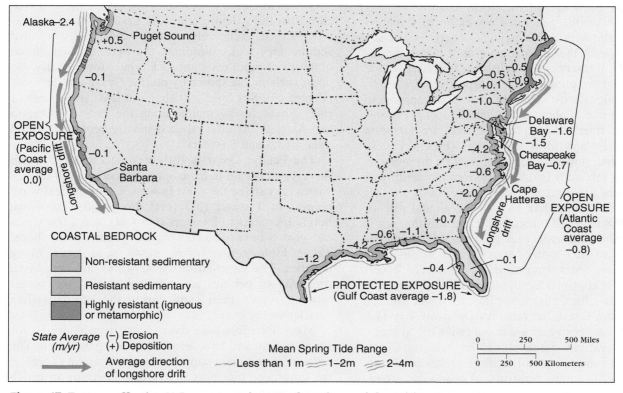

Figure 17 Factors affecting U.S. coasts and rates of erosion and deposition.

Map showing United States coastal bedrock type (*red, yellow,* and *blue colors*), the mean spring-tide range (*light blue lines*), degree of exposure, and average direction of longshore drift (*purple arrows*). The map also shows the average rate of erosion (−) or deposition (+) between 1979 and 1983 in meters per year for each coastal state and average rate for each coastal region.

385

The Atlantic Coast

Figure 17 shows that the U.S. Atlantic Coast has a variety of complex coastal conditions:

- Most of the Atlantic Coast is exposed to storm waves from the open ocean. Barrier islands from Massachusetts southward, however, protect the mainland from large storm waves.

- Tidal ranges generally increase from less than 1 meter (3.3 feet) along the Florida coast to more than 2 meters (6.5 feet) in Maine.

- Bedrock for most of Florida is a resistant type of sedimentary rock called *limestone*. Most of the bedrock northward through New Jersey, however, consists of nonresistant sedimentary rocks formed in the recent geologic past. As these rocks rapidly erode, they supply sand to barrier islands and other depositional features common along the coast. The bedrock north of New York consists of very resistant rock types.

- From New York northward, continental glaciers affected the coastal region directly. Many coastal features, including Long Island and Cape Cod, are glacial deposits (called *moraines*) left behind when the glaciers melted.

North of Cape Hatteras in North Carolina, the coast is subject to very high-energy waves during fall and winter when powerful storms called *"nor'easters"* (northeasters) blow in from the North Atlantic. The energy of these storms generates waves up to 6 meters (20 feet) high, with a 1-meter (3.3-foot) rise in sea level that follows the low pressure as it moves northward. Such high-energy conditions seriously erode coastlines that are predominantly depositional.

Sea level along most of the Atlantic Coast appears to be rising at a rate of about 0.3 meter (1 foot) per century. Drowned river valleys, for instance, are common along the coast and form large bays (Figure 18). In northern Maine, however, sea level may be dropping as the continent rebounds isostatically from the melting of the Pleistocene ice sheet.

The Atlantic Coast has an average annual rate of erosion of 0.8 meter (2.6 feet), which means that sea is migrating landward each year by a distance approximately equal to the length of your legs! In Virginia, the loss is over five times that rate at 4.2 meters (13.7 feet) per year but is confined largely to barrier islands.

Erosion rates for Chesapeake Bay are about average for the Atlantic Coast, but rates for Delaware Bay [1.6 meters (5.2 feet) per year] are about twice the average. Of the observations made along the Atlantic Coast, 79% showed some degree of erosion. Delaware, Georgia, and New York have depositional coasts despite serious erosion problems in these states as well.

The Gulf Coast

The Mississippi River Delta, which is deposited in an area with a tidal range of less than 1 meter (3.3 feet), dominates the Louisiana–Texas portion of the Gulf Coast. Except during the hurricane season (June to November), wave energy is generally low. Tectonic subsidence is common throughout the Gulf Coast, and the average rate of sea level rise is similar to that of the southeast Atlantic Coast, about 0.3 meter (1 foot) per century. Some areas of coastal Louisiana have experienced a 1-meter (3.3-foot) rise during the last century, due to the compaction of Mississippi River sediments by overlying weight.

The average rate of erosion is 1.8 meters (6 feet) per year in the Gulf Coast. The Mississippi River Delta experiences the greatest rate, averaging 4.2 meters (13.7 feet) per year. Erosion is made worse by barge channels dredged through marshlands, and Louisiana has lost more than 1 million acres of delta since 1900. Louisiana is now losing marshland at a rate exceeding 130 square kilometers (50 square miles) per year.

Although all Gulf states show a net loss of land, and the Gulf Coast has a greater erosion rate than the Atlantic Coast, only 63% of the shore is receding because of erosion. The high average rate of erosion reflects the heavy losses in the Mississippi River Delta.

The Pacific Coast

The Pacific Coast is generally experiencing less erosion than the Atlantic and Gulf Coasts. Along the Pacific Coast, relatively young and easily eroded sedimentary rocks dominate the bedrock, with local outcrops of more resistant rock types. Tectonically, the coast is rising, as shown by marine (wave-cut) terraces (Figure 19). Sea level still shows at least small rates of rise, except for segments along the coast of Oregon and Alaska. The tidal range is mostly between 1 and 2 meters (3.3 and 6.6 feet).

The Pacific Coast is fully exposed to large storm waves, and is said to have *open exposure*. High-energy waves may strike the coast in winter, with typical wave heights of 1 meter (3.3 feet). Frequently, the wave height increases to 2 meters (6.6 feet), and a few times per year 6-meter (20-foot) waves hammer the shore! These high-energy waves erode sand from many beaches. The exposed beaches, which are composed primarily of pebbles and boulders during the winter months, regain their sand during the summer when smaller waves occur.

Many Pacific Coast rivers have been dammed for flood control and hydroelectric power generation. The amount of sediment supplied by rivers to the shoreline for longshore transport is reduced, resulting in beach starvation in some areas.

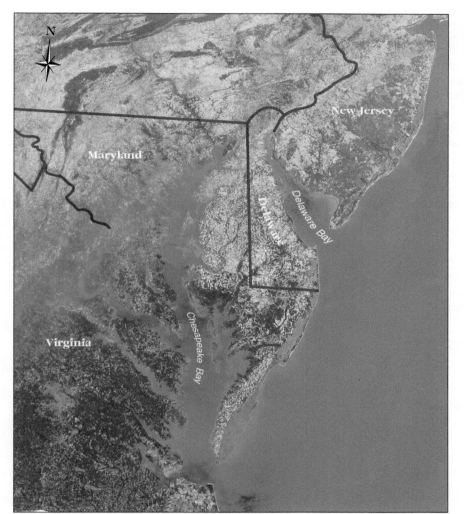

Figure 18 Drowned river valleys.

Satellite false-color image of drowned river valleys such as Chesapeake and Delaware Bays along the east coast of the U.S., which were formed by a relative rise in sea level that followed the end of the Pleistocene Ice Age.

Figure 19 Marine (wave-cut) terraces.

Each marine terrace on San Clemente Island offshore southern California was created by wave activity at sea level. Subsequently, each terrace has been exposed by tectonic uplift. The highest (oldest) terraces near the top of the photo are now about 400 meters (1320 feet) above sea level.

With an average erosion rate of only 0.005 meter (0.016 foot)[4] per year and only 30% of the coast showing erosion loss, the Pacific Coast is eroded much less than the Atlantic and Gulf Coasts. Nevertheless, high wave energy and relatively soft rocks result in high rates of erosion in some parts of the Pacific Coast. In some parts of Alaska, for example, the average rate of erosion is 2.4 meters (7.9 feet) per year.

Of the Pacific states, only Washington shows a net sediment deposition. The long, protected Washington shoreline within Puget Sound helps skew the Pacific Coast values (Figure 17). Although the average erosion rate for California is only 0.1 meter (0.33 foot) per year, over 80% of the California coast is experiencing erosion, with rates up to 0.6 meter (2 feet) per year.

> U.S. coastal regions are affected by many variables, including composition of the coastal bedrock, degree of exposure, and tidal range. Most U.S. coastal regions are experiencing erosion.

---

[4]0.005 meter is equal to 5 millimeters (0.2 inch).

Hard Stabilization

Coastal residents continually modify coastal sediment erosion/deposition in attempts to improve or preserve their property. Structures built to protect a coast from erosion or to prevent the movement of sand along a beach are known as **hard stabilization**. Hard stabilization can take many forms and often results in predictable yet unwanted outcomes.

Groins and Groin Fields

One type of hard stabilization is a **groin** (*groin* = ground). Groins are built perpendicular to a coastline and are specifically designed to trap sand moving along the coast in longshore transport (Figure 20). They are constructed of many types of material, but large blocky material called **rip-rap** is most common. Sometimes, groins are even constructed of sturdy wood pilings (similar to a fence built out into the ocean).

Although a groin traps sand on its *upstream side*, erosion occurs immediately downstream of the groin because the sand that is normally found just downstream

Figure 20 Interference of sand movement.

Hard stabilization like the groin shown here interferes with the movement of sand along the beach, causing deposition of sand upstream of the groin and erosion immediately downstream, modifying the shape of the beach.

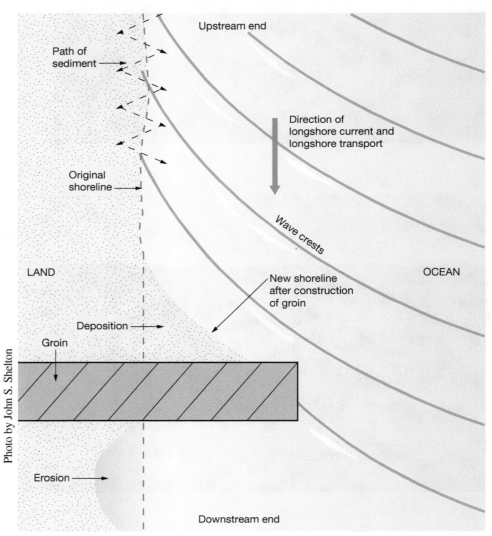

388

of the groin is trapped on the groin's upstream side. To lessen the erosion, another groin can be constructed downstream, which in turn also creates erosion downstream from it. More groins are needed to alleviate the beach erosion, and soon a **groin field** is created (Figure 21).

Does a groin (or a groin field) actually retain more sand on the beach? Sand eventually migrates around the end of the groin, so there is no additional sand on the beach; it is only *distributed differently*. With proper engineering, an equilibrium may be reached that allows sufficient sand to move along the coast before excessive erosion occurs downstream from the last groin. However, some serious erosional problems have developed in many areas resulting from attempts to stabilize sand on the beach by the excessive use of groins.

Jetties

Another type of hard stabilization is a **jetty** (*jettee* = to project). A jetty is similar to a groin because it is built perpendicular to the shore and is usually constructed of rip-rap. The purpose of a jetty, however, is to protect harbor entrances from waves and only secondarily does it trap sand (Figure 22). Because jetties are usually built in closely spaced pairs and can be quite long, they can cause more pronounced upstream deposition and downstream erosion than groins.

Breakwaters

Figure 23 shows a **breakwater**—hard stabilization built parallel to a shoreline—that was constructed to create the harbor at Santa Barbara, California. California's longshore drift is

Photo by John S. Shelton

Figure 21 Groin field.

A series of groins has been built along the shoreline north of Ship Bottom, New Jersey, in an attempt to trap sand, altering the distribution of sand on the beach. The view is toward the north, and the primary direction of longshore current is toward the bottom of the photo (toward the south).

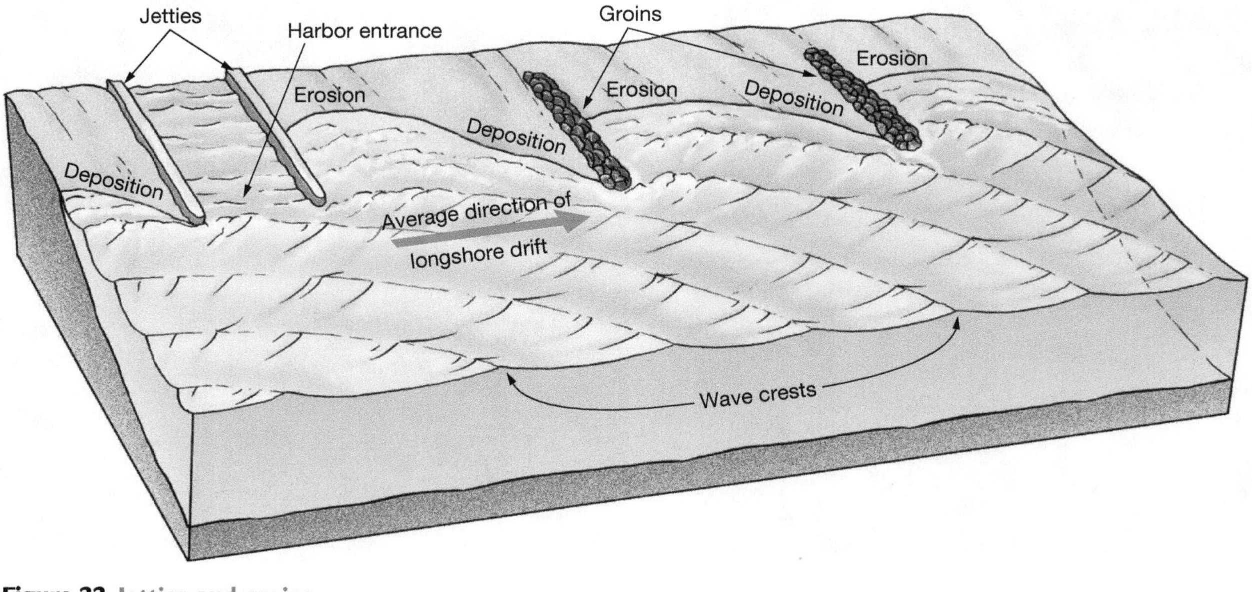

After Tarbuck, E. J., and Lutgens, F. K., *Earth Science*, 5th ed., Merrill Publishing Company, 1988

Figure 22 Jetties and groins.

Jetties protect a harbor entrance and usually occur in pairs. Groins are built specifically to trap sand moving in the longshore transport system and occur individually or as a groin field. Both structures cause deposits of sand on their upstream sides and an equal amount of erosion downstream.

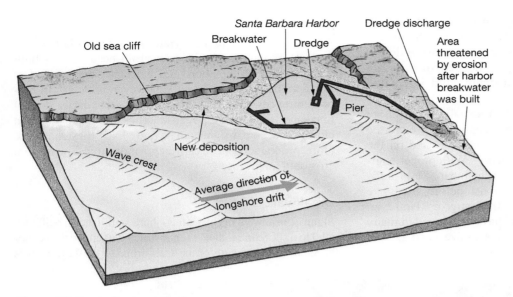

Figure 23 Santa Barbara Harbor.

Construction of a breakwater at Santa Barbara Harbor interfered with the longshore drift, creating a broad beach. As the beach extended around the breakwater into the harbor, the harbor was in danger of being closed off by accumulating sand. As a result, dredging operations were initiated to move sand from the harbor downstream, where it helped reduce coastal erosion.

predominantly southward, so the breakwater on the western side of the harbor accumulated sand that had migrated eastward along the coast. The beach to the west of the harbor continued to grow until finally the sand moved around the breakwater and began to fill in the harbor (Figure 23).

While abnormal deposition occurred to the west, erosion proceeded at an alarming rate east of the harbor. The waves east of the harbor were no greater than before, but

the sand that had formerly moved down the coast was now trapped behind the breakwater.

A similar situation occurred in Santa Monica, California, where a breakwater was built to provide a boat anchorage. A bulge in the beach soon formed upstream of the breakwater and severe erosion occurred downstream (Figure 24). The breakwater interfered with the natural transport of sand by blocking the waves that used to keep

(a)

(b)

Figure 24 Santa Monica breakwater.

(a) The shoreline and pier at Santa Monica as it appeared in 1931. (b) The same area in 1949, showing that the construction of a breakwater to create a boat anchorage disrupted the longshore transport of sand and caused a bulge of sand in the beach.

the sand moving. If something was not done to put energy back into the system, the breakwater would soon be attached by a tombolo of sand, and further erosion downstream might destroy coastal structures.

In Santa Barbara and Santa Monica, dredging was used to compensate for erosion downstream from the breakwater and to keep the harbor or anchorage from filling with sand. Sand dredged from behind the breakwater is pumped down the coast so it can reenter the longshore drift and replenish the eroded beach.

The dredging operation has stabilized the situation in Santa Barbara, but at a considerable (and ongoing) expense. In Santa Monica, dredging was conducted until the breakwater was largely destroyed during winter storms in 1982–1983. Shortly thereafter, wave energy was able to move sand along the coast again, and the system was restored to near-normal conditions. When people interfere with natural processes in the coastal region, they must provide the energy needed to replace what they have misdirected through modification of the shore environment.

Seawalls

One of the most destructive types of hard stabilization is the **seawall** (Figure 25), which is built parallel to the shore along the landward side of the berm. The purpose of a seawall is to armor the coastline and protect landward developments from ocean waves.

Once waves begin breaking against a seawall, however, turbulence generated by the abrupt release of wave energy quickly erodes the sediment on its seaward side, causing it to collapse into the surf (Figure 25). Where seawalls have been used to protect property on barrier islands, the seaward slope of the island beach has steepened and the rate of erosion has increased, causing the destruction of the recreational beach.

A well-designed seawall may last for many decades, but the constant pounding of waves eventually takes its toll (Figure 26). In the long run, the cost of repairing or replacing seawalls will be more than the property is worth, and the sea will claim more of the coast through the natural processes of erosion. It's just a matter of time for homeowners who live too close to the coast, many of whom are gambling that their houses won't be destroyed in their lifetimes.

Alternatives to Hard Stabilization

Is it better to preserve the houses of a few people who have built too close to the shore at the expense of armoring the coast with hard stabilization and destroying the recreational beach? If you own coastal property, your response would probably be different from the general beachgoing public. Because hard stabilization has been shown to have negative environmental consequences, alternatives have been sought.

Of course, one alternative to the use of hard stabilization is to restrict construction in areas prone to coastal erosion. Unfortunately, this is becoming less and less an option as coastal regions experience population increases and governments increase the risk of damage and injuries

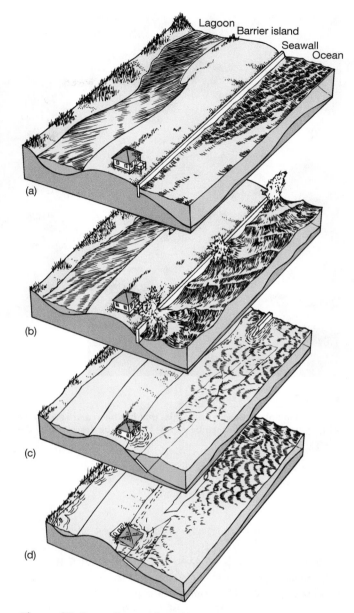

Figure 25 Seawalls and beaches.
When a seawall is built along a beach (such as on this barrier island) to protect beachfront property **(a)**, a large storm can remove the beach from the seaward side of the wall and steepen its seaward slope **(b)**. Eventually, the wall is undermined and falls into the sea **(c)**. The property is lost **(d)** as the oversteepened beach slope advances landward in its effort to reestablish a natural slope angle.

because of programs like the *National Flood Insurance Program (NFIP)*. Since its inception in 1968, NFIP has paid out billions of dollars in federal subsidy to repair or replace high-risk coastal structures. As a result, NFIP has actually *encouraged* construction in exactly the unsafe locations it was designed to prevent![5] Further, many homeowners spend large amounts of money rebuilding structures and fortifying their property.

[5]Recent changes in regulations of the Federal Emergency Management Agency (FEMA), which oversees NFIP, are intended to curb this practice.

APT photos

Figure 26 Seawall damage.

A seawall in Solana Beach, California, that has been damaged by waves and needs repair. Although seawalls appear to be sturdy, they can be destroyed by the continual pounding of high-energy storm waves.

STUDENTS SOMETIMES ASK ...

I have the opportunity to live in a house at the edge of a coastal cliff where there is an incredible view along the entire coast. Is it safe from coastal erosion?

Based on what you've described, most certainly not! Geologists have long known that cliffs are naturally unstable. Even if the cliffs appear to be stable (or have been stable for a number of years), one significant storm can seriously damage the cliff.

The most common cause of coastal erosion is direct wave attack, which undermines the support and causes the cliff to fail. You might want to check the base of the cliff and examine the local bedrock to determine for yourself if you think it will withstand the pounding of powerful storm waves that can move rocks weighing several tons. Other dangers include drainage runoff, weaknesses in the bedrock, slumps and landslides, seepage of water through the cliff, and even burrowing animals.

Even though all states enforce a setback from the edge of the cliff for all new buildings, sometimes that isn't enough because large sections of "stable" cliffs can fail all at once. For instance, several city blocks of real estate have been eroded from the edge of cliffs during the last 100

years in some areas of southern California. Even though the view sounds outstanding, you may find out the hard way that the house is built a little too close to the edge of the cliff!

However, policy has recently shifted from defending coastal property in high hazard areas to removing structures and letting nature reclaim the beach. This approach is called **relocation**, which involves moving structures to safer locations as they become threatened by erosion. One example of the successful use of this technique is the relocation of the Cape Hatteras Lighthouse in North Carolina (Box 2). Relocation, if used wisely, can allow humans to live in balance with the natural processes that continually modify beaches.

Hard stabilization includes groins, jetties, breakwaters, and seawalls, all of which alter the coastal environment, cause erosion and deposition, and result in changes in the shape of the beach.

BOX 2   People and Ocean Environment

THE MOVE OF THE CENTURY: RELOCATING THE CAPE HATTERAS LIGHTHOUSE

In spite of efforts to protect structures that are too close to the shore, they can still be in danger of being destroyed by receding shorelines and the destructive power of waves. Such was the case for one of the nation's most prominent landmarks, the candy-striped lighthouse at Cape Hatteras, North Carolina, which is 21 stories tall—the nation's tallest lighthouse and the tallest brick lighthouse in the world.

The lighthouse was built in 1870 on the Cape Hatteras barrier island 457 meters (1500 feet) from the shoreline to guide mariners through the dangerous offshore shoals known as the "Graveyard of the Atlantic." As the barrier island began migrating towards land, its beach narrowed. When the waves began to lap just 37 meters (120 feet) from its brick and granite base, there was concern that even a moderate-strength hurricane could trigger beach erosion sufficient to topple the lighthouse.

In 1970, the U.S. Navy built three groins in front of the lighthouse in an effort to protect the lighthouse from further erosion. The groins initially slowed erosion, but disrupted sand flow in the surf zone, which caused the flattening of nearby dunes and the formation of a bay south of the lighthouse. Attempts to increase the width of the beach in front of the lighthouse included beach nourishment and artificial offshore beds of seaweed, both of which failed to widen the beach substantially. In the 1980s, the Army Corps of Engineers proposed building a massive stone seawall around the lighthouse but decided the eroding coast would eventually move out from under the structure, leaving it stranded at sea on its own island. In 1988, the National Academy of Sciences determined that the shoreline in front of the lighthouse would retreat so far as to destroy the lighthouse and recommended its relocation. In 1999, the National Park Service, which owns the lighthouse, finally authorized moving the structure to a safer location.

Moving the lighthouse, which weighs 4395 metric tons (4830 short tons), was accomplished by severing it from its foundation and carefully hoisting it onto a platform of steel beams fitted with roller dollies. Once on the platform, it was slowly rolled along a specially designed steel track using a series of hydraulic jacks. A strip of vegetation was cleared to make a runway along which the lighthouse crept 1.5 meters (5 feet) at a time, with the track picked up from behind and reconstructed in front of the tower as it moved. During June and July 1999, the lighthouse was gingerly transported 884 meters (2900 feet) from its original location, making it one of the largest structures ever successfully moved.

After its $12 million move, the lighthouse now resides in a scrub oak and pine woodland 488 meters (1600 feet) from the shore. Although it now stands further inland, the light's slightly higher elevation makes it visible just as far out to sea, where it continues to warn mariners of the hazardous shoals. At the current rate of shoreline retreat, the lighthouse should be safe from the threat of waves for at least another century.

Relocation of the Cape Hatteras Lighthouse, North Carolina.

Chapter in Review

- *The coastal region changes continuously.* The *shore* is the region of contact between the oceans and the continents, lying between the lowest low tides and the highest elevation on the continents affected by storm waves. The *coast* extends inland from the shore as far as marine-related features can be found. The *coastline* marks the boundary between the shore and the coast. The shore is divided into the *foreshore*, extending from low tide to high tide, and the *backshore*, extending beyond the high tide line to the coastline. Seaward of the low tide shoreline are the *nearshore* zone, extending to the breaker line, and the *offshore* zone beyond.

- *A beach is a deposit of the shore area*, consisting of wave-worked sediment that moves along a wave-cut bench. It includes the *recreational beach, berm, beach face, low tide terrace*, one or more *longshore bars*, and *longshore trough*. Beaches are composed of whatever material is locally available and coarser beaches have steeper slopes.

- *Waves that break at the shore move sand perpendicular to shore* (toward and away from shore). In *light wave activity, swash dominates the transport system* and sand is moved up the beach face toward the berm. In *heavy wave activity, backwash dominates the transport system* and sand is moved down the beach face away from the berm toward longshore bars. In a natural system, there is a *balance between light and heavy wave activity*, alternating between sand piled on the berm (*summertime beach*) and sand stripped from the berm (*wintertime beach*), respectively.

- *Sand is moved parallel to the shore, too.* Waves breaking at an angle to the shore create a *longshore current that results in a zigzag movement of sediment called longshore drift* (longshore transport). *Each year, millions of tons of sediment are moved from upstream to downstream* ends of beaches. Most of the year, *longshore drift moves southward along both the Pacific and Atlantic shores* of the United States.

- *Erosional-type shores are characterized by headlands, wave-cut cliffs, sea caves, sea arches, sea stacks, and marine terraces* (caused by uplift of a wave-cut bench). Wave erosion increases as more of the shore is exposed to the open ocean, tidal range decreases, and bedrock weakens.

- *Depositional-type shores are characterized by beaches, spits, bay barriers, tombolos, barrier islands, deltas, and beach compartments.* Viewed from ocean side to lagoon side, barrier islands commonly have an ocean beach, dunes, barrier flat, and salt marsh. Deltas form at the mouths of rivers that carry more sediment to the ocean than the longshore current can carry away. *Beach starvation* occurs when the sand supply is interrupted. *Beach replenishment* (beach nourishment) is an expensive and temporary way to reduce beach starvation.

- *Coasts can be classified as either primary or secondary coasts. Primary coasts include those developed by nonmarine processes*; they include land erosion coasts, subaerial deposition coasts, glacial deposition coasts, volcanic coasts, coasts shaped by earth movements, and ice coasts. *Secondary coasts include those where the nonmarine character has been destroyed by marine processes*; they include wave erosion coasts, marine deposition coasts, and coasts formed by marine biological activity.

- *Shorelines can also be classified as emerging or submerging based on their position relative to sea level.* Ancient wave-cut cliffs and stranded beaches well above the present shoreline may indicate a *drop in sea level relative to land*. Old drowned beaches, submerged dunes, wave-cut cliffs, or drowned river valleys may indicate a *rise in sea level relative to land. Changes in sea level may result from tectonic processes causing local movement of the landmass or from eustatic processes changing the amount of water in the oceans or the capacity of ocean basins.* Melting of continental ice caps during the past 18,000 years has caused a eustatic rise in sea level of about 120 meters (400 feet).

- *Sea level is rising along the Atlantic Coast* about 0.3 meter (1 foot) per century, and the average erosion rate is −0.8 meter (−2.6 feet) per year. *Along the Gulf Coast*, sea level is rising 0.3 meter (1 foot) per century, and the average rate of erosion is −1.8 meters (−6 feet) per year. The Mississippi River Delta is eroding at 4.2 meters (13.7 feet) per year, resulting in a large loss of wetlands every year. *Along the Pacific Coast*, the average erosion rate is only −0.005 meter (−0.016 foot) per year. Different shorelines erode at different rates depending on wave exposure, amount of uplift, and type of bedrock.

- *Hard stabilization, such as groins, jetties, breakwaters, and seawalls, is often constructed in an attempt to stabilize a shoreline. Groins* (built to trap sand) and *jetties* (built to protect harbor entrances) widen the beach by trapping sediment on their upstream side, but erosion usually becomes a problem downstream. Similarly, *breakwaters* (built parallel to a shore) trap sand behind the structure, but cause unwanted erosion downstream. *Seawalls* (built to armor a coast) often cause loss of the recreational beach. Eventually, the constant pounding of waves destroys all types of hard stabilization. *Relocation* is a technique that has been successfully used to protect coastal structures.

Key Terms

Backshore
Backwash
Barrier island
Bay barrier (bay-mouth bar)
Beach
Beach compartment
Beach face
Beach replenishment (beach nourishment)
Beach starvation
Berm
Breakwater
Coast
Coastline
Delta

Depositional-type shore
Drowned beach
Drowned river valley
Emerging shoreline
Erosional-type shore
Eustatic sea level change
Foreshore
Groin
Groin field
Hard stabilization
Headland
Jetty
Longshore bar
Longshore current

Longshore drift (longshore transport)
Longshore trough
Marine terrace
Nearshore
Offshore
Primary coast
Relocation
Rip current
Rip-rap
Sea arch
Sea cave
Sea stack
Seawall

Secondary coast
Shepard, Francis
Shore
Shoreline
Spit
Stranded beach deposit
Submerged dune topography
Submerging shoreline
Summertime beach
Swash
Tombolo
Wave-cut bench
Wave-cut cliff
Wintertime beach

Questions and Exercises

1. To help reinforce your knowledge of beach terminology, construct and label your own diagram similar to Figure 1 from memory.

2. Describe differences between summertime and wintertime beaches. Explain why these differences occur.

3. What variables affect the speed of longshore currents?

4. What is longshore drift, and how is it related to a longshore current?

5. How is the flow of water in a stream similar to a longshore current? How are the two different?

6. Why does the direction of longshore current sometimes reverse in direction? Along both U.S. coasts, what is the primary direction of annual longshore current?

7. Describe the formation of rip currents. What is the best strategy to ensure that you won't drown if you are caught in a rip current?

8. Discuss the formation of such erosional features as wave-cut cliffs, sea caves, sea arches, sea stacks, and marine terraces.

9. Describe the origin of these depositional features: spit, bay barrier, tombolo, and barrier island.

10. Describe the response of a barrier island to a rise in sea level. Why do some barrier islands develop peat deposits running through them from the ocean beach to the salt marsh?

11. Discuss why some rivers have deltas and others do not. What are the factors that determine whether a "bird's-foot" delta (like the Mississippi Delta) or a smoothly curved delta (like the Nile Delta) will form?

12. Describe all parts of a beach compartment. What will happen when dams are built across all of the rivers that supply sand to the beach?

13. Define the characteristics of the two major categories of Shepard's classification of coasts, and list the subcategories of each.

14. Compare the causes and effects of tectonic versus eustatic changes in sea level.

15. List the two basic processes by which coasts advance seaward, and list their counterparts that lead to coastal retreat.

16. List and discuss four factors that influence the classification of a coast as either erosional or depositional.

17. Describe the tectonic and depositional processes causing subsidence along the Atlantic Coast.

18. Compare the Atlantic Coast, Gulf Coast, and Pacific Coast by describing the conditions and features of emergence-submergence and erosion-deposition that are characteristic of each.

19. List the types of hard stabilization and describe what each is intended to do.

20. Draw an aerial view of a shoreline to show the effect on erosion and deposition caused by constructing a groin, a jetty, a breakwater, and a seawall within the coastal environment.

Coastal Waters and Marginal Seas

From Chapter 12 of *Introduction to Oceanography*, Tenth Edition, Harold V. Thurman, Alan P. Trujillo.

Coastal Waters and Marginal Seas

Coastal lagoon. Sailboats drift in a placid lagoon between lush green islets at Tobago Cays in The Grenadines. Although lagoons can be formed by a variety of processes, most were created during the worldwide rise in sea level that followed the most recent Ice Age.

Key Questions

- How does the coastal ocean vary in terms of salinity, temperature, and currents?
- How are estuaries created and what kinds of estuaries exist?
- Why are coastal wetlands important?
- Why is the circulation pattern in the Mediterranean Sea so unusual?
- What characteristics do marginal seas exhibit?

The answers to these questions (and much more) can be found in the highlighted concept statements within this chapter.

"All the rivers run into the sea, yet the sea is not full."

—From *Ecclesiastes*, 1.7

Coastal waters and their adjoining marginal seas are filled with life, commerce, recreation, and fisheries. Of the world fishery,[1] about 95% is obtained within 320 kilometers (200 miles) of shore. Coastal waters also support about 95% of the total mass of life in the oceans. Further, coastal estuary and wetland environments are among the most biologically productive ecosystems on Earth and serve as nursery grounds for many species of marine organisms that inhabit the open ocean. In addition, these waters are the focal point of most shipping routes, oil and gas production, and recreational activities.

Coastal waters are also the conduits through which land-derived compounds must pass to reach the open ocean. Numerous chemical, physical, and biological processes occur in these environments that tend to protect the quality of the water in the open ocean. Human activities, however, are increasingly altering coastal environments. Coastal waters are the final destination of much of the waste products of those living on the adjacent land.

Coastal Waters

Coastal waters are those relatively shallow-water areas that adjoin continents or islands. If the continental shelf is broad and shallow, coastal waters can extend several hundred kilometers from land. If it has significant relief or drops rapidly onto the deep-ocean basin, on the other hand, coastal waters will occupy a relatively thin band near the margin of the land. Beyond coastal waters lies the open ocean.

Because of their proximity to land, coastal waters are directly influenced by processes that occur on or near land. River runoff and tidal currents, for example, have a far more significant effect on coastal waters than on the open ocean.

Salinity

Fresh water is less dense than seawater, so river runoff does not mix well with seawater along the coast. Instead, the fresh water forms a wedge at the surface, which creates a well-developed **halocline**[2] (Figure 1a). When water is shallow enough, however, tidal mixing causes fresh water to mix with seawater, thus reducing the salinity of the water column (Figure 1c). There is no halocline here; instead, the water column is **isohaline** (*iso* = same, *halo* = salt).

Freshwater runoff from the continents generally lowers the salinity of coastal regions compared to the open ocean. Where precipitation on land is mostly rain, river runoff peaks in the rainy season. Where runoff is due mainly to melting snow and ice, on the other hand, runoff always peaks in summer.

Prevailing offshore winds can increase the salinity in some coastal regions. As winds travel over a continent, they usually lose most of their moisture. When these dry winds reach the ocean, they typically evaporate considerable amounts of water as they move across the surface of the coastal waters. The increased evaporation rate increases surface salinity, creating a halocline (Figure 1b). The gradient of the halocline, however, is reversed compared to the one developed from the input of fresh water (Figure 1a).

Temperature

Sea ice forms in many high-latitude coastal areas where water temperatures are uniformly cold—generally greater than $-2°C$ (28.4°F) (Figure 1d). In low-latitude coastal regions, where circulation with the open ocean is restricted, surface waters are prevented from mixing thoroughly, so maximum surface temperature may approach $45°C$ (113°F) (Figure 1e). In both high- and low-latitude coastal waters, **isothermal** (*iso* = same, *thermo* = heat) conditions prevail.

Surface temperatures in mid-latitude coastal regions are coolest in winter and warmest in late summer. A strong **thermocline**[3] may develop from surface water being warmed during the summer (Figure 1f) and cooled during the winter (Figure 1g). In summer, very-high-temperature surface water may form a relatively thin layer. Vertical mixing reduces the surface temperature by distributing the heat through a greater volume of water, thus pushing the thermocline deeper and making it less pronounced. In winter, cooling increases the density of surface water,

---

[1]The term *fishery* refers to fish caught from the ocean by commercial fishers.

[2]Recall that a *halocline* (*halo* = salt, *cline* = slope) is a layer of rapidly changing salinity.

[3]Recall that a *thermocline* (*themo* = heat, *cline* = slope) is a layer of rapidly changing temperature.

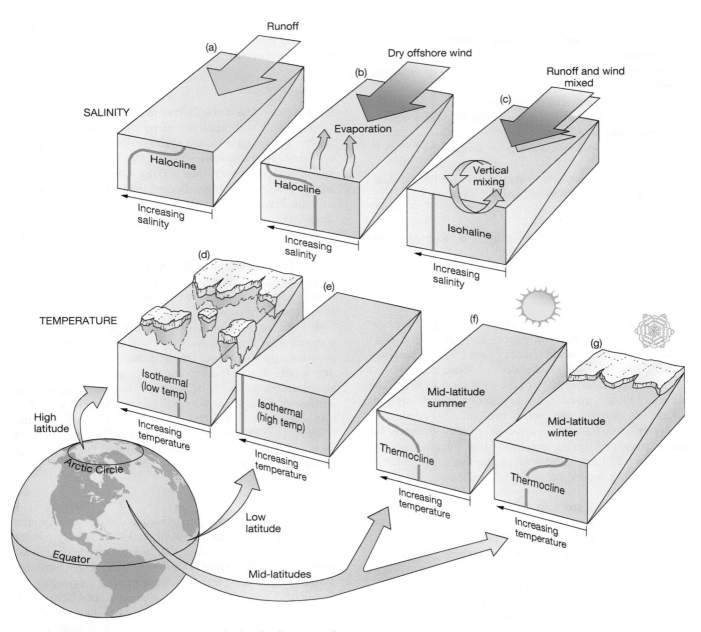

Figure 1 Salinity and temperature variation in the coastal ocean.

Changes in coastal salinity (*top row*) can be caused by the input of freshwater runoff (**a**), by dry offshore winds causing a high rate of evaporation (**b**), or by both (**c**). Changes in coastal temperature (*bottom row*) depend on latitude. In high latitudes (**d**), the temperature of coastal water remains uniformly near freezing. In low latitudes (**e**), coastal water may become uniformly warm. In the mid-latitudes, coastal surface water is significantly warmed during summer (**f**) and cooled during the winter (**g**).

which causes it to sink, thus creating an isothermal water column.

Prevailing offshore winds can significantly affect surface water temperatures. These winds are relatively warm during the summer, so they increase the ocean surface temperature and seawater evaporation. During winter, they are much cooler than the ocean surface, so they absorb heat and cool surface water near shore. Mixing from strong winds may drive the thermoclines in Figures 1f and 1g deeper and even mix the entire water column, producing isothermal condi-

tions. Tidal currents can also cause considerable vertical mixing in shallow coastal waters.

Coastal Geostrophic Currents

Recall that *geostrophic* (*geo* = earth, *strophio* = turn) *currents* move in a circular path around the middle of a current gyre. Wind and runoff create geostrophic currents in coastal waters, too, where they are called **coastal geostrophic currents**.

Wind blowing parallel to the coast piles up water along the shore. Gravity eventually pulls this water back toward the open ocean. As it runs downslope away from the shore, the Coriolis effect causes it to curve to the right in the Northern Hemisphere and to the left in the Southern Hemisphere. Thus, in the Northern Hemisphere, the coastal geostrophic current curves *northward* on the western coast and *southward* on the eastern coast of continents. These currents are reversed in the Southern Hemisphere.

A high-volume runoff of fresh water produces a surface wedge of fresh water that slopes away from the shore (Figure 2). This causes a surface flow of low-salinity water toward the open ocean, which the Coriolis effect curves to the right in the Northern Hemisphere and to the left in the Southern Hemisphere.

Coastal geostrophic currents are variable because they depend on the wind and the amount of runoff for their strength. If the wind is strong and the volume of runoff is high, then the currents are relatively strong. They are bounded on the ocean side by the steadier boundary currents comprising the open-ocean gyres.

An example of a coastal geostrophic current is the **Davidson Current** that develops along the coast of Washington and Oregon during the winter (Figure 2). Heavy precipitation (which produces high volumes of runoff) combines with strong southwesterly winds to produce a relatively strong northward-flowing current. It flows between the shore and the southward-flowing California Current.

The shallow coastal ocean adjoins land and experiences changes in salinity and temperature that are more dramatic than the open ocean. Coastal geostrophic currents can also develop.

Estuaries

An **estuary** (*aestus* = tide) is a partially enclosed coastal body of water in which freshwater runoff dilutes salty ocean water. The most common estuary is a river mouth, where the river empties into the sea. Many bays, inlets, gulfs, and sounds may be considered estuaries, too. All estuaries exhibit large variations in temperature and/or salinity.

The mouths of large rivers form the most economically significant estuaries, because many are seaports, centers of ocean commerce, and important commercial fisheries. Examples include Baltimore, New York, San Francisco, Buenos Aires, London, Cairo, Tokyo, and many others.

Origin of Estuaries

The estuaries of today exist because sea level has risen approximately 120 meters (400 feet) since major continental glaciers began melting 18,000 years ago. These glaciers covered portions of North America, Europe, and Asia during the Pleistocene Epoch, which is more commonly referred to as the *Ice Age*. Four major classes of estuaries can be identified based on their origin (Figure 3):

1. A **coastal plain estuary** forms as sea level rises and floods existing river valleys. These estuaries, such as Chesapeake Bay in Maryland and Virginia, are called *drowned river valleys.*

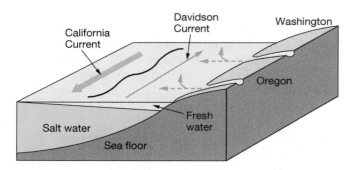

Figure 2 Davidson coastal geostrophic current.

The Davidson Current is a coastal geostrophic current that flows north along the coast of Washington and Oregon. During the winter, runoff produces a freshwater wedge (*light blue*) that thins away from shore. This causes a surface flow of low-salinity water toward the open ocean, which is acted upon by the Coriolis effect, curving to the right.

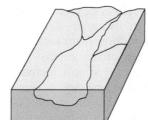
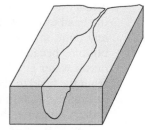
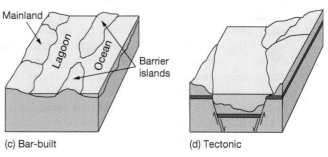

Figure 3 Classifying estuaries by origin.

Diagrammatic views of the four types of estuaries based on origin. **(a)** Coastal plain estuary. **(b)** Glacially carved fjord. **(c)** Bar-built estuary. **(d)** Tectonic estuary.

2. A **fjord**[4] forms as sea level rises and floods a glaciated valley. Water-carved valleys have V-shaped profiles, but fjords are U-shaped valleys with steep walls. Commonly, a shallowly submerged glacial deposit of debris (called a *moraine*) is located near the ocean entrance, marking the farthest extent of the glacier. Fjords are common along the coasts of Alaska, Canada, New Zealand, Chile, and Norway (Figure 4a).

3. A **bar-built estuary** is shallow and is separated from the open ocean by sand bars that are deposited parallel to the coast by wave action. Lagoons that separate *barrier islands* from the mainland are bar-built estuaries. They are common along the U.S. Gulf and East Coasts, including Laguna Madre in Texas and Pamlico Sound in North Carolina.

4. A **tectonic estuary** forms when faulting or folding of rocks creates a restricted downdropped area into which rivers flow. San Francisco Bay is in part a tectonic estuary (Figure 4b), formed by movement along faults including the San Andreas Fault.

Water Mixing in Estuaries

Generally, freshwater runoff moves across the upper layer of the estuary toward the open ocean, whereas denser seawater moves in a layer just below toward the head of the estuary. Mixing takes place at the contact between these water masses.

Estuaries can be classified based on the way freshwater and seawater mix, as shown in Figure 5:

1. **Vertically mixed estuary**—A shallow, low-volume estuary where the net flow always proceeds from the head of the estuary toward its mouth. Salinity at any point in the estuary is uniform from surface to bottom because river water mixes evenly with ocean water at all depths. Salinity simply increases from the head to the mouth of the estuary, as shown in Figure 5a. Salinity lines curve at the edge of the estuary because the Coriolis effect influences the inflow of seawater.

2. **Slightly stratified estuary**—A somewhat deeper estuary in which salinity increases from the head to the mouth at any depth, as in a vertically mixed estuary. However, two water layers can be identified. One is the less saline, less dense upper water from the river, and the other is the more saline, more dense deeper water from the ocean. These two layers are separated by a zone of mixing. The circulation that develops in slightly stratified estuaries is a net surface flow of low-salinity water toward the ocean and a net subsurface flow of seawater toward

the head of the estuary (Figure 5b), which is called an **estuarine circulation pattern**.

3. **Highly stratified estuary**—A deep estuary in which upper-layer salinity increases from the head to the mouth, reaching a value close to that of open-ocean water. The deep-water layer has a rather uniform open-ocean salinity at any depth throughout the length of the estuary. An estuarine circulation pattern is well developed in this type of estuary (Figure 5c). Mixing at the interface of the upper water and the lower water creates a net movement from the deep-water mass into the upper water. Less-saline surface water simply moves from the head toward the mouth of the estuary, growing more saline as water from the deep mass mixes with it. Relatively strong haloclines develop at the contact between the upper and lower water masses.

4. **Salt wedge estuary**—An estuary in which a wedge of salty water intrudes from the ocean beneath the river water. This kind of estuary is typical of the mouths of deep, high-volume rivers. No horizontal salinity gradient exists at the surface because surface water is essentially fresh throughout the length of—and even beyond—the estuary (Figure 5d). There is, however, a *horizontal* salinity gradient at depth and a very pronounced vertical salinity gradient—a halocline—at any location throughout the length of the estuary. This halocline is shallower and more highly developed near the mouth of the estuary.

The mixing pattern within an estuary may vary with location, season, or tidal conditions. In addition, mixing patterns in real estuaries are rarely as simple as the models presented here. For example, Chesapeake Bay, which is one of the most intensely studied coastal bodies of water on the planet, often exhibits complex and poorly understood mixing patterns. In some cases, Chesapeake Bay exhibits upstream surface flow accompanied by downstream deep flow, which is exactly the opposite flow pattern than would normally be expected. In other cases, periods of downstream flow have been observed throughout all depths of the bay. In still other cases, even more complex patterns develop, such as a surface and bottom flow in one direction separated by a mid-depth flow in the opposite direction, or landward flows along the shores and seaward flows in the central portions of the estuary.

Estuaries were formed by the rise in sea level after the last Ice Age. They can be classified based on origin as coastal plain, fjord, bar built, or tectonic. Estuaries can also be classified based on mixing as vertically mixed, slightly stratified, highly stratified, or salt wedge.

---

[4]The Norwegian word *fjord* is pronounced "FEE-yord" and means a long, narrow sea inlet bordered by steep cliffs.

(a)

(b)

Figure 4 Estuaries.

(a) A Norwegian fjord, which is a deep glacially formed estuary that has been flooded by the sea.
(b) Aerial view of San Francisco Bay in California, which is a tectonic estuary that was created by faulting.

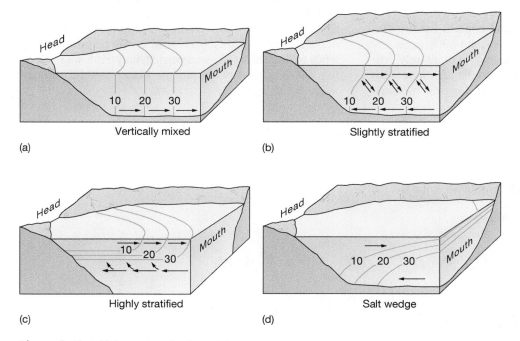

(a)

Vertically mixed

(b)

Slightly stratified

(c)

Highly stratified

(d)

Salt wedge

Figure 5 Classifying estuaries by mixing.

The basic flow pattern in an estuary is a surface flow of less dense fresh water toward the ocean and
an opposite flow in the subsurface of salty seawater into the estuary. Numbers represent salinity in
‰; arrows indicate flow directions. **(a)** Vertically mixed estuary. **(b)** Slightly stratified estuary.
(c) Highly stratified estuary. **(d)** Salt wedge estuary.

Estuaries and Human Activities

Estuaries are important breeding grounds and protective nurseries for many marine animals, so the ecological well-being of estuaries is vital to fisheries and coastal environments worldwide. Nevertheless, estuaries support shipping, logging, manufacturing, waste disposal, and other activities that can potentially damage the environment.

Estuaries are most threatened where human population is large and expanding, but they can be severely damaged where populations are still modest, too. Development in the Columbia River estuary, for example, demonstrates how a relatively small population can damage an estuary.

Columbia River Estuary   The Columbia River, which forms most of the border between Washington and Oregon, has a long salt-wedge estuary at its entrance to the Pacific Ocean (Figure 6). The strong flow of the river and tides drive a salt wedge as far as 42 kilometers (26 miles) upstream and raise the river's water level over 3.5 meters (12 feet). When the tide falls, the huge flow of freshwater [up to 28,000 cubic meters (1,000,000 cubic feet) per second] creates a freshwater wedge that can extend hundreds of kilometers into the Pacific Ocean.

Most rivers create floodplains along their lower courses, which have rich soil that can be used for growing crops. In the late 19th century, farmers and dairymen moved onto the floodplains along the Columbia River. Eventually, protective dikes were built to prevent the annual flooding. Flooding brings new nutrients, however, so the dikes deprived the floodplain of the nutrients necessary to sustain agriculture.

The river has been the principal conduit for the logging industry, which dominated the region's economy through most of its modern history. Fortunately, the river's ecosystem has largely survived the additional sediment caused by clear cutting by the logging industry.

The construction of over 250 dams along the river and its tributaries, on the other hand, has permanently altered the river's ecosystem. Many of these dams, for example, do not have salmon ladders, which help fish "climb" in short vertical steps around the dams to reach their spawning grounds at the headwaters of their home streams.

Even though the dams have caused a multitude of problems, they do provide flood control, electrical power, and a dependable source of water, all of which have become necessary to the region's economy. To aid shipping operations, the river receives periodic dredging of sediment, which brings an increased risk for pollution. If these kinds of problems have developed in such sparsely populated areas as the Columbia River estuary, then larger environmental effects must exist in more highly populated estuaries, such as Chesapeake Bay.

Chesapeake Bay Estuary   Chesapeake Bay, which formed by the drowning of the Susquehanna River (Figure 7), is a large coastal plain estuary that is about 320 kilometers (200 miles) long and 50 kilometers (30 miles) wide at its widest point. Most of the fresh water entering the bay comes from its western margin via rivers that drain the slopes of the Appalachian Mountains. About 15 million people live near this estuary.

Chesapeake Bay is a slightly stratified estuary that experiences large seasonal changes in salinity, temperature, and dissolved oxygen. Figure 7a shows the estuary's average surface salinity, which increases oceanward. The salinity lines are oriented virtually north–south in the middle of the bay because of the Coriolis effect. The Coriolis effect causes flowing water to curve to the right in the Northern Hemisphere, so seawater entering the bay tends to hug the bay's *eastern* side, and fresh water flowing through the bay toward the ocean tends to hug its *western* side.

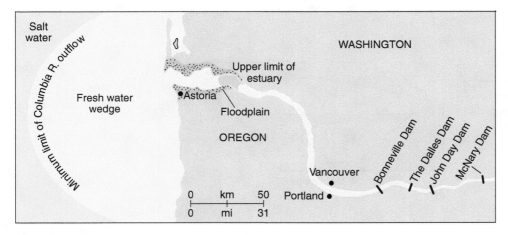

Figure 6 Columbia River estuary.

The long estuary at the mouth of the Columbia River has been severely affected from interference by floodplains that have been diked, by logging activities, and—most severely—by hydroelectric dams. The tremendous outflow of the Columbia River creates a large wedge of low-density fresh water that remains traceable far out at sea.

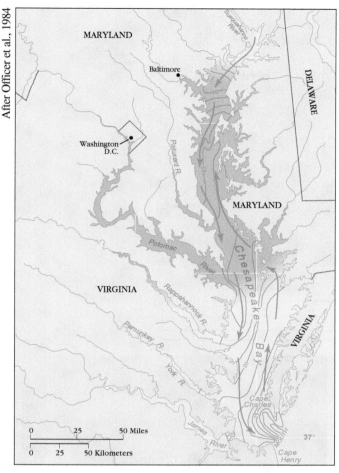

(a)

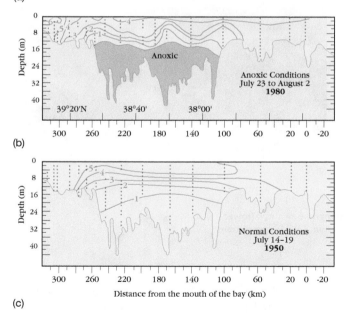

(b)

(c)

Distance from the mouth of the bay (km)

Figure 7 Chesapeake Bay.

(a) Map of Chesapeake Bay, showing average surface salinity (*blue lines*) in ‰. The purple area in the middle of the bay represents anoxic (oxygen-poor) waters. **(b)** Profile along length of Chesapeake Bay showing dissolved oxygen concentration (in ppm) during July–August 1980, indicating deep anoxic waters (*purple*). **(c)** Comparison profile showing normal dissolved oxygen concentrations (in ppm) during July 1950.

With maximum river flow in the spring, a strong halocline (and *pycnocline*[5]) develops, preventing the fresh surface water and saltier deep water from mixing. Beneath the pycnocline, which can be as shallow as 5 meters (16 feet), waters may become **anoxic** (*a* = without, *oxic* = oxygen) from May through August, as dead organic matter decays in the deep water (Figure 7b). Major kills of commercially important blue crab, oysters, and other bottom-dwelling organisms occur during this time.

The degree of stratification and extent of mortality of bottom-dwelling animals have increased since the early 1950s. Increased nutrients from sewage and agricultural fertilizers have been added to the bay during this time, too, which has increased the productivity of microscopic algae (algal blooms). When these organisms die, their remains accumulate as organic matter at the bottom of the bay and promote the development of anoxic conditions. In drier years with less river runoff, however, anoxic conditions aren't as widespread or severe in bottom waters because fewer nutrients are supplied.

Coastal Wetlands

Wetlands are ecosystems in which the water table is close to the surface, so they are typically saturated most of the time. Wetlands can border either fresh water or coastal environments. Coastal wetlands occur along the margins of estuaries and other shore areas that are protected from the open ocean and include swamps, tidal flats, coastal marshes, and bayous.

The two most important types of coastal wetlands are **salt marshes** and **mangrove swamps**. Both are intermittently submerged by ocean water and both have oxygen-poor mud and accumulations of organic matter called *peat deposits*. Marshes support a variety of grasses and are known to occur from the Equator to latitudes as high as 65 degrees (Figure 8a and b). Mangroves are restricted to latitudes below 30 degrees (Figure 8a and c).

Wetlands are some of the most highly productive ecosystems on Earth and provide enormous economic benefits when left alone. Salt marshes, for example, serve as nurseries for over half the species of commercially important fishes in the southeastern United States. Other

---

[5]Recall that a *pycnocline* (*pycno* = density, *cline* = slope) is a layer of rapidly changing density. A pycnocline is caused by a change in temperature and/or salinity with depth.

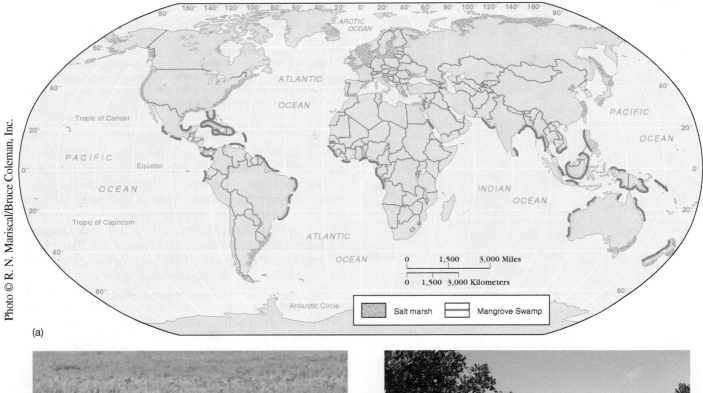

(a)

(b)

(c)

Figure 8 Salt marshes and mangrove swamps.

(a) Map showing the distribution of salt marshes (higher latitudes) and mangrove swamps (lower latitudes). (b) Salt marsh along San Francisco Bay at Shoreline Park, California. (c) Mangrove trees on Lizard Island, Great Barrier Reef, Australia.

fishes, such as flounder and bluefish, use marshes for feeding and protection during the winter. Fisheries of oysters, scallops, clams, eels, and smelt are located directly in marshes, too. Mangrove ecosystems are important nursery areas and habitats for commercially valuable shrimp, prawn, shellfish, and fish species. Both marshes and mangroves also serve as important stopover points for many species of waterfowl and migrating birds.

Wetlands are amazingly efficient at cleansing polluted water. Just 0.4 hectare (1 acre) of wetlands, for example, can filter up to 2,760,000 liters (730,000 gallons) of water each year, cleaning agricultural runoff, toxins, and other pollutants long before they reach the ocean. Wetlands remove inorganic nitrogen compounds (from sewage and fertilizers) and metals (from groundwater polluted by land sources), which become attached to clay-sized particles in the wetland mud. Some nitrogen compounds trapped in sediment are decomposed by bacteria that release the nitrogen to the atmosphere as gas and many of the remaining nitrogen compounds fertilize plants, further increasing the productivity of wetlands. As marsh plants die, their remains either accumulate as peat deposits or are broken up to become food for bacteria, fungi, and fish.

Serious Loss of Valuable Wetlands

Despite all the benefits they provide, over half of the nation's wetlands have vanished. Of the original 87 million hectares (215 million acres) of wetlands that once existed in the conterminous United States (excluding Alaska and Hawaii), only about 43 million hectares (106 million acres) remain. Wetlands have been filled in and developed for housing, industry, and agriculture, because people want to live near the oceans and because they often view wetlands as unproductive, useless land that harbors diseases.

Other countries have experienced similar losses of wetlands, too. In fact, scientists estimate that 50% of wetlands worldwide have been destroyed in the past century. The Philippines, for example, has lost 70% of its original mangrove cover.

To help prevent the loss of remaining wetlands, the U.S. Environmental Protection Agency established an Office of Wetlands Protection (OWP) in 1986. At that time, wetlands were being lost to development at a rate of 121,000 hectares (300,000 acres) per year! Currently, the rate of wetland loss has slowed to 8100 hectares (20,000 acres) per year and the agency's goal is to minimize the loss of wetlands to the point that there is no net loss of wetlands in the U.S. The OWP actively enforces regulations against wetlands pollution and identifies the most valuable wetlands so that they may be protected or restored.

A rise in sea level is predicted to exacerbate the loss of wetlands. Even using a conservative estimate of sea level rise over the next 100 years of 50 centimeters (20 inches), it is estimated that 38% to 61% of existing U.S. coastal wetlands would be lost. Some of this wetland loss, however, would be partially offset by new wetland formation on former upland areas, although even under ideal circumstances not all lost wetlands would be replaced.

> Coastal wetlands such as salt marshes and mangrove swamps are highly productive areas that serve as important nurseries for many marine organisms and act as a filter for polluted runoff.

Lagoons

Landward of barrier islands lie protected, shallow bodies of water called **lagoons** (see Figure 3c). Lagoons form in a bar-built type of estuary. Because of restricted circulation between lagoons and the ocean, three distinct zones can usually be identified within a lagoon. A *freshwater*

zone lies near the mouths of rivers that flow into the lagoon. A *transitional zone* of brackish[6] water occurs near the middle of the lagoon. A *saltwater zone* lies close to the entrance (Figure 9a).

Salinity within a lagoon is highest near the entrance and lowest near the head (Figure 9b). In latitudes that have seasonal variations in temperature and precipitation, ocean water flows through the entrance during a warm, dry summer to compensate for the volume of water lost through evaporation, thus increasing the salinity in the lagoon. Lagoons actually may become hypersaline[7] in arid regions, where the flow of seawater cannot keep pace with the lagoon's surface evaporation. During the rainy season, the lagoon becomes much less saline as freshwater runoff increases.

Tidal effects are greatest near the entrance to the lagoon (Figure 9c) and diminish inland from the saltwater zone until they are nearly undetectable in the freshwater zone.

Laguna Madre

Laguna Madre is located along the Texas coast between Corpus Christi and the mouth of the Rio Grande

---

[6]Brackish water is water with salinity between that of fresh water and seawater.

[7]Hypersaline conditions are created when water becomes excessively salty.

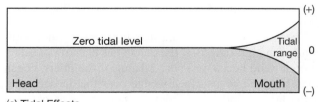

(a) Geometry

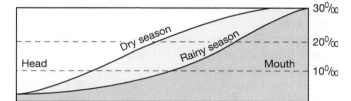

(b) Salinity

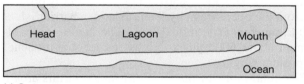

(c) Tidal Effects

Figure 9 Lagoons.

Typical geometry **(a)** salinity **(b)** and tidal effects **(c)** of a lagoon.

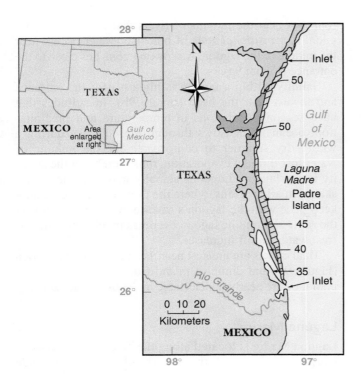

28°

N

TEXAS

MEXICO Area enlarged at right *Gulf of Mexico*

Gulf of Mexico

27°

Inlet

50

50

Gulf of Mexico

TEXAS

Laguna Madre

Padre Island

45

40

35 Inlet

26°

Rio Grande

0 10 20
Kilometers

MEXICO

98°   97°

Figure 10 Laguna Madre summer surface salinity.

Map showing geometry of Laguna Madre, Texas, and typical summer surface salinity (in ‰).

(Figure 10). This long, narrow body of water is protected from the open ocean by Padre Island, a barrier island 160 kilometers (100 miles) long. The lagoon probably formed about 6000 years ago as sea level approached its present height.

The tidal range of the Gulf of Mexico in this area is about 0.5 meter (1.6 feet). The inlets at each end of Padre Island are quite narrow (Figure 10), so there is very little tidal interchange between the lagoon and the open sea.

Laguna Madre is a hypersaline lagoon and much of it is less than 1 meter (3.3 feet) deep. As a result, there are large seasonal changes in temperature and salinity. Water temperatures reach 32°C (90°F) in the summer and fall below 5°C (41°F) in winter. Salinities range from 2‰ when infrequent local storms provide large volumes of fresh water to over 100‰ during dry periods. High evaporation generally keeps salinity well above 50‰.[8]

Because even salt-tolerant marsh grasses cannot withstand such high salinities, the marsh has been replaced by an open sand beach on Padre Island. At the inlets, ocean water flows in as a surface wedge *over* the denser water of the lagoon and water from the lagoon flows out as a *subsurface* flow, which is exactly the opposite of the classic estuarine circulation.

[8]Recall that normal salinity in the open ocean averages 35‰.

Marginal Seas

At the margins of the ocean are relatively large semi-isolated bodies of water called **marginal seas**. Most of these seas result from tectonic events that have isolated low-lying pieces of ocean crust between continents, such as the Mediterranean Sea, or are created behind volcanic island arcs, such as the Caribbean Sea. These waters are shallower than and have varying degrees of exchange with the open ocean, depending on climate and geography; as a result, salinities and temperatures are substantially different from those of typical open ocean seawater. Let's examine some of the more important (and unusual) marginal seas that border the Atlantic, Pacific, and Indian Oceans.

Marginal Seas of the Atlantic Ocean

The Atlantic Ocean has several large marginal seas, including the Mediterranean Sea, the Caribbean Sea, and the Gulf of Mexico.

The Mediterranean Sea The **Mediterranean** (*medi* = middle, *terra* = land) **Sea** is actually a number of small seas connected by narrow necks of water into one larger sea. It is the remnant of the ancient Tethys Sea that existed when all the continents were combined about 200 million years ago. It is over 4300 meters (14,100 feet) deep, and is one of the few inland seas in the world underlain by oceanic crust. Thick salt deposits and other evidence on the floor of the Mediterranean suggest that it nearly dried up about 6 million years ago, only to refill with a large salt water waterfall (Box 1).

The Mediterranean is bounded by Europe and Asia Minor on the north and east and Africa to the south (Figure 11a). It is surrounded by land except for very shallow and narrow connections to the Atlantic Ocean through the Strait of Gibraltar, and to the Black Sea through the Bosporus, which is roughly 1.6 kilometers (1 mile) wide. In addition, the Mediterranean Sea has a human-made passage to the Red Sea via the Suez Canal, a waterway 160 kilometers (100 miles) long that was completed in 1869. The Mediterranean Sea has a very irregular coastline, which divides it into subseas such as the Aegean Sea and Adriatic Sea, each of which has a separate circulation pattern.

An underwater ridge called a **sill**, which extends from Sicily to the coast of Tunisia at a depth of 400 meters (1300 feet), separates the Mediterranean into two major basins. This sill restricts the flow between the two basins, resulting in strong currents that run between Sicily and the Italian mainland through the Strait of Messina (Figure 11a).

Mediterranean Circulation Atlantic Ocean water enters the Mediterranean as a surface flow through the Strait of Gibraltar to replace water that rapidly evaporates in the very arid eastern end of the sea. The water level in

BOX 1   Research Methods in Oceanography

WHEN A SEA WAS DRY: CLUES FROM THE MEDITERRANEAN

The Mediterranean Sea is surrounded by land except for its shallow connection to the Atlantic Ocean through the Strait of Gibraltar, which is only about 14 kilometers (9 miles) wide. Analysis of sea floor sediments from the Mediterranean Sea suggest that it must have nearly dried up at least once (and perhaps several times) in its history.

About 6 million years ago, a drop in sea level or tectonic activity at the Strait of Gibraltar cut off circulation from the Atlantic Ocean—in effect, creating a dam. With the inflow of the Atlantic Ocean eliminated, the arid climate and resulting high evaporation rates caused the Mediterranean Sea to nearly evaporate in just a few thousand years. As the seawater evaporated, the dissolved substances began to precipitate out of the water, leaving thick layers of evaporite minerals on the sea floor. Up to 4000 meters (13,100 feet) of salt can be found in parts of the Mediterranean, suggesting that the basin may have partially filled and dried up several times during this period. At the same time, unusual gravel deposits washed in from the continents and shallow-water carbonate algal mats called *stromatolites*

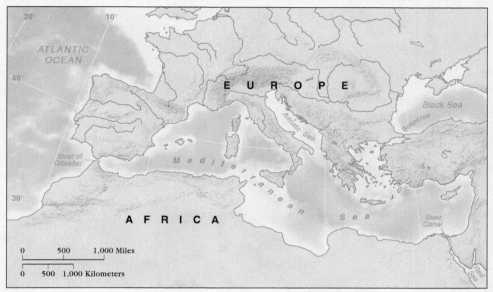

The Mediterranean Sea.

(*stromat* = covering, *lithos* = stone) also formed. Other supporting evidence for the drying of the Mediterranean Sea includes changes in climate, fossil evidence, and even deep notches cut into the surrounding river valleys. Eventually, most of the water evaporated, leaving a hot, salty, desiccated basin floor far below sea level.

About a half million years later, erosion, further tectonic activity, or a rise in sea level caused the dam at Gibraltar to breach and the Mediterranean started to refill with seawater. The waterfall that spilled into the Mediterranean was probably the largest ever to exist and is estimated to have been 1000 times larger than the flow of all rivers in the world. At that rate, the Mediterranean would have again been full of seawater in only 100 years. Nonetheless, the clues to its history of drying out are preserved in its sea floor sediments.

---

the eastern Mediterranean is generally 15 centimeters (6 inches) lower than at the Strait of Gibraltar. The surface flow follows the northern coast of Africa throughout the length of the Mediterranean and spreads northward across the sea (Figure 11a).

The remaining Atlantic Ocean water continues eastward to Cyprus. During winter, it sinks to form what is called *Mediterranean Intermediate Water*, which has a temperature of 15°C (59°F) and a salinity of 39.1‰. This water flows westward at a depth of 200 to 600 meters (660 to 2000 feet) and returns to the North Atlantic as a *subsurface* flow through the Strait of Gibraltar (Figure 11b).

By the time Mediterranean Intermediate Water passes through Gibraltar, its temperature has dropped to 13°C

(55°F) and its salinity to 37.3‰. It is still denser than even Antarctic Bottom Water and much denser than water at this depth in the Atlantic Ocean, so it moves down the continental slope. While descending, it mixes with Atlantic Ocean water and becomes less dense. At a depth of about 1000 meters (3300 feet) its density equals that of the surrounding Atlantic Ocean, so it spreads in all directions (Figure 11b). It has been detected in deep waters as far north as Iceland.

Circulation between the Mediterranean Sea and the Atlantic Ocean is typical of closed, restricted basins where evaporation exceeds precipitation. Low-latitude restricted basins such as this always lose water rapidly to evaporation, so surface flow from the open ocean must replace it. Evaporation of inflowing water from

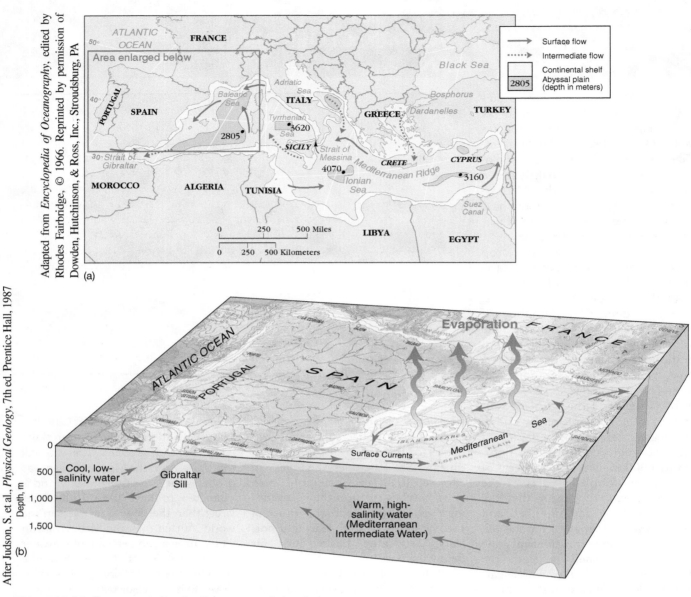

Adapted from *Encyclopedia of Oceanography*, edited by Rhodes Fairbridge, © 1966. Reprinted by permission of Dowden, Hutchinson, & Ross, Inc., Stroudsburg, PA

After Judson, S. et al., *Physical Geology*, 7th ed. Prentice Hall, 1987

Figure 11 Mediterranean Sea bathymetry and circulation.

(a) Map of the Mediterranean Sea region showing its subseas, depths, sills (underwater ridges), surface flow, and intermediate flow. (b) Diagrammatic view of Mediterranean circulation in the Gibraltar Sill area.

the open ocean increases the sea's salinity to very high values. This denser water eventually sinks and returns to the open ocean as a subsurface flow.

This circulation pattern, which is called **Mediterranean circulation**, is opposite that of most estuaries, which experience estuarine circulation where fresh water flows at the surface into the open ocean and salty water flows below the surface into the estuary. In estuaries, however, fresh water input exceeds water loss to evaporation, whereas evaporation exceeds input in the Mediterranean.

STUDENTS SOMETIMES ASK ...
How can Mediterranean Intermediate Water sink if it's so warm?

While it is true that warm water has low density, remember that *both* salinity and temperature affect seawater density. In the case of the Mediterranean Intermediate Water, it has high enough salinity to increase its density despite being warm. Once its density increases enough, it sinks beneath the surface and retains its temperature and salinity characteristics as it flows out through the Strait of Gibraltar into the North Atlantic.

High evaporation rates in the Mediterranean Sea cause it to have a shallow inflow of surface seawater and a subsurface high-salinity outflow—a circulation pattern opposite that of most estuaries.

The Caribbean Sea   The **Caribbean Sea** is separated from the Atlantic Ocean by an island arc called the Antillean Chain. Composed of the islands of Cuba, Hispaniola, Puerto Rico, and Jamaica, the *Greater Antilles* form the northern boundary of the Caribbean Sea. The *Lesser Antilles* extend in an arc from the Virgin Islands to the continental shelf of South America. The deepest connection between the Caribbean and the Atlantic Ocean is the Anegada Passage east of the Virgin Islands, with a maximum depth near 2300 meters (7550 feet); many other channels approach that depth. The Caribbean Sea is divided into four major basins from east to west: the Venezuela, Colombia, Cayman, and Yucatán basins, all of which reach depths in excess of 4000 meters (13,100 feet) (Figure 12a).

Circulation Patterns   The *Guiana Current*, entering the Caribbean through channels between the Lesser Antilles islands, represents a portion of the *South Equatorial Current* that moves northwest along the Guiana Coast of South America. It has a temperature between 26°C and 28°C (78.8°F and 82.4°F) and a salinity between 35.0‰ and 36.5‰. This relatively thin mass of water passes into the Caribbean Sea through the shallow channels north and south of St. Lucia Island and mixes in a 1:3 ratio with *North Atlantic Water*. This current becomes the *Caribbean Current*, which travels about 250 kilometers (155 miles) north of the Venezuelan coast, continues generally west over the deepest portion of the Caribbean Sea, and finally turns north and passes through the Yucatán Strait into the Gulf of Mexico. Surface velocities as high as 4.5 kilometers (2.8 miles) per hour have been measured in the main axis of the Caribbean Current, but typical surface velocities usually average less than half that speed.

The easterly component of the trade winds blowing along the coast of Venezuela and Colombia sets up a surface flow away from the coast that produces shallow *upwelling* (movement of deep water to the surface). Most of the water rising to the surface comes from depths of less than 250 meters (820 feet). The upwelling water is cold and contains high concentrations of nutrients, which, in the presence of sunlight, result in relatively high biological productivity at the surface.

Water Masses   There are four readily identifiable water masses in the Caribbean Sea. Two are relatively warm surface masses found above 200 meters (660 feet) depth, and two are deeper masses characterized by lower temperature. The salinity of *Caribbean Surface Water* is determined by the rate of evaporation versus the amount of precipitation and runoff; it is generally above 36‰ during the winter, partially because of the upwelling of high-salinity water. Moving northward, the surface salinity decreases to values generally less than 35.5‰.

Extending from the southeast to the northwest of the Caribbean Sea near the Yucatán Strait is a thin, sheet-like, high-salinity layer called the *Subtropical Underwater*. Located at depths as shallow as 50 meters (164 feet) in the southeast, it dips to a depth of 200 meters (660 feet) near the Yucatán Strait. The maximum salinity within this sheet follows the axis of flow for the Caribbean Current and exceeds 37‰ in the Yucatán Strait; salinity decreases away from the flow axis. Directly beneath the Subtropical Underwater, following the main flow axis, is a low-salinity water mass called the *Subtropical Intermediate Water*. Identification of this water mass is based on a salinity minimum that falls below 34.7‰ in the southeast and becomes less detectable at the Yucatán Strait (Figure 12b).

Deep below the surface, *North Atlantic Deep Water* enters the Caribbean primarily through the Anegada Passage between the Virgin Islands and the Leeward Islands of the Lesser Antilles, and through the Windward Passage between Cuba and Hispaniola. Characterized by a salinity slightly less than 35‰ and a temperature just above 2°C (35.6°F), this water spreads out as *Caribbean Bottom Water* and can be identified by an oxygen maximum layer that reaches values in excess of 5 parts per million.

The Gulf of Mexico   The **Gulf of Mexico** is tectonically much less complex than the adjoining Caribbean Sea. Surrounded by a wide continental shelf, this relatively broad basin reaches a maximum depth in excess of 3600 meters (11,800 feet). The Gulf of Mexico is connected to the Caribbean Sea by the Yucatán Strait, which reaches a maximum depth of 1900 meters (6200 feet); its only connection with the Atlantic Ocean is through the Straits of Florida, which reach depths approaching 1000 meters (3300 feet).

Taken together, the Caribbean Sea and the Gulf of Mexico have an unusual geometry of a series of deep basins that are connected by passageways similar to the Mediterranean Sea. This relationship, plus the fact that they exist in an area of high evaporation, is why these two bodies of water are often collectively referred to as the "American Mediterranean."

Circulation Patterns   The Caribbean Current passing through the Yucatán Strait loops clockwise, producing a dome of water in the Gulf of Mexico that stands 10 centimeters (4 inches) higher than the Atlantic water southeast of Florida. This elevated sea level causes an intense flow known as the *Florida Current* to pass through the Straits of Florida. It joins with water carried north by the *Antilles Current* and flows north along the coast of Florida (see Figure 12a).

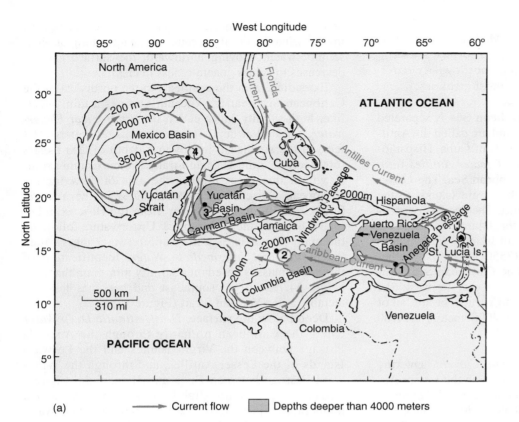

West Longitude

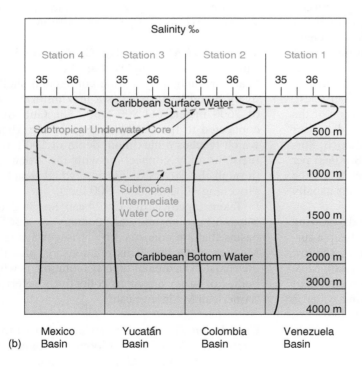

Figure 12 Bathymetry, surface circulation, and salinity profiles in the Caribbean Sea and the Gulf of Mexico.

(a) Location map showing major surface currents and bathymetry. Circled numbers represent stations shown in part (b). (b) Vertical salinity profiles and water masses at four stations marked on the location map in part (a). The central cores of the Subtropical Underwater and the Subtropical Intermediate Water can be identified on the profiles as maxima and minima, respectively.

The *Loop Current* is a significant feature of the Gulf of Mexico's surface circulation. Figure 13a shows the relationship of the current flow direction to the topography of the 20°C (68°F) isotherm surface in the southeastern Gulf of Mexico. Much of the surface water entering the Gulf of Mexico through the Yucatán Strait loops around the temperature contour in a clockwise flow and heads toward the Straits of Florida. After passing through the Yucatán Strait, surface water characteristics can be identified during the winter to a depth of 90 meters (295 feet) and, during the summer, to 125 meters (410 feet), which marks the depth at which seasonal temperature changes extend. Generally, the surface temperature just off the Yucatán coast ranges from 24° to 27°C (75° to 81°F), whereas temperatures along the northern Gulf Coast range between 18° and 21°C (64° and 70°F) (Figure 13b).

Water Masses The Subtropical Underwater is still identifiable as a salinity maximum north of the Yucatán Strait at a depth of 100 to 200 meters (330 to 660 feet). The boundary between the upper water (containing the surface water and Subtropical Underwater) and the deep water is marked by the 16°C (61°F) isotherm at a depth of about 200 meters (660 feet). Intermediate Water entering through the Yucatán Channel below 850 meters (2800 feet) can be identified by a salinity minimum throughout the Gulf of Mexico. The core of the Intermediate Water can be identified throughout the Gulf at depths as shallow as 550 meters (1800 feet), but its identity is lost passing through the Straits of Florida. Salinity and temperature increase very slightly toward the bottom of the basin.

Figure 13 Gulf of Mexico Loop Current.

(a) Location map showing depth of 20°C (68°F) temperature surface and clockwise flow of Gulf of Mexico Loop Current. Block diagram of the Loop Current (*inset*) shows Loop Current flow around the "dome" of water that directly overlies the "bowl" representing the depth of the 20°C temperature surface; the vertical scale is greatly exaggerated. **(b)** February 26, 1988 NOAA 9 satellite infrared image of sea-surface temperature in the Gulf of Mexico. The 20°C temperature surface that forms the "bowl" in part (a) intersects the ocean surface where the two lightest shades of blue meet. The Loop Current flows clockwise around the warm water that "fills" the "bowl," then moves off through the Straits of Florida. Note that the warm water that forms the "dome" reaches temperatures in excess of 26°C (79°F) (*red color*).

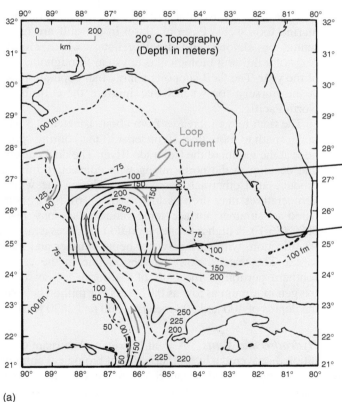

(a)

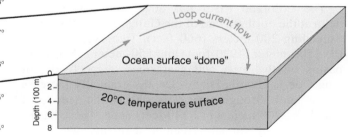

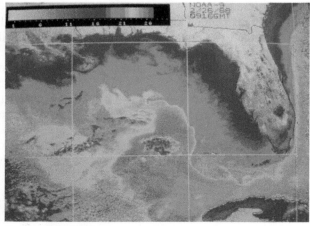

(b)

Courtesy of NOAA

Marginal Seas of the Pacific Ocean

Two of the most important marginal seas in the Pacific Ocean are the Gulf of California (which lies between Baja California and mainland Mexico) and the Bering Sea (which lies between Alaska and Russian Siberia).

The Gulf of California   The narrow, northwest–southeast trending **Gulf of California**[9] extends from near the Tropic of Cancer at its open southern end to the north at the mouth of the Colorado River, which is the main river system draining into it (Figure 14a). About a half-dozen smaller rivers also empty into the Gulf from the east, carrying water from the Sierra Madre Occidental across a broad coastal plain that forms its western margin. From this coastal plain, which is on the North American Plate, a continental shelf extends as far as 50 kilometers (30 miles) from shore. The shelf terminates at an average depth of about 100 meters (330 feet). The western side of the Gulf, which is on the Pacific Plate, does not have a wide shelf; instead, it is characterized by steep rocky slopes.

The Gulf of California is one of the most recently created seas on Earth. Tectonically, it was formed as the East Pacific Rise spreading center migrated northward, rifting Baja California away from mainland Mexico about 6 million years ago. Today, active sea floor spreading still occurs along segments of the mid-ocean ridge that underlie the central portion of the Gulf and continue to enlarge the sea.

The Colorado River has developed a significant delta at the northern end of the Gulf, with depths rarely exceeding 200 meters (660 feet). Two exceptions are the 1500-meter (4920-foot) and 550-meter (1800-foot) basins on the west and east sides, respectively, of Angel de la Guarda Island. Depths gradually increase to the south through a series of basins, the deepest of which is 3700 meters (12,140 feet) deep. These basins are created by spreading center segments, which are separated by sills that generally extend up to 400 meters (1300 feet) above the basin floor. The sills represent east–west trending offsets (transform faults/fracture zones) of spreading centers.

The character of the northern Gulf of California has changed dramatically since the completion of Hoover Dam in 1935. Before the dam was built, the Colorado River provided an annual average flow of almost 18 billion cubic meters (23 billion cubic yards) of water, which carried 147 million metric tons (161 million short tons) of suspended sediment per year to the Gulf. Since 1935, however, the average annual flow has been reduced to less than 8 billion cubic meters (10 billion cubic yards) of water and about 14 million metric tons (15 million short tons) of sediment. In recent years, no Colorado River water (or sediment) makes it to the Gulf; instead, the water is diverted to supply the water needs of many southwest municipalities, depriving the Gulf of an important source of land-based nutrients. The drainage systems on the eastern side of the basin have relatively small flow volumes, and many are intermittent owing to the arid nature of their drainage basins.

Circulation Patterns   Seasonal winds control surface circulation in the Gulf of California. A low-pressure atmospheric system in summer located over the northern end of the peninsula develops winds that drive the surface water from the Pacific into the Gulf. This flow produces upwelling along the steep rocky coast of the Baja peninsula. During the winter months, the low-pressure system is located on the mainland east of the Gulf. These winter winds produce upwelling along the mainland side. Upwelling produces a bloom of rich **plankton** (*planktos* = wandering), which are microscopic, free-floating organisms that abound in nutrient-rich waters. **Phytoplankton** (*phyto* = plant, *planktos* = wandering) are microscopic algae that photosynthesize and are the base of most marine food webs. Phyroplankton in the gulf are represented by diatoms and dinoflagellates, which are the basis of a thriving biological ecosystem throughout most of the year. The Gulf supports a large fish population and is the nursery for whales that migrate there from the North Pacific.

The tidal range increases from about 1 meter (3.3 feet) in the south to more than 10 meters (33 feet) during spring tides at the mouth of the Colorado River. The tidal currents that develop in the north, along with convective mixing, produce an isothermal water column during the winter. Temperatures may drop as low as 16°C (61°F), as compared to summer surface temperatures that may reach 30°C (86°F). A high rate of evaporation produces a marked stratification, with surface water being warmer and more saline. The water below the thermocline in the central southern portion of the Gulf of California possesses an oxygen minimum as low as 0.01 parts per million between the depths of 400 and 800 meters (1300 and 2620 feet).

Hydrothermal Vents   A joint Mexican–American expedition discovered a hydrothermal vent biological community along the mid-ocean ridge in the Guaymas Basin during the summer of 1980, only three years after the first hydrothermal vent biocommunity was discovered in the Galápagos Rift in the eastern Pacific. In 1982, the vent biocommunity was observed and sampled during a dive of the submersible *Alvin* (Figure 14b). Since that time, many other hydrothermal vent biocommunities in the Gulf have been identified and observed along segments of active spreading centers. Because the newly forming mid-ocean ridge is so close to areas of high sediment input, many hydrothermal vents are covered by sediment.

The Bering Sea   The **Bering Sea**, on the northern margin of the Pacific Ocean, extends to 66 degrees north latitude

---

[9]The Gulf of California is also known as the Sea of Cortez or the Vermillion Sea.

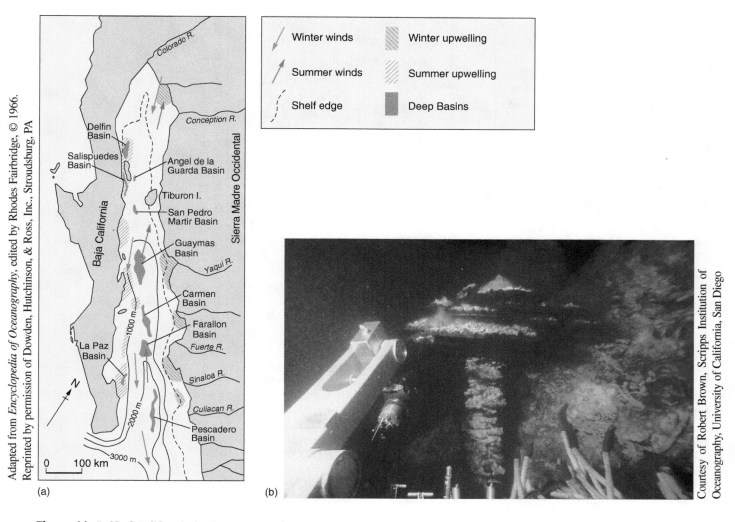

Adapted from *Encyclopedia of Oceanography*, edited by Rhodes Fairbridge, © 1966. Reprinted by permission of Dowden, Hutchinson, & Ross, Inc., Stroudsburg, PA

Legend:

Winter winds	Winter upwelling
Summer winds	Summer upwelling
Shelf edge	Deep Basins

Map labels: Colorado R., Conception R., Delfin Basin, Salispuedes Basin, Angel de la Guarda Basin, Tiburon I., San Pedro Martir Basin, Guaymas Basin, Yaqui R., Carmen Basin, Farallon Basin, Fuerte R., La Paz Basin, Sinaloa R., Culiacan R., Pescadero Basin, Baja California, Sierra Madre Occidental, 1000 m, 2000 m, 3000 m, 0 100 km, N

(a)   (b)

Courtesy of Robert Brown, Scripps Institution of Oceanography, University of California, San Diego

Figure 14 Gulf of California bathymetry and seasonal circulation.

(a) Map showing location and major rivers that drain into the Gulf of California. Basins within the Gulf increase in depth from north to south. Winds that reverse on a seasonal basis produce winter upwelling on the east side of the Gulf and summer upwelling on the west side. **(b)** Pagodalike structure of a hydrothermal vent atop a sediment mound that covers a spreading center in the Guaymas Basin. Tubeworms and *Alvin's* mechanical "arm" can be seen in the foreground.

and has the shape of a triangle with a curved base formed by the volcanic island arc of the Aleutian Islands (Figure 15). A broad continental shelf with depths less than 200 meters (660 feet) extends off the Siberian and Alaskan coasts, but most of the rest of the basin is deeper than 1000 meters (3300 feet). The deepest part of the basin is located in the western half of the sea, and fully 90% of the sea is either less than 200 meters (660 feet) in depth or more than 1000 meters (3300 feet) in depth. Except where it is cut by the Bering Canyon at the end of the Alaska Peninsula, the continental shelf drops off very abruptly into the deep basin at slopes of up to 5 degrees.

Circulation Patterns   The major surface flow of water into the Bering Sea occurs between the Komandorski Islands of Russia and Attu Island, which is the most westerly of the Aleutian Islands of Alaska. Here the *Alaskan Current*, flowing in a westerly direction south of the Aleutian chain, converges with northward-moving water of the western Pacific and flows through the passages into the Bering Sea. A small counterclockwise gyre is set up north of the Komandorski Islands, while a clockwise rotation develops to the north of the eastern end of the Aleutians. The main flow continues to the east until it reaches the broad Alaskan shelf and then follows this shelf edge to the north. A portion of this northward flow passes between St. Lawrence Island and the east Siberian coast before crossing the Bering Strait into the Arctic Ocean. Tidal currents dominate the shallow Alaskan shelf region, but a persistent northward-flowing current resulting from the runoff of fresh water from the Alaskan coast flows at speeds up to 10 kilometers (6 miles) per hour along the coast and through the Bering Strait (Figure 15).

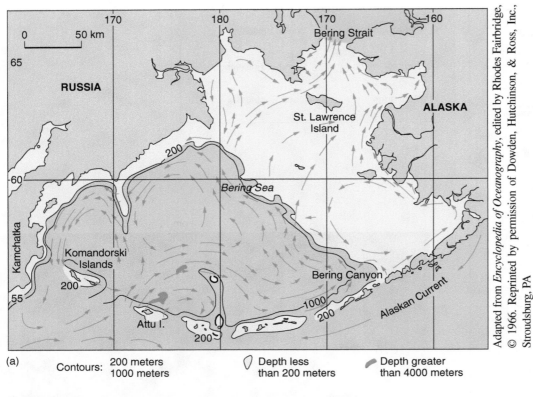

(a) Contours: 200 meters 1000 meters | Depth less than 200 meters | Depth greater than 4000 meters

Adapted from *Encyclopedia of Oceanography*, edited by Rhodes Fairbridge. © 1966. Reprinted by permission of Dowden, Hutchinson, & Ross, Inc., Stroudsburg, PA

Figure 15 Bering Sea bathymetry and surface circulation.

Location map showing bathymetry and surface circulation in the Bering Sea. Note that much of the Bering Sea is either shallower than 200 meters (660 feet) or deeper than 1000 meters (3300 meters).

Marginal Seas of the Indian Ocean

Marginal seas of the Indian Ocean include the narrow Red Sea and the broader Arabian Sea and Bay of Bengal.

The Red Sea   The **Red Sea** extends more than 1900 kilometers (1200 miles) north of the narrow Strait of Bab-el-Mandeb (Gate of Tears) to the northern tip of the Gulf of Suez, the western branch of the Red Sea that separates the Sinai Peninsula from the African mainland. Forming the eastern boundary of the Sinai Peninsula is the Gulf of Aqaba, which is an eastern branch at the northern end of the Red Sea (Figure 16).

Extending from 12 degrees to 30 degrees north latitude, the Red Sea lies in a highly arid region and is characterized by surface waters of unusually high temperature and salinity. Broad reef-covered shelves no more than 50 meters (164 feet) deep drop off sharply to a gently sloping surface at about 500 meters (1640 feet), which eventually leads into a central trough with depths from 1500 meters (4920 feet) to more than 2300 meters (7500 feet).

Geologic evidence indicates the Red Sea formed primarily during the past few million years by intracontinental rifting. Similar to the origin of the Gulf of California, the Red Sea is in the initial stages of ocean basin formation, which will continue as the plates containing the Arabian Peninsula and the African mainland rift apart. New oceanic crust and an active spreading center underlie the Red Sea.

Circulation Patterns   Sill depth at the Strait of Bab-el-Mandeb is only 125 meters (410 feet) compared to a maximum depth of more than 1000 meters (3300 feet) over parts of the Red Sea. Across this shallow sill, the basic circulation is dominated by a high rate of evaporation, which exceeds 200 centimeters (79 inches) per year. Because of this water loss, surface water from the Indian Ocean flows through the Gulf of Aden into the Red Sea. As this surface flow moves north, its density increases as evaporation increases its salinity. The dense water sinks and returns as a subsurface flow to the sill and out into the Gulf of Aden. This outflowing warm, saline water sinks rapidly until it finds its equilibrium depth (based on density) and then spreads out into the Indian Ocean. This pattern of circulation (Figure 16b) is similar to that of the Mediterranean Sea (see Figure 11b).

Because of the arid conditions in the region, the surface water in the Red Sea reaches a salinity of 42.5‰ and a temperature of 30°C (86°F) during the summer months. Below a depth of 200 meters (660 feet), a uniform mass of water extends to the bottom throughout most of the Red Sea. This deep-water mass has a temperature of 21.7°C (71°F) and a salinity of 40.6‰.

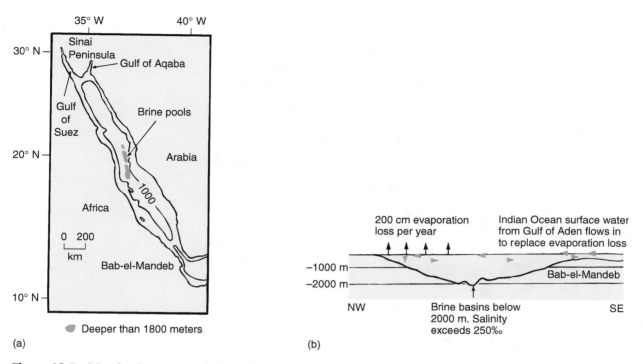

Figure 16 Red Sea bathymetry and circulation.

(a) Map showing location and bathymetry of the Red Sea, including location of brine pools. (b) Cross-section view of the mouth of the Red Sea, showing circulation between the Red Sea and the Indian Ocean.

Brine Pools In 1966, investigators aboard the Woods Hole Oceanographic Institution research vessel *Chain* studied a series of deep basins in the central Red Sea that had been previously noted to contain extremely high-salinity and high-temperature water masses. At about 21 degrees north latitude, two major basins were found—the Discovery Deep to the south and the Atlantis II Deep to the north. These and other similar basins contain *brine pools* with temperatures in excess of 36°C (96.8°F) and salinities as high as 257‰! These brine pools, because of their high salinity, have densities great enough to keep them in their basins and prevent them from mixing with overlying surface waters.

The brine pools are formed from hydrothermal circulation of seawater in the hot, porous oceanic crust. The sediments associated with the brine pools have concentrations of salts and metals that give them a great potential for future mining. In addition, there is also enrichment in the crust beneath the sediment, thereby enhancing the economic potential of this area. The Discovery Deep contains the first hydrothermal springs to be discovered. This discovery provided the impetus to initiate the search that led to the discovery of the hydrothermal vents along the Galápagos Rift in 1977.

The Arabian Sea The **Arabian Sea** is the northward extension of the Indian Ocean between Africa and India (Figure 17).

Circulation Patterns Surface currents in the Arabian Sea are dominated by *monsoon winds*[11] that blow from the northeast from November until March, when the *southwest monsoon* begins to develop. The air carried onto the continent during this southwest monsoon contains large quantities of water and produces heavy precipitation in the coastal regions.

During the *northeast monsoon* (winter), the surface current moves south along the west coast of India and turns west at about 10 degrees north latitude. Here, some of the surface water flows into the Gulf of Aden and the rest turns south along the Somali coast to converge with the *North Equatorial Current*. When the southwest monsoon begins in the summer, the North Equatorial Current disappears, and a portion of the *South Equatorial Current* flows north along the Somali coast as the *Somali Current*. This strong seasonal current flows with velocities in excess of 11 kilometers (7 miles) per hour and continues along the coast of Arabia and India in a clockwise pattern until it reaches 10 degrees north latitude. Here, it becomes the *Southwest Monsoon Current* and replaces the North Equatorial Current. Because of the alignment of winds relative to the African and Arabian coasts, significant upwelling occurs during the southwest monsoon.

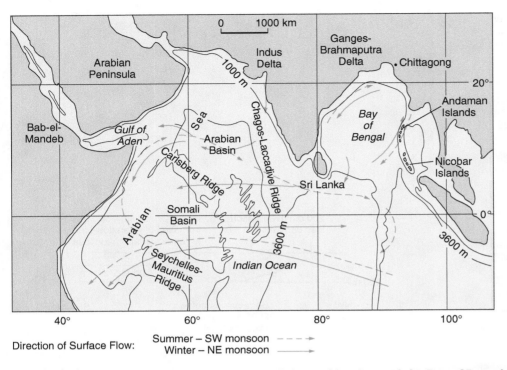

Figure 17 Bathymetry and surface circulation of the Arabian Sea and the Bay of Bengal.

Map showing location, bathymetry, and surface circulation of the Arabian Sea and the Bay of Bengal, both of which are affected by seasonal monsoon winds.

Surface salinities north of 5 degrees north latitude in the Arabian Sea are generally above 36‰ during the northeast monsoon. The Somali coastal region surface salinity may fall below 35.5‰ because of dilution by the South Equatorial Current and upwelling during the southwest monsoon. During the rainy season, surface salinities of less than 35‰ can be found as a result of dilution due to precipitation and runoff. Surface temperatures in the central region reach a maximum of 28°C (82°F) in June and a minimum temperature of 24°C (75°F) in February.

Below 200 meters (660 feet), the salinity decreases to values near 35‰ until an abrupt salinity maximum of 35.4‰ to 35.5‰ develops at depths above 1000 meters (3300 feet). This salinity maximum represents the flow of water into the Arabian Sea from the Persian Gulf and the Red Sea. The temperature of the Red Sea water ranges from 9°C to 10°C (48°F to 50°F). Red Sea water can also be identified by the low concentration of dissolved oxygen (0.45 parts per million) at about 790 meters (2600 feet) off the Somali coast. Interestingly, hydrogen sulfide has been observed on the continental slope at depths where this oxygen minimum occurs in the northern Arabian Sea.

Bay of Bengal The **Bay of Bengal** is a large body of water bounded by India and the island of Sri Lanka on the west, and by the Malay Peninsula and the Andaman-Nicobar Island Ridge to the east (Figure 17). A significant continental influence is exerted on this body of water by the runoff from the Ganges and Brahmaputra rivers at the extreme north end of the bay.

Circulation Patterns The currents in the Bay of Bengal are also dominated by the monsoon wind system. During the southwest monsoon, a clockwise rotation is established within the Bay; this circulation is accompanied by upwelling along the east Indian coast. With the development of the northeast monsoon in November, the circulation reverses and forms a counterclockwise gyre. At Chittagong in southeast Bangladesh, a seasonal change in the sea level of 1.2 meters (4 feet) occurs as a result of monsoon wind changes.

The surface salinity in the Bay of Bengal seldom exceeds 34‰. During the southwest monsoon, particularly during late summer when the rainfall is the greatest, the runoff from the Ganges, Brahmaputra, and other rivers along the coast of Burma and India dilute the water and reduce surface salinity. As a result, salinity values as low as 18‰ can be observed at the extreme north end of the Bay. The major influence of this dilution is observed along the Indian coast; it is less significant away from shore.

STUDENTS SOMETIMES ASK ...

Which nation on Earth would experience the greatest impact of a rise in sea level?

Of all the nations on Earth, Bangladesh, with a population of over 127 million, is under the greatest threat if a significant sea level rise occurs. This is because more than 80% of Bangladesh is built on a low-lying delta within a few meters of sea level, and it is regularly devastated by storm surges associated with tropical cyclones, particularly during the southwest monsoon. Even a small rise in sea level (like that predicted due to global warming) will severely impact the country. Other low-lying small islands will certainly be impacted, but they don't have the population size that Bangladesh does.

The characteristics of marginal seas are influenced by their tectonic origin, location, circulation, and physical processes, all of which affect water temperature and salinity.

Chapter in Review

- *Coastal waters support about 95% of the total mass of life in the oceans*, and they are important areas for commerce, recreation, fisheries, and the disposal of waste. *The temperature and salinity of the coastal ocean vary over a greater range than the open ocean* because the coastal ocean is shallow and experiences river runoff, tidal currents, and seasonal changes in solar radiation. *Coastal geostrophic currents are produced from freshwater runoff and coastal winds.*

- *Estuaries are semienclosed bodies of water where freshwater runoff from the land mixes with ocean water.* Estuaries are *classified by their origin* as coastal plain, fjord, bar built, or tectonic. Estuaries are also *classified by their mixing patterns* of fresh and salt water as vertically mixed, slightly stratified, highly stratified, and salt wedge. *Typical circulation in an estuary consists of a surface flow of low-salinity water toward its mouth and a subsurface flow of marine water toward its head.*

- *Estuaries provide important breeding and nursery areas for many marine organisms* but often suffer from human population pressures. The *Columbia River Estuary*, for example, has degraded from agriculture, logging, and the construction of dams upstream. In *Chesapeake Bay*, an anoxic zone occurs during the summer that kills many commercially important species.

- *Wetlands are some of the most biologically productive regions on Earth. Salt marshes and mangrove swamps are important examples of coastal wetlands.* Wetlands are ecologically important because they remove land-derived pollutants from water before it reaches the ocean. Nevertheless, human activities continue to destroy wetlands.

- *Long offshore deposits called barrier islands protect marshes and lagoons.* Some lagoons have restricted circulation with the ocean, so water temperatures and salinity may vary widely with the seasons.

- *Marginal seas are relatively large semi-isolated bodies of marine water often formed by tectonic processes that isolate patches of ocean crust or that are forming new ocean basins.* For example, the Mediterranean is a remnant of the ancient Tethys Sea, which has been closing up as the plates containing Africa and Europe move closer together. Both the Gulf of California and the Red Sea are geologically young seas produced by sea floor spreading rifting apart adjoining landmasses.

- *Marginal seas typically are shallower than the open ocean and have varying degrees of restricted circulation.* Circulation in the Mediterranean Sea is characteristic of restricted bodies of water in areas where evaporation greatly exceeds precipitation. Called *Mediterranean circulation, it is the reverse of estuarine circulation.* In other marginal seas, salinities may fall below those of normal seawater because of large influxes of river runoff.

- *Seasonal wind patterns like those found in the Gulf of California cause coastal upwelling and high biological productivity.* An extensive shelf on the northeast side and a deep basin to the southwest are characteristic of the *Bering Sea* north of the Aleutian Islands. Many important commercial fisheries exist in this sea. *The Arabian Sea* to the west of India and the *Bay of Bengal* to the east have circulation patterns controlled by monsoon winds.

Key Terms

Anoxic
Arabian Sea
Bar-built estuary
Bay of Bengal
Bering Sea
Caribbean Sea
Coastal geostrophic current
Coastal plain estuary
Coastal water
Davidson Current

Estuarine circulation pattern
Estuary
Fjord
Gulf of California
Gulf of Mexico
Halocline
Highly stratified estuary
Isohaline
Isothermal
Lagoon

Mangrove swamp
Marginal sea
Mediterranean circulation
Mediterranean Sea
Phytoplankton
Plankton
Red Sea
Salt marsh
Salt wedge estuary
Sill

Slightly stratified estuary
Tectonic estuary
Thermocline
Vertically mixed estuary
Wetland

Questions and Exercises

1. For coastal oceans where deep mixing does not occur, discuss the effect that offshore winds and freshwater runoff will have on salinity distribution. How will the winter and summer seasons affect the temperature distribution in the water column?

2. How does coastal runoff of low-salinity water produce a coastal geostrophic current?

3. Based on their origin, draw and describe the four major classes of estuaries.

4. Describe the difference between vertically mixed and salt wedge estuaries in terms of salinity distribution, depth, and volume of river flow. Which displays the more classical estuarine circulation pattern?

5. Discuss factors that cause the surface salinity of Chesapeake Bay to be greater along its east side, and why periods of summer anoxia in deep water are becoming increasingly severe with time.

6. Name the two types of coastal wetland environments and the latitude ranges where each will likely develop. How do wetlands contribute to the biology of the oceans and the cleansing of polluted river water?

7. What factors lead to a wide seasonal range of salinity in Laguna Madre?

8. List the evidence that exists to support the idea that the Mediterranean Sea completely dried up in the geologic past.

9. Describe the circulation between the Atlantic Ocean and the Mediterranean Sea, and explain how and why it differs from estuarine circulation.

10. Describe how coastal upwelling in the Gulf of California is related to seasonal winds.

11. Compare and contrast the circulation between the Red Sea and the Indian Ocean to that between the Mediterranean Sea and the Atlantic Ocean.

12. Explain why Red Sea water that flows into the Indian Ocean at a depth of 125 meters (410 feet) sinks to 1000 meters (3300 feet) before spreading throughout the Arabian Sea.

13. Describe the relationship between surface circulation and monsoon winds in the Bay of Bengal.

Index

Page references followed by "f" indicate illustrated figures or photographs; followed by "t" indicates a table.